Essays on the Art of Chaucer's Verse

Basic Readings in Chaucer and His Time
Christian K. Zacher and Paul E. Szarmach, *Series Editors*

Writing After Chaucer
Essential Readings in Chaucer and the Fifteenth Century
edited by Daniel J. Pinti

Chaucer's Dream Visions and Shorter Poems
edited by William A. Quinn

Essays on the Art of Chaucer's Verse

Edited by
Alan T. Gaylord

Routledge
New York • London

Published in 2001 by
Routledge
29 West 35th Street
New York, NY 10001

Published in Great Britain by
Routledge
11 New Fetter Lane
London EC4P 4EE

Routledge is an imprint of the Taylor & Francis Group.

Printed on acid-free, 250-year life paper.
Manufactured in the United States of America.

10 9 8 7 6 5 4 3 2 1

Library of Congress Cataloging-in-Publication Data

Essays on the art of Chaucer's verse / edited by Alan T. Gaylord.
p. cm. – (Basic readings in Chaucer and his time ; v.3)
Includes bibliographical references.
ISBN 0-8153-2951-2
1. Chaucer, Geoffrey, d. 1400–Versification. 2. English language–Middle English, 1100–1500–Versification. I. Gaylord, Alan T. II. Series.

PR1951 .A78 2001
821'.1–dc21

00-065299

Contents

PREFACE

The present volume displays in its twentieth-century essays certain practices which need to be explained as being part of what might be called the campaign for decent order and good sense within prosodic analysis.

Spelling

Above all, the spelling of r–i–m–e. Chaucer and his French sources spelled the word *rime* or *ryme.* The addition of the (silent) "h" to make the grapheme, "r**hy**me," is a later addition by scholars looking to classical Greek (which has no connection to Chaucer's verse at all). From the *New Princeton Encyclopedia of Poetry and Poetics*: "The spelling 'rhyme' became common in Eng. in the 17th c.; the earlier Ren. and ME spelling, "rime," derives from OF *rime, ritme* < Med. Lat. *rithmi* < Lat. *rithmus, rhythmus* < Gr. *rhythmos.* In Eng. the spelling *rime/ ryme* for vernacular, accentual, rhymed verse was preserved to ca. 1560 . . . . *rhyme* subsequently won out, though the (historically correct) spelling rime has never entirely disappeared." (T.V.F. Brogan in NPEPP 1994, 1053) I hope any future writer on Chaucer's prosody will adopt the "historically correct" spelling, *rime,* which does, indeed, appear in most modern dictionaries as a variant.

Furthermore, a number of terms which prosodists too much in the shadow of classical prosody have spelled "antiquely"–for example, "cæsura," and "anapæst"–are now spelled (but not for the first time) *cesura, anapest,* etc.

Terminology

The progression of essays displays a great variety of words describing metrics, prosody, and poetry. In most cases, terms that might strike the student at first as exotic or incomprehensible, should become clearer after further reading. Adding editorial definitions in brackets at each occurrence seemed otiose, especially when the essay in question was in progress of defining and using the term (but definitions-in-brackets have been added in a few cases). A lexicon or glossary of "hard words" was also rejected as threatening to become a ponderous imitation of what might better be at the elbow of any serious student of the subject; that is, the NPEPP, as named above.

A. Gaylord
Hanover, N.H.

INTRODUCTION

It often makes people positively angry to be told that the greatest part, if not the whole, of the pleasure-giving appeal of poetry lies in its sound rather than its sense, or, to speak with extreme exactness, lies in the manner in which the sound conveys the sense. No "chain of extremely valuable thoughts" is poetry in itself: it only becomes poetry when it is conveyed with those charms of language, metre, rhyme, cadence, what not, which certain persons disdain.

–George Saintsbury[1]

Viewed one way, what holds most of the contributors here together is their agreement that Chaucer criticism has tended, and still tends, to treat Chaucer as if he were a writer in prose. True, the statement begs the question of the definition of prose, but the basic point is clear enough, and I'll open it up it three ways:

1. Chaucer has been treated as a writer of prose: his versification has been ignored. Versification is a formalist category, and formal, along with structural, analysis bespeaks an assurance about *what is there* that no longer can be taken seriously.
2. His versification has been ignored because as a formalist or mechanical aspect it is kept separate from *poesis*–the latter linked to metaphor, image, and insight, and the diction necessary to convey such matter; the former linked to devices for setting the poet's matter off as recognizably entertainment or art, and for delivering unobtrusively the more important parts. Poesis has nobility and soul; Hallmark cards have versification. One soars, the other jingles. This may seem curious at first, since part of the modernist credo was to insist on the unity of form and content. Verbal categories like diction and image were privileged, and verbal practices, like rhythm and rime, were ignored–or declared (or assumed) not to be within the "organic" package. As Barney puts it, with a touch of irony: "In the age of free verse . . . the pedantry of classically based versification, with its Victorian claim of Science, number, rigor, came to be stifling."

   In short, the concept of "the Aesthetic" was often devalued or debunked. It either was accused of irresponsible flights into imaginary safe havens of formal beauty, or assumed to be fixated on prettiness/attractiveness even more than on Beauty–i.e., fixated on secondary, even trivial aspects of a kind of discourse that needed analysis in terms of historical, social, and political contexts.

3. The demoting of the Aesthetic is in part a reaction to "New Critical" analysis of versification, where sound and sense were believed to be organically related and mutually enhancing. Patterns of sound, like patterns of diction, were discovered to have an iconic sense, that is, realized a meaning that was beyond prose-analysis: "a poem should not mean, but be"; which is to say, that patterns of sound were not objects for translation or decoding but vital elements in a gestalt which would be more deeply experienced (emphasis on "experience") as each element was perceived, felt, absorbed. The negative reaction was to devalue a project whose intense vagueness, it was thought, too easily degenerated into statements like: "the repeated sibilants in this line provide an uneasy suggestion of anger . . . or seduction . . . or secrecy," and so forth.

   Furthermore, the element of rhythm has probably been neglected because–at least, in the Western world–poetry is seldom recited in public any longer, and seldom memorized, and those critics who write about poetry (consequently?) do not seem have been reading aloud what they hear, or to be hearing it clearly in their inner ears, or feeling it in their bones. (I am aware that "poetry readings" on many American campuses are alive and well, and well attended, Deo gratias, though these are almost always selections from the poet-reader's own work. It is an interesting phenomenon, with deep but narrow effect–that is, I am not aware of parallel programs on campuses with public readings of non-contemporary poetry, though I would be glad to learn of any.) Things are not made any better by the fact that serious studies of historical metrics are produced largely by specialists, scholars of Linguistics, whose conflicting conclusions have not yet been successfully translated into the somewhat more available discourses of literature and literary criticism. Or to put it more sharply, the concept of Linguistics most literary critics think they are working with has little relationship to the Linguistics of linguists!

And so: on the one hand, we have "the bean-counters," those metrical specialists who count, measure, quantify, and seem (to the unwashed) to be treating verse as just another aspect of linguistic constituent analysis; and on the other hand we have students whose personal "default mode" in metrical production seems to be *The Night Before Christmas* or Dr. Seuss, as I learn when I ask them to write their own modern imitations of portraits from the General Prologue (a response quite natural, if very restricted and simplistic).

It is not, to be sure, that students everywhere have been deprived of courses in which the elements of poetry are discussed and illustrated; but the particular problem here is that even the brightest, most level-headed, and most imaginative textbooks do not treat with any thoroughness if at all the poetics of medieval verse, Chaucer's in particular. As far as modern prosodic analysis is concerned, the problem can be traced back to influential New-Critical guides like Brooks and Warren's *Understanding Poetry*; for it could be argued (and I do argue) that the elaborate kit they provide there for the serious student's dissection of verse has very few tools appropriate for the narrative modes and poetic forms of, say, the *Canterbury Tales* or the *House of Fame*. Most prosodic systems that are being taught are based on post-medieval subjects and assumptions.

In response to this national and cultural situation, most of the writers in this volume are classroom teachers who utilize a variety of strategies for realizing the aural textures of the Chaucerian text. Chickering, for example, teaches a course in Chaucer whose objectives are outlined as "to read *Troilus and Criseyde* aloud in Middle English for personal enjoyment and, while doing so, to develop a sharp ear and eye for its best poetic effects" (Chickering 1998, 96).

The volume is not assembled as a manifesto against those who do not swing with Chaucer's swing, and yet the occasion is portentous. For the first time, it has become possible to gather together on this topic essays by leading scholars and critics who have been working separately (there is no Academy of Prosody, let alone an annual series of meetings, conferences, seminars, or other sessions on the topic), but who share a conviction that Chaucer's versification is artful, pleasurable, and deserving of much, much more attention than it has erstwhile received. And so here we are.

I said at the beginning that "viewed one way," we are held together by our conviction that most Chaucer criticism treats Chaucer as if he were a writer in prose. That is the negative, or polemic, way. Another way, demonstrated with all the variety of the personalities and approaches of these essays, is the positive one of showing just how intricate and how essential the analysis of Chaucer's verse can be–as essential as breath and body, as a soul expressed by material sounds and movements of a song or story.

My intention in what follows is to discuss the essays by Tyrwhitt and Saintsbury in some detail, partly to explain why such ancient pensioners are included in the present symposium, and partly and more importantly to introduce some of the major themes and issues that will be developed and argued in all the other essays. Then, proceeding in the order in which they appear, I will introduce the rest of the essays and place them, their arguments, and their approaches, within the context of the theory and practice of Prosody.

PART ONE: HISTORICAL AND THEORETICAL ESSAYS

An Essay on the Language and Versification of Chaucer. Part the Third

Thomas Tyrwhitt (1730–1786)

Thomas Tyrwhitt, son of a clergyman, was educated at Eton and Queen's College, Oxford, and worked in government. William Prideaux Courtney's article in the *Dictionary of National Biography* notes that his post as deputy secretary of war was "not incompatible with residence for most part of the year at Oxford." While a Fellow at Merton he pursued his studies, gaining a reputation as one learned not only in Greek and Latin, but also "in almost every European tongue," and (remarkably) in English literature as well. It was while he was clerk of the House of Commons that he began to publish, using his philological knowledge, early dealing with questions of authenticity of various passages from Shakespeare. He retired from government duties in 1768, "and spent the remaining years of his life almost wholly among his books." He bequeathed to the British Museum a personal collection of classical authors of about 900 volumes. An obituary in *Gentleman's Magazine* noted that "the profundity and acuteness of his remarks on Euripides, Babrius, Chaucer, Shakspeare and the Pseudo-Rowley, bear sufficient witness to the diligence of his researches and the force of his understanding" (cited in Windeatt 1984, 117).

His Chaucer edition, published anonymously in 1775, was frequently reprinted, and, truth be told, egregiously plagiarized in his lifetime,[2] enjoying in one form or another absolute authority until Skeat's editions appeared about 100 years later–no other edition of Chaucer can match such longevity. Note that Tyrwhitt, though a Merton Fellow, was not a teacher and did not directly address the beginning student. Perhaps one could describe his edition as the last, and greatest, piece of antiquarian scholarship devoted to Chaucer. Not until Skeat's editions did Chaucer take up residence in the classroom. But Tyrwhitt was so respected at Oxford that in 1798 the Delegates of the Clarendon Press arranged a fine reprinting of the first edition, in two quarto volumes, with a portrait of Tyrwhitt and an "Advertisement" that explained that in so doing they desired "to shew every respect on the part of the University to Mr. Tyrwhitt's name and abilities" (sig. [iv]^{r}).

There are several ways to read his introductory Essay's third part, on "the Versification of Chaucer," and several values to derive therefrom. I do *not* recommend one way, which might be called the Cautionary and Condescending way, and which would take comfort in identifying the limits to Tyrwhitt's criticism and the limited literary resources available to him (the MS. of the Pearl Poet, for example, had not yet been re-discovered; he did not have available to him the early, and excellent, Hengwrt and Ellesmere MSS. of the Canterbury Tales[3])–in order to commend our modern scholars for their superior knowledge and achievements. Instead, I recommend the following themes or topics to follow in the course of reading:

1. *The classical inheritance of Chaucerian criticism (for better or worse)*. Whatever formal training in the analysis of verse Tyrwhitt received, it would have dealt solely, of course, with Greek and Latin, though in his ear and under his eyes would also have been the heroic couplets of Pope and Dryden, the intricate metrical forms of rime and the sonorous blank verse of Milton, and the plays–in rime, blank verse, and prose–of Shakespeare. It is fascinating to watch for the places where classical and English poets are quoted.

   We see him explaining in n. 42 how "all the nations of Roman Europe" have derived their "poetic measures" from the iambic and trochaic rhythms of Latin. Without even protesting that English is a Germanic, not a Romance language, and that the Germanic and Romance branches of proto-Indo-European developed quite different prosodies, one need only point out that medieval Latin (considered a mongrel, debased form of Latin by the classicists) had largely developed an accentual, not quantitative, mode of scansion for its verse. Tyrwhitt knows this in the abstract, but evinces no capacity to deal with that mode except to say it often can be taken as quantitative!

The point here is to note how absolutely the terms of classical prosody are carried along in this essay: measures; iambs; trochees; until: " . . . instead of a Dimeter Iambic, it is a Dimeter Trochaic Catalectic." And so forth.

It will be instructive watching him carry along, develop, and apply the classical concept of meter. This topic, absolutely central to his editorial work as we shall see, introduces a theme which resounds through virtually every essay in this volume. One can begin with section IX, where we are told that "the most considerable part of Chaucer's works" was composed in the "Heroic" meter. He did not feel it necessary to remind his readers that the term, "Heroic," for iambic pentameter couplets was fairly recent, named by Puttenham in the 16th and by Dryden in the 17th centuries, and brought to perfection by Pope in the 18th (when it of course could be used in translating Homer [NPEPP 1993, s.v. "Heroic Couplet," 522–24]).

His next step is to lay down this axiom: "the correctness and harmony of an English verse depends entirely upon its being composed of a certain number of syllables, and its having the accents of those syllables properly placed" (sec. X). It is an axiom that will be picked over in subsequent essays, especially by Saintsbury, Gaylord, Pearsall, Guthrie, and Barney, but it seems unexceptionable until one begins to inquire more closely what the "certain number" is that must be allowed, and what "properly placed" must mean, let alone what an "accent" is. And is "proper" another word for "absolute rigor"? For we will read further on, that "I have no conception myself that an heroic verse, which wants a syllable of its complement, can be musical, or even tolerable."

Shadowing the classical argument, which comfortably appeals to vernacular Romance examples in French and Italian, is the somewhat contrary situation of native English (Germanic) verse. It is a separate line of study to watch Tyrwhitt glance off the domain of alliterative verse–from the "Saxon" in which he cannot "discover any material distinction of . . . Poetry from Prose, except a greater pomp of diction, and a more stately kind of march" (n. 40)–a wonderful sentence, not at all foolish, if insufficiently informed, and metaphorically if unintentionally richly suggestive . . . for a march is a very definite realization of rhythm based on quite precise "measures"–and then reaching to Langland, which he has read with no apparent thrill of affinity, confessing himself unable to "reduce to any certain Metre" those lines (n. 57). The classicist will thus have the hardest time finding this kind of literature "poetic."

2. *The task of the editor of Chaucer.* This topic follows naturally out of the first, at any number of points. Tyrrwhitt is called the father of modern editors for his insistence on returning to and critically examining all available manuscripts. His

method is that of the "best text," a provocative phrase (now); as Windeatt puts it: "Tyrwhitt holds with his 'best MSS.' where they seem self-evidently best" (124), and the critical question centers on the determination of what is "self-evident" (see Donaldson 1966, 114–16). If the logical circularity seems inevitable, one can at least see where Tyrwhitt's circle begins–with, I think, his twin convictions that Chaucer is an English master of verse, and that a master will write "harmonious verse." As one follows him carefully from his text, down to the elaborate excursuses of his footnotes, and back, it will be seen that he is comparing MSS as carefully as he can, leading him to conclude that the text of the *Canterbury Tales*, at least, is "not in any case radically corrupt." And so one arrives at a critical crossroads, or the "cross," that is, the *crux*–for the question arises as to what the editor must do when he finds, amidst good lines, a bad one (a "crux") and concludes that the scribe, not the poet, is to blame. For Chaucer "was not ignorant of the laws of metre" (sec. XII). Note the classical/Neo-Classical term, "laws"–which will be revived and redefined in linguistic approaches to verse, as in "generative prosody" (see Gaylord and Guthrie in this volume).

But he remains a conservative emender, not happy to go against a consensus of "the best MSS." and able to secure another kind of help by attention to the question of word stress ("accent") and the role of "*e*-feminine" in determining pronunciation and syllable count. His treatment of these latter questions in secs. XV–XVII (with their notes) is remarkable ("astute," says Windeatt).

Tyrwhitt was not the first to emend–all editors since Caxton had emended, though quite often without comment or explanation–but Tyrwhitt's reasoned explanation of the rationale and procedures for responsible emendation bring us into the world of modern editing (see Windeatt 1984, "Emendation: Editorial Practices," 125–34). Very large in his program, then, is the matter of versification, for it is often in the process of emendation that a line becomes correct, which is to say "harmonious." And for all his rigor, he never hides the fact that his judgments, based on careful accumulation of evidence, must be supported by "taste"–another Neo-Classical term that brings us to the third and final "way" of approaching his work.

3. *"Tasting the poetry": the eye and the ear.* How does Tyrwhitt experience (taste) the poetry of Chaucer? To what extent could he apprehend its verbal textures? It is hard to imagine. He would have been unlikely to have had systematic understanding of the major vowel-shifts that occurred between the age of Chaucer and of Shakespeare. There is little evidence as to how, and when, Chaucer might have been read aloud in any community Tyrwhitt would have known. And he does not seem to use the verb, "sounds," when he describes a Chaucerian verse. Which accounts, I think, for his careful attention to the issues of syllabification and accent. If much of his phonology might have been incorrectly "modern" he could still approximate the movement and even the impetus of a verse. But when one asks about rhythmical variety in Chaucer (not with reference to metrical "exceptions"), and about expressiveness, one is largely in

search of inferences–there seem to be no axioms to cover such matters. Tyrwhitt is attempting to describe the abstract pattern of Chaucer's verse in accordance with those "laws" of poetic meter he is confident Chaucer obeyed; he is not trying to imagine how Chaucer might have recited his poetry, or even (it seems) how the verse might take life within a reader's imagination.

It is particularly instructive, then, to have a close look at his "grammatical and metrical analysis" of the first 18 lines of the General Prologue (sec. XVIII). It will be seen that there is only a small difference between the words of this text and that, say, of the *Riverside Chaucer* (Chaucer 1987). "Serve" instead of "ferne" at line 14 is the only substantive change. "Sound" is involved in the sense that most of the commentary is directed to the matter of syllabification, and, hence, the "hearing" of a harmonious line. Prosodically, he marks what will later be called "stress maximums," and does not distinguish between a major and a minor stress–so one cannot be sure if he "hears" these lines in a tick-tock or sing-song manner, or modulates them according their lexical and syntactical hierarchies (note accent marks on "with," "to," "is," etc.; note the handling of line V). But the subject is one of "numbers" (another term taken from classical prosody); and one can count just as well with the eyes as hear with the ears–perhaps even more accurately. Of the "style" of the passage, to use a favorite term of the New Critics, or of its "register"– a term from linguistic Stylistics–there seems to be no report whatsoever. An editor, then, is like the King's Taster–one who personally assures that the meats at board are wholesome, properly composed, and (in the Miltonic sense) innocuous; and who can safely assume that what is served to the king will be exquisite, so that identifying "taste treats," the mensuration of delight, will not be his business.

Perhaps, then, the Tyrwhitt essay starts us on our way towards a consideration of the art of Chaucer's work by concentrating in a preliminary (and editorial) way on the basis of that art (which was sometimes a synonym for it): his craft.

Chaucer's Prosody
George Edward Bateman Saintsbury (1845–1933)

"As a critic," writes D. Nichol Smith in the DNB entry, "Saintsbury was pre-eminently a 'taster' who said what it was he liked, and why he liked it." This is a sense of taste somewhat diverging from Tyrwhitt's, for it includes a strong sensuous intuition and an approach emphasizing a gusto that never strays far from the corporeality of verse, from its heft and limberness.

Immediately, a program of instructive comparisons is suggested. Tyrwhitt was an editor, a solitary worker in rare books and manuscripts, and one who walked carefully in the service of (Neo-Classical) metrical laws; Saintsbury (no less a scholar, and also an editor) was a journalist, a teacher, and a prolific literary critic and reviewer, and one who danced in the appreciation of a meter and its music. (I begin my "Scanning" essay with a quote from him, which charmingly and revealingly connects his classical training with his social dancing even as it shows him responding with both body and mind to the movement of a verse.) In the methods of Tyrwhitt one finds a patient stamina that supports his meticulousness, and a strength displayed in the copious exhibits of his readings and researches; in Saintsbury, one is almost bowled over, or at least carried along as in a torrent, by the unceasing and yet not careless *energeia* of the man.[4] The record of his literary career, from his longevity to his unceasing activity and productivity, bears out what the chapter included here displays.

The son of a secretary-and-superintendent of the Southampton docks, Saintsbury was sent off to King's College School, London, and then entered Merton College, Oxford (where Tyrwhitt had been a Fellow a century earlier), studying the classics. After graduating, he was a schoolmaster for eight years, while reading widely in French literature, but then returned to London in 1876 "to live by his pen." And one may well say, reviewing the list of his subsequent books and articles, that the floodgates were therewith opened.

By his own definition, he was a journalist for the next 20 years, during which time, he said, "I must have written the equivalent of at least a hundred volumes." But then, in 1895, he was appointed to a chair of Rhetoric and English literature (a fairly new category in Britain for that time, as in the United States) at the university of Edinburgh, and for the next 20 years completed the final phase of his professional life. And Smith writes, that "the big books which he had long wanted to write now followed one another with surprising rapidity." It is relevant to note that the first of these was *A Short History of English Literature*, followed by *History of Criticism and Literary Taste in Europe from the Earliest Texts to the Present Day*, in three volumes, and then *History of English Prosody from the Twelfth Century to the Present Day*, in three volumes (is there anyone alive who would even contemplate writing a similar work, with similar scope, today?). The relevance comes from the way this sequence illuminates his methods and concerns as a prosodic critic.

The history of English literature now demands attention as one of the major themes of the essays in this volume, both in terms of a context in which Chaucer is to be placed, and a body of convictions as to what that literature is all about, where it has come from and where it is going (Saintsbury is given to metaphors which show a set of not very complex Darwinian assumptions about the "evolution" or "natural history" of versification). Both Tyrwhitt and Saintsbury take for granted, rest upon, a classical background (but neither is richly informed in the realm of medieval Latin literature, sacred or secular), and each is remarkable for examining as closely as possible the French and Italian influences on Chaucer's poetry. Neither is enamored of "the metrical school of alliteration"; both see Chaucer as bringing accentual/syllabic verse (which they define in their own ways) to its first stage of perfection.

As to the nature of this "accentual/syllabic verse," a reader of Saintsbury's chapter will likely be intrigued, puzzled, perhaps enlightened, more likely exasperated, by the remarks, hints, definitions to be found there. As Dorothy Richardson Jones observes, Saintsbury had a peculiarly sensitive ear: "he had an unusual ear that heard feet and line divisions"; he said that even as a schoolboy he would read "'scanningly': . . . that method of reading aloud 'with accompaniment of handbeat'" (Jones 1992, 244). And he insisted, if equivocally, that quantity (how long it took to pronounce a syllable) and accent(how much emphasis a syllable received) somehow combined in the practice of Chaucer and, thereafter, of the best poets. But how should we understand the categories, "long" and "short," then? His entry in his *Manual of English Prosody* is typical–and I also consider it endearingly nonsensical, like Alice's Red Queen who can think of so many impossible things before breakfast:

> Long and Short . . . represent two values which . . . are invariably, unmistakably, and at once, distinguished by the ear; and the combining of which . . . constitutes the feet . . . of metrical rhythm. . . . "Does length," some people ask, "really mean 'duration of time' in pronouncing?" This question . . . seems to the present writer unnecessary. We need not decide what makes the difference between "long" and "short"; it is sufficient that this difference unmistakably exists, and is felt at once. Whether it is due to accent, length of pronunciation, sharpness, loudness, strength, or anything else, is a question in no way directly affecting verse. The important things are, once more, that it exists; that verse cannot exist without it. (Saintsbury 1930, 287)

Strictly speaking, this is neither logical proof nor abstract theory. It is f-u-d-g-e. It depends upon Saintsbury's classical education, which included a taxonomy of feet (iambic, etc.), and which provided the basis of scansion; and it develops from his conviction that he could *hear* feet in the recitation of poetry. Thus he will write, in this chapter, that "Chaucer has found an English prosody already thoroughly broken to the use of foot-divisions and their arrangements in metrical groups. . . . Now, there is no more doubt. The tuner [of the English lyre] has come." But this is less a theoretical statement than an interpretation of literary history, supported by his own palpable logic: Eureka!: see it or (better) hear it! It is *there.*

Here is a typical sentence such a position will generate: "there can, to any reader with a careful eye and a good ear, be no question about the immense gain of fluency and exactness combined which *Troilus* shows." Note the naming of a reader and the appeal to the eye/ear of commonsense taste/judgment. The fact that he is exactly right about the *Troilus* is not the point, here; rather, we are looking at the grounds for his methods. A more famous sentence: "You may call a thing an octosyllable, or an iambic dimeter, or a four-beat verse, but the *thing* is the same and unmistakable." But this is not a statement of moderate compromise; it is more fudge. For in his preface, had he not written firmly that "the central idea of this book" is "that feet or 'spaces' are the integers, the grounds, the secret, of English prosody"(ix)? The *thing* was a prosody of feet.

As a corrective to and explanation of the map of the prosodic terrain Saintsbury waltzes or marches through, Brogan's essay on modern concepts of the foot can be consulted (NPEPP 1993, 417–20). But even after this, I would suggest that Saintsbury has great value today precisely because of his intuitions and his affinities. These are scattered everywhere, and should be gathered like brilliant wildflowers; for example, his long paragraph on the advantages of the deca- or hendecasyllabic couplet ("heroic verse" again), beginning "In fact it would have been very extraordinary if the heroic had not 'separated itself from the heap' . . ." is one of those descriptions that every lover of poetry should want to read and re-read.

Many of his observations are within the category he calls a "rhetorical prosodic," consisting of "devices . . . to enhance the beauty of sound"–which enlarge the category of versification beyond syllabification and meter to other elements of art. The consideration of "rhetoric" can lead one to the different levels of address–usually some literary version of what is remembered or understood as oratorical strategies; and this relates even more largely to the oral and the colloquial, not only in terms of the notion of decorum, where word-choice and syntactical configurations are marked for class, dignity, personality, and audience, but also various markings for performative aspects like intonation, emphasis, nuance (tone), tempo/pace/impetus, and so forth. (It is a category that Knight draws upon in his chapter.) It is this performative sense of verse in action–supple, various, surprising, and satisfying–that Saintsbury hears (in his mind) and helps us hear. One is not required to use his particular calipers and measuring tape, but the *thing*, unmistakable if (finally) unmeasurable, dances before our ears: just like the line from the *Roman de la Rose* that Saintsbury puts on his title page: "Ainsi karoloient illecques." (The *karole* here is a courtly dance of the 13th century.) And so they foot it lustily.

Scanning the Prosodists: An Essay in Metacriticism

Alan T. Gaylord, Dartmouth College

The first page or two of this essay, in which I define where I started my "scanning" in 1976, can also serve to introduce the purpose of the present volume and to define some of the questions raised, terms used, and procedures followed. Which is not to say that everyone now works the same way in dealing with prosody! Some, for example, still find it convenient to use the analytic terminology that originated with the study of Greek poetry; others are more comfortable with the language of modern Linguistics. Some are concerned to emphasize the creative links between French and/or Italian poetry; others wish to connect Chaucer more strongly to native and traditional English poetry. But what is extraordinary, I believe, is that every essay after Saintsbury, except for Knight's, has been published after 1976. In 1976 I was distressed to see so few critics and scholars dealing with Chaucer's versification, and on the whole was not enthusiastic about the ones that did. In twenty years or so, there has been no revolutionary change in the priorities of critics as a whole, but Chaucer studies have gone through some major changes that help to account for the quality and the importance of what is anthologized here.

My essay begins with the question of the authenticity of the texts usually made the basis for scansion, which leads to the issue of codicology and manuscript-study. What attracted me to such questions was my connection to one of the scholarly enterprises that was about to encourage some new directions. For a few years later a new type of Chaucer edition began to be published: a browse through the post-1978 items under "Chaucer" in this volume's "Works Cited" will make an interesting survey. The appearance of the Variorum Project (I was working on the *Knight's Tale*) brought together a large number of British and American scholars–some experts in the field of editing, some newcomers–and set forward a series of seminars and consultations centering, at the start, on the study of Chaucer's manuscripts. At the same time, the third edition of "Robinson's Chaucer" was about to emerge as *The Riverside Chaucer*; and for the first time, this was a large collaborative effort (guided by Larry Benson). There would follow a series of editions, each of which re-thought and re-argued the question of Chaucer's poetry and the evidence of Chaucerian manuscripts. All of these minds, these energies, these researches revitalized the literary examination of Chaucerian "texts" (the word put into quote marks to indicate that post-modern theory tended to support what was being discovered about manuscript "authority," or the lack thereof). More than ever, the student of Chaucer found it necessary to begin work at this level.

Also important during these years was a widespread interest in questions of "orality" and "performance." Chaucer's age was of interest as transitional between a (largely) non-literate culture and a culture of readers–first of manuscript books, and later, of printed ones. The question of "hearing" Chaucer needed to be theorized and reconsidered (see, for example, Leicester 1980–the date is significant). This process is still very much in motion, but it has encouraged greater interest in performative approaches to the poetry, such as the enterprises of The Chaucer Studio (see also Bowden 1988 and Gaylord 1990).

My essay sets up five categories for my "metacritical" overview: TEXT; PRONUNCIATION; METRICAL PATTERN; VERSIFICATION; and POETIC EFFECT. I was largely seeking information and instruction which, I complained, was either deficient in its theoretical assumptions or inadequate in its practical applications. But now, every one of the post-Saintsbury essays gathered herein works centrally in some or all of the five categories; makes sense, adds to our knowledge, and–each in its own way–satisfies my call for the prosodic critic as one who will "identify a pattern of sounds in motion, a regular and expressive succession which is part of the order of verse and a major component of its effectiveness."

My initial definition of "prosody" (in its literary aspect) as "the theory and practice of versification" has provided the basic organization of the gathering of the essays here: "Historical and Theoretical Essays" and "Essays on Prosodic Practices" (with a transitional category added, partaking of both theory and practice).

Chaucer's Meter: The Evidence of the Manuscripts

Derek Pearsall, Harvard University

As Pearsall 1984 and Pearsall 1985 demonstrate, Derek Pearsall had recently completed a considerable amount of Chaucer-editing when he wrote this essay; and of course he has been editing Middle English literature all along (see, for example, Pearsall 1977). He begins by talking (one can hear him) about the editorial assumptions of Skeat, whose opinions on the way Chaucer should be read out loud would be appalling if anyone tried to take them seriously. Pearsall does not, but the larger point has to do with what one finds in the manuscripts and how one decides what to do with it. Which leads to a central concern, Chaucer's "system of versification," where Pearsall takes a position against rigidity. The definition of that system is one many of the authors here re-examine–some supporting what Robert Frost called "loose iambics," some supporting a much tighter and more rigorous description of metrical "laws." As we shall see, the question of rigor is important for an editor (as Tyrwhitt illustrates) in deciding what to emend, and why; it also has some bearing for readers on the question of "hearing" Chaucer, and of defining his "art" as more or less "natural," or more or less "artificial."

It is also helpful that Pearsall's teacherly and scholarly breadth includes a great deal of work in two important parts of English early literary history: the so-called "nativist" traditions of verse, largely alliterative (see Pearsall 1970 and 1977); and post-Chaucer verse, especially Lydgate's (see Pearsall 1970 and 1997), where Chaucerian imitations and echoes, whether knowing or imprecise, can give back instructive if prismatic images of the earlier prosody (the manuscripts are, after all, themselves 15th-century witnesses).

Prosody and the Study of Chaucer: A Generative Reply to Halle & Keyser

Steven R. Guthrie, Agnes Scott College

Guthrie illustrates precisely that kind of more recent student whose study of Chaucerian prosody includes linguistic metrical theory, and he thus updates my preliminary examination in 1976 of generative metrics. Since Halle and Keyser did not specialize in medieval literature, Guthrie can use their approach (a machine he notes that had "one moving part") and modify it in light of his readings of medieval French verse. He will be arguing not so much for relaxation in Chaucer's observation of metrical laws, as for a different perception of their basis, which he takes to be a syllabic measure permissive, or even generative, of (as he puts it) "weak-position ternary rhythmic prominences"–which is to say, anapests. Such a notion would have been abhorrent to Tyrwhitt and Saintsbury, though quite at home within a "nativist" metric like the alliterative long line.

Guthrie's strategy of argument is distantly related to that of Baum 1961, except that the lists Baum includes seem like posies he has gathered from his rambling reading; whereas Guthrie is working his way through 8,110 lines from the Corpus Christi MS of the *Troilus* (Chaucer 1978). But even this is a first step. What he is establishing is the "lightness" of the typical line, and that leads to the reaffirmation of "an iambic foot" within the Chaucerian norm, and, most importantly–after a comparison with the prosody of Shakespeare's sonnets–to the proposition that "Chaucer's stress contour . . . suggests the background presence of the Romance line . . . . He was writing for an audience, himself included, whose ear-training included a powerful exposure to Romance cadences, and who found those cadences pleasing."

In a comparison between possible French (Machaut) or Italian (Boccaccio) models, Guthrie wishes to demonstrate that Chaucer is more like Machaut, although he insists Chaucer does go his own way (he has developed further in this direction in Guthrie 1991 & 1995);[5] but it is interesting to see him taking the phenomenon of the "lightness" of lines and identifying a "cursus" movement in the two authors, in which the "iambic pulse" is temporarily suspended "in favor of a rising rhythm in the major phrase as a whole." This is a suggestive observation, partly because it approaches the linguistic phenomenon of intonation–an extremely difficult feature to get at via historical linguistics (Guthrie's little illustration of a scheme where the lines "build to a crest and then break" actually looks a little like what Bollinger displays in his intonational studies).

Guthrie ends with some observations on the way Chaucer's lines should be realized performatively; the discussion is brief but suggestive, and fits in with the renewed attention to what I will call *literary orality*–not at all an oxymoron in Chaucer, as Guthrie helps show and as we have continued to discover during the last ten years.

Chaucer's *Troilus*: Meter and Grammar

Stephen A. Barney, University of California, Irvine

This is the most detailed and most technical of the essays in this book, and non-specialists (those who are not editors?) might be inclined to pass it by. But it makes a major contribution to a thematic sub-set in this collection, the discussions of Chaucer's verse by scholars who have spent time editing it. In Barney's case, the occasion was his edition (a task, as he explains, that rather fell to him, and then *on* him) of Chaucer's *Troilus and Criseyde* for *The Riverside Chaucer* (Chaucer 1987)–the edition that is probably the most widely used by students today, and that has the most "authority" (if only by virtue of its being quoted most widely) of all extant editions, in or out of print. Six years later Barney published his book of studies, among which this essay is the third chapter, as "partly apologetic, partly reflective, partly corrective, partly argumentative spillings over from that editorial work" (2).

It is important to note, then, that versification was only one of the topics he discussed, for in the transition from theoretical discussions to practical analyses "the art of Chaucer's verse" is taken to include many things besides its rhythms and metrical forms. And this is as it should be (as long as versification does not get edged out altogether), especially as one begins to see how intricately the topic of versification is related, as both Guthrie and Barney illustrate, to grammar, to syntax (not exactly the same things, but close enough). After all, expressive poetic language is an exquisite adjustment between a particular syntactical configuration and a formal structure to highlight, or foreground, a word or phrase–a more than usual emphasis, a more than usual implication: versification is a kind of semantic ordering that depends on *paralanguage*, that "extra stuff" beyond, which is largely the stuff of emotion.

Barney is emphatic that those who believe Chaucer uses (here, in the *Troilus*) "the meter traditionally called iambic pentameter" are *right*– "in fact," he says. "The basic principles of Chaucer's meter were correctly worked out a century and more ago, and should be relied upon by the textual critic." So it would be a useful exercise for any student of verse to watch Barney develop his language and the stages of his argument–to see what passes as "evidence" here, and how it is assembled in the service of what he at one point describes as "precisionist metrics." It is assembled with a personal reflectiveness (with all its intimations of vulnerability and fragility), and yet a careful decisiveness . . . as if we were sitting by a Swiss watchmaker who was talking out loud, really to himself, as he artfully put the cogs and wheels and other pieces of a mechanism together as we watched: which then ticked loudly, and began to keep time. True, it is hard to imagine one's usual introductory class in Chaucer sitting raptly while the question of final *-e* is worked through, line by line, example by example. But there it is: the primal demonstration, at hand, up close. How to learn about the principle of *difficilior lectio* and Occam's razor, all in one practical application.

Well into his discussion, Barney makes an observation that might freeze the blood of the well-intentioned beginner: that, perhaps, "acquiring the grammar, the phonology, and the textual expertise necessary for grasping Chaucer's usage is simply too hard." And his list: "To study Chaucer's sounds requires more or less ample knowledge of a number of things, including Old English, Anglo-Norman, Italian, Latin, paleography, Middle English dialectology, phonology, and accidence, as well as modern linguistic, text-critical, and metrical theory in several languages and profound knowledge of Chaucer's text in all its forms." He is actually criticizing the would-be prosodic critic, not the beginning student, yet is not trying to be hyperbolic: the correct study of Chaucer's versification, as he goes on to demonstrate, involves just about everything–backwards, forwards, and sideways (diachronic and synchronic). If the devil is in the details, so, it would appear, is the angel: it depends how one puts the pieces together. Barney gives us the cogs, the gears, the springs . . . and the working watch.

PART TWO: ESSAYS COMBINING HISTORY, THEORY, AND CLOSE READING

"I kan nat geeste": Chaucer's Artful Alliteration

Richard H. Osberg, Santa Clara University

In commissioning this new essay, I wanted to have interrogated the double life of the prosodic term, *alliteration*–at once, part of the descriptive array of a kind or "school" of late medieval English poetry supposedly so different from Chaucer as to define his prosodic "Other," and yet also a "musical" term describing a feature of color, or texture, or "ornamentation" all poets might display in their craft. It was intriguing to see how seldom the topic was explored with any rigor in discussions of Chaucer versification, and Osberg takes this fact as his beginning. Of course it is important to unriddle the appearance of those two famous alliterating passages which do appear in KnT and LGW, and Osberg treats these passages definitively by reaching back into the cultures of popular poetry, defining the metrical norm of the fourteenth-century poems of the "alliterative revival," and classifying the kinds of poetic register where alliteration was likely to appear in a wide array of types. Because he has worked with the metrics of non-Chaucerian metrical literature like the "Harley lyrics" of MS Harley 2253 (Osberg 1984) and, most recently, of Middle English *Pearl* (Osberg 1996a), Osberg can re-examine Chaucer's practice within a wide, varied, and detailed context. We see in his analytic techniques the blending of linguistic/philological terminology with that kind of close reading often carelessly called "New Critical": it is really a sensuous engagement with the physical body of poetry adjusted to the day-in, day-out requirements of classroom teaching.[6] It thus becomes a model for the process in which a Stylistic (linguistic) examination can begin with counting, classification, and generic and historic comparisons, and modulate, finally, into what in the Eighteenth Century might have been called "Beauties criticism": the demonstration and appreciation of what (Saintsbury smiles) is most fully *there.*

Natural Music in Middle French Verse and Chaucer

James I. Wimsatt, University of Texas

In the book from which this chapter is drawn, Wimsatt is summarizing a lifetime of close reading and scholarly research into the sources and cultural colleagues of Chaucer in France. And he develops most fully a term which he takes from Deschamps, "natural music" (cf. J. Wimsatt 1991a), turning it into a major prosodic category that will define those aspects of Chaucer's versification that are *lyric.* In this, he takes a direction quite different from Osberg or Chickering, and attempts a corrective to the assumption that Chaucer's art of versification is entirely a means of acoustically enhancing a *narrative.* The "music" that Wimsatt finds in the versification he examines has a different origin and a different impulse:

"That the principle of a non-mimetic, non-expressive relationship of the sounds to the verbal meaning applies to the phonetics of the poetic text as well as to any musical notation provided for the text is a main tenet of this study." The "expressive" element that is a reflex of what we might call the prosodic proverb, "the sound must seem an echo to the sense" (it actually derives from Pope), is deliberately being turned on its head. Lyrical versification "expresses" pleasing but abstract sound-patterns, much more literally "musical" than the looser use of the term by sentimental prosodists.

Wimsatt's section, "Natural Music in Machaut's 'Remede' and Chaucer's 'Troilus'," is a tour de force of clearly defined theory carefully applied in close reading. He is careful not to press too far ("of course, much goes beyond the Machauvian mode . . ."), but it is still far enough: Chaucer does not lose his narrative aspects, but he gains a great deal of the lyrical. To say that "despite their narratives both [Machaut's and Chaucer's poems] have fundamental lyricality," is to plant a flag in the heartland of the *Troilus*, and Wimsatt has done his own counting: the *Troilus* is seen to have "fifty-six developed lyric passages, amounting to 1,532 lines (of 8,238) essentially non-narrative." That would amount to more than 18% of the poem.Thus he can analyze the appeal to "ye loveres" in I. 22–51 as "a type of love lyric common in Middle French verse," whose "standard imagery and repetitive conventional diction again make it appropriate to speak of a pattern that matches the abstract design of the phonetics and the grammar."

Not the least of Guthrie's and Wimsatt's contributions is to help us look more closely at the prosody of Machaut, though neither tries to make Chaucer into a copy of Machaut; both are actively aware of the major differences between medieval French and medieval English that shape the versification. It is in such work that the topic of prosody is most fully realized: in comparisons that go beyond source-hunting to explore the unique creative processes of a poet like Chaucer as he translates, "to make his Englissh sweete upon his tonge."

The Joy of Chaucer's Lydgate Lines

Emerson Brown, Jr., Vanderbilt University

Emerson Brown's essay arrives in this gathering after having been out on the road barnstorming, and it seemed appropriate in light of certain themes of our volume not to sandpaper off its accompanying marks of oral delivery. Those road-events utilized the talents (perhaps they are one) of the teacher and the performer, and like so many of our contributors, Brown makes an argument born out of teaching encounters (see his "Diverse Folk Diversely They Teach," in Gibaldi, ed. 1980). Yet it is not simply a matter of its gusto, its memory of good times; there is also in it a kind of transgressive scholarship at work, a carnivalesque attack on those prosodists (headpieces filled with straw, perhaps) who are too tightly buttoned. Here is a *jeu* in outrageosity by one who has often raised his voice on Chaucer Studio tapes (SummT, FranklT, MerchT), but also reasoned at length in a variety of essays on the *Merchant's Tale* (see esp. Brown 1978 & 1979).

Our "symposium" in this anthology is, of course, after the fact; but one can imagine what our authors (if brought together at their ease at the Tabard) might wish to go on to say to each other in the liveliest manner about "loose" and "strict" iambics, about correctness and laxness in metrics and prosodic realizations.

The so-called "Lydgate line" is problematic not only for its failure to alternate stressed and unstressed syllables, but also for losing a syllable altogether at an awkward moment. And yet there are such lines–not a great many of them–where the manuscript witnesses give no authority for emendation, and the precisionists must fall back on their faith that Chaucer would not so deliberately break the metrical rules. On the other hand, there are any number of lines in Chaucer with fillers and/or word orders that provide exactly that norm of alternating stresses; which is to say, that his practice seems generally to avoid the "broken-backed" line. All the more reason, then, to puzzle over the meaning of those instances where his practice does not. To some editors, it is simply a matter of letting the roughness ride, as either an instance of Chaucer being a bit lax, or of following a norm more elastic than some would accept. But to Brown, these instances are part of "the delight in the unexpected that is so much a part of medieval life." And it seems that many of them are that kind of surprise that startles the reader/hearer into awareness–a feature, if you will, that calls for us to look even as it stumbles before us. It's all part of the rhythmic idiolect of a master: *it don't mean a thing if it ain't got that swing*. It might be relevant to note that Emerson Brown is also a semi-professional jazz clarinetist.

Scansion is a word and a practice that, along with old words from fusty days like "parse," is not likely to find favor now with student or teacher. Yet used well in prosodic studies, a scansion serves as the visual surrogate for a vocal rendition or realization, encouraging that kind of close-reading that is also close-imagining and close-hearing. Brown is an elegant demonstrator-performer with that instrument, too.

PART THREE: **ESSAYS ON PROSODIC PRACTICES**

Theme, Prosody, and Mimesis in the *Book of the Duchess*
Winthrop Wetherbee, Cornell University

He has translated Latin works (see Wetherbee 1973), and written on Chaucer and the *poets* (Wetherbee 1984, a book about the *Troilus*), but this is the first time Wetherbee has written specifically about matters of versification–the hope is that his example will encourage many others who, like him, have been dealing for years with matters of versification in their classrooms, and have much they could say to us.

In dealing with the *Book of the Duchess,* Wetherbee is in the category of Chaucer's early, very nearly his earliest, verse, but that fact is not the center of his concern, even though he is willing to offer, in passing, some agnostic remarks about influence and independence as far as French "sources" are concerned. His focus, however, is on prosodic behavior–the particular movements and developing phonological texture of the poem as it supports and expresses the theme(s).

In taking seriously the prosody of the *Book of the Duchess,* even though it is normally judged an early work, Wetherbee either ignores the descriptive notion of a beginner-poet or captures and re-defines it. Seizing upon the portentous phrase, "a maner song,/ Withoute noote, withoute song" (that is, "a kind of song, but with neither singing nor music"), he shows us a young poet who is going to experiment with the relation between movement and meaning in a way quite different from his continental models/sources.

Many of the effects Wetherbee discusses, especially "pacing, enjambment, and the use of hypermetrical lines," are considered for the large part to be "subliminal"; that is, they contribute to the emotional force and thematic structure of the poem without calling attention to themselves. Certainly the dreamer-narrative is not aware of them. But what about the reader? Here we touch upon an important issue in prosodic "close reading": are we describing elements readers will notice and are expected to take specific pleasure in? Probably not, although most prosodic critics will be able to name certain instances–for example, "Therefore he loved gold in special," A444–where a kind of foregrounding is apparent, even if one avoid technical nomenclature and speak of the line's dexterity, its brilliant placement, the devastating irony of the feminine-rime, "speciál."

In Wetherbee's analysis, at any rate, there can be no doubt as to Chaucer's awareness of the behavior of his versification: the Chaucerian prosody is found to be "conscious, intricate, and carefully adapted to the representation of the delicate psychological process the poem describes." How this works can be seen particularly well in Wetherbee's treatment of the poem's "more or less obsessive energy" that "overflows from one line into another." His definition of enjambment is nicely to the purpose: "the isolation at the beginning of one line of a striking word or short phrase that bears a close syntactic relation to the previous line"; it helps keep the focus, not on the metrical peculiarity, but on the syntactical-semantic positioning of words, phrases, and lines. It is a kind of energy, in such details, that works against the inherited conventions of poem-making and lyric forms. In Wetherbee's words, these details amount to "calculated gestures, ways of calling attention to an underlying existential level of experience which the poem's rhetoric and conventions tend to obscure." The overall achievement is a "generous prosody," in which, finally, "prosody and therapy have become as nearly as possible one and the same."

The Making of ***Troilus and Criseyde***
David Wallace, University of Pennsylvania

Because Wallace is one of the few scholars to deal with Italian authors of the Trecento not at arm's length but inside the very language of their works, and because he has mastered both late-medieval Italian history and the forms, styles, and developments of Italian verse, his essay here, a chapter from his *Chaucer and the Early Writings of Boccaccio*, will have great and basic value for any student of Chaucer wanting to broaden an understanding of his "Italian period." In addition, there is a strong theme that organizes part of Wallace's argument which deals with the versification of Boccaccio's eight-line stanza, *ottava rima*, compares it tellingly with the poetry of Dante, and shows how Chaucer responded, imitated, and adapted what he found in the *Filostrato*. Thus the theme of "translation" as it relates to versification gets another treatment, and we are brought now to consider things Italian as we earlier had considered things French.

A good deal of the early discussion is designed to illustrate how well Chaucer understood the Italian poetry he was translating, and the concentration is on word, phrase, and idiom. In fact, it would seem that Chaucer made a rather deliberate choice in using Boccaccio as a narrative source a good deal more than a poetic: "Chaucer's imagination rarely seems to have been swayed simply by the rhythms of Boccaccio's verse." This is the sub-theme to follow, worked out over the course of the essay. And here, quite appropriately, Chaucer is discovered as deliberately avoiding "prose" as Wallace formulates the response: "the extraordinary counterpointing of syntax against meter which generates or is generated by the distinctive prose-like movement of [Boccaccio's] verse . . . caused Chaucer considerable misgivings."

There will be many illustrations of the movement of the verse within the two poets' stanzas. The long and the short of it is Wallace's description of Boccaccian prosody as that of a relative beginner in contrast to that of the more experienced Chaucer. Much of the "prose-like movements" in Boccaccio will be discovered to be a consequence of enjambment and cesuras: there is an intuitive point where syntax that overruns line endings too often can seem to obliterate the vessel of (perceivable) form. One has, then, prose by default (realizing that "prose" elsewhere can be artfully written–considerably more than, other than, poetic incompetence).

Wallace will take one step further, in thematizing the concept of prose. He observes that, "for a more sophisticated, first-hand understanding of *curteisie* and for standards of versification which might attest to such understanding" Chaucer turned to Dante and the French poets: "The *Filostrato's* imperfect control of courtly terminology complements its imperfect versification: both imperfections attest to a lack of *mesure*. . . ." (135). It is a brilliant and suggestive formulation, and deserves to provoke other studies along the same lines.

Chaucer's Witty Prosody in the General Prologue
Charles A. Owen, Jr. (1914–1998)

It is good to have been able to commission a work from "the Dean of modern prosodic studies," one which sums up, clarifies, and extends further the series of essays over the last 33 years that Owen has been producing on Chaucer's prosodic wit. No one has ever looked so closely at the versification of the General Prologue, and with such particular and knowledgeable attention to its extraordinary prosodic vitality. But here is another point about "close reading": if an approach to poetry's effects is to be called, loosely, "New Critical" for its ingenuity in discovering that "every little movement has a meaning of its own," that every molecule of a piece of poetry trembles with implicitness, vibrates with nuance, dances within its binary ironies of yes-and-no . . . then Owen's approach is not New Critical. His subject, indeed, is wit, but he reminds us that this is not a synonym for every moment in the poetry: "In much of his poetry [Chaucer] was not trying for special effect, simply for a sense of measured, not monotonous language. This sense gave the special prosodic effect when it did occur the impact of surprise, of wit."

As his argument proceeds, it will be noted that, in a different emphasis from those who hold for "precisionist metrics," Owen will stress Chaucer's sense of prosodic adventure–his experimentation, and his challenging the reader with the surprises of his wit (these, of course, calibrated in their intensity: one could imagine a Wit-Scale ranging from a quiet *Ah there, Chaucer*, at a certain point, to an involuntary exclamation . . . or just a silent putting of the book down and staring into space for a moment). Now it may appear, once he gets started in earnest, that we are back to DayGlo prosody, where every nubble shines in the dark; but there is a distinction always operative between the elements of craft that are there, but not normally to be noticed, and the elements of craft that are witty (for an extreme demonstration of this distinction compare his almost-but-not-quite-nonplussed reading of the Knight's Yeoman with his discussion of the wit-saturated portrait of the Prioress). It is just that in this once-for-all examination, one finds elements both of the taxonomic inventory, and the phenomenological itinerary: one is pulling out drawers and opening the doors of the Cabinet of Wonders, even as one is making one's way steadily from entrance to egress.

By now, if one has been reading all the essays in order, it will seem very natural that Owen is attentive to the varying, sometimes conflicting, witness of the manuscripts; it is a separate area of his continuing researches that are here integrated with the tasks of prosody (see esp. Owen 1991, and his three essays on Chaucer's manuscripts that are listed there). These represent his grounding (if that is the right word for such a shifty/shifting thing) in textual reality; and he proceeds through many more levels of particularity, each with its appropriate terminology and applications. Many thumbs are put in; many plums are pulled out. The General Prologue becomes an extravagant Christmas pudding, so filled with nuts and fruits and other tasty things, that one fears repletion (I suspect that the essay will need to be used in segments, or revisited at intervals).

Yet the essay is not simply a demonstration of the intensely considered detail; we must substitute for the plum-pudding the image of a mosaic, for these details are always being disassembled from a pattern whose brilliance becomes clearer as we put the pieces back. And Owen attends to the putting-back: his architectonic concerns are continuous and come to the fore as he examines that part of the Prologue that follows the portraits. At his conclusion, structural analysis becomes thematic, as he rounds off his discussion with an elegant two-part movement: first, the end comes around to the beginning, as Chaucer's apology becomes a virtual paraphrase of the art of versification, invoking "the cousinship of words and deed." This can have the specific meaning of onomatopoeia; or it can extend to the subject of this essay, the many ways in which "'Everich a word' can by sound, rhythm, grammar, rhetoric more fully 'telle the tale'"; second, the art is seen as "enabling" Chaucer's continued experimentation in the subsequent tales precisely because our readerly attentions have been so challenged, so stimulated, and so gratified–the ending is not a closing but an opening; we are not finished, the Tales will not be completed, Chaucer will not live to put everything together. Nor, God love him, will Charles Abraham Owen, Jr.

Comic Meter in the ***Miller's Tale***
Howell Chickering, Amherst College

How could we not have an essay of prosodic analysis of the *Miller's Tale*, so full of life that it practically jumps off the page? The challenge here would seem to consist in describing what's funny without making a fool of oneself; but Chickering has devised the central question that allows close analysis to partake in the general play. For he asks, could this be just as amusing if it were in prose ? (Which of course is how most critics have handled it.) And he asserts his fundamental prosodic axiom: "In the hands of a good poet, form is less a limitation than an energizing opportunity to make meanings that wouldn't be there in prose."

His essay gives us a chance to see how his particular interest in the witness of manuscripts can work; that is, he believes in "unpunctuating Chaucer" (see Chickering 1990), and suggests that in so doing we come to stand at the same starting point as the medieval reader, who almost never would find punctuation in a manuscript's text. It is actually a penchant that rises as much from the classroom as the study, and reminds us that, just as we have an emendation (group plural) of editors among these essays, so also do we have a tasting of teachers, who have developed many of their convictions about Chaucer's verse by reading him aloud with their students (we are given a further glimpse into his and his colleagues' classrooms, with special attention to the virtues of assigned memorization, in Chickering 1998).

I have been compiling a list of Chaucerian lines and sequences that every prosodic critic should have to deal with before receiving their license; one of these is surely

> And seyde fy allas what have I do
> Te hee quod she and clapte the wyndow to

In which case, Chickering not only gets his license but a certificate of commendation.

The Nun's Priest's Tale
Stephen Knight, University of Wales, Cardiff

Knight, whose essay is, comparatively speaking, fairly early, has the distinction of being the dove who returns to the Ark: after him, things began to flourish. (Although it must be said, for all of his complaint that few have been paying attention to the "mechanics" of the poem, that 25 years later the situation is still about the same, even though the bibliography on the tale has burgeoned. Some crops are slow to ripen.) He is significant for integrating a topic that had newly come to prominence, situated between Stylistics and New Criticism, for Rhetoric as a formal subject had always made some critics nervous, precisely because it seemed "mechanical," formulaic, not to have drunk deeply at Poetry's well. Yet within medieval studies, it was imperative to study this product of formal training in the schools, with its ramifications into preaching, Law, and certain types of poetry. And Knight brings the topic all the way home by including rhetorical considerations within his overall review of the versification.

It may be rather less easy to see in this essay (the final chapter in his book), but he also maintains a position, or a distinction, with regard to his analytic method and that of (linguistic) Stylistics (the issue is addressed directly in his Introduction). He defends his mode of discourse, which comes out of the classroom and university lecturing, even though it might seem impressionistic and incomplete: "One of the results of the linguist's concern with total and objective description is that when linguists use their techniques to move toward literary criticism they seem to achieve little" (p. xv). Whether or not this is still true today, here is not the place to inquire; in Knight's essay, however, we see a discursive method that moves through the poem, quoting a good deal, not offering dissection or extended analysis, but rather a few observations that are appropriate for each passage. It is a method related to what Owen and Chickering are doing, but with fewer extreme close-ups. Not a single line is marked out for scansion, yet his responses are full of remarks on the effects of the prosody (e.g., "The pauses and the varying rhythms of the lines help to create the colloquial effect"; and so forth)–one wishes a recording of his reading of the passages could have been included, to complete his demonstrations (there is even one place where he says to his readers, "If you read the passage aloud, etc."–the next best thing to hearing him say it).

Some readers of this essay, especially those in the throes of the Tales's critical bibliography for the last twenty-five years, may wish a heavier conclusion or a louder, may hope to see The Meaning of Everything Explained, especially since there seems to be a consensus (50.01 percent of all readers) that this may be the Tale that deserves the dinner, so should it not have not only Great Lines but Great Meanings? But observe two things about Knight's method: one, is that he wishes to open not close, to advance discussion not cut it off, and to invigorate further encounters with the poem; two, is that the aim is enjoyment as a form of edification. He does, however, have a position on the poem, he finds it a piece written in a "holiday" mood, one that is supremely playful: "I cannot see that this play anywhere has an implicitly moral side, except to warn us not to take ourselves too seriously." Let the prosodists take such a conclusion to heart! Whereas Knight exhibits an approach to versification which aims at the measure of mirth. And vice versa.

NOTES

[1]From an essay on Tennyson in *Corrected Impressions*; cited in Priestly 1924, 149.
[2]The plagiarist, a notorious one, was publisher John Bell, who included "Chaucer's Works" (T.'s edition) as the first 14 volumes of a 109-volume set of *The Poets of Great Britain from Chaucer to Churchill.* For an account of that plagiarism, and Tyrwhitt's angry but resigned response in a letter to *Gentleman's Magazine* (June 1783), see Muscatine 1963, 50. One of the best, and most measured, assessments of Tyrwhitt's achievements as an editor remains Hammond 1908, especially 206–10. She lists all the editions before Skeat that used his material and his name, and those that used the material without attribution (206).
[3]Tyrwhitt identified the MSS. he "collated, or consulted," and Windeatt lists them, indicating the five he seems regularly to have collated–"these were the best manuscripts available to him" (Windeatt 1984, 122–4). I note that of the ten fifteenth-c. manuscripts for collations provided in editions from the Chaucer Variorum, only two–Cambridge University Dd.4.24 and British Library Lansdowne 851–were among Tyrwhitt's regular collations.
[4] J.B. Priestly has written a fine appreciation of Saintsbury, including some words on the Saintsbury style that deserve to be quoted: "The two most characteristic features of his style are, of course, his extraordinary use of parenthesis, clause within clause like the carven globes in the Oriental toys, and his uncommon use of literary allusion. . . . His parenthetic manner is simply the result of a full mind, anxious to leave nothing unsaid on the subject in hand, working with little space at its command. . . . Mr. George Saintsbury, the enthusiastic lover of letters, begins the sentence with a smashing hyperbole, but is immediately checked by Professor Saintsbury, the scholar, who points out some exception, a reservation, or what not; the enthusiast promptly shakes off his interrupter, and gives a side-cut at those for whom it should be necessary to state such reservations, etc.; so the scholar immediately hints that there is something to be said for them; and so it goes on" (Priestly 1924, 148).
[5]An interesting development not apparent in the present essay is adumbrated at the end of Guthrie's essay in "Meter and Performance in Machaut and Chaucer" (Baltzer 1991); I quote from it here to indicate how his metrical ideas have continued to develop, and to point towards his creative use of some Bakhtinian approaches in his latest (1995) prosodic essay: "From one perspective, then, the French rhythmic effects were Chaucer's way of hedging his bets. From another, they were simply a part of the process of translation. From yet another, which is beyond the scope of this paper, they were part of a dialogic, complication-abrogation relationship with his sources that he never resolved and that contributed an enriching tension to all of his work" (94).
[6]Osberg, himself both a poet and an editor, has the additional advantage of having produced a *Sir Gawain and the Green Knight* for classroom use: a facing-page edition with a new text and a modern translation in (alliterative) verse (Osberg 1990).

Part One:
Historical and Theoretical Essays

Thomas Tyrwhitt

Essay on the Language and Versification of Chaucer. Part the Third*

Before we proceed in the third and last part of this Essay, in which we are to consider the Versification of Chaucer, it may be useful to premise a few observations upon the state of English Poetry antecedent to his time.

§ I. That the Saxons had a species of writing, which differed from their common prose, and was considered by themselves as Poetry (39), is very certain; but it seems equally certain, that their compositions of that kind were neither divided into verses of a determinate number of syllables, nor embellished with what we call Rime (40). There are no traces, I believe, to found of either Rime or Metre in our language, till some years after the Conquest; so that I should apprehend we must have been obliged for both to the Normans, who very early (41) distinguished themselves by poetical performances in their Vulgar tongue.

The Metres which they used, and which we seem to have borrowed from them, were plainly copied from the Latin (42) rythmical verses, which, in the declension of that language, were current in various forms among those, who either did not understand, or did not regard, the true quantity of syllables; and the practice of Riming (43) is probably to be deduced from the same original, as we find that practice to have prevailed in Ecclesiastical Hymns, and other compositions, in Latin, some centuries before Otfrid of Weissenberg, the first known Rimer in any of the vu1gar European dialects.

§ II. I wish it were in my power to give a regular history of the progress which our Ancestors made in this new style of versification; but (44), except a few lines in the Saxon Chronicle upon the death of William the Conquerour, which seem to have been intended for verses of the Modern fashion, and a short Canticle, which, according to Matthew Paris (45), the blessed Virgin was pleased to dictate to Godric, an Hermite near Durham, I have not been able to discover any attempts at Riming Poetry, which can with probability be referred to an earlier period than the reign of Henry the second. In that reign Layamon (46), a Priest of Ernleye near Severn, as he calls himself, translated (chiefly) from the French of Wace (47), a fabulous history of the Britons, entitled "Le Brut," which Wace himself, about the year 1155, had translated from the Latin of Geffrey of Monmouth. Though the greatest part of this work of Layamon resemble the old Saxon Poetry, without Rime or metre, yet he often intermixes a number of short verses, of unequal lengths but riming together pretty exactly, and in some places he has imitated not unsuccessfully the regular octosyllable measure of his French original.

§ III. It may seem extraordinary, after these proofs, that the art of Riming was not unknown or unpractised in this country in the time of Henry II, that we should be obliged to search through a space of above an hundred years, without being able to meet with a single maker of English Rimes, whom we know to have written in that interval. The case I suspect to have been this. The scholars of that age (and there were many who might fairly be called so, in the English dominions abroad [48] as well as at home) affected to write only (49) in Latin, so that we do not find that they ever composed, in verse or prose, in any other language. On the other hand they, who meant to recommend themselves by their Poetry to the favour of the great, took care to write in French, the only language which their patrons understood; and hence it is, that we see so many French poems (50), about that time, either addressed directly to the principal persons at the English court, or at least written on such subjects as we may suppose to have been most likely to engage their attention. Whatever therefore of English Poetry was produced, in this infancy of the art, being probably the work of illiterate authors and circulating only among the the vulgar (51), we need not be much surprised that no more of it has been transmitted down to posterity.

§ IV. The learned Hickes, however, has pointed out to us two very curious pieces, which may with probability be referred to this period. The first of them is a Paraphrase of the Gospel Histories, entitled *Ormulum* (52), by one *Orm*, or *Ormin*. It seems to have been considered as mere Prose by Hickes and by Wanley, who have both given large extracts from it; but, I apprehend, every reader, who has an ear for metre, will easily perceive that it is written very exactly in verses of fifteen syllables, without Rime, in imitation of the most common species of the Latin Tetrameter Iambic. The other piece (53), which is a moral Poem upon old age, &c. is in Rime, and in a metre much resembling the former, except that the verse of fifteen syllables is broken into two, of which the first should regularly contain eight and the second seven syllables; but the metre is not so exactly observed, at least in the copy which Hickes has followed, as it is in the *Ormulum*.

§ V. In the next interval, from the latter end of the reign of Henry III, to the middle of the fourteenth century, when we may suppose Chaucer was beginning to write, the number of English Rimers seems to have increased very much. Besides several, whose names we know (54), it is probable that a great part of the anonymous Authors, or rather Translators (55), of the popular Poems, which (from their having been originally written in the Roman, or French, language) were called Romances, flourished about this time. It is unnecessary to enter into particulars here concerning any of them, as they do not appear to have invented, or imported from abroad, any new modes of Versification, by which the Art coud be at all advanced (56), or even to have improved those which were before in use. On the contrary, as their works were intended for the ear more than for the eye, to be recited rather than read, they were apt to be more attentive to their Rimes than to the exactness of their Metres, from a presumption, I suppose, that the defect, or redundance, of a syllable might be easily covered in the recitation, especially if accompanied, as it often was, by some musical instrument.

§ VI. Such was, in general, the state of English Poetry at the time when Chaucer probably made his first essays. The use of Rime was established; not exclusively (for the Author of the "Visions of Pierce Ploughman" wrote after the year 1350 (57) without Rime,) but very generally; so that in this respect he had little to do but to imitate his predecessors. The Metrical part of our Poetry was capable of more improvement, by the polishing of the measures already in use as well as by the introducing of new modes of versification; and how far Chaucer actually contributed to the improvement of it, in both or either of these particulars, we are now to consider.

§ VII. With respect to the regular Metres than in use, they may be reduced, I think, to four. First, the long Iambic Metre (58), consisting of not more than fifteen, nor less than fourteen syllables, and broken by a *Cæsura* at the eighth syllable. Secondly, the Alexandrin Metre (59), consisting of not more than thirteen syllables, nor less than twelve, with a *Cæsura* at the sixth. Thirdly, the Octosyllable Metre; which was in reality the antient Dimeter Iambic. Fourthly, the Stanza of six verses; of which the first, second, fourth, and fifth, were in the complete Octosyllable Metre; and the third and last catalectic, *i.e.* wanting a syllable, or even two.

§ VIII. In the first of these Metres it does not appear that Chaucer ever composed at all, (for, I presume, no one can imagine that he was the author of Gamelyn,) or in the second; and in the fourth we have nothing of his but the Rime of Sire Thopas, which, being intended to ridicule the vulgar Romancers, seems to have been purposely written in their favourite Metre. In the third, or Octosyllable Metre (60), he has left several compositions; particularly, "an imperfect Translation of the *Roman de la Rose,"* which was, probably, one of his earliest performances; "the House of Fame;" "the Dethe of the Duchesse Blanche," and a poem called his "Dreme": upon all which it will be sufficient here to observe in general, that, if he had given no other proofs of his poetical faculty, these alone must have secured to him the pre-eminence, above all his predecessors and contemporaries, in point of Versification.

§ IX. But by far the most considerable part of Chaucer's works is written in that kind of Metre which we now call the Heroic (61), either in Distichs or in Stanzas; and as I have not been able to discover any instance of this metre being used by any English poet before him, I am much inclined to suppose that he was the first introducer of it into our language. It had long been practised in France, in the Northern as well as the Southern provinces; and in Italy, within the last fifty years before Chaucer wrote, it had been cultivated with the greatest assiduity and success, in preference to every other metre, by Dante, Petrarch, and Boccace. When we reflect that two of Chaucer's juvenile productions, the Palamon and Arcite, and the Troilus, were in a manner translated from the *Theseida* and the *Filostrato* of Boccace (62), both written in the common Italian hendecasyllable verse, it cannot but appear extremely probable that his metre also was copied from the same original; and yet I cannot find that the form of his Stanza in the Troilus, consisting of seven verses, was ever used by Boccace, though it is to be met with among the poems of the King of Navarre, and of the *Provencal* Rimers (63). Whichever he shall be supposed to have followed, whether the French or Italians, it is certain that he coud not want in either language a number of models of correct and harmonious versification; and the only question will be, whether he had ability and industry enough to imitate that part of their excellency.

§ X. In discussing this question we should always have in mind, that the correctness and harmony of an English verse depends entirely upon its being composed of a certain number of syllables, and its having the accents of those syllables properly placed. In order therefore to form any judgement of the Versification of Chaucer, it is necessary that we should know the syllabical value, if I may use the expression, of his words, and the accentual value of his syllables, as they were commonly pronounced (64) in his time; for without that knowledge, it is not more probable that we should determine justly upon the exactness of his metres, than that we should be able to cast up rightly an account stated in coins of a former age, of whose current rates and denominations we are totally ignorant.

§ XI. Let us consider a moment, how a sensible critic in the Augustan age would have proceeded, if called upon to examine a work of Ennius (65). When he found that a great proportion of the verses were strictly conformable to the ordinary rules of Metre, he would, probably, not scruple to conclude that such a conformity must have been produced by art and design, and not by mere chance. On the other hand, when he found, that in some verses the number of feet, to appearance, was either deficient or redundant; that in others the feet were seemingly composed of too few or too many syllables, of short syllables in the place of long, or of long in the place of short; he would not, I think, immediately condemn the old Bard, as having all at once forgotten the fundamental principles of his art, or as having wilfully or negligently deviated from them. He would first, I presume, enquire, whether all these irregularities were in the genuine text of his author, or only the mistakes of Copyists: he would enquire further, by comparing the genuine text with other contemporary writings and monuments, whether many things, which appeared irregular, were not in truth sufficiently regular, either justified by the constant practice, or excused by the allowed licence of the age: where authority failed, he would have recourse, but soberly, to etymology and analogy; and if after all a few passages remained, not reducible to the strict laws of Metre by any of the methods above-mentioned, if he were really (as I have supposed him) a sensible critic, he would be apt rather to expect patiently the solution of his difficulties from more correct manuscripts, or a more complete theory of his author's versification, than to cut the knot, by deciding peremptorily, that the work was composed without any regard to metrical rules.

§ XII. I beg leave to pursue the same course with respect to Chaucer. The great number of verses, sounding complete even to our ears, which is to be found in all the least corrected copies of his works, authorises us to conclude, that he was not ignorant of the laws of metre. Upon this conclusion it is impossible not to ground a strong presumption, that he intended to observe the same laws in the many other verses which seem to us irregular; and if this was really his intention, what reason can be assigned sufficient to account for his having failed so grossly and repeatedly, as is generally supposed, in an operation, which every Balladmonger in our days, man, woman, or child, is known to perform with the most unerring exactness, and without any extraordinary fatigue?

§ XIII. The offences against metre in an English verse, as has partly been observed before, must arise either from a superfluity or deficiency of syllables, or from the accents being improperly placed.

§ XIV. With respect to the first species of irregularity, I have not taken notice of any superfluities in Chaucer's verses, but what may be reduced to just measure by the usual practices (66) of even modern Poets. And this, by the way, is a strong proof of his real attention to metrical rules; for otherwise, if he had written without any restraint of that kind, a certain proportion of his deviations from measure must, in all probability, have been on the side of excess.

§ XV. But a great number of Chaucer's verses labour under an apparent deficiency of a syllable, or two. In some of these perhaps the defect may still be supplied from MSS. but for the greatest part I am persuaded no such assistance is to be expected (67); and therefore, supposing the text in these cases to be correct, it is worth considering whether the verse also may not be made correct, by adopting in certain words a pronunciation, different indeed from modern practice, but which, we have reason to believe, was used by the author himself.

For instance, in the Genitive case Singular and the Plural Number of Nouns (which, as has been remarked above, in the time of Chaucer had the same expression), there can be no doubt that such words as, shoures, ver. 1. *croppes,* ver. 7. *shires,* ver. 15. *lordes,* ver. 47, &c. were regularly pronounced as consisting of two syllables. Whenever they are used as monosyllables, it must be considered as a Poetical Licence, warranted however even then (as we may presume from the natural progress of our language) by the practice of inaccurate speakers in common conversation.

In like manner, we may be sure that *ed,* the regular termination of the Past Tense and its Participle, made, or contributed to make, a second syllable in the words, *perced,* ver. 2. *bathed,* ver. 3. *loved,* ver. 45. *wered,* ver. 75, &c. (68) The first step toward reducing words of this form to Monosyllables seems to have been to shorten the last syllable, either by transposing the final letters, as in–*wolde,* ver. 144. *saide,* ver. 763. &c. or by throwing away the *d,* as in–*coste,* ver. 1910. *caste,* ver. 2083, &c. In both these cases the words still remained of two syllables, the final *e* being sounded as an *e* feminine; but they were prepared to lose their last syllable by the easy licence of changing an *e* feminine into an *e* mute, or of dropping it entirely, according to the modern practice.

§ XVI. But nothing will be found of such extensive use for supplying the deficiencies of Chaucer's metre as the pronunciation of the *e* feminine; and as that pronunciation has been for a long time totally antiquated, it may be proper here to suggest some reasons for believing (independently of any arguments to be drawn from the practice of Chaucer himself) that the final *e* in our antient language was very generally pronounced, as the *e* feminine is at this day by the French.

With respect to words imported directly from France, it is certainly quite natural to suppose, that, for some time, they retained their native pronunciation; whether they were Nouns substantive, as, *hoste,* ver. 753. *face,* ver. 1580, &c.–or Adjectives, as, *large,* ver. 755. *strange,* ver. 13, &c.–or Verbs, as, *grante,* ver. 12756. *preche,* ver. 12327, &c. and it cannot be doubted, that in these and other similar words in the French language, the final *e* was always pronounced, as it still is, so as to make them dissyllables.

We have not indeed so clear a proof of the original pronunciation of the Saxon part (69) of our language; but we know, from general observation, that all changes of pronunciation are usually made by small degrees; and therefore, when we find that a great number of those words, which in Chaucer's time ended in *e,* originally ended in *a,* we may reasonably presume, that our ancestors first passed from the broader sound of *a* to the thinner sound of *e* feminine, and not at once from *a* to *e* mute. Besides, if the final *e* in such words was not pronounced, why was it added? From the time that it has confessedly ceased to be pronounced it has been gradually omitted in them, except where it may be supposed of use to lengthen or soften (70) the preceding syllable, as in–*hope, name,* &c. But according to the ancient orthography it terminates many words of Saxon original, where it cannot have been added for any such purpose, as, *herte, childe, olde, wilde,* &c. In these therefore we must suppose that it was pronounced as an *e* feminine, and made part of a second syllable; and so, by a parity of reason, in all others, in which, as in these, it appears to have been substituted for the Saxon *a.*

Upon the same grounds we may presume, that in words terminated, according to the Saxon form, in *en,* such as the Infinitive modes and Plural numbers of Verbs, and a great variety of Adverbs and Prepositions, the *n* only was at first thrown away, and the *e,* which then became final, continued for a long time to be pronounced as well as written.

These considerations seem sufficient to make us believe, that the pronunciation of the *e* feminine is founded on the very nature of both the French and Saxon parts of our language; and therefore, though we may not be able to trace the reasons of that pronunciation in all cases so plainly as in those which have been just mentioned, we may safely, I think, conclude with the learned Wallis (71), that what is generally considered as an *e* mute in our language, either at the end or in the middle of words (72), was antiently pronounced, but obscurely, like the *e* feminine of the French.

§ XVII. The third kind of irregularity, to which an English verse is liable, is from the accents being misplaced. The restoring of Chaucer's words to their just number of syllables, by the methods which have been pointed out above, will often be of signal service in restoring his accents also to their proper places; but further, in many words, we must be cautious of concluding too hastily that Chaucer accented the same syllables that we do. On the contrary, I am persuaded that in his French words he most commonly laid his accent according to the French custom (upon the *last* syllable, or the *last but one* in words ending in *e* feminine), which, as is well known, is the very reverse of our practice. Thus in ver. 3. he uses *licoúr* for *líquour;* ver. 11. *coráges* for *coúrages;* ver. 22. again, *coráge* for *coúrage;* ver. 37. *resón* for *réason;* ver. 77. *viáge* for *vóyage;* ver. 109, 10. *viságe–uságe* for *vísage–úsage;* ver. 14o. *manére* for *mánner;* ver. 186. *laboúre* for *lábour;* ver. 204. *prelát* for *prélate;* ver. 211. *langáge* for *lánguage;* ver. 212. *mariáge* for *márriage;* ver. 216. *contrée* for *coúntry;* and so through the whole work.

In the same manner he accents the last Syllable of the Participle Present, as, ver. 885, 6. *weddíng–comíng* for *wédding–cóming;* ver. 903. *livíng* for *líving;* ver. 907, 8. *comíng–cryíng* for *cóming–crýing;* ver. 998. *brenníng* for *brénning,* &c. and as he does this in words of Saxon as well as of French growth, I should suppose that the old Participle of the present tense, ending in *and,* was originally accented upon that syllable, as it certainly continued to be by the Scottish Poets a long time after Chaucer. See Bp. [Gavin] Douglas, Virgil p. 18. ver. 18. Sprynggánd; ver. 51. Beránd; p. 27. ver. 49. Fleánd; p. 29. ver. 10. Seánd.

These instances are all taken from the Riming syllables (where a strong accent is indispensably necesary) in order to prove beyond contradiction, that Chaucer frequently accented his words in the French manner. But if he followed this practice at the end of his verses, it is more than probable that he did the same in the middle, whenever it gave a more harmonious flow to his metre; and therefore in ver. 4. instead of *vértue,* I suppose he pronounced, *vertúe;* in ver. 11. instead of *náture, natúre;* in ver. 25. instead of *avénture, aventúre;* in ver. 46. instead of *hónour, honoúr,* &c.

It may be proper however to observe, that we are not to expect from Chaucer that regularity in the disposition of his accents, which the practice of our greatest Poets in the last and the present century has taught us to consider as essential to harmonious (73) versification. None of his masters, either French or Italian, had set him a pattern of exactness (74) in this respect; and it is rather surprising, that, without rule or example to guide him, he has so seldom failed to place his accents in such a manner, as to produce the cadence best suited to the nature of his verse.

§ XVIII. I shall conclude this long and (I fear) tedious Essay, with a Grammatical and Metrical Analysis of the first eighteen lines of the Canterbury Tales. This will afford me an opportunity of illustrating at once a considerable part of that Theory, which I have ventured to propose in the preceding pages, with regard to the Language and Versification of Chaucer. The remainder I shall take occasion to explain in a few notes upon particular passages.

* * * * *

THE BEGINNING OF THE CANTERBURY TALES.

I. (1)*Whánne* that Ápril with his (2)*shoúres* (3)*sóte*
II. The droúghte of Márch hath (1)*pérced tó the* (2)*róte,*
III. And (1)*báthed* évery véine in (2)*swíche* (3)*licoúr,*
IV. Of whíche (1)*vertúe* engéndred ís the floúr;
V. Whan Zéphirús eke wíth his (1)*sóte* bréthe
VI. (1)*Enspíred* háth in évery hólt and héthe
VII. The téndre (1)*cróppes,* and the (2)*yónge* sónne,
VIII. Háth in the Rám his (1) *hálfe* coúrs (2)*yrónne,*
IX. And (1) *smále* (2)*foúles* (3)*máken* mélodíe,
X. That (1)*slépen* (2)*álle* níght with ópen éye,
XI. So príketh (1)*hém* (2)*natúre* in (3)*hír* (4)*coráges;*
XII. Than (1)*lóngen* fólk to (2)*gón* on pílgrimáges,
XIII. And (1)*pálmer'es* fór *to* (2)*séken* (3)*stránge* stróndes,
XIV. To (1)*sérve* (2)*hálwes* (3)*coúthe* in sóndry lóndes;
XV. And spécially̋ from évery (1)*shíres* énde
XVI. Of (1)*Englelónd* to Cánterbúry (2)*they wénde,*
XVII. The hóly blísful mártyr fór to séke,
XVIII. That (1)*hém* hath (2)*hólpen,* whán that théy were (3)*séke.*

COMMENTARY

I. 1. *Whanne,* SAX. Hwænne, is so seldom used as a *Dissyllable* by Chaucer, that for some time I had great doubts about the true reading of this line. I now believe that it is right, as here printed, and that the same word is to be pronounced as a *Dissyllable* in ver. 703.

> But with these relikes whanne that he fond–

Thanne, a word of the same form, occurs more frequently as a *Dissyllable.* See ver. 12260. 12506. 12721. 13924. 15282. 2. Shoures, Dis[syllable]. *Plural number.* See §XV.–3. *Sote.* See ver. V.

II. 1. *Perced,* Dis. *Participle of the Past Time.* See above, § XV.–2. *Rote;* root.

III. I. *Bathed,* Dis. See II. 1.–2. *Swiche,* such; from *Swilke,* SAX.–3. *licoúr,* FR. has the accent upon the *last* syllable, after the French mode.

IV. 1. *Vertúe,* FR. may be accented in the same manner. There is another way of preserving the harmony of this verse, by making *whiche* (from *whilke,* SAX.) a *Dissyllable.* See ver. 1015. 3921. 5488. 6537. *Vertúe* may then be pronounced, as it is now, with the accent on the *first;* the second syllable being incorporated with the first of *engendred.*

V. 1. *Sote, swote, swete;* sweet, Dis. See ver. 3219. 3699. 3724. 3765. 3790.

VI. 1. *Enspired,* Tris. *Part.* of *Past Time.*

VII. 1. *Croppes,* Dis. *Pl. N.* as *shoures.* 1. 2.–2. *Yonge,* Dis. See ver. 213. 666. 1013. 3233, 73. It is used as a *Dissyllable* in the *Ormulum.* Col. 230.

> That wás god bísne fúl i wís till úre *yúnge* génge.

Stronge and *Longe* are pronounced in the same manner. See ver. 2375. 2640, 6. 3069. 3438. 3682.

VIII. I. *Halfe,* or *Halve,* Dis. The original word is Halfen. So *Selve,* from *Selven,* is a *Dissyllable,* ver. 2862. 4535. 2. *Yronne;* Run. *Part. of the Past Time,* with the Saxon prepositive article *ge,* which in the MSS. of Chaucer is universally expressed by *y,* or *i.* In this Edition, for the sake of perspicuity, *y* only is used.

IX. 1. *Smale,* Dis. See ver. 146. 2078. 6897. 10207.–2. *Foules,* Dis. as *Shoures.* 1. 2.–3. *Maken;* make. *Plural Number of the Present Tense.* . . .

X. 1. *Slepen,* as *Maken.* IX. 3.–2. *Alle,* Dis. See ver. 76. 348. 536. 1854. 2102.

XI. 1. *Hem;* Them. It is constantly used so by Chaucer. 2. *Nature* should perhaps be accented on the *last* syllable (or rather the *last but one,* supposing it a *Trisyllable),* after the French manner, though in the present case the verse will be sufficiently harmonious if it be accented on the *first.* That Chaucer did often accent it after the French manner appears from ver. 8778. 9842. 11657. 11945. 12229. In the same manner he accents *Figúre,* ver. 2037. 2045. *Mesúre,* ver. 8132. 8498. *Asúre, Statúre,* ver. 8130, 3. *Peintúre,* ver. 11967. *Aventúre,* ver. 1188. 1237. *Creatúre,* ver. 2397. 4883. and many other words of the same form, derived from the French language.–3. *Hir;* Their. The Possessive Pronoun of the third Person Plural is variously written, *Hir, Hire, Her,* and *Here;* not only in different MSS. but even in the same page of good MSS. There seems to be no reason for perpetuating varieties of this kind, which can only have taken their rise from the unsettled state of our Orthography before the invention of Printing, and which now contribute more than any real alteration of the language to obscure the sense of our old Authors. In this edition, therefore, *Hir* is constantly put to signify *Their;* and *Hire* to signify *Her,* whether it be the Oblique case of the Personal Pronoun *She,* or the Possessive of the same Pronoun.–4. *Corages,* FR. is to be accented on the *Penultima.* See §XVII and also ver. 1947. 2215. To the other instances quoted add, *Avantáge,* ver. 2449. 4566. *Brocáge,* 3375. *Foráge,* ver. 3866. *Lináge,* ver. 4270. 5419. *Serváge,* ver. 1948. 4788. *Costáge,* ver. 5831. *Paráge,* ver. 5832.

XII. 1. *Longen* as *Maken.* IX. 3.–2. *Gon,* Infinitive Mode of *Go,* terminated in *n* according to the Saxon form. . . .

XIII. 1. *Pálmer'es,* Dis. the *e* of the termination being cut out by Syncope, as it generally is in *Plural Nouns* of *three* Syllables, accented upon the *first,* and in the *Past Tenses* and their *Participles of Verbs,* of the same description, ending in *ed.* The reason seems to be, that, where the Accent is placed so early, we cannot pronounce the final syllables fully, without laying more stress upon them, than they can properly bear.–2. *Seken* as *Gon.* XII. 2.–3. *Strange,* Dis. FR. See §XVI.

XIV.1. *Serve,* Dis. from *Serven,* the *n* being thrown away before *h.* See §XVI.–2. *Halwes,* Sax. halghes. The Saxon *[yogh]* is changed into *w,* as *in sorwe, morwe,* and some others; though it generally passes into *y.* The derivatives from this same word afford us instances of both forms; *Holyness, Holyday,* All-*Hallows*-day.–3. *Couthe;* known, *The Participle of the Past Time* from *Connen,* to know. . . .

XV.1. *Shires,* Dis. *Genitive Case Sing.* See §XV.

XVI. 1. *Englelond,* Trisyllable, from the Saxon Englalanda.–The last foot consists of three syllables.

–to Cán | terbúr | y they wénde.

See above, n. 66.

XVIII. 1. *Hem;* Them. See XI. 1.–2. *Holpen,* the *Participle of the Past Time* from the Irregular Verb *Help.* . . . –3. *Seke;* Sick. As Chaucer usually writes this word *Sike,* we may suppose that in this instance he has altered the Orthography in order to make the Rime more exact; a liberty, with which he sometimes indulges himself, though much more sparingly than his contemporary Poets. The Saxon writers afford authorities to justify either method of spelling, as they use both *Deoca* and *Dioca.*

I have hitherto considered these verses as consisting of *ten* syllables only; but it is impossible not to observe, that, according to the rules of pronunciation established above, all of them, except the 3d and 4th, consist really of *eleven* syllables. This is evident at first sight in ver. 11, 12, 13, 14, and might be shewn as clearly, by authority or analogy, in the others; but as the *eleventh* syllable, in our versification, being unaccented, may always, I apprehend, be absent or present without prejudice to the metre, there does not seem to be any necessity for pointing it out in every particular instance.

NOTES

*From "An Essay on His Language and Versification," *The Poetical Works of Geoffrey Chaucer.* 2 vols. Part III. Rpt. with corrections. Oxford: The Clarendon Press, 1798. [Notes 1–38 appeared with parts I and II.]

[39]The account which Beda has given of Cædmon [Eccl. Hist.1. iv. c. 24.] is sufficient to prove this. He repeatedly calls the compositions of Cædmon *carmina–poemata–*and in one place, *versus:* which words in the Saxon translations are rendered, *Leoth,–Leoth songes,* or *songes–*and *vers*: and *ars canendi* is translated, *Leoth cræft* or *sang cræft.*

Asser also, in his Life of Alfred, speaks of *Saxonica poemata* and *Saxonica carmina* [p. 16. 43.] and most probably the *Cantilenæ per successiones temporum detritæ,* which Malmesbury cites in his History, 1. 11. p. 52, were in the Saxon language. The same writer [1. v. de Pontif. edit. Gale.] mentions a *Carmen triviale* of Aldhelm (the author of the Latin Poem *de Virginitate,* who died in 709,) as *adhuc vulgo cantitatum*; and he quotes the testimony of King Alfred, in his *Liber manualis* or *Hand-boc,* as saying, "that no one was ever equal to Aldhelm in English Poetry."

[40]Both these circumstances are evident from the most cursory view of the several specimens of Saxon Poetry, which Hickes has exhibited in his Gram. Ang. Sax. c. xxi. and they are

allowed by that learned writer himself. Unwilling however, as it should seem, to leave his favourite language without some system of versification, he supposes, that the Saxons observed the quantity of syllables in their verses, "though perhaps," he adds, "not so strictly as the Heroic Greek and Latin Poets."

He gives three reasons for this supposition. 1.) Because they did not use Rime. 2.) Because they transposed their words in such an unnatural manner. "Hoc autem cur facerent Anglo-Saxonum Poetæ, nulla, ut videtur, alia assignari causa potest, quam quæ, ut idem facerent, Græcos et Latinos poetas coegit; nempe Metri Lex." 3.) Because they had a great number of dissyllable and polysyllable words, which were fit for metrical feet.

However specious these reasons may appear, they are certainly far from conclusive, even if we had no monuments of Saxon Poetry remaining; but in the present case, I apprehend, the only satisfactory proof would have been to have produced, out of the great heap of Poetical compositions in the Saxon language, some regular metrical verses; that is, some portions of words, similar to each other in the nature and order of their component syllables, and occurring either in a continued series, or at stated intervals. If all external proofs of the nature of the Roman Poetry were lost, a few verses of Virgil or Horace would be sufficient to convince us, that their metres were regulated by the quantity of syllables; and if Cædmon had really written in a metre regulated by the quantity of syllables, a few of his lines must have afforded us the same conviction with respect to the general laws of his versification.

For my own part, I confess myself unable to discover any material distinction of the Saxon Poetry from Prose, except a greater pomp of diction, and a more stately kind of march.

Our ancestors affected a certain pomp of style in all their compositions. *Angli* (says Malmesbury, 1. i. p. 13.) *pompatice* dictare amant. And this affectation, I suspect, was the true cause of their so frequently inverting the natural order of their words, especially in Poetry. The obscurity arising from these inversions had the appearance of Pomp. That they were not owing to the constraint of any metrical Laws (as Hickes supposes) may be presumed from their being commonly used in Prose, and even in Latin Prose, by Saxon writers. Ethelwerd, an Historian descended in the fifth degree from King Ethelred [inter Script. post Bedam, p. 831-850.], is full of them. The following passage of his history if literally translated, would read very like Saxon Poetry. "Abstrahuntur tunc | ferventes fide| anno in eodem | Hibernia stirpe | tres viri lecti; | furtim consuunt lembum | taurinis byrsis; | alimentum sibi| hebdomadarium supplent; | elevant dies | per vela septem totidemque noctes," &c.

We do not see any marks of studied alliteration in the old Saxon Poetry; so that we might attribute the introduction of that practice to the Danes, if we were certain, that it made a part of the Scaldic versification at the time of the Danish settlements in England.

However that may have been, Giraldus Cambrensis [Descr. Camb. p. 889.] speaks of *Annomination,* which he describes to be what we call *Alliteration,* as the favourite rhetorical figure of both the Welsh and English in his time. "Adeo igitur hoc verborum ornatu duæ nationes, Angli scil. et Cambri, in omni sermone exquisito utuntur ut nihil ab his eleganter dictum, nullum nisi rude et agreste censeatur eloquium, si non schematis hujus limâ plene fuerit expolitum." It is plain that Alliteration must have had very powerful charms for the ears of our ancestors, as we find that the Saxon Poetry, by the help of this embellishment alone, even after it had laid aside its pompous phraseology, was able to maintain itself, without Rime or Metre, for several centuries. See Dr. Percy's Essay on the Metre of Pierce Plowman's Visions. Rel. of Antient Poetry, vol. ii.

[41]I cannot find that the French Antiquaries have been able to produce any Poetry in any of the dialects of their language, of an earlier date than the Conquest of England, or indeed than the beginning of the XIIth Century. However we read of a Thibaud de Vernun, Canon of Rouen, who, before the year 1053, "multorum gesta Sanctorum, sed et S[anc]ti Wandregesili, a sua latinitate transtulit, atque in communis linguae usum satis facunde refudit, ac sic, *ad quamdam tinnuli rythmi similitudinem, urbanas ex illis cantilenas edidit*" [De

Mirac. S(anc)ti Vulframni. Auctore Monacho Fontanell. tempt. Will. I. ap. Dacherii Acta SS. Ord. Ben. t. iii. p. 379.] It is probable too, that the "*vulgares cantus,*" which, according to Raimond de Agiles [Gesta Dei, p 180.], were composed against Arnoulph, a Chaplain of the Duke of Normandy, in the first Croisade, were in the French language; and there can be little doubt that William IX, Duke of Aquitain, upon his return from Jerusalem in 1101, made use of his native tongue, when "*miserias captivitatis suæ, ut erat jocundus et lepidus, multotiens retulit rythmicis versibus cum facetis modulationibus.*" Ord. Vital. 1. x. p. 793. The History of the taking of Jerusalem, which is said to have been written by the Chevalier Gregoire Bechada, of Tours in Limoges, "*maternâ linguâa, rythmo vulgari, ut populus pleniter intelligeret,*" [Labbe, Bibl. Nov. t. ii. p. 296.] has not yet been brought to light; so that probably the oldest French Poem of any length now extant is a translation of the *Bestiarius by* Phillipe de Thaun, it being addressed to Aliz (Adeliza of Louvain) the second Queen of our Henry I.

There is a copy of this Poem among the Cotton MSS. Nero. A.v. The authors of the *Histoire Littéraire de la France,* t. ix. p. 173–90. suppose it to have been written about 1125, that is, thirty years before *Le Brut,* which Fauchet had placed at the head of his list of French Poems.

I shall take occasion in another place to shew, that the real author of *Le Brut* was Wace (the same who wrote the *Roman de Rou,*) and not Wistace, as Fauchet calls him.

[42] The Latin Rythmical verses resembled the Metrical in the number of syllables only, without any regard to quantity. "Arma cano virumque qui primus Trojæ ab oris" would pass for a very good Rythmical Hexameter. The greatest part however of these compositions were in imitation of the Iambic and Trochaic metres; and in them, if the Accents fell luckily, the unlearned ear would often be as well pleased as if the laws of Quantity were observed. The two Rythmical Hymns quoted by Beda [De Metris, edit. Putsch. p. 2380.] are sufficient to prove this. The first, he observes, "ad instar Iambici metri pulcherrime factus est."

O rex æterne Domine
Rerum creator omnium, &c.

The other is "*ad formam metri Trochaici.*"

Apparebit repentina dies magna Domini
Fur obscurâ velut nocte improvisos occupans.

In the former of these Hymns, "*Domine,*" to a modern ear at least, sounds as well as "*nomine*;"–and in the latter, "*dies*" and "*velut,*" being accented upon their first Syllables, affect us no other wise than "*dices*" and "*velum*" would have done.

From such Latin Rythms, and chiefly those of the Iambic form, the present Poetical measures of all the nations of Roman Europe are clearly derived. Instead of long and short Syllables, the Feet of our Poetry are composed of Syllables accented and unaccented, or rather of Syllables strongly and less strongly accented; and hence it is, that we have so little variety of Feet, and consequently of Metres; because the possible combinations of Syllables accented and unaccented are, from the nature of speech, much more limited in point of number, than the combinations of long and short Syllables were in the Greek and Latin languages.

[43] We see evident marks of a fondness for Rime in the Hymns of S. Ambrosius and S. Damasus, as early as the fourth Century. One of the Hymns of Damasus, which begins,

Martyris ecce dies Agathæ
Virginis emicat eximiæ, &c.

is regularly rimed throughout. Prudentius, who had a more classical taste, seems studiously to have avoided Rimes; but Sedulius and Fortunatus, in the fifth and sixth Centuries, use them frequently in their Hymns. See their works, and an Hymn of the latter ap. Fabric. Bib. Med. Ætat. v. FORTUNATUS.

The learned Muratori, in his Dissertation *de Rythmicâ Veterum Poesi* [Antiq. Med. Ævi, Dissert. xl.] has collected together a vast heap of examples, which prove that Rimes were very generally used in Hymns, Sequences, and other religious compositions in Latin, in the VIIth, VIIIth, and IXth Centuries; so that for my own part I think it as probable, that the Poets in the vulgar languages (who first appeared about the IXth Century) borrowed their Rimes from the Latin Poetry of that age, as it is evident that they did the forms of their versification.

Otfrid of Weissenberg, the earliest Rimer that is known in any of the modern Languages, about the year 870, calls Rime, in the style of the Latin Grammarians, *Schema omæoteleuton* [Præf. ad Liutbert. ap. Schilter. Thes. Antiq. Teuton, t. i. p. 11.] And when the Monk, who has been cited in n. 41. says, that Thibaud de Vernun composed his Songs "*ad quamdam tinnuli rythmi similitudinem,*" he must mean, I think, that he composed them "in imitation of [Latin] jingling Rythm." I say, *Latin,* or at least some *foreign,* Rythm, because otherwise he would rather have said *in rythmo tinnulo.* The addition of the epithet *tinnulus* seems to shew plainly enough, that *Rythmus* alone did not then signify what we call *Rime.*
[44]William of Malmesbury [de Gest. Pont Angl. l. iii. p. 271.] has preserved two Riming verses of Aldred, Archbishop of York, which that Prelate threw out against one Urse, Sheriff of Worcestershire, not long after the Conquest. "Hatest thou Urse–Have thou God's curse." "*Vocaris Ursus–Habeas Dei maledictionem.*" Malmesbury says, that he inserts this English, "*quod Latina verba non sicut Anglica concinnitati respondent.*" The Concinnity, I suppose, must have consisted in the Rime, and would hardly have been thought worth repeating, if Rime in English had not then been a novelty.

The lines in the Saxon Chronicle, to which I mean to refer, are in p. 191. ed Gibs. The passage begins,

> Lastelas he let thyncean,
> And earme men swithe swencean–

All the lines are not in Rime; but I shall set down a few, in English characters, which I think coud not have chimed together so exactly by mere accident.

> Thet he nam be rihte
> And mid mycelan un–rihte
> Of his leode
> For littelre neode–
> He sætte mycel deor-frith,
> And he lægde laga ther with–
> He forbead tha heortas,
> Swylce eac tha baras;
> Swa swithe he lufode tha hea-deor
> Swylce he wære heora fæder.
> Eac he sætte be them haran,
> That hi mosten freo faran–

The concluding lines are–

> Se æll–mihtiga God
> Kithe his saule mild–heortnisse
> And do him his synna forgifenesse.

The writer of this part of the Chronicle (as he tells us himself, p. 189.) had *seen* the Conquerour.

[45] Hist. Angl. p. 100. Godric died in 1170, so that, according to tradition, the Canticle was prior to that period. The first Stanza being incorrectly printed, I shall only transcribe the last.–

> Seinte Marie, Christes bur,
> Meidenes clenhad, moderes flur,
> Diliee mine sennen, rixe in min mod,
> Bringe me to winne with selfe God–

Hoc Canticum (says M. P.) *potest hoc modo in Latinum transferri.*

> *Sancta Maria, Christi thalamus,*
> *virginalis puritas, matris flos,*
> *dele mea crimina, regna in mente meâ,*
> *duc me ad fælicitatem cum solo Deo.*

Upon the authority of this translation I have altered *pinne* (as it is in the print) to *winne,* The Saxon "w" is often mistaken for a p.

[46] This work of Layamon is extant among the Cotton MSS. Cal. A. ix. A much later copy, in which the author, by a natural corruption was called *Laweman,* was destroyed by the fire. There is an account of both copies in Wanley's Cat. MSS. Septent. p. 228, and p. 237.

The following short extract from fol. 7, 8. containing an account of the Sirens, which Brutus met with in his voyage, will serve to support what is said in the text of this Author's intermixing Rimes with his prose.

> Ther heo funden the Merminnen,
> That beoth deor of muchele ginnen.
> Wismen hit thunchet ful iwis,
> Bineothe thon gurdle hit thunceth fisc.
> Theos habbeth swa murie song,
> Ne beo tha dai na swa long,
> Ne bith na man weri
> Heora songes to heran–

[47] The French Clerk, whom Layamon professes to have followed in his history, is called by Wanley [Cat. MSS. Sept. p. 228] *Wate*; as if poor *Maistre Wace* were doomed to have his name perpetually mistaken. Fauchet, and a long string of French Antiquaries, have agreed to call him *Wistace.* I shall here, in justice to *Maistre Wace,* (for whom I have a great respect, not only as a very antient but as a very ingenious Rimer,) state my reasons shortly for believing, that he was the real author of that translation in French verse of Geffrey of Monmouth's Romance, which is commonly called *Le Brut.*

In the first place his name is distinctly written in the text of three MSS. of very considerable antiquity. Two of them are in the Museum, viz. *Cotton.* Vitell. A. x. and *Reg.* 13 A. xxi. The third is at Cambridge, in the Library of Bennet College, n. 58. In a fourth MS. also in the Museum, *Harl.* 6508. it is written *Gazce,* and *Gace,* by a substitution of G for W, very usual in the French language.

Secondly, in the MS. abovementioned of Layamon's history Cal. A. ix. if I may trust my own eyes, the name is *Wace;* and not *Wate,* as Wanley read it. The Saxon "t" is not very unlike a c. What Layamon has said further, "that this Wace was a French Clerk, and presented his book to Alienor, the Queen of Henry" [the Second,] agrees perfectly well with the date of *Le Brut* (in 1155, according to all the copies) and with the account which Wace himself, in his *Roman de Rou,* has given of his attachment to Henry.

Thirdly, in a subsequent translation of *Le Brut,* which was made by Robert of Brunne in the beginning of the XIVth Century, he repeatedly names *Mayster Wace,* as the author (or rather translator from the Latin) of the French History. See *Hearne's* App. to Pref. to *Peter Langtoft,* p. xcviii.

In opposition to this strong evidence in favour of *Wace,* we have nothing material, except the MS. of *Le Brut* quoted by Fauchet *[de la Langue Françoise,*1. ii.], in which, according to his citation, the author is called *Wistace.* The later French writers, who have called him so, I apprehend, have only followed Fauchet. The Reader will judge, whether it is not more probable, that the writer of the MS. or even Fauchet himself, may have made a little slip in this matter, than that so many MSS. as I have quoted above, and the successive testimonies of LAYAMON and ROBERT OF BRUNNE, should have concurred in calling the author of *Le Brut* WACE, if that had not been his true name.

I will just add, that *La vie de Seint Nicholas,* which is frequently quoted by *Hickes* [Gr. A. S. p. 146. 149. et al.] was probably a work of this same *Wace,* as appears from the following passage. [MS. Bodl. 1687. v. 17. from the end.]

Ci faut le livre *mestre Guace,*
Qil ad de Seint Nicholas fait,
De Latin en Romaunz estreit
A Osberd le fiz Thiout,
Qui Seint Nicholas mout amout.–

And I should suspect, that *Le Martyre de St. George en vers François par Robert Guaco,* mentioned by M. Lebeuf as extant in the Bibl. Colbert. Cod. 3745 [Mem. de l'Acad. D.J. et B.L. t. xvii. p. 731.] ought to be ascribed to the same author, as *Guaco* is a very strange name. The Christian name of Wace was *Robert.* See Huet, Orit. de Caen, p. 412.

[48]The following passage of Roger de Hoveden [p. 672.] gives a striking description of the extent of the English dominions in the time of Richard I. *Sciendum est quod tota terra, quæ est ab Anglia usque in Hispaniam, secus mare, videlicet Normania, Britannia, Pictavia, est de dominio Regis Angliæ.* The Kings of France at that time were not possessed of an inch of territory upon the coasts of the Ocean.

[49]It will be sufficient to name John of Salisbury, Peter of Blois, Joseph of Exeter, Gerald Barry, Nigell Wireker, Geffrey Vinsauf. I should add to this list Walter Map, if there were not a tradition, not entirely destitute of probability, that he was the author of the *Roman de Saint Graal* in French. I find this in an old MS. of Tristan, Bib. Reg. 20. D. ii. p. antep. *Quant Boort ot conte laventure del Saint Graal, teles come eles estoient avenues, eles furent mises en escrit, gardees en lamere de Salibieres, dont Mestre Galtier Map l'estrest a fair son livre du Saint Graal, por lamor du roy Herri son sengnor, qui fist lestorie tralater del Latin en Romanz.* The adventure of the *Saint Graal* is plainly written upon a very different plan from the other Romances of the Round Table, and is likely enough to have come from an Ecclesiastick, though rather, I confess, from a graver one than Walter Map may be supposed to have been. The French Romance, from which our Romance called "*Mort d'Arthur*" is translated, seems to be an injudicious jumble of *Le Brut, Lancelot, Tristan,* the *Saint Graal,* and some other Romances of less note, which were all, I apprehend, originally separate works.

[50]*Le Bestiaire,* by *Philippe de Thaun,* addressed to Queen Adelisa; *Le Brut* and *Le Roman de Rou,* by *Wace,* have been mentioned above. Besides the *Roman de Rou,* there is another Chronicle of Normandy in French verse by *Maitre Beneit,* compiled by order of Henry II. MS. *Harl.* 1717. The same *Beneit* was, perhaps, the author of the *Vie de St.Thomas, MS. Harl.* 3775. though he there calls himself

"Frere Beneit, le pecheour,
"ove les neirs dras"–

At the end of a copy *of Le Brut,* Bib. *Reg.* 13 A. xxi. there is a Continuation of the History to the death of William II, in the same Metre, by a *Geffrei Gaimar,* which escaped the observation of Mr. Casley; and at the end of another copy, *Vitell.* A. x. the History is continued by an anonymous author to the accession of King John.

Richard I composed himself in French. A specimen of his Poetry has been published by Mr. Walpole, Cat. of Royal Authors, v. i. And his Chancellor, William Bishop of Ely (who, as has been observed before, "was totally ignorant of the English language"), was by no means behindhand with his Master in his encouragement of French Poets; for of this Bishop the passage in Hoveden is to be understood, which Mr. Walpole has applied to the King himself. It is part of a letter of Hugh Bishop of Coventry, who, speaking of the *Bishop of Ely,* says, that HE, "*ad augmentum et famam sui nominis, emendicata carmima et rythmos adulatorios comparabat, et* de regno Francorum *cantores et joculatores muneribus allexerat, ut de illo canerent in plateis; etjam dicebatur ubique, quod non erat talis in orbe.*" Hoveden, p. 103.

[51]To these causes we may probably impute the loss of those Songs upon Hereward (the last perhaps of the Saxon heroes,) which, according to Ingulphus, "were sung about the streets" in his time. Hist. Croyl. p. 68. Robert of Brunne also mentions "a Rime" concerning Gryme the Fisher, the founder of Grymesby; Hanelok [*sic*] the Dane; and his wife Goldeburgh, daughter to a King Athelwold; who all now, together with their bard,

> –illacrymabiles
> Urgentur ignotique longâ
> Nocte.–

See Translation of Peter of Langtoft, p. 25. and Camden's Brit. p. 569.

[52]The Ormulum seems to be placed by Hickes among the first writings after the Conquest [Gram. Ang. Sax. c. xxii. p. 165.], but, I confess, I cannot conceive it to have been earlier than the reign of Henry II. There is a peculiarity in the author's orthography, which consists in doubling the Consonants; e. g. brother, he writes, *brotherr*; after, *afterr*, &c. He has done this by design, and charges those who shall copy his book to be very careful to write those letters twice, which he has written so, as otherwise, he assures them, "they will not write the word right." Hickes has taken notice of this peculiarity, but has not attempted to explain the author's reasons for it; and indeed, without a more perfect knowledge than we now probably can have of the Saxon pronunciation, they seem totally inexplicable. In the few lines, which I think it necessary to quote here as a specimen of the Metre, I shall venture (first begging Ormin's pardon for disregarding his injunction) to leave out the superfluous letters, and I shall also for my own ease as well as that of the reader transcribe them in modern characters. The first lines of Wanley's extract from MS. *Bod.* Junius. I. [Cat. Codd MSS. Septent. p. 59.] will answer my purpose as well as any other.

> Nu, brother Walter, brother min after the fleshes kinde,
> And brother min i Cristendom thurh fulluht and thurh trowthe,
> And brother min i Godes hus yet o the thride wise,
> Thurh that wit hafen taken ba an reghel boc to folghen
> Under kanunkes-had and lif swa sum Sant Awstin sette,
> Ic hafe don swa sum thu bad, and forbed [MS.: *forthed*] te thin wille,
> Ic hafe wend intil English godspelles halighe lare,
> After that little wit that me min Drihten hafeth lened–

The reader will observe, that, in calling these verses of fifteen syllables, I consider the words–*kinde, trowthe, wise, sette, wille, lare*–as dissyllables.

The laws of Metre require that they should be so considered, as much as *folghen* and *lened:* and for the same reason *thride* in ver. 3 and *hafe* in ver. 6 and 7 are to be pronounced as consisting of two syllables.

It is the more extraordinary that neither Hickes nor Wanley should have perceived that

Ormin wrote in Metre, as he himself mentions his having added words for the sake of *filling* his *Rime,* or *Verse,* for he calls it by both those names in the following passages:

> Ic hafe sett her o this boc among Godspelles wordes
> All thurh me selfen manig word, the *Rime* swa to fillen–

And again,

> And ic ne mihte noht min *fers* ay with Godspelles wordes
> Wel *fillen* all and all forthi sholde ic wel ofte nede
> Among Godspelles wordes don min word, min *fers* to *fillen*–

It is scarce necessary to remark, that *Rime* is here to be understood in its original sense, as denoting the whole verse, and not merely the consonancy of the final syllables. In the second quotation *fers,* or *verse,* is substituted for it as a synonymous term. Indeed I doubt whether, in the time of Ormin, the word *Rime* was, in any language, used singly to convey the idea of Consonant terminations.

[53]A large extract from this Poem has been printed by Hickes [Gram. Ang. Sax. c. xxiv. p. 232.], but evidently from very incorrect MSS. It begins thus:

> Ic am nu elder thanne ic wes
> A wintre and ec a lore;
> Ic ealdi more thanne ic dede,
> Mi wit oghte to bi more.

[54]Robert of Gloucester and Robert of Brunne have been mentioned already. To these may be added Richard Rolle, the hermite of Hampole, who died in 1349, after having composed a large quantity of English rimes. See Tanner, Bib. Brit. Art. HAMPOLE.–Laurence Minot, who has left a collection of Poems upon the principal events of the former part of the reign of Edward III. MS. *Cotton.* Gal Ba.E. ix.–Within the same period flourished the two Poets, who are mentioned with great commendations by Robert of Brunne [App. to Pref. to Peter Langt. p. xcix.] under the names "Of Erceldoun and of Kendale." We have no memorial, that I know, remaining of the latter, besides this passage; but the former I take to have been the famous Thomas Leirmouth, of Ercildoun (or Ersilton, as it is now called, in the shire of Merch.) who lived in the time of Edward I, and is generally distinguished by the honourable addition of "The Rhymour." As the learned Editor of "Ancient Scottish Poems, Edinburgh, 1770," has, for irrefragable reasons, deprived this Thomas of a Prophecy in verse, which had usually been ascribed to him, [see Mackenzie, Art. THOMAS RHYMOUR.] I am inclined to make him some amends by attributing to him a Romance of "Sir Tristrem;" of which Robert of Brunne, an excellent judge! [in the place above cited] says,

> Over gestes it has th'esteem,
> Over all that is or was,
> If men it sayd as made THOMAS.

[55]See Dr. Percy's curious *Catalogue of English Metrical Romances,* prefixed to the third Volume of *Reliques of ancient Poesy.* I am inclined to believe that we have no English Romance, prior to the age of Chaucer, which is not a translation or imitation of some earlier French Romance. The principal of those, which, being built upon English stories, bid the fairest for having been originally composed in English, are also extant in French. A considerable fragment of *Hornchild,* or *Dan Horn* as he is there called, is to be found in French Alexandrines in MS. *Harl.* 527. The first part of *Guy of Warwick* is in French, in the octosyllable metre, in MS. *Harl.* 3775. and the last part in the same language and metre in MS. Bib. *Reg.* 8 F. ix. How much may be wanting I have not had opportunity to examine. I have never seen *Bevis*

in French; but Du Fresnoy, in his *Biblioth. des Romans,* t. ii. p. 241. mentions a MS. of *Le Roman de Beuves de Hantonne,* and another of *Le Roman de Beuves et Rosiane, en Rime;* and the Italians, who were certainly more likely to borrow from the French than from the English language, had got among them a Romance *di Buovo d'Antona* before the year 1348. Quadrio, Storia della Poesia, t. vi. p. 542.

However, I think it extremely probable that these three Romances, though originally written in French, were composed in England, and perhaps by Englishmen; for we find that the general currency of the French language here engaged several of our own countrymen to use it in their compositions. Peter of Langtoft may be reckoned a dubious instance, as he is said by some to have been a Frenchman; but Robert Grosseteste, the famous Bishop of Lincoln in the time of Henry III was a native of Suffolk, and yet he wrote his *Chasteau d'Amours,* and his *Manuel des Pechées* in French. [Tanner's Bib. Brit, and Hearne's Pref. to Rob. of Gloucester, p. lviii.]–There is a translation of *Cato* in French verse by *Helis de Guincestre,* i.e. Winchester, Ms. *Harl.* 4388. and a Romance also in French verse, which I suppose to be the original of the English *Ipomedon* [Percy's Cat. n.22.] by *Hue de Rotelande,* is to found in MS. *Cotton.* Vesp. A. vii.–A French Dialogue in verse, MS. *Bod.* 3904. entitled, "*La pleinte par entre mis Sire Henry de Lacy Counte de Nichole et Sire Wauter de Bybelesworth par la croiserie en la terre Seinte,*" was most probably composed by the latter, who has also left us another work in French prose. [See his article in Tanner, Bibl. Brit.]–Even as late as the time of Chaucer, Gower wrote his *Speculum meditantis* in French, but whether in verse or prose is uncertain. John Stowe, who was a diligent searcher after MSS. had never seen this work [Annals, p. 326.]: nor does either Bale or Pits set down the beginning of it, as they generally do of the books which they have had in their hands. However, one French Poem of Gower's has been preserved. In MS. *Harl.* 3869. it is connected with the *Confessio Amantis* by the following rubric: "Puisqu'il ad dit cidevant en Englois par voie d'essample la sotie de cellui qui par amours aime par especial, dirra ore apres en Francois a tout le monde en general une traitie selonc les auctours, pour essampler les amants marriez, au fin q'ils la foi de leurs seints espousailles pourront par fine loialte guarder, et al honeur de dieu salvement tenir." Pr. *Le creatour de toute creature.* It contains LV Stanzas of 7 verses each, in the last of which is the following apology for the language:

"Al'universite de tout le monde
Johan Gower ceste Balade envoie,
Et si jeo nai de Francois la faconde,
Pardonetz moi qe jeo de ceo forsvoie;
Jeo suis Englois, si quier par tiele voie
Estre excuse–."

Chaucer himself seems to have had no great opinion of the performances of his countrymen in French. [Prol. to Test. of Love, ed. 1542.] "Certes (says he) there ben some that speke theyr poysy mater in Frenche, of whyche speche the Frenche men have as good a fantasye, as we have in hearing of French mennes Englyshe." And he afterwards concludes, with his usual good sense. "Let then Clerkes endyten in Latyn, for they have the propertye of science and the knowinge in that facultye; and lette Frenchmen in theyr Frenche also endyte theyr queynt termes, for it is kyndly to theyr mouthes; and let us shewe our fantasyes in suche wordes as we lerneden of our dames tonge."

[56]It was necessary to qualify the assertion, that the Rimers of this period "did not invent or import from abroad any new modes of Versification," as, in fact, Robert of Brunne (in the passage referred to in n. 54.) has mentioned three or four sorts of verse, different from any which we have hitherto met with, and which appear to have been much cultivated, if not introduced, by the writers who flourished a little before himself. He calls them *Couwee, Strangere, Enterlace,* and *Baston.* Mr. Bridges, in a sensible letter to Thomas Hearne [App. to Pref. to Peter Langt. p. ciii.] pointed out these terms as particularly "needing an explana-

tion;" but Thomas chose rather to stuff his book with accounts *of the Nunnery at Little Gidding,* &c. which cost him only the labour of transcribing. There can be little doubt, I think, that the Rimes called *Couwée* and *Enterlacé* were derived from the *Versus Caudati* and *Interlaqueati of* the Latin Rimers of that age. Though Robert of Brunne in his Prologue professes not to attempt these elegancies of composition, yet he has intermixed several passages in Rime *Couwée;* [see p. 266. 273, 6, 7, 8, 9, et al.] and almost all the latter part of his work from the Conquest is written in Rime *Enterlacée,* each couplet riming in the middle as well as at the end. [This was the nature of the Versus *Interlaqueati,* according to the following specimen, MS. *Harl.* 1002.

> Plausus Grecorum | lux cecis et via claudis |
> Incola celorum | virgo dignissima laudis.]

I cannot pretend to define the exact form of the Rime called *Baston,* but I dare say it received its appellation from the Carmelite, *Robert Baston,* a celebrated Latin Rimer in the reigns of Edward I. and II. [See Tanner, Bibl. Brit. in v. and Hearne's Pref. to Fordun, p. ccxxvi. et seq.] His verses upon the battle of Bannockburn, in 1313, are printed in the Appendix to Fordun, p. 1570. They afford instances of all the whimsical combinatians of Rimes which can well be conceived to find a place in the Latin heroic metre.

As to Rime *Strangere,* I suspect (upon considering the whole passage in Robert of Brunne) that it was rather a general name, including all sorts of *uncommon* Rimes, than appropriated to any particular species.

Upon the whole, if this account of these new modes of Versification shall be allowed to be any thing like the truth, I hope I shall be thought justified in having added, "that the Art coud not be at all advanced by them."

[57]This is plain from fol. 68. edit. 1550. where the year 1350 is named, as a year of great scarcity. Indeed, from the mention of the Kitten in the tale of the Rattons, fol. iii. iiii. I should suspect that the author wrote at the very end of the reign of Edward III, when Richard was become heir apparent.

The Visions *of* (i. e. *concerning*) Pierce Ploughman are generally ascribed to one *Robert Langland;* but the best MSS. that I have seen, make the Christian name of the author *William,* without mentioning his surname. So in MS. *Cotton.* Vesp. B. xvi. at the end of p. 1. is this rubric. "Hic incipit secundus passus de visone *Willilmi* de Petro Plouhman." And in ver. 5. of p. 2. instead of, "*And sayde;* sonne, *slepest thou?*" the MS. has, "*And sayde;* Wille, *slepest thou?*" See also the account of MS. *Harl.* 2376. in the Harleian Catalogue.

I cannot help observing, that these Visions have been printed from so faulty and imperfect a MS. that the author, whoever he was, would find it difficult to recognize his own work. However, the judgement of the learned Doctors, Hickes and Percy, [Gram. A. S. p. 217.–Rel. of Anc. Poet. v. ii. p. 260] with respect to the laws of his versification, is confirmed by the MSS. Each of his verses is in fact a distich, composed of two verses, after the Saxon form, without Rime, and not reducible to any certain Metre. I do not mean to say, that a few of his verses may not be picked out, consisting of fourteen and fifteen syllables, and resembling the metre used in the *Ormulum;* and there are still more of twelve and thirteen syllables, which might pass for very tolerable Alexandrines: but then, on the other hand, there is a great number of his verses (warranted for genuine by the best MSS.) which cannot, by any mode of pronunciation, be extended beyond nine or ten syllables; so that it is impossible to imagine, that his verse was intended to consist of any determinate number of syllables. It is as clear that his Accents, upon which the harmony of modern Rythms depends, are not disposed according to any regular system. The first division of a verse is often Trochaic, and the last Iambic; and *vice versâ.* The only rule, which he seems really to have prescribed to himself, is what has been taken notice of by his first Editor, viz. "to have three wordes at the leaste in every verse whiche beginne with some one letter." Crowley's Pref. to Edit. 1550.

[58]The most perfect example of this metre has been given above, n. 52, from the *Ormulum.* Each verse is composed of fifteen syllables, and broken by a *Cæsura* at the eighth, which always terminates a word. The accents are so disposed upon the even syllables, particularly the eighth and fourteenth, as to produce the true Iambic Cadence.

The learned reader will recollect, that the *Political verses,* as they are called, of Tzetzes, and others, who wrote when the Greek versification was become Rythmical instead of Metrical, are *chiefly* of this form. See Du Cange, v. POLITICI VERSUS. And it is remarkable, that, about the time of our Orm, Ciullo d'Alcamo, a Poet of Sicily, where the Greek was still a living language, [Montf. Palæog. Gr. 1. vi.] made use of these verses of fifteen syllables, intermixed with Hendecasyllables, in the only production of his which has been preserved. Raccolta dell' Allacci, p. 408–16. The first Stanza is quoted by Crescimbeni, [Istor. d. V. P. 1. i. p. 3.] who however labours very much to persuade us that the verses in question ought not to be considered as verses of fifteen syllables, but as containing each of them two verses, the one of eight and the other of seven syllables. If this were allowed, the nature of the verse would not be altered: [See before, sec. iv] but the supposition is highly improbable, as by that distribution there would be three verses in each Stanza not riming. In what follows, Crescimbeni shews very plainly that he had not adverted to the real nature of Ciullo's measure, for he compares it with the noted tetrameter, "Gallias Cæsar subegit, Nicomedes Cæsarem," which is a *Trochaic,* whereas these verses of Ciullo are evidently *Iambics,* like those of Orm.

I suspect, that, if we coud recover the genuine text of Robert of Gloucester, he would be found to have written in this Metre. It was used by Warner, in his *Albions England* (another Chronicle in verse) in the latter end of Q. Elizabeth's reign; and Gascoigne about the same time *[Instruction concerning the making of verse in Eng.* Signature U. ii] speaks of the couplet, consisting of one verse of twelve and another of fourteen syllables, as *the commonest sort of verse* then in use. It may be proper to observe, that the metre, which Gascoigne calls a verse of fourteen syllables, is exactly the same with what is called above a verse of fifteen syllables; just as the French Alexandrin may be composed indifferently of twelve or thirteen syllables, and the Italian Hendecasyllable of ten, eleven, or even twelve. The general rule in all these kinds of verse is, that, when they consist of the greater number of syllables, the superfluous syllables, as they may be called, are never accented.

[59]Robert of Brunne, in his translation of *Peter of Langtoft,* seems to have used the *Alexandrin* verse in imitation of his Original; but his Metre (at least in Hearne's copy) is frequently defective, especially in the latter part of his work, where he affects to rime at the *Cæsura* as well as at the end of his verse. The Alexandrin metre is generally agreed to have been first used in the *Roman d'Alexandre,* by Lambert li Cors and Alexandre de Bernay, toward the latter end of the twelfth Century. Du Verdier, Bibl. p. 780. Fauchet, 1. ii. A late French Antiquary (M. L'Eveque de la Ravaliere,) in his history *Des Revolutions de la Langue Françoise,* p. 165. has combated this opinion, upon the authority of some Alexandrin verses, which he has discovered, as he supposes, in the *Roman de Rou.* I shall only observe, that no such verses are to be found in a very good MS. of the *Roman de Rou,* Bib. *Reg.* 4 C. xi. and I very much suspect that upon an accurate examination they will appear to have been not the work of *Wace,* but of some later author. A similar mistake of an interpolation, or continuation, for the original work has led another very able Antiquary of the same nation to place the *Roman de Rou* in the fourteenth Century. Mem. de l'Acad. des I. et B. L. tom. xv. p. 582. There can be no doubt, that *Wace* wrote the *Roman de Rou* about the middle of the twelfth Century. See before, n. 47.

They who attend only to the length of the Alexandrin verse, will naturally derive it from the Trimeter Iambic rythms, which were in frequent use in the beginning of the twelfth Century. See Orderic. Vital. 1. ii. p. 404. 409, 410. 415, et al. But when it is considered, that the *Cæsura* at the sixth syllable, so essential to the Alexandrin metre, was hardly ever observed in the Trimeter Iambic, it will seem more probable, I think, that the inventor of the Alexandrin took for his model, what has been called above, the long iambic, but, for some reason or other, retrenched a foot, or two syllables, in the first hemstich.

[60]Though I call this the Octosyllable Metre from what I apprehend to have been its original form, it often consists of nine and sometimes of ten syllables; but the eighth is always the last accented syllable.

The oldest French poems, to the latter end of the twelfth Century, are all in this metre; but upon the invention of the Alexandrin, the octosyllable verse seems by degrees to have been confined to the several species of lighter compositions, in which it is still used. Here in England, Robert of Brunne, in his Preface to his translation of *Le Brut* [App. to Pref. to Peter Langtoft, p. c.] calls it *"light rime,"* in contradistinction to "strange rime," of which he has just enumerated several sorts [see n. 56.]; and says, that he wrote in it "for luf of the lewed man:" and Chaucer himself speaks of it in nearly the same terms in the beginning of the third book of the *House of Fame.*

"God of science and of light,
Apollo, thurgh thy grete might
This little last book now thou gye;
Not that I will for maystrye
Here art potential be shewde;
But, for the ryme is *light and lewde,*
Yet make it somewhat agreable,
Though some verse fayle in a syllable."

The learned Editor of a part of the Canterbury Tales [London, 1737, 8vo.] has quoted this passage [Pref. p. xxv.] as proving, "by Chaucer's own confession, that he did not write in equal measure."

It certainly proves, that he did not write in equal measure *in this particular poem* of the House of Fame; but it proves also, that he knew well what the laws of measure were, and that he thought that any deviation from them required an apology. Is it just to conclude, because Chaucer has owned a neglect of those laws in one work, written in light metre, and in which he formally disclaims any exertion of art [ver. 4, 5.] that therefore he has been equally negligent of them in his other works, written in the gravest metre, and in which he may reasonably be supposed to have employed his utmost skill of versification? In the Troilus, for instance, [b. v.] he has a solemn prayer, "that none miswrite, or *mismetre* his book." Can we suppose that it was not originally written in Metre?–But I shall not enter any further into the general argument concerning Chaucer's versification, which will more properly be discussed in the text. My business here was only to prevent the reader from coming to the question with a preconceived opinion (upon the authority of the learned Editor above-mentioned) that "Chaucer himself," in this passage of the House of Fame, "has put the matter out of dispute."

To return again to the Octosyllable Metre. Its constitution is such, that the first syllable may often be dropped without much prejudice to the harmony of the verse; and as far as I have observed, that is the syllable in which Chaucer's verses of this kind generally fail. We have an instance in the first line of the passage quoted above–

God of science and of light–

sounds as well (to my ear at least) as

Thou God of science and of light–

according to Mr. Urry's correction. The reason, I apprehend, is, that the measure, though of another sort, is still regular: instead of a Dimeter Iambic, it is a Dimeter Trochaic Catalectic.

But no such liberty can be taken in the Heroic Metre without totally destroying its harmony; and therefore when the above-mentioned learned Editor says [Pref. p. xxvi.] that the numbers of Chaucer "are always musical, whether they want or exceed their complement," I doubt his partiality for his author has carried him too far. I have no conception myself that an heroic verse, which wants a syllable of its complement, can be musical, or even tolerable. The line which he has quoted from the Knightes Tale [ver. 1228 of this Edition],

Not in purgatory but in helle–

however you manage it; (whether you make a pause; or give two times to the first syllable, as he rather advises;)–can never pass for a verse of any form. Nor did Chaucer intend that it should. He wrote (according to the best MSS.)–

Not *only* in purgatory but in helle.

[61]The Heroic Metre with us, as with the Italians, is of the Iambic form, and consists of ten, eleven, or twelve syllables; the tenth, however, being in all cases the last accented syllable. The French have the same Metre; but with them it can scarce contain more than eleven syllables, as their language has few (if any) words, in which the accent is laid upon the Antepenultima. Though we have a great number of such words, we seldom use the verse of twelve syllables. The extraordinary difficulty of riming with three syllables is a sufficient reason for excluding it from all works which are written in Rime, and in Blank Metre the two unaccented syllables at the end make the close of the verse heavy and languid. Milton, for the sake of variety of measure, has inserted a very few of these verses, which the Italians call *Sdruccioli*, in his heroic poems; but they are more commonly and, I think, more properly employed in Dramatic compositions, where a continued stateliness of numbers is less requisite.

The generical name for this Metre in Italy is *Endecasyllabo;* and the verses of ten and twelve syllables are distinguished by additions; the former being called *Endecasyllabo tronco,* and the latter *Endecasyllabo sdrucciolo.* This proves, I think, that the verse of eleven syllables was the primitive metre, and principally used, as it still is, in Italy; and it will appear hereafter, if I am not mistaken, that the greatest part of Chaucer's heroic verses, when properly written and pronounced, are in this measure.

[62]It is so little a while since the world has been informed, that the Palamon and Arcite of Chaucer was taken from the *Theseida* of Boccace, that it would not have been surprising if another century had elapsed without our knowing that our countryman had also borrowed his Troilus from the *Filostrato* of the same author; as the *Filostrato* is more scarce, and much less famous, even in Italy, than the *Theseida.* The first suspicion which I entertained of this theft was from reading the title of the *Filostrato* at large, in *Saxii* Hist. Lit. Typog. Mediolan. ad an. 1498, and I afterwards found, in Montfaucon's Bibl. MSS. t. ii. p. 793. among the King of France's MSS. one with this title: "*Philostrato, dell' amorose fatiche di Troilo per Gio Boccaccio.*" See also Quadrio, t. vi. p. 473. I had just employed a person to procure me some account of this MS. from Paris, when I had the good fortune to meet with a printed copy in the very curious Collection of the Reverend Mr. Crofts. The title is "Il Fylostrato, che tracta de lo innamoramento de Troylo e Gryseida: et de molte altre infinite battaglie. Impresso nella inclita cita de Milano per magistro Uldericho Scinzenzeler nell anno M. CCCC lxxxxviii. a di xxvii. di mese de Septembre, in 4°." By the favour of the learned owner (who is as free in the communication, as he has been zealous in the collection, of his literary treasures) I had soon an opportunity of satisfying myself, that Chaucer was to the full as much obliged to Boccace in his Troilus as in his Knightes Tale.

The doubts which Quadrio mentions [t. vi. p. 474.], whether the *Filostrato* was really a work of Boccace, are sufficiently answered, as he observes, by the concurring testimony of several antient MSS. which expressly name him as the author. And it may be remarked, that Boccace himself, in his Decameron, has made the same honourable mention of this Poem as of the *Theseida;* though without acknowledging either for his own. In the introduction to the Sixth Day, he says, that "Dioneo inseme con Lauretta *di Troilo et di Chriseida* cominciarono cantare," just as afterwards, in the conclusion of the Seventh Day, we are told, that the same "Dioneo et la Fiammetta gran pezza cantarono insieme *d'Arcita et di Palemone.*"

[63] See *Poesies du Roi de Navarre,* Chans. xvi. xviii. xxvii. xxxiii. lviii. The only difference is, that the two last verses, which in Chaucer's Stanza form a distinct couplet, are made by Thibaut to rime with the first and third. In a MS. of Provençal poetry (in the Collection of the Reverend Mr. Crofts), I find one piece by Folket de Marseilles, who died about 1213, in which the Stanza is formed exactly agreeable to Chaucer's.

This Stanza of seven verses, being first introduced, I apprehend, by Chaucer, was long the favourite measure of the Poets who succeeded him. In the time of Gascoigne it had acquired the name of *Rithme royall; and surely,* says he, *it is a royall kinde of verse serving best for grave discourses.* [Instruction concerning the making of verse. Sign. U. 1. b.] Milton, in some of his juvenile compositions, has made the last verse of this Stanza an Alexandrin. As the *Theseida* and the *Filostrato* of Boccace are both written in the Octave Stanza, of which he is often, though improperly, called the inventor [see Pasquier, *Recherches,* 1. vii. c. 3.] it seems extraordinary that Chaucer should never have adopted that Stanza. Even when he uses a Stanza of eight verses (as in the Monkes Tale), it is constituted very differently from the Italian Octave. I observe, by the way, that Chaucer's Stanza of eight verses, with the addition of an Alexandrin, is the Stanza in which Spenser has composed his *Faery Queen.*

[64]Mons. l'Eveque de la Ravaliere, in his Discourse *de l'ancienneté des Chansons Françoises,* prefixed to the *Poësies du Roi de Navarre,* has the same observation with respect to the old French poets. *Leur Poësie* (says he, p. 227.) *marque combien ils respectoient cette régle* [of exact riming]; *mais pour en juger aujourd'hui,* ainsi que de la mesure de leurs Vers, *il faut prononcer les mots comme eux:*–He is vindicating the antient French bards from an unjust and ignorant censure of Boileau, in his *Art Poet.* Chant. i. So that, it should seem, a great Poet is not of course a judicious Antiquary. See . . . [the] censure of Chaucer's verse by our Dryden, who was certainly a *great Poet.*

[65]Though Ennius died not an hundred and fifty years before what may be called the age of Augustus, his language and versification are so different from those of Ovid, for instance, that I much question whether his poems were better relished, or even understood, by the vulgar Romans in that age, than the works of Chaucer are now by the generality of readers. However a great many of his verses are as smoothly turned as those of Ovid himself, and it is well known, that Virgil has not scrupled to incorporate several of them into his divine Æneid. At the same time, whoever casts an eye over the Fragments of his Annals, as collected by Columna, Hesselius, and others, will find frequent examples of all the seeming irregularities alluded to in the text.

[66]It is unnecessary to trouble the Reader with an enumeration of Syncope, Apostrophus, Synecphonesis, &c.

Quicquid habent telorum armamentaria vatum.

They may all, I think, be comprehended in our language under this one general principle, that an English verse, though chiefly composed of feet of two syllables, is capable of receiving feet of three syllables in every part of it, provided only one of the three syllables be accented.

In short, whoever can taste the metrical harmony of the following lines of Milton, will not be embarrassed how to dispose of the (seemingly) superfluous syllables, which he may meet with in Chaucer.

P. L. ii. 123. Óminous | conjecture on the whole success.
302. A pil | lar of státe |; deep on his front engraven–
658. Celestial spir | its in bón | dage, nor the abyss–
v. 495. No inconvenient di | et, nor tóo | light fare.
vii. 122. Things not revealed, which the invis | ible king–

[67]I would not be thought to undervalue the MSS. which I have not seen, or to discourage those who may have inclination and opportunity to consult them. I only mean to say, that, where the text is supported (as it generally is in this Edition) by the concurrence of two or three good MSS. and the sense is clear and complete, we may safely consider it as tolerably correct. In the course of the Notes, I shall have occasion to point out several passages, in which either the disagreement of the good MSS. or the obscurity of their readings, makes a further enquiry absolutely necessary in order to settle the text.

[68]It appears from the Preface to the last Edition of Chaucer's Works, Lond. 1721, that Mr. Urry, the undertaker of that Edition, had the same opinion with respect to the pronunciation of the final syllables in this and the last mentioned instance; and that it was his intention to distinguish those syllables, *whenever they were to be pronounced,* by printing them with an *i,* instead of an *e;* as, *shouris, shiris, percid, lovid* &c. As such a distinction is entirely unsupported by the MSS. and must necessarily very much disfigure the orthography of the language, I cannot think that an Editor has a right to introduce it upon ever so plausible a pretence. A shorter and (in my opinion) a less exceptionable method would have been to have distinguished the syllables of this sort, *whenever they were to be contracted,* by adding a sign of Syncope, thus; *shoure's, shire's, perce'd, love'd.* But after all a reader, who cannot perform such operations for himself, had better not trouble his head about the Versification of Chaucer.

Mr. Urry had also discovered, that the final *e* (of which I shall treat more at large in the next Section) often made a syllable in Chaucer's verse; and (according to the Preface quoted above) he "always marked with an accent, when he judged it necessary to pronounce it; as, swetè, halvè, smalè, ver. 5, 8, 9." I have the same objection to this mark that I have to innovations in orthography; and besides, that it would be apt to mislead the ignorant reader (for whom only it can be intended), by making him suppose that the *e* so marked was really to be accented, whereas the true *e* feminine is always to be pronounced with an obscure evanescent sound, and is incapable of bearing any stress or accent.

[69]This is owing to the Saxons not having left us any metrical compositions, as has been observed before, §1. Hickes complains [Gr A. S. c. xxiii. §. 7.], "that it is difficult to know of how many syllables a Saxon verse sometimes consists, for this reason among others, *quod non constat quomodo voces in* e *fæminino vel obscuro terminatæ pronuntiandæ sunt in carmine.*" He might, perhaps with more propriety, have complained, that it is difficult to know how words ending in *e* feminine are to be pronounced in a Saxon verse, because it is uncertain of how many syllables any of their verses consisted. I have mentioned in the text two cases of words abbreviated, in which I think we might conclude from general reasoning that the final *e* was pronounced. As this Theory, with respect to these words is entirely confirmed by the practice of Orm (the most authentic metrical composer that we have in our antient language) it would not perhaps be unreasonable to infer, that the practice of Orm, in other words of Saxon original, in which the final *e* is pronounced, is consonant to the old Saxon usage. However that may be, the practice of Orm must certainly be admitted to prove, that such a pronunciation prevailed at least 150 years before Chaucer.

[70]In most of the words in which the final *e* has been omitted, its use in lengthening or softening the preceding syllable has been supplied by an alteration in the Orthography of that Syllable. Thus, in–*grete, mete, stele, rede, dere,*–in which the first *e* was originally long, as closing a syllable, it has (since they have been pronounced as Monosyllables) been changed either into *ea,* as in–*great, meat, steal, read, dear;* or into *ee,* as in–*greet, meet, steel, reed, deer.* In like manner the *o* in–*bote, fole, dore, gode, mone,* has been changed either into *oa,* as in–*boat,*

foal; or into *oo,* as in–*door, good, moon.*

[71]Gram. Ling. Ang. e. i. §. 2. "Originem vero hujus *e* muti, nequis miretur unde devenerit, hanc esse judico: Nempe, quod antiquitus pronunciatum fuerit, sed obscuro sono, sicut Gallorum e fœmininum." He afterwards adds: "Certissimum autem hujus rei indicium est ex antiquis Poetis petendum; apud quos reperitur illud *e* promiscuè vel constituere vel non constituere novam Syllabam, prout ratio carminis postulaverit." So that, according to this judicious writer, (who has confessedly searched much deeper into the formation of vocal sounds in general, and the pronunciation of the English language in particular, than any of our other Grammarians,) I might have assumed, as certain, the point, which I have been labouring in the text (by arguments drawn from reason and analogy) to render probable.

There is much more to this purpose in Wallis, *loc. cit.* which I should transcribe, if I did not suppose that his book is in the hands of every one, who is likely to be curious upon this subject. I will only take notice of one passage which may be wrested to his disadvantage. From considering the gradual extinction of the *e* feminine in our language, and observing that the French, with whom he conversed, very often suppressed it in their common speech, he has been led to predict, that the pronunciation of it would *perhaps shortly* be disused among them as among ourselves. The prediction has certainly failed; but, notwithstanding, I will venture to say, that, at the time when it was made, it was not unworthy of Wallises sagacity. Unluckily for its success, a number of eminent writers happened, at that very time, to be growing up in France, whose works, having since been received as standards of style, must probably fix for many centuries the antient usage of the *e* feminine in Poetry, and of course give a considerable check to the natural progress of the language. If the age of Edward III had been as favourable to Letters as that of Louis XIV; if Chaucer and his contemporary Poets had acquired the same authority here, that Corneille, Molière, Racine, and Boileau, have obtained in France; if their works had been published by themselves, and perpetuated in a genuine state by printing; I think it probable, that the *e* feminine would still have preserved its place in our Poetical language at least, and certainly without any prejudice to the smoothness of our Versification.

[72]The reasoning in the text concerning the final *e* is equally applicable to the same vowel in the middle of words. Indeed (as Wallis has observed, *loc. cit.*) "vix uspiam in medio dictionis reperitur *e* mutum, quod non ab origine fuerit finale." If therefore it was pronounced while final, it would probably continue to be pronounced notwithstanding the addition of a syllable. If it was pronounced in *swete, trewe, large, riche,* it would be pronounced *in swetely, trewely, largely, richely.* [See ver. 123 and 3219, ver. 775 and 3692, ver. 2740 and 3034, ver. 1014 and 1913.] In another very numerous set of words (French Verbals ending in *ment)* the pronunciation of this middle *e* is countenanced, not only by analogy, but also by the still subsisting practice in the French language. So Chaucer certainly pronounced the words, *jugement,* ver. 780. 807. 820. *commandement,* ver. 2871. 2981. *amendement,* ver. 4183. *pavement, avisement,* ver. 4505, 6. Even Spenser in the same Canto (the 8th of B. v.) uses *attonement* and *avengement,* as words of four syllables: [St. 21. 8.-30. 5.] and Wallis takes notice that the middle *e* in *commandement* was pronounced in his time.

[73]It is agreed, I believe, that, in our Heroic Metre, those Verses, considered singly, are the most harmonious, in which the Accents fall upon the even Syllables; but it has never, that I know, been defined, how far a verse may vary from this its most perfect form, and yet remain a verse. On the *tenth* (or riming) syllable a strong Accent is in all cases indispensably required; and in order to make the line tolerably harmonious, it seems necessary that at least *two more* of the *even* syllables should be accented, the *fourth* being (almost always) one of them. Milton however has not subjected his verse even to these rules; and particularly, either by negligence or design, he has frequently put an unaccented syllable in *the fourth* place. See P. L. b. iii. 36. 586. b. v. 413. 750. 874.

[74]It has been suggested above, that Chaucer probably copied his Heroic Metre from Boccace. But neither Boccace nor any of the older Italian Poets are exact in the disposition of their accents. Though their Hendecasyllable Metre is allowed by the best Critics to be

derived from the Trimeter Iambic Catalectic, the perfection of it has never been determined, like that of our Heroic Metre, to consist in the conformity of its Accents to the pure Iambic measure. Quadrio, L. ii. Dist. iii. c. iv. Part. i. Nor does the King of Navarre always dispose his Accents more agreeably to our present notions. It is probable, I think, that some fundamental differences in the three languages may have led each of the three nations to prefer a different form of constructing the same kind of verse.

George Saintsbury

Chaucer's Prosody*

We now come to what would have been regarded, not so very long ago, as the starting-point, but what is in reality only the center (if not even the real end) of the first stage of our inquiry–the prosody of Chaucer. Something of what has to be said as to his relations with his forerunners and older contemporaries will fall best into the Interchapter which follows this book, but something also must be said here. Then we may give, in our usual fashion, a survey of the actual prosody of Chaucer's actual works, a survey which will not neglect the modern theories about them wholly, and which will always admit, for quoting, the most modern texts, but which will be mainly based on very many years' actual reading of Chaucer and Chaucer's predecessors and followers. After this it will be convenient to make a minuter study of foot- and verse-arrangement, syllabic values, rhyme, and the like. I may add that though, as will be seen, I cannot agree with the principles on which some of the Chaucerian fringe has been cut off the garment, I shall confine myself, in the *text* of this chapter, to the matter of Dr. Skeat's *Student's Chaucer* and the *Globe* edition (I prefer the latter, on the whole, as presenting a text rather less "made up" according to theory).

Those who have done me the honor to read the preceding pages will have a tolerably clear idea of what any man of fair education, and of interest in poetry, had, as prosodic data, about the seventh decade of the fourteenth century, towards the end of which Chaucer probably began. And certain slight additions can be made from internal evidence as to what he personally and actually had before him. Such a man, or such a poet, might belong to either (or to both) of the two great schools of purely metrical and purely alliterative prosodians. We know that, as a matter of practice, Chaucer, "a southern man," belonged to the former, and from the famous disclaimer of "rym ram ruff" (I give Gascoigne's form in his *Notes.* The MSS. of the *Parson's Prologue* seem to vary between *rum* and *rom*), we may not unfairly conclude that he belonged to it as a matter of positive preference. What sort of prosodic models he had before him in English we may judge from the Auchinleck MS., apparently written some twenty years before, and the Vernon MS., apparently written not ten years after, his probable *début.* The contents of both of these have been elaborately analyzed and discussed in the preceding pages. He would find in them[1] octosyllabic couplets and Romance sixes, the staples of English verse; but he would also find a very large number of more elaborate stanzas–the whole reducible, though never as yet by any preceptist reduced, to a system of foot-division, or of accent-grouping, according to taste.

But he had more means, material, machinery, at his disposal than those furnished by the pure vernacular. That he could have written bilingually, as Gower did with complete ease if not with complete scholarship, in English, French, and Latin, there is no evidence one way or another; that he did not so write there is at least the evidence that no such writing exists. But as every educated man of his generation still necessarily was (though according to the great passage of Trevisa[2] things were actually changing) he was perfectly familiar with French, which, as it happened, had for a century and more betaken itself to extremely elaborate, very strict, and in some cases very beautiful arrangements of prosodic form. And his earliest probable stage was occupied with direct translations and almost as direct imitations of French poetry. If not a Latin scholar–few people in his day deserved that name out of Italy, if many in it–he was familiar with Latin classical authors to some extent, and with the Dark and Middle Age writers to a large one. In particular, the Vulgate, and the hymns and services of the church, he must have known by heart. Everything points to his having, in somewhat later days, had a direct knowledge of Italian, which already possessed in Dante the greatest, and in Petrarch and Boccaccio two of the most formally accomplished, of European men of letters, in prose and verse, for a thousand years past. (Chaucer's remarks on Dante in the *Legend,* if accidentally felicitous, are one of the oddest examples of accidental felicity in criticism.) His linguistic literary equipment is not likely to have extended further, but this was a sufficiently wide range.

The *Romaunt of the Rose,* which is usually put in the front of Chaucer's works, is one of those which have fallen under the suspicion of modern scholars for reasons, many of which do not touch our subject, while the principal one that does touch it seems impossible of argument.[3] To be as accommodating as may be, however, let us say that the English *Romaunt of the Rose,* whether Chaucer's or not, displays with rare exceptions, though perhaps with those exceptions, no very great advance upon, and even no very great difference from, precedent octosyllabic couplet work, especially such (the great majority) as is translated from French.

The author or authors seems or seem to have sufficiently realized the first secret of music in this meter–the overrunning of the line; and less fully the second, that of the overrunning of the couplet. The third, the putting of a full stop at the end of the first line, which relieves the variety of the verse paragraph, is also known. There is a little, but not much, equivalence (more than in Gower, less than in most of his romances): but there is very little, if anything, of the other secret, which Chaucer afterwards learnt so thoroughly, of alternating lines of strict and full iambic cadence with those where a monosyllabic foot at the beginning turns that cadence to trochaic. Nor is there much understanding of pause-variation, though sometimes we find a full stop early in the line.[4] The value for us of the whole piece, however, is lessened by the preciseness with which (in part at least) it keeps to its original. The languages were by this time close enough to each other to make this easy, and when there was any difficulty it scarce required the wit of a Chaucer to supply such a *cheville* as

> An emperesse or *crowned* queen

for

> D'estre emperieris ou roine

(though it may be observed that "crownèd" is a distinct improvement to the sound, if not to the sense of the line), or

> The *lusty* folk that danced there

for

> Ainsi karoloient illecques.

On the whole, however, the poem is fairly free from the abominable stock-stuffings–"verament," "everichone," and the like–which are so frequent elsewhere. But it has little new for us.[5]

The so-called "Minor Poems" of the French period, the majority of which are fortunately unchallenged, have more. The use of elaborate, and even very elaborate, stanzas was, as we know well, not itself a novelty; we have them in very fair perfection, and in very great variety, as far back as the Harleian *Lyrics,* which were pretty certainly written half a century, and may have been written the best part of a century, before Chaucer's time. But with rare exceptions, most of which have been pointed out, these stanzas do not run quite easily, and the exceptions themselves are due rather to inspiring force of subject–to a little passing gust of poetry in feeling–than to assured craftsmanship. Now, as has been said above, the French had for more than a century been writing elaborate forms of poetry most sedulously, and had turned out, in several different kinds of continuous stanza, and in the smaller integers of triolet, rondeau, ballade, and the like, the most artificial perhaps, but certainly not the least artful and artistic, of poetic arrangements.

In what is sometimes supposed to be his very first work, the *A B C*–in what certainly may be his first as well as any other–there are divers noteworthy things. Like the *Romaunt,* it is a direct translation; but, unlike the *Romaunt,* it does not follow the prosody of its original, but innovates in a remarkable way. That original is in a twelve-line stanza of octosyllables rhymed *aabaabbbcbbc*. Chaucer shortens the stanza and lengthens the line, using eight decasyllables rhymed *ababbcbc*.[6] Now this instinctive and early striking out for the great staple line of English poetry is a prosodic fact, the importance of which cannot be overrated. It had for centuries been one of the staples (it was perhaps the oldest of all) in French, and it corresponded (with the necessary difference in the two languages) to the hendecasyllable which had established itself as the staple of Italian. But though there had been, as we have seen, sporadic examples of it, and even of its couplet, in English, it had never been staple, had never been used continuously and deliberately, had never even made frequent appearance. Yet Chaucer, as to the manner born, seems to have hardly the slightest difficulty with it. That he is a beginner is perhaps shown by the facts, not merely that he wields it with less varied ease than later, but that he writes it with some severity. There is possible trisyllable equivalence in one or two places

> Haven of refute, of quiete and of reste,

and

> Ever hath myn hope of refut been in thee,

where, of course, some folk would apply their rule of elision before liquids, and scan "hav'n" and "ev'r." He has some double rhymes that are not feminine, such as "never" and "ever" where the same note may be made if any one likes. He does not appear to trouble himself with the French decasyllabic caesura at the fourth syllable, for though it sometimes appears, it is quite as often absent. Indeed, as we see from Gascoigne–much later but almost as early as we have an opportunity of seeing anything of the kind–a rational idea grew up (even in times which had the superstition of this caesura) that it was less binding in stanza than in couplet. Still, where he dares a full, or very strong, stop in the middle of a line, it is generally at this fourth syllable.

This last point brings us to the consideration of a new class of prosodic characteristics, which it has been hardly worth while to consider earlier, the class which may be called rhetorical-prosodic; where devices are employed, not immediately or not wholly for versification, but as they might be employed in prose, to enhance the beauty of sound. These, except of a very rudimentary description, can only be found when a language and its writers have arrived at a certain point of accomplishment. Such a thing as the sharp pull-up just noticed[7] is itself of them, though on the more prosodic side. Two others to be mentioned now incline rather to the rhetorical. One of these, the least noticeable, though neither is unnoticeable here, is the well-known reduplication of synonyms, as in

> Haven of refute, of quiete and of reste,

which has nothing whatever to correspond to it in the French. Still more noteworthy is the first sign of that *epanaphora*, or trick of beginning successive lines with the same word or words, which Chaucer afterwards indulged in very freely, and which his successors, including even the earlier Elizabethans, not seldom abused:

> O verrey light of eyen that ben blynde,
> O verrey lust of labour and distresse.

The *Complaint unto Pity*, even if it be not (as some again think), and as it may very well be, the actually earliest, and even if it be (as some also think) a translation of a French poem not yet identified, has an even higher interest. For here we have, beyond reasonable doubt, the first English piece in the great Rhyme-royal, or seven-lined stanza of decasyllables rhymed *ababbcc,* which Chaucer afterwards brought to such perfection, and which long held the premier place among our stanza forms. His pitching on it, and his preference of it, are fresh proofs of his instinctive genius for prosody. It is not, indeed, a stanza-of-all-work. But it can do several things well, and one thing, the expression of clangorous cry, it can do supremely. It is odd that, this being so, the very first example of it should be in so suitable a subject; for the expression itself is not very successful. The poet's instinct is true, but his craftsmanship is as yet incomplete. It can hardly be quite accidental that the MS. variations in the piece are unusually numerous and serious, not least from our special point of view. Some of them, if original, would certainly show that Chaucer's prosody was not born full grown, in which, indeed, there would be nothing remarkable but the reverse.[8]

Still on the mounting hand is the interest of the *Book of the Duchess.* Nobody disputes its genuineness, or its solidarity, or its earliness, and it is in the octosyllabic couplet, so that we are able to study Chaucer's handling, of the most popular English meter before his day, undisturbed by any quibbles or irrelevances. He has by no means reached the mastery of it which he afterwards showed in the *House of Fame*, but which he did not care, elsewhere or later still, to exhibit at all. Yet he is already far above the level of the bulk of his predecessors. As in the *Romaunt*, and as we should expect, the model is the non-equivalenced one of *The Owl and the Nightingale*, not the equivalenced one of *Genesis and Exodus.* But it displays the catalectic [end-shortening]-trochaic alternation. Once (ll. 471–472) we find a curious identical rhyme ("song" and "song" in the same sense), which is followed by a pretty lyric or strophe-arrangement–an onzain divided into five and six, and rhymed *aabbaccdccd.* And, a little out of the strict prosodic road, we may note the ease with which the verse is made subservient to conversation, partly by the obvious device of splitting the couplets between the interlocutors, and sometimes by the slightly more daring one of splitting a line between them; but never, I think, by running on one speech into a line and then beginning another in the same, which is the crowning grace.[9]

There is more metrical experiment in the curious composite poem called the *Complaint of Mars,* where Chaucer has rather scandalized some of his admirers by celebrating an intrigue between Princess Isabel of Castille, Duchess of York, and John Holland, Duke of Exeter. The proem and the story are in rhyme-royal; but the "Complaint" itself is in a nine-line stanza[10] of some complexity, decasyllabically lined, and rhymed *aabaabbcc,* which may be regarded either as a six-line body with a triplet coda, or as a triplet with three couplets strung to it, or as rhyme-royal with two lines (2nd and 5th) inserted. It is by no means unimportant to observe that in both these stanza-meters the couplet itself plays a very large part. These forms gave him ample exercise in both forms of it–the strophes of the *Complaint* stanza in the "enjambed," the final couplets of rhyme-royal in the "stopped."

The *Parliament of Foules* is wholly rhyme-royal, with a splendid piece of cadence[11]–the first great thing, perhaps, in Chaucer–at the opening, others later, and a very pretty "roundel,"[12] "Now, welcome, summer," which may be the earliest example of these forms in English.

The remainder of the minor poems, whether they be all of one time or not, and discarding the minor questions of authenticity, supply interesting evidences of Chaucer's metrical *Wanderjahre.* Especially interesting is the collection of fragments, which older copyists seem to have taken as a *coda* to the *Complaint of Pity,* but which Professor Skeat groups as a *Complaint to his Lady.* The first, consisting of two stanzas of rhyme-royal, strikes me (I dare say it has struck others) as of real value in connection with the development of the quatorzain or English sonnet by Wyatt and Surrey, just when there was a renewed study of Chaucer. It is followed by certain experiments in terza rima,[13] which have interest of the same kind, in redoubled measure, as affecting the answers to two questions of extreme importance: "Why did Chaucer, at a time when he was evidently under very strong Italian influence, not make further experiments in this favorite meter of the 'great poet of Italy'?" and "Why has this meter never really acclimatized itself with us?" The double answer is, of course, obvious: "Because he found, and because all have found, that it would not do." The rest, and the bulk of the piece (if we may so call it), is in ten-line stanzas, a sixain tipped not with triplet "unicorned" like that of the *Mars* poem, but with a quatrain of decasyllables rhymed *In Memoriam* fashion–as a whole *aabaabcddc.*[14]

Annelida–to use the old form (the double *n* is prettier and there is MS. authority for it)–*and Arcite,* a beautiful poem, has a frame, or rather a long beginning and a single stanza end, of rhyme-royal, which was evidently Chaucer's metrical standby at this time; but nearly half of it, between the beginning and the end, has remarkable variations. First, we get the nine-line *Mars* stanza, arranged in two corresponding blocks, which Professor Skeat very justifiably calls "strophe" and "antistrophe." Each of four of the niners is followed by a fifth,[15] which consists of sixteen lines in batches of four-three octosyllables and a decasyllable, rhymed *aaab, aaab, bbba, bbba*–and a sixth,[16] which is Chaucer's only attempt at the ringing internally rhymed carol arrangement.

Of the rest, the half-jocular, half-angry, rebuke to Adam, his scrivener, is a rhyme-royal stanza; "The Former Age" is in decasyllabic octaves rhymed *ababbcc*;

and the rest, including the *Complaint of Venus,* are ballads and roundels, except the "Proverbs of Chaucer," which are quatrains of eights rhymed alternately. The lessons of these early poems are quite clear and easy to disengage. Chaucer has found an English prosody already thoroughly broken to the use of foot-divisions and their arrangement in metrical groups, and he does not attempt any startling innovations or reformations upon it as far as feet go. He uses, on the whole, the severe forms, except in his predilection (which was to continue) for an occasional monosyllabic opening foot. In meters, however, he is decidedly eclectic and experimental, and calls both French and Italian to his aid. He practices the old octosyllabic couplet, but does not seem to have any great fancy for it: and he practices the new French artificial forms, but without very much eagerness or very brilliant success. On the other hand, he hits (in the seven-lined stanza with end-couplet, the "rhyme-royal") on a form which evidently suits him, and which, not merely by the effect of his example, holds a very great place in English poetry for the two next centuries. Moreover, he shows in his handling of these various vehicles distinct mastery, and a great freedom from the two faults–straggling looseness and wooden precision–which had characterized most earlier verse.

But it is important to notice that both in diction and versification–more particularly in that adaptation of the two which was later to be his great glory–he as yet shows no very brilliant accomplishment. The opening of the *Parliament of Foules* is the chief exception, and there are few more. If these poems stood alone to his credit, it is but merely trivially obvious to say that he would hold no great place in English poetry. It would be strictly and critically correct to say: "Here was a man who seemed to have a surer prosodic grasp than any previous writer; one who showed the definite constitution of English prosody, but not much more."

All this makes the final outcome of this period, in the completed and substantive work belonging to the next, a most interesting thing. The delightful romance of *Troilus and Creseide* has been abundantly illustrated, in respect of its indebtedness of matter, by the very painful and very useful industry (here quite in place) of the modern scholar. It is–in another department of strictly literary criticism from that which we are pursuing–a great document against the idle notion that Chaucer disliked, despised, and depreciated Romance itself. But here we are busy only with its form. As such, it is the finished work–the diploma-piece, such as but few diploma-pieces are–of that period itself. Chaucer has preferred the prosodic form, which in his 'prentice period he had already selected, that of rhyme-royal, and of this preference merely as such, or of the qualifications of the stanza, there is no need to say any more than has been said. But of his accomplishment in it there is much more. The earlier pieces had been scarcely of substance enough individually, or of variety enough taken as a whole, to show the capacities of the meter, and Chaucer had in them done little more than produce "copies of verses," such as, let us say, the author of the "copy of verses" generally does *not* produce. Here he had buckled to quite a different task. This is not the place to dilate upon the extraordinary interest of the Troilus story–that story which, hardly suggested in the classical Tale of Troy, took form, so far as we know, under the hands of Benoît de Sainte-More, was continued by Guido delle Colonne, and Boccaccio, and taken up by Chaucer himself, Henryson, Shakespeare, and Dryden, in a fashion which has left us a group of compositions by greater and lesser masters, hardly one of which is negligible, and most of which are great. Chaucer's is not one of the exceptions, and the greatness is due in large measure to qualities which come fairly under our purview, whether as pure prosodic matter or as what we have called rhetorical-prosodic; in other words, in respect of versification and diction.

As to the first point, there can, to any reader with a careful eye and a good ear, be no question about the immense gain of fluency and exactness combined which *Troilus* shows. It is not even necessary to use the text in which the obliging hand of Professor Skeat has judiciously restored, and perhaps in a few cases supplied, readings according to the strictest orthodoxy of the final *e*, and similar things, or that less composite one with which, in the "Globe" edition, Professor M'Cormick has given us a useful companion. The comparatively unregenerate *textus receptus* of the Moxon one-volume edition will be quite satisfactory to any one with such an eye and such an ear. The stanzas "set," in the dancing sense, to themselves and each other with an accomplished grace; they carry out the combined figures, if not with such perfect accomplishment as in the possibly later *Prioress's Tale,* at any rate with a great advance in it over the earlier examples of the meter. But besides this we begin to get–what we got rarely or not at all earlier–those single lines or short batches of perfected prosodic and symphonic beauty, which are the *sine qua non* of really great poetry. How caressing is the throb and soar of the *Cantus Troili* in the first book:–

> If no love is, O God, what fele I so ?
> And if love is, what thing and which is he ?
> If love be good, from whennes comth my wo ?

No matter whether Italian or French, or his own soul taught him this melody; the point is that he has *found* it–that it is there.

Turn the leaves over at random and come to such a line as iv. 816–

> The mighty tresses of hir sonnish heres,

and see how he varies the vowel sound; dip again and you will again find. But, of course, the crucial examples of this, as of other excellence in the poem, are the three famous passages, first of Cressida's surrender–the universally known

> And as the newe abaysshed nightingale–

the magnificent address of the desolate lover to the palace also desolate, and the conclusion. Up to this time, though the lyre of English prosody is pretty well built and quite capable of producing musical sounds, it has never been thoroughly in tune, could never be quite trusted to apply concord and discord alike for the total production of harmony. Now, there is no more doubt. The tuner has come. But perhaps his main instrument of adjustment is, after all, his diction–his command of the famous "gold dew-drops of speech,"[17] already to no small if not to the fullest extent. We find it in occasional epithets and phrases ("Fortune, executrice of *wierdes,*" etc.) where the trick-combination of Latin and Saxon vocabulary is evidently known and practiced; but still more in the purple patches, the set passages already indicated and others. The compass of rhyme-royal, as has been hinted, is not quite so wide as its appeal is poignant. But Chaucer knows already how to make the best of both in a way never surpassed by any of his successors, and perhaps only equaled by Sackville in his two little masterpieces.[18]

Still the compass *is* rather narrow, and a very much smaller person than Chaucer must have found this out in writing eight thousand lines of it. At any rate he deserted the measure in his two next poems, poems where the interest still heightens, prosodically and otherwise. He had found out, no doubt, that it is not very well suited for narrative, save of a very brief or a very discursive character, dealing little with action and character, and that it is (unless willfully burlesqued and parodied in mock-heroic) as deficient in lightness as it is full of pathos and gravity. Now both the poems which he proceeded to write were narrative, and the first of them had a strong satiric tendency. For it, he fell back once more on the old octosyllabic couplet–for the last time, but also with far the best success. The *House of Fame* is in the good sense a very comfortable poem, and it is by no means least comfortable prosodically.[19]

At the beginning of the Third Book Chaucer makes a curious apology,[20] echoed with much better reason by many of his fellows, for his meter. As a matter of fact he manages the light and lewed rhyme very agreeably. His verses that omit a syllable hit the very genius of English poetry, and, though their lesson was at one time lost or slighted, helped Milton and Dyer and Coleridge to keep the precious torch alight. But he was evidently not quite satisfied with it, as appears not merely from the apology, which might be a mere piece of manners, or even of fun, but still more from the fact that he left the piece unfinished, and most of all from the other fact that he never again attempted the form. I do not know, sorry as I should be not to have the *House of Fame*, that he was wrong. The meter is crisp, fresh, and alive; the "failing" syllable gives variety and more freshness, and the poet uses effectively the device above referred to of finishing the sense of a paragraph at the first line of a couplet. But in avoiding the "lubricity" of the French original–the way in which the couplets slip away without mark or "bite," and which Gower has thoroughly transferred–the author has incurred a certain lack of ease, of fluency and fluidity. I think myself that there are some decasyllables in it, (*E.g.* i. 12; iii. 1967), as there had been in the work of the kind turned out by other practitioners; whether there are or not, Chaucer must have felt the cramp and "fidget" of so short a unit, for after it he turned definitely to the longer one, and usually, though not always, to the couplet form of it.

As to the origin of this, there have been great but perhaps unnecessary searchings of heart, which have as usual even obscured the true objects of search. Everybody with some small knowledge of old French knew, of course, that the decasyllable itself, in long batches of mono-rhymed (or mono-assonanced) lines, is perhaps the oldest of all meters in French, and is certainly the staple meter of the oldest extant French literature. But this knowledge implied the other, that the French, before Chaucer's time, did not often or largely use it in couplets, though the octosyllabic couplet had been one of their staples for centuries. It was therefore a great relief to some, though one not in the least needed by others, when a poem[21] by Guillaume de Machault, Chaucer's certain model in some things, was discovered in this meter.

Now I do not think it in the least necessary to doubt that Chaucer knew this poem, and perhaps others, and that their existence was not without some influence on his adoption, if not creation, of the great English epic, satiric, almost pan- (or pam-) poetic vehicle. But I am quite certain that he might have devised it independently of Machault, and I am by no means certain that he did not do so. It is one evil of the accent or beat theory that it obscures attention to the syllabic constitution of the line. If that attention is used properly, I am quite certain that not only decasyllabic lines but decasyllabic couplets, rude, and sometimes not so very rude, in English poems before and sometimes long before Chaucer, are unmistakable. I have called attention to these often here, but the matter is important enough to justify their repeated citation, especially as there is hardly a point which has been more generally overlooked, and which is received with more incredulity when presented.

In fact it would have been very extraordinary if the heroic had *not* "separated itself from the heap," to employ once more the precious phrase for which we must ever thank our sometimes Shylock Guest [*History of English Rhythms*]. On our own general hypothesis of the application of the metrical molds of French and Latin to the rhythmical matter of English blended with them, and of the resulting constitution of all forms that really suited that language, it could not but do so. But there is a stronger reason in the peculiarly loose and *molybdine* character of these earliest stages of English prosody, while the rigid syllabicism of French lessened the same chance there. A Frenchman *might* deliberately say to himself, "We have been using the decasyllabic line and the octosyllabic couplet for ages; so let us 'combine our information' and use the decasyllabic couplet which we already have in *laisse* and stanza." But he was not likely to stumble into this latter by accident and then, seeing that he had stumbled upon a good thing, to keep it on purpose. Many an Englishman, on the other hand, had, as we have shown, done the first, and an Englishman who was Chaucer was not at all unlikely to do the latter. The irregularity even of the more rigid octosyllabic distich, the elasticity of the equivalenced one, made such things as those which have been quoted certain to occur, when one remembers the almost uncanny virtues of the decasyllable itself, the way in which it has, in one form or another, imposed itself upon every great literary nation in Europe (except the Spaniards) as the most capacious of sense that will give a thoroughly satisfactory continuous medium for sound.[22] But besides all this

Chaucer had another strong reason for adopting the decasyllabic couplet, which was this, that he had actually been writing it for years at the close of each of his rhymes-royal. He had written more than a thousand such couplets in *Troilus,* he had written numbers in other poems, and, as has been seen, some of his most apparently elaborate stanzas resolve themselves in part into a mere sequence of decasyllabic couplets. And such a master, at once of rhetoric and poetry, could not fail, with such practice, to see its extraordinary advantages, though no doubt he saw these, as he shows them, more and more till the end. The heroic gives that elbow-room which the octosyllable denies; it retains the attraction, without imposing too much of the tyranny, of rhyme; it avoids the blocky and broken-up character of stanza writing; it gives in every particular room enough, and not too much room, for authentically prosodic and prosodic-rhetorical exercise and ornament; it is easy in a general way, without the fatal fluency and facility of the octosyllable itself; it offers much less temptation to the *cliché* and the *cheville*–the stereotyped padding and the cut-and-dried tag. And lastly, though even genius could hardly discover this at once, it provides opportunity for a variety of adjustment and appeal which is marvelous and almost endless. Nothing can speak more highly for Chaucer's metrical genius itself–though of course he had a certain advantage in the paucity of models before him–than the fact that he never put himself under articles, either to the enjambed or to the stopped couplet, as poets of other ages have in turn done. If there is one secret that he does not seem to have fully discovered, it is the virtue of the full stop within the line. But even he had to leave something for others.

He took to this couplet, anyhow; and while the whole of the *Legend of Good Women* (barring the inset Ballade) is in this meter, the exceptions in the *Canterbury Tales* are but exceptions. The *Man of Law's, Clerk's, Prioress's,* and *Second Nun's Tales* are in rhyme-royal, and the *Monk's* in octaves, while the *Rhyme of Sir Thopas,* for obvious reasons of parody, is in Romance sixes. But all the rest, and all the prologues and interim conversations which frame the whole, are in heroics, or as the old phrase better put this variety, "riding rhyme."[23] To expatiate on the delights of all is for the historian of English Literature, not for the historian of English Prosody. It is, however, within our competence to point out that the *Legend of Good Women,* though it lacks the astounding variety in accomplishment of the *Prologue,* the splendor of the best parts in the *Knight's Tale,* and the humorous flexibility of the comic stories, already shows remarkable command of the capacity of the meter for narrative purposes. The *Prohemium* in particular, where the poet has elbow-room, and can run over a wider gamut than in renderings of the pathetic stories of the "martyrdom" of the dames and damsels of old, is a most remarkable thing in its adaptation of the almost infant meter to the needs of irony, of description, of fancy, of argument, and of debate. When a metrical child is thus brought up in the way it should go, it is likely to go far.[24]

But the arrangement and examination of larger prosodic forms, though an indispensable part of our duty, and perhaps that which demands most space, is scarcely the most important part. Of that most important part the consideration of the general prosodic *effect* is itself a subdivision: the rest concerns the very vital matters of foot-constitution, quantity or accent, line-arrangement, rhyme, and the like. And here the difficulty which besets all this earlier part of our inquiry reaches its acutest stage.

That difficulty is plumply and plainly this, *that we have no means of ascertaining with any certainty what, exactly, Chaucer wrote*; by which I do not mean to touch anew on the *eternum vulnus* of the genuine and spurious works. What I mean is that in the case of the things most certainly and indisputably Chaucer's–the Prologue, say, or the *Knight's Tale*, or the *Rhyme of Sir Thopas*–we cannot, except by guesswork, decide what exact words Chaucer wrote, and still less in what exact spelling he wrote them. The stages of the history of the text are briefly and roundly three. We have a large number of early MSS., and we have some fairly early printed editions which are allowed by the most fastidious scholar to have their weight. But I do not think that any of the extremest of fanatics or fantastics has ever suggested that we have a line of Chaucer's own handwriting in the MSS.: while even Caxton's print is shut off by some seventy years from the possibility of Chaucer having supervised the printing.

Then we have a further number of printed editions only–possessing no authority whatever except what they may have derived from MSS., and dating partly from the times when Chaucer was still a great name but had not been actually studied at all, partly from the later times when even those who thought him a genius had made up their minds that he did not know how to scan. During this time, naturally, there grew up and flourished–it had begun even in the fifteenth century, and among the MSS. themselves–a process of arbitrarily "mending" Chaucer, of putting in words to fill up the nine-syllable lines and compensate for the misunderstood final *e,* of altering in order to correct what was thought false accent, and the like. Let us remember that even Tyrwhitt (who did more service to Chaucer than almost all other Chaucerians with "weight for age") printed–

> *A* twenty bokes clothed in black or red.

But Tyrwhitt himself began a new order, and the new order (as the "Board School," if not the "Christian" child, and as almost "the grey barbarian" knows) has gone very far and very fast. The editions of Chaucer now current are constructed[25] with a view of piecing together from this MS. and that, even (where the MSS. will not help) from this printed text and that "critical" text, things that shall comply with the notions as to Middle English grammar, prosody, and pronunciation, which have been excogitated by guesswork, or, if that seem too uncivil, by inferential hypothesis, during the last half century or more. Now in reference to these "critical" texts there is always an irrefutable logical *aporia* lying in wait. Any single MS., however bad, *may* be a copy at first or second-hand, careful or careless, of the original. A blending of two or three or more is less and less likely to represent any actual original at all.

But it may be said, "This is blasphemy against classical scholarship as well, and you do not intend that, surely?" To which I reply, "Certainly not," though I confess that even in the name of this–the true–"scholarship" things are sometimes done at which a tolerably lachrymose angel would shed floods of tears. But between this and the so-called "scholarship" of philologists in modern languages, and in English perhaps most of all, there are differences of the gravest and the most multiple kinds. That the one is the fruit not of centuries but of millennia of study, mistake, reparation of mistake; and the other a thing scarcely of yesterday, is not very much, though it is something. That, however they may fight about details, there is very general agreement among the classical scholars on important points, and a chaos of discordance among the others, may not be much, though it is a little more. The main and almost hopeless differences are other than these, and infinitely more important. In the first place, we know that nearly all Greek and Roman literature, if not all, was written by persons who were regularly instructed in their own language; that grammar, composition, and prosody formed part of Greek education from a very early time, and were transferred to Rome bodily almost before Roman literature, properly so called, so much as began. That is to say, all the texts we have, including even the redactions of such poets as Homer and Hesiod, were every one written and revised on definite principles–principles recognized, taught, learnt, and therefore beyond all doubt discoverable, with sufficient pains, from the examination of a sufficient number of instances.

Nor is this all. Not only do we know that there was such instruction; that it was given and that it was received; that the results were exposed to pretty sharp grammatical and rhetorical criticism; but we actually possess the documents and the instruments of this criticism and that instruction. We have in Dionysius Thrax for Greek and in Varro (incomplete as he is) for Latin, grammatical treatises representing the earlier part of the century before Christ, when the great period of Latin was just beginning, and when, though the greatest periods of Greek were over, its laws and lessons were only the more jealously preserved, studied, and handed down. We have a mass of documents for both stretching over the whole later period; we have the help of untiring *déblayage*–clearing away of rubbish–on the part of Renaissance scholars; and we have three whole centuries of unremitting attention to the matter, given by some of the acutest minds of Europe, and by a vast body of persons, all of whom have been from their youth trained up in the received and ascertained orthodoxy of the subject.

Now look on the other picture. *There was up to Chaucer's time absolutely no school-instruction even with English as a vehicle, let alone any school-instruction in English itself.* We know from the invaluable and should-be famous passage of his contemporary Trevisa[26] that, until the great alteration of social conditions by the Black Death, English boys learnt Latin and other things at English schools *in and by French.* There is not the very faintest spark of evidence that Chaucer ever received the smallest instruction from anybody how to spell an English word, to decline an English noun or verb, to construct an English sentence, or to modulate an English line. It is, on the contrary, about as certain as anything of which we have not positive evidence can be, that he never had anything of the sort, and that his successors for a generation or two never had anything of the sort. The earliest grammatical and rhetorical dealings with English that we have date from the sixteenth century; the earliest prosodic observations from its latter end.

On the one hand, therefore, the classical "scholar's" problem is to discover the positive and doctrinal principles of a body of documents–

I. Which were originally written under such principles;
II. Which were, in at any rate some cases (not of course in all), transcribed by persons acquainted with, and instructed in, these principles;
III. Which include formal treatises stating, explaining, and illustrating these principles themselves, and to no small extent coinciding with the period of original writing, to a much larger with that at which the documents were transcribed.

On the other hand, the Middle English "scholar's" problem is to discover the positive and doctrinal principles of a body of documents–

I. Which were written when there is no evidence that any such positive or doctrinal principles existed, and all but a certainty that they did not;
II. Which were transcribed by persons under the same deprivation or limitation;
III. Which include no pedagogic treatise dealing with the matter.

I think that to rub this contrast in any further would be an insult to the intelligence of the reader.

But though, while the art and labor of the classical scholar consists in revising documents according to a norm, capable to at least some extent of being independently and authoritatively established, that of the modern scholar too often consists in extracting from documents a norm according to his own taste and fancy, and then according to his own taste and fancy refashioning the documents in obedience to the norm, not all even of this latter's work is of such a perilous sort. Paleography, though easily abusable, is a real science of a kind, and can refer to outside and independently contributed evidence. Some documents are dated; and the forms in them are dated likewise by real external and internal evidence, not "hariolation." And lastly, in our present department of Chaucer particularly, some scholars have taken the troublous but most thankworthy method of printing the MSS. themselves, of giving us the real property in so far as it exists. A great deal more than we can at all wish is still left to guess on the part of those who like guessing, and to confession of uncertainty on the part of those who do not. But on the whole, we can make out something, and can even say of this something, "'twill serve."

To take, then, those points which have been noticed above in order, there can be no dispute (except mere logomachy) about the general and so to speak *prima facie* metrical character of Chaucer's prosody. You may call a thing an octosyllable, or an iambic dimeter,[27] or a four-beat verse, but the thing is the same and unmistakable. So, too, the various stanza forms are identical under any dress of words, and so is the great staple meter of the *Canterbury Tales,* whether you call it "riding rhyme," or "heroic couplet," or "rhymed decasyllables," or "rhymed five-beat lines," or anything else that the wit or the perversity of man has invented or may invent. Whatever each *libentius audit,* it is *there*–unmistakable, fully constituted, corresponding to things of the same kind written five hundred years after Chaucer went to his grave. In each case we shall have a good deal more to say about these forms in the next Interchapter and in the Appendix. For the present they are *data.*

Ascending or descending to the next stage, there is matter for more legitimate controversy about the composition of the *lines* which themselves compose these forms. The old and long prevalent idea that Chaucer could not scan was based upon, or rather was but another form of, the idea that he could not count; and this itself, though partly the result of mere ignorance of the value of syllables, especially of the final *e,* had a second cause in the obstinate heresy, finally formulated as orthodoxy by Bysshe, that the syllabic composition of English lines was arithmetically positive and unalterable.

Now, as it happened, Chaucer, the first great named and known poet of English, had, by good luck–though he undoubtedly leant, as we have said, towards the principle of fixity rather than towards the principle of equivalent substitution–handed in evidence, unchallengeable except by ignorance, that he was *not* of this opinion. In regard to his octosyllables there could indeed never have been a mistake about the fact, and it was even very difficult, in face of Milton's adoption of the practice in perhaps his most melodious and certainly his most popular poems, to stigmatize it as improper. It *was* so stigmatized, of course, by the fanatics of syllabic regularity. But the actual presence of seven-syllable lines–set it down as you liked to substitution of trochaic for iambic rhythm, *anacrusis* [unaccented extra-metrical syllables at beginning of a line], monosyllabic feet, "reversal of beat," "omission of thesis," stick on it any earthly or unearthly ticket you pleased–this actual presence remained unmistakable and undeniable, alike as to its existence in great poets, and its enjoyment by well-qualified readers.

That he took the same liberty with the decasyllable (followed, though more sparingly, again by Milton) was for a long time much less clearly perceived, and I believe is still denied or blinked by some people, while it is obvious that the disapproval of it by the neo-classic critics would have been still more severe. For myself, I have long ceased to have the slightest doubt of the fact, which Professor Skeat has established by an invulnerable array of quotations. It *is* the fact; and what is more, it would be extremely surprising if it were not. The thing had, as we have seen, been usual in the octosyllable for centuries, and it was certain to extend itself to the longer meter, when at last this came to be tried on the great scale. I am, however, far from thinking, despite the mighty authority of its two great practitioners, that it is a desirable license: and I would have resisted the evidence if I could. Instead of adding beauty, as the companion license does in the octosyllable, it appears to me to give (with the very rarest exceptions, if with any) an ugly jolt and jar in continuous verse, and complete destruction of all harmony in the stopped couplet. The fact is, as I have ventured to express it already elsewhere, that the octosyllable treads too closely on the heels of the decasyllable to allow the latter to contract its own stride. It may extend with advantage–with very great advantage: but that is a different matter, and to it we may come, just observing that in stanza-work Chaucer is not prone to avail himself of this license, and for very obvious reasons.[28]

The same prejudice which prevented critics and readers in the neo-classic period from observing or, if they observed, allowing Chaucer's cutting the line short would have extended, and did extend, to his lengthening it; and this too is not dead. That there are trisyllabic feet, as I should call them, accented syllables with more than one unaccented between them as I suppose the accent-people would be obliged by their etiquette to put it, (some of them call it "a double thesis"), I have no more doubt than I have that there are monosyllabic feet or nine-syllable lines. I even think that there are a great many more of them, that they are in fact of constant occurrence. And though this makes for my own general theory, I am rather surprised at it, and am forced to admit that a good many of these feet are of a fairly "squeezable" character. The squeezableness, which is important, may fitly introduce something (to be again and again of course supplemented with something more) on one of the great questions of English prosody.

That question is: When we meet in older English poetry–there is not much controversy about the fact, though there may be some about the law, in regard to the poetry of the nineteenth century–what has just been called a trisyllable foot, are we to set it down as really such; or to account for it by actual Elision; or to adopt a middle course and set it down to Slur? And let it be observed (to follow the excellent method of Aristotle and of *The Art of Pluck*) that by Trisyllabic Foot I mean a collection of syllables in which full though not necessarily the same value is given to each; by Elision the actual *crushing out* of one so that the foot becomes dissyllabic; and by Slur,[29] the compromise which hurries over one syllable, if it does not quite elide it.

Any unfaltering answer to the question, at this our present time of the close of the fourteenth century, is made difficult by a certain peculiarity of spelling which pervades (though by no means consistently) the MSS. and the early printed editions from the close of the fifteenth till late into the sixteenth. These writers and printers did not use the ugly apostrophe, which invaded English books in the seventeenth century, and persevered into the eighteenth, under the influence of a definite theory of scansion, which in turn it undoubtedly strengthened. But they did run the two words together in the case of articles, prepositions, and sometimes even pronouns. Just as we find in Wyatt and Surrey "tembrace" and the like, so, a hundred years earlier, we find in Chaucer sometimes (not always) "thestat," "tharray," etc., and even "in thalyghte" for "in *thee* alyghte." Now is this also a matter of theory–a sprout of the idea that the three syllables *ought to be two*? Or does it express a real custom of pronunciation? Were these two words–not merely the first, which might be and in some MSS. is, "the state," but "tharray" where there is no way out of the difficulty–so pronounced?

I do not believe they ever were; but even from my point this by no means settles the question. I do not, in the same way, believe that a man ever let such a monster pass the door of his lips as "monstrorrendinformingens," but I feel sure that Vergil *scanned* "monstrum horrendum, informe, ingens," so. Was there anything similar in Chaucer or was there not?

The arguments for Elision are, first, the spelling; secondly, the undoubted belief of generations, not so far from Chaucer's own time, that there *was* elision; thirdly, the fact that it exists abundantly and obtrusively, one may say, in the two *grammaticæ,* the two accomplished literary languages, Latin and French, which Chaucer and others knew.

The arguments for Slur are, first, the usual ones for any compromise; secondly, that even unquestionable trisyllable feet are undoubtedly pronounced somewhat quicker than dissyllabic; thirdly, that English is notoriously addicted to slurring and clipping in pronunciation, from the extreme cases of Chiselhampton and Cirencester and Cockburnspath to the lesser ones of Southwell and Southwark.

Those for actual trisyllable feet may seem weaker at first, but to me they become stronger and stronger the more they are considered. One which is, to me, almost sufficient, is purely historic, and so in reality, if not in appearance, the most solid possible. It is drawn from the earliness and the persistence of the undisputed trisyllable foot in English. Nobody denies the presence in Anglo-Saxon of groups of syllables which would naturally, if not necessarily, pass into it when meter was substituted for mere rhythm. Its presence in *Genesis and Exodus* (if not even earlier) and other poems of the mid-thirteenth century is undeniable. In all folk-song and ballad-writing it perseveres, while the persistent and ferocious persecution of it, and the critical disapproval of it, for two hundred years and more, cannot drown it or burn it or bury it. Earth and water and fire may combine against it, but it abides victoriously in the air, the element of poetry, and descends again at the right time.

The second is more controversial, but to me quite satisfactory. It is only by means of this mixture of trisyllable feet that the extraordinary variety and charm of English poetry–a thing acknowledged by those who are not Englishmen as well as by those who are–can be attained; and it has been almost invariably by those who used them most that the attainment has been most successful and complete. Nay more, just as it has been said of the Jews in Spain, and of other persecuted races and families elsewhere, that by changing names they avoided the persecution directed against them, so the trisyllable foot survives at the very time when it seems to have disappeared in folk-song and theatrical verse. The Bysshes, and even the Johnsons, cannot prevent persons with an ear from reading the apostrophe with the syllable it has vainly tried to expel, and giving value to the *i* and *y* syllables to which they impotently refuse value. Such a captain of the heathen or heretic host as Pope himself selects a line which derives most of its beauty from a trisyllable foot, as his own favorite among his own productions ("The freezing

Tanais through a waste of snows"): and Shenstone (in the *Essays),* forty years at least before Coleridge, vindicates the "dactyl" in English poetry.

Another point of no inconsiderable interest in connection with the length of Chaucer's lines opens the question, "Did he ever use the Alexandrine, or line of normally twelve syllables?" I think he did, as in the examples given below, and I am not much affected by the general failure to take this view, with its consequent adjustments by syncope or elision or other devices. For, in the first place, it matters to the theories of those who deny that they should deny it; and it does not matter to my theory at all that I should assert it. Secondly, the lines–or some of them–scan much better as Alexandrines. Thirdly, it is reasonable that in the process of "separation from the heap" this form also should be tried, especially considering the great prominence of it in French poetry, which was always more or less a model. Fourthly, we see historically that there is–at least up to Dryden and sometimes since–a constant tendency to take the Alexandrines as an "easement," now and then, to the decasyllable.[30]

We come now to yet another point of great importance, the question how Chaucer manages the individual syllabic values which make up his feet or his accent-groups.[31] In the great majority of words this "accent" is mainly, though not wholly, identical with that of the present day, and it is not necessary for any decently-bred modern Englishman who is acquainted with that *secret de Polichinelle,* the value of the final *e,* to accept any unfamiliar pronunciation in order to get the full metrical and rhythmical value of Chaucer's lines. Whether the vowels were then differently pronounced or not I do not know; there is practically no evidence on the subject of any kind that I can admit. But it is certain that if the *actual* sound has changed, the *relative* values of the different sounds have not. Where we should expect a long vowel before a single consonant we find it, and we often find that where a short vowel sound comes before two consonants it can take the place of a long, though not invariably. The really and constantly short vowels of modern English are, as a rule, short also, unless some special stress be laid on them. These are rules; but to them we find two considerable classes of exceptions, which have mainly become obsolete in English. One of these concerns proper, especially classical proper, names, the other words in which the French accent is retained.

It is, indeed, not at all improbable that these two classes are really, at least in origin, one. The peculiarity of French accentuation, or rather the dogma of it, is well known, and Professor Ker, among others, has rightly drawn attention to the very peculiarly pronounced values which French, like Low Latin, gives to Latin words (*The Dark Ages,* [202 sq]). It is obvious that Chaucer follows the same system, and that he is followed by all English poets down at least to Spenser, who was a very fair scholar in the classical languages. Milton is about the first to give the correct quantification. Earlier writers not only shorten naturally long vowels and lengthen short, but even make a cretic [Gr: 'long at both ends'] out of *Minerva,* as Baudelaire does out of *Francisca.*

More indubitably, though I think not more really, French is the constant valuation of such words as "manèr," "entraìl," etc., according to their French rather than their English value.

And so we come to one of the hottest of the ash-places, the question of rhyme, on which, however, I do not propose to say much. Although I absolutely refuse to accept the *y-ye* test, as in the very slightest degree valid for establishing authenticity, until the Bradshavians give up *Sir Thopas,* I believe that Chaucer probably avoided these rhymes, just as a modern English poet with delicate ear avoids the rhyme of "or" and "ore."[32] Otherwise, and with the large exception of that freedom of shifting the accent which has just been noticed, and which enables him to make a rhyme of "squire" and "supper" ("squyer" and "soper"), his rhymes are for the most part quite modern and normal. Many of them are, of course, double rhymes, thanks to the *e.* But I have always thought that the excision of this exuberance, or excrescence, which was certainly going on in Chaucer's own time, was probably much helped by the popularity of "riding rhyme" in which the doubling is rarely if ever good, save to produce special and exceptional effects. It is scarcely necessary to say that, in common with all poets up to at least the middle of the seventeenth century he avails himself of the full syllabic value of words in -*ion* and similar endings; or that, though the modern utter abhorrence of an identical rhyme, even with changed sense does not appear in him, he is not very prone to indulgence in it.

NOTES

[*]Reprinted from *A History of English Prosody from the Twelfth Century to the Present Day.* 3 vols. London: Macmillan and Co., 1906–10. I.143–77.

[1]As the perversity of some readers is only not incalculable, let me prevent it by observing that I do not mean by "them" the two MSS., but their contents. Some of those of the Auchinleck are mentioned in *Sir Thopas.*

[2]This will be referred to again; see n. 26 below.

[3]I repeat regretfully, respectfully, but peremptorily and irrevocably, that it is impossible to argue with persons who say that Chaucer never rhymes *Y* to *ye,* and then admit that he did in *Sir Thopas,* and say that it can easily be explained. Of course it can–by the fact that if he ever made a rule of the kind at one time he broke it at another–and in no second way. This unfortunate *lubie* of the late Mr. Bradshaw must, I suppose, be allowed to have its day; it will cease to be in time, like other things of the same kind. Meanwhile, let it be now observed that the various discussions about the English *Romaunt,* and the way in which its parts are chopped and changed by this and that distributor, are characteristic. In this book we do not rope-dance, but keep to solid paths, and where the paths are not solid we do not care to walk.

[4]*E.g.* 6322: "As I. For I never come in toune." Near this are some lines which *I* should take as slipped decasyllables.

[5]An extract, however, may be desirable:–

Hir heer was as yelowe of hewe
As ony basyn scoured newe,
Hir flesh [as] tendre as is a chike,
With bente browis smothe and slyke;
And by mesure large were
The openyng of hir yen clere;

Hir throte also white of hewe
As snowe on braunche snowed newe.
Of body ful wel wrought was she,
Men neded not in no cuntre
A fairer body forto seke.
And of fyn orfrays hadde she eke

Hir nose of good proporcioun,
Hir yen grey as is a faucoun;
With swete breth and wel savoured,
Hir face white and wel coloured,
With litel mouth and rounde to see;
A clove chynne eke hadde she,
Hir nekke was of good fasoun,
In lengthe and gretnesse by resoun,
Withoute bleyne, scabbe, or royne;
Fro Iersalem unto Burgoyne
Ther nys a fairer nekke, i-wys,
To fele how smothe and softe it is.
A chapelet so semly oon
Ne werede never mayde upon.
And faire above that chapelet
A rose gerland had she sett.
She hadde [in honde] a gay mirour,
And with a riche gold tresour
Hir heed was tressed, queyntely.
Hir sleves sewid fetously,
And forto kepe hir hondis faire
Of gloves white she had a paire.
And she hadde on a cote of grene
Of cloth of Gaunt, withouten wene.

ll. 539–574.

[6]*E.g.*–

Al myghty and al mercyable Queene,
To whom that al this world fleeth for socour
To have relees of sinne, of sorwe, and teene!
Glorious Virgine, of alle floures flour,
To thee I flee confounded in errour.
Help, and releeve, thou mihti debonayre,
Have mercy on my perilous langour!
Venquisshed me hath my cruel adversaire.

[7]As in l. 12–

Axeth thyn helpe. Thyn herte is ay so free.

[8]A single line (50) will give us a curious and capital instance of what is called critical editing. Of the seven MSS. which Professor Skeat collates, two give–

Thanne leve I alle thees vertues sauf pitee;

two–

Then leve we al vertues saue oonly pite;

three–

Then leve all vertues saue onely pite.

Now none of these will scan according to the orthodox values of the final *e*. So you take the text of the first group and spell it according to the others, and you get

Then leve I al thise virtues sauf pite.

But we ought to give a whole stanza–

Pite that I have sought so yore ago
With herte sore and ful of besy peyne,
That in this worlde was never wight so wo
With-oute dethe; and if I shal not feyne,

My purpos was to Pite to compleyne
Upon the crueltee and tirannye
Of Love, that for my trouthe doth me dye.

[9]Or outrage, according to the famous *perruque* critic of *Hernani.* A short couplet batch, chosen to show the *dialogue,* and the onzain, may follow:–

"Sir," quod I, "wher is she now ?"
"Now!" quod he, and stynte anoon.
Therwith he wex as deed as stoon
And seyde, "Allas, that I was bore!
That was the los, that her-before
I tolde the that I hadde lorn;
Bethenk how I seyde herbeforn;
'Thow wost ful litel what thou menest;
I have lost more than thou wenest!'
God wot, allas! right that was she!"
"Allas! sir, how? what may that be?"
"She ys deed! "
"Nay!"
"Yis, by my trouthe!"
"Is that your los? by God, hit is routhe!"
And with that worde right anoon
They gan to strake forth; al was doon
For that tyme, the hert-huntying.
ll. 1297–1312.

I have of sorwe so grete woon
That joye gete I never noon,
Now that I see my lady bright,
Which I have loved with al my myght,

Is fro me deed and is a-goon.
Allas, Deeth, what ayleth thee
That thou noldest have taken me,
Whan thou toke my lady sweete
That was so fayr, so fresh, so fre,
So good, that men may wel se
Of al goodnesse she had no meete.

ll. 475–485

[10]To whom shal I then pleyne of my distresse?
Who may me helpe ? Who may my harm redresse?
Shall I compleyne unto my lady fre?
Nay, certes! for she hath such hevynesse,
For fere, and eek for wo, that, as I gesse,
In litil tyme it wol her bane be.
But were she sauf, it were no fors of me!
Alas ! that ever lovers mote endure,
For love, | so ma | ny a pe | rilous a | venture!
ll. 191–98.

[11]The lyf so short, the craft so long to lerne,
Thassay so hard, so sharp the conquerynge,
The dredful joye, alwey that slit so yerne;
Al this mene I be love, etc.

[12]Now welcom, somer, with thy sonne softe,
That hast this wintres weders overshake
And driven a-wey the longe nyghtes blake.

Lines 1 and 2 repeated *twice* and 3 *once,* woven ingeniously with others into *thirteen* and rhymed *abbabab–abbabb.*

[13] Hir name is Bountee, set in womanhede,
Sadnesse in youthe and Beautee pridelees
And Plesaunce, under governaunce and drede;

Hir surname eek is Faire Rewthelees,
The Wyse, y-knit un-to Good Aventure,
That, for I love hir, she sleeth me giltelees.

[14]My dere herte and best beloved fo,
Why liketh yow to do me al this wo,
What have I doon that greveth yow, or sayd,
But for I serve and love yow and no mo?
And whilst I lyve I wol ever do so;
And therfor, swete, ne beth nat yvel apayd.
For so good and so fair as [that]* ye be
Hit were right gret wonder but ye hadde
Of alle servantes, bothe of goode and badde;
And leest worthy of alle hem, I am he.
*Supplied by Professor Skeat.

[15]Now cer | tes, swe | te, thogh | that ye
Thus cau | seles | the cau | se be,
Of my | dedly adver | sitee,
Your man | ly re | soun oght | e it to | respite,

and so on to sixteen.

[16] My swete foo, why do ye so, for shame?
And thenke ye that furthered be your name,
To love a-newe, and ben untre | we? Nay!
And putte you in sclaunder now and blame,
And do to me adversitee and grame,
That love you most–God, wel thou wost!–alway ?
Yet turn ageyn, and be al pleyn som day,
And then shall this, that now is mis, be game,
And al foryive, whyl that I li | ve may.

This, of course, is interesting to compare with "E. I. O." and "The Nut-Browne Mayde," and to note the shortened and, as it were, "pulled up" effect of the places marked. Chaucer, though not ill, was not supremely well at these *carillon* numbers. Yet some have even called the piece "Pindaric," and it is certainly both ingenious and pleasing. . . .
[17]Might not this admirable phrase have saved its poor author, whoever he was, from dismissal of the piece as "a poor stanza," and a "poor imitation of the style of Lydgate" ? Even if he stole it from somebody else, he gave it rightly to the right person, wobble and "wamble" as his poor verses may.
[18]To illustrate the *karole*–the musical dance above noticed–take these stanzas–

And when that he was slayn in this manére
His lighte goost ful blisfully is went
Up to the holwnesse of the eighte spere,
In convers leting everich element:
And ther he saugh with ful avisement
Th'erratik sterres, herkning armonye
With sounes fulle of hevenissh melodye.

And down from thennes faste he gan avise
This litel spot of erthe that with the see

Embraced is, and fully gan despise
This wrecched world, and held al vanité
To réspect of the pleyne felicite
That is in hevene above. And at the laste,
Ther he was slayn his loking down he caste,

And in himself he lough right at the wo
Of hem that wepen for his deth so faste,
And dampned al our werk, that folwen so
The blinde lust the whiche that may not laste,
And sholden al our herte on hevene caste.
And forth he wente, shortly for to telle,
Ther-as Mercúrie sorted him to dwelle.

Swich fyn hath tho this Troilus for love!
Swich fyn hath al his grete worthinesse!
Swich fyn hath his estat reál above!
Swich fyn his lust, swich fyn hath his noblesse!
Swich fyn, this false worldes brotelnesse!–
And thus bigan his loving of Criseyde
AsI have told and in this wise he deyde.
ll. 1807–34

[19]I am particularly anxious not to multiply differences with Professor Skeat. But surely it is very misleading to say, true enough as all the statements are: "The four-accent meter was commonly known before Chaucer's time," that "it was used by Robert of Brunne in 1303, in the *Cursor Mundi* and in *Havelok,"* being, however, "of French origin." All these statements are, I say, true; but how very far do they fall short of the whole truth! The "four-accent meter," octosyllabic couplet, or iambic dimeter, is practically the staple meter of English verse from Layamon to Hampole, both included. Layamon himself, a century before Robert, the author of *Genesis and Exodus,* and the author of *The Owl and the Nightingale,* a vast proportion of the romancers, and a vast proportion of the religious verse-makers all alike use it. And further, to say that "it occurs in the *Roman de la Rose,"* though again quite true, obscures the fact that, long before Lorris, it had been used by Chrestien and the other French authors of the Arthurian poems, that it is the staple of the Renart cycle, of the *Fabliaux,* of the *Romans d'aventures* generally. All this Professor Skeat knows as well as I do, and did know long before I knew it. But his readers do not know in one case out of a hundred, and they could hardly learn it from his words.

[20] Nat that I wilne, for maistrye
Here art poetical be shewed;
But, for the rym is light and lewed,
Yit make hit sumwhat agreable,
Thogh som vers faile in a sillable.

There is yet another prosodic reference in the *House of Fame,* which has been the occasion of so much discussion that it may perhaps best be treated here at some little length. This is where the eagle, in his amusing and very unceremonious talk with Chaucer, observes that the poet has never yet received any favors from Venus or Cupid–

And neverthelesse hast set thy wyt
(Although that in thy heed ful lyte is)
To make bookes, songes, or dytees
In ryme or *elles in cadence.*

Now what, it is asked, is this "cadence" which is so opposed to "rhyme"? "Alliteration" of course, say some. Without being in a hurry to answer them, let us cite two other "classic places." One of these is from Gower *(Conf. Am.* iv. 2414)–

> And Heredot in his science
> Of meter, of rime, *and of cadence,*
> The firste was of which men note.

The other is Wyntoun's (*Orig. Cron.* Bk. v. ch. xii. 4336)–

> Had he cald Lucyus Procuratoure
> Whare that he cald hym Empyrowre,
> That had mare grevyd the *cadens*
> Than had relevyd the sentens.

The mere quotation of these side by side ought to show that, at any rate, "alliteration" was not a *specific* meaning of "cadence" known to and used by the three writers; and it seems to me to show that none of them can have, by cadence, meant alliteration at all. We do not know that Chaucer wrote any alliterative verse; and we do know the *ad infinitum* cited *locus* suggesting that he did not. Whomsoever and whatsoever Gower meant by "Heredot" (Mr. Macaulay has no note dealing with the passage) he most certainly did *not* mean that any of the ancients whom he is cataloguing wrote like Langland. And, as a matter of fact, the substitution of "Procurator" for "Emperor" need not "grieve" alliterative verse at all, so that Wyntoun certainly did not refer to it and did refer to "cadence" in ordinary sense. In one or other form of this last I myself see no reason whatever to doubt that the word is used in all three. . . .

[21]The *Complainte après la bataille de Poitiers.* See Tarbé's ed., Paris and Rheims, 1849, p. 89; and Professor Skeat's *Chaucer,* iii. 383.

[22]The French Alexandrine is the only (and only an apparent) exception. I do not, of course, mean that the Spaniards did not use the decasyllable. But they continued to prefer the "short line" as a staple, especially in drama.

[23]If any one wishes to know why I say "better," let him look at a really good horseman *walking* his horse.

[24]It was certain that the discovery of two versions of the *Prologue to the Legend* would lead to conflicting theories as to last and first, and it has done so. Metrically there is no striking difference: or rather the differences are *cross,* and cancel one another.

[25]It has been already said that the *Globe*–though it still indulges in those extraordinary family-trees of MSS., which look like diagrams of Euclid that have had bombs thrown into their middles–is less eclectic and "improving" than some others.

[26]Anybody who wants this may find it in Morris and Skeat's *Specimens,* vol. ii. p. 241.

[27]I would fain enter a protest against a practice–common with the compilers of ordinary English grammars and composition-books, and not unknown among those of better breed–of speaking of this line and the next greater as iambic *tetrameters* and *pentameters.* This numeration is quite contrary to the recognized practice of classical prosody, and likely to cause confusion, especially in the use of the word "pentameter."

[28]The "Lydgatian" monosyllable at the caesura, which Professor Skeat reluctantly admits as an exception, I reject. The examples given by him are so few that they are fairly dismissible as copyists' mistakes. And I must respectfully protest that the lines in Tennyson's *Vision of Sin,* "Then methought," etc. are no parallel to Chaucer's "acephalous" experiments. Here the meter is dexterously changed, in a solid block or strophe, to trochaic.

[29]I have, as will have been sufficiently evident, no objection to, but a great liking for, classical terms when they are necessary or even convenient. But with so excellent an English word as "slur," which exactly expresses the English practice, I can see no excuse for *Synizesis.*

[30]We shall trace the further use of this line–venerable from its achievements in Greek and French–later; but it may not be improper to say at once that it seems to me *only* an easement, not a staple, in English. I think it may be well here to give specimens, not only of it, but of the other anomalous or debated lines just mentioned.

Alexandrines:–

Westward, | right swich | ano | ther in | the op | posit; *K.T.* 1036.

where, of course, those who like may scan–

Westward, | right swich | anoth | 'r in thop | posit,

if they will, though no MS. is quoted for the contraction.

Others are in some of the places (*W. of B. T.* 231; *F. T.* 158, 286; *Som. T.* 462) where they wish to pronounce *benedicite* "bendisty" or "bencity," in spite of the fact that it must have the full five-syllable value in *K. T.* 927. See also *Sq. T.* 20, 75, 480, 515–16.

Acephalous lines:–

Passim: the well-known one cited above from the *Prologue* and usually mended–

Twen | ty bo | kes clad | in blak | and reed

with

And | a cok | kow sit | ting on | hir hand, *K. T.* 1072.

will do well enough.

As for the Lydgatian "breakback," the examples quoted by those who believe in it are such as–

My tale is doon for my wit is thinne. *M. T.* 438.

and

I mean of Mark, Mathew, Luke, and John. *Prol. Mel.* 33.

For my own part, I am perfectly certain that Chaucer's prosodic wit was never so thin, and his ear never so thick, as to write the first; while in the second, Marke is admittedly possible, and supported by MS. and early print while both are easily mended with syllables that copyists were quite likely to slip, especially when Lydgate himself had misled them.

[31]I must, I am afraid, repeat once more that I entirely exclude the previous or subsequent question as to the *cause* of this value, whatever it is. I shall only say that Chaucer is one of the main sources of evidence in favor of the position that, whether there is quantity in English, or no quantity but only accent, accent is certainly one of the main agencies in English for the creation of the thing which *I* call quantity.

[32]He does it only when he cannot help it, or can help it at such an expense that the game is not worth the candle; but he does not regard it as he regards a rhyme of "Leonora" and "before her," or of "Helen" and "willing."

Alan T. Gaylord

Scanning the Prosodists: An Essay in Metacriticism*

"English prosody has tended to be a subject for cranks."
–John Hollander, *Vision and Resonance*[1]

"I am sure that attention to prosody never barred or spoiled attention to poetry, except in those who have been made unpoetical from the beginning."
–George Saintsbury, *A History of English Prosody*[2]

"Certainly an important aspect of literary criticism is the behavior of literary critics."
–Seymour Chatman, *A Theory of Meter*[3]

To show how Chaucer moves, and in moving, moves us: is that not what the study of his prosody should do? Should it not identify a pattern of sounds in motion, a regular and expressive succession which is part of the order of verse and a major component of its effectiveness?

I use "should" in these questions, because my aim in this essay is to do more than describe prosodic criticism as it is currently being practiced. I wish to analyze the various methods that have been used and then evaluate what has been achieved, because I think Chaucer studies tend to pay too little attention to his versification, in large part because what has been done thus far has not given us what we need. "Metacriticism," as I understand it, is the criticism of criticism; therefore, I shall aim to expose the language and working assumptions of prosodic criticism, identify the major areas which comprise its discipline, inquire into the theory and the practice of the generally acknowledged prosodic "authorities," and sum up where we have come to, and where we should go next. The aim of metacriticism should be to improve the naming of parts and the using of tools, towards helping better criticism emerge. Thus, although I shall consider many critics, my aim is not systematically to find them wanting; to do so would be presumptuous and foolish. As a field, Chaucerian prosodic criticism can provide both instruction and delight–in varying measure–to those who explore it. Nevertheless, that criticism helps us most, which grows the best; and so we must inquire periodically what it has done, is doing, and can, and should, do now.

I. Prosody: Theory

My general definition of prosody will be "the theory and practice of versification." The term came originally from the Greek, and was adopted by those whose approach to poetry had been influenced–directly or indirectly–by a classical education. This kind of definition is in the process of dying out, along with the education, as another is being supplied by linguists: those "features [which] include pitch, stress, length, and, often, syllabicity."[4] The latter definition does not necessarily have anything to do with poetry, but should be of great interest to literary prosodic studies. To indicate philological and linguistic domains of the definition, however, is only one way of getting at some basic differences which underlie contemporary problems in terminology and method. For example, the following quotation does much more than illustrate the classical legacy of prosody; it illustrates a style, or a set of values, which is not as extinct as might first appear:

> More than forty years ago, I was reading the *Odyssey* one evening in a set of Oxford rooms, on the ground-floor looking into Merton Street. Somebody had a wine not far off; and the respectable "Slap" (whom Oxford men of my generation will remember) had brought his "noise" to the spot according to custom. Just as I came to the Song of the Sirens, they were playing a certain waltz of the day, well known to me (for like the unfortunate hero of a contemporary comic ditty I was "very fond of dancing") as *The Cornflower*. And it struck me, as I listened to the slow voluptuous music, and read the famous line with the clinging *u* sound pervading it, and rendered poignant by the sharper *i*'s and *o*'s and *a*'s–
>
> Δευρ´ αγε νυν, πολυαιν´ Οδυσευ, μεγα κυδος [´Αχαιων],
>
> with how little truncation (of the last word only) it could be adjusted–*spaced*–to the waltz-tune itself, different as it is from that of the natural hexameter. I do not mean to say that I elaborated a theory of prosody at the age of eighteen. But I had, even before that, been accustomed to scan (and if possible to scan in different ways) the poetry of which I was, and ever have been, an unsatiated and insatiable lover; and by degrees things shaped themselves. (Saintsbury 1906, I, ix–x)

At first blush, the passage may seem elegiac, redolent, like an ancient gardenia discovered between the leaves of an old book. If there are many things in this scene to smile at, let modern readers ignore at their peril the reminder that an "insatiable love" of poetry preceded that theory of prosody. True, it could at times confuse the issues (as Saintsbury tried to fudge distinctions between quantity and accent in his theory). But etymology implies what has been disciplined, when scholarship moves from *philology* to *linguistics*. The question of love becomes irrelevant. Temperature and temperament have changed, and–as the following passage suggests–have changed absolutely:

> We propose to view meter as the encoding of a simple abstract pattern into a sequence of words. This is achieved by establishing a correspondence between

> the elements constituting the pattern and specific phonetic (or phonological) properties of the word sequence. The study of meter must therefore be composed of two separate parts, namely, the study of abstract patterns and the study of the correspondence rules which enable a given string of words to be viewed as an instance of a particular abstract pattern.
>
> It is perfectly conceivable that the increase in complexity due to the need to invoke the third rather than the second alternative of the correspondence rule (52bii) should be a fraction of that resulting from the invocation of the second alternative. Such questions, however, can be answered only when a massive body of verse has been subjected to the type of analysis proposed. (Halle & Keyser 1971, 140 & 177)[5]

I do not intend, however, to suggest simply that prosodic criticism has developed linearly in 65 years, from classical to linguistic bases, but rather to indicate two attitudinal extremes–call them subjective and objective, if you will–which have distinguished methodologies over the years (for Saintsbury there was Jakob Schipper; for Halle and Keyser, Ian Robinson). Both claim to be inductive, to be attending to the observable data without prejudice, and to be talking about the poetic art of versification. And yet, not only do these attitudes fail to complement each other (as we might hope they could), they also cannot agree upon what is there. My suspicion is, that such failure to cooperate in the advancement of knowledge rises from a larger indifference in the critical community, so that neither side has been called to account for its methods, working definitions, aims, or assumptions.

Let us move closer to the question of "what is there." I provide below fifteen excerpts from the General Prologue to the *Canterbury Tales.* All are poetry, some are more "poetic" than others. Some are regularly cited when Chaucer's craft is discussed, and some are distinctive illustrations of his ironic wit. All should be familiar, though not all are remarkable. Each excerpt, however, contains several problems for the prosodist, some elementary, others quite sophisticated. I invite the reader to scan the list, characterize the prosodic issues, and then check against my own questions which follow in the reduced type. My statement of the questions is seldom innocent, of course, and what may have seemed to me to warrant a simple response of "Yes, of course," may provoke from others a snort of dissent. At any rate, I provide a summary of the critical issues, after the detailed inventory.

Excerpts

1. The holy blisful martir/ for to seke
   That hem hath holpen when that they weere seeke (17–18)[6]

2. In lystes thryes/ and ay slayn his foo (63)

3. And I seyde/ his opynyon was good

What sholde he studie/ and make hym seluen wood (183–84)

4. And ouer al/ ther as profit sholde aryse
Curteys he was/ and lowely of seruyse (249–50)

5. Twenty bookes/ clad/ in blak/ or reed
Of Aristotle/ and his Philosophye (294–95)

6. Ful redy hadde he/ hise Apothecaryes
To senden hym/ his drogges/ and his letuaryes (425–26)

7. For gold in Phisyk. is a Cordial
Ther fore/ he loued gold in special (443–44)

8. She koude muchel/ of wandrynge by the weye
Gattothed was she/ soothly for to seye (467–68)

9. That if gold ruste/ what sholde Iren do (500)

10. And for to drynke strong wyn/ reed as blood (635)

11. For curs wol sle/ right as assoillyng sauyth
And also/ war hym of a significauit/ (661–62)

12. But ye be murye/ I wol yeue yow myn heed (782)

13. Ne studieth noght ley hond to/ euery man (841)

14. He seyde/ syn I shal bigynne the game
What welcome be the Cut in goddes name (853–54)

15. And he bigan/ with right a murye cheere
His tale anoon/ and seyde as ye may heere (857–58)

Questions

1. What is the proper punctuation for this couplet, and is the virgule to be ignored? What is the significance of the *rime riche* in "seke" and "seeke"? Are there only two major stresses in the second line ("holpen" and "seeke")? Does the spelling of "weere" indicate unusual stress, or shall we emend to Ellesmere's "were"? How should this couplet be scanned? Is it in iambic pentameter? Are terminal -e's at line ends to be pronounced?
2. Is there a syllable lacking; or should "thryes" be two syllables? How expres-

sive is the assonance in this line? Is there a spondaic fourth foot?

3. What is the rhythm of 183? What is its intonation, particularly around "I" and "good"? Should we spell "opinioun" as in El? Why? How is 184 to be scanned? How many syllables are "studie" and "and," taken together? Which word receives the greater stress in "what sholde"?
4. How many syllables in 249? Why didn't Chaucer begin 250: "He was curteys"? Should the back diphthong in "lowely" be given extended stress, or drawl?
5. Shall the virgules be ignored? Is 294 a "headless" line? How can we tell? Should there be a cesural pause after "bookes"? How many major stresses in 295? Does "Aristotl(e)" elide with "and"? Should "his" in 295 receive any kind of stress? Should it be "promoted" to equal the stress in the second syllable of "Philosophye"?
6. How many unstressed syllables at the end of 425? Which receives more stress, "hadde" or "he"? Is there a cesural pause after "he"? Are there as many syllables in 426 as in 425? How many syllables in "drogges"? Should the line be emended to Ellesmere's "To sende him drogges and his letuaries"? (Robinson so emends in his edition.) Why?
7. What pauses, if any, within this couplet? How many major stresses in 443? How many stresses on "cordial," and which syllable has the main stress? How are the "d" of "cordial" and the "c" in "special" pronounced? How do we know? Should this couplet be made to sound rhythmically regular or irregular? What should its tempo be?
8. How many syllables in "koude"? Where is the stress in "muchel"? Should we accept other MSS.'s "muche"? How many major stresses in 467? Should the rhythm of 467 imply a line of anapests? Should "by" be promoted to any kind of stress? Is 468 a "headless" line? Or does the "Gat tothid" of Petworth MS. suggest that "tothed" is two syllables? Where are the stresses in "Gattothed"? Is it significant that the Hengwrt scribe has written it as one word? Is this an example of the notorious "broken-backed" line: x / | x / | / | x / | x /(x) ?
9. El has "shal" for "sholde," and Robinson adopts. Is either reading preferable? How many syllables in "ruste"? Should "ruste" be one syllable, with a marked pause after, counting as the arsis [weak position] of a reversed foot? Is "what" stressed? Are "gold" and "ruste" equally stressed? Should "if" be promoted? Why or why not?
10. El has "drynken"–a better reading? How many syllables in "drynke"? (Note Petworth MS., "drink.") Where are the major stresses? Should "for" be promoted? Does the addition of "for" suggest Chaucer was counting syllables? Is the assonance significant here?
11. What is the rime? Do both lines have the same number of syllables? How many major stresses in 662? How many syllables in "significauit," and where are the stresses? Where are the pauses in this couplet?
12. Is there any elision between "murye" and "I"? Does 782 tend towards anapests? Which receives the more stress, "But" or "ye"? Should this line be

emended towards regularity (adapting something like Harleian MS. 7334's "But ye be murye smyteth of myn heed")? Why or why not?

13. How should this line be punctuated? El has one virgule, following "noght"–does either MS. offer thereby any prosodic guidance? How many syllables in "studieth" and how should it be pronounced? Are there seven major stresses in this line–or how many? Where are the pauses? Should the prose rhythm of this line be marked enough so as to suggest no metrical pattern?
14. Is 853 metrically regular? Is "seyde" to be two syllables, or does the pause after it count as the arsis of the next foot? Is "I" equally stressed with the second syllable of "bigynne"? Or do we not worry about regularity in light of the colloquial character of the prose rhythm of this couplet? In 854, Robinson follows El's "a goddes name": What would be the argument for taking El's "a" over Hg's "in," and is the difference at all significant? Is the unevenness of 853 resolved by the apparent metrical regularity of 854?
15. Is this couplet very markedly a succession of iambic feet? Do the monosyllables contribute to this effect? Does the enjambment help keep it from turning into sing-song? Is the final -e of "cheere" in 857 to be pronounced, or to elide with "His" in the next line? El reads "and seyde in this manere" (which Robinson does not follow). Does this difference have implications for prosodic interpretation?

Everyone who has read these lines from the General Prologue has given some kind of answer, willy-nilly, to many of the questions I have raised above–at least by proxy, through accepting a critical text which has done some of the answering for readers. But if one were to set about to make some sense of the issues involved, one would have to grapple more systematically with those questions of fact and interpretation which I outline below under separate headings.

TEXT. As the excerpts from Hengwrt, an early fifteenth-century manuscript, make abundantly clear, the lines do not "look" like the poetry we have been accustomed to see. Not only do they lack the prosodic cues of contemporary punctuation, but they lack the authenticity which most texts of verse are presumed to possess. The prosodist is handicapped by having to deal with reports about, rather than words directly from, the poet. He deals with overlapping, even opposing versions. *There is no such thing as Chaucer's own line.* There are only scribal versions of it.[7] Hence, the prosodist faces the problem of circularity. Before one can analyze a text, one must decide which is "best"–and frequently that best derives from a prosodic analysis which begs the question of authority. Emendation–its validity and scope–is a problem no prosodist can avoid, even if pretending to (simply ask him which text has been used, and why).

PRONUNCIATION. Having decided what text to adopt, the prosodist must decide how much it tells us about pronunciation. Unless one is resolutely a-historical, it will be necessary to see, also, what phonology and historical linguistics can tell about the quality and placement of vowels; the articulation of consonants; the relationship between orthography (scribal) and pronunciation; prose and poetic "facts" and conventions concerning medial and final -*e*'s; and the stress system of late-fourteenth-century London Middle English. Needless to say, every time the prosodist scans a line or reads it to others, a position has been taken–or fallen into–on all of these extraordinarily complex matters.

METRICAL PATTERN. If the prosodist does more than report how the line that has been established and sounded as determined resembles examples of modern meter, it will be necessary to discover what the metrical conventions were for a poet of Chaucer's tongue and environment. Here the problem of terminology will be acute, since old terms or new shed only particular beams of light on particular phenomena. To adopt one set of terms is not to see, or to rule out, certain other details. Upon taking a stand on meters, the prosodist must further declare the relationship found between metrical abstractions and their realization in lines of verse, deciding what regular/irregular, metrical/unmetrical mean, and illustrating by reference to a coherent set of "rules" drawn from the verse, which cannot be so strict as to require many exceptions, or so loose as to blur the distinction between poetry and prose. In short, our prosodist will have to scan, coherently and persuasively.

VERSIFICATION. Such scansion will have to build into the description of a working system. The prosodist must tell us what is "typical" in Chaucer's prosody, and pay special attention to the place of rime in Chaucerian couplets and stanzas. Again, we will wish to see how the rime works, and have identified what would be "normal" and what "remarkable" in a rime, or "simple" and "complex," as the range of riming and its relationship to the movement of the verse are defined. The scansion will have to open up into the larger question of architectonics; i.e., the prosodist must show not only how Chaucer writes lines but also how he builds them into larger units. And any detailed and extended description will have to be related to semantic and rhetorical facts, since the pace, stress, and force of a line, the "how" of its saying, is a function of the "what" of its meaning.

POETIC EFFECT. If the prosodist is working with Chaucer because the "best text" and variety of verses are assumed to belong to great, or even very good poetry, it will be necessary to go further. Does the scansion help explain that excellence? Does the art of Chaucer include his prosody? The critic must show us what grounds there are for suggesting Chaucer intended to be admired for his versification; we must be shown "beauties" and special effects, verified in terms of medieval aesthetics. In short, versification must marry interpretation, in order to beget a "best" reading.

These five headings I have discussed outline the facts, assumption and aims which, it is my claim, no prosodic critic can avoid. Every single question, from the largest to the most minute, which I noted for the excerpts above from the General Prologue, cannot be answered responsibly without first coming to terms with *all* of these issues.

Let us say now, in summary, what it is we expect literary prosodic analysis of verse to accomplish: it will identify three coordinate categories: a) meter; b) [prose] rhythm; and c) performance. The first will be a set of norms for the positioning of stressed and unstressed syllables; the second will be the way a given line or passage should be imagined as spoken, with stresses marked according to conventions of speech and the requirements of sense; and the third will be a rendition of the line or passage in the "prosody" (in the linguistic sense) which an interpreter might provide. To apply these categories to Chaucer's verse, the prosodic critic must decide a) whether Chaucer recognized a set of norms for verse in English which he and we would agree in labeling "meters"; b) whether he intended a "prose rhythm" to intersect with a metrical concept, i.e., to play off speech rhythms against metrical pattern; and c) whether he conceived of a particular recital or delivery for fullest effect.

Satisfactory prosodic analysis, then, should be able to answer a), then nicely describe b) in the light of a), to the end of enhancing our imagination of c). That is to say, criticism will consider the specific *form* of the line, passage, or poem, and then its possible *performance*.[8]

Now this kind of prosodic analysis certainly does not look like a new idea. Those taught to read poetry through some version of Brooks and Warren will recognize immediately the principle of *expressive variation* which any schoolboy is supposed to be able to demonstrate in the verses of Shakespeare, Pope, Keats, Tennyson, Yeats, Frost, or anyone else writing metrical verse, and which Paul Fussell has made the very foundation of his work in *Poetic Meter and Poetic Form* (1965). But if the idea is well established, its realization in the prosodic criticism of Chaucer's verse is quite rare. Students who undertook to find answers to the questions itemized above for the 15 excerpts would not find them in any one place; and if they read as much of the body of prosodic criticism concerning Chaucer's verse as could be discovered, I do believe that they would conclude they were worse off than if they had never begun. It is not that they would fail to find intelligent and concerned critics, or even that they would not enjoy this article or that book, but the net result would be that they would discover they had attempted to enter a house with many doors but no connected walls, roof, or floor.

In their *A Prosody Handbook* Karl Shapiro and Robert Beum write:

> In recent decades, the study of poetry has focused intensively on the SEMANTIC elements of the poem, and prosody has been somewhat neglected. Between the analyses of critics whose main interest lies in allusiveness and connotation, and of critics who are interested primarily in "myth" or in the "history of ideas," the MEDIUM of poetry–the moving sound stream, the song-stuff–has become an unfashionable subject. (Shapiro & Beum 1965, 3)

It may be symptomatic that this book, while mentioning Chaucer briefly, never examines his verses. At any rate, the authors' remarks, aimed generally at "the study of poetry," seem all too applicable to Chaucer studies, more than ten years later. Even though we know the accepted truisms about the unity of form and content, Chaucerian scholarship seems disadvantageously dual. Chaucer's mind–his meanings, his masks, his moods, his modes–are being analyzed with subtlety and learning. Whereas Chaucer's craft, the body of his art, lies a-moldering. What is vital in one part is moribund in another. In effect, most contemporary criticism of Chaucer's art treats him *as a master in prose.* Perhaps the problem stems from the difficulty of establishing a rational and coherent prosodic criticism, answerable to the facts and our latter-day needs; or perhaps it rises from the behavior of the critics themselves. Let us see.

II. Prosody: Practice

A good place to begin is with a boundary marker of a decade ago, Tauno F. Mustanoja's review essay, "Chaucer's Prosody," in *Companion to Chaucer Studies* (Rowland 1979). Useful as this was in annotating a bibliography which extended from Child's "Observations on the Language of Chaucer" (1863) to Halle and Keyser's "Chaucer and the Study of Prosody" (1966), it did not begin to cry the alarum it should have over the state of the art.

Implicit in the concluding paragraphs of that essay are two interesting points: first, that there have been no major critical or scholarly breakthroughs in this century; and second, that there is nothing alarming about this fact: "Generations of modern readers have enjoyed reading Chaucer in the traditional way outlined in the nineteenth century, and will probably continue to read him along the same lines at least for some time to come" (77). Philologia still reigns, and neither modern aesthetics nor linguistic science has been able to topple her from the throne. It is not surprising, then, to find works from the nineteenth century, obscure German dissertations, and articles 30 or 40 years old cited in the same paragraphs and given equal weight, for the aim of the essay is to characterize those specialized studies upon which the venerable editions of Skeat and Robinson so solidly rest. Hence: "The works of Kaluza, Wright, Jordan, Wyld, and Luick on historical phonology, or on both phonology and morphology, have served generations of philologists and are still valuable or even standard" (59). There is little hint that most of these would prove stultifying to the general reader or the enthusiast of poetry. And what Mustanoja should have added is that they are standard because few trouble to consult or correct them.

Take, for example, that work which Mustanoja says "is still considered the standard guide to Chaucer's language and versification"(59): Bernhard ten Brink's *The Language and Metre of Chaucer* (1901).[9] It is certainly appropriate to honor the memory of Professor ten Brink, since his scholarship was formidable, and Kluge's "Biographical Notice" (pp. xxi–xxvi) is impressive. Nevertheless, there is virtually nothing about this monument to suggest that it can now exercise that mobility which would allow it to be a guide to Chaucer's prosody.

Ten Brink approaches Chaucer as the originator of "classical metre," and although the adjective refers here to the tradition of English verse, it clearly is intended to link Chaucer to a tradition of "heroic verse" which began in Greek and

Latin and continued in the Germanic tongues, advancing in Anglo-Saxon, and being polished and developed in Middle English. By Chaucer's time, "heroic verse" is what others would call iambic pentameter; this is how ten Brink describes its relative, "the normal short line":

> Between every two stressed syllables, or beats (thesis, 'Hebung'), there is invariably an unstressed or weak element (arsis, 'Senkung'). The first stress is, as a rule, preceded by an anacrusis ('Auftakt'), so that in its complete form the rhythm of the verse is iambic. The anacrusis may, however, be suppressed (208).

As we shall see, this statement is curiously similar to what Halle and Keyser would work out, from quite different directions (and cf. the paragraph quoted from them, above). The methodology belongs to classical scholarship and expects to reach precision and order. Hence, one must cope with phrases like these: "syncope of consonants with consequent synaeresis" (177); "actual crasis is rare" (182); and "contraction is the elision of *e* in the negation *ne*, when accompanied by aphaeresis of a consonant in cases where it was the rule already in O.E." (187). Now these are less obfuscatory than intractable. They describe something clearly–although it is a something erroneously perceived as closely related to Latin verse–yet without expediting our approach to a line of poetry as we might wish to read it for ourselves or to others. ten Brink lays out a series of meticulously classified and numbered paragraphs which describe "rules" which derive from laws, and which admit of some, but not too many (note the "invariably" above), exceptions. He clearly understands a "rule" to be a summary of a great many phenomena, inductively observed, but the reasoning which led to the rule, or the general laws behind them, and the salient illustrations of the evidence, are entirely omitted. The effect is like examining some bulky engine in a museum, once designed, we are told, to perform some useful task, but whose precise function and workings are now obscure.

The old machine, however, is not wholly inert. It can still provoke some mischief, if not damage. For it defends the assumption that editor-philologist knows best. Chaucer is to be rescued from his scribes. One either shows how a line may be "regularized" by "syncope, synaeresis and synizesis" (209), *or one emends.* Since "anapestic or trochaic rhythm is foreign to the metre," offending syllables and intractable lines are to be pruned or correctly rehabilitated. Rules may have exceptions, but laws are not to be "jarred": "Personally, when in reading a Chaucerian poem in heroic metre I come upon a verse without anacrusis, I experience a jarring sensation for which I should be loth to make the poet responsible" (215).

Ten Brink, then, gives us an objective system and a false science. His assumptions about text, pronunciation, and metrical pattern are at best out of date. Chaucer is not a "heroic" poet, and the more strictly classical philology is brought to bear on his verse, the more it warps the exemplar. On the question of architectonics and of poetic effect, ten Brink is mute, obviously feeling such "subjective" matters are beyond the scope of his treatment. Yet this kind of approach to prosody does not carry within it a methodology for bridging the gap. The point is not that ten Brink was insensitive. The admiring evidence of his colleagues is that he combined, as in his *History of English Literature*, "first-hand knowledge as to technical detail, fine literary appreciation, and suggestive genius." As a prosodist, however, he did not develop a method which could do all it should.

The tribute I have just quoted is from Eleanor Prescott Hammond's *Chaucer. A Bibliographical Manual* (Hammond 1908, 556), a work noted only briefly in Mustanoja's essay, and yet of such importance to the study of prosody that it could be said to *supersede* that essay, even though it was published 60 years earlier. Given the static condition of prosodic criticism, the serious student must still start with her superb review of the issues in section VI of her manual, "Linguistics and Versification" (464–509), especially the review essay, "On the Language and Verse of Chaucer" (481–91). I suspect that it was within the terms of her critical analysis that the book was written which many consider the "authority" on Chaucer's prosody.

That book was Paull F. Baum's *Chaucer's Verse* (Baum 1961), called by Mustanoja "a sensitively written and highly informative account of Chaucer's versification"(60). It is explicitly an attempt to build on the conservative good sense of Hammond in the light of the major scholarly achievement since her time of John Matthews Manly and Edith Rickert, in their 8-volume edition of *The Text of the Canterbury Tales* (Manly & Rickert 1940). Thus Baum will lead off by saying (prematurely, I think) "By now . . . most of the texts (except for the Minor Poems) seem to be as near definition as we are likely to come and it is time for a fresh start" (4).

The fact that Baum's book seems to dominate the field of prosodic criticism is a prime illustration of what I have claimed is the unsatisfactory state of the art. For it is a book of parts and particles. Despite its promising major divisions into "Meter," "Prosody," and "Art Poetical," the overall treatment is eccentric. It is written tersely, in a kind of scholarly shorthand. Despite Baum's displeasure with the specialists who have written on the subject, his book cannot be treated either as a general introduction to the subject or an essential aid for the undergraduate. It must be read as a commentary on what already has been written, as a series of notes, and as a preliminary collection of data–some immediately useful, and some irreducibly obscure.

It represents a version of Chaucerian criticism which is a reaction to hypermodernism, and hence imputes merit to a poetry characterized as un-intense, uncomplex, straightforward, often plain, even careless: "he was not so much a virtuoso as a good craftsman . . . . Felicities came easily, or, if not, he was content to press on with a second-best. In short, his versification has the same uneven qualities–from the highest on down–as his whole work" (112–13).

If one is overweary with rigoristic considerations, this insouciance can be refreshing. It can strike one like a revelation of commonsense. Here is a basic description of the foundation of Chaucer's metrical patterns:

> The language which Chaucer used, which he spoke and heard, was a Germanic language with definite lexical accent; and when he composed in verse his

> language was still the same. When he read his poems to himself and when he recited them aloud to others, it was still the language of his normal speech adapted to metrical patterns as he understood them. How he read the verse of his contemporary French poets we can only guess. We must assume that he was aware of its syllabism, but it does not follow that he adopted it as his prime metrical principle; and if he had tried, even so his ear would not have been satisfied with making a line of verse out of just only ten syllables. The syllables would have to afford a recognizable series of repeated units determined by the conventional accents of his words– an iambic pattern, te-tum te-tum, varied by all the devices of unequal stress, of pause and time values, of phrasal and syntactic patterns, that he could find (9–10).

He means, as I understand him, that Chaucer intended his writing to be a natural extension of his talking, which put stress on meaningful words; and in his verse counted syllables, but not too rigorously, combining this with a preference for an iambic pulse. Therefore Baum is willing to allow the possibility of tri-syllabic feet, dactyls and anapests, in scanning lines, but does not insist on it. In other words, syllabic *-e* may or may not be pronounced, but not merely to gain ten syllables. Halle and Keyser might claim that Baum is anticipating their positional/stress-maxima theory, although Baum will say, a few paragraphs later: "But finally now, however he may have come to it, Chaucer's line is a series of five iambs" (11).

It is this conservative sense of ease which keeps Baum's practical criticism so persuasive. Like the poet he conceives, he does not try too much and hence does not often fail. As a prosodic glossator, his hand is firm and clear. But as a *doctor scientiae,* he gives us neither lore nor language to carry away and use ourselves.

For example, there is the matter of evidence. Baum's method is to give lists, as in discussing "acephalous" lines (a term he quirkily thinks "less gruesome" than "headless"): he displays single lines all in a row, often in groups of three, but reaching in one case–nine–syllabled lines where "a conjunction seems to have fallen out, thus spoiling a balance" (25)–the number of ten, all from different works. He is quite accurate in describing the effect of this method: "The prosodist must be prosaic and statistically dull" (53). Perhaps this is so, although the problem is compounded when Baum stirs lumpy samples of "statistics" into his discourse. Because they are samples, gathered from all over, they are not really "scientific," particularly since no single place is exhaustively examined or completely inventoried. (And reviewers complained they could not tell how or why he scanned many of the lines the way he did.) The prosodist, says Baum, "accepts his handicap with fortitude" (53). His readers may prove less patient.

His discussion of rime, in fourteen pages, is not well integrated, in that he makes no attempt to relate the poet's practice in riming to his practice in meter. Very few will wish to read him closely here. Chaucer's rime, as a function of his wit, is not even touched. The aggregation of examples can help one to begin thinking about categories of rime–feminine in particular–but cannot contribute a great deal to the inquiry he quite properly calls for: "In sum, it is not a question of vindicating Chaucer's accuracy in riming . . . so much as illustrating both his latitude on the side of convenience and his artistic results in choosing and rejecting" (41).

That prescription alone would require a fuller treatment than Baum provides.

It is in his last chapter, "Art Poetical," that Baum will attempt to give some larger sense of the poet at work. His opening statement carries on his theme consistently, but now his language is more transparently problematic:

> Chaucer was first of all a narrative poet. His main interest, and ours, is in the story and its adjuncts, the people and their surroundings, which make the story something more than a bald and unconvincing narrative. The 'poetry' is therefore diffused . . . . All narrative poets have liked to heighten the narrative and refresh the reader, here and there, with fine things, purple inlays, which are meant frankly as embellishments. (80)

What's purple is 'poetry'; that gray stuff in between is Chaucer's 'verse.' The dichotomy strikes me as absurd if taken as a general principle, occasionally halfway accurate, quite often dead wrong. It applies fairly well, to be sure, to the few samples Baum chooses for analysis, especially to "set pieces" like the Boethian hymn to Love in the *Troilus*. It leads him, in ascending steps, through Anelida's *Compleynt*, to the *Parlement of Foules*: "in ease and smoothness it equals and probably surpasses anything he ever did, as well as in its varied mingling of lyric and narrative, of descriptive and conversational passages. It is purple all through" (101–02).

Putting the *Parlement* at the top of his list is significant. For that, Baum floods the ground with his own kind of statistics, but wades through them with a brusque "it goes without saying that all these repetitions, echoes, and interweavings contribute markedly to the lyrical mood and effect of the poem" (106). After a hasty plot summary and theme analysis, he concludes by ascending into his own purple haze: "Chaucer has lavished [here], as nowhere else, all his art of poetry. . . . If ever Beauty is Truth, here it is; and it is enough." Baum is negatively capable, then, of inferring that at the top of his form Chaucer may stand in the same light as Keats. But for the rest, "his business was to tell a story that would please a none too exigent audience, and for this he created a style and a method of versifying which were perfectly suited to his aim" (116).[10]

Baum has consistently wished to discourage those who would not give Chaucer a "critical" appreciation; or as D. S. Brewer put it in his review: "Mr. Baum is very anxious that we should not praise Chaucer too much." But in so rigidly separating "poetry" from adequate verse, he has done prosodic criticism a disservice. Brewer's summary is telling: "Mr. Baum seems to imagine Chaucer telling anecdotes to commercial travelers. The old image of an artless, genial, bawdy Chaucer, *un vrai business-man*; having been driven by modern scholars out of the poetry as a whole, has been lodged in the versification." (Brewer 1963, 397 & 398)

Since Baum is least effective, even embarrassing, as a critic when attempting to deal positively with Chaucer's accomplishments, we must look to a piece of negative criticism to find him at his best: the first Appendix of his book, headed "The Rhythmical or Four-Beat Heresy." Here his easy handling of scholarship, his unpedantic grasp of literary history, and his good sense stand him in good stead.

Bearing the brunt of his attack is James G. Southworth, whose work I shall discuss more fully below, but who stood for Baum as the proponent of a theory of Chaucer's prosody which was "rhythmical" rather than "metrical." Although the terms could be confusingly handled, what Southworth seemed to mean was that Chaucer modeled his lines after "natural speech rhythms" and did not follow a rigid iambic standard; in fact, his long lines were taken to be composed of four main stresses, much like those in the English alliterative tradition. In addressing himself to this part of Southworth's work, and not to other extensions which I shall discuss, Baum very neatly ties it to that argument of Northrop Frye, in *Anatomy of Criticism*, that a "four-stress line seems to be inherent in the structure of the English language" (Frye 1969, 251), and also to the small but not insignificant "nativist" school of thought which extends back to the early nineteenth century. That it should be called a "heresy" helps identify Baum's voice as the chief representative of orthodox "establishment" prosodic criticism.

Baum accomplishes two useful things in this Appendix. He makes clear the distinction between meter and rhythm, between "base" or norm, and "the rhythmical sound of the lines"–"the rhythm being, as always, the resolution of conflict between scansion and the natural prose enunciation" (123). That is, declaring what metrical pattern a poet had in mind did not mean that every line was expected to be its absolute realization. The theme of variation on a pattern leads Baum to his other important point: that if a four-stress line appears in all sorts of poetry–nursery rimes, medieval Latin verses, modern marches and dance music–it does not follow that iambic pentameter is "really" a four-stress line: "The decasyllable is not a popular but a sophisticated, a literary form; and obviously ten is not readily divisible into four" (125). And he continues:

> That the decasyllable may *appear* to have sometimes a four-beat movement there are two good and sufficient reasons: (1) the need for relief from the monotony of consistently repeated iambs, and (2) the number of unemphatic monosyllables and of polysyllables with secondary accent. These two work together to afford variations which are both natural and inevitable. Together they support rather than contradict the five-stress iambic pattern. To argue otherwise is to reverse logic. (125)

Other prosodists have added, that the concept of "ictus" supports this argument; i.e., an "ictus" is a *comparative* stress, when a syllable will receive somewhat greater stress than the one before or after it, and yet not necessarily a stress maximum. Those who scan using secondary and tertiary stress markings will be identifying ictus. With this concept, the norm of five stresses will still be approximated, if not precisely realized:

1795 So preye I god that noon myswryte the.
Ne the mysmetre for defaute of tonge.[11]

The first line would seem to have five stresses and be a regular iambic pentameter, whereas the second exhibits four main stresses. There is an ictus, however, on "for," which has more stress than the preceding *-tre* or the following *de-*, if less than "tongue."

If Baum can establish these basic points comfortably in brief compass, he has still only left the way clear for a task which others than he must perform. For to declare prosodic variations permissible within the poet's craft is not to demonstrate what those variations accomplish, unless variety itself is the only aim. Towards the possible marriage of versification and interpretation, Baum's attitude is remarkably ascetic, if not celibate.

It is at this point that it makes most sense to turn again to James G. Southworth, for his main quarrel is with orthodox scholar-critics who have obscured the poetic effects in Chaucer's prosody: "Chaucer's music, rightly apprehended, is superb. A straightjacketed iambic reading obscures its variety" ("Chaucer's Prosody," p. 96). Southworth apparently came to this conviction after deciding that final -e's were not to be pronounced in the poetry, just as they were not in the common speech; inevitably this would roughen lines previously scanned as smooth decasyllables, requiring a new theory of prosody. Such a theory was described in three separate monograph/essays, which can be treated as a whole: *Verses of Cadence. An Introduction to the Prosody of Chaucer and His Followers* (Southworth 1954); *The Prosody of Chaucer and His Followers. Supplementary Chapters to* Verses of Cadence (Southworth 1962); and "Chaucer's Prosody: A Plea for a Reliable Text" (Southworth 1964). The first book contains the fullest attack on "conventional wisdom" in describing and dealing with Chaucer's poetry–and is the one Baum responded to; the second has the most on the prosodic implications of manuscript punctuation; and the third, the article, restates with very little modification the basic tenets of the earlier studies.

I have already given a general description of his "heresy"; let us see now how the theory works in practice. Consider the following lines, as Southworth prints them in *The Prosody of Chaucer* (1962) from the opening of *The booke of the Duchesse:*

    I have grete Wonder/ by this lyghte
How that I lyve/ for day ne nyghte
4 I may not slepe/ wel nygh noght
I have so many/ an ydel thoght.

It is very important to this counterview to get back to manuscripts–in this case, Bodleian Fairfax 16–because the "establishment" editors are accused of foisting a false prosody upon us through their emendations and synthetic texts.[12] In this case, the virgule (/) becomes important, and also the spelling. Robinson, for example, deletes the final -e in "grete," line 1, in his edition.

Then Southworth says, "the foregoing lines can be forced into an iambic pattern, or almost:

x /   x   / x / x   /
I have gret won der be this lyght

 x   / x / x   / x   /
How that I lyve for day ne nyght

x / x / x /   x   /
I may not sle-pe wel nyghe noght

x / x / x x / x   /
I have so ma-ny an y-del thoght" (34).

Although he has here provided no more than a metrical frame, he apparently feels that this is the way the iambicists might try to read it, incredible as that may seem; for: "the mechanical piano quality of this is deadening" (34), and "my quarrel with those who adhere to an over-simplified prosody for Chaucer is that they obscure the superb rhythmical effects that Chaucer achieves" (14). "They speak of his infinite variety and read him aloud with a monotonous drone that denies the presence of variety" (4). Notice that finding the metrical pattern in this case is assumed to be the same thing as finding (imposing) the prose rhythm, and also as performing the line. By my earlier formula, then, a)= b)= c). It would be easy to accuse Southworth of setting up a straw man, but since his aim is the laudable one of discovering expressive variation, let us see how he directs us to a "proper" reading of these same lines:

2 3   3   3 2 3 2   1
x /   /   / / / x   /
I have grete wonder/ be this lyghte

 2   4 3 2   2 3   2 3
 /   / x /   / /   x /
How that I lyve/ for day ne nyghte

2 4 3 3   3 2   1
x / / /   / x   /
I may not slepe/ wel nygh noght

2 3 3 3 2   3 2 2   1
x / x / x   x / x   /
I have so ma-ny/ an y-del thoght

Over each vowel, the x or / indicates unstressed or stressed syllables (and stress is for him simply loudness). The numbers refer to levels of pitch, "4 for high level, 1 for the lowest level, and 3 and 2 for the intermediate ones" (34). The virgule indicates "single-bar juncture," keeping the voice-level high, with "slight pause." In effect, he wishes to *stress* the lines as in "normal" prose (he does not explain the puzzling series of stresses he assigns in line 1), and use the cues of *punctuation* for intonation. The lines thus have both "stress" and "tune." "Nyghte" in line 2 is at a higher level than lyghte" of 1, to indicate enjambment. The resultant pattern of half-lines is "rhythmical," not syllabic, allowing him to argue that final -e is not to be pronounced.

The lines certainly are various as he scans them for us, but are they metrically various? What the devil is the meter of which they are a variation? What is the pattern, or the norm, against which the poet makes his lines? It looks very much as if Southworth conceives of "metrical pattern" purely as speech-in-prose, with two slight additions: the rime, about which he says virtually nothing, and the configurations at ends of lines which seem to scan according to cadences identified from Latin prose. The cadences became attenuated as Chaucer developed, he thinks, and were probably not conscious additions anyway. So we are left with speech itself, "prose rhythm," with a kind of border of rime. And the best manuscript for this is the Hengwrt: "Hengwrt indicates the speech rhythms more clearly and accurately than the others. English speech, unlike that of French, has a wave-like quality" (67).

Southworth, then, having persuaded himself that the lines ebb and flow, rise and fall, like waves, but do not march in feet, is also convinced that the manuscript markings can be elegant directions for performance. Some manuscripts are subtler than others–perhaps they represent delicate tunings to match the poet's revising ear. They are signs, not so much of variations–since the norm is so loose as to be virtually non-existent–but of rhetorical emphases. In one of the lines cited above from the General Prologue:

> 18 That hem hath holpen/ whan that they weere seeke,

Southworth observes that Additional MS. 5140 omits "that," and so can be scanned:

```
\    /   x   /  \    \    /     x     /
That hem hath holpen/ whan they weere seek(e).
```

He thus answers none of the questions I raised earlier about the line (question #1 above), but introduces a different marking for scansion (presumably to show primary and secondary stresses–though why "hath" and "-en" of "holpen" are not both unstressed is not clear) in order to aver: "the omission kills any iambic pattern" (66). That is quite a confusion of terms, however, since an iambic *pattern* would be

```
  x   /  x    /  x    /  x    /  x    /
That hem hath holpen whan that they weere seek(e)
```

but few would insist on actually reading the line that way. The loss of a syllable is an irregularity (unless, then, "weere" became two syllables), but pertains to the question of whether, or when, Chaucer omitted syllables from his verses. The loss of a syllable certainly does not kill *any* variant of the iambic pattern. The line is still irregular, even with the "that," for which there is manuscript authority. The use of a curious manuscript, fairly late, "contaminated," of no special interest, is typical (Lansdowne MS. 851, which also omits the "that," is more available in the Six-Text edition).

Having argued that the manuscripts tell us more about prosody than previous editors have allowed, Southworth must now explain the variations among them. And so the best manuscript turns out to be the one that provides the subtlest hints for performance. As a sample:

> The Hengwrt also introduces an element of suspense. In line 69: *And of his poort/ as meke/ as is a mayde*, Ellesmere and Add. 5140 have no virga [virgule] after *meke*. The slight pause that the virga indicates gives a sly twist to what follows. (67)

For a more extended illustration, one may consult Southworth's comparative reading of the Squire's portrait, as pointed by El and by Hg. "The pointing of Hengwrt gives a subtler and wittier reading than does Ellesmere" (64). A close look may be sufficient to demonstrate the absurdity of this kind of treatment, inserting into these energetic, cantering lines the most curious hesitations, gulps, winks, and nudges.

This basic error in taking scribal marks as poetic messages rises in large part from misusing a slender monograph by Peter Clemoes, *Liturgical Influence on Punctuation In Late Old English and Early Middle English Manuscripts* (Clemoes 1952). In that, the intonational markings that come from music, Gregorian chant, and rhythmical prose are identified. Southworth translates these to be the "virgas" which Clemoes defines as "an acute accent when adopted for musical notation. It indicated one note in a rising melody" (4); and the "punctum," "a grâve accent when adopted for musical notation. It indicated one note in a descending melody" (4). These are the basis for "down-up" pointing. Although Southworth admits–he has to!–that most scribes in later centuries did not understand the original use of these markings, he still thinks he has found some that do. Yet Clemoes only intended his work as an introductory sketch, and hardly considers late-medieval manuscript pointing at all. Not only does he say "in the fifteenth century the system was in decay" (12)–the time when the Chaucerian mss. were produced–but he also suggests, at least for fourteenth- and fifteenth-century prose, that the system became adapted "to its increasingly logical structure" (19). And this would be my suspicion about scribal punctuation–that it is *logical*, or *syntactical*–and even that, minimally–before it is rhetorical or (in the linguistic sense) prosodic. That is, the least concern of the scribe in his scriptorium or study would have been a conception of poetic performance. Clarity might be an aim, and here the virgule and other markings could be seen as functions of the basic charge of the scribe to deliver a text that looked attractive and was adequately legible. Few scribes, however, would be declaiming, or performing, what they were copying. If they had done so, we ought to have found more signs on the leaves of surviving manuscripts of the inkstand having been knocked over.

There are too many contradictions, gaps, and distortions in Southworth's theories for them to have much influence on the course of prosodic criticism. He had the misfortune, I think, of insisting on the importance of two areas–textual criticism and Linguistics–where his scholarship was provocative but superficial. There may still be a case to make for prosodic revision employing those disciplines, but he did not make it well. Since he was never seriously challenged nor debated, his arguments have the blurred and repetitive quality of a man speaking to himself. Too many distractions cloud his reasoning, such as the idea of Latin cursus explaining part of the metrical pattern, or the use of the temporalist's musical notation for scansion, or the seizing upon a few anachronistic accidentals as the foundation for a substantial case. Furthermore, the four-beat "heresy" seems to fade as he keeps writing, so that one is hard put to find exactly what Southworth thinks is the metrical pattern behind Chaucer's versification. It begins to look as if there is none, and that we have been given, finally, an artist who writes in *rimed prose.*

It is hard to tell, looking out into the world of scholarship, whether these arguments were much read at all. Certainly they were lightly reviewed. Baum's avuncular confrontation of the "heresy" seems to have guaranteed the impenitent the awful punishment, not of the stake, but of silence. And yet much of the heretical critique of orthodox prosodic criticism asked questions which are not easily answered. It was inevitable that another would come to urge those questions again. We turn now to Ian Robinson, *Chaucer's Prosody, A Study of the Middle English Verse Tradition* (Robinson 1971).

Like a good theological disputant, Robinson is a clever wielder of the *tu quoque* argument, implying that Baum is a representative of a long but mistaken line of scholars who stem from the arch-heretic, Thomas Tyrwhitt–that eighteenth-century editor of Chaucer who amended the text in the conviction that its "numbers" must be regular. Robinson will not reject the syllogism that the prosodists before him have assumed: "good poets write metrically, Chaucer is a good poet, therefore Chaucer writes metrically" (10), but he will provide an anti-establishment definition of "metrically." He will argue: 1) Chaucer did not count his syllables like a Frenchman; 2) did not write in strict iambics; 3) only pronounced "silent" -e's when he sought poetic effect; 4) did not use variable accent in order to be read "regularly." As regards the basic metrical pattern, Robinson will defend a modified position, one which loosens up the academic "rules," without quite destroying them, even as it sharpens, clarifies, and modifies the "four-beat heresy":

> In more than three-quarters of the lines of *The Canterbury Tales*, there are two rhythmic groups of approximately equal length which balance each other after the manner of alliterative lines. The ordinary number of stresses or beats per half-line is two and this is, again, ordinary enough to create an expectation and make

us read with two stresses per half-line where we have a choice. (154)

The major divisions of his book, originally a Cambridge dissertation, are three. Part One presents "Criteria" for understanding Chaucer's meters. Part Two includes four related "Investigations," dealing with Chaucer's prosodic terminology, the interpretation of "final *-e*," the issue of "variable stress," and the evidence of "manuscript punctuation." Part Three comprises "Readings"–first of Chaucer, then of "the English Chaucerians," and finally of "the last Chaucerians" (poets from Hoccleve to Wyatt)–as demonstrations of his theories.

He argues correctly that evidence in these matters cannot be flat or final, and he is particularly good in reminding us of the leaps of faith one must make to read Chaucer with medieval sounds. He has, instead, two appeals: one, the intuitive, that a better reading will *feel* better and be acknowledged by a modern reader when he sees and understands "the sound of sense" more fully–for "Middle English lives if at all as an extension of modern English" (71); two, the historical, that the modern intuition can be supported by fifteenth-century manuscript evidence and the verses of the English Chaucerians. He believes he is in the realm of literary criticism, an aesthetic and rhetorical art, rather than exact science, so that the formula of F. R. Leavis may apply: "where the best one can hope for is to say . . . 'This is so, isn't it?' hoping for a reply of the form 'Yes, but . . . '" (17). To which formulation the truculent reviewer is moved to add, "NO. Because . . ."

"What do you need to know to read Chaucer?" Robinson asks, and quickly leads a sacred cow to slaughter: "the insistence on the old vowels tends . . . to lead away from Chaucer's poetry rather than into it . . ." (22). He recommends instead "simply opening the book, without editorial guidance. . . do not be persuaded by the authority of the scholars into using archaic sounds unless you can make them natural and feel at home in them" (29). It is a startling argument, and yet a misleading one, because his quarrel is less with historical phonology than with the importance usually accorded it. He wishes to argue that rhythms are more accessible than sounds. His point is that by concentrating on "quaint sounds" one makes Chaucer sound like a dead poet. Instead, Chaucer could be read like Shakespeare, who is rarely performed with sixteenth-century sounds. The emphasis should be on getting the rhythms right. They, he implies, are more expressive, more meaningful, than the sounds, and are what one should know. Those who have always bridled at the unexplained assurance of the sound charts in the standard editions will enjoy his attacks. But the overall argument is tendentious, and the results could be barbarous. His treatment does not attempt to see what Chaucer might like to do with patterns of sound (where surely diphthongs, tense or slack vowels, "short" or 'long" vowels, front or back vowels, the articulation of consonants, add up to an important series of aesthetic discriminations), nor does it deal with the crucial matter of rime. For as we shall see, rime will be de-emphasized, to give more stress to rhythm. I suspect he intends the student to approximate a vowel system much like what Robinson or Donaldson give in their editions, but to be very relaxed about it, not to "correct" pronunciation and to consider the system a convenience rather than a necessity.[13]

As Robinson attacks over-assurance in historical phonology, so does he attack conventional wisdom concerning the analysis of iambic pentameter. It is essential for his argument to start fairly close to general Linguistics, identifying rhythm as a pattern of stress built around the "phrase," a grouping of meaningful syllables about a primary accent. And a crucial step: "it is a deeply-ingrained habit of English speech and prose to work in two-beat phrases" (43). Although there is not a great deal of evidence for this in his book, and a thorough-going response to his claim would need to examine his assertion with some care, Robinson takes it as so important that he promotes his definition of "phrase" to include a wider meaning: "I shall use 'phrase' for the half-line, the coalescence of the two smaller units, as well as for the smaller units themselves" (42). This is the step which allies him with Southworth and, as he notes, Frye. It allows him to reach easily over to what Saintsbury called the "under-hum" of English alliterative verse, "a sort of singing in the ears, rather than any tune,"(Saintsbury 1906, I, 73) and to utilize the vocabulary of Marjorie Daunt, who has shown "how characteristic it is for alliterative verses to work with phrases that are ordinary syntactic units, to be pronounced with whatever rhythms they would have in speech or prose" (Daunt 1947, 43). He particularly likes her phrase, "poetry . . . was made with *pieces of language*." Thus, the "half-line" becomes the matrix for native English rhythms, and the analysis of alliterative poetry will be directly relevant to analysis of most English verse, the medieval in particular. It will offer an alternative to the academic analysis of the five-beat line, and to norms of syllable and accent. The "foot" of strict iambic analysis now becomes the looser "phrase" (in his more limited definition) and the line becomes–in Chaucer's prosody–an interesting fusion of half-lines and normally decasyllabic verse.

To clear the way further, Robinson offers his "Investigations." The first one, on terminology, focuses on Chaucer's own distinctions between "ryme" and "prose," and his understanding of "geeste," "metres," and "vers." By reminding us of the development of ME "rym" out of Latin *rithmus,* through OF *rime,* he quite properly links riming to accentual medieval Latin poetry, and concludes that "regularly metrical verse in feet' will best describe what Chaucer writes. But this is transparently tendentious, for he emphasizes in the rhythm-rime definition what the OED calls "measured motion, time, proportion" to make room for his subsequent work with "feet" and crypto-alliterative half-lines, and so almost completely ignores "similarity of the terminal sounds." Surely this is to stand Chaucer's practice, not on its feet, but its head. Of course Robinson must make Chaucer what Saintsbury called a "beat-man," a pulse-and-accent man, to fit him within "a tradition of regularly metrical accentual verse" (79); but not to *start* with Chaucer's contract in rime, not to pay due attention to the fact that (except for rime royal) every two lines will have "similarity of terminal sound," is to leave untreated too large an area of Chaucer's craft. For a discussion of rime belongs in a book on meters: the expectation and the necessity of rime influences matters of tempo, enjambment and cesura, and periodic structure.

The next investigation, in the spirit of Southworth, attacks the sounding of "some now mute final -e's" for the purpose of iambic regularity. The whole question is a crazed teapot in which scholars have been brewing tempests for several centuries. Robinson is no exception. His technique, in encountering philological scholarship, is to attack the question of certainty (which, narrowly conceived, is always easy to do with historical evidence), affect agnosticism, and emerge with license to choose as he thinks best. He does not try to rule out the sounding of all final -e's (and he should speak of medial -e's more than he does), for he is not too far from received opinion: "Chaucer, as a contemporary of Gower, is exactly where we might expect to find him, at the critical point where -e is in process of disappearance but sometimes still seems to be sounded" (97). This leaves the door ajar. Arguing that the sound of such an -e was a "tiny vestigial sound," he wishes to "replace a grammatical criterion for the sounding of possible -e's with a stylistic one." So he finds "it might be retained for *sentence*, deliberate or formal speech of any sort, or proverbial phrases" (101). In other words, not used to "regularize" a line, but to give rhetorical emphasis. He doesn't like putting -e's at the end of riming words: "They make him sound stilted, sing-song, and artificial" (108). Again, this is special pleading. He means they make Chaucer sound less like Langland. Quite so–they link him more to the French continental tradition. Nevertheless, Robinson's examples are very good, in that they show us how well certain lines work when -e's *are* pronounced. Thus:

A 4269 "A, falsë traitour! falsë clerk!" quod he,

from the *Reeve's Tale*, "gets the feeling" of the Miller's reply in "the heavily lagging emphasis on the repeated *false*" (106). He omits, however, such examples as:

A 3279 And heeld hir(e) hardë by the haunchëbonës–

which is how I'd pronounce it: a line that gallops along lustily. The *harde* sounds as an adverbial ending, but it and its line are certainly not an example of sententiousness, deliberation, or formal speech! So readers will have to test for themselves, to see if there are other comic, quick, or informal examples of sounding final or medial -e's. I suspect Chaucer liked iambics more than Robinson will allow.

His next investigation is into the received dogma of "variable stress." Again, he attacks historical orthodoxy by arguing that there is no *proof* that English of Chaucer's day was comfortable in pronouncing certain words with the accent on either syllable ("nature," for example, or "vertu"). His aim will be to allow "trochaic substitutions," particularly in the final foot, which plays hob with the usual way of perceiving the iambic pentameter line, allowing him to redefine it as an accentual line, grouped around stresses not necessarily rising to a final iamb. Here he wishes to persuade by examples. Thus:

A 1773 Fy

/ / x
Upon a lord that wol have nó mércy̆;

/ x /

seems to read better as he scans it thus, than "... no mercy," although some readers may wish to draw the final foot into something of a spondee. On the other hand:

A 45 he loved chivalrie,
Trouthe and honour, fredom and curteisie,

does not convince me at all pulled into Robinson's half-line scheme:

/ x x
he loved chivalri(e)

/ x / x / x x / x x
Trouth(e) and honour fredom and curteisi(e).

(I presume he does not pronounce final -e of chivalrie/curteisie.) To me, the passage read this rum-ram-ruf way stumps in like a soldier from the wrong campaign. The verse has been set up to flow into these great words with dignity, eloquence, and–I think–compelling *smoothness*. Hence,

/ x / x
"chivalrie,"

the two accents for the noble word, and the familiar trochee-iamb combination,

/ x x /
"trouth(e) and honour,"

to rivet those related terms together, even as the English *troth* is joined to the continental *honour*, with the tense, high back-vowel of *-our* cooperating with the stress. Also,

/ x x / x / x
"fredom and curteisiё"

again, same pattern, slightly extended, capitalizing on the expectation of rime, and sonorously linking the quintessential chivalry and courtesy.

Thus, Robinson discovers some lines where the final foot does seem to be reversed, but he has hardly found a principle. He continues to ignore the function of rime in taking precedence, in some cases, over speech-accent, and conveniently ignores the possibility that to do so has been a perfectly normal convention in poetry in virtually any language we investigate.[14]

Robinson's final investigation is designed to bring a corrected literary history to his aid through the science of diplomatics. Like Southworth, he is convinced that scribal punctuation in the manuscripts–which Manly and Rickert omitted entirely–has something important to tell us: "The biggest group of *Canterbury Tales* manuscripts that punctuate verse at all do so by an occasional mark quite obviously meant to stop the reader at places where not to pause would ruin the sense" (137); nevertheless, "there are about a dozen manuscripts" which manifest "a strong connection between care in copying and spelling, and the use of metrical punctuation" (139). "Care" is a weasel word, of course, and Robinson knows that the majority of the MSS. he cites, besides being late in the fifteenth century, are usually deemed "unimportant to editors." (His list may be consulted on p. 140.) He calls "the punctuating manuscripts a central tradition." They "create the different expectation that Chaucer's lines are to go in half-line phrases as well as lines. . . . So the phrase-balancing which is so central to the alliterative tradition is as much a part of the structure of this verse as the iambic meter" (144, 145). This completes his thesis. The issue is fascinating, indeed, but the evidence simply will not do what he wishes it to do.

It is not surprising to find him choosing the tournament scene from the *Knights Tale* for extended illustration, for it is a passage (A 2597–2614) which imitates the native "epic" style through the gesture of alliteration. Citing the system of virgules from the Ellesmere, Robinson purports to find the half-line structure emerging. A close reading, however, will show that many of the lines lack the patterns of the alliterative tradition; that many "halves" are strangely divided (as in 2599, 2606, 2609); and that some lines are not punctuated at all. Furthermore, a check with the manuscript will show that Robinson has ignored the distinction between free-standing and "attached" virgules (those which are descenders from terminal letters like "-t"), the latter not necessarily a sign of punctuation at all. From this example, a student would be hard put to say what the half-lines were, and how the "halves" could be felt to be "balanced." It is also hard to see that the force of a reading would be enhanced if one took the points marked by virgules as cesural pauses. Finally, it is strange to find Robinson here citing the Ellesmere MS., which he has said previously was inferior to the Hengwrt because he suspected the scribe "of using the virgule as symmetrically as possible to improve the look of the page" (140). Comparison with the Hengwrt would show, in fact, that the punctuation does not exactly correspond, and yet is no more, and no less, symmetrical.[15]

No, the truth of the matter is that the punctuation system cannot be used to help us read the Chaucerian lines "metrically." Let us take an example from another place in the *Knights Tale*, one that intends no special effects. It is from the middle of Theseus' "light" speech on the god of Love, A 1806–10. The transcriptions below are from those same two authoritative MSS.–the Hengwrt and the Ellesmere–generally agreed to be by the same scribe, consulting, in these two cases, different, but related, exemplars:

Hg But this is yet-/ the beste game of alle
El But this is yet-/ the beste game of alle

Hg That she/ for whom/ they haue this Iolitee
El That she/ for whom they han this Iolitee

1808 Hg Kan hem ther fore/ as muche thank as me
El Kan hem ther fore/ as muche thank/ as me

Hg She woot namoore/ of al this hoote fare
El She woot-/ namoore/ of al this hoote fare

Hg By god/ than woot-/ a cokkow of an hare
El By god/ than woot a Cokkow of an hare

1806. Clearly an attached virgule in both MSS.
1807. In Hg, virgule after "she" markedly smaller than after "whom."
1808. In El, virgule after "thank" might be considered attached, but in fact stands clear.
1809. In El, attached virgule ("woot").
1810. In Hg, attached virgule ("woot") but not in El. MSS. agree on "of," which F.N. Robinson silently emends to "or" in his edition.

What conclusions can we draw here? First, that the MS. punctuation is very far from modern conventions, with no final pointing at all. Second, that the MSS. are close in their punctuation, saving the troublesome matter of attached virgules. If they are excluded, the MSS. are in large agreement, save for 1807, but the case of 1806 suggests the decision may be arbitrary (note that terminal "-t" does not always have an attached virgule–see 1809 Hg and 1810 El). If we were to assert that roughly the same practice here obtained, would we have demonstrated thereby that a metrical reading in half-lines was being forwarded? I fail to see how that could be defended, unless we a) ignored Hg and took El (contrary to Robinson's practice, and to the idea of a "central punctuating tradition"); b) ignored attached virgules; and c) called a half-line whatever segment occurs on either side of the virgule. In which case, 1806 has no half-lines, or the attached-virgule here coincides with a regular punctuation mark. Note also the shape of the "half-lines": two beats and three in 1806; one and three (or four) in 1807; two and three in 1808; two and three in 1809; and one and three in 1810. Assuming that half-lines are "balanced" over the chasm of a cesura, do these divisions give us the best balancing points? Possibly for 1806, although a pause anywhere in that line strikes me as artificial; possibly for 1807, although the restrictive clause suggests there be no effective pause; possibly for 1808, although there should be as much–or as little–pause before "ther fore" as after; probably not for 1809; and probably for 1810, although not as a "balance": for 1809 and 1810 flow together into one long phrase, with the asseveration, "by god," dropped in by the way.

It is curious about the matter of cesuras. Chaucer surely uses them, but not in the way the punctuation is supposed to suggest. Robinson, for all his talk about balancing half-lines, says virtually nothing about the function of cesura. These five lines have hardly any noticeable (rhetorical) pauses in them, and resist being turned into a four-beat pattern. Lines 1806–09 are very close to being regular iambic pentameter, and do have five stresses, although line 1810 has a pyrrhic fourth foot.

When Robinson comes to his prosodic demonstrations, in a chapter titled "Readings," he gives special attention to Theseus's "majestic speech" at the conclusion of the *Knights Tale,* A 2994–3034. Arbitrarily, he displays "the half-line punctuation of the Hengwrt manuscript." Two things are wrong with this: first, his transcription has a number of errors in it, including the lumping together of free-standing and attached virgules, and the original has *more* virgules than Robinson reports; second, although some lines do break easily into halves, many do not, and many do not go easily with the cesuras his method implies. Here, however, we come to a major point.

Robinson's claim from the very start is that his method will *work,* that his way of pointing will enhance the force and sense of the poetry: "Never trust an expert on meter unless he improves your reading of a poet" (175). Perhaps it would be more persuasive to hear him read the passages out loud, for his written directions do not very often produce–for me–satisfactory results. I think this mode of analysis, therefore, accomplishes two things. It quite rightly attacks the oppressive bookishness of the philological tradition–and, indeed, Robinson begins his work by complaining about the "wooden" effect of an old Linguaphone recording of Chaucer done by H. C. Wyld. (And unfortunately, he could have cited even more recent examples from recordings without spoiling his point.) But what follows from all this is something else: if bookishness is an ill in discussing Chaucer's prosody, *can more bookishness be the cure*? The time may arrive, I am suggesting, when a prosodic critic, as he turns from meter and prose rhythm to comment on performance, must step away from the printed page and provide for us some real version of the sounds he is imagining. (In my fantasies, I see the advertising for future books on prosody including samples on tape or records of the critic reading Chaucer; then if one liked the sample, one would buy the book–to see how it was done, and to learn how to do it oneself.)

To sum up: Robinson's method with Chaucer's prosody does not work very well. At those points where he concentrates on lines and passages, gets off his hobbyhorse, and shows us what is going on, how movement and meaning go together, he is very winning. But all too often those quiet moments of intense regard are disturbed by the larger needs of the argument, which must press on to a greater battle. But there is no greater battle. The foe is really little more than the collective foibles of philological scholars, which deserve chastisement and correction, to be sure, but which can hardly be displaced in favor of a counter-theory whose version of literary history is distorted, and whose critical practice is eccentric.

It is probably all right for us to speak of Chaucer's standard meter as "iambic pentameter," as long as we make it clear what the label suggests for prosodic analysis. Historically, we must be catholic, not exclusive or partial. We must not characterize Chaucer as being ready to discuss Tennyson's scissors. We must not show him constructing his verse to match an identifiable and previously legislated set of "rules" for respectable English poetry. We must never, never confuse the generic term "iambic pentameter" with the prescriptive habit of placing iambs in every foot. Nor must we insist on finding, waiting for our critical calipers, little blocks of feet in every line. But we will insist upon the difference between Chaucer's practice and the so-called alliterative tradition. And we will say that he was writing poetry, which *was* artificial, even in the ways in which it affected the "natural." It had a strong relationship to speech, but a poetic relationship.

"Loose iambics" (Robinson's phrase, but also Ezra Pound's, and Robert Frost's) may do well as a label if one is concerned to underscore the variety and flexibility of Chaucer's practice, and if one realizes that the terminology is part of the critic's and reader's optical apparatus for peering closely at something which was there prior to, and not because of, our special equipment. Saintsbury liked the popular phrase, "riding rhyme," which does not work so well in an age of motor-cars. And it is tempting to think twice about a term George Young (1928) proposed to no avail: "Recalling the original connection of verse with dancing, the name 'cinquepace' suggests itself."(14) 'Tis a good woolsack term–a cinquepace from the cinqueports–verie ffrenshe and verier English, with kinetic implications which are healthy. Yet one hardly dances to Chaucer's meters. And who would be the first to write of The Art of Cinquing in Poetry? No, we stick with "the goddam Iamb" (Ezra Pound) as fact and fiction . . . for the time being.

Robinson goes just that much farther than Southworth, casts just enough more light, to let us see that he has brought us to a dead end. Having been reviewed not intensely, but adequately and thoughtfully (Pyle 1973 and Owen 1974) his book can now be allowed to sink into a decent obscurity–if we could only be sure that prosodic criticism would continue with the work of revision and renewal.

But criticism has that frustrating Looking-Glass capacity for running in place. In the next year, a book was published which advanced not at all, displaying a method and an attitude that belonged to a critical temper even more conservative than Baum's. Norman E. Eliason's *The Language of Chaucer's Poetry. An Appraisal of the Verse, Style, and Structure* (1972) is not about language or poetry or Chaucer in any way that is more than intermittently useful. Least of all does it contribute to our understanding of Chaucer's prosody. Of the book's major divisions, "The Sound of the Verse" is 44 pages; "The Style," 77; and "Chaucerian Structure," 108. Since the latter sections deal hardly at all with prosody, one can see that little more than $\frac{1}{6}$ of the book treats the subject.

The reasons for this seem to stem from certain preferences in critical method which are only next door to prejudice. First, Eliason's kind of analysis, he says, "has never been tried before–that is, applied broadly to Chaucer's poetic art as a whole instead of to some small facet of it" (12). The intention, if not the claim, sounds all right–holistic criticism, we might think; but in practice, it turns out to be an exercise in partiality rather than comprehensiveness. For example, he does not wish to consider the subjects of Chaucer's humor and his irony–which are hardly "small facets," and are surely inextricably connected to the question of language. His decision thus leaves some significant blind spots in his critical gaze. What seems to be holistic, in fact has all too many holes.

It displays a most unsatisfactory attitude towards illustration and evidence. The first section of the book, "The Sound of the Verse," makes the claim that the poetry "is capable of producing an auditory effect so delightful that it alone may content us" (17). The first 18 lines of the General Prologue are then quoted, followed by this revealing paragraph:

> Stripped of its embellishing details, all that this very long sentence says is that in spring people like to go on pilgrimages, especially to Canterbury. Yet we are not bothered by this. The sound rather than the sense is all that matters, reaching a peak of auditory enchantment in [lines 15–17 are quoted]. . . . Chaucer rarely beguiles us thus and never more flagrantly (17).

And that is all. Or rather, not quite all. In place of a conventional Index, at the end of his book Eliason provides an inventory of all the lines and passages in Chaucer's works which he has commented upon. Thus, on the General Prologue, we find these listings: "[verse] *1*–couplet structure [pp.]45–6; *1–2* scansion of 51–2; *1–18* sound of 16–18; trueness of riming 41–3; regularity of meter 47; artificial style 116; *1–100* large number of double rimes 43; *12* scansion of 51; *17* object of pilgrimage 234; *17–18* Chaucer's use of identical rime 43"–and that *is* all.

This sample makes a point about the whole: Eliason does not favor the close view, and does not really have a critical language for illustrating how style and sense come to the same thing. To strip the opening as he does is to read as a Neo-Augustan critic. Note the reductionist's telling phrase, "all that this very long sentence says." Why *is* it "very long"? And does none of those details "say" anything? And how do we decide that "the sound . . . is all that matters"? And why should Chaucer be beguiling us "flagrantly" (a really impossible phrase)? And why is this passage more lusciously delightful than any other? No answer. This is *je ne sais quoi*, not holistic, criticism.

If one goes into Eliason's special index for more light on the issues, little will be shed. We are told in one place that Chaucer provides variety in couplets and run-on lines and that the effect, if not the intention, is to "soften the rime"–as if too many "obvious" couplets would not only chime but bruise. Nothing is said about why there should be a run-on line in this place rather than that. The "scansion" given for lines 1 and 2 is simply an illustration to show how the rigorists would scan it, and other lines are not scanned or marked. We are told there are no "untrue" rimes in the first 18 lines, but the effect of the rime pairings is not discussed. And so on. If one looked up the point about "identical rime" at line 17–18, he would find this: "The trueness of the riming is enhanced by Chaucer's . . . use of identical rime, like *seke: seke* (seek: sick), for which he evidently had neither any special fondness nor any special aversion" (43). Again, that is all. It is not enough, by any means; or it is too much. But it shows vividly how little interest Eliason has in what might normally be considered the criticism of poetry.

One begins to see that the first examination any prosodic critic should be required to take is on the General Prologue. It is here that his method, his presumptions, his heuristic skills, his wit and wisdom, and his power can be evaluated and compared with those of others. On that basis, one is sorely tempted to put aside *The Language of Chaucer's Poetry* without further ado, and I must say that it takes a large increment of patience and good will to keep reading.

For what is revealed at first is only enlarged and extended later. Eliason's broad considerations are reductive and tendentious when argued. His procedures are arbitrary, tending towards caprice. For example, his discussion of Chaucer's meter is arbitrary in sturdily advancing a summary of received opinion with a there's-no-real-problem-here manner, and capricious in giving us no single place where the meter is illustrated and graphed. The problem is less that he is misleading in nudging prickly questions into the corner than that he leaves us empty-handed: "If Chaucer's meter is described as a line of five (or four) stresses falling on alternate syllables and if metrical stress is not expected to match up exactly with speech-stress, there is little irregularity that needs comment, save the cesura" (53). Not only, what does this mean, but also, what can it do? What about that "speech-stress," then? How does it work, and how far does it stretch away from the metrical "rule," and where, and why? Deponent sayeth not.

It is painful to realize that this section has virtually nothing to say about the real sound of the verse. "How did he himself recite his verse? Did he emphasize the meter, beating it out strongly and insistently and producing a tum-ta, tum-ta effect that would appall us today? I suspect he did" (55). And one may well be appalled–but by the absence, not the presence, of the holistic method. For would not a larger view have surveyed the evidence Chaucer provides throughout his poetry for the imitation of speech and dramatic recital, for the hints he gives of the kinds of talking he wishes to produce? Could Chaucer have recited the *Troilus* in a tum-ta, tum-ta fashion (which sounds trochaic, anyway)? Put Pandarus on that rocking horse? Or droned and "beat out" the vivacious passage describing Alisoun in the *Miller's Tale*? Eliason will tell us about the diction of that passage, which he clearly admires, but nothing about how it should sound. Very clearly, his preference is for a reading, not a hearing, and his best critical observations will serve those who hold the book mute in their hands.

The last fifteen pages of the section on "The Style" deal with the *Troilus.* (Here is another examination every prosodist should have to take.) Curiously, Eliason likes the poem, but in his fashion, and that fashion excludes a number of essential categories. Like so many of those who react to the poem as a whole, he effectively treats it as if it were written in prose (I suspect part of the allure of that theory which classifies the poem as a novel comes from its releasing the critic from prosodic obligations). And he treats the characters as figures in a romanticized history rather than as fictional personae. For all his touting of Chaucer's craftsmanship, his discussion of "love talk" is in terms of Criseyde doing and thinking this, Troilus feeling that, Pandarus proposing this and that. The aesthetic distance is ignored, the poetic effect oversimplified. The discussion of talking does not for one minute relate the amorous dialogue to the shape of line and stanza. We are told in one place that there is much "colloquial" style in the poem, but given no analysis or demonstration (and hence learn nothing more about tum-ta, tum-ta). Eliason does not explore the significance of his passing observation that "there is not much action in Chaucer's stories–and least in the best of them" (99). Although he views Chaucer as a clear, lively, fresh, uncomplicated master of narrative, he nowhere broods on the contradiction. Perhaps the "action," at least in the *Troilus*, lies in the very life of the dialogue and the speeches (including the narrator's)? Here is a cue for the prosodist to come forward and explain. But not in the pages of *The*

Language of Chaucer's Poetry. As Saintsbury earlier observed, the *Troilus* is the high point in development of the seven-line stanza later called rime royal, and one might expect some extended discussion of the way Chaucer moves in and through the 1,177 stanzas he wrote there. All Eliason can do, in a single paragraph, is to say that the stanzas exhibit structural variety (44–45), and then proceed to discuss the behavior, not of the verse, but of the characters.

The Year's Work in English Studies (1974) suggested that Eliason's book might be "of some value perhaps to a beginner" (108). Pursuing that "perhaps," this is what I would say to any such beginner: "Read this book quickly. When you find something interesting, let it start you off on your own train of thought, or, better, send you back to the text. It will probably be most useful as a debunker and an irritant. But you must also remember that it is not very accurate. Some kinds of scholarship it knows very well, others it ignores entirely. It apparently knows little about really close reading, or does not enjoy the process. Because it tends to skim over the surface of things, it will not even characterize the general nature of the poetry precisely. Unless you already agree with its arguments, you are not likely to be convinced. And although it claims to draw our attention to Chaucer's craftsmanship, it is most memorable when discussing what Chaucer did not or could not do."

Actually, for beginners, I should much prefer to recommend a book I have reviewed elsewhere, Stephen Knight's *The Poetry of the Canterbury Tales* (1973). Of limited scope, the book has something to say, often very brief, about each tale, and seems directly aimed at the non-specialist and the student. Its basic principle is crucial:

> At all times he has been recognized as a fine storyteller and a master of description. The remarkable thing about all these views of Chaucer is that they could be just as valid if he had written in prose: very little criticism treats him as a man working with the special methods and the special powers of the poet. (vii)

This is quite accurate. As a remedy, Knight recommends that the student learn "to read Chaucer aloud," for this "will often reveal patterns of meaning in the sound and tone of a passage" (viii). Successive chapters will draw attention to some of these patterns. As Knight's introductory glossary of terms shows, the constituents to be discussed include Diction, Syntax, Word-Order, Enjambment, Rime-Linking, Rime-Breaking, Assonance, Alliteration, Metrical Features, Rhetoric, Levels of Style, and Imagery. It will be seen that all of these can be gathered under the heading of Prosody–a term Knight does not single out–especially for the critic who is aiming to account for Poetic Effect. There is no hint of any problem in summing these up and applying them to analysis, nor does Knight attempt to explain why there has been so little prosodic criticism heretofore. It is a matter of an emphasis to be shifted, but within a scholarly domain taken to be available, comfortable, and non-controversial. F. N. Robinson's text is used, "all good editions of the poetry contain a section on . . . pronunciation" (viii), and in *The Canterbury Tales* "Chaucer uses as his norm a line of ten syllables with five iambic feet" (x). Not only is there no Counter-Reformation here, but Luther has not been heard of–and the Devil may not exist. Or at least the children don't need to hear about him.

The Poetry of the Canterbury Tales displays attendant virtues and vices from its attempt to live prosodically within postlapsarian Eden. In its artificially quiet atmosphere, one can stroll with the lecturer past each tale, pausing before those moments "which are the most striking" (xii). The "test" on the General Prologue is passed with flying colors: Knight's survey is the best of the books we have covered. The method throughout is relaxed, impressionistic, genial, and intelligent. Here is a sample, concerning the following lines from the *Clerk's Tale:*

> There stood a throop, of site delitable,
> In which that povre folk of that village
> Hadden hir beestes and hir herbergage,
> And of hir labour tooke hir sustenance,
> After that the erthe yaf hem habundance.

> There is a striking contrast between the simple, largely monosyllabic body of the lines and the elegant rime words: the "throop" becomes a "village," for example. This appears to be a deliberate prosodic linking of the court and the village, for as the action moves into the village in the next stanza, the whole line becomes basically monosyllabic, and the rime words are also simple: "man," "alle," "kan," "stalle," "calle," "sighte," "highte." It is a subtle prosodic modulation, which links the court and the village, rather than harshly juxtaposing them: it both stresses the difference between the two worlds and acts out in poetry the type of transition that Griselda will have to make. (84)

The "deliberate prosodic linking of the court and the village" is a striking idea, certainly not simple-minded. Whether or not one is persuaded, the point requires an attention to what the poetry is doing that is entirely valid. Note that none of the lines is scanned (some word on 203 might have been helpful); Knight only discusses those features he deems most important in a given extract. In discussing some lines of what musicians might call "passage work," from the *Miller's Tale*, 3307-11, he notes the function of good prosody in an unremarkable series:

> This is straightforward narrative, and less striking than many passages in the tale. Yet here we find a remarkable variety of rhythm that keeps the poetry mobile and interesting. We have a pause in the first line, a stress to open the second and an assonance in "werkes . . . wirche;" the third line lets four stresses fall close together in "This goode wyf went." The fourth line has a stress irregularity in "Hir forheed shoon" and the last line alliterates strongly. These features stop the poetry falling into the sort of doggerel regularity that Chaucer's contemporaries found it almost impossible to avoid. The poetry does not strike us vividly, it makes no specific meaningful implications, as it may elsewhere. Yet it is the work of a master, writing riming couplets with a colloquial, forceful effect that creates the

impression of a natural speaking voice. (33)

It can thus be seen that he covers a wide range of prosodic features, from journeyman lines to special effects, and for each such perception we may give thanks, if only because their kind are so rarely discovered elsewhere.

On the other hand, these are inconclusive fruits from his horticulture. The trouble with roaming in his flimsily enclosed garden is that it does not really equip a beginner to carry on in the real, much more bitterly controversial, world outside–much less warn him about its real nature. What would happen to beginners who put down Knight and picked up Southworth, or Ian Robinson? They would have to think either they or the author had gone mad. Certainly, nothing at all in Knight's book equips one to respond to the others rationally. For the review of the poems there had not stressed underlying issues or assumptions. Perhaps for such a book such a technique is understandable, but it abandons its clergeouns to get their throats cut the first time they go out alone.

To be fair to Knight, he observes that he had not touched on many important aspects of the poetry, and refers his readers to a list of books for "Further Reading." I was somewhat surprised to find there these words: "Ian Robinson's very recent *Chaucer's Prosody* . . . discusses in detail Chaucer's prosodic habits and what has been said about them in the past" (200). Can Knight have read the book himself? It is a little like St. Augustine saying to his Hippo congregation, "Fellow named Pelagius has written on original sin and freedom of the will, really covered the ground, you should look him up"–with a straight face. More to the point, Knight lists another book of his which will contain "much greater detail."

That book is *Rymyng Craftily. Meaning in Chaucer's Poetry* (1973), and concentrates on five studies: (chapter 1) "Anelida and Arcite and the Parlement of Foules," (2) "Troilus and Criseyde: Minor Characters and the Narrator," (3) "The Knight's Tale," (4) "The Manciple's Tale and the Franklin's Tale," and (5) "The Nun's Priest's Tale." There is also an Appendix which lists most (but not all) of the rhetorical figures Knight employs in his analysis, or at least "The Easy Ornaments"–those "types of verbal complexity and emphasis" which he transmits from Geoffrey de Vinsauf, with brief illustrations from Chaucer.

Even in this book, Knight has no pretensions to completeness. He aims, rather, at "a full understanding of Chaucer's power as a poet," and this may be derived from a few extended studies of "poems of different sorts written at different stages" (xvii). That power consists of "extended and subtle meaning" which is "transmitted in exquisitely judged and finely modulated poetry" (233). The key word is "modulated," which refers to "the movement of the verse"–and "movement of the verse" will entail prosodic and rhetorical analysis. Knight, as he begins, will identify those critics–and they are usually very good ones–whose interpretations he accepts. For he will advance no new readings of *what* a poem means. Rather, he will elaborate the *how,* concentrating on the expressive, or the mimetic, achievements of Chaucer. His commentaries are thus useful supplements to what has already been written, and particularly good when they look closely at passages which interpretive essays have touched only lightly.

It will be useful at this point to consider a portion of a poem which Knight and several others of our critics treat, as a means of comparing them with each other, and of seeing what he can accomplish. For the very elaborateness of *Anelida and Arcite* in structure and meter calls for a prosodic accounting. Here is a stanza, from the Fairfax MS. 16:

> 272 My suete foo/ why do ye so for shame
> And thenke ye/ that furthered be your name
> to love a newe/ and ben vntrew/ nay
> And put yow/ in sclaunder now/ and blame
> 276 And do to me. aduersite. and grame
> that love yow most. god. wel thou wost always
> yet come ayein. and be al pleyn som*me* day
> And turne al this. that hath be mys. to game
> 280 And al for-yeve. whil that I lyve. May
> (Chaucer 1878, Part II, pp. 164 & 166)

Once again, in this transcription from a fifteenth-century MS., we see the many differences between a medieval original and the modern critical texts most critics take for granted, and can sense how much prosodic matters must depend upon textual scholarship.[16] The poem, or fragment of a poem, is not much read today, and for obvious reasons: what little narrative interest it may contain is overshadowed by the completion of its "matere" in the *Knight's Tale*, and its lyric convolutions seem more curious than convincing: a mechanical canary with a broken spring. All the more reason, then, to look to the critics for a description of its significance, with an application of its behavior to the study of Chaucer's prosody. However, when we turn to most of the volumes at hand, we discover more about their authors' proclivities than Chaucer's poetry.

Baum responds to the *Anelida* as if it were a bizarre piece of engineering. All of his attention, in his section of analyses called "Art Poetical," is paid to the construction. He provides an inventory of lines, parts, stanzas, and rimes, from which one who did not know the poem could learn that "altogether there are 141 end rimes and 36 internal rimes, or 177 riming words," for example, but could learn nothing at all about the poem's texture or argument. The three-page discussion concludes: "There was nothing like it before; one would be hard pressed to find anything like it since." (One is reminded of the more pungent formulation by the film critic, James Agee: "the goddamndest thing I ever did see.")

Ian Robinson will have nothing to do with the poem, presumably because he concentrates on the *Canterbury Tales*, and possibly because he would consider it a ridiculous deviation from the less mannered "English" tradition. His sole reference is highly oblique, an aside while brushing Gower out of the way: "Gower is always trying to be a Great Poet (an affliction from which Chaucer made an almost complete recovery after *Anelida and Arcite*) . . ." (181). This sounds like wit, but may only be an echo of student evasiveness: one cannot tell from it whether or not our critic has read the poem carefully, or is only repeating the received wit of others.

Eliason's treatment is very typical, stemming from his theme that "the most conspicuous characteristics of Chaucer's meter and rime are, on the one hand, their remarkable regularity and, on the other hand, their apparent simplicity and naturalness" (37). Fair enough, but one would expect the *Anelida* to be cited to give background, or contrast, or qualification to the "apparent" in that sentence. Instead, Eliason points to the poem as a kind of sport, a strange, perhaps even grotesque, begonia stuck in a pot in an obscure corner of a shed otherwise devoted to petunias. He quotes the heavily edited version of Robinson, and then slips away with nothing more than this:

> The poem remains a mystery to critics, who can make nothing of it except as a dazzling display of technical virtuosity. Very likely its unfinished state indicates Chaucer's feeling that such displays were not worth his time or effort (38).

It is something of a relief, after the other critics have shown us their empty pockets, to turn to the sober generosity of Knight. His *Rymyng Craftily* provides the first sustained discussion of the poem, stanza by stanza, in terms of theme, form, and mood. He does not attempt to make of the poem something more than it is–in fact, he concludes that it is a "failure"–but he does try to evaluate its achievement in large part as an experiment in "the movement of the verse."

Let us take another stanza from the *Anelida*, this time as Knight quotes it from Robinson's edition:

> When Theseus, with werres longe and grete,
> The aspre folk of Cithe had overcome,
> With laurer corouned, in his char gold-bete,
> Hom to his contre-houses is he come;
> For which the peple, blisful al and somme,
> So cryëden that to the sterres hit wente,
> And him to honouren dide al her entente.[17]

He writes of this "packed narrative":

> The short phrases and the forceful epithets that characterize Chaucer's denser style are visible here; it is a vigorous stanza and, though the last line is a little weak and the last phrase in the fifth line rather slack, it is more successful as a whole than the stanzas of the invocation [which he has previously discussed]. The movement of it is direct; it is by no means ornate in style, and when we compare this stanza with its source in Statius . . . we can see how faithfully Chaucer has presented the vigorous and solid tone of the Latin. (6)

Following this, he provides four lines from Statius, without translating or identifying the citation; and says: "The paraphrasing of the Latin seems to give to Chaucer's verse a much firmer form than is achieved when he translates from French in *The Romaunt of the Rose* . . . ."(7)

If in this kind of discussion Knight does not try to cover as much ground as in his *The Poetry of the Canterbury Tales,* it cannot be said that he thereby digs much deeper. Tone and general effect ("vigorous," "rather slack," not "ornate," "solid") seem to be what is of most importance. "Crisp" and "brisk" are two of his favorite descriptive words, and he can overuse them. When he makes Chaucer begin to sound like a bite of celery, he has inadvertently reminded us of the perils of "affective" prosodic analysis. Curiously, the technique more often than not brushes against prosodic matters, but only on the way to something else. The lines are not scanned. Cesuras are infrequently remarked, or indirectly indicated insofar as phrases may be called "short." There is some attention paid to stanza-organization and the demands of rime (and there was more in preceding paragraphs), and yet virtually nothing about the meter can be descried, beyond a haze of adjectives dike "forceful" and "direct." Knight does not comment on the implications of "Cithe" (a one-syllable version of three-syllabled "Cithia" two stanzas later); he does not solve the difficulties in line 24, which seems to have too many syllables, requiring apocopation unless it is a tri-syllabic foot–along with a very heavy final three syllables; and he does not tell us how to read line 28, which limps unless provided a somewhat unusual elision–and even then wavers with some uncertain stresses.

With a second look, a certain skepticism grows. Is there really "vigor" here? It looks rather as if Chaucer is falling over his own feet. And it does seem that the villain–as "contre-houses" for Statius' *domos patrias* shows–is the Demon of Pedantic Translation. To say that the last line "is a little weak" is not enough. The "that to the sterres hit wente" is a Statianism, not vintage Chaucer; he would learn later to follow the *vestigia* from a greater distance. That kind of line will not be found in the *Knight's Tale.*

In fact, without seeming to condescend, one may re-read these stanzas somewhat more severely, and make some observations on Chaucer's practice when he is sticking to his Latin. His first rule of thumb seems to be syllabic, as the "Cithe" of l. 23 or the "alle" of 42's "Fulfilled of largesse and of alle grace" indicate. There are accentually "regular" lines like 40, with its iambs in "That al the ground about her char she spradde," but there are more irregular lines, like 41's proto-trimeter: "With brightnesse of the beaute in her face." More important, the differences between regular and irregular lines do not depend on expressive discriminations or rhetorical emphases. One is aware, rather, of the stanza-form as the "problem," which is "solved" with inevitable signs of labor or compulsion. The intelligence at work here is clearly interesting–remarkable, even–but it has not yet shown where its genius may best stride forth.

And there is another matter. Knight says nothing about the text as he follows–not without a few errors–Robinson's edition. In so doing, he offers a clear instance of the dangers the critic faces when he tries close reading of a text dubiously construed. Robinson's textual notes offer no specific commentary on these lines. He observes generally that the Bodleian's Fairfax MS. 16 was the base text, "for orthographical reasons," but advises us that other readings have been substituted "where they appear more probable," and also that "a number of final -e's have been supplied for grammatical regularity" (901). Anyone who takes a few minutes with the

Chaucer Society's parallel texts will discover:

1. The scribe who wrote Fairfax 16 cared not for final -e's: the last two lines of the stanza rime "went/entent" and Robinson silently emends. The scribe, however, did believe in the cesural virgule, whether there was a cesura or not, and every line of the poem has one virgule, no more, medially placed. There is, of course, no other punctuation in that MS., and Robinson's pointing is entirely his own.
2. Robinson emends the original MS. reading of "the laurer" in l. 24 to "with laurer"–a sensible correction, but done silently.
3. More importantly, Knight follows Robinson's "corouned" from Fairfax, but does not remark that other MSS. have "crowned." This has implications for scanning the line.
4. Robinson adopts a reading, "cryëden"–giving us firm guidance with his diacritical marks–but this has little MS. authority, appearing only in Caxton's text (notably corrupt in a number of places, as in l. 25: "Home to his contre hool is come"). There are other solutions, and most include making two syllables out of the plural, "sterres." None makes it a particularly mellifluous line, however.
5. The last line remains metrically problematic in all the MSS., a point worth remarking. No better "solution" exists, and that does seem to tell us something unambiguously about Chaucer's practice.

Surely the moral of this sortie into the manuscripts is that one had better be careful to locate just where the text is that is the supposed object of discussion, especially in matters metrical, where so much depends upon the interpretation of scribal vagaries and the multiplicity of MSS. For a modernized critical text provides modern cues for what a poem looks and sounds like which are not always discovered to the medieval originals. When one digs down, then, to discover the base, or strikes out to discover the true location of a poem, one would be well advised to have the guidance, if not the company, of both philologists and linguists.

Knight does not think so, for other reasons. His Introduction takes particular notice of Linguistics, with reference to the account to be given of any poetic passage. A few notes cite selected books and articles on Linguistics and literary criticism, although nothing is cited for the medieval period. His primary distinction seems to be that a literary critic may proceed intuitively and partially, while a linguist must "work toward a full and objective account of a passage" (xv). I think he has microlinguistic structural analysis chiefly in mind, although he does not say so. As a description of the chasm between disciplines, it hardly will do, but serves instead to confirm his own resolve to "jump off" with intuitions and deal "with the more subtle issues" (xvi)–which rather begs the question. With this brief glance, Knight then moves on to his chosen work with no more reference to linguistic or modern philological scholarship. But he is thus quite consistent. Baum mentioned Trager and Smith's intonational markings only to express cautious interest and deep reservations, and did not try to utilize any tools other than what he had inherited from classical prosody. Mustanoja's essay noted Halle and Keyser's essay on Chaucer's Prosody (which I will discuss below), but also declared the time was not ripe; and Eliason cited two brief entries in encyclopedias, after declaring that "recent attempts to adapt these techniques to problems of interest to literary critics have thus far proved disappointing, stirring up much critical theorizing but in practice achieving trivial results" (9)[18] So the job of integrating literary and linguistic prosodic studies, as far as both the orthodox and heretical critics are concerned, is for someone else to do. Or perhaps our critics are more like Roman and Eastern churches, in which case the Linguist is the Turk. But the Turk cannot be ignored in our metacritical review.

III. Prosodic Studies and Linguistics

"Middle English studies are overdue for a reappraisal of their traditional concerns and methods in the light of recent developments in general linguistic theory," writes Charles Jones, in his *An Introduction to Middle English* (1972). Since it is clear that most who have written about Chaucer's prosody have not been trained in modern Linguistics, it is not surprising that the (relatively) new discipline should be so mis-represented. I trust we can look forward to a day when a humanist/philologist will no longer devote a few casual opening remarks to dismissing Linguistics as irrelevant, implying or openly saying that linguists are insensitive to poetry, or that they want to do things that are of little moment to poets or their readers. It may well be true that we do not yet have applications to Chaucer of linguistic analysis which non-linguists can find useful. (I should like to remind the reader, however, that much the same is true for the literary applications of those non-linguistic prosodists we have reviewed.) But surely the literary prosodic critic must try to keep current about what is happening, and even play, if not work, with some of the new ideas and methodologies being developed by this alien culture (which, I suspect, may prove less and less alien to succeeding generations of graduate students and young scholars, as Rome falls but the Empire continues).

For example, it is all very well to speak of prosodic "fictions," and to be content with a binary system of stress/non-stress when we describe metrical patterns, but what is stress? Do we all mean the same thing when we use the term in our analysis? Demonstrably, we do not.[19] If nothing more, Linguistics can help us re-evaluate our terminology. I do not anticipate literary prosodists eventually taking over all the descriptive apparatus and formulations of a linguist; the assumption is naive. Nor do I even think it is helpful to suggest that a literary prosodist should work like a linguist. Rather, being informed of this developing science, working in dialogue with it, future critics may borrow from, play off against, complement, react to, or argue with its practitioners, as they go about their own business.

This is not to say that any work which purports to bring Linguistics and Chaucer's poetry together should automatically be acclaimed. It needs to be approached with the same suspicion and charity as any other kind of criticism. Especially will this be true during these confused years when representatives from the two cultures (literary and linguistic) are insufficiently informed about each other.

As a sample of the linguistic approach, I want to mention in passing Merle Fifield's *Theoretical Techniques for the Analysis of Variety in Chaucer's Metrical Stress* (1973). It is really a sketch, taking off from the Trager-Smith four-levels-of-stress theory, and Chomsky-Halle generative rules for the phonology of surface structure. Fifield shows us how one might postulate a series of iambic types, generated from four-level rules, for Chaucer's poetry, and points to some areas where prosodic analysis might be enriched by such a linguistic approach. And yet she seems to feel the job can only be indicated, rather than executed: "Until a humanly endowed English robot stalks out of Computerbury toward the Tabard, a dubious boon, the full examination of Chaucer's prosody by the generative method remains improbable" (36). Indeed, her generative analyst sounds more like Tantalus than Prometheus; and one who loves Chaucer more than abstract science may be pardoned for quitting the scene rapidly, before the dubious boon is lowered. The trouble with this attempt is that it wrongly describes what must be accomplished to perform an adequate literary-linguistic study; one need not turn into a computer or a robot to combine science and art. As long as such claims are made, the literary folk will remain unreconciled and unedified.

One step further on, stands a monograph with a prepossessing title, which a student of the orthodox school of prosodic criticism might write upon conversion to Linguistics, or a linguist might write who is trying to think kindly of poetry. But Jack Conner's *English Prosody from Chaucer to Wyatt* (1974) promises more than it can deliver. It turns out to be an adventure in speculative phonology, to the end of validating the iambic line in early English poetry. Its genesis, the author tells us, lay "in a question asked by Professor R. W. Zandvoort when he was editing *English Studies.* In another connection, I had mentioned in passing that Chaucer regularly released his final consonants; Professor Zandwoort wanted to know who had ever demonstrated that, and I could not say" (7).

Conner will defend these four theses:

1. In Middle English, in the East Midlands dialects which coalesced to form Standard English, every word-final consonant was released with a vowel-like sound (voiced or voiceless) which was so conspicuous that it could serve as a weak syllable between stronger syllables.
2. The vowel-like sounds so produced were available to poets of the fourteenth and fifteenth centuries so that, if they chose to do so, they could use these phonetic syllables as metrical syllables.
3. During the transition from Middle English to Early Modern English (say, between 1475 and l550) the mode of articulation in the emerging Standard English was changed–no doubt by imperceptible degrees–so that eventually the vowel-like sounds of consonantal release were no longer so conspicuous that they could be perceived and apprehended as syllables, and so were no

longer available as metrical syllables in the making of verse.

4. The change of mode of articulation progressed at different rates in different parts of the speech-community; but the present state of knowledge does not permit more precise statements about it.

As a consequence, the prose rhythm of the following lines from the General Prologue:

> 12 Than longen folk to goon on pilgrymages
> And palmeres for to seken straunge strondes;[20]

could be rendered as follows (i.e., if pronounced in normal, nonmetrical speech–where "uh" represents that unstressed "vowel-like sound" [schwa]):

> Than-uh longen-uh folk-uh to goon-uh on-uh pilgrymages-uh
> And-uh palmeres-uh for-uh to seken-uh straung(e)-uh strondes-uh.

If we feel like Englishmen Italianate while talking this way, we are not far from the mark: "audible explosions similar to those of Modern Italian," says Conner (65). He does not say the verse itself would be pronounced this way. Rather, he argues that such an abundance of syllables allows us a) to worry only about the words, not the spellings, in medieval texts (for whether a scribe writes "than" or "thanne," its normal pronunciation would have been "than-uh"); and b) to pronounce only those "vowel-like sounds" which will create a line that is "rhetorically and esthetically most expressive of the author's meaning" (72). One will not find here any new evidence showing that that "best line" should be a version of iambic pentameter; Conner thinks it should be, and wishes to show that with so many syllables to choose from, one will have an easy time (getting ten or eleven syllables, that is; iambics won't come any easier). Presumably, one reads each line twice, deciding the first time which vowel-like sound will be repressed in the performance. One's linguistic competence will give the available syllables, and one's prosodic conventions, the choice. But Conner's book, in spite of its title, gives us absolutely no news at all about what those prosodic conventions were for Chaucer, or where they came from.

I suspect that Conner's argument, on linguistic grounds alone, will seem remarkably silly.[21] But even if all scholars were to receive it as new gospel, the reader of Chaucer would be very little illumined about Chaucer's prosody. Someone else would have to explain how many syllables to select, or what system of stress to use, and someone else would surely have to explain what is "rhetorically and aesthetically most expressive." In his Foreword, Conner criticizes Ian Robinson for advising readers to sound -e's in rime only if they sound right: "Surely," he says disdainfully, "we can deal more justly with Chaucer's prosody than to make it conform to our own" (7). I fail to see that his end result is much different from Robinson's.

But these are preliminaries. We must advance now to a more prominent example of the intersection of Linguistics and medieval literature.

The practice of prosodic analysis has had the extreme misfortune of getting its scarf caught in the passing wheels of transformational-generative linguistics, and has severely strained, if not broken its neck. It is not entirely clear why Chaucer had to be the poet submitted to analysis in Morris Halle and Samuel Jay Keyser's *Chaucer and the Study of Prosody*, unless we take the words I have italicized in the following quotation as hinting a larger study to come: "We propose to characterize the accentual-syllabic meter known as iambic pentameter in the form *in which it was first used by Geoffrey Chaucer*" (Halle & Keyser 1966, 187). And indeed, the same authors published *English Stress. Its Form, Its Growth, and Its Role in Verse* five years later (Halle & Keyser 1971).[22] That included a major section on "The Evolution of the English Stress System," with a separate treatment of "Late Middle English Stress" (97–109), and also a concluding section on "A Theory of Meter," whose treatment of "Iambic Pentameter" (164-80)[23] scanned the Clerk's portrait from the General Prologue "to illustrate the metrical theory developed here." The authors have decided that the standard English iambic pentameter line began with Chaucer, they don't say why, so a study in generative metrics must needs pay close attention to its starting point. (Nevertheless, neither of the authors appears to have had special training, or current research interests, in the poetry of Chaucer.)

By having Chaucer's be the chiefest corpus dissected, the linguists force the philologists and literary critics of the old school to take a position on a matter they might have preferred to ignore. For the situation is highly controversial and very fluid. Halle and Keyser's book–listed as "forthcoming" in their article–cited two criticisms of their initial theories[24] and promised that "a more direct and detailed reaction" would be "forthcoming" (which came forth in Halle & Keyser 1971). Indeed, the bibliographies of many books and articles on Linguistics are liberally studded with such notes to "forthcoming" work, and since virtually none of the subsequent debate has been much interested in Chaucer, it all adds up to a worrisome distraction. Wimsatt, in arguing in friendly but trenchant fashion, made many of his points with lines from Chaucer, although his scansions strike me as quite clumsy. And so it goes. Those who write on this new metrical approach look back to Halle and Keyser's first article, and that means they quite often deal with Chaucerian lines. I have placed in a note those articles which stem from their first, to give some idea of the ramifications of the discussion.[25] For our purposes, surely, it is important to decide whether Chaucer has been kidnapped by the generative metricists and needs rescuing; or has gone some place where we should follow; or can be trusted to return home on his own, dragging his tales behind him.

Would that someone, at the very start of all this, had insisted that Halle and Keyser get their background clearly determined before moving ahead. For example, their first note in their first essay says, somewhat confusingly, "All quotations come from the *Concordance* from *The Complete Works of Geoffrey Chaucer*, ed. F. N. Robinson (Boston, 1933)" (Halle & Keyser 1966, 187). What does that second "from" mean? The text for the *Concordance* is the Globe edition of Chaucer, originally 1898; perhaps they mean that they found their quotations in the *Concordance* and used Robinson for the actual text. But why, in 1966, use the unrevised 1933 edition? These are basic questions, I believe, first, because the 1933 edition did not have the Manly-Rickert text for reference, and second, because Robinson has had his own theory of Chaucer's prosody, which governs his punctuation, including the frequent use of that heavy juncture-marker, the semi-colon (not known to Chaucer), and the addition or subtraction of final -e's. By basing their metrical demonstration on a distinctively "modern" critical text, which is yet out of date, Halle and Keyser have started to row out to sea in a leaky boat.

Let us look at what actually happens when Halle and Keyser read and scan Chaucerian lines. Here is an example of their modified procedures, from *English Stress,* reproducing their markings:

```
         /  /          /                  /
Ful thredbare was his ov[ereste] courtepy;
 W S      W    S  W  S  W         S  W  S

                       /                  /
For he hadde get[en hym] yet no benefice,
 W  S  W        S     W       S  W  S  W SX

                /                  /
Ne was so worldly for to have office.
 W  S   W    S     W  S  W  S   W SX

                     /                /     /
For hym was lev[ere have] at his beddes heed
 W    S   W   S       W       S  W   S   W   S

          /     /      /      /      /
—Twenty bookes, clad in blak or reed,
  W  S W    S  W     S  W   S  W   S

      /                      /
Of Aristotl[e and] his philosophie,
 W  S W S       W     S  W  S W  SX

          /      /         /           /    /
Than robes riche, or fith[ele, or] gay sautrie.
  W   S W    S     W  S      W      S  W   SX
```

(179)

(The authors supply no discussion of what they have done at this point, having previously explained their symbols.) The accents, as over "thredbare," indicate "fully stressed vowels," and secondary or tertiary stresses are not marked. Those syllables that are bracketed (in the original, indicated by attachments under the line) indicate the assignment of more than one syllable to a position. The W and S symbols mark the "Weak" and the "Strong" positions, the latter always even-numbered. X indicates extra, unstressed syllables at the end of lines. The dash in 294 indicates the omission of a syllable in the weak initial position. The single underline refers to the formulation of their "abstract metrical pattern" (169), and indicates that a vowel which is not fully stressed appears in the S position (by rule, the line is still metrical); the double underline indicates that a fully stressed vowel appears in a W position, but is not, however, a linguistically defined "stress maximum" because it does not contain "a stressed syllable located between two syllables with lesser stress." Therefore, while some lines are more metrically "complex" than others, none is discovered to be unmetrical.

Two things may be noted about their practice. First, what prosodists have called extra-metrical syllables are allowed and declared metrical within this scheme, which is stress-positional but not strictly syllabic. We are not told why this should be the rule for Chaucer. Yet it is silently presumed that the terminal -e in "thredbare," "overeste," "hadde," and "have" was *not* to be pronounced. What looks to be a system for allowing Chaucer a good deal of flexibility does not give us the rules for pronouncing unstressed syllables, and takes for granted a system of orthography which comes from the modern editor.

Second, the implications for performance are not clear. It is a subject in which Halle and Keyser are not directly interested, since they address themselves to the description of a "structure." The job of marking out secondary accents (as with "courtepy" and "benefice") is left to us, as is the assignment of pitch and juncture. They do not tell us why they earlier marked "SObrely" in l. 289, but "courtePY" in 290, which would weaken the rime effect;[26] nor do they explain why they give more stress, in 291, to "geten" than to "yet," or even "no." I don't think "clad" in 294 would be stressed equally with "blak" and "reed."

When the same passage is compared with F. N. Robinson's example, on p. xxxvi of his revised edition, it can be seen that it represents an intermediate position. Robinson marks the "metrical" stresses, and hence is confusingly conservative. He has placed an accent, in effect, over *every one* of what Halle and Keyser would call the S positions, or the ictus of every iamb. Hence:

/ / / / /
292 Ne was so worldly for to have officë.

Students should not be allowed to perform the line this way. Nor does Robinson intend they should. Nevertheless, even though he says that Chaucer will sometimes reverse the stress in feet, and "it will be understood, of course, that the metrical accents varied in strength," his illustration will almost always mislead the student. For it *looks* like a scansion, even if it is meant to be a picture of a metrical pattern, superimposed on rhythmical lines of poetry. In which case, Halle and Keyser's

/ /
Ne was so worldly for to have office

is greatly preferable in indicating the stress maxima in the line, allowing "was," "for," and "have" to receive secondary or tertiary stress as would be the case with any piece of prose. By this system, the *pronunciation* of the line is not "poetic"; the poetry is inferred through the cumulative intuition of the metrical norm, expressed in the syllabic consistency and the rimes, or in other aspects not discussed here, like rhetoric and imagery. We have, then, "prose spoken in verse" (my reduction)–

a definition some prosodists would find easy to accept, once the terms were defined. I think it is an extreme position, not sensitive enough to Chaucer's poetic "register,"[27] but it is to be preferred to a system that tends towards doggerel.

After all this, it is understandable if the old-school prosodist concludes there is little from this direction he really needs to attend. When Mustanoja glanced at the 1966 article by Halle and Keyser, the debate had scarcely begun, nor had *English Stress* appeared, so it was hardly imprudent to say "its usefulness will have to be proved in actual practice" (71). He did suggest, however, that their theory "will probably satisfy the needs of linguists better than those of students of literature," which may encourage one to dismiss their work out of hand. As a prime example of such a conclusion taken to a posture of witty disdain, there is the brief survey by Thomas Cable, who asserts: "It is not too much to say that generative prosody has been properly discredited, nor too soon to predict that it will go the way of structural prosody, taking with it the arrows, brackets, symbols, and perhaps the distinct expository style. . . . Like the Andromeda Strain, generative prosody will eventually mutate into something harmless and float away." (Cable 1972, 228 & 231) One appreciates the exasperated cleverness, yet it ridicules serious work while characterizing it inaccurately: it points to essays like Wimsatt's in *College English* as "incisively" criticizing the Halle-Keyser theory–while in fact Wimsatt insisted (see the "Discussion" reported in Chatman 1971, 219) that "the system is more flexible than any other, less committed, and more consistent." Wimsatt was its critic precisely because he acknowledged its considerable potential.

At the very least, I should think the student of Chaucerian prosody owes this ongoing discussion the courtesy of open-minded attention.[28] One quite new to the field might be encouraged to plunge into the essays edited by Donald C. Freeman in *Linguistics and Literary Style,* in which the reprinted essay by Halle and Keyser assumes significance within a fuller context of related issues (Freeman 1970). If it is true that generative metrics, or structural and transformational Linguistics, have yet to throw bright light on Chaucer's verse, primarily because the linguists' *philology* has been defective, it is also true that they are raising questions and challenging assumptions which no student of Chaucer can afford to ignore. On the one hand, there are the ancillary disciplines from philology which the literary critic has depended upon, and these are clearly in need of correction or amplification, whether it be phonology, textual criticism, or scansion. On the other hand, there is the area of Stylistics, a large domain with plenty of room and a great many possibilities, but–thus far–almost totally uninhabited by Chaucerian pioneers. To construct a "grammar of style" for Chaucer's verse seems to me an interesting and possible task, in which one can cooperate with linguists without capitulating to them. The generative-metrical sense of "rules" is appropriate in such an inquiry, as one attempts to define what Chaucerian meter is, after determining the attendant problems of medieval pronunciation and stress; and so is the linguistic issue of "metrical complexity" which yet remains for extended study, after appropriate texts have been determined.

At the moment, however, the sense that Linguistics is some kind of competing enterprise for the philologist literary-critic is not unhealthy, if the results tend towards the release of energy and the retirement of unsubstantiated authority (Linguistics, for example, has quite properly killed any further possibility of speaking of quantitative or durational scansion in English verse). Clashes at the frontier seem to be in terms of warring languages, or terminology, and this, certainly, is a good thing. The literary critic, old-style, must no longer feel secure in putting down the curious science of Linguistics and then relying on the doubtful science behind his own "humanism," in such petrified notions as "feet," "iambs," "cesuras," and so forth (they are the gods we have found it necessary to invent). I should like to see a kind of criticism develop in which the literary and linguistic study of prosody could be united–as in the study of rime, where the literary critic could inveigle the structuralist to raise his segmental gaze to the longer unit of couplets, stanzas, and series of lines, and where the prosodic implications of rimed couplets could be fully accounted for in terms of stress, rising meter, rhetorical devices of contrast, tempo, logic, enjambment, and wit.[29] In the Frankensteinian laboratory of my fantasy, I construct a future Paragon of Prosody, who will think like Chomsky and write like Saintsbury.

IV. Future Studies

Neither literary nor linguistic criticism has done enough yet with Chaucer's verse. The explanation should now be at least partially clear. The old science, which produced so many of those authoritative works now gathering authoritative dust, wished to investigate Chaucer systematically as a contribution to our understanding of the history of the English language and of the progress of the arts.[30] When it came time to read particular poems of Chaucer, however, their schemes and terms proved more of a barrier than a bridge to appreciation. Furthermore, for reasons I do not entirely understand, those of their students who adventured into literary and practical criticism (by which I mean close reading and individual explication) seemed to be governed by the conviction that, while Chaucer may have been a great poet, he was only a mediocre versifier. That is to say, when one reviews as much of the corpus of prosodic criticism as possible, and wonders why there is so little of it, and even less–in terms of what is being written about other poets–that is really good, one must conclude that the field has been depressed by the unvoiced assumption, *that the job is not worth doing.*

Another way of putting it is to say that there is little value perceived in such studies, referring not only to the economics of the profession but to its meager system of recognition and positive reinforcements. It is surely no coincidence that there are a very small number of recordings of Chaucer for sale today, and virtually none coming to market; and that the Modern Language Association has never, to my knowledge, scheduled a meeting which featured a symposium of performances, i.e., a time when different people would come together to read Chaucer out loud and discuss what they were doing. And in an age in which the critic must gain note through ingenuity in interpretation or rigor in exotic science, it must be admitted that prosodic criticism is but a hand-maiden. It is not likely to have direct influence in any discourse on meaning, and is required in any case to harmonize its findings with meanings which others have already identified.[31]

The remedy for this parlous situation is not to utter a professional Bull, proclaiming Chaucer great enough to support (and reward) greater industry in searching out the seeds of his genius; nor to institute a section in the Graduate Record Examination on scanning Chaucer; nor even (though still a nice idea) to require all doctoral candidates to perform a Canterbury Tale as part of their orals. No. Chaucer's versification, happily, will not decay if neglected, but it will shine if noticed. Its virtues will not resist the inquisitive eye, especially of those "unsatiated and insatiable lovers" who will allow things to "shape" themselves "by degrees" as affection and curiosity stimulate each other. Perhaps it will be enough to describe the kinds of inquiries which can still be pursued as novelties, or as necessary revitalizations of what has too long lain dormant. And perhaps we can hope that the next reviewer of the prosodic field will marvel at all the elegant voices attesting the eloquence of Chaucer's verses.

Towards that happy state, this abbreviated list of questions and issues.

TEXT. The Variorum Chaucer will eventually publish a facsimile of the Hengwrt ms. with a transcription which includes a corrected version of the Ellesmere. On this basis, one can try to account for differences and similarities between these two related MSS. and relate such evidence to prosodic issues. There is room for more discussion of Ian Robinson's thesis that Chaucer's followers tell us, through their imitations of his verse, a good deal about his own practice, but this must be based on responsible textual scholarship. A close study of Fairfax MS. 16, in terms of text and prosody, and varieties of poetry, should be interesting. *The Virgule and Medieval Prosody* will never be a best-seller, but it could be a useful monograph. In a larger sense, there is work to be done in describing the extent to which fifteenth-century MSS. were and were not books-intending-to-be-performed, i.e., a set of prosodic cues. There is also a need for comprehensive work on Chaucerian texts other than the *Canterbury Tales,* which is at least a long-term project of the Chaucer Variorum. Whether we need facsimiles beyond El and Hg should be debated; corrections of the Chaucer Society transcriptions will be forthcoming.

PRONUNCIATION. Historical Linguistics purports to have a good deal to tell medieval scholars, but its work is just beginning, and its results must be translated into the critical community. Chomsky and Halle's formulations of stress rules need more review and debate, bringing together both literary and linguistic historians. The performer needs to decide how precisely he should try to reproduce the sounds of Chaucer, and capture the nuances of intonation. The English critic should know more about current theories of syllabic/stress bases in late-medieval French. In fact, the total environment of speech sounds in Chaucer's day should be identified and integrated, so that the prosodist can be brought up to date on the sounds of Anglo-Norman, Parisian French, Church Latin, school Latin, and

Italian. All of these sound, stress, and syllabic systems had relevance to the development of Chaucer's verse. A prosodic inventory of Chaucerian and Middle-English readings currently available on records and tapes would also be useful, particularly if it provided guidelines for future productions and stimulated the demand. Its main purpose would be to assess the quality of the sounds available and identify the prosodic assumptions that seem to have guided them.

METRICAL PATTERN. To establish Chaucer's conception of meter we need a much richer contribution from continental and insular literary history. In the list of books from the library of William Ravenstone, left to St. Paul's school in 1358, and to which (Edith Rickert argues) Chaucer could easily have had access, there appear such titles as the *Magnum Doctrinale,* "a grammar in verse"; John of Garland's *Accentarius,* a poem "on accent in poetry"; Gregory of Huntingdon's *Regulae versificandi;* a *Liber accentus,* which might have been Priscian's *De accentibus;* and so on–in other words, a rather hefty collection of reference works on Latin prosody, along with volumes of Horace, Persius, Juvenal, Vergil, Ovid, Lucan, and Statius (cf. *Troilus,* V.1792). This is "proof" of nothing, but has implications worth exploring (Rickert 1948, 122–26). More than terms or texts, however, we need demonstrations. The contemporary world of Latin verse has scarcely been related to Chaucer's linguistic environment. We need a kind of "source study" which will illustrate for us the mixture of quantitative theory and accentual practice in medieval Latin verse, and which will help us hear its rhythmic variety and evaluate its influence. We could use more study of *macaronic* verse, where several languages are blended and one prosody confronts, or is overwhelmed by, another. Likewise, musicology can make a contribution–not to give us the old, effete metaphor of the "music" of Chaucer's verse, but to tell us what sorts of musical rhythms actually abounded, and how they were fitted to different kinds of poetry.

The area of translation should offer much prosodic information, on somewhat the same principle as macaronic verse. If French verse was rimed syllabics without an accentual pattern, we must pay more attention to what Chaucer's most literal translations from the French sound like, as compared with his loosest. We must try to characterize the prosodic universes of French and Italian poetry, since they represent alternatives Chaucer apparently quite deliberately chose between. We could use careful prosodic analyses of Guillaume de Lorris, Jean de Meun, Guillaume Machaut, Eustache Deschamps, and Jean Froissart. I have not seen the same for Boccaccio, even though his hendecasyllabic stanzas would seem much more important metrically to Chaucer than the abundantly studied verse of Dante. (I say nothing here about German and Flemish verse, because they seem less relevant to Chaucer, yet news from those areas might prove very interesting.) And of course, the metrics of the "native," or alliterative, verse have been so prominent in the arguments of the "heretics" that a good deal more theology remains to be worked out–based more firmly, it is to be hoped, on historical and textual grounds. We need more discussion of a question too often lightly handled: what would be the "normal" exposure of a young page of bourgeois origins to the meters of popular poetry? It is not an easy matter to be precise about. For the very young, there must surely have been the equivalent of jump-rope rimes, jingles, proverbs, and a rather luxurious undergrowth of sturdy "English" phrases, tags, songs, riddles, charms, and curses to scramble about in. But this hardly argues a predilection for alliterative verse, itself rather exotic and strictly mannered in its day. Separate prosodic studies of Langland, of the Pearl Poet, and of Gower should offer important comparative systems. Gower seems potentially the most interesting, since he links Anglo-Norman and medieval Latin to the English literary scene; the question I find intriguing is whether he and Chaucer might represent rather separate aesthetic assumptions, in that one is writing a book to be read with the ears, the other, with the eyes. (I am thinking that perhaps the Ellesmere MS. represents a Gower-like editorial supervision which distinguishes it from the Hengwrt–i.e., metrical pattern taking precedence over prose rhythm.)

VERSIFICATION. Some of the tools most needed for a survey of Chaucer's practice are badly out of date. But a new Concordance and Rime Indices must wait upon a textual consensus. Also very vexing is the matter of the dating of Chaucer's works. There has been little new work on this topic, and it may not be possible to do much more than sift over old evidence towards new speculation. But the question of Chaucer's prosodic development falls flat if it cannot lean upon a reliable structure of dating. Within the poetry as a whole, there is more work to be done on assessing the prosodic vocabulary and allusions which crop up all over, always within the framework of the literary artifice. But surely we can never pay too much attention to that moment when Chaucer ostentatiously plays the poet . . . and produces doggerel. I am beginning to think that the *Thopas* is one of the few ends which can be pulled out from the tangled ball of prosody. We should pay more attention to what it implies about metrical pattern and versification, and to all its many hints about what kind of prosodic models Chaucer knew best, what his attitude towards excessive regularity was, and how he played with rime for sound, structure, and wit. The *Thopas* is his *Peri Bathous.* In it, Chaucer virtually invents the word "dogerel," as far as the MED can tell. And sends it up, with high hilarious art. (For a recent discussion in the right direction, see Burrow 1971, 122–6.) Then again, if I am correct in suggesting that the *Nun's Priest's Tale* comes closest to fulfilling the poet's own conditions for winning the "soper" (Gaylord 1967), then it should yield happy results to the prosodic critic, being a prime example of *doing* what it is. It also provides a happy hunting-ground for the critic seeking to integrate rhetorical and prosodic analyses. And like the *Thopas,* it is a pill to purge melancholy, and should be pecked right up by every practicing prosodist for health and good cheer.

POETIC EFFECT. We need to put versification back into the glossary of those who have regularly discussed Chaucer's style. Expressive variation, metrical complexity, and what Fussell calls "density" are all pleasant and interesting subjects, and since they require that close attention be given to poetry, their pursuit should be encouraged. But in order to accomplish a significant increase in what I might call "total" prosodic criticism, an important change must take place: "performance" must be more eagerly anticipated and put closer to the center of the critical enterprise. (I wish the MLA would give an Annual Award to a Prosodic Critic for "Best Performance.") For concentration on form permits a variety of useful descriptions, without coming close to an accounting of the life of the verse as it is perceived in time and motion. Literary and linguistic attention to performance must be fine-tuned, of course; it must involve something further than reciting the *Miller's Tale* in a loud voice, or swooning through the beginning of the Prologue to the *Legend of Good Women,* or curling the lip while reading the Friar's portrait. The notion of "effect" must not be taken for granted; it must be placed–at least initially–within its day and age. If, as I believe, Chaucer's poetry is more kinetic than sensuous, it follows that the movement of his verse will be mimetic, or gestural–it will give the impression of a job accomplished, a race well run. It will be at once a game and a contest, it will be an *agon* (in several fitts). If we change things about, and say the meaning (the "prose sense") is the music, then the verse *dances* to that music.

It cannot be easy to show how this is so. A critic confined to the written word will have to devise a vocabulary for helping the reader imagine, not what he is reading, but what he should be hearing. So the critic should have some sense of himself as an absurdity, a heavy bear of theory, climbing towards the hive. (I say this because solemnity seems to be the chief occupational hazard of prosodists.) But what he needs most of all is a faith in that honey almost within his grasp. The poetic effects of Chaucer's verse are abundant, and sweet to the taste.

The subject of Chaucer's prosody is a great thing–not because the critic is great, but because the poetry is.

NOTES

*Essay reprinted with permission from *Chaucer Review* 11 (Summer 1976): 22–82.

[1]Hollander 1975, viii.

[2]Saintsbury 1906, ix–x.

[3]Chatman 1965, 197.

[4]Lotz 1972, 1. Cf. Crystal 1969, 5: "pitch, loudness and duration." προσοδια: "that which is added to song"; προσωδιαι came to mean "the signs used to mark the accents" in "the final codification of traditional Greek accentuation," "which included the marks for the rough and smooth breathings" (Firth 1948, 5); Palmer (Palmer 1970) argues that Firth was the founder of linguistic prosodic analysis, and hence the originator of its non-aesthetic definition. For a general explanation, see R. H. Robins, "Aspects of Prosodic Analysis," in Palmer 1970, 188–200. Note that this is from a particular "school," and that many other linguists prefer the term "supra-segmental." For a fuller treatment, originally done under the direction of Noam Chomsky, see Langendoen 1968.

The very important essay by James Craig La Drière, on "Prosody," in the *Princeton Encyclopedia of Poetry and Poetics* 1974, manages to keep separate and yet related the definitions of literary and linguistic prosody: 669–77. The enlarged edition also includes essays in its Supplement on "Generative Metrics" and "Metacriticism." [But see note on *New Princeton Encyclopedia* 1993, in the Intro. to the present vol.–Ed.]

[5]I don't imply for a minute that Mssrs. Halle and Keyser love their work any less than Saintsbury. I am talking about criticism, not critics, and the style, not the motives, perceived within its practice.

[6]For reasons which should become clear later, I have followed the text of the Hengwrt, or Peniarth, MS., from the Six-Text Print in Chaucer 1869. When not otherwise noted, subsequent quotations will be from Chaucer 1957.

[7]For a helpful introductory survey, see Donaldson, "The Manuscripts of Chaucer's Works and Their Use," in Brewer 1975, 85–108.

[8]I follow here the terminology of Roger Fowler, who is in turn trying to summarize literary and linguistic consensus, in "Linguistic Theory and the Study of Literature," in Fowler 1966, 8.

[9]Mustanoja recommends the (untranslated) third edition, *Chaucers Sprache und Verskunst* (1920), ed. E. Eckhardt. ten Brink had died in 1892.

[10]Cf. Hammond 1908: "For when we speak of Chaucer's freshness and simplicity, it is his freedom from just such beautiful sophistications that we mean–a freedom which befits the man who was first, last, and always the storyteller and but incidentally the singer" (p. 488).

[11]The Campsall MS., from Chaucer 1882, 295. Line 1976 is one of the most significant among the few where Chaucer speaks openly of versification. (Robinson's ed. follows Campsall's version.) How extraordinarily ironic that the MS which Robinson took as his base text, Corpus Christi College, Cambridge 61, reads: "So prey I *to* god that non myswrite the./ Ne the *this* mysmetre for defaute of tonge" (Chaucer 1895, 293). I have italicized those added words, the first otiose and the second nonsensical, which quite effectively mis-meter the two lines.

[12]It is a little disheartening, then, to discover that in comparison with the Chaucer Society's transcription of Fairfax 16, Southworth's version shows six minor changes in these four lines, which he fails to note. Nor is it clear why he should have spelled this work *The Boke of the Duches,* which appears in none of the MSS.

[13]It is certainly true that if we look to modern phonology for reassurance to correct Robinson, we are not likely to find much that is specific. Lass and Anderson, *Old English Phonology* (1975), write: "As far as we can tell, historical investigation does not permit us to recover much more than grossly binary (i.e. classificatory) specifications. . . . When it comes to 'pronunciation,' i.e. the specification of what would have to be n-ary feature coefficients, we must simply say that we have no relevant information, and cannot even conceive how we might get it, short of a time machine" (203). Cf. Wolfe 1972, *Linguistic Change and the Great Vowel Shift in English* : "I do not wish to make any claim about . . . exact phonetic quality, since I do not think it possible to determine this with any accuracy for an earlier stage of the language for which we lack not only instrumental records but even impressionistic description of the sounds"(p. 2). The prosodist should realize however, that the linguists are being punctilious in telling us they cannot show us exactly how Chaucer would have sounded as he read. But such a precise description is not what prosodic critics look for in trying to get at the major sound qualities and contrasts, any more than they try to determine the tempo, tone, expressive pauses, or gestures Chaucer might have adopted in reciting his verses. Robinson is perhaps more agnostic than is warranted.

[14]In the category of fairly definite Chaucerian evidence, there are words like Palamon and Arcite in the *KnT,* which are spelled alternately Palamoun and Arcita, where the accent is to be shifted to pronounce the names within the lines or at the end, depending on rime, or to change the syllable count for the meter.

[15]For an instructive comparison, note the "carefully punctuated" Fairfax MS. 16, already cited, whose stanza from the *Anelida* will be studied below. The scribe obviously felt there should be at least one virgule, possibly one cesura, in each line and yet just as clearly is not responding to the *poetic* pointing needed. Any attempt to read that stanza as a construction of half-lines is obviously in trouble.

[16]For a discussion of the extraordinary Fairfax 16 MS. in the Bodleian Library, Oxford, see Hammond 1908, 333–35, 338–39.

[17]Ed. Robinson, p. 304. Knight did not include Robinson's marks over "cryeden" which I have added here.

[18]Ian Robinson has written a book attacking the work of Noam Chomsky: *The New Grammarian's Funeral* (1975).

[19]Cf. Crystal, *Prosodic Systems*: "recent research has shown that it is facile to expect that such a phenomenon as stress can be identified with a single phonetic feature" (29).

[20]The text for these lines is from Manly & Rickert 1940, III, 3; for Conner will find theirs a "definitive" edition for reasons of his own–stemming from his belief that the word, but not its spelling, is what is most important to recover. Only get the right words in order, and final -e's and MS. punctuation will be inconsequential.

[21]Surely the first of the four points quoted above is in heaviest weather? The whole question of what "released with a vowel-like sound (voiced or voiceless)" means is fudged. To be convincing for the purposes of prosody, Conner would have to show us a voiced sound. He never really does–and intriguing speculation about a voiceless release unobtrusively turns into "voiced or voiceless," as if either one would work. Not so. Furthermore, persuasive evidence for his sweeping theory is virtually non-existent. Even if he is on to something, a much fuller job must be done. Like most polemicists, he characterizes the evidence available to the conventional school over-gloomily. I don't think the case of the final -e is quite as chaotic as he insists. It is not clear, for example, that he has spent any significant time comparing the authoritative manuscripts of the CT.

[22]This was built, in turn, out of the transformational sortie into Historical Linguistics, Chomsky & Halle 1968, *The Sound Pattern of English,* and on those authors' "Nuclear Stress" rule.

[23]Also, abridged and slightly modified, in W. Wimsatt 1972, 217–37.

[24]W. Wimsatt 1970 and Magnuson & Ryder 1970. Wimsatt's essay has been reprinted in Chatman 1971, 197–215, where it is followed by a report of the "Discussion of Wimsatt's Paper," 215–20.

[25]Halle and Keyser's "Illustration and Defense," already cited, restates their "modified theory" (as in *English Stress*) and then responds in considerable detail to the critiques of Wimsatt and of Magnuson and Ryder. On the whole, they feel their modifications have answered the important criticisms, and find no need for further change or retreat. In the same number of *College English,* Joseph C. Beaver reviews their theory and Magnuson and Ryder's, finding for the former, but adding some further rules of his own, responding more complexly to shifting stresses and the "promotion" of secondary or tertiary stresses (Beaver 1971, 177–97). After that, Magnuson and Ryder reply to Halle and Keyser's opening response, and to Beaver's remarks. They, too, appear to have modified their original "alternative," but, while responding favorably to many of Beaver's suggestions, still consider Halle and Keyser's theory too accommodating.

In "Computers and the History of Prosody," Dilligan & Lynn (1973) describe how they programmed an IBM 370/155 computer to scan Chaucer's verse, according to the Halle and Keyser modified theory (*English Stress*); their data come from a 1,000-line sample, using Robinson's revised text, based on the first 100 lines of *Anelida, PF, MillT, MLT, WB, PrT,* and *T&C,* Bks. I, III, and V. Their procedure took no account of subsequent criticisms or modifications, and clearly must be suggestive rather than definitive; such results seem particularly useful in providing some preliminary graphs of metrical complexity.

Those who debate the theories of Halle and Keyser with greatest gusto are undoubtedly also those who read the journal *Poetics* with greatest care. Founded for the study of the theory of literature, heavily informed by new developments in Linguistics, *Poetics* devoted a separate number to essays by Beaver, Klein, Hascall, Guéron, Bernhart, and Magnuson on "Generative Metrics" (#12, 1974). None of these essays, however, discusses Chaucer's prosody.

The entry under "Generative Metrics" in the Supplement to the *Princeton Encyclopedia of Poetry and Poetics* (1974) is by Joseph C. Beaver, himself a chief adapter of the Halle-Keyser system; his account summarizes their theory and some of its competing alternatives, and cites some other sources not discussed in my essay (pp. 931–33). [In the revised 1993 *Encyclopedia,* the same entry is now written by the Dean of Metrists, T.V.F. Brogan – Ed.]

[26]The reason would appear elsewhere in the book, as rules are devised for the assignment of stress to various morphemic segments–"sobrely' and "courtepy" being two different kinds of words. But note the assumption that the "prose rhythm" does not interact or get modi-

fied by metrical expectations, an assumption I find highly debatable.

[27]Cf. Seymour Chatman's quite contrary position: "Meter is a form of 'organized violence' of poetic technique by which the poet disrupts normal stereotyped linguistic habits in order more effectively to convey his own fresh and unique message" (Chatman 1965, 211).

[28]We have had altogether too many examples of premature responses like Ronald Sutherland's "Structural Linguistics and English Prosody," which reassures his audience that the new science at best only need add a few useful accessories to the same old good-enough Brooks-and-Warren New-crit-8 (Sutherland 1958). The essay was out of date before it was published, and provides a picture of Linguistics which, I dare say, would be misleading today.

[29]There is one resource for the study of rime which deserves close study but is not widely available: Masui 1964: *The Structure of Chaucer's Rime Words. An Exploration Into The Poetic Language of Chaucer.* The aim is to study "the totality of all the relations of rime words which establish themselves as nuclei in the line-structure of Chaucer's poetry" (v). The range of scholarship blends material from the philology of ten Brink, Kaluza, and the like to the structural linguistics of Jespersen. The text is F. N. Robinson's second edition. The care and amplitude of the whole study carry off the attempt to harmonize a body of material which is not inherently in agreement. And it is much more than an updated body of lists and categories; the author is well read in literary criticism and the whole range of English poetry to the present, and his Part II, "The Semantic and Stylistic Structure of Chaucer's Rime Words" (269ff.) contains much good stylistic discussion. The study is not directly interested in meter, but its analysis of the structural significance of rime has central relevance to prosodic criticism.

[30]Jakob Schipper 1910, *A History of English Versification*: "The study of English Meter is an integral part of English Philology . . . indispensable to the investigator of the history of the language. . . . As an aid to the study of English literature in its aesthetic aspects the science of meter is no less important. It exhibits the gradual development of the artistic forms of poetical composition, explains the conditions under which they took their rise, and by formulating the laws of their structure affords valuable help in the textual criticism of poems which have been transmitted in a corrupt or imperfect condition" (1).

[31]A recent work shows how nonchalantly the question of prosody may be disposed of on the way to other things, even in a time when the critic is aware of some of the prosodic issues being debated. Elliott 1974, *Chaucer's English,* is "a conducted tour along some of the more interesting highways and byways of Chaucer's English: his use of colloquialisms and slang, technical language, literary terms, proper names, oaths, and the like" (9). It is a book about the vocabulary and diction of a poet, then, and only indirectly about his poetry. As such, it is full of lore and useful perceptions. Nevertheless, for reasons that are not spelled out, the first chapter "endeavors to provide with a minimum of technicalities the more important facts of Chaucer's pronunciation and grammar and a few hints about his prosody" (9). Elliott's assurance in such matters matches that of his compatriot, Knight. Even though he cites Southworth and Robinson, here and there a linguist, and Mustanoja's work (but not Halle and Keyser's), all's well in the world. A fact is a fact, and Kökeritz may be summarized to tell us what sounds *were*; but when there is doubt, then "objective criteria are hard to establish" (27), and the principle seems to be *Do As You Please.* And then we come upon this very revealing transitional sentence: "No matter how the modern reader approaches Chaucer's verse, he will soon become delighted," etc. Careful prosodic analysis seems to be an option which the beginner may pass by, although somewhere, someplace, there would seem to be someone who is doing precise work with it. The "hints" of this chapter refuse to apply further directions. It is the Looking Glass syndrome (which would be, of course, "déjà vu all over again").

Derek Pearsall

Chaucer's Meter: The Evidence of the Manuscripts*

Talking about meter is a hazardous business. For one thing meter is very important. Though it might easily slip one's mind, given that nine-tenths of the critical writing on Chaucer never mentions the fact, Chaucer's poetry is written in verse, and the way we read that verse and respond to its musicality, whether in our heads or when reading aloud, is presumably an important part of our interpretation of and response to its meaning. Another hazard, given that the matter is an important one, is that rational debate is even more difficult than usual, since interpretation must in the end be based on an intuitive "feel" for the music of Chaucer's verse, and none of us is going to be very ready to allow that someone else's intuitive feel is better than our own, or to be easily persuaded out of our very good opinion on the matter. There is the evidence of the manuscripts, which will be the subject of this paper, but instinct, ingrained habit, prejudice, and the determination to prove one's opinion right are more potent shaping forces, and are the reason that discussions of meter always end in tight-lipped fury and the painful recognition that one's colleagues are not as likable or intelligent as one had thought. A third hazard is the role of meter in the determination by editors of unoriginal readings. An editor does not have to have a theory of meter in order to edit a verse text, but, in an area where theories are increasingly hard to come by, it is possible to have a theory of meter, and editors usually avail themselves of the opportunity. The editor's theory of meter thus becomes entrenched in the text, acquires something of the sacramental quality of the text, and comes to be even more strenuously defended as a recovered rather than a perceived reality. The subject seems to be one that invites intransigence. The following discussion, which will confine itself to the pentameter couplet of the *Canterbury Tales,* will attempt a greater flexibility.

For a long time there has been a theory of meter behind the practice of Chaucerian editors, one which has therefore exerted considerable influence upon the way in which Chaucer is read. The best and clearest statement of this theory, as always, is by Skeat, in his general introduction to the six-volume Oxford Chaucer (Chaucer 1894, "Versification," lxxxii–xcvii). Skeat was not immune to the influence of fanciful theories, and he flirts for a while with a notion of speech-waves and a law of monopressures derived from an anonymous tract published in Edinburgh of which he was surely wrong to say that it "deserves to be better known" (lxxxiv). But he does not allow this to interfere much with his analysis, which has the kind of Skeat-like pragmatism that makes it seem not a theory at all. He finds, from his reading of the Old French ten-syllabled line, that there were sixteen possible varieties of the line, allowing for the addition of an extra unstressed syllable at the cesura or line-end, the omission of the unstressed syllable at the line-beginning or cesura, and the permissible permutations of these four kinds of license. He considers that Chaucer "freely accepted" the principle of adding a syllable at the cesura or line-end (the so-called feminine ending), that he "allowed himself to accept" the principle of dropping the unstressed syllable at the line-beginning (the "headless" line), but that he "disliked" all four types of line in which the unstressed syllable at the cesura was omitted (the "Lydgate" or "broken-backed" line).

Skeat's language is delightfully disingenuous: what Chaucer "allowed himself to accept" is clearly something that Chaucer accepted against his better judgment, or, more properly, against Skeat's better judgment, and the way is clear for the editor to remove as many of these unfortunate evidences of indulgence as he decently can. With the Lydgate line, Skeat's distaste is as marked as the "dislike" that he attributes to Chaucer. Such lines, he says, "introduce a most disagreeable jerk into the middle of the line, such as he very rarely allows" (lxxxviii), adding that Lydgate, nevertheless, "did not shrink from these unmelodious forms." Lydgate's failure to shrink from it may have been, to Skeat, a sufficient condemnation of the practice, though the line he quotes, presumably one of the worst he could find, does not seem to me unspeakable:

> Up he roos maugre all his foon.[1]

It is clearly difficult to talk about single lines out of context.

Later in his introduction, Skeat returns to a discussion of the Lydgate line, as if bracing himself for a disagreeable task. It is a license, he repeats, "of which Lydgate availed himself to a painful extent" (xcii). Of Chaucer he says:

> It is clear that his ear disliked it; yet there seem to be just a few cases that cannot fairly be explained away, the MSS. being sadly unanimous. It is better to learn the truth than to suppress what we should ourselves dislike. (xcii)

The line he quotes as an example of the sad truth of Chaucer's betrayal of his good ear is *Merchant's Tale*, E (IV) 1682:

> My tale is doon:–for my wit is thinne.[2]

He admits that this cannot be mended (without conjectural emendation based on meter, that is): the *done* offered by the two worst manuscripts is, as he says, "impossible." With another problem line, *Melibee,* B 2141 (VII.951), Skeat allows the truth to be ever so slightly obscured, if not suppressed:

I meane of Marke, Mathew, Luk, and John.

"Four MSS," he comments, "have a tag after the *k* in *Mark*; hence I have printed *Mark-e.* But I fear it can hardly be justified" (xcii). One could not reasonably ask for more honesty, except that Skeat might have mentioned that one of the manuscripts with a tag is the Ellesmere (San Marino, California, Henry E. Huntington Library, MS. 26.C.9), which had such a profound influence generally on Skeat's view of Chaucer's text and meter in the *Canterbury Tales.* Nor could one ask for a better demonstration of the way in which an editorial assumption becomes enshrined in his text, even though he acknowledges that his assumption is insecurely based. And there is, to be sure, absolutely nothing wrong with the line: the meter is perfectly apt to the rhetorically emphatic syntax of the list of evangelists.

Skeat quotes two other Lydgate lines as "unsatisfactory." One is *Monk's Tale,* B 3384 (VII.2194), which he does not cite, but which appears in his text thus:

"Goth bringeth forth the vessels," [tho] quod he.

He emends as indicated, citing in his note lines B 3391, 3416, 3418, where the plural *vessels* is similarly spelt. I'm sorry to say that F.N. Robinson, in his edition, shows no such scrupulousness, and simply emends *vesseles* without comment or textual note. The line is not one that we are going to like, I must admit, but we might be prepared to admit a certain metrical license at the junction of direct speech and speech prefix (much as in alliterative verse speech-prefixes are often extra-metrical), where the pause in the continuity of sense might accommodate a metrical pause.

The second line that Skeat quotes as unsatisfactory is *Monk's Tale,* B 3535 (VII.2346)–he is using Fragment B for nearly all his examples:

And Hermanno, and Thymalaö.

It is impossible to imagine what this line could have deteriorated from, or why a scribe might have made a mistake with it. It is evidently what Chaucer wrote, and he accepted the Lydgate line and the metrical stress on *and* in the context of a list of these strange-sounding foreign names, and as part of the desire to encode the correct pronunciation of Thymalao, and the correct rime, in the metrical structure of the line. No one has emended this line.

Another interesting feature of Skeat's discussion of meter is his emphasis upon the medial pause, for which he found manuscript support in the care and regularity with which the virgule is inserted in the Ellesmere MS to indicate the cesura.[3]

It was for this reason that he welcomed Chaucer's practice of introducing an extra unstressed syllable at the cesura, particularly when this syllable was a light one such as an inflexional final -e. Not only that, but he considered that normal elision, as of -en, or -er, or final -e with following initial vowel or h-, was inhibited at the cesura, so that an extra unstressed syllable was often created in this way. In this Skeat departed from the strict rules of elision and scansion established by ten Brink[4] and read lines such as the following with greater freedom:

> Which that my fader in his prosperitee.
> (B 3385, VII.2195)
>
> That god of heven hath dominacioun.
> (B 3409, VII.2219)

Skeat even added final -e's to his copy-text (the Ellesmere) so as to create the kind of line that he liked, the most famous example being the second of the opening two lines of the *General Prologue:*

> Whan that Aprille with his shoures sote
> The droght of Marche hath perced to the rote.

Neither Hengwrt (Aberystwyth, National Library of Wales, MS. Peniarth 392D) nor Ellesmere has this final -e for *March,* and it is completely unetymological. Note also how Skeat has added an -e to *Aprill* in the first line, though in that case the purpose is to convert a headless line, which we remember is the kind of line Chaucer occasionally allowed himself to accept but would evidently not allow in the very first line of his great poem, into a line with reversal of the first foot and in no danger of turning into the dreaded Lydgate line, whatever the pronunciation of *Aprille* (Hengwrt has *Aueryll,* Ellesmere *Aprill*).

Skeat's fondness for the medial pause has to do with his general opinion that Chaucer's verse should be read slowly and with deliberation, with careful attention to feminine endings both at cesura and at line-end. (An analogy that he does not mention might be with the pronunciation of the alexandrine of French classical drama.) He explains his opinion thus:

> We may believe that, in old times, when poetry was recited by minstrels to large assemblies, the enunciation of it was slow and deliberate, and the pauses were longer than when we now read it to a friend or to ourselves . . . . The minstrel's first business was to be understood. Many speakers speak too fast, and make too short pauses, till experience teaches them better. (xc)

The generalization about minstrel delivery seems to me to be mistaken: I cannot imagine a slow and deliberate enunciation of a tail-rime romance like *Sir Launfal,* where speed is essential to the bright, bitty, and trivial nature of the narrative performance. There is nothing to sustain deliberation. Chaucer knew this style exactly and catches it with unerring precision in *Sir Thopas:* the reader of these jog-trot tail-rime stanzas invariably finds himself going faster and faster, as if the accelerator were stuck. But I think Skeat is right about the Chaucerian pentameter, and it is quite possible to believe that one of Chaucer's purposes, especially after his early work in the short couplet, was to slow down English verse, and to make it capable of bearing a richer cargo of meaning. His introduction of the pentameter, the type of verse which most of all resists the compulsive onward drive of traditional English meters such as the four-stress alliterative line and popular ballad meter, may be seen as an important element in this strategy.

Skeat's emphasis on the medial pause seems therefore to be well-judged, and it seems a little inconsistent of him to be so severe on the Lydgate line, or at least the good Lydgate line, especially when he accepts that the cesura may on quite numerous occasions necessarily preserve final -e from elision (xci), as in this line from the *Nun's Priest's Prologue* (B 3989, VII.2799)

> Than had your tale al be told in vayn.

The effect of hiatus is not unlike that of the Lydgate line, which is perhaps one reason why the stricter metrists of the fifteenth and twentieth century have taken advantage of the liberal sprinkling of final -e's in early manuscripts to emend the line and read as follows:

> Thanne haddë yourë tale be toold in veyn

or

> Thanne haddë your tale al be toold in veyn.

The first is presumably the reading of the line intended by revisers in the group of heavily editorialized manuscripts represented by Corpus Christi College, Oxford, MS. 198, British Library MS. Lansdowne 851 and the Petworth MS, (the latter is the reading explicitly preferred by Sisam)[5] both have a metronome-like regularity and neither it seems to me can bear comparison with the naturalness and syntactic adequacy of the line as first quoted.

One has to accept, perhaps, that there are various kinds of medial pause, including both genuine hiatus and also the sense of deferred continuity or demurral which is what I think Skeat really prefers, that delicious drawing out of a half-sounded final -e or of a complex consonant cluster that recognizes artifice and self-conscious pleasure in musicality at the same time that it defers to the insistence of the line and the continuity of sense. The opening lines of the *General Prologue* will illustrate the variety of Chaucer's techniques:

Whan that Aprill with his shoures soote
The droghte of March hath perced to the roote
And bathed every veyne in swich licour
Of which vertu engendred is the flour. . . .

At the same time there should be no persistent loitering, and the practice of many readers, of always giving full syllabic value to feminine endings and even of supplying them when they are not there, becomes in the end a kind of strait jacket. I have heard readers go on with the next lines,

Whan Zephirus eek with his sweete breeth(-ë)
Inspired hath in every holt and heeth(-ë)
The tendre croppes. . . .

The effect is to deny rather than to defer continuity, and to overemphasize line-end at the expense of Chaucer's daring enjambment.

One should also recognize, even whilst acknowledging the potential importance of the medial pause, that flexibility and variety are even more important considerations for Chaucer. At times his verse can move with frenetic speed, and the passage that everyone would go to as an example, the breathtaking finale in the bedroom of the *Reeve's Tale,* is notable for the infrequency of feminine endings, the complete absence of headless or Lydgate lines, and the almost complete swallowing of the medial pause in the headlong onrush of the verse.

The system of versification that Skeat outlined for Chaucer, though in his own practice it was modified by his own admirable pragmatism, became subsequently more rigid, and was reinforced in the paragraphs on versification in a hundred introductions to texts of Chaucer, and in an editorial practice that tended to follow Skeat closely. It was the increasing rigidity of the system that I think goaded James G. Southworth and Ian Robinson into asserting that Chaucer did not write pentameter, that his verse was not indeed metrical at all, but rhythmical, and came from essentially the same mold as traditional alliterative verse (Southworth 1954 & 1962; Ian Robinson 1971). Their view depended on their belief that final -e was never sounded in Chaucer's versification, a belief that has been conclusively shown to be false on several occasions (Donaldson 1948; Samuels 1972; Burnley 1982), and also on an eccentric interpretation of the prosody of Chaucer's followers. The usual view is that the secret of his versification was lost with the loss of sounded final -e, already an archaic practice in his own day, and that English poets tended to revert to the older traditional semi-alliterative type of measure, described by C. S. Lewis as "a long line divided by a sharp medial break into two half-lines, each half-line containing not less than two or more than three stresses" (Lewis 1938; for further discussion of fifteenth-century prosody, see Pearsall, ed. 1962, intro. 59–62; and Pearsall 1970, *John Lydgate* 60–63). Here is an example from the fortunately little known poet George Ashby, who purports to be writing rime royal:

At the ende of Somer, when wynter began
And trees, herbes and flowres dyd fade,
Blosteryng and blowyng the gret wyndes than
Threw doune the frutes with whyche they were lade.
(Opening lines of "A Prisoner's Reflections," in Ashby 1899)

Southworth and Robinson argue, on the contrary, that Chaucer's followers really understood Chaucer's versification and it is nineteenth-century scholars who have got it wrong. Southworth scans Chaucer using musical notation, producing for instance the reading of the opening lines of the *General Prologue,* as they appear in Ellesmere (figure 1).[6] I hope (in my reading aloud) that I am not doing an injustice to Southworth's reading of these lines, though I do, I admit, find it difficult to conceive of an injustice being done to a reading so bad. His claim, in opposing a system of versification that he sees as being over-rigid and mechanical, is that Chaucer must be read more naturally, in accord with the rhythms of prose and colloquial speech ("it is the movement of a highly developed English speech," Southworth 1954, 91). This of course is the interpretation generally offered of the scansion of alliterative verse–that it is a highly wrought version of speech, with the syntactical and rhythmical patterns of speech to some extent formalized and systematized, and that it is, to that extent, strictly speaking non-metrical.

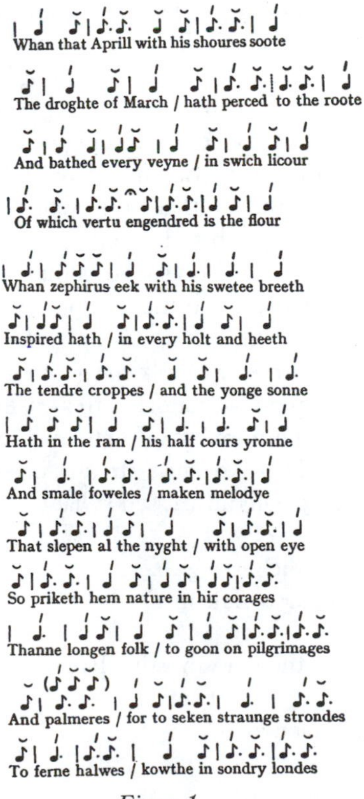

Figure 1

I have to make it clear at this point that I know exactly what "metrical" means in relation to English verse. A metrical system posits the existence of a regular line, or regularly repeated pattern of lines, with an arbitrarily fixed number of stresses regularly disposed, the regularity of disposition being temporal, and based on the isochronous interval. Such a metrical system may be *accentual* (what Coleridge propounded in his preface to "Christabel" as his "new" principle) or *syllabic:* to be more exact, and simpler, there may be less or more regularity in the distribution of unstressed syllables. This, of course, does not affect in any way the almost unlimited local variations that may be worked in individual lines, in the interests of rhythm, by rhetorical and syntactic patterning, often in tension with and counterpointed against the metrical pattern. Alliterative verse is non-metrical because the rhythmical interest is found, as Bliss points out, "not in the more or less exact accommodation of the speech-material to the metrical pattern," but in the variation in the patterns of individual half-lines, which are themselves "selected from among the rhythms which occur most commonly in natural speech" (Bliss 1962, 29). Whether this remains entirely true of later Middle English alliterative verse, and whether there is not there some accommodation to the increasingly dominant metrical forms of verse, would be another question, and the answer would certainly take in the process already alluded to by which the "metrified" four-stress alliterative or semialliterative line infiltrates the Chaucerian pentameter.

It would be possible to acknowledge that there is already influence of this kind being exerted upon Chaucer. I did, after all, in a moment of high excitement on the very first page of my book on *Old English and Middle English Poetry,* call the alliterative four-stress line "the secret power and anvil of the pentameter" (Pearsall 1977, 1). The audacity and freedom of Chaucer's handling of the pentameter may have something to do with tunes that were ringing in his head from older forms of English verse. If it were this inheritance that Southworth was genuinely trying to draw attention to, there would be much to be said for his iconoclasm. But reading according to his system of musical notation suggests that what he is doing, without realizing it, is simply to reduce Chaucer to the compound four-stress meter which, with its close affinities with dancing, marching, and popular music, lies at the root of all English popular verse. It is the meter of folk song and nursery rime, and is characterized by regularity of primary and secondary stresses, frequent absence of intermediate unstressed syllables, and a primacy of metrical stress over speech rhythms which allows, for instance, for things like pause-stresses in secondary positions. Here is an example where the intermediate unstressed syllables are mostly present:

> Up the airy mountains, down the rushy glen,
> We daren't go a-hunting for fear of little men.

And here is an example where they are mostly absent:

> Deedle deedle dumpling, my son John,
> Went to bed with his trousers on. . . .

Once this jingly meter is in your head it is very difficult to get it out, and even the most orthodox pentameter will collapse into its jog-trot rhythms:

> Clóse by those méads, for éver crowned with flówers,
> Whére Thames with príde survéys his rising tówers,
> Thére stands a strúcture of majestic fráme,
> Whích from the néighbouring Hámpton takes its náme.

I mangle thus these lines from Pope (*The Rape of the Lock* 3.1–4) as a terrible warning against any attempt to argue a "rhythmical" reading, in Southworth's sense of the term, of Chaucer's verse.

It remains true, though, that the over-rigid interpretation of Chaucer's pentameter that Southworth was reacting against was itself a distortion of Chaucer's versification. As Manly and Rickert pointed out in 1940:

> Current theories of Chaucer's versification are based, not upon the text as found in the MSS, or as established by critical processes, but upon the artificial text made regular by all the devices at the disposal of the scholar. (Manly & Rickert 1940, 2: 40)

It has always been possible for editors to produce regular decasyllabic lines by selection among the variants offered by the manuscripts, whose scribes, indeed, were often prompted by the same concern for regularity. But study of the text as it is presented in the Hengwrt manuscript, which has a special claim to textual authority that is now generally recognized, and to an only slightly lesser extent in the Ellesmere manuscript, which has been rather unfairly impugned by the editors of the Variorum Chaucer, including me, compels one to recognize a difference in metrical practice between what must be Chaucer's and what must be his editors'. The freedom and generosity in the conception of the rhythmical possibilities of the pentameter, the audacity of variation and experimentation, and the subtle sense of the relation between rhetorical and syntactical impetus and rhythmical variation, are surely positive characteristics of the creative poet at work, while the mending and smoothing of lines to produce a mechanically regular syllable count or alternation of stressed and unstressed syllables, at the expense of natural speech rhythms, are surely likely to be characteristic of the improving scribe or editor.

A statement like this needs to be backed up with specific examples, and the examples I shall give will all be from the *Nun's Priest's Prologue* and *Tale,*[7] where a small but significant number of emendations continue to be made by editors for the sake of meter, and more particularly for the sake of restoring a more regular decasyllabic line. I begin with two lines I allowed myself, in the Variorum edition, to emend (to adopt Skeat's phrase), but which I now think need no emendation:

> "I crye on the mynystres," quod he
> (B 4233, VII.3043)

Ellesmere and most other manuscripts add *out* after *crye*, and are followed by all modern editors. This certainly makes for smoother meter, but the Hengwrt reading, with the abrupt break in the line created by the inhibition of elision, could be seen as conveying more emphatically the outrage of the speaker. Both phrases, *crye on* and *crye out on*, seem to be equally idiomatic. The second line appears thus in Hengwrt:

> As man that was affrayd in his herte
> (B 4468, VII.3278)

Ellesmere and most other manuscripts have *affrayed*, for obvious metrical reasons, and are followed by all modern editors. Chaucer uses both forms, *affrayd* and *affrayed*, but a case for *affrayd* could be made here on the grounds that the sustaining of the stressed syllable that is necessary to carry the voice over the following hiatus adds emphasis to the key word in the line.

The examples that follow might be regarded as clearer examples of the mending of meter in Ellesmere. Ellesmere is followed by all editors in "improving" the following headless line,

> For a preestes sone yaf hym a knok
> (B 4504, VII.3314)

by adding *that* after *For*. Ellesmere alone has this reading; the two usages, *for* and *for that*, are equally idiomatic. The following Lydgate line, or at least the Lydgate line effect created by inhibition of elision at the cesura,

> Who so wol seke Actes of sondry Remes
> (B 4326, VII.3136)

is restored to syllabic regularity by Ellesmere, which adopts the reading *seken,* with full infinitival ending, for *seke,* as do most modern editions. Yet the line is perfectly readable in Hengwrt. Simple syllable counting seems to be the reason for the change that Ellesmere makes in this line,

> Than is a Clokke or any Abbey Orlogge
> (B 4044, VII.2854)

by substituting *an* for *any*. Most modern editors follow Skeat's lead in adopting the Ellesmere reading, even though elision of the final *y* of *any* with the initial vowel of *abbey* (which is pronounced with the accent on the second syllable, of course), will produce a perfectly regular line for those who want it. Ellesmere also removes the extra syllable in the following rather striking line,

> A dong Carte wente as it were to donge lond
> (B 4226, VII.3036)

by omitting *wente*. Skeat followed suit, but other modern editors have been happy to accept the line as it appears in Hengwrt and other early manuscripts.

Sometimes the editor of Ellesmere makes problems for himself, as for instance in this line, where he shows his usual pedantic concern for removing the contracted form of the third person singular:

> Comth of the grete superfluitee.
> (B 4117, VII.2927)

The line, now thought to have too many syllables with the substitution of *cometh* for *comth*, is further emended by the omission of *the* and the substitution of the ungrammatical strong form of the adjective. The line now reads,

> Cometh of greet superfluytee

which is sufficient in itself to deny the Ellesmere editor much of an ear. What modern editors do, characteristically, is to adopt the uncontracted form from Ellesmere (or more likely from Skeat, who has exerted a powerful influence on subsequent editors), but to ignore the other Ellesmere emendations in the line. They possibly assume that *cometh* is contracted in pronunciation if not in spelling.

Ellesmere, however, for all the comments I have made, here and elsewhere,[8] on its editorializing propensities, is on the whole very close to Hengwrt. Indeed, there are one or two occasions when the *eek*'s which were fairly liberally thrown around by fifteenth-century editors in their attempts to regularize meter appear in Hengwrt but not Ellesmere:

> Ran Cow and calf and eek the verray hogges.
> (B 4575, VII.3385)

> The hope and pryde eek of hire enemy.
> (B 4594, VII.3404)

To be consistent, I suppose I should be suspicious of these *eek*'s, but then, there are good Lydgate lines and bad Lydgate lines, and these would be bad ones. A nice illustration of the positive value of Ellesmere for understanding Chaucer's meter is provided in a line that appears in a portion of the *Nun's Priest's Prologue* not present in Hengwrt:

> Ye quod oure hoost by Seint Poules belle
> (B 3970, VII.2780)

Modern editors have had a good deal of trouble with this line, which they have mended by reading *hooste* for *hoost*, a form which appears elsewhere in Chaucer with syllabic final -e, but not in this line in any important manuscript, or by reading *seinte* for *seint*, a form which is found in the heavily editorialized British

Library MS. Harley 7334, but which itself needs a great amount of special pleading. Editors are clearly desperate to avoid the Lydgate line, but it seems to me here not only acceptable but superior, with appropriate emphasis given to the first word of the Host's oath by its position after the mid-line break.

The testimony of Hengwrt and Ellesmere combined is thus formidable, and the most striking examples of editorial emendation based on an over-rigid theory of the regularity of Chaucer's versification come where the joint testimony of the two manuscripts is rejected. The following headless line,

> And of many a maze ther with al
> (B 4283, VII.3093)

is emended by nearly all editors by the addition of *eke* after *And*, a reading picked up from Cambridge University Library MS. Dd.4.24, which alone of all reputable manuscripts has it. The same manuscript provides the reading (*Ipassed*) that Skeat adopts in order to eliminate another headless line,

> Was complet and passed were also (B 4379, VII.3189)

though later editors have been content to accept the line (*complet* may be accented on either syllable in Chaucer). A harder case is this Lydgate line in Hengwrt:

> And when the fox say that he was gon.
> (B 4608, VII.3418)

The hiatus comes between fox and *say* (as often, the virgule in Hengwrt and Ellesmere, inserted here between *say* and *that,* is completely arbitrary and misleading), and the line is by no means difficult, given the possibility of drawing out the final double consonant of *fox.* But some modern editors, including F. N. Robinson, prefer to pick up the reading *the cok* for *he* from Dd.4.24, which gives good meter, with stress reversal after the cesura, and possibly better sense.[9] This emendation is certainly preferable to that of Skeat, who adopted *igoon* for *gon* from Harley 7334, a manuscript that still had some shreds of respectability hanging about it in his day, even though Chaucer's normal form would be *agon.*

Resistance to the quasi-Lydgate line created by inhibition of elision at the cesura has induced many modern editors into accepting the various remedies offered by fifteenth-century editors. Nearly all accept the insertion of *wolde* before *han* in the second line here:

> Was lyk an hound and wolde han maad arest
> Up on my body and han had me ded
> (B 4090–91, VII.2900–01)

even though the artificial raising of *and* in the original Hengwrt-Ellesmere line produces an appropriately petulant stridency into Chauntecler's account of his dream. Nearly all editors accept *answered* from editorializing manuscripts such as Corpus 198 and Harley 7334 in their desire to avoid mid-line hiatus in the following line:

> The hostiler answerde hym anon.
> (B 4219, VII.3029)

The virgule after *hostiler* in Hengwrt and Ellesmere, though I have said that the positioning of the virgule in these manuscripts has no general authority, might suggest that *answerde* was to be pronounced, unusually, with the accent on the first syllable, to produce a rather nice Lydgate line. Elsewhere, two successive lines present similar problems to metrical purists:

> And preyde hym his viage to lette
> As for that day he preyde hym to byde.
> (B 4274–75, VII.3084–85)

In the first line few modern editors have adopted the early expedient of picking up *preyed* from manuscripts such as Corpus 198 and Dd.4.24 in order to avoid the hiatus of *preyde hym*, but most adopt *for to lette* for *to lette*. It may be that they are accepting the hiatus in the early part of the line and are simply doubtful about the pronunciation of the final -e of *viage*, but the suspicion remains that they are introducing the extra syllable in order to avoid the hiatus. In the second line, nearly all editors–though not Robinson in this case–accept the reading *abyde* for *byde* offered by large numbers of manuscripts and so avoid hiatus.

Finally, two lines with extra syllables might be mentioned as examples of the embarrassment afforded to editors by the apparently irregular versification sanctioned by Hengwrt and Ellesmere. The first,

> And in this Cart heere he lyth gapyng upright
> (B 4232, VII.3042)

is metrically unusual, but Sisam, in his excellent edition of the *Nun's Priest's Tale*, has suggested that it may be effective in conveying the impression of "hurried and excited speech" (Chaucer 1927, 41). Other modern editors have little time for such niceties, and most follow manuscripts such as Corpus, Lansdowne, and Petworth in omitting *heere*, even though, from the textual point of view, there is no plausible explanation of the generation of the reading of Hengwrt and Ellesmere from the variant. Similarly, in this line,

> But herkneth to that o man fil a gret mervaille
> (B 4266, VII.3076)

nearly all editors avoid metrical irregularity by omitting *herkneth*, the authority again being Dd.4.24. Other manuscripts, such as Corpus 198, Lansdowne, and

Petworth, tinker with the line in different ways, in their attempt to produce a regular decasyllable. The omission of *herkneth* is difficult to justify from a textual point of view, since there seems no good reason why the word should have been introduced by a scribe. Its presence can be defended in terms of the "dramatic effect in reading" that it creates, as Manly and Rickert suggest; and Sisam thinks it may be one of the "extra-metrical asides" that Chaucer sometimes allows when narrative and dramatic discourse converge. (Manly & Rickert 1940, 4: 515; Chaucer 1927, 42)

Inevitably, the many examples that have been given above of editorial management of Chaucer's meter will seem mechanically isolated out of context, and it is true that surrounding lines would have to be quoted and talked about to demonstrate fully the value of the scansion offered. Ideally, the whole poem would have to be read aloud. But even in this abbreviated manner of presentation it is possible to see how Chaucer's versification, or what can reasonably be inferred to be Chaucer's versification, has been misrepresented by generations of editors and metrists. Whether it is the editors who mislead the metrists, or vice versa, it would be hard to say, but both seem to have an interest in devising systems that obscure the freedom, variety, and flexibility of Chaucer's meter.

NOTES

*Reprinted with permission from *Medieval Literature: Texts and Interpretation*, ed. Tim William Machan (Binghamton: Medieval and Renaissance Texts and Studies, 1991), pp. 41–57.

[1]The line is from Lydgate's *Siege of Thebes*, and appears as line 2195 in the edition of A. Erdmann, EETS, 108 (London: Oxford University Press, 1911). Skeat quotes from an earlier edition.

[2]Quotation, here and in the following examples, is from Skeat's text and not from his introduction. Alternative fragment numberings refer to the edition of F. N. Robinson (Chaucer 1957), which is used for all other quotations from Chaucer, unless otherwise indicated.

[3]I have myself found no impelling reason to share Skeat's respect for the positioning of the virgule in the Ellesmere manuscript (nor for that matter in Hengwrt): it is sometimes unusually apt, often not so, and is clearly scribal in origin. G.B. Killough, in a valuable essay on "Punctuation and Cesura in Chaucer" (Killough 1982), concludes likewise that the virgule is scribal, but considers that the placement is highly regular, and in accordance with well-established tradition.

[4]ten Brink 1901: *The Language and Metre of Chaucer*. For an account of the history of the study of Chaucer's meter, with full bibliography, see Mustanoja 1979. See also the very useful essay by Gaylord 1976, "Scanning the Prosodists: An Essay in Metacriticism."

[5]Chaucer 1927. All references, here and subsequently, to variant readings in MSS and printed editions of lines from the *Nun's Priest's Tale* are detailed and discussed more fully in my edition of *The Nun's Priest's Tale* (Chaucer 1984a).

[6]Southworth 1954, 66–67. Reproduced by permission from J.G. Southworth, Verses of Cadence: An Introduction to the Prosody of Chaucer and His Followers (Oxford: Basil Blackwell, 1954), 66–67.

[7]All quotation, of text and variant readings, is from Chaucer 1984a. Supplementary quotation from Ellesmere is from the collation of Ellesmere given in P.G. Ruggiers, ed., Chaucer 1979.

[8]E.g., in Chaucer 1984a, 97–99, and in *The Canterbury Tales* (Chaucer 1985, 10–14). I think the Variorum editors have felt themselves under pressure to denigrate Ellesmere as part of their determination to defend Hengwrt. It is not necessary: the differences between the two are clear enough, and Ellesmere remains an exceptionally good witness.

[9]It is worth recalling here that Dd.4.24, as the best representative of the alpha tradition, has often been thought to preserve, on occasions, original but rejected Chaucerian readings ("first shots"). See Chaucer 1984, 99–100.

Steven R. Guthrie

Prosody and the Study of Chaucer: A Generative Reply to Halle & Keyser*

"Chaucer and the Study of Prosody," published in 1966 by Morris Halle and Samuel Jay Keyser, is the ground-breaking document in the field of generative metrics. During the past twenty years, Halle & Keyser as it is called has been attacked, defended, revised by the authors, and modified elsewhere, and it remains a point of reference for discussions of pentameter theory.[1] What has not been questioned–strange but true–is its adequacy as a description of Chaucer's meter.[2] The responses to Halle & Keyser have been based on studies of Renaissance and post-Renaissance texts, and Halle and Keyser themselves, being primarily concerned with the general theory (and also perhaps able to sympathize with the general scramble for higher ground), have shown no interest in redirecting the discussion toward Middle English. There is nothing intrinsically wrong with the kind of apples-to-oranges comparison that has come about as a result. Apples may properly and profitably be compared to oranges if one's interest is in describing fruit, and that kind of interest is at the heart of M.I.T.-school linguistics. The problem in this case is simply that the account of apples is flawed, and that has sent the ensuing discussion off course.

My purpose here is to summarize the results of a generative analysis which both responds to Halle & Keyser and offers applications to a range of Chaucerian concerns, most immediately the old *endecasillabo-décasyllabe* debate. I will argue that, while Chaucer's line is iambic pentameter if Shakespeare's is, Chaucer's is not the Renaissance pentameter it has been supposed to be since Tyrwhitt. It differs from Renaissance pentameter by virtue of a Romance presence so strong as to constitute a motive rhythmic force in the poetry, and a presence, moreover, which seems to be specifically French rather than Italian or generic Romance. In *Troilus and Criseyde*, composed more or less directly from an Italian source and at the height of what used to be called Chaucer's Italian period, the key rhythmic affinity is not for the English pausing line or for the *Filostrato* but for the Middle French *décasyllabe* of Machaut. This has consequences for pentameter theory and also for the ways in which we read Chaucer.

In its overall effect, the Halle & Keyser study reconfirmed the Nineteenth Century's reading of Chaucer as a Renaissance or post-Renaissance pentametrist on the order of Gascoigne or Gray. In a 1000-line sample, Halle and Keyser found 99 percent of Chaucer's lines to be consistent with a metrical rule which forbids the placement of a linguistic *stress maximum* (a syllable of greater stress than either adjacent syllable; the idea goes back to Jespersen) at any *weak* (odd-numbered) metrical position.[3] The other 1 percent of lines Halle and Keyser rejected as unmetrical, suggesting scribal error as the likely source of the vagrancy and dismissing the thought that Chaucer might have produced such lines on purpose, or even by accident (Halle & Keyser 1966, 214). The Halle & Keyser results were confirmed by Karen Lynn in 1978, but in view of the size of her sample (also 1000 lines), Lynn labeled her conclusions tentative (p. 118).

The caution was justified, but it is doubtful that a larger sample would have produced better results. The cruel irony of the situation is that the method itself is almost completely unsuited to the subtleties of Chaucer's meter. The Halle & Keyser machinery is designed, on premises inherited from nineteenth-century metrics, to weed out precisely those rhythms which are of central importance in Chaucer. The key to Chaucer's variational system lies in its permission of weak-position ternary rhythmic prominences (anapests), and the majority of these involve purposeful violations of the stress-maximum principle. The Halle & Keyser machinery is able to detect such violations–that is its one moving part–but it is unable to discuss them and thus unable to explore possible relationships between them and other elements of the prosody.

A few illustrations will be in order. The following lines from *Troilus and Criseyde* would be dismissed as unmetrical by Halle and Keyser:

So fer am I from his *help* in derknesse	1.18
Than thynketh he though I *praunce* al byforn	1.221
And seyde lord so ye *lyue* al in lest	1.330
Al were it wist but in *pris* and vp born	1.375
Sire al *this* shal be don quod Pandarus	2.1459
O moral gower this *book* I directe	5.1856

In these lines, weak-position stress maxima (italicized) create a tendency toward ternary rather than binary rhythmic prominences within major phrases (roughly, cesuras). Like cadences occur in 2.2 percent of the lines in *Troilus and Criseyde.*

In the next three lines, by contrast, there are similar cadences, but they appear at the ends of major phrases:

By my *wil* // she sholde al be thyn to morwe	1.861
O lady myn // that I *loue* // and na more	5.229
As he *rood* // forby places of the town	5.563

Like cadences occur in .7 percent of the lines in *Troilus and Criseyde.* They are not ruled out by Halle & Keyser, which does not count stress maxima at major phrase boundaries, but neither is their existence acknowledged in any way. In fact, the same underlying metrical principle is reflected in all nine lines, but it is applied more radically in these last three.

In Shakespeare's *Sonnets* there is no clear example of a similar cadence at a major-phrase boundary. Medially there are a few instances ("No, I *am* that I am, and they that level," Son. 121.9), occurring almost once in 100 lines, or at about the rate predicted by Halle & Keyser. In *Troilus and Criseyde,* however, they occur at a combined 3 percent level in both orientations and outnumber any other type of stress variation except the phrase-initial trochee. Even at 3 percent we are still in the presence of a low-level phenomenon, but my contention is that within a highly principled and finely tuned metrical system, low-level phenomena may be disproportionately important. Most of the lines above, even out of context, will be immediately familiar to readers of Chaucer, and it is difficult to support a metrical theory which refuses to consider them. An approximate parallel in a study of Shakespeare would be the rejection of characteristic lines like "Resembling strong *youth* in his middle age" (Son. 7.6), which comprise a 4 percent phenomenon. It is less that the lines from *Troilus and Criseyde* are memorable because they come at important junctures in the poem than that they, and the junctures they mark, are made conspicuous by the unusual rhythms in them.

What is needed for a study of Chaucer, then, is an analytical machinery capable of making fine distinctions and comparisons among a variety of low-level rhythmic phenomena, and also capable of reserving judgment on what it observes until the observation is complete.

My argument is based on an analysis of *Troilus and Criseyde* using Paul Kiparsky's stress-tree apparatus, which views stress as both relative and hierarchical within the domain of the major phrase.[4] This choice of method reflects my assumption that the study of meter is essentially the study of syntax; that is, its aim is to describe the ways in which linguistic stress patterns, the rhythmic components of actual words and phrases, work to produce both a metrical norm–an anticipated recurrence of stress–and a range of permissible variation from that norm.[5] The linguistic line is of course the focus of any generative method, and the distinctions, basic to Kiparsky's theory, between linguistic stress and metrical accent (ictus), and (therefore) between meter and performance, are generally accepted now, at least in principle, by linguists and traditional prosodists alike. Kiparsky's method, however, of those current, is most thorough in its syntactic approach and thus best able to make the fine distinctions I have asked for; and it is also the only one which permits the iambic foot to be treated as a linguistic reality rather than a purely arbitrary metrical template. The value of this approach will appear in the following discussion.

Under the terms just outlined, the metrical *system* of a poet (the term seems to have originated with Robert Bridges [Bridges 1921, 2]), his rhythmic idiolect or prosodic encephalogram, is defined by the particular patterning constraints he observes, and these differ from poet to poet, within pentameter and even among contemporaries. What is metrical in Shakespeare is not necessarily metrical in Chaucer and vice versa.

The limitation of Kiparsky's theory as published is that it considers only absolute constraints. It is capable of observing, for example, that of the following four weak-position stresses, (a.) and (b.) are permitted in Shakespeare but not (c.) or (d.):

a. Resembling strong *youth* in his middle age	Son. 7.6
b. Feed'st thy *lights* flame with self-substantial fuel	Son. 1.6
c. *To the *Gar*den of Bliss, thy seat prepar'd	Milton PL 8.299
d. *By my *wil* she sholde al be thyn to morwe	TC 1.861

(The example from Chaucer is mine; Kiparsky illustrates the same constraint with a line from Wyatt, who, "in rebuilding the pentameter line . . . had not yet hit on a principle" which later poets followed [Kiparsky 1977, 206]. Chaucer's practice destroys this argument, but Kiparsky was unaware of Chaucer's practice except as reported by Halle & Keyser.) But Kiparsky's theory is not interested in the relative overall frequencies of (a.) and (b.) or in their tendencies, if any, to concentrate at particular positions in the metrical line. This represents a tactical decision on Kiparsky's part, one which in some respects weakens the results of his study. It does not represent a weakness of the analytical machinery, which is perfectly capable of recording relative and positional constraints, and which will be put to that use in my discussion.

The base text for my analysis was the Parkes-Salter facsimile of the Corpus Christi MS. of *Troilus and Criseyde*.[6] I emended 162 lines on the basis of the published transcriptions of other manuscripts (primarily the concurrence of St. John's, Campsall, and Harleian 2280) where evidence of scribal error in Corpus was particularly strong (St. John's is in Chaucer 1894–95; Harleian 2280 and Campsall are in Chaucer 1894). Lines missing from Corpus I omitted from the sample, which thus includes 8110 lines. I rejected no line peremptorily on metrical grounds. The analysis of *Troilus and Criseyde* is supported by similar analyses of Shakespeare's *Sonnets,* Boccaccio's *Filostrato,* Machaut's *Jugement dou Roy de Behaingne,* and the *Chanson de Roland.*

Troilus and Criseyde seemed a logical choice because of its length and coherence, whatever one's view on the stages-of-composition issue. I chose Corpus because the Parkes-Salter facsimile was at hand. I preferred a base manuscript to a published edition for two reasons: first, I wanted to avoid either being swayed by or caviling at modern pointing (there is for example in Halle & Keyser 1966, 203–based on Robinson–a curious note about semi-colons as clause markers); second, I wanted to bypass the metrical regularization that still occurs in published editions of the poem.

This second issue seems important enough to warrant a digression. Here is one example of the phenomenon, extreme in degree but representative in kind. For line 5.382, Corpus and St. John's have essentially the same reading: "As rauenes qualyn or shrichyng of thise owles" (St. John's has *qualin*). Other manuscripts have *qualm* for *qualyn,* and this rendering appears in all modern editions. There is no note in Robinson, but his glossary defines *qualm* as "plague, pestilence; death; loss, damage; croak (of raven)." Baugh's gloss is similar, and Root's note on the line appears to seal the matter: "Qualm, croaking; see NED s.v. Qualm, sb. 2." (Chaucer 1957; Chaucer 1963; Chaucer 1926)

But the OED entry to which Root refers is this: "qualm sb2 Obs. rare [App. imitative; cf. G. galm sound, noise.] Croak. 1374 Chaucer Troylus v. 382 Augurye of thise fowles . . . As ravenes qualm or schrychynge of this owles." No other citation is given. Under the circumstances, "Obs[olete]. rare" must rank as one of the choicest understatements in modern lexicography.

The word is certainly mimetic, but the *m* of *qualm* is suspect for the simple reason that ravens have no lips. *Qual-*, on the other hand, is very much like the sound that English ravens apparently began making in the sixteenth century. The only editorial disadvantage of the gerund *qualyn* is that it introduces an extrametrical syllable into the line, a practice traditionally held to be un-Chaucerian. In fact, in *Troilus and Criseyde* at least, extrametrical syllables are quite rare, but it may be sounder editorially to grant the poet his rare variation, here and elsewhere, than to deprive him of it.

The following sequence of events seems plausible: Chaucer wrote *qualyng* (parallel with *shrichyng*), which he either coined or borrowed from the colloquial repertoire; nervous scribes shortened the suffix to *-yn/-in* as it remains in Corpus and St. John's; another scribe, finding *qualin* unfamiliar or the row of minims difficult to interpret or the meter in jeopardy, wrote down *qualm* as the nearest approximation in his vocabulary. So far we are within the realm of normal medieval scribal practice, but the sequel is another matter. Against the evidence of their own best texts from Beta (Root) or Gamma (Robinson, Baugh), supported in each case by the manuscript of highest regard in the other group, modern editors have canonized the reading, and in the process have added a phantom word to the dictionary, for the sole purpose of regularizing a line. (The same criticism does not apply, at least in the same way, to Fisher, who worked from Campsall [Chaucer 1989]).

Most such liberties now, like this one, are probably inadvertent, a result of the unreflective adoption of nineteenth-century readings or assumptions rather than of any modern traditionalist conspiracy. And the great majority of them affect syllable count rather than stress pattern. My strong impression is that in the latter regard, a study based on one of the modern editions would have produced substantially the same results as the study based on Corpus. Still, a new edition of the poem which systematically went behind nineteenth-century assumptions would be welcome, and I mention the problem for that reason.

To return to the metrical study, the first order of business is to come to grips with what many have found unprovable or self-evident or both, the metrical norm. (In Chaucer's case this will also prove to be one of the last orders of business.) If Chaucer's line is iambic pentameter, it will give evidence of a ten-syllable norm and an iambic foot. The first condition is easily established, even despite the fluidity of Chaucer's vowel structure: in lines without final *-e* or any other potential variable-vowel phenomenon (either elision in the broadest sense or diaresis), the decasyllabic base is firm.[7]

The second issue is more controversial. What, after all, is an iambic foot? Seymour Chatman has argued that the division of lines into feet is "purely notional" and has no discernible relationship to language: "I have never been able to discover a good reason for assuming that a metrical accent has any closer connection with the zero that it follows than with the one that it precedes" (in Sebeok 1960, 161)–in other words, for calling a line iambic rather than trochaic. Chatman prefers to abandon the foot-concept entirely, retaining only a binary metrical grid WSWSWSWSWS, without internal boundaries.

Actually, the presence of an iambic foot in either Chaucer or Shakespeare is quite clear if the foot is seen as a linguistic unit–since poems, and meters, are built of words–rather than as an abstraction imposed on the line from without. The closest embodiment of the iambic foot in English is the iambic lexical word (*estat, abood, forsook, meschaunce, deuyn*), and in the poetry we call iambic, these words are position-bound. They may appear in WS metrical orientation–with the grain of the meter–but not in SW orientation. (In Donne there are rare and highly visible exceptions.) Trochaic words are not so bound in iambic meter. Thus the familiar trochaic inversion, at the beginning of a line or after a cesural break, is easily the most common rhythmic variation in English verse.

Iambic lexical words, however, are relatively uncommon in English. In Chaucer they are outnumbered by lexical trochees (*double, louynge, purpos, woful*) by a ratio of 8:5. But there is another important source of iambic word-shapes in the language. Chaucer's poetic English is composed mainly (76 percent) of monosyllables, and major-class monosyllables (nouns, verbs, adjectives, and some adverbs) tend to carry with them unstressed proclitic particles, so that the shape of a resultant *proclitic group* is iambic: *an hous, this fissh, to loue, haue seyde, and peyne, so cleere.* These proclitic groups, or phonological as opposed to lexical words, are also position-bound, not absolutely but to a high degree, in English verse (99 percent in Chaucer). In French and Italian meters, constraints on the placement of iambic word-shapes are much looser, and that is why those meters are syllabic rather than foot-syllabic. Iambic meter, then, arises in the patterning of iambic shapes against the metrical grid, and the answer to Chatman's objection is that the language itself tends toward an iambic rhythmical inertia and the iambic foot is abstracted from the language.[8]

The metrical systems of both Chaucer and Shakespeare operate within this basic definition of the line, and in many respects the two systems are similar. They also differ in a few important ways, which are crucial for the study of Chaucer.

Difference number one: the overall figures on weak-position stress are dissimilar in the two poets. In Shakespeare's *Sonnets,* weak-position stresses of all types occur at the rate of 16.3 per hundred lines, 11.1 per hundred if we leave out the universally accepted phrase-initial trochaic inversions.[9] In Chaucer the figure is 6.4 per hundred, or 5.2 leaving out trochaic inversions. In terms of sheer numbers, then, Chaucer's line is more regular than Shakespeare's, and from a Renaissance perspective this seems puzzling in view of Chaucer's weak-position anapests. A line which observes the metrical norm so strictly ought not to permit such far-flung variations from it. The difficulty vanishes, however, if we escape the Renaissance perspective. Then the obvious suggestion–that the overall strictness and the peculiar variational system may somehow be related in Chaucer–will be seen to be correct.

Difference number two: Chaucer's line, as many people have noted, is unusually light for an English pentameter, "underweighted" to use Hammond's term (Hammond 1927, 20). Shakespeare's line averages 3.92 stresses and Chaucer's 3.5. (To anticipate the upcoming argument, Boccaccio's line averages 4.02 stresses and Machaut's 3.56.) The difference of approximately half a stress between Chaucer and Shakespeare may seem inconsiderable, but a little arithmetic will suggest its consequences over several hundred or several thousand lines of verse. Chaucer's line is spare, Shakespeare's is dense.

The emerging picture is of two pentameter lines which operate on different rhythmic principles, and this is confirmed (difference number three) by the tendencies of the two variational systems. To begin with, there is one important rule which is absolute in Shakespeare but only relative in Chaucer. It involves the ternary rhythms I have mentioned, and from a theoretical standpoint it involves an issue which has been a primary focus of generative metrical discussion. Halle and Keyser claimed, in effect, that weak-position ternary prominences are inadmissible within major phrases, in Chaucer and in iambic verse generally. Kiparsky showed that they are permitted in Shakespeare within major phrases, but he concluded that they are inadmissible–in Shakespeare and in iambic verse generally–at phrase boundaries (Kiparsky 1977, 206). In Shakespeare's system, then, the first of the following two lines is metrical but not the second:

No, I *am* that I am, // and they that level	Son. 121.9
*By my *wil* // she sholde al be thyn to morwe	TC 1.861

The second line, a hypothetical construction in Shakespeare, is of course an actual line of verse in Chaucer, and if the variation is metrical in Chaucer, then it should not be excluded from a general theory of pentameter. Granted, a theory which incorporates it will not directly correspond to Renaissance practice, but there is no reason it should, being after all a statement of the essential range of the line and not a report on one of its epochal manifestations. (Even within the Renaissance, Kiparsky has been forced to make allowance for the wide differences between Shakespeare and Milton by granting each poet his separate stronghold within pentameter [Kiparsky 1977, 215 & 216].) It may be wondered whether there is any advantage in having a general theory at all under these circumstances. I can think of one immediate advantage: it will allow us to view some of Frost's signature cadences ("One by *one* // he subdued his father's trees") as pedigreed variations rather than as (at best) willful eccentricities or (at worst) signs of the twentieth-century breakdown of English meter.

Chaucer's permission of the weak-position stress in TC 1.861 is consistent with the relatively high frequency in his verse of lines like TC 1.221, "Than thynketh he // though *I praunce* al by forn." Similar lines are also metrical in Shakespeare (Son. 121.9 above), but they occur nearly three times as often in Chaucer.

Conversely, the most characteristic Shakespearean variations are relatively rare in Chaucer:

a. Feed'st thy *light*'s flame // with self-substantial fuel
b. Resembling strong *youth* // in his middle age
c. Be thou the tenth *Muse*, // ten *times* more in worth
(Sonnet 1.6; 7.6; 38.9)

In each of these lines, a weak-position stress is immediately preceded or followed by a major-class word in the same major phrase. Halle and Keyser, apparently following ten Brink, assume level stress in similar phrases and return them to the catchall of the metrical norm. Clearly these lines differ from "Than thynketh he though I praunce al byforn," but just as clearly they differ from "The curfew tolls the knell of parting day," and if they are dismissed as merely normal, we lose the chance to talk about their differences. There are significant differences even among these lines, but the important thing for this discussion is that such phrases add density to the line, and they are frequent in Shakespeare and rare in Chaucer. Final *-e* has some bearing on the matter–major-class word stresses less often abut one another in Chaucer's English–as does the fact that Chaucer's poetic language is adjective-poor compared to Shakespeare's. (Note, however, that this is a stylistic issue; the adjectives are there in the natural language.) But these are not the whole explanation. Chaucer is capable of producing similar compressions ("And men criden in the strete se Troilus" [TC 2.612]; "ffor wonder laste but nyne nyght neuer in towne" [TC 4.588]), but they are less often to his purpose.

Difference number four concerns the positional constraints of the two systems. In Shakespeare the line-initial trochaic inversion is the most common stress variation (32 percent of all weak-position stresses). Second most common is stress at the half-line, in position 5 (22 percent). At positions 3, 7, and 9, stress levels are approximately equal (15 percent each). In Chaucer the stress contour is much different. The highest frequency of weak-position stress, by far, is not at position 1 but at position 7 (42 percent of all weak-position stresses). Positions 1 and 3 (19 percent and 20 percent) are approximately equal, position 5 (15 percent) is somewhat lighter, and position 9 (4 percent) is lightest. There are differences at the strong positions as well, and the most important of these is that, while Shakespeare's stress curve remains nearly level at positions 6 and 8 (.64 and .66 stresses per line), Chaucer's drops off sharply from .63 per line at position 6 to .51 at position 8. Something happens in the second half of Chaucer's line that does not happen in Shakespeare.

The prosodic import of these figures is clear. Shakespeare's stress contour suggests an underlying form of the kind that Northrop Frye has proposed for English verse (and that C. S. Lewis has proposed for Chaucer): a five-foot, four-stress hybrid in which the Native pausing line is a strong background presence (Frye 1969, 251 f.; Lewis 1938). Chaucer's stress contour, however, suggests something quite different; it suggests the background presence of the Romance line, with its characteristic tendency toward stress at positions 4, 7, and 10.

One last point of contrast, related in principle to these others, lies in the conduct of the line where no weak-position stress is present. This point will be illustrated to better effect later on, and I will leave it in abeyance for now.

In Chaucer and Shakespeare we have two systems of iambic pentameter, neither of which is exactly *the* pentameter. Chaucer's is not a Renaissance line but a medieval one, which means, for a poet in his circumstances, that it is Romance-clad. I do not mean that Chaucer was trying to write syllabics; the iambic foot is as strong in his verse as in Shakespeare's, and more concrete. But he was writing for an audience, himself included, whose ear-training included a powerful exposure to Romance cadences, and who found those cadences pleasing. His new metrical line must be kept fairly simple, in order to be comprehensible, and the variations he permitted must be recognizable and must be limited strictly enough to preserve the balance of the line. His approach to the problem was to make a virtue of necessity. He worked close to the foot-model he had abstracted from his natural language, and having defined it carefully–having established the proclitic group as his unit of measure–he was able to use it as well to vary the line by playing Romance rhythms against the normal iambic pattern. The next question, and I recognize that it is an old and haggard one by now, is whether his line owes more to French or to Italian.

Unlike some of the really stirring controversies of our age, such as the one over final *-e*, this particular debate has never exactly flourished. Thomas Tyrwhitt summarized the general modern consensus in 1785: Chaucer, he said, began with the French poets and moved on to the Italian ones, who appear to be more influential in his mature work, although the two Romance meters are so similar that either one would have served (Chaucer 1798, 51–2). Occasionally there have been more impassioned arguments, mostly on the Italian side. The best-known and most persuasive of these is Hammond's, and its prime exhibit is a comparison of the following lines from the *Filostrato* and *Troilus and Criseyde:*

> Tu savio, tu amico, tu sai tutto — Filo. 2.33
> But thow wis thow woost thow maist thow ar al — TC 1.1052[10]

But compare the two lines. Boccaccio's is a fairly normal *endecasillabo;* Chaucer's is the only line in *Troilus and Criseyde* with three weak-position stresses. Boccaccio's phrases are paroxytonic–the main stress falls on the penultimate syllable–while Chaucer's are oxytonic. If in this line Chaucer has intentionally imitated the *endecasillabo*, he has done the job about as well as his resources will allow, and he has had to stretch his metrical system some distance in order to do it at all. That there should now and then be mimicry of the source in a poem like *Troilus and Criseyde* seems only natural, and in this line I would be inclined to say that Chaucer *evokes* the Italian, but Hammond has cited the line as evidence of a deep rhythmic *influence*, and that is quite a different matter. The prosodic difference in focus here is a function of linguistic differences between Italian and English, but that is just the point. Chaucer was an excellent student of his own language, and he must have known what it would cost him to wring Italianate rhythms from it with any degree of consistency. Rather than force such a continuous uphill battle, in his search for prosodic materials he gravitated instead toward French.

A statistical comparison of the three medieval lines sheds some light on the matter. For the Italian sample, the choice of the *Filostrato* was obvious.[11] For the French, I chose Machaut's *Jugement dou Roy de Behaingne*, a *dit* of only moderately *longue haleine* (2079 lines) in a 1010–10–4 linked stanza, rimed a-a-a-b, with the b-rime becoming the next a-rime. I simply ignored the four-syllable lines in my count.[12] A patchwork sample from Machaut's 150-odd decasyllabic lyrics would probably have done just as well, but it seemed prudent to use the narrative sample that was available, and *Behaingne* has the advantage that Chaucer was certainly aware of the poem.[13]

As in Chaucer, position 7 is the principal locus of weak-position stress in Boccaccio (38 percent of all weak-position stresses) and Machaut (55 percent), but in terms of phrase structure, Chaucer's line more closely resembles Machaut's:

Gli occhi lucenti e l'angelico viso	1.28.8
A sè la donna, con seco propose	1.37.3
Ch'alla non mabbia la vita levata	2.7.8
So fer am I from his help in derknesse	1.18
Thanne thynketh he though I praunce al byforn	1.221
Knew ich hire aught for my loue telle me this	1.864
Par un matin cointement m'acesmay	10
Biau, cler, luisans, nès et purs, sans froidure	14
Quant mes regars celle part guenchissoit	18

Stresses occur at position 7 in all these lines. In Chaucer and Machaut they are oxytons, and in Boccaccio they are paroxytons (and in line 1.28.8 a proparoxyton). In Machaut 80% and in Chaucer 88 percent of position-7 stresses mark major or minor phrase boundaries, as opposed to 40 percent in Boccaccio. This means that position-7 prominences tend to be more conspicuous in a decasyllabic line in Chaucer or Machaut than in an endecasyllabic line in Boccaccio. The difference, again, is lingual, but it is no less prosodically real for that. Add to it the overall weights of the three lines at both strong and weak positions–4.02 stresses in Boccaccio, 3.56 in Machaut, and 3.5 in Chaucer–and the rhythmic affinity of Chaucer's line becomes even clearer. Obviously Chaucer's weak-position stresses occur at comparatively low frequencies, but again, I am arguing for French presence, not Chaucerian syllabism, and it will be worth repeating my earlier claim that in a finely tuned metrical system, low-level rhythmic phenomena may be disproportionately important. The seventh-position prominences in the lines from Chaucer are effective variations because they are conspicuous in the line, harmonious with the overall tendencies of the metrical system, and recognizable to the audience.

One point needs clarifying. I have called Chaucer's line decasyllabic rather than endecasyllabic, despite its frequent rimes in final *-e* (for example in TC 1.18 above), which are often presented as evidence of Italian influence. Chaucer's *-e*, however, is far from the full-voweled Italian endings; if syllabic in rime, it is much closer to the French *-e caduc*. If Chaucer were truly after Italianate endings, then we would expect to see in *Troilus and Criseyde* endecasyllabic rimes like *náture : státure*, but no such rimes occur.

There is another important way in which Chaucer's verse resonates with Machaut's, and it involves the conduct of the line within the metrical norm, that is, where no weak-position stress is involved. This territory has not been explored in any systematic way. Kiparsky simply allows that a linguistic W may appear freely over a metrical S, and Halle and Keyser in effect say the same thing. The following lines will illustrate Chaucer's practice:

And preieth for hem *that ben in the* cas	1.29
In euery peril *which that is to* drede	1.84
Aftir hir cours *ay whil that thei were* wrothe	1.140
And lif is lost *but ye wol on me* rewe	1.462
ffor whan men han wel cryde than wol they rowne	4.587
And that ye me wolde as youre brother trete	5.134

In these lines, there are no misplaced stress maxima or, indeed, misplaced stresses of any kind (except for the initial trochee in line 1.140). In fact, there is no strong linguistic stress at all in a string of four or five or even in one case (5.134) seven syllables. In seemingly neutral territory like this, traditional prosodic wisdom would have us "tilt" the line toward the metrical pattern to keep the iambic rhythm thumping along (W. Wimsatt 1970, 785). This is a performance prescription and not strictly a metrical statement at all, but the practice has been so general as to prejudice metrical analysis, which is precisely why lines like these have failed to receive the attention due them. In these lines, Chaucer suspends the iambic pulse temporarily in favor of a rising rhythm in the major phrase as a whole. Similar stress patterns, involving rows of proclitics, are rare in Shakespeare and Boccaccio but common in Chaucer and Machaut. In Chaucer they are concentrated in the second half of the line (which helps to explain the relative lightness of position 8 in his verse), culminating in rime stress, and they resemble the cursus movement of Modern French, in which the primary unit of stress is the major phrase. If Chaucer were less skilled or differently motivated as a rhetorician, if we could depend on finding a main clause in the first half of his line and a full stop at the end, then it might be argued that these extended phrases are rhetorically motivated–padding, in short–and their prosodic effects accidental. Such is not the case, and the alternative is to recognize that the lowly classes of function words can be as important prosodically as the grander classes of nouns and notional verbs.

The degree to which cursus movement was established in fourteenth-century French is uncertain.[14] It appears (based on the metrical patterning of proclitic groups) that minor-phrase or nexus stress remains real in Machaut, but it also appears that Machaut was aware of the phonological changes occurring in his natural language and that he encouraged in his poetic language a tendency toward cursus movement. The following lines display his strategy:

Si liement et de si grant revel	JRB 22
« Oci Oci.» Et je le sievi tent	27
Uns chevaliers de moult trés noble arroy	50
Par leur rigour et par leur bel accueil	313

Machaut's line differs from the Old French *décasyllabe* in several important ways, illuminated by comparison with the *Chanson de Roland*.[15] In the Old French poem, the line is relatively heavy, averaging 3.98 stresses as opposed to 3.56 in Machaut, and the binary pulse is relatively strong, with 87 percent of stresses appearing in strong metrical positions, as opposed to 78 percent in Machaut (82 percent in Boccaccio). Cesura is fixed at position 4, unlike in Machaut, where it is movable. The metrical form of *Roland*, defined by cesural placement (with allowance for epic cesura following an extrametrical syllable), is the *décasyllabe ordinaire*, and this is a discrete metrical form in Old French (see Verrier 1932, 119–79). In Machaut, however, this and other Old French forms–the inverted *ordinaire*, with cesura at position 6; the *décasyllabe lyrique*, with first-position stress and fourth-position cesura; and (rarely) the *décasyllabe à césure médiane*, that is, at position 5–alternate at close quarters within the same poem. Machaut's purpose, apparently, is to provide a varied rhythmic movement, rather than the strong binary pulse of Old French, and lines like those cited above help to enforce this movement. The important thing is that the enforcement is syntactic: the rhythmic structure of these lines does not depend on the emerging phonological characteristics of the natural language but abets them by means of conscious prosodic contrivance.

A similar movement appears in the lines cited from Chaucer. My guess is that extended phrases like these are designed to encourage in performance a rising rhythm in the phrase, in the form of an accumulation of undisposed rhythmic emphasis, psychologically realized as suspense, resolved by rime. This movement may not be precisely "rhythmic" in the sense in which C. S. Lewis and others use the term,[16] but it is movement nonetheless, and it is purposeful. Lines in which it occurs do not gracefully ripple,

	whil		thei		wrothe
ay		that		were	

but neither are they becalmed; they build to a crest and then break:

wrothe
were
the
that
whil
ay

This schematic is meant to convey metrical tension, arising from the suspension of anticipated recurrence, one of whose potential physical realizations is what might be called a *grading* rather than a leveling of stress.

This kind of movement occurs within what is usually considered the metrical norm, but it is as important to Chaucer's metrical system as are his characteristic patterns of weak-position stress. It is also highly consistent with those patterns: in both corners of the prosody, effort is made to lighten the stress load of the second half of the line, and to emphasize both the unusual stresses at position 7 and the obligatory ones at position 10.

Chaucer's line is strict overall: the syllabic norm is strongly enforced, and the frequency of weak-position stresses is relatively low. The line is also surprisingly light overall, even given the presence of final *-e* as a metrical wild card, and it is especially light at position 8. It avoids the typical 4–8–10 stress pattern of later pentameter, tending instead toward a 4–10, 6–10, or 4–6–10 movement. Its characteristic variations, both within and without the norm, reinforce this tendency. Weak-position stress is concentrated at position 7, tending there to echo the 4–7–10 pattern of the French *décasyllabe ordinaire.* Strong position unstress is an important tendency especially in the second half of the line, and frequently both positions 6 and 8 are occupied not by stresses but by proclitic words, with the result being a rising rhythm in the entire major phrase. In its English version of cursus movement, and in its characteristic weak-position stresses, Chaucer's line resembles Machaut's, and my guess is that Chaucer strategically adapted Machaut's metrical style as flavoring for his own line. (It is no safer or more accurate to say Middle French than to say Machaut. Machaut is Middle French, and Deschamps and Froissart are laborers in his vineyard.)

In one respect–the presence of final *-e*–phonological differences between Middle and Renaissance English help to determine the prosodic differences between Chaucer and Shakespeare. It should be noted, however, that the status of final *-e* in Chaucer's natural language (not in his poetic language) is conjectural. He may have been using an already largely archaic form for prosodic purposes. Certainly final *-e* is more a factor in his pentameter than in his tetrameter verse, which is dense, or cluttered, by comparison. Wherever the truth lies on this matter, it is worth pointing out that in large part Chaucer's metrical system is still accessible to Modern English. The restrictiveness of the pentameter line, against which we moderns have railed, results to some degree from constraints imposed by the Renaissance, and the metrical experiments of Frost and others (including the earlier experiments of Shelley and Browning) should be seen as attempts to recover the full range of the line, rather than as attempts to escape from it.

How does all this affect the ways in which we should read Chaucer? I would like to offer two kinds of speculation, one for criticism and one for performance. First, as to criticism, I think that on the whole we have dismissed Machaut too lightly, or accepted him too grudgingly, as an influence on Chaucer. There are Kittredge's old notes (Kittredge *MLN* 1915 & *PMLA* 1915); there is James Wimsatt's work based on line correspondences (Wimsatt 1968 and 1976); and there is a recent assortment of articles and dissertations linking the two poets in one way or another. But in (for example) Muscatine's highly regarded *Chaucer and the French Tradition*, there is only passing mention of Machaut (Muscatine 1969). And it is only very recently that the first English translation of any of Machaut's narrative poems has appeared.[17] To put it simply, Machaut has seemed frivolous and tedious to us, and he may have seemed so to Chaucer, but I think there is a reasonable chance that he did not, and there is certainly room for work on the subject.[18]

Second, as to recitation. This is more difficult to do in writing, and I agree with Alan Gaylord's call for a new emphasis on actual oral performance as one aspect of prosodic study.[19] Chaucer's meter, as I have discussed it, takes no brief from performance tradition, but it does have suggestions to make for oral reading. First, we should not read Chaucer as though he were coming downstairs bump-bump-bump on the back of his head. W. K. Wimsatt claimed that in neutral territory he could "tilt" the line toward the metrical norm *"without violence* to any linguistic given" (W. Wimsatt 1970, 785; emphasis his), but he was responding to Halle & Keyser, which did not even consider the rhythmic tendencies of the norm. There *are* linguistic givens involved, and a thumping iambic rhythm often violates Chaucer's purpose.

We should not, on the other hand, read Chaucer as though he were writing Gregorian Chant, or a pausing line, or blank verse. Nor will the normal rhythms of modern spoken English do him justice. There is a complex and coherent rhythmic movement in the poetry, for which we have strong syntactic evidence, and it makes more sense to observe that movement in recitation than to invent some other mode of delivery.

We should not slide over the strange-sounding anapests. They do not occur very often, but when they do they are purposeful, and English poetry would be poorer without the lines in which they appear. The case of Milton is instructive in this regard. There is a class of lines in Milton at which prosodists fumed throughout the nineteenth century:

To the Garden of Bliss, thy way prepar'd	PL 8.299
By the waters of life, where'er they sat	PL 11.79

In these lines and others, Milton violates a cardinal rule of Shakespearean pentameter which says, thou shalt not place a phrase like *the garden* (proclitic plus trochaic word) in SWS metrical orientation. Kiparsky showed that such cadences have a comprehensible syntactic basis in Milton, and it will come as no surprise to modern Miltonists that they have a comprehensible literary one as well: they derive from Italian cadences. Chaucer does not often do Italian cadences; his signature variations are roughly similar to Milton's in the degree of their departure from Shakespeare, but Chaucer's come from French. The moral is that when proud Bayard has his moment–"Than thynketh he // though I *praunce* al byforn"–we should allow him his gait as well. I have only occasionally heard a perfectly iambic rendering of this line: "Than *thynk/*eth *he/* though I/praunce *al/* by*forn*." More often I have heard this: "Than *thynk/* eth *he,/* [rest] *though/* I praunce *al/* by*forn*"–as though it were a Lydgate line with a trisyllabic fourth foot. Neither reading will do. Nor does it seem possible to resolve the line into four equal time intervals between stresses. Isochronist theory is often attractive, for example in the case of Wyatt, but it is much less attractive in Chaucer's case, because Chaucer is extremely finicky about his syllable count. A close correspondence between vocalic unit and metrical position indicates that a poet is interested in an abstract kind of duration; the syllable, not the second, is his unit of measure. In other words, "though I *praunce*" remains an anapest, despite all attempts at rescue. Similarly, when Pandarus says, "Were it for my suster al thy sorwe / By my *wil* she sholde al be thyn to morwe," it is wrong to offer him meter-saving emphasis on *my* in the second line (as opposed to whose?). His real message is that his *will* is efficacious; that is where the emphasis falls and that is where it belongs.

Rime stress is important, notwithstanding Chaucer's verse paragraphy; the characteristic movement of the line helps to enforce it. There is the tendency, already noted, toward an overall rising rhythm in the second half of the line, and there is a very strong tendency toward phrase stress in riming position. Chaucer is, as ten Brink said, a master of enjambment (ten Brink 1901, 227), but only within very strict limits. There is no real pressure toward full endstop, but neither are there the radical enjambments of Shakespeare's late blank verse, to say nothing of Milton's. Nearly always there is major or minor phrase closure at the end of the line. The strong Germanic suffix deserves emphasis–"So fer am I from his help in *derknesse*"–as, I think, does even the very rare enjambed pronoun: "That in science so expert was that *he* / Knew wel that Troie sholde destroied be" (1.67–68). This is prosodic showmanship, and it demands both emphasis and pause.

Among the issues either mentioned in passing or ignored completely in this discussion–final *-e*, variations in syllable count–the most important, or farthest reaching, is that of the role of the individual line in the construction of the larger unit, the verse paragraph. The subject remains to be explored systematically, and the line-analysis presented here, while useful in itself, should also be seen as a step in that direction.

One final note, and this is patently obvious but it is also the root of most nineteenth-and twentieth-century problems of prosodic analysis including those inherent in Halle & Keyser: we should remember that Chaucer read Guillaume de Lorris, Benoit, Boccaccio, Machaut, and Gower. He did not read Shakespeare, Tennyson, Johnson, Gascoigne, or Gray. What is remarkable is that, single-handed, he fashioned a metrical line which has endured for 600 years and whose potential has yet to be exhausted by English poets.

NOTES

*Reprinted with permission from *Chaucer Review* 23, 1 (1988): 30–49.
[1]The principal but by no means only documents in the controversy, in addition to Halle & Keyser 1966, are these: Halle & Keyser 1971 (retreating from the syntactic argument of the original paper); Beaver 1971 (supporting and modifying Halle & Keyser); Magnuson & Ryder 1970 (employing feature-complexes of syllables); Magnuson & Ryder 1971; Chisolm 1977 (modifying Magnuson-Ryder); Kiparsky 1975; Kiparsky 1977; Hayes 1983 (modifying Kiparsky). Halle & Keyser, Magnuson-Ryder, Kiparsky, and Hayes stand as separate theories. Mention should also be made of an article by Mieko Ogura, "Metrics of Chaucer: An Analysis Based on the Kiparsky Theory" (Ogura 1979). Ogura lists some of the cadences discussed in this paper, but does not explain them or note their divergence from Kiparsky's model. Ogura's scansions are sometimes puzzling. For example, *ydel* is analyzed as an oxyton (*ydél*) and *Duchess* 144 is oriented to the metrical pattern "Bid hym / crepe in- / to the / body," when in fact the line is headless, with a feminine rime (*bódy* : *ródy*). Ogura's conclusion, that "the constraints on mismatches become severer in an orderly way from Chaucer's early poetry to his late poetry" (14), will need to be tested. My strong impression is that certain variations become less frequent, but that there is no particular change in the kinds of constraints observed.
[2]W. K. Wimsatt's objection to Halle & Keyser, in "The Rule and the Norm: Halle and Keyser on Chaucer's Meter" (1969), has to do with performance criteria and not with meter as such. Wimsatt's argument will be discussed later in this essay.
[3]Halle & Keyser 1966, 197; and 1971, 169. Jespersen's discussion is in "Notes on Metre" (1900), rpt. in Chatman and Levin 1967.
[4]Kiparsky, 1977. In the notation, the linguistic stress tree (similar to the trees often used for syntactic analysis) appears above the line of verse, and the metrical pattern appears below:

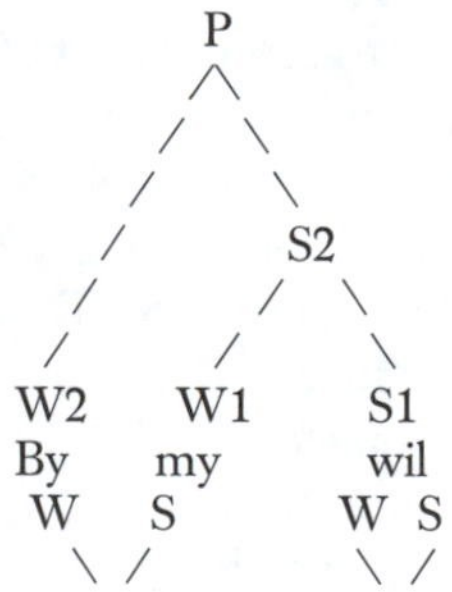

The surface stress pattern (here WWS) appears immediately above the verse line. The crucial feature of the tree is its binary Weak-Strong branching, which expresses stress relationships at increasing levels of syntactic complexity. Here the node S2, composed of W1 and S1, represents the proclitic group, *my wil.* The phrase node P, composed of W2 and S2, represents the entire cesural phrase.
[5]Given the role of syntactic relationships in Kiparsky's theory, the relative stress levels of different classes of words are important to know, and these are not self-evident in Middle English. For example, do demonstratives, relatives, and auxiliary verbs count as major-class words, particles, or intermediate classes? On this subject and other technical matters beyond the physical scope of this paper, see my 1985 Brown University dissertation, "Chaucer's French Pentameter."
[6]M. B. Parkes and Elizabeth Salter, intros., Chaucer 1978. For convenience, I have adopted the lineation of the Chaucer Society transcription (Chaucer 1894–5). Again for convenience, I used my copy of the transcription as a working copy, having corrected on its pages

its 116 substantive scribal errors.

[7]Derek Brewer has proposed a more limited version of the same test in which only lines with syllabic *-e* are disregarded. See "The Grain of the Text," in Carruthers & Kirk 1982, 126.

[8]Roman Jakobson similarly proposed the proclitic group as foot-model in Czech iambics. See "Toward a Description of Macha's Verse" in Jakobson 1979, 441.

[9]My study of Shakespeare is based on the *Sonnets,* ed. Hyder Rollins (Shakespeare 1944). I rejected the tetrameter sonnet number 145 and line 2 of number 146.

[10]Hammond 1908, 486. I have given the line from *Troilus and Criseyde* as it appears in Corpus Christi. Most recently to the same effect, see Kean 1983.

[11]The study is based on Vittore Branca's edition (Boccaccio 1964–), vol. 2. In the analysis of French and Italian verse, I was interested in overall stress contours, and not in the finer distinctions it was necessary to make for Chaucer and Shakespeare. Therefore I used a sample of 625 lines (lines 1–625) from the *Filostrato.*

[12]The study is based on Ernest Hoepffner's edition (Machaut 1908), vol. I. Again, I used a 625-line sample (the first 625 decasyllable lines in the poem). Chaucer may indeed have looked at Benoit while writing *Troilus and Criseyde,* but Benoit's *Roman* is octosyllabic and thus has no bearing on a metrical argument.

[13]See James Wimsatt 1968, 155–62. There is also the short (58 lines) "Complainte a Henri," which Skeat pointed to as evidence of French influence on Chaucer's earlier heroic couplet. See Chaucer 1899–1900, 3: 383.

[14]There is no previous treatment that I know of fourteenth-century French verse. The general consensus is that cursus movement was present to a high degree by the sixteenth century. See Pope 1952, 82; and Klausenberger 1970, 11–12. On the same issue and on nexus and cursus typology generally, see Pulgram 1970, 24–39.

[15]I have used T. Atkinson Jenkins's edition, *La Chanson de Roland* 1924.

[16]Lewis 1938, 32. Lewis expresses the typical English opinion that French poetry is unrhythmic. Tyrwhitt felt the same way about Old English.

[17]R. Barton Palmer, trans., *The Judgment of the King of Bohemia* [Machaut 1984]. James Wimsatt and William Kibler have completed a new edition, with facing-page translations, of *Behaingne* and the *Remede de Fortune,* which will be published by the University of Georgia Press in 1988 [Machaut 1988–Ed.].

[18]There are encouraging signs, however, in two books now in progress, one by James Wimsatt on Chaucer and his French contemporaries, and another by William Calin on Machaut and medieval England. [See James Wimsatt 1991b and Calin 1987–Ed.]

[19]Gaylord 1976, 76. Gaylord's article is well worth reading ten years later, especially for anyone whose exposure to Chaucerian prosodies has been limited to Tauno Mustanoja's "Chaucer's Prosody" (in Rowland 1979, 65–94).

Stephen A. Barney

Chaucer's *Troilus*: Meter and Grammar*

Because editing Chaucer depends so largely on our understanding of the meter of his poetry, a treatment of editorial method must grapple with the question of meter. Windeatt wrote an article on the *Troilus* meter that resolutely endorses the opinion announced by Puttenham, explained by Tyrwhitt, elaborated by Child, ten Brink, Kittredge, Baum, and Halle and Keyser, and assumed by all modern editors of his texts, and as far as I know by nearly all modern scholars who trouble to argue the point except for J. G. Southworth and I. A. Robinson (Windeatt 1977).[1] These *auctores* do not settle the question by their mere weight, but in fact they are right, and Windeatt presents the argument well. I need not repeat his remarks, abbreviated somewhat in the section on "Metre" in his edition (Windeatt 1984, 55–64), but would emphasize one thing and correct another.

The thing worth emphasizing is the way an assumption about meter–that Chaucer in *Troilus* uses, with a tolerable, expedient, and comprehensible set of variations, the meter traditionally called iambic pentameter–fits so well. I think modern Chaucer editors all subscribe, in a more relaxed way, to ten Brink's dicta because those assumptions make sense out of a countless array of variants. It is simply inconceivable, for example, that the various traditional findings about Chaucer's final *-e*, which underlie any premise about meter, are generally wrong: the historical evidence (the strong and weak adjective inflections, the subjunctive vs. indicative differences, the sounded *-e(n)* of the infinitive, etc.) and the metrical evidence simply concur too often to admit any other hypothesis.[2] The argument is not circular: it is an argument in which reasonable hypotheses about grammar and reasonable hypotheses about meter reinforce each other so firmly that contrary hypotheses become incredible. It would be incredible, for example, to deny that Chaucer ended an infinitive with *-e(n)*, because in all but extremely rare cases the assumption provides for ordinary iambic pentameter and makes good rimes.

It is likewise incredible to deny *Troilus* ordinary iambic pentameter, with its recognized variation, because it accounts for so regular a set of expected inflections.

Further, Windeatt is right to point out certain lines in *Troilus* as giving special evidence about meter: those lines in which *all* the manuscript witness agrees on syllabification. Many studies of Chaucer's meter, including Halle and Keyser's, have relied on Robinson's text for their evidence. This happens to yield roughly the right results because Robinson's theory of meter is more than roughly right. In the case of *Troilus* the procedure happens to make sense because Robinson did not need to alter his base text, the Corpus manuscript, very much: I count forty-one instances in the first five hundred lines of the poem in which spellings Robinson altered (or in one or two cases, I altered in my Riverside Chaucer edition) would affect the meter–about one every twelve lines. For this count I do not include as affecting meter final *-e's* at line-end or in elision before a vowel or *h.* (In all, there are 105 alterations of spelling in these five hundred lines.) To these forty-one instances should be added twenty in which Cp readings that are rejected on critical (including metrical) grounds would affect the meter. This brings the rate up: once every eight or so lines Robinson and I alter the base manuscript in a way that affects the syllabification. No detailed study of meter can rely on texts like ours and all other editor's which depend on metrical assumptions for their establishment. Child, ten Brink, and Kittredge of course went directly to the manuscripts for their studies.

Thus Windeatt attempts to find lines in *Troilus* in which all manuscripts agree–at least in the syllabification. Of such lines it can be said that no better witness exists of Chaucer's meter. Windeatt lists a few of these lines in his article (1977, 46 & 51) and more in his edition (1984, 56).[3] He says in both essays that in these lines "the syllabic content is the same in all manuscripts." Unfortunately this is not true: of the thirteen lines, only one–or two, if *eithre* before a vowel is reckoned as if it were *either* (4.1033, Ph)–has no syllabic variation in the manuscripts, namely line 1.771. In the following list, the minority variants that could alter the syllabification follow the colons. I assume, as I think one must (and as Windeatt seems to), that the context of the word, perhaps admitting elision, should not influence the list–elision is one of the metrical properties under investigation. However, I do not list syllabic variants at line end, because these do not concern any relevant theory of meter except for particular theories of line-end phonology.

So: 1.551 *Allas: Allace* S^1; 2.264 *word: worde* J (and 5 other manuscripts), also *inwardly: endewardly* Dg; 2.341 *swich: suche* R H^3 H^5, *siche* S^2, *suiche* S^1, also *youre: your* J (and 6 other MSS); 3.849 *god: gode* H^3, also *to-forn: to-forne* D S^2 H^3, also *shal: shalle* S^2; 3.918 *pitous: pitinous* D, *pitouse* S^1; 4.297 *this: this in* A; 4.954 *despeir: dispaire* H^1 (and 5 other MSS); 4.988 *were: wer* H^2, also *rather: rathere* Cl, also *an: ane* S^2; 4.1058 *suffiseth: suffisethe* A, also *right: righte* A, also *ynough: ynoughe* A S^2; 4.1605 *Allas: Allace* S^1; 5.47 *nyl: nylle* S^2, also *rather: rathere* Cl Gg.

In fact these variants are trivial, and the Chaucerian readings are obvious in them all; nevertheless a rigorous study of meter requires exactitude. It is tedious work to find lines in which there are no syllabic variants, but a few years ago I examined the first thousand lines of the poem, starting with the seven manuscripts printed by the Chaucer Society and examining the rest on film (I have now checked all in photographic reproductions), and uncovered four or five lines (including Windeatt's one correct instance, 1.771) in which there are no syllabic variants in the manuscripts (not considering the printed editions). I believe these are the only four perfect examples in the first thousand lines:

> 1.268 This Troilus of every wight aboute
> 1.482 Fro day to day in armes so he spedde
> 1.770 Why nay quod he by god and by my trouthe
> 1.771 What nat as bisyly quod Pandarus

To these may be added one other, in which manuscript R omits the *i* of *curacioun:*

> 1.791 That of thi wo is no curacioun

These lines have variants (I have not counted line-end variants): 268 *of: and* Cl H^5, *on* H^4, *with* H^2 Ph; 770 *by: be* (in both instances of the word, in several manuscripts); 771 *bisyly: prevely* H^5; 791 *thi: the* Gg; *is: nys* H^4. None of these variants affects meter.[4]

These five lines, like practically any string of, say, six to ten words, can be read so as to support a theory of a four-stress meter, but they also support what is much harder to organize: iambic pentameter. Windeatt is right to notice that the principle of *difficilior lectio* [the more difficult reading] operates metrically as well as lexically: the most complex metrical hypothesis that fits the facts is the right one. This seems to invert, but finally confirms, Occam's razor: the most complex metrical hypothesis is also the simplest. From a study of these lines, and lines like those listed in the last footnote, we can conclude that a line like

> The double sorwe and peyne of Troilus to tellen

or

> The double sorwe and peyne to tellen

is unChaucerian (whether or not Chaucer wrote it by mistake or deliberately flouted his normal practice); that a line like:

> The double sorwe that of Troilus to tellen

is improbably but just conceivably Chaucerian; and that:

> The double sorwe of Troilus to tellen,
> The double sorwe of Troilus for to tellen,

or

Double sorwe of Troilus to tellen,*
Double the sorwe of Troilus for to tellen

and so forth are unobjectionable, while

The double harm Troilus now telleth**

is suspect because of the adjacent stresses *harm Tro-* (without a "compensating" extra light syllable). Note that a theory of meter must be able rigorously and consistently to reject unmetrical lines; that is, to "generate," as linguists say, only metrical lines. Although recent editors are more tolerant of headless (*) and Lydgatian (**) lines and the occasional extra weak syllable than ten Brink and Kittredge were, the basic principles of Chaucer's meter were correctly worked out a century and more ago, and should be relied upon by the textual critic. When a modern editor emends his base text *causa metri*, the puzzled reader should first turn to Kittredge's *Observations on the Language of Chaucer's Troilus* (1891) for an explanation.

Still we constantly hear Chaucerians saying that such-and-such an editor follows too naively the Victorian table-thumping notions of meter, preferring one manuscript over another or making emendations because of a wrongly over-precise view of Chaucer's wonderfully flexible line. Again, such remarks are generally made by the way, accompanied by no evidence or simply wrong evidence. Of course Chaucer's line *is* wonderfully flexible, but it is so–like Shakespeare's, Milton's, Pope's, and Wordsworth's–within fixed constraints. In his justly famous replies to Southworth (1948 and 1949), and again more influentially in his edition of Chaucer's poems (Chaucer 1975, 1017), E. Talbot Donaldson, to name a formidable scholar, seems to license a view of Chaucers phonology much looser than his own editing practice depends on:

> In the last analysis, perhaps the most that can be said about final *e* is that it is pronounced or silent according to the demands of the meter.

A great deal more can be said about final *-e*, as Donaldson himself knew and asserted.[5] Why should he and others make such statements? And why are there no contrary voices, arguing that ten Brink or Robinson or Manly and Rickert were not strict enough?

Several reasons suggest themselves. Perhaps under all lies a natural reactive or cycling process in the history of scholarship. The Chaucerians a generation before us inevitably raised their banners over territory that had been claimed a generation and more before them by Kittredge, F.N. Robinson, Young, Koch, Root, even Child, Saintsbury, Lounsbury, ten Brink. Children slay their parents; as the findings of Germanic philology became less and less exciting, more and more refined, the field must have seemed overprecise and tedious. In the age of free verse, as Eliot's own essays show, the pedantry of classically based versification, with its Victorian claim of Science, number, rigor, came to be stifling.[6] Too much attention to metrical technique would draw energy away from more important critical activity.

Two other minor causes of the modern discomfort with the classic description of Chaucer's meter can be suspected. First, notoriously, the first line of the first work by Chaucer that we normally read is metrically difficult. Second, most treatments of meter naturally dwell on exceptions and oddities and irregularities, giving a false impression to the beginner.

Among more serious causes of the modern disapproval of precisionist metrics, three are more technical. The first lies beyond the scope of my knowledge, the possibility that the meter of *Troilus* differs from that of others of Chaucer's poems. Possibly Chaucer developed his mastery of the *Troilus* line over a number of years, and then magisterially, like (I am told) Shakespeare, gave himself more license in later poems. Second, each rigorous rule about Chaucer's versification that might be announced seems to find its exception. Wimsatt's distinction between the "rule" and the "norm" can help (W. Wimsatt 1970), but some residue of doubt about particular cases can cloud the whole enterprise. And third, we are never certain, given scribal activity, that what Chaucer wrote has been preserved.

Before treating these last two causes, I would suggest a final one: acquiring the grammar, the phonology, and the textual expertise necessary for grasping Chaucer's usage is simply too hard. Of course Donaldson himself cannot be accused of this, but most writers who criticize F.N. Robinson's idea of meter simply avoid the trouble of learning what one needs to know. Most writers on Chaucer's meter, for example, use an edited text, usually Robinsons, as their basis. Hence they describe (and then criticize!) Robinson, not Chaucer or the scribes; the procedure is inept. To study Chaucer's sounds requires more or less ample knowledge of a number of things, including Old English, Anglo-Norman, Italian, Latin, paleography, Middle English dialectology, phonology, and accidence, as well as modern linguistic, text-critical, and metrical theory in several languages and profound knowledge of Chaucer's text in all its forms. A student may well be unhappy in the face of these requirements, but the fact that understanding Chaucer's language is difficult is no argument that the attempt should not be made, or that we should attend to the arguments of the incompetent.

A randomly selected stanza from *Troilus* can demonstrate the difficulties of metrical analysis. The first one my eye falls on in the Riverside edition is 3.1793–99:

> For soth to seyne, he lost held every wyght,
> But if he were in Loves heigh servise–
> I mene folk that oughte it ben of right.
> And over al this, so wel koude he devyse
> Of sentement and in so unkouth wise
> Al his array, that every lovere thoughte
> That al was wel, what so he seyde or wroughte.

In preparing the Riverside edition, I saw no need for a textual or explanatory note to these lines, but provided a gloss to the rather difficult second sentence: "And moreover, he knew so well how to order (*devyse*) all his behavior (*array*) feelingly (*Of sentement*) and in so striking a way (*unkouth wise*) that lovers thought all was well done, whatever he said or did."

I would call this a perfectly regular iambic pentameter stanza in rime royal. This observation may seem patently wrong, and it needs defending from a reasonably naive point of view ("reasonably" in not arguing, for example, that *folk* is monosyllabic or that the first syllable of *Loves* has prominence over the second). In our naïveté let us first assume that this text is not only correct, but that it was written just so by Chaucer, who here intended to spell his text to reflect both his grammar and his sounds–even knowing that it would be folly to assume that Chaucer or any scribe invariably spelled with these goals in mind. It still may seem to require great leaps of faith to squeeze iambic pentameter from these lines. (I agree with the modern tendency to be skeptical of the notion of metrical feet, hence iambs, in English verse, but the notion does little harm and one may substitute the phrase "five stress alternating rhythm" or some such for "iambic pentameter.")[7] But the lines have an Augustan regularity of meter, with of course an infinite number of potential phonic realizations by any reader.

First consider the number of syllables in each line. If we start by guessing that every vowel or adjacent pair of vowels, including *y*, forms the nucleus of a single syllable (this will not always be true), then the lines above have 12, 12, 11, 13, 11, 13, and 12 syllables. Since this seems hopelessly unpentametric, we quickly adduce the familiar rules about elision before vowels and some words beginning with *h*. We don't know what Chaucer's elided vowels sounded like, but we do know that some sort of suppression or slurring or simply "not counting" of them, in the manner of the rigorously syllabic French and Italian poets (and the rigorously syllabic Orm), produces a syllable count of much greater apparent uniformity. Eliding, then, the final vowels of *seyne, were, oughte, koude*, and *seyde* (but not eliding the vowel of *so*, which in fact can be elided but rarely is) we arrive at counts of 11, 11, 10, 12, 11, 13, 11. The *b* and *c* rimes of the stanza are all feminine, and invoking the principle that a final unstressed syllable in a line "doesn't count," does not disrupt the hypothesis of iambic pentameter, we have counts of 11, 10, 10, 11, 10, 12, 10. Finally let us assume, the trickiest assumption so far, that certain polysyllabic words in certain contexts can have a reduced syllable count with a presumed slurring, especially words with *er*. (Here we need elaborate this property of meter so far, but a full account would be much more complex and would admit of variation and exceptions.) Hence *every* and *lovere* count as two syllables (the final *-e* of *lovere* is variable anyway), and *over* as one. Now our counts are 10, 10, 10, 10, 10, 10, 10. With three assumptions we can produce lines that are not decasyllabic, but that "count" as decasyllabic for metrical purposes. What keeps the erection of these three assumptions from being merest *petitio principii* is the fact, abundantly attested, that these same assumptions allow for, "generate," thousands of metrically decasyllabic Chaucerian lines. Doubtless Child, who first stated with rigor the grammatical and phonological principles that underlie the modern scansion of Chaucer, was influenced by Augustan versification when he (following Tyrwhitt) formulated his initial hypothesis (roughly, that Chaucer's verse was like Pope's), but the hypothesis is confirmed by its effects. The proof is comparable to the proof of the heliocentric solar system: whereas we lack confirmable knowledge of the efficient or final causes, the formal and material causes integrate with such consistency and simplicity that contrary hypotheses are incredible. The principle is economy.

The precise stress Chaucer would have given his syllables is unknowable. Still, the hypothesis of an alternating stress conforms well with such other hypotheses about English in 1385 as the prominence of a root syllable over an inflectional ending, or the prominence of a noun over an article–such hypotheses as historical phonology finds inescapable to account for the development of sounds as represented in spelling. In the stanza we are examining, a hypothesis of iambic pentameter would call forth little objection, even with a modern stressing of the words, except in a few places.

The stress on the second vowel of *servise* turns out to be regular in Chaucer, and we know that words borrowed from French behave differently from native words. *Array* and *devyse* are the same, less noticeable because we still accent the second syllable, presumably somehow conscious that the first syllables of these words are prefixed. The stress on the first syllable of *unkouth* is the least obvious, but (examining the *Concordance*) we find it is used elsewhere in Chaucerian pentameter in only these places:

> So unkouth and so riche, and wroght so wel (KnT 2497)
> So unkouthe, and swiche fresshe contenaunces (SqT 284)
> In many an unkouth, glad, and dep matere (Tr 2.151)

Assuming these texts are right (the Globe Chaucer reads *so* for *swiche* in SqT 284, making an easier rhythm), we cannot say that Chaucer accents the second syllable of *unkouth,* nor by the way can we say that *so* regularly elides its vowel before *unkouth.*

If we have the word stress right, what about the phrasing? We commonly presume that such "function" words as prepositions, articles, conjunctions, often pronouns, the copulative, auxiliaries, and the like, bear less stress than "lexical" or "notional" words like nouns, verbs, and adjectives. Applying this norm still leaves a number of ambiguous sequences in the stanza. In *he lost held,* which of the last two words, if either, is prominent? How do we scan *But if he were*? Or *that oughte it ben*? Or *al this*? Or *so wel koude he*? Or *and in so*? Or *what so*? We should first notice that these seven ambiguously stressed sequences seem many, but that in fact the great majority of stresses in the stanza are obvious. If we invoke another principle, that ambiguous sequences should be stressed, for metrical scansion if not for reading, to conform with the pattern of the majority of unambiguous sequences, then we are left with a residue of one sequence that would conform to a regularly alternating pattern only with wrenching, namely *Al his* at the opening of line 1798, "Al his array, that every lovere thoughte."[8] (We could add *what so* without affecting the argument.)

Hence, marking with italics syllables that are suppressed in the meter (however they are pronounced), and marking with an acute accent every syllable that is unambiguously prominent, and with a grave accent every syllable that can conform to iambic meter even though it is of ambiguous stress, we have:

For sóth to séyn*e*, he lòst held év*e*ry wíght,
But ìf he wèr*e* in Lóves héigh servíse–
I méne fólk that oùght*e* it bèn of ríght.
And óv*e*r al thìs, so wèl koud*e* hè devýse
Of séntemént and ìn so únkouth wíse
Ál his arráy, that év*e*ry lóver*e* thóughte
That ál was wél, what sò he séyd*e* or wróughte.

Only the inverted first foot of the sixth line, always recognized as a permitted variation in the iambic line, mars the regular appearance of this scansion. (Note that, as usual at least in the Romance and Germanic languages, the latter part of the line tends to be more obviously regular.) Arguably a dramatic reading based consistently on this scansion, obviously avoiding a mechanical thumping isochronicity and overemphasis of stress, would respect Chaucer's rhythm as well as any other reading.

These results would be persuasive if the only relevant evidence were *The Riverside Chaucer*. More assumptions about syllabification and stressing would have to be made, and certain licenses and even some rare unconforming lines would have to be tolerated, but the huge majority of lines could be scanned as regular iambic pentameter. But alas, the question of Chaucer's meter cannot be settled without raising much more severe difficulties. These require a deeper scrutiny of the evidence, and I hope I may be pardoned in what follows for adopting commonsensical shorthand locutions instead of scientifically rigorous formulation.

The first problem is, how can we account for the many apparent exceptions to the usual set of metrical rules? Lines of good grammar, well attested, in no obvious way unChaucerian, do not conform to even a fully elaborated treatment of regular scansion. Such exceptional lines are, indeed, so rare as not to weigh substantially against the hypothesis of iambic pentameter. Still, an editor and a student of the detail of Chaucer's verse need to know whether certain lines are unlikely to be Chaucer's, or whether certain irregularities may be deliberate breaches of the norm for rhetorical effect, or whether certain lines are simply authentic Chaucerian mistakes or instances of carelessness.

On page 1017 of his edition Donaldson (Chaucer 1975) gives a few instances of exceptions to his generalizations about the pronunciation of final *e*, and scans the lines:

|Swich ár | rogánc | cë ís | nat worth | an hén | (WBT 1112)
|Yit hád | dë hé | but 1í | tel gó1d | in cóf | rë (GP 298)

|He coú | dë sóng | es mák(e) | and wél | endí | të (GP 95)

The last two are not "exceptions," but rather instances of common variation. Sometimes Chaucer seems to treat *coude*, like some other common auxiliary verbs, as metrically monosyllabic, doubtless in keeping with a London apocope of an *-e* that is historically organic. In the General Prologue these lines may be examples:

Wel koude she carie a morsel and wel kepe (130)
In felawshipe wel koude she laughe and carpe (474)
Ther koude no man brynge hym in arrerage (602)

This last line might scan with dissyllabic *koude* and a triplet (extra unstressed syllable) late in the line, but this would miss the interesting stress thrown on *hym*. But these lines in the General Prologue, along with the one Donaldson quotes, more likely have dissyllabic *coude:*

Ther koude no wight pynche at his writyng (326)

(The Globe Chaucer reads *pynchen*, but the variance is irrelevant, especially if we recognize that the *-en* of an infinitive often is slurred, especially before vowels, as if it were *-e* elided. An editor is helpless before this phenomenon, and might as well follow the base manuscript.)

Of alle deyntees that men koude thynke (346)
(An instance only if *men* is singular, the indefinite pronoun; otherwise the *-e* is the regular plural form.)
He koude rooste, and sethe, and broille, and frye (383)
She koude muchel of wandrynge by the weye (467)

(Here we need to know that *muchel* is usually monosyllabic–in scansion–before a vowel, and that the *-e* of a present participle/gerund is a rare instance in Chaucers grammar of a purely free inflectional variation.)

He koude bettre than his lord purchace (608)

The rest of the *koude*s in the General Prologue are indeterminate because they precede a vowel or unaspirated *h*. In what follows I call such metrically indeterminate words "ambiguous." If the *Concordance* is right (in my experience it reflects the Globe Chaucer with great accuracy), then of the nineteen instances of *koude* in *Troilus,* only one has a reasonable claim to being monosyllabic, and that one is not free of doubt:

Ymagynen ne kouthe how to be bet (2.836)

(The Globe reads "Imaginen ne coude how to be bet.") Sometimes, but not often, an *-e* elides before the *h* of *how*, presumably of middling aspiration. This evidence suggests that Donaldson errs in saying that *coude* is generally monosyllabic. It further suggests, by the way, that *Troilus* more carefully preserves the historically expected sounded *-e* in this word. This might be a matter of chance, or of Chaucer's changing usage, or of a different (more careful) usage on the part of those scribes on whom the Globe edition (and hence the *Concordance)*, and Robinson's and my editions, are based, or of the habits of the modern editors, including me. I suspect that the last two are the prime causes: I will return to this issue.

The other example that Donaldson calls an exception and I would call a regular variation,

> Yit hadde he but litel gold in cofre,

may be scanned to sound the *-e* on *hadde*, which sometimes happens. But it is not common, and I know of no other instance of dissyllabic auxiliary or main verb *hadde* before a vowel or unaspirated *h*, that is, with hiatus. The line performs well if we scan it as headless, throwing a nice rhetorical accent on *Yit.* (Here I contradict the scansion indicated on p. xliv of the *Riverside Chaucer* as well.) So read, the line conforms to a pattern of rhythm and syntax that expresses an aspect of the distinctive voice of the General Prologue, the voice of one seeming to refine and negate what he has just seemed to observe:[9]

> And though that he were worthy, he was wys
> But sikerly she had a fair forheed
> Yet wolde he have a ferthyng, er he wente
> But he was lyk a maister or a pope
> But greet harm was it, as it thoughte me
> And yet he semed bisier than he was
> And yet he was but esy of dispense
> And yet he hadde a thombe of gold, pardee
> And yet this Manciple sette hir aller cappe
> And yet hadde he but litel gold in cofre

Well, we have to remove the *And* from this last line to report what Chaucer wrote, but I think he would have written it so, had the syntactic context permitted an *and:* the preceding line is "But al be that he was a philosophre." The line is headless, of regular meter. Donaldson's last example really is exceptional:

> Swich arrogance is nat worth an hen

Such words as *arrogance* regularly have four syllables, but the hiatus of sounded *-e* before following *is* breaks the rule of elision. No cesura or rhetorical excuse saves the scansion. To claim that sounding the *-e* gives the word appropriate haughtiness would be desperate. Chaucer may have written it, as any poet who writes many lines will write a few that are irregular or abnormal in terms of his own usage, but the line arouses ready suspicion in anyone accustomed to scribal variation in Chaucer manuscripts. Chances are very good that some scribe altered *nis* to *is*. Manly and Rickert report that five manuscripts read *nys* here. An editor would rightly read *is*, but the ideal examiner of meter, ideally learned, would keep in mind the possibility of a corruption.

Donaldson then gives three lines "in which final *e* is suppressed" where "there is probably no other reason than the demands of the meter" (p. 1017).

|For hé | was lá | të cóm(e) | from hís | viá | gë (GP 77)

|In hóp(e) | to stón | den ín | his lá | dy grá | cë (GP 88)

|Hir nós(e) | tretís, | hir ´y | ën gréy(e) | as glás | (GP 152)

The words in question are *come* (past participle), *hope*, and *nose*. The past participle *come(n)*, not standing before a vowel or unaspirated *h* or at line end, occurs according to the *Concordance* only seventeen times in the first fragment of the Canterbury Tales and *Troilus*. Of these instances, five would read more smoothly, assuming iambic pentameter, if the word were monosyllabic: the one Donaldson quotes, and

Bretful of pardoun comen from Rome al hoot (GP 687)
Was come to Atthenes his felawe to visite (KnT 1194)

of difficult meter in any reading, and

For sith the day is come that I shal dye (KnT 1732)
To Troie is come this woful Troilus(Tr 5.197)

Three different explanations are possible, if we are to retain the hypothesis of iambic pentameter. Chaucer may vary his intended pronunciation of this word, even though we would expect a strong verb to end in *-e* or *-en* in the past participle. Hence Baugh lists *have* and *come* among "certain common words" that "were often pronounced as monosyllables" (Chaucer 1963, xli). Or the printed texts (Globe, Donaldson, Robinson, Riverside) may err. Or these lines may exemplify a recognized license in Chaucer's lines, an occasional "triplet" or extra light syllable between stresses. Given only this evidence, which of the three is most likely cannot be determined, but the fact that the monosyllabic usage is uncommon in *Troilus* (one out of nine instances) but common in the first fragment (five out of eight) makes me suspect that the second explanation has some weight, not out of editorial fault but because the scribal situation differs. In my experience, the past participle of strong verbs rarely lacks its expected ending, but a full account of the facts would require an elaborate study. Another consideration would make such a study difficult. Possibly very common participles like *come* or *sene* (no dissyllabic instances in mid-line in *Troilus*) lose their *-e* more readily than other participles, like *yronne*, on the analogy of common verbs like *hadde*. But such a phenomenon would be hard to pin down, because of the great rarity of uncommon strong past participles in metrically unambiguous positions. No instances occur, for example, of *yronne*(*n*) in metrically unambiguous situations, unless we use rimes as evidence of final *-e*, a flawed procedure.

In any case, the possibility that these are mere triplets deters us from concluding that we hear this inflectional *-e* only at the whim of meter. Donaldson's second example involves the monosyllabic noun *hope*, which in fact according to the *Concordance* preponderates over dissyllabic *hope* eight (GP 88, KnT 1512, 1925, ClT 1181, FrankT 1170, Pity 27, Tr 2.7, 5.348) to five (KnT 2435, WBT 994, SqT 488, FrankT 924, CYT 870) in unambiguous cases, even though the dissyllabic form (OE *hopa*) would be expected. Comparable would be the word *name* (OE *nama*), of similar frequency, where I find twenty-one instances of dissyllabic pronunciation and four of monosyllabic, none in *Troilus*. *Love* (OE *lufu*) is similarly variable, usually monosyllabic. A little research can convince us that these nouns with historically expected *-e* are simply variable in Chaucer's metrics, with preponderance of one or the other syllabification depending on the individual word. The syllabification of these nouns affects a very small proportion of Chaucer's lines, and we may simply accept such variation, as the traditional account of Chaucer's meter does, while recognizing that the evidence of rimes indicates that the dissyllabic sounding was "standard" when Chaucer is otherwise free of metrical constraints, as at line end.

Nose (OE *nosu*) behaves the same way: of nine metrically unambiguous examples (four in Fragment A of the *Romaunt*) only three are pronounced dissyllabically, if the *Concordance* preserves Chaucer's text. It is true that we pronounce these words variously depending on the metrical context; it does not follow (to quote Donaldson again) that "perhaps the most that can be said about final *e* is that it is pronounced or not according to the demands of the meter." The existence of variable nouns (and adjectives) with "organic," historically expected *-e* by no means obviates what we can determine about the much more frequent cases of inflectional *-e*, and these (the endings of weak and plural adjectives, subjunctives, first person singulars, plural verbs, infinitives, weak preterit first and third singulars, strong past participles) are so consistent as to allow one to speak of rules and exceptions.

To exemplify the regularity of Chaucerian final *-e* in meter let us examine a sample of his corpus. Probably the most consistent feature of Chaucer's inflectional use of *-e* is the rule that infinitives end in *-e*(*n*). The presence or absence of the *-n* complicates the study, so we may need to rule out all instances of infinitives followed by a vowel or unaspirated *h*, rule out, that is, the possibility of elision; scribes may well not be trusted to preserve or omit an *-n* with sufficient care. (In fact, the Corpus scribe is very careful with these spellings.) Also to make such a study work we need to assume a great deal about other aspects of Chaucer's meter.

Even so, let it not be charged that we thereby fall into a vicious circle, making a claim about a certain metrical phenomenon which depends on another claim about another metrical phenomenon, with neither phenomenon free of doubt. If a pair of mutually dependent hypotheses can be jointly confirmed, they are at least jointly tenable, and because in metrical studies the actual dependence of one feature on another is incredible (for example, we cannot believe that the *-e* of a first person singular verb depends on the phenomenon of elision), those same hypotheses are severally tenable. In any case, each feature of Chaucer's syllabification and stress can be isolated in metrical contexts otherwise undisputed.

For our sample let us use the first thousand lines of *Troilus* as preserved in the Corpus manuscript (I will return to the problem of which text we can use to study meter), that is, lines 1–1008 (Corpus omits lines 859 and 890–96). Of the 384 infinitives that I caught in this sample, nearly half, 177, fall at line end, and these we shall for the moment set aside. Why so high a proportion of infinitives fall at line end probably results from a natural syntactic retraction of them to the ends of phrases and clauses, especially when they occur with auxiliaries and the quasi-auxiliary *gan,* as well as from their general ease of riming. Much more striking is the fact that only four times does an infinitive begin a line:

> Preyen for speed al sholde I ther fore sterue (1.17)

and lines 514, 522, 688. Syntactic retraction mildly discourages line-initial infinitives, but the major cause is Chaucer's unwillingness to begin a line with a stressed syllable–that is, to make a headless line or invert the first foot: lines 17 (if *Preyen* is dissyllabic) and 514 have initial trochees; line 522 (*Know all*), where Corpus omits the expected *-e* of *Know,* may have demoted stress on *Know*; line 688 (*Mistrusten*) is normal with an unstressed prefix.

Of the 207 non-line-end infinitives, a sizable number seem to disrupt the hypothesis of metrically sounded *-e*(*n*), but in every case with very rare exceptions these verbs fall into explicable and predictable patterns. First are a number of verbs, some very frequent, whose stem ends in a vowel or (if *ey/ ei* is a diphthong) a diphthong. The spelling and phonological history of these verbs suggests that their final *-e* does not appear when the vowel is a monophthong (*be/ben, go/gon/goon, the* ["prosper"], *do/don/doon, see/se/sen* ["see"]–these words already show assimilation in Old English, and never had a final *-e*), and that the final *-e* of verbs whose stem ends in *ey/ei* is variable (*seyne* 12, 591–these two may be petrified inflected infinitives–*seyn* 396, 398, 512, 514, 804; *sey* 451; *seye* 492, 574, 672; *say* 931; *Preyen* 17; *prey* 48; *deyen* 306; *deye* 573, 758, 930; *dyen* 674; *dye* 728; *wrey* 329; *leye* 559; *pleye* 671; *slen* 815, 823; *unwre* 858) except that words borrowed from French whose stem ends in *i/y* seem to retain *-e* regularly as far as this sample shows (*crye* 750, 806; *espye* 193; *multiplie* 486, 546). In these lists I have included line-end as well as medial infinitives. Assuming elision of *-e* before an initial vowel or unaspirated *h,* only five irregularities occur in this sample. Typical lines are

> To prey for hem that loues seruauntz *be* (48)
> And trewelich it sit wel to *be* so (246)
> That neuere thoughte hym *seen* so good a syghte (294)
> I dar wel *seyn* in al that Troilus (396)
> That so ken *leye* oure Iolite on presse (559)

That certein for to *dyen* in the peyne (674)

Most of the instances of infinitives in *ei/ey* are at line end.

Some of the lines are not perfect iambic pentameter–

Ben worthi to *be* brent felle and bones (91)
(usually emended but a tolerable Lydgatian line)
Nas neuere yet seyn thyng to *ben* preysed derre (174)
(a typical extra unstressed syllable in mid-line)–

but only in the following five would one be tempted to alter Corpus's spelling so as to show better meter:

Hym self to *wrey* at hem he gan to *smyle* (329)
Was ay on hire that fairer was to *sene* (454)
That as hire Ioies moten *ouergone* (846)
To hym behoueth first *unwre* his wownde (858)
Here after may thy comfort *be* also (945)

The first one and last two of these apparent exceptions to the elision rule can be accounted for by refining the rule to exclude stressed vowels from obligatory elision (Robinson and Riverside respell *wrey* of 329 as *wrye* merely for clarity). *Sene* in 454 rimes with *Polixene* and breaks the provisional rule that infinitives whose stem ends in a monophthong have no syllabic *-e* before or after the last *n.* The *Concordance* indicates that this verb not uncommonly breaks the rule, and it should be treated as an exception. It may be a petrified vestige of the inflected infinitive with *to.* In 846, *ouergone* rimes with *euerechone*; Corpus seems to miswrite both these words (Robinson and Riverside both omit both *e*'s); a plural *euerechone is* unlikely.

The infinitive *have* has two forms, spelled *haue* or *han* in the Corpus manuscript. In this sample, Corpus only twice spells the word *haue* before a consonant where one would expect a monosyllable to preserve iambic rhythm:

For who so list haue helyng of his wownde (857)
For by my trouthe in loue I dorste haue sworne (906)

Only these two, if they are properly dissyllabic and not just scribal misrepresentations of *han*, instance dissyllabic *have* not at line end. A parallel oddity involves the word *love*(*n*).The infinitive occurs nine times, including lines 388, 392, 520, 798, 817, and 986. Three times it is spelled with an *-e* where meter calls for a monosyllable:

To loue swich oon and if he dede his cure (369)
More than my self wole loue yow to my laste (537)
(Corpus often spells *wole* for regular wol)
A man to loue tyl that hym list to leue (686)

We can only view these as exceptions, and probably we do best to construe the unsmooth *haue*'s as properly *han*'s, and the unsmooth *loue*'s as simply unsmooth, instances of extra unstressed syllables at mid-line. That *love* so often shows this oddity suggests, if the whole corpus bears out this sample, that it was the first infinitive in London English, whose stem ends in a consonant, to sound right as a monosyllable.

Setting aside infinitives at the end of the line, and setting aside the words treated above–*be, go,do, the, see, seyn, preyen, deyen, wreyen, leyen, pleyen, slen, unwre, have, love*–we find sixty-seven infinitives in *-e* or *-en* that fall before a vowel or unaspirated *h*, and forty-one that fall before a consonant. In addition to these, six infinitives, treated below, are in one way or another irregular as spelled by Corpus.

I think Chaucer sometimes permits an infinitive in *-en* to slur, as if it were *-e* in elision, before a vowel or unaspirated *h*. But in this sample only one instance occurs:

> But gan to *preisen* and lakken whom hym leste (189)

This can be read as offering an extra unstressed syllable, but Robinson and I drop Corpus's *-n*. I now think this was wrong of us, and accept slurring, or (less probably) syncope.[10] Otherwise–and I was surprised to see this–no instance of *-e* or *-en* among these sixty-six cases before a vowel or unaspirated *h* would tempt an editor to alter *-e* to *-en* or *-en* to *-e*: Corpus spells just as an editor would who meant to display the hiatuses and elisions that permit regular iambic meter:

> That I haue myght to *shewe* in som manere (33)
> *To graunte* hem soone owt of this world to pace (41)
> He wolde *smyle* and *halden* it folye (194)

The consistency in this matter of the Corpus scribe responsible for these thousand lines might well encourage a modern editor who wished to add or subtract an *-n causa metri.*

Why this scribe spells so "well"–that is, so consistently to reveal grammar and meter–cannot be determined. Obviously, as the other manuscripts show (especially the twelve not in the group Cp Cl J H[1]), such practice was not common among fifteenth-century scribes. My guess would be that the Corpus scribe had a "carefully" written exemplar–that is, one very like his own text–that he was very careful, and that he understood the principles of Chaucer's meter. The last possibility raises the question whether Corpus was regularizing Chaucer's irregular sounds. The proposition is incredible: it would assume that a few other scribes (like that of Ellesmere and Hengwrt, if one scribe wrote both) performed the same acts of regularizing, in the same way, and it would assume a vast scribal rewriting in a text that otherwise shows few signs of corruption.

The firmest evidence that Chaucer sounded the *-e* and *-en* of his infinitives lies in the forty-four instances before consonants (except unaspirated *h*). To avoid giving the impression that regularity is a minority phenomenon, I will quote the first ten instances:

> For which for *to departen* softely (78)
> Now vp now down gan hem to *whilen* bothe (139)
> At which the god of loue gan *loken* rowe (206)
> To *seruen* loue which so soon kanne (234)
> The yerde is bet that *bowe*[*n*] wole and wynde (257)
> (the *n* of *bowen* is erased or effaced in the manuscript; either spelling is regular)
> But for to *tellen* forth in special (260)
> Ascaunces what may I nat *stonden* here (292)
> And thoughte he wolde *werken* pryuely (380)
> Loo next this vers he may it *fynde* here (399)
> May *liken* yow so beth to me benigne (431)11

As spelled by the Corpus scribe, all but two of these lines are hard to scan except as regular iambic pentameter. In line 206, as often (but probably not in line 234), the noun *loue* is either monosyllabic or given an added unstressed syllable–like the infinitive, the noun is variable, as we saw above.[12] In line 234 the scribe omits the *-e* regularly expected for the adverb *soone* (OE *sona*): in the twenty-one unambiguous instances in *Troilus,* all are smoothly dissyllabic in context. These lines are all iambic pentameter with sounded *-e*(*n*) on the infinitives.

The six apparently irregular infinitives are these:

> As for to *honour* hir goddes ful deuoute (151)
> But gan to *preisen* and lakken whom hym leste (189)
> To *folowen* hym that so wel ken yow lede (259)
> God goodly to whom *serue* I laboure (458)
> . . . oon that sholde
> *Know* al thi wo al lakked hir pitee (522)
> That I shal neuere mo *discoueren* the (675)

In 151 and 522 the scribe omits an *-e* whose presence would not affect the meter (*to* before *honour* shows regular elision). In Corpus's spelling system these are errors. Line 189 was discussed above. Line 259 seems to resemble it–dropping the *-n* would mend the meter–but the medial vowel is liable to be slurred (the word is often spelled *folwen*; cf. *sorwe, borwe, morwe, holwe, halwen*) and the line is regular. So is 675; the first *e* of *discoveren* likewise may be slurred (cf. *covred, hyndren, ordred, offren, profren*). Line 458 could be smoothed by adding *-n* to *serue,* but I consider the line corrupt in Corpus and print *and* after *I.* None of these instances disturbs the hypothesis of iambic pentameter and infinitives in *-e*(*n*).

Seven other lines of apparently irregular or strained meter, not involving the infinitive itself, occur:

To herknen of Palladion the servyce (164)
(I emend *Palladion* the to *Palladions*)
First to hiden his desire in muwe (381) (headless)
I wol parten with the alle thi peyne (589)
(*alle*, singular, is usually spelled *al*; headless)
Ther as he felle that couth loken wide (629)
(regular grammar would be represented by *fel, couthe*)
That toucheth loue that ought ben secree (744)
(*oughte* would be expected)
And on the morwe pulle it as blyue (965)
(the Corpus scribe and two others omitted *vp* after *it*)
I hope of this to maken a good ende (973)
(Chaucer writes a metrically inferior line; two scribes attempted to improve it by adding *right* or *ful* before *good*)

Only the last instance provokes doubt about Chaucer's meter.

We have observed that 177 of the 384 infinitives in our sample corpus fall at the end of a line. The meter of the lines is not in question in these instances. Their ambiguous endings are hard to determine, but the words with which they rime should have an appropriately sounded *-e* or *-en* if our hypothesis is correct. Let us examine these, again omitting from consideration those infinitives that traditional historical phonology indicates are difficult: *be, go, do, the, see, seyn, preyen, deyen, wreyen, leyen, pleyen, slen, have, love*, and their compounds.

First let us examine infinitives that rime with verbs. Far the most abundant are those that rime with other infinitives, all *ex hypothesi* sounding their final *-e*(*n*). I count fifty-five of these,[13] far above what would be expected in a random distribution. Only nouns rime more frequently with infinitives than infinitives do. The other verb forms that traditionally are thought to sound *-e* or *-en* in Chaucer's verse are plural verbs, first person singular present tense verbs, first and third person singular preterit weak verbs, subjunctive verbs, (variably) present participles, (variably) imperatives, past participles of strong verbs, and (variably) second person singular preterit strong verbs.

In our sample all but the last two are found riming with infinitives:

plural verbs (10 instances): lines 3, 131, 145, 148, 217, 344, 565, 565, 705, 763.
1 sg. present verbs (6): 7, 15, 342, 406, 752, 1000.
1, 3 sg. weak pret. verbs (3): 261, 312, 477.
subjunctive verbs (3): 226, 693, 829.
present participles (3): 71, 743, 853.
imperatives (1): 957.

In every case but one the Corpus scribe writes the expected *-e(n)*; the exception is the omitted *-e* on *tellyng*, line 743. Verb forms in which we do *not* expect *-e* or *-en* are the second and third person present indicative singular, first and third person singular strong preterit, second person singular weak preterit, and weak past participle. No instance of these riming with an infinitive occurs in our sample. I take this as incontrovertible proof of the *-e(n)* of Chaucer's infinitives, and further of the actual pronunciation of *-e* at line end when it occurs.

We generally expect adverbs, except for some common ones like *ful* and *wel*, to end in *-e*. Ten times in the first thousand lines infinitives rime with adverbs: 121, 387, 399, 534, 629, 667, 669, 748, 821, 965. The words in question are *here, inne, faste, wide, sore, more, blyue*.

Adjectives are notoriously more difficult. Two instances of an adjective with "organic" *-e, dere*, rime with infinitives (30, 54). Adjectives with inflectional *-e* include those in plural use (11: lines 130, 160, 233, 264, 288, 561, 698, 840, 910, 912, 914), weak adjectives (rare at line end: only one instance riming with an infinitive, in substantive use, at line 209), and, variably, predicate adjectives, although this class is uncertain and some of these may be adverbs or simply irregular (5: lines 97, 229, 358, 547, 553). *Leene* (line 553) and *a fere* ["afire"] (line 229) may have organic *-e*, and the latter is probably best construed as an adverb (Robinson takes it as a petrified dative [Chaucer 1957, xxxii]; it surely was dative in origin); the other three instances have the word *allone*, of therefore suspect form (possibly adverbial). The evidence here imperfectly supports the hypothesis, but the preponderance of plural adjectives in rime with infinitives suggests that both have *-e*.

Our hypothesis is confirmed so consistently without them that I hesitate to introduce the infinitives that rime with nouns. Many nouns are variable, and from the list that follows some are sometimes found without *-e*. But that all of them can have *-e* can be determined by examining their use in unambiguous mid-line instances. Nearly all of them, it can be said, nearly always have *-e*; I think the italicized ones always do in Chaucer, although I have not hunted hard through the texts:[14] peyne 9, 508, 674 *trauaille* 21 ese 28, 43 manere 33 grace 42, 370, 907 *perseueraunce* 44 *plesaunce* 46 matere 53, 265 dede ["deed"] 93 drede 95, 501, 529, 775 *chere* 124, 280 side 185 *compaignie* 191 *folye* 194 *whippe* 220 lawe 223, 1003 kynde 238, 254, 265, 979 wise 275, 363, 697 *noblesse* 287 syghte 294 herte 307 while 328, 718 tyme 351 *mynde* 365 muwe 381 hewe 461 *cure* 469 *preue* 470, 690 *sorwe* 485 *morwe* 487 hede ["heed"] 501 *cheyne* 509 *daunce* 517 brede ["breadth"] 530 laste (dative?) 537 blisse 623 Pandare 624 *amete* ["Admetus"] 664 Eleyn 677 speche (dative?) 702 *wile* 719 nede 772, 863 wrecche 798, 889 synne 824 *lite* 826 helle 872 welle 873 *heuene* 878 *place* 905 (only monosyllabic in the famous rime at Sir Thopas 781) *feuere* 916 tyde 954 *vice* 987 *awe* (dative?) 1006.

Corpus misspells only one of these, *Eleyn* (677), which is variable and here should have its *-e*. The noun *whippe* (220) is too infrequent to show how Chaucer normally sounds it, as is *brede* (530), monosyllabic in its only other unambiguous use (KnT 2916). *Nede* more often has one syllable than two in unambiguous cases (it is a monosyllable in Old English, variably feminine or neuter). The whole set of nouns riming with infinitives displays Chaucer's tendency to sound in full the potential endings of variable words when they fall at the end of a line, where even words like *hire* and *oure* can be dissyllabic.

The significance of these findings can best be felt when we consider rime-words in our sample that do *not* rime with infinitives (again excluding the list above: *be, go, do,* etc.): cas, was, thus, down, distruccion, knyght, natheles, town, entencioun, corn, man, yet, Troilus, yow, pryuely, therby, is, this, I, myghtily, renoun, amys, whom, from, sailleth, Pandarus, vs, deeth, iwys, allas, shal, redy. Why not? Because these words have no *-e* or extremely rare *-e* either in their stem or–in the case of nouns–in their case inflections.

To sum up the argument: lines that have been taken as exceptions to the traditional statements–those of ten Brink, Robinson, and Baum, for example–about Chaucer's meter are usually not exceptional, but in some very rare cases some lines break some firm rules, either because the text is corrupt or because Chaucer nodded. Some variability in Chaucer's syllabification is recognizable and predictable both phonologically and historically, but it is restricted in its occurrence and not difficult to adjust for at reading speed. Even in the spelling of a scribe–that of the early part of the Corpus manuscript–infinitives, which exemplify Chaucer's inflectional *-e(n)* show the expected ending and even spell the expected ending with great consistency. Only the infinitive *love* disturbs the symmetrical distribution of the grammatical ending with metrical norms, and that word only three times out of several hundred infinitives. Chaucer nowhere in a large sample rimes an infinitive with a word without *-e(n)*. In short, this can be said about Chaucer's *-e*: infinitives have it.

This brief study of Chaucer's infinitives would have to be extended in several directions to provide a comprehensive account of his accidence and metrics. Such a full study has never been done. Fortunately, editors have been well enough instructed, by general accounts of Middle English grammar and by a large number of partial studies of Chaucer's metrics, to do their work. There remain areas of uncertainty and a good number of particular problems, but the terrain has been roughly mapped, and so many indices of Chaucer's usage conform so well with one another that editors can deal with all but a few textual situations with confidence.

I see two further central problems in Chaucerian metrics, aside from the problem of "exceptions" treated above. The problem of non-decasyllabic and non-iambic lines I will treat below. The other problem is, on what text do we base our study of meter? The answer is, unfortunately, on no extant text. Even if we had Chaucer's autographs, we would doubtless find that his system of spelling represented a complex compromise between his actual pronunciation (itself surely variable), his grammar, his own and others' spelling conventions, and his occasional efforts to clarify such metrical phenomena as elision and slurring. Obviously the scribes would tend to increase rather than reduce those features of spelling that obscure the phonology and metrics of the lines. Students of meter can only operate with a text in two stages "reconstructed": first by the scribe, who reworks Chaucer's or another scribe's spelling, and then by the investigator, who must attempt to uncover the intended sounds through the mask of scribal spelling.

For an example let us return to the stanza treated above, this time spelling it as the Corpus scribe does:

> For soth to seyne he lost helde euery wyght
> But if he were in loues heigh seruise
> I mene folk that oughte it ben of right
> And ouere al this so wele koude he deuyse
> Of sentement and in so vnkoude wise
> Al his array that euery louere thoughte
> That al was wel what so he seyde or wroughte
> (3.1793–99)

So the stanza is printed in *The Riverside Chaucer* with these changes: *helde/held, ouere/over, wele/wel, vnkoude/unkouth.* We should set aside variations that we may agree are graphemic and not even potentially phonetic (u/v, "thorn"/th, ee/e, gh/h/ "yogh", i/y, oo/o, ay/ai/ey/ei, f/ff/F, rr/r, ll/l, y/ "yogh", -es/-ys, s/c, c/k, some common abbreviations, and the like). So doing, we find the following variations among the manuscripts (Caxton's and Thynne's editions, here the only printed authorities, are too late to be worth much for metrical study):

line 1793: *sothe* A H^{3} H^{2} Ph; *seyn* J Cl R H^{4} H^{1} D H^{2} Ph Gg H^{5}, *sey* S^{2}; *loste* A D, *lorn* H^{2} Gg H^{5}, *loue* Ph; *held* J Cl H^{4} H^{1} S^{1} H^{2}, *hold* R, *had* H^{2} Ph, *hade* Gg; *euery* S^{2}, *of eury* Ph; *wyghte* A D.

line 1794: *Bot* S^{2}; *yif* J Gg, *euere* Ph; (*were*:)*was* Ph; *heyghe* Cl, *hye* R A H^{2} Ph; *hih* H^{4} D^{1} H^{3} H^{5}, *hey* Gg.

line 1795: *meen* H^{3}; *folke* H^{3}; *that* om. H^{5}; *ought* R H^{4} H^{1} D S^{2} S^{1} H^{2} Ph Gg H^{5}, *oughten* H^{3}; (*it*:)*to* A, *hit* Ph; *be* R S^{2} H^{3}, *bene* A H^{2} Ph; (*of*:)*by* R, *be* H^{4} H^{3}, *a* A; *righte* D.

line 1796: *ouer* J Cl R H^{4} A D S^{1} H^{3} H^{2} Gg H^{5}, *oure* S^{2}; *alle* H^{1} A D S^{2}; *wel* J Cl R H^{4} D H^{3} Gg H^{5}; (*koude he*:) *he couth* R, *he cowde* H^{3}; (*koude*:) *couth* D S^{2}, *coud* S^{1}, *couthe* H^{2} Ph.

line 1797: *sentmont* A, *ientilnes* H^{5}, *sentementis* Ph; *and* om. H^{5}; (*so*:) *nan* R, *to* H^{3}; *unkouth* J A S^{2} S^{1} H^{3} Gg H^{5}, *unkow* Cl, *uncouthe* R H^{1} H^{2} Ph, *uncouth a* D.

line 1798: *Alle* J A; *euere* H^{5}; *louer* R H^{1} A D S^{2} S^{1} H^{3} H^{2} H^{5}; *thoght* R H^{4} S^{2} S^{1} H^{2} Ph H^{5}

line 1799: *alle* A D S^{2}; *wele* A D S^{2} S^{1} Ph, *loue* H^{2}; (*what*:) *that* R H^{2} Ph; (*so*:) *euere* H^{2} Ph; (*he*:) *be* S^{2}; *said* A D S^{1} H^{2} Ph, *wroght* R H^{4} S^{2} S^{1} H^{3} H^{2} Ph Gg, *thought* H^{5}.

(Windeatt wrongly reads in line 1793 *holde* for *helde* H3 and *hald* for *held* H5.)

No edition of the poem would print this mass of minor variation; Windeatt–except for his base manuscript, Cp–rightly prints only "substantive" variants, not variations of spelling, and therefore not variants involving final *e*. The first thing to observe, then, is that metrical studies cannot depend on editions.

A great deal of the clutter has no bearing on questions of meter, chiefly because of elision, and also because many of the variants have the same syllabification and stress. Whether Chaucer wrote or "meant" *seyn* rather than *seyne* in line 1793 is of no moment, because the word is followed by *he* which at least for metrical purposes absorbs the *-e* in elision. (I think Chaucer would usually sound the *-e* of *seyne* because *soth to seyne* is a common phrase which seems to preserve an old inflected infinitive.) Even so, much of the variation does matter:

1793	For soth to seyne he lost helde euery wyght
	sothe loste wyghte
	loue
1794	But if he were in loues heigh seruise
	heyghe
1795	I mene folk that oughte it ben of right
	meen folke *om.* oughten righte
1796	And ouere al this so wele koude he deuyse
	alle wel he couth
	he cowde
1797	Of sentement and in so vnkoude wise
	sentmont *om.* unkouth
	sentementis uncouth a
1798	Al his array that euery louere thoughte
	Alle louer thoght
1799	That al was wel what so he seyde or wroughte
	alle wele euere be wroght
	loue thought

An editor or student might think only twenty-four places in this stanza require a decision. Nearly every place not before a vowel or unaspirated *h* and not a simple monosyllable like *he*, *in*, *so*, *of*, *was* presents a metrically differentiated choice of readings. What to do?

One possibility would be to follow the base manuscript. But unless we assume that the scribe writes exactly what Chaucer wrote, and that Chaucer invariably spelled so as to reflect the meter he wished to pronounce, we know that the spelling of any manuscript will not reveal the meter. These two assumptions are incredible.

Another possibility would be to spell each word according to a majority of manuscript readings. Either the word–take *soth* for example–would be spelled *soth* here because most manuscripts *at this place* read *soth*, or spelled *soth* because the word (in this grammatical context?) is so spelled by *Troilus* manuscripts or Chaucer manuscripts most of the time (if it is). A computer could make these determinations, but it would be useless because the majority readings, by either method, would only tell how a majority of scribes spell the word most of the time–it would tell little about how Chaucer would pronounce the word. A similar argument weighs against deciding on the "right" spelling according to some stemmatic, text-critical principles. Textual criticism has a hard enough time determining substantive readings with confidence, and is helpless before the accidentals of spelling.

I see no way to proceed if we wish to describe the meter of a line, other than to determine as best we can by other criteria how Chaucer's words in their various grammatical uses normally sound. If those other criteria generate a meter that is self-consistent throughout *Troilus*, or throughout Chaucer's poems, and furthermore a meter that shows a reasonable orderliness of repetitions (not merely something like "a line of five to thirty syllables"), then it may be accepted. Of course this method is the one adopted as the classical description of Chaucer's language and meter, from the time of Child and ten Brink. The other criteria are the histories of the individual words and the rules of accidence derivable from general Middle English grammar and–finally–from the symmetry of correspondence between hypotheses about grammar and hypotheses about meter. Applying these criteria yields a text very close to that of Corpus, and even closer to the text printed in the Riverside edition.

The criteria necessary to apply here to generate regular Chaucerian meter, traditionally called iambic pentameter, are not many. The nouns *soth*, *wyght*, *folk*, and *right* are regularly monosyllabic, as in Old English, and *sentement* from French has regularly this spelling. The weak past participles *lost* and *unkouth* (weak in form) regularly have no *-e*. The strong singular adjective *al* regularly has no *-e*. Monosyllabic *heigh*, in weak position after a possessive, is exceptional, but this adjective has so various an array of spellings that it should be considered simply variable (See Samuels 1972, 447, & Burnley 1982, 173). The first person singular verb *mene* has its expected *-e*, as do the weak preterite third person verbs *oughte* (*n*)(plural), *koude* (weak in form), *thoughte*, *seyde*, *wroughte*. The adverb *wel* is monosyllabic, as in Old English. Slurred *louere* was discussed above; agent nouns in *-er*(*e*)are variable. The other variants that affect the meter–*that* and *and* omitted, *loue* for *lost*, *he couth*(*e*) for *koude he*, *sentementis* for *sentement*, *loue* for *wel*, and *euere* for *so* (if a consonant follows)–cannot be excluded from consideration on grammatical grounds: these are substantive variants whose discrimination is the business of textual criticism.

Except for *heighe*, which would form a triplet if it were so pronounced, the expectations of etymology and grammar are fulfilled in this stanza as spelled in Corpus with two alterations, from *vnkoude* to *unkouth*, for grammar, and from *wele* to *wel.* If we chose manuscript H[3], six alterations would be required; if we chose A, seven; if we chose Cl (with *heighe*), none. Cps and Cls low frequency of unhelpful spellings has promoted them to the status of something like copy texts for the editors. A full study of Chaucer's meter might well begin with those two manuscripts, carefully and conservatively emended in places where strong evidence recommends other spellings.

The last major problem with Chaucer's meter is the classic one of both those lines which are not decasyllabic (or hendecasyllabic with feminine endings), and those lines whose patterns of stressed and unstressed syllables fail to maintain the regular alternation expected of iambic meter. The first group includes headless lines, lacking an unstressed syllable at the beginning; Lydgatian or broken-backed lines, lacking a weakly stressed syllable somewhere in mid-line and hence throwing two strongly stressed syllables together; and lines with extra weakly-stressed syllables in mid-line, that is, lines with triplets. The second group may be extended to include lines with "inverted feet," that is, lines of regular syllable count but uniambic stress pattern. Examples from the Riverside edition (with unsounded vowels in parentheses, and syllables promoted to stress by the metrical context marked with a grave accent):

> Fór it wér(e) a lóng digréssión (Tr 1.143) (headless)
> Ne sémed ít that shé òf hym róughte (1.496) (Lydgatian)
>
> x x
> Nas név(e)re yét seyn thýng to ben préysed dérre (1.174)
>
> (with triplet)
>
> x x
> Préyen for spéed, al shóld(e) I thérfor(e) stérve (1.17)
>
> (inverted, as are the next two)
>
> x x
> But yé lóver(e)s, that báthen ìn gladnésse (1.22)
>
> x x
> So fér am Í from his hélp ìn derknésse (1.18)

Our modern tolerance for these variations from iambic pentameter accords with their frequency in Chaucer: we least like Lydgatian lines, then headless ones, and triplets and inverted-stress lines scarcely trouble us when they are infrequent. Hence most editors "correct," with manuscript support, the examples of headless and Lydgatian lines given above . . . but do not tinker with the others. The rhythmic effect of lines with (mid-line) inverted stress of course resembles that of Lydgatian lines, but modern readers and editors reconcile themselves to spondees and pyrrhics, if the syllable count is right, as easily as they do to dactyls and anapests.

As the textual notes to the Riverside edition of *Troilus* show, headless and

Lydgatian lines are a major cause of scribal activity and editorial difference. Several scholars, including Kittredge and Baum, have dealt with these phenomena, but none has treated these lines systematically as they appear in a single unedited manuscript.

Corpus has these lines among its first thousand (to the right I give the Riverside reading when it differs in meter):

143	For it were a long disgression	
145	But the Troian gestes as they felle	
261	Of this kynges sone of which I tolde	
286	Shewed wel that man myght in hire gesse	
310	Ouer al thing he stood for to biholde	Riverside: alle
381	First to hiden his desire in muwe	
483	That the grekes as the deth him dredde	
490	That the hote fire of loue hym brende	
563	And art now falle in deuocioun	in: in som
589	And with angre don his wo to falle	
603	I wol parten with the alle thi peyne	
646	Loue ayeins the which wo so defendeth	
555	I that haue in loue so oft assayed	
649	Ek the ne aughte net ben yuel appayed	
728	Sholde falle or elles soone dye	He sholde
761	No quod Pandarus therfore I seye	
767	Dorste thow that I tolde in hire ere	
811	Twenty wynter that his lady wiste	
820	Of that word took hede Troilus	
860	Were it for my suster al thy sorwe	

A few lines in Corpus readable as headless I omit here because obvious spelling changes (*sterelees* for *sterlees* and the like) make them regular (lines 411, 416, 617 might be added to the list). A few more lines could be added if respelled according to Corpus's principles or altered on text-critical grounds. I may have missed a few or mis-scanned a few, but if this list of twenty lines is close to right, we might judge that Chaucer, as represented by this sample from the Corpus scribe, admits about two percent of headless lines.

These lines in the same sample from Corpus seem to me Lydgatian:

91	Ben worthy to be brent felle and bones	for to brennen
161	Palladions feste for to holde	Palladiones
496	Ne semed it that she of hym roughte	
539	Though neuere more thing ye me heete	byheete
681	But telle me plat what is thenchesoun	
812	That neuere yet his lady mouth kiste	he kiste
824	But bothe don vnmanhod and synne	a synne
829	To whom Pandare answerde if the like	answered

Again I omit a few lines where obvious spelling changes or slips of the pen affect the meter (96, 176, 234, 453, 583, 817). These are not very many instances, and of the eight six are so altered in the Riverside edition as to remove their Lydgatian scansion (I now think 829 need not have been altered). If this sample is typical, we would have to say that technically hypometric Lydgatian lines in Chaucer are rare, even though lines with a Lydgatian rhythm– clashing stresses because of inversion–are not uncommon.

It follows from these observations that the traditional description of Chaucer's verse as iambic pentameter is right, given the occasional licenses of inverted stress and extra syllables, of headless lines, and rarely of Lydgatian lines. Manuscripts like Corpus reveal by their spelling a meter that is rigorously consistent both with itself and with reasonable hypotheses about the sounds of words. The consequences of these findings for editing the text of Chaucer involve intricate complexities, and I will conclude with a few examples of the use of our knowledge of meter to determine what Chaucer wrote.

Among the twenty headless lines listed above, some or all major editors since Skeat (Skeat, McCormick, Root, Robinson, Baugh, Donaldson, Fisher, Windeatt) adopt readings from manuscripts other than Corpus that give non-headless readings in eight cases–lines 143 (all editors), 261 (all), 483, 563, 589, 649, 761, 820– and in three lines I too adopted readings, for grammatical or other text-critical reasons, that are non-headless (310, 555, 728). Only nine of the headless lines attract the consensus of modern editors.

Let us examine the first two headless lines of Corpus to exemplify how scribes and editors react. I list only variants that affect the syllabification of the lines (and omit the early printed texts):

143 For it were a long di(s)gression Cp Cl A H^5
For it were a longe discrecioun H^1 D S^2 Dg
For why it were a long disgressioun S^1 H^2
For why it were a longe disgrescioun Ph
For it were heere a long disgressioun J Gg
For it were here a longe disgressioun H^3
For it were right a long dygrescyoun R
For whi it were of to long discuscioun H^4
(Windeatt wrongly reads *ofte* for *of to*)

The *-e* of *longe* has no justification, so the manuscript groups are Cp Cl A H^5 H^1 D S^2 Dg, S^1 H^2 Ph, J Gg H^3, R, and H^4. As usual, these groups are not consistent with any scheme of manuscript families. In this part of the text, Root's *alpha* consists of H^2 Ph H^4, his *beta* of J Gg H^5 H^3 R, and his *gamma* of the rest, Cp Cl A H^1 D S^2 Dg (he regards S^1 as a *beta* manuscript contaminated by *gamma*). Only the *gamma* group looks right, with the intrusion of H^5, and of course I would argue that this group coheres here possibly because it is a real manuscript family, with its own hyparchetype, but perhaps simply because it preserves, as often, Chaucer's original text.

If we discount the manuscript reading *discrecioun* found in H^1 A H^5 as obviously wrong, any of these readings is plausible, although H^4 has rough meter. For me the decision to print the reading of Cp + was easy: it not only has the support of the most reliable manuscripts, especially Cp Cl H^1, but it also makes sense as the original from which the variants arose. An examination of the variants for headless lines as represented in Windeatt's apparatus will quickly reveal that headless lines elicit an unusual number of variant readings, usually in conflict with themselves and usually bland additions which make as if to smooth the meter. At least among the *Troilus* manuscripts we have evidence that some scribes did hear the meter of Chaucers lines, however falteringly, and made efforts to emend headless lines to regular decasyllables. This example is typical: the variants radiate from a presumed original in "split transmission," and no obvious reason suggests itself for why any of the non-Cp variants should have elicited the others. If J [St. Johns College, Cambridge, L.1] were the original, as all the editors but me have agreed, why should we have the other variants? Scribal substitution and omission of all kinds are abundant, and often inexplicable, but here the most trustworthy manuscripts permit a rational judgment.

The second line has provoked no disagreement among the editors:

145 But the Troian gestes as they fell(e) Cp J H^4 H^1 A S^2 Dg H3 Gg H^5
(D reads *Troians*; J has *all* interlin. after *gestes*)
But the Troiane gestes as they felle Cl S^1 Ph
But the troianes gestes as the fell(e) R H^2

The *-e* on *Troian* cannot be right, and I would think the three scribes had no intention of spelling it to be sounded. But the *-es* of R H^2 makes good sense, is partially supported by the *-s* of D, and could yield a rather strained non-headless line. If the *-es* represents an effort to smooth the meter (the J interlineators *all* scarcely helps), better expedients are at hand–the addition of any vapid syllable before or after *But* (*of* or *for* would do) would add a head to the line. The variants from Corpus are very weakly supported, no radiation of variants appears, and the *-es* may well have been induced by the neighboring *-es* of *gestes.* The editors rightly accept the headless line.

In *The Riverside Chaucer* only two of Corpus's Lydgatian lines in our sample remain. Again I record only variants that affect the syllabification:

496 Ne semed it that she of him roughte Cp Cl H^1 A
D S^2 Dg S^1 Gg
Ne semed(e) it as that she of him roughte J R H^4
H^5
Ne semyd hit as she of hit roght H^2 Ph (H^3 *out*)

All editors but me follow J R H^4 H^5. The reading of H^2 Ph gives poor grammar, and it arguably derives from J +, making a pretty good division between Root's *gamma* (here Cp +) vs. *alpha* and *beta*, with only Gg escaping from *beta* to *gamma*. Root's explanation for how the presumably mediate version, *gamma*, can oppose agreement of the earliest and latest versions is complex but conceivable; in any case it is not at issue now. The only question is, can we admit this well but imperfectly attested Lydgatian line?

Two considerations weighed with me: first, given a close decision I would (in optimism) side with the base manuscript; and second, the line in Corpus might be considered (in eclecticism) a *difficilior lectio* from the metrical point of view. This latter reason can weigh only lightly, because we cannot be sure how hard the average scribe tried to fix his exemplar's meter, or how well he understood Chaucer's system. We cannot suppose a scribe would deliberately create a Lydgatian line, but enough evidence of scribal tinkering with meter exists to let us think a scribe could "correct" a rare Chaucerian broken-backed line.

I retained the other Lydgatian line from Corpus with more confidence:

681 But telle me plat what is thenchesoun

The editorial problems of this line are treated in a later chapter, and I need not repeat my reasoning toward their solution.

In concluding I would reaffirm the need for deeper study of Chaucer's meter, for the sake of a better-founded literary criticism, textual criticism, and theory of phonology and meter. The science seemed to stop with the generation of Kittredge, whose work was inevitably incomplete. Obviously we should turn to mechanical word-processing for future exploration in the detail required. Proper study of meter can only rely on complete collation of the spellings of all the authorities, and few have the patience, even with the advent of microfilm, to undertake such labor–let computers do it for us.

NOTES

*Reprinted with permission from *Studies in Troilus: Chaucer's text, meter, and diction*, Medieval texts & studies, 14 (East Lansing: Colleagues Press, 1993), pp. 77–114.

[1]A very full bibliography on prosody is Brogan 1981: *English Versification, 1570–1980: A Reference Guide.* In spite of its title, this contains annotated references to the study of Chaucerian and Middle English meter. Also especially useful are the bibliographies compiled by Rae Ann Nager: "English: II. Bibliographical," in W. Wimsatt 1970; and "A Selective Bibliography of Recent Work in English Prosody" 1977 in *Style.* See also Gaylord 1976, "Scanning the Prosodists." Chaucerians should be familiar with ten Brink, *Chaucers Sprache und Verskunst* (Leipzig: Weigel, 1884), with revised editions by Kluge, 1901, and Eckhardt, 1920, and a translation of the 1901 edition by Smith (ten Brink 1901); and also Baum 1961. I would single out one admirable anthology of essays on meter, *The Structure of Verse: Modern Essays on Prosody* (Gross 1979), which reprints Otto Jespersen's brilliant "Notes on Metre" (pp. 105–128) from *Linguistica* (Copenhagen: Levin & Munksgaard, 1933), an essay that anticipates practically everything worthwhile in the modern study of meter, including Halle & Keyser's seminal essay (1966).

I should mention some more recent and valuable studies of meter, especially Chaucer's, that treat in more sophisticated ways topics less humble than my own (that is, my concern with what an editor needs to know). Typical of the intricacies of recent general studies of prosody from a linguistic and statistical point of view are Hayes 1984, "The Phonology of Rhythm in English"; Giegerich 1985, *Metrical Phonology and Phonological Structure* ; and Tarlinskaja 1984, "Rhythm-Morphology-Syntax-Rhythm" (all with full bibliographical notes). A series of articles by Minkova persuades me that final *-e*'s preservation or loss in English has to do with euphony and rhythm: Minkova 1987, "The Prosodic Character of Early Schwa Deletion in English," with refs. to her earlier work. Stanley's 1989 ruminations on Hoccleve's meter give the impression of a human being responding to poetry. Studies on the meter of the alliterative long line have bearing on *-e:* see especially Duggan 1988; Cable 1991, ch. 3: "Fourteenth-Century Meter: Final *-e.*"

[2]See for example Samuels 1972, and Burnley 1982. These excellent studies of Chaucer's phonology are aware of the need to work from actual manuscript readings; most studies of Chaucer's meter are vitiated by ignorance of this fact.

[3]Tr 1.551, 771; 2.264, 341; 3.849, 918; 4.297, 954, 988, 1033, 1058, 1605; 5.47. Now three other studies perform similar, equally persuasive examinations of meter in Chaucer (and Hoccleve) by locating lines in which the manuscripts offer little if any syllabic variation: Derek Brewer 1982; Jefferson 1987; and Cowen 1987.

[4]A future student of Chaucer's meter might welcome a list of lines, besides those listed from Windeatt above, in which the manuscripts *almost* agree on syllabification: Book I, lines 35, 58, 191, 215, 303, 326, 480, 519, 551, 778, 901, 970. With these and Windeatt's lines the total to work with comes to twenty-nine in the first thousand lines. More lines show syllabic variation, but are not likely to contain a final *-e* even when it appears in a scribes spelling (except at line end): Book I, lines 15, 29, 30, 32, 39, 40, 86, 114, 142, 164, 348, 466, 483, 554, 568, 591, 617, 645, 653, 678, 684, 721, 730, 773, 779, 780, 790, 811, 834, 845, 853, 871, 924, 927, 960. From these lines an inductive account of Chaucers meter might begin.

[5]Good brief accounts of the lexical and grammatical occurrences of *-e* are in the section "Language and Versification" by Davis in Chaucer 1987, pp. xxix–xlv); the same author's "Notes on Inflexions" in Davis 1979, pp. xv–xx; and the section on versification in Baugh's edition (Chaucer 1963, pp. xl–xlii). Baugh also says that *-e* is always pronounced at line-end and often before a cesura, but "otherwise it is pronounced when the meter requires it" (p. xli). He means doubtless only that students should pronounce the *-e*'s in his edition only when the meter requires, but even this is wrong and misleading. We need to distinguish truly *variable* words and inflectional endings, whose *-e* (for good historical reasons) may or may not be sounded in different contexts, from a number of classes of words and inflectional endings in which the presence or absence of *-e* is a matter of rule, and hence which are *irregular* when the rules are broken.

[6]But Eliot of course said "There is no escape from meter; there is only mastery": "Reflections on *Vers Libre*" (Eliot 1917).

[7]In "Prosody and the Study of Chaucer," Steve R. Guthrie ably defends the idea of iambs in Chaucerian meter (Guthrie 1988, 35–36). His study is based on the Corpus *Troilus* manuscript and contains valuable observations. Sometimes I doubt his ear: he thinks *wil* in *Troilus* 1.861 must have priority of stress over *my:*

Were it for my suster al thy sorwe
861 By my wil she sholde al be thyn to morwe

He writes (p. 46), "it is wrong to offer him meter-saving emphasis on *my* in the second line (as opposed to whose?)." Well, as opposed to his hypothetical sister's, or to Criseyde's, or best, as opposed to public opinion–no matter what they may say, by my will she shall be yours. I distrust metrical arguments that *depend* on such judgments of "rhetorical" or "performance" or "sense-context" stress, even though such judgments must be made.

[8]The principle is W.K. Wimsatt's (1970, 785) and is developed by Guthrie (1988, 41–44).

[9]After writing this I came upon Donaldson's essay which makes a similar point, "Adventures

with the Adversative Conjunction in the Gen. Prol. . . . " (Benskin & Samuels 1981).

[10]On the question of *-e* and *-en* see Smither's 1983. The Corpus distribution of *-e* and *-en* tends to counter Smithers's conclusions, and I further doubt his exclusion of the "trisyllable foot" from Chaucers practice. I hope to treat this problem in another place.

[11]The other instances are in lines *486*, 587, 589, 592, 614, *623*, 629, 648, 668, 690, 698, 702, *703*, 734 *gladen*, 738, *747*, 751, 763, *784*, *789*, 794, 799, 808, 813, 838, 865, 978, *989 peyne*, 990. Italicized numbers indicate infinitives spelled with *-e* rather than *-en*.

[12]Apart from the discussion above, on the exceptional noun *love* see Kitttredge 1891, 368 & 372; and McJimsey 1942, 113–14.

[13]Infinitives riming with other infinitives occur in lines 11, 12, 83, 84, 142, 144, 190, 192, 235, 236, 256, 257, 277, 278, 295, 297, 300, 301, 310, 313, 389, 390, 391, 392, 426, 427, 443, 445, 446, 503, 504, 510, 511, 562, 564, 596, 598, 650, 651, 671, 672, 685, 686, 688, 691, 755, 756, 806, 808, 848, 850, 865, 866, 869, 871.

[14]The detailed study by McJimsey 1942 treats Chaucer's use of *-e* in monosyllabic nouns, as far as it can be determined from the Globe (and *Concordance*) text and Robinson's first edition (1933). She examined all the monosyllabic nouns for which the edited lines give evidence of the presence or absence of *-e*. Her net is too wide; she does not take proper account of elision before unaspirated *h*. Even so, her conclusions are congruent with mine. Her findings for my list of nouns that rime with infinitives follows. In parenthesis I list the number of times in Chaucer's works (excluding *Romaunt*) in which the word seems *not* to have *-e* according to McJimsey.

A. Nouns normally with *-e* but sometimes without it: peyne (3), ese (1), grace (6), dede ["deed"] (1), drede (2), side (1), lawe (2), kinde (2), wise (5), while (4), hewe (1), preue (4), hede ["heed"] (4), speche (2), nede (12), wrecche (1), synne (2), helle (1), welle (2), tyde (2), vice (1).

B. Nouns always with *-e*: chere, whippe, mynde, wile, lite.

C. Nouns often with *-e*: sighte, herte, tyme, last, bliss.

McJimsey inexplicably does not treat the words muwe, cure, cheyne, awe.

Part Two:
Essays Combining History, Theory, and Close Reading

Richard H. Osberg

"I kan nat geeste": Chaucer's Artful Alliteration

Unlike the poetry of Shakespeare, Spenser, Dryden, Dante, Petrarch, and Boccaccio, Chaucer's verse has never received modern systematic analysis with regard to his alliterative practices.[1] This lacuna in the study of Chaucer's prosody is due in part, one suspects, to the older received notion of alliterative verse (poetry composed with "lel lettres loken"–the poetry of the Gawain-poet, William Langland, and the *Gest Historiale of the Destruction of Troy*, for instance) as northern and western, anti-French and anti-Ricardian, as in John Speirs' classic 1958 study of such verse: the *Non-Chaucerian Tradition.* Because Chaucer's Parson is a "Southren man" who "kan nat geeste 'rum, ram, ruf' by lettre," the assumption seems to have been, so too Chaucer must have regarded alliteration as a northern mannerism: rustic, provincial, inferior. Such prejudice about the speech of northern men would not have been unique; in his interpolation in Higden's *Polychronicon* concerning the development of English, John Trevisa notes of northern England that "vplondisshe men wil likene hym self to gentil men and fondeth with greet besynesse for to speke frensce."[2] For most readers, then, Chaucer does not alliterate at all, or if he does, does so only in passages appropriate to an imitation of northern alliterative long-line verse.[3]

Although the present essay confines itself largely to alliteration in *The Canterbury Tales,* it aims to show that alliteration and phonological foregrounding (that is, instances in which the "melos" of the verse obtrudes on the reader's attention) are far more frequent and artful in Chaucer's verse than has been recognized heretofore. Once freed from the assumption that Chaucer's alliteration is a response solely to northern romance conventions, we can see alliteration in Chaucer as a continuum of phonological habits (ornament, "poetic" texture, and subtle effects of rhetoric and signification) which, more than simply being a minor chord in Chaucer's "music,"[4] demonstrates a variety of resonances that range from high seriousness to parody.[5]

In another, more subtle gesture of disdain for alliterative verse, Chaucer has Harry Bailly suppress Chaucer-the-pilgrim's "rym dogerel" by inviting him to demonstrate whether "thou kanst tellen aught in geeste" (VII 933),[6] as if to say, "rime is certainly beyond you, but perhaps you can alliterate," and indeed, two passages in Chaucer's poetry that exhibit an unusual density of alliteration,[7] the tournament scene in "The Knight's Tale" and the sea-battle in "The Legend of Good Women," have been often described as simulacra of the alliterative romance tradition,[8] or, as Paull Baum suggests, "a deliberate imitation of the Anglo-Saxon long line" (Baum 1961, 56). Nonetheless, a close examination of these two passages in the light of Thomas Cable's and Hoyt Duggan's recent elucidations of the metrical principles governing alliterative verse[9] makes it even more unlikely that Chaucer has for the northern alliterative long-line verse what Dorothy Everett called a "good ear."[10]

The description of the tournament in "The Knight's Tale" has long been cited as evidence that Chaucer knew and imitated the northern alliterative long- line (critical discussion of these passages may be found in Jacobs 1972; Baum 1961, 55–59; Elliott 1974, 103; Blake 1969; and Fries 1985, 58–59):

> *Ther* is namoore to seyn, but west and est
> *In goon* the **s**peres ful **s**adly in arrest;
> *In gooth* the **sh**arpe **s**pore into the **s**yde.
> *Ther* seen men who kan juste and who kan ryde;
> *Ther* **sh**yveren **sh**aftes upon **sh**eeldes thikke;
> *He feeleth* thurgh the herte-spoon the prikke.
> Up **spr**yngen **sp**eres twenty foot on highte;
> *Out goon* the **s**werdes as the **s**ilver brighte;
> The **h**elmes they to**h**ewen and toshrede;
> *Out* b*rest* the **b**lood with **st**ierne **st**remes rede;
> With **m**yghty **m**aces the **b**ones they to**b**reste.
> *He* **th**urgh the **th**ikkeste of the **th**rong gan **th**reste;
> *Ther* **st**omblen **st**eedes **st**ronge, *and* doun gooth al,
> *He rolleth* under foot as dooth a bal;
> *He* **f***oyneth* on his **f**eet with his tronchoun,
> *And* **h***e hym* **h***urtleth* with his **h**ors adoun;
> *He* thurgh the body is hurt and sithen take,
> Maugree his heed, *and* broght unto the stake.[11]

Stephen Knight remarks of this passage: "It is not alliterative poetry, it just sounds rather like it. Chaucer could no doubt have written a thumping piece in the metre of the alliterative *Morte Arthure* had he chosen to, but here as elsewhere suggestion is the purpose of his stylistic modulation."[12]

A comparison of Chaucer's description of the naval engagement in the *Legend of Good Women* with two similar accounts, one in alliterative long-lines, one in alliterative accentual-syllabic meter, further demonstrates how inconclusive is the evidence for the influence of alliterative long-line verse on Chaucer's poetry. On 30

August 1350, off Winchelsea, King Edward III won a significant naval encounter against the Castilian fleet under the command of Charles de la Cerda. In the alliterative *Morte Arthure*, "the Spaniards" who leap overboard at line 3700 have also been thought to allude to the sea battle off Winchelsea.[13] A comparison of this account with Laurence Minot's poem on the same subject and Chaucer's description of a naval engagement between Octavian and Anthony reveals much about Chaucer's alliterative practices.

After the ships grapple, the battle described in the alliterative *Morte Arthure* proceeds with armed knights boarding:

> Brushes boldly on borde   brenyed knightes,   rush, armed
> Out of botes on borde,   was busked with stones,   pelted
> Bete down of the best,   bristes the hatches;
> Some gomes through-gird   with godes of iron,   kights pierced, goads
> Gomes gaylich cledde   englaimes wepenes;   clad, make slimy
> Archers of England   full egerly shootes,
> Hittes through the hard steel   full hertly dintes!   strikes, mortal
> Soon ochen in holly   the hethen knightes,   completely cuts down
> Hurt through the hard steel,   hele they never!   heal
>
> (*Morte Arthure* 1984)

Although there is little agreement about the metrical details of alliterative long- line verse, the salient features include a four-stress line (this is accentual verse, in which metrical stress and lexical stress coincide) broken by a notable cesura, the first half-line containing (usually) two alliterating stressed syllables (staves), the second half-line (usually) one alliterating and one non-alliterating stave; the patterns aa / ax ; aaa / ax ; axa / ax ; aax / ax and xaa / ax predominating. Lines are linked by alliterative recurrence (b, g, and h-vocalic alliteration here). All the salient features enumerated by Duggan are present in these lines:

1. Alliterative patterns aa / ax ; aaa / ax ; axa / ax ; aax / ax and xaa / ax

> Then **b**rothly they **b**eker   with **b**ustous tackle;   aa / ax
> **B**rushes **b**oldly on **b**orde   **b**renyed knightes,   aaa / ax

2. Alliteration always falls on a stressed syllable (coincides with normal prose phrasal stress):

> Out of **b**ótes on **b**órde,   was **b**úsked with stónes, aa / ax

3. Distinct half-lines with cesura and 4. Each half-line has two staves separated by dips:

> **B**éte dówn of the **b**ést, / **b**rístes the hátches;   axa / ax

4. In the B verse, there are two lifts and one to three dips; if two or three dips are filled, only one can contain two or more syllables:

(1) was **b**úsk |(2) ed with |(3) stónes

By contrast, Chaucer's description of the Battle of Actium in *The Legend of Good Women* seems merely to hint at this alliterative meter:

And in the se   it happede hem to mete.
Up goth the trompe,   and for to **sh**oute and **sh**ete,
And peynen hem   to **s**ette on with the **s**unne.
With **g**rysely soun   out **g**oth the **g**rete **g**onne,
And **h**eterly they **h**urtelen   al atones,
And from the top   doun come the grete stones.
In **g**oth the **g**rapenel,   so ful of crokes;
Among the **r**opes **r**enne   the sherynge-hokes.
In with the **p**olax   **p**reseth he and he;
Byhynde the mast   begynnyth he to fle,
And **out** ageyn,   and dryveth hym **o**verbord;
He **s**tyngeth hym   upon his **s**peres ord;
He rent the **s**eyl   with hokes lyke a **s**ithe;
He **b**ryngeth the cuppe   and **b**iddeth hem be **b**lythe;
He **p**oureth **p**esen   upon the haches slidere;
With pottes ful of lyme   they **g**on to**g**idere;
And thus the longe day   in fyght they spende . . .

Removed from their accentual-syllabic metrical context, most of these lines do not, in fact, resemble alliterative long lines. Alliterative patterns are rare or unmetrical: ax/ax, xa/xa, xx/aa, aa/xx; many lines have only three staves; one second half-line has three alliterative staves. Even within the accentual-syllabic tradition, however, Chaucer so frequently places in a position of ictus a word that normally does not have lexical stress–a pronoun or a preposition, for instance– that some scholars have read Chaucer as an accentual poet, as Arthur Wayne Glowka recounts:

A scanner intent on finding four-stress lines in *The Canterbury Tales* . . . has little trouble scanning fairly pleasant four-stress verse:

Whán that Áprill with his shóures sóote
The dróghte of Márch hath pérced to the róote,
And báthed every véyne in swích licóur
Of whích vertú engéndred is the flóur (I 1–4)

The scansion suppresses the bumps, however slight, of the scannable prepositions *with* in line 1 and *to* in line 2, the quantifying determiner *every* in line 3, and the

> linking verb **is** in line 4, but strong-stress meter allows such strings of unstressed syllables between stressed ones. . . . In such a performance of these lines, it is interesting to note the strings of three unstressed syllables in the lines (where the forgotten stresses are) and their position in regard to the strong stresses. Chaucer varies their position, and although he was thinking of fives, his ear varied arrangements of fours. The lines that we have here offer the unstressed strings after the second, the third, the first, and the third stresses in each line respectively.
> (Glowka 1991, 80)

When Elliott notes that the meter of lines I 2605, 2612, and 2615 resembles that of regular alliterative long lines:

Ther shyveren shaftes   upon sheeldes thikke;
He thurgh the thikkeste   of the throng gan threste;
And he hym hurtleth   with his hors adoun;

he is actually noting that the string of three unstressed syllables happens to fall around the cesura, occasioned by prepositions occupying the third foot stress position, 2605 and 2616 following exactly the same syntactical structure of sub-verb / prep noun adj (adv). It would be surprising, were Chaucer deliberately imitating four-stress alliterative long lines, not to find a greater number of such lines, but in this passage from the Knight's tale such strings fall, as Glowka notes of the lines in the GP, in a fairly random distribution, two in the first ictus position, five in the second, four in the third and five in the fourth; two lines have five strong stresses.

What is surprising, then, in the passage from *The Legend of Good Women* is that in eleven of these lines, the second half-line contains a dip of three syllables (at the fourth ictus position), for instance:

1   2   3   4   5
He bryngeth the cuppe / and biddeth hem be blithe.

These second half-lines all resemble a single kind of alliterative second half-line in which a dip of three unstressed syllables alternates with one of one. Such second half-lines do occur in alliterative verse, of course, the first unarguable instance in *Sir Gawain and the Green Knight* occurring in line 62, "Fro the king watz cummen with knyghtes into the halle." This high concentration of strings of unaccented syllables at the fourth ictus position (11 of 17 lines, 64 percent) suggests that here indeed Chaucer was attempting a metrical echo of the "swing" of alliterative verse, although not necessarily that of the alliterative long-line romance.

Norman Blake sensibly suggests that these two alliterating passages in Chaucer's poetry may respond to a much larger range of alliterative work, both poetry and prose, which Chaucer was far more likely to have known than the alliterative long-line romances (Blake 1969, 164); and the metrical "swing" of Chaucer's alliterative verse seems comparable to the "swing" of Laurence Minot's account of *Espagnols sur la mer*:

Thai sailed furth in the Swin in a somers tyde — the river Zwin; time
with trompes and taburns and mekill other pride — trumpets and drums; great

When thai sailed westward, tho wight men in were, — those strong; war
thaire hurdis, thaire ankers hanged thai on here. — bulwarks; anchors
Wight men of the west neghed tham nerr — approached nearer and nearer
and gert tham snaper in the snare–might thai no ferr — made; stumble; get away
Fer might thai noght flit, bot thare most thai fine, — flee; die (come to an end)
and that thai bifore reved than most thai tyne. — what; plundered; lose
(Minot 1996, ll. 1–2, 13–8, p. 61)

Note particularly Minot's reliance on half-lines with three dips, deployed as both first ("Fer might thai noght flit") and second half-lines ("and mekill other pride"). These extended dips, which create the "swing" of Minot's verse, seem to be what, in his lines on the Battle of Actium, Chaucer gestures toward by clustering three lexically unstressed syllables at the fourth ictus position. Another characteristic of Minot's alliterative verse is the tendency to alliterate only within the half-line ("and gert tham **sn**aper in the **sn**are–might thai no ferr"), a tendency also common in Chaucer's lines (e.g. "Up goth the trompe, and for to **sh**oute and **sh**ete").

Of non-metrical stylistic features, Elliott and Everett note the occurrence of a number of words either unique to these passages, "herte-spoon," "toshrede," "stomblen," and "tronchoun," or rare in Chaucer's lexicon. Despite alliterative phrases like "helm tohewen," however, only two traditional alliterative collocations occur in Chaucer's two battle descriptions and also in alliterative long-line poems: "Ther *shyvеren* shaftes upon *sheeldes* thikke," which occurs as "thaire *sheldes* war *shiferd* and helms rifen / Ful stalworth strakes war thare gifen" in *Ywaine* (3539–40), and as "*scheuyrde scheldes*" in *Guy of Warwick*, 8153 and elsewhere (Oakden 1935; II: 300, 336). In the Battle of Actium, another single alliterative collocation is shared with alliterative poems (*stongen* wyth a *spere*, *Tolous*, 645; with *spere ystonge*, *Octavien* I, 962 [Oakden 1935; II: 338]). Note, too, that characteristic alliterative long-line diction, "buernes," "derffe," "dyntes," "ferlies," for instance, is not to be found in Chaucer's lines.

In addition to the density of alliteration, however, Chaucer's battle passages also exhibit a stylistic use of repetition (particularly anaphora) and parallelism that does seem to echo alliterative long-line practice, as exhibited, for instance, in the following lines from the *Gest Hystoriale of the Destruction of Troy*:

In this shall faithfully be founden, to the fer ende,
All the dedis bydene as thai done were: — utterly
How the groundes first grew, and the grete hate,
Bothe of torfer and tene that hom tide aftur, — hardship, grief, befell
And here fynde shall ye faire of the felle peopull: — fierce
What kynges ther come of costes aboute; — qualities
Of dukes full doughty, and of derffe erles, — doughty
That assemblid to the citie that sawte to defend; — assault
Of the Grekys that were gederet, how gret was the nowmber,

How mony knightes there come, and kynges enarmede,
And what dukes thedur droghe for dedis of were; — thither
What shippes there were shene, and shalkes within, — men
Bothe of barges and buernes that broght were fro Grese: — knights
And all the batels on bent the buernes betwene;
What duke that was dede through dyntes of hond,
Who fallen was in fylde, and how it fore after.
Bothe of truse and of trayne the truth shalt thu here, — truce, guile
And all the ferlies that fell, unto the ferre ende. — marvels

(Gibbs 1966; lines 78–95)

The repetition of such parallel syntactical elements as *All the dedis*; *And all the batels*; *all the ferlies* and *Bothe of torfer and tene*; *Bothe of barges and buernes*; *Bothe of truse and of trayne* as well as *How the groundes*; *how gret was the nowmber*; *How mony knightes*; *how it fore after* and *What kynges ther come*; *And what dukes thedur droghe*; *What shippes there were*; *What duke that was dede*, creates a rhetorically elevated style that Chaucer might be thought to echo in his own use of anaphora and parallelism: *Ther is, Ther seen, Ther shyveren, Ther stomblen; In goon, In gooth; Out goon, Out brest.* Anaphora, however, also characterizes numerous stanzas in Boccaccio, as, for example, stanza 90, describing how the noble spectators survey the field of battle:

E similmente assai chiaro notava
l'opere di ciascuno e 'l suo ferire;
e chi la morte per onor cercava,
e chi temeva per gloria morire,
e chi più arte en la battaglia usava,
e chi aveva o più o meno ardire,
e chi schifava e chi facea niente,
tutto vedea in sé tacitamente.

(Boccaccio 1964, II: 526)

[And likewise one notes clearly the deeds of each one and the wounding of others, and who searches for death with honor and who fears to die with glory, and who uses the greater art in battle, and who possesses more boldness and who less, and who flinches and who did nothing–all was witnessed within, silently.]

Other stylistic characteristics of alliterative long-line verse noted by Oakden (the use of an infinitive in the second half-line preceded by a word beginning with the required alliterative sound, e.g., "That assemblid to the citie *that sawte to defend*"; tags like "all the batel *on bent*" and "the *truth* shalt thu *here*"; a fondness for beginning a line with "For . . ."; and the absolute use of the adjective) simply do not occur in Chaucer's lines, although they do find ample play in Chaucer's "Tale of Sir Thopas" as discussed later. In fact, Chaucer's alliterative practice here is not dissimilar from that of the riming romances. Compare, for instance, this battle description from a riming romance of Charlemagne, "The Sege off Melayne":

Thay **f**ruschede in **f**ersely for Goddis sake; charged; fiercely
Grete strokes **g**ane thay **g**yffe and take,
With **w**ondis **w**erkande **w**yde. painful
Bot yitt the **S**arazens with thayr **s**peris
Full ferre on **b**akke oure **b**atelle **b**erys push our army far in retreat
And knyghtis **f**elde undir **f**ete.
(Shepherd 1995, 278)

N.F. Blake comments on Chaucer's alliterative passages, "These two passages do raise the question why Chaucer should have used such a concentration of alliteration here. We tend to be surprised at this concentration only because we forget or are unaware of how much alliteration Chaucer did in fact use in his poetry" (Blake 1969, 165). These two passages have been singled out at least in part, I suspect, on the basis of generic considerations–tournaments and sea-battles are common topoi of alliterative long-line romances. However, other common alliterative topoi, for instance the famous "storm-topos," simply do not seem in Chaucer to have elicited an alliterative response.[14] The alliterative density of the sea battle and tournament scenes appears much less distinctive, however, when seen in the larger context suggested by Blake, including Latin, French, and Italian practice, a context in which Chaucer's alliteration emerges as a significant aspect of his prosody.

I. The Alliterative Environment in the Late Fourteenth Century

That Chaucer might have known something of the alliterative long-line is perhaps not as far-fetched an idea as Blake would have it; in the precincts of St. Paul's in the 1390's someone, perhaps John Tickhill, was writing unrimed alliterative verse which survives as "A Byrd in Bishopswood" (Kennedy 1987); and as early as 1375, in "The Lament for Sir John Berkeley"–"He reweld him o reson, he rested on right, / He was a housholder, a hunter ful hiende" (38–39)–rimed alliterative verse is associated with the landed gentry (Turville-Petre 1982). The rimed alliterative poetry of Laurence Minot,[15] celebrating the victories of Edward III in Scotland and France from 1333 to 1352, might have been familiar to Chaucer, as might the well-established tradition of devotional alliterative prose.[16] There was as well in the fourteenth century a strong tradition of rimed verse with alliteration of the stressed syllables, in the courtly lyrics of MS Harley 2253 for instance (1325–1350, probably near Hereford or perhaps Ludlow), and in the religious and devotional materials of the Vernon (Bodl. 3938, c. 1385) and Simeon manuscripts (BM Addit. 22283, late 14th c.) both in lyric and prose.[17]

For so well-read a poet as Chaucer, alliteration was undoubtedly merely one color in the Latin rhetorical spectrum; in Vergil he would have discovered the alliterative ornamentation of syllables, the sibilance of Hybla's bees, for instance:

Hyblaeis apibus florem depasta **s**alicti
saepe levi **s**omnum **s**uadebit inire **sus**urro. (*Eclogues*: 1.54–55; ed. Fairclough)
[willow blossoms sipped by Hybla's bees shall often with gentle hum soothe you to sleep].

Other instances are less onomatopoeic: the apples of Amaryllis, "cui **p**endere sua **p**atereris in arbore **p**oma" (*Eclogues* 1.37: "for whom you let the apples hang on their native trees"); and the refrain line of Eclogue VIII, "**D**ucite ab urbe **d**omum, mea carmina, **d**ucite **D**aphnim (line 68): "Bring Daphnis home from town, bring him, my song". Lucretius also provides examples of alliterative ornamentation:

cogit uti fiat spisso **c**ava **c**orpore **c**ircum (*De Rerum Natura* 6.127; ed. Smith 1975) : "compels the cloud more and more in every direction to form a hollow with a thick crust all around")
Semina quae **f**aciunt **f**lammae **f**ulgere colores. (*De Rerum Natura*, 6.213: "pour forth seeds which make the colors of flame to lighten")[18]

Lucretius also uses alliteration for onomatopoeic effects:

. . . **d**iscludere **t**urris,
disturbare **d**omos, avellere **t**igna **t**rabesque *(De Rerum Natura*, 6.240–41: "[thunderbolts] split open towers with a stroke, overturn houses, tear out beams and rafters").

Closer to hand, perhaps, he might have discovered models in what may be termed popular battle poetry, in both English and Latin:

To the kyng edward hii **f**asten huere **f**ay;
fals wes here **f**oreward so **f**orst is in may.
(Robbins, ed. 1959, 15; ". . . false was their promise as frost is in May")

Francia **fl**os **fl**orum, caput olim nobiliorum,
Jam contra mores leopardus tollit honores.
Subpedito **fl**orem, rapio **fl**orentis honorem,
Flos **f**ueram, **f**ormido **f**eram cum jubare veram.
(Wright, ed. 1859, I: 40)

[France is the flower of flowers, the capital once of those of nobler birth. Now, against his nature, the leopard carries off the honors. I supply the flower, I seize the glory of him that prospers. Once I was the flower; now I fear the real beast with its splendor.]
(Trans. from Minot 1989, 96)

Besides such popular poetry, there was, too, an alliterative tradition in what might be termed the clerkly or "art" poetry in Latin and Anglo-Norman:

> **P**etre, **p**iis **p**lausibus **p**ro **p**etra **p**unito,
> **P**laudat **p**ræsens **p**opulus **p**ectore **p**olito;
> (Wright & Halliwell 1845, II: 20)
>
> [Peter, with purified hearts the people here give reverent praise for the rock once slain.]

> **S**oule **s**u, **s**imple, e **s**aunz **s**olas,
> **s**eignury me **s**omount **s**ojouner
> (Wright & Halliwell 1845, II: 256)
>
> [Should I suffer alone, free and without solace, his lordship bids me to remain.]

Alliterative ornament may be found as well in French courtly poetry, either as an extended exercise, as it is in the opening lines of Froissart's first ballade:

> **J**one, **j**oians, **j**olie et amoureuse,
> **B**onne, **b**elle, **b**ien faite et **b**ien parlans,
> **S**age, **s**oués, courtoise et gra**ti**euse,
> **L**ie, **l**oyaus, **l**egiere et avenans,
> **F**rance, **fr**ice, **f**aitice et trés plaisans,
> **D**ame d'onneur, de bien enluminee,
> **D**ame **d**igne d'estre en tous lieus amee:
> (Quoted in James Wimsatt, *Chaucer* 1991b, 184–85)
>
> [Young, joyful, pretty, and loving, good, beautiful, well-formed, and well-spoken, smart, gentle, courteous, and gracious, happy, loyal, easy, and agreeable, noble, animated, shapely, and very pleasant, a lady of honour, shining with goodness, a lady worthy to be loved everywhere; trans. Wimsatt]

or in isolated lines:

> S'ai bien **c**uesi
> Quant j'ai en **c**oer tel flourette en**c**eri
> Qui **s**ans **s**emen**c**e et **s**ans **s**emeur o**ss**i
> **P**remierement hors de terre a**pp**ari.
> (James Wimsatt, *Chaucer* 1991b)
>
> [Thus I have well chosen when I have cherished in my heart such a flower (the daisy), which first appeared from the earth without seed and without being sown.]

It is not surprising, perhaps, that Chaucer's portraits of courtly ladies (and their country cousins) tend to alliterative ornament. Italian, too, offered models for imitation. Alliteration in Dante, Petrarch, and Boccaccio, particularly of non-initial syllables, might well have caught Chaucer's eye and ear (see Robey 1988):

> la **qu**ale e'l **qu**ale, a **v**oler dir lo **v**ero: "and both, to tell the truth" (*Inferno* ii, 22)
> **le l**ingue **l**or non **si s**entono **s**tanche: "their tongues are never weary" (*Inferno* xxii, 90)
> ve**d**ilo an**d**ar pien **d**'ira e **di dis**d**egno: "see him go full of wrath and disdain" (*Trionfi* 1.1.98)
> con**t**ra **tutt**a **T**oscana **t**enne un pon**t**e: "against all Tuscany held a bridge" (*Trionfi* 4.1.81)
> a **p**ianger **p**iù che non **f**aremmo **f**orse: "to weep more than we would, perhaps" (*Teseida* 2.27)
> e **f**ece **l**oro il **l**oro a**ff**ar pa**l**ese: "and make their business manifest to them" (*Teseida* 2.53)

It is in the context of this larger range of sources, I will argue, that we should look to discover the complexities of alliterative practice in Chaucer's verse. The parallels drawn below between alliterative passages in Chaucer's work and passages from other traditions are not intended to suggest specific sources for Chaucer's poetry. Rather, they will, I hope, suggest the very broad range of alliterative conventions available to Chaucer in the 1380's and 1390's, conventions which he assimilated and evoked for particular aesthetic ends.

II. Traditional Collocations and the Inferred Rules of Alliteration

The earliest study of Chaucer's alliteration examined his use of traditional collocations and alliterative formulae, and this work was the basis for Oakden's catalogue of those formulae shared between Chaucer and the body of alliterative verse and prose. Oakden found 279 alliterative phrases in Chaucer, 98 of which are also to be found in Gower. Chaucer shares the largest numbers of phrases, however, with poems of the alliterative revival (191 phrases) and the riming romances (164 phrases).[19] Not surprisingly, these are the most traditional collocations: "toun and tour," "wepyng and wo," "jangle as a jay," "make amend," and so forth. Such formulae seem to serve two purposes in Chaucer's prosody. In the first instance, Chaucer uses formulas to bridge the cesura:

> Which that he **l**ovede   moore than his **l**yf (I 3222)
> With **l**okkes crulle   as they were **l**eyd in presse (I 81)
> And though that he were **w**orthy,   he was **w**ys (I 68)
> And sende hym **d**rynke,   or elles moste he **d**eye (VII 2042)
> For be he **l**ewed man,   or ellis **l**ered (VI 283)

This practice is, however, much less common than is the use of formulas for rime words:

My gold caused my mordre, *sooth to sayn* (VII 3021)
Thy mynde is lorn, thou *janglest as a jay* (II 774)
But shortly for to *telle* is myn *entente* (I 1000)

Sometimes it is the case, as McClumpha noted (1906,35), that the second term of the formula has its accent shifted from the alliterative syllable to the rime syllable:

It were to me a *gret guerdoun* (RR 2611)
But sikerly she hadde a *fair forheed* (I 154)
Certeyne *dayes* and *duracioun* (I 2996)

In the deployment of such collocations, alliteration is simply a happenstance, and it can be generally argued that lines with two alliterating syllables in Chaucer probably do not constitute phonological foregrounding, even though in certain instances such "twice-struck" alliteration (I am indebted to Alan Gaylord for this coinage) can provide rhetorical "italics" as it were or be itself the by-product of certain rhetorical tropes familiar to medieval writers from such texts as the *Rhetorica ad Herennium* of Pseudo-Cicero[20]:

1. "Traductio" or "polyptoton"–"a class of figures which repeat a word or words by varying their word-class (part of speech) or by giving different forms of the same root or stem." (This, p. 967, and subsequent definitions are from NPEPP.)

Ther was no *boond* with which men myghte him *bynde* (VII 2072)
He *let* his *lyf*, and there I *lete* hym dwelle (VII 306)
O *cursed* synne of alle *cursednesse* (VI 895)

2. "Iteratio" or "Ploce"–"the genus of figures for word repetition, with or without intervening words, generally in close proximity" (NPEPP, 916).

He seyde he *lovede* and was bi*loved* no thyng (V 946)
That my *wyl* was his *willes* instrument (V 568)
Hir child *cride*, and she *cride* pitously. (II 919)

3. "Antimetabole"–"A species of chiasmus, or word repetition in reverse" (NPEPP, 79).

Forsaketh synne, er synne yow forsake (VI 286).
For hote of cold, for cold of hote, I dye (TC 420)
[A rhetorical figure not caught out of Petrarch's "e tremo a mezza state, ardendo il verno," which it translates.]

4. "Antanaclasis"–"repetition of a word with a shift in meaning" (NPEPP, 968).

The *Creatour* of every *creature* (VIII 49)

Nonetheless, some lines in Chaucer which exhibit extensive alliteration arise neither from traditional collocation nor from rhetorical figure:

axxaa Or **h**oord of apples leyd in **h**ey or **h**eeth (I 3262)
aaxxa **F**ledden for **f**ere, whan the wode was **f**alle (I 2930)
aaaxa Of **br**as they **br**oghten **b**emes, and of **b**ox (VII 3398)
aabab How **m**anye **m**yghte she have in **m**ariage (III 23)

Setting aside the use of traditional alliterative collocations, Chaucer's use of alliteration as part of the "music" of the verse resembles in large part that of Shakespeare, Spenser, and Dryden; that is, in particular lines, stressed syllables alliterate, but alliteration is neither a structural principle nor a sustained device, although a number of axioms can be inferred from Chaucer's practice:

1. The alliterative syllable generally coincides with lexical stress:

Hou **m**yghte David **m**ake thee so **m**aat (II 935)
And **pr**echest on thy bench, with yvel **pr**eef (III 247)
To **wh**om she **h**adde al **h**ool hir **h**erte yive (V 1450)

1a. Occasionally, syllables without lexical stress but promoted by ictus alliterate (e.g., "hem," "he," "to," "with"):

And do al th*yn* entente and th*y* corage (IX 164)
And **b**reketh b*othe* **b**owes and the leves (I 1639)

1b. Occasionally, syllables with tertiary stress in polysyllables, especially when promoted by ictus, alliterate:

Com **f**orth now, with thyne eyen **c**olumbyn!
How **f**airer **b**een thy **b**restes than is wyn! (IV 2141–42)

2. There is some evidence that Chaucer allows vocalic alliteration:

Fulfild of **i**re and **o**f in**i**quitee (I 940)
For **ou**t and **ou**t he **i**s the worthi**e**ste (TC II 739)
Til **b**othe the **ey**r and **e**rthe **b**rende (Fame 954)

2a. Occasionally, "h" apparently alliterates with initial vowels as it does in alliterative long-line poems:

With **a**ll her **oo**st, **e**rly and late (RR 5859)
Heven, **e**rthe, and **e**ke the see (Fame 846)
But maketh **h**oundes **e**te hem in despit (I 947)

3. Chaucer does not distinguish consonantal clusters; s alliterates with sp, st, sw; c [k] alliterates with cl, cr; and so on. (Apparently even the distinct phonemes sh and th alliterate with s and t, as McClumpha notes, a variety of weak or "eye" alliteration):

As though a storm sholde **br**esten every **b**ough (I 1980)
[br with b]
That **fr**othen whit as **f**oom for ire wood (I 1659) [fr with f]
Thus **s**at, thus **sp**ak, thus **sp**an; this was hire chere (LGW 1762)
[s with sp]
Shoon as the burned gold with **str**emes **br**ighte (V 1247)
[sh with str; b with br]

4. Alliteration may link several lines:

A **b**rooch she **b**aar upon hir **l**owe co**l**er,
As **b**rood as is the **b**oos of a **b**okeler. (I 3265–66)

4a. A single syllable in a line alliterates with one or more in the subsequent or previous line:

That **s**wymmen **f**ul of **s**male **f**ishes lighte,
With **f**ynnes rede and **s**kales **s**ylver bryghte (PF 188–89)
His **m**yrie **m**en co**m**anded he
To **m**ake hym bothe **g**ame and **g**lee (VII 839–40)
That foughten **b**reme as it were **b**ores two.
The **b**righte swerdes wenten to and fro (I 1699–1700)

4b. Lines may exhibit more than one alliterative syllable (recalling the older forms, aabb, abab, abba, etc).

Ful **m**any a **m**ayde, **b**right in **b**our (VII 742)
Un**t**o the **t**emple, as reson **w**as, they **w**ende.
The **s**ervice **d**oon, they **s**oupen al by **d**ay. (V 296–7)

5. Chaucer alliterates syllables in ictus position (thesis) with those in non-ictus position (arsis), a prosodic feature also called "hidden alliteration," e.g.:
*S*omme **s**eyden thus, *s*omme **s**eyde "it **sh**al be **s**o" (I 2516)
And gees*t*ours for *t*o **t**ellen **t**ales, (VII 846)
. . . no thyng dorste he **s**eye
Save in his **s**onges **s**om**w**hat **w**olde he wreye
His **w**o . . . (V 943–45)

This last example also suggests the possibility of "eye" alliteration in Chaucer, for of course "wreye" [r] does not alliterate with "wo" [w].

III. Alliterative Passages in *The Canterbury Tales*

Alliteration is one stylistic barometer of ceremony, solemnity, and high seriousness and also, obviously, of their abuses in satire and parody. Chaucer's use of alliteration responds to particular rhetorical and poetic situations at both ends of this register. Within these broad categories, however, stylistic effects in general and the density of alliteration in particular are clearly governed by the rhetorical context, demands of characterization, and other subtle requirements. Studies of alliterative clusters also point to specific rhetorical results, and the literary context is a good check against isolated prosodic study. McClumpha identifies 124 passages in which "alliteration is closely related to subject-matter" (51), including passages from a number of sources now thought to belong to the Chaucer apocrypha. Some of these passages, however, do not exhibit the density of alliteration that would warrant consideration here. While it is useful to quote a number of examples of alliteration simply to demonstrate the high incidence of the figure in certain passages, such examples run the danger of suggesting that Chaucer always ornamented his lines–in reality, of course, there are many passages in which few if any of these prosodic effects are to be found.

A. High Style Address

Blake suggests religious prose as the stylistic ground against which to hear Chaucer's alliteration, but the Parson's identification of alliteration with the North suggests another source, the Cycle Plays of York. Richard II visited York in 1397 for the express purpose of seeing the plays (Wickham 1959, I: 223), in which prophets, judges, clerks, and wise women all speak in alliterative verse (even in otherwise non-alliterative plays) through virtue of their degree, their high style mirroring both the solemnity, the ceremoniousness of the occasion, and the dignity of rank.[21] Chaucer's Miller, of course, knows Pilate's voys, "By armes, and by **b**lood and **b**ones, / I kan a **n**oble tale for the **n**ones" (I 3125–26), an alliterative echo, perhaps, of the York *Pilatus*:

> For sir Pilate of Pounce as prince am Y preved,
> As renke moste royall in richeste array,
> Ther is no berne in this burgh has me aboute hevyd,
> But he sekis me for sovereyne, in certayne Y saie,
> To knawe.
>
> (Beadle 1982, 283)

(Compare, for instance, the praise of Henry VII spoken by "Salamon" at the entry into York in 1486 discussed below.) Such self-aggrandizing alliterative bombast also marks Octavyan's introductory speech in the otherwise non-alliterative Chester play of the Nativity:

> I, **p**reeved **p**rince most of **p**owere,
> under **h**eaven **h**ighest am I **h**ere;
> **f**ayrest **f**oode to **f**ight in **f**ere,
> noe **f**reake my **f**ace may **fl**ee.
> All this **w**orld, withowten **w**ere–
> kinge, prynce, **b**aron, **b**atchlere–
> I may *d*estroy in great *d*angere
> through vertue of my *d*egree.[22]
> (Chester 1974, 104)

Tyrants rant because their corruption of the language of office is a clue to their abuse of the office itself. At the other end of the spectrum, address to persons of dignity, too, are marked rhetorically by alliteration. Even that otherwise sober exponent of the plain style, John Trevisa, in his dedicatory letter to Lord Berkeley, rhapsodizes in high-style alliterative prose:

> **W**elthe and **w**orship to my **w**orthy and **w**orshipful **l**ord sir Thomas, **L**ord of **B**erkley. I John Trevysa youre priest and youre **b**edman o**b**edient and **b**uxom to **w**orche youre **w**ille **h**olde in **h**ert and **th**enke in **th**ought and **m**ene in **m**ynde youre **m**edeful **m**enyng and **sp**eche that ye **sp**ake and **s**eide that ye wold haue englissh translacioun. (*The Burghley Polychronicon*, MS. HM 28561, f. 24a)

Much of this mannered alliteration is secondary to rhetorical tropes; there is a good deal of *traductio* and *iteratio* here to be sure, and Trevisa quickly moves into the plain style. This distinctive alliterative high style is not, in fact, unique to generally alliterative works;[23] in the *Ludus Coventriae*, for example, *Contemplacio* speaks an alliterating high style not shared by other characters:

> **C**ryst conserve this **c**ongregacion
> fro **p**erellys **p**ast, **p**resent and future,
> and the **p**ersonys here **p**leand, that the **p**ronunciacion
> Of here **s**entens to be **s**eyd mote be **s**ad and **s**ure.
> (Block 1922, VIII, lines 1–4)

Like *Contemplacio*, the Eagle of the House of Fame decorates his more sententious comments in alliteration:

> "A **h**a," quod **h**e, "**l**o, so I can
> **L**ewedly to a **l**ewed man
> **S**peke, and **sh**ewe hym **s**wyche **s**kiles
> That **h**e may **sh**ake hem **b**e the **b**iles,

> So **p**alpable they **sh**ulden **b**e.
> But telle me **th**is, now **p**raye y **th**e,
> How **th**inketh **th**e my conclusyon?" (865–71).

Like Polonius, who "will use no art" (despite his preceding antimetabole, "'tis true 'tis pity; / And pity 'tis 'tis true," followed by the "f" alliteration of "A foolish figure! / But farewell it . . ."), the Eagle forswears "termes of philosophie," "figures of poetrie," and "colors of rethorike" (857–59), although his triumphant finale not only alliterates but contains both philosophic terms (Teager 1932) and a nearly impenetrable metaphor, "shake hem be the biles"; which Skeat explains: "The eagle characteristically says that his reasons are so 'palpable,' that they can be shaken by the bills, as men shake others by the hand" (Chaucer 1894, III: 26). The Eagle of course loves to hear himself talk; the "shaken" of his "bird-idiom" (Kittredge's term; see Chaucer 1987, n. to these lines) might well also suggest an image of terrified Geoffrey shaking in the Eagle's bill, an image underscored by the alliteration.

It is, however, as Sharon Farmer has shown, particularly women who are, at least in the Latin clerical tradition, endowed with the ability to deploy affective rhetoric: "The stress on feminine persuasive power . . . remained constant: from the time of Ermengard to the time of Thomas of Chobham male clerical writers persistently emphasized the ability of women to use spoken language–sweet words and eloquence–to soften men's hearts."[24] In Chaucer's *Knight's Tale*, the widow of Cappaneus, the eldest of the women accosting Theseus and demanding justice, begins in a solemn plain style befitting the gravity of her situation and the seriousness of her petition:

> "Lord, to whom Fortune hath yiven
> Victorie, and as a conqueror to lyven,
> Nat **g**reveth us youre **g**lorie and youre honour,
> But we bi**s**eken mercy and *s*ocour.
> Have mercy on oure wo and oure distresse!
>
> "Som drope of pitee, thurgh thy gentillesse,
> Upon us wrecched wommen lat thou falle,
> For, certes, lord, ther is noon of us alle
> That she ne hath been a duchesse or a queene."

The occasional alliteration employed here, "**g**reveth . . . **g**lorie" and "bi**s**eken . . . *s*ocour," gives no hint, however, of the sudden effervescence of alliteration in the following lines, as the Theban widow deploys all her rhetorical skills to soften the Athenian's heart:

> "I, wrecche, **w**hich that **w**epe and **w**ayle thus,
> *W*as whilom **w**yf to **k**yng *C*appaneus,
> That **s**tarf at Thebes–**c**ursed be that day!–

And **a**lle **w**e that been in this *a*rray
And maken **a**l this **l**amentacioun,
We **l**osten **a**lle oure **h**ous*b*ondes **a**t that toun,
Whil that the **s**eege ther*a***b**oute **l**ay.
And yet now the **o**lde **C**reon–**w**eyl*a***w**ay!–
That **l**ord is now of Thebes the **c**itee,

“*F*ul**fi**ld of **i**re and **o**f *i*n**i**quitee,
He, **f**or de*s*pit and **f**or his tirannye,
To **d**o the **d**ede **b**odyes vi**l**eynye
Of **a**lle oure **l**ordes whiche that **b**een y**s**lawe,
Hath **a**lle the **b**odyes **o**n an **h**eep y**d**rawe,

“And **w**ol *n*at **s**uffren **h**em, by **n**oon a**ss**ent,
Neither to **b**een y**b**uryed nor y**b**rent,
But maketh **h**oundes **e**te hem **i**n despit.” (I 931–47)

Here, the interjection, “weylaway,” might well serve as the alliterative template, with “l”, “w” and initial assonance controlling eleven of sixteen lines; the widows’ collective grief is provided a verbal echo–not, to be sure, “swich cry ne lamentacion . . . of ladyes maad whan Ylion / Was wonne” (VII 3355–57), nor yet, when Nero burned Rome, the cries of “senatoures wyves / For that hir husbondes losten alle hir lyves” (VII 3371–72)–but a measured rhetorical attempt to move Theseus to pity through the power of eloquence. Note, too, the way in which sibilance sounds insistently, not always on accented syllables to be sure, but nonetheless, finally coming to a head in “suffren . . . assent,” two words which encapsulate the rhetorical situation of the speech–the ladies suffer, and they desire Theseus’ assent to redress their grievances.[25]

Another instance of a woman using alliteration for persuasive rhetorical ends is to be found in the *Clerk’s Tale* in Griselda’s plea to Walter that she be allowed to return to her father’s house not naked but wearing such clothes as she wore before her marriage:

“**L**at me nat **l**yk a **w**orm go by the **w**eye.
Re**m**embre yow, myn owene **l**ord so deere,
I **w**as youre **w**yf, though I un**w**orthy **w**eere.

“Wherfore, in **g**erdon of my **m**aydenhede,
Which that I **b**roghte, and noght agayn I **b**ere,
As voucheth **s**auf to yeve *m*e, to my **m**eede,
But **s**wich a **s**mok as I was **w**ont to **w**ere,
That I ther**w**ith may wrye the **w**ombe of **h**ere
That **w**as youre **w**yf. And **h**eer take **I** my **l**eeve
Of yow, myn **o**wene **l**ord, *l*est **I** yow greve.”

No mere verbal echo of its source here, as is, for instance, the "p" alliteration of these lines from the KnT:

> The crueel Ire, reed as any gleede;
> The pykepurs, and eek the pale Drede (I. 1997–98)
> [Videvi l'Ire rosse come fuoco
> E la Paura pallida in quel loco (VII. 33–34)]

The alliteration in Griselda's response to Walter has no counterpart in Chaucer's French and Latin sources (noted by Adams 1972, 531). Although alliteration, indeed eloquence itself, is in Chaucer's version of this scene ancillary to Griselda's ethical stance–she remains unchanged in the face of Walter's cruel capriciousness–Chaucer's alliteration seems a deliberate heightening of the rhetorical and affective power of Griselda's speech: she is bringing to bear on Walter all the persuasive powers at her command. In response to Walter's declaration that he intends to take another wife, there is, in fact, an implied rebuke in her "God shilde swich a lordes wyf to take / Another man to housbonde or to make" (IV 839–40), and the alliterative peroration (especially the linkage of "leeve," "lord," and the unstressed but subtly underlined "lest") serves to heighten the emotional intensity of her speech–she is on the brink of "grieving" Walter by breaking her promise to "sey nat 'nay.'"

The affective power of Griselda's alliterative eloquence overflows in a narrative emphasis that underlines Walter's "routhe," however cruelly withheld, as well as that pity felt by the populace at large:

> "The **s**mok," quod he, "that **th**ou hast on thy **b**ak,
> Lat it be **s**tille, and **b**ere it forth with **th**ee."
> But **w**el unnethes **th**ilke **w**ord he spak,
> But **w**ente his **w**ey, for routhe and for pitee.
> Bi**f**orn the **f**olk hir**s**elven **s**trepeth **sh**e,
> And in hir **s**mok, with **h**eed and **f**oot al bare,
> To**w**ard hir **f**adre **h**ous **f**orth is she **f**are.
>
> The **f**olk hire **f**olwe, **w**epynge in hir **w**eye,
> And **F**ortune ay they cursen as they goon. (IV 890–98)

Particularly effective here is the device of *iteratio*, or stanza linking, through the "f" alliteration, an impetus leading directly to Fortune, whose turning wheel Griselda's circumstances seem to exemplify. Moments of emotional intensity are frequently underscored with alliteration; in the Wife of Bath's construction of nostalgia, for instance, alliteration is simply one of several poetic devices, including internal rime, consonance, and assonance, which help create a sense of emotional realism:

> "**St**ibourn and **st**rong, and joly as a pye.
> How kou*d*e I **d**aunce to an harpe smale,

And **s**ynge, y**w**is, as any nyghtyngale,
Whan I had **dr**onke a **dr**aughte of **sw**eete wyn!
Mete*ll*ius, the fou*l*e cher*l*, the **sw**yn,
That **w**ith a staf birafte his wyf hir lyf,
For she *d*rank **w**yn, thogh I ha*dd*e been his wyf,
He shol*d*e nat han **d**aunted me fro **d**rynke!”

In these lines, alliteration is part of a complex tissue of phonological features that signal emotional richness,[26] as can be seen as well in the *Franklin's Tale* in Arveragus's reaction to Dorigen's mis-plighted “troth”:

“**T**routhe is the hyeste thyng that man may kepe”–
But **w**ith that **w**ord he **b**rast anon to **w**epe,
And seyde, “I yow for**b**ede, up peyne of **d**eeth,
That **n**evere, whil thee **l**asteth **l**yf ne **b**reeth,
To **n**o *w*ight **t**elle thou of this aven**t**ure–
As I may **b**est, I **w**ol my **w**o en**d**ure . . . ”

In addition to characterizing the intensity of Arveragus's distress, alliteration here helps identify syntactical and rhetorical structures. Especially interesting is the “b” alliteration (“brast,” “forbede,” and “breeth”–suggesting the explosive force of Arveragus's grief), which helps to give the superlative “best” its ironic juxtaposition with “the hyeste thyng”–dishonor may be endured “best” in silence.

B. Courtly Life and Courtly Ladies

The courtly life as it is depicted in the world of romance, particularly by the Franklin, “a burel man,” who “lerned nevere rethorik, certeyn,” seems to attract alliterative ornament. The magician of Orleans shows Aurelius:

. . . er he **w**ente to **s**o*p*eer,
Forestes, **p**arkes ful of **w**ilde deer;
Ther **s**augh he **h**ertes **w**ith hir **h**ornes **h**ye,
The gretteste that **e**vere were **s**eyn with **y**e.
He **s**augh of **h**em an **h**ondred **s**layn with houndes,[27]
And **s**omme with arwes **b**lede of **b**ittre woundes.
He **s**augh, whan **v**oyded were thise **w**ilde deer,
Thise **f**auconers upon a **f**air ry**v**er,
That **w**ith hir **h**aukes **h**an the **h**eron **s**layn. (V 1189–97)

The description of the illusions presented by the sorcerer continues to line 1202 in densely alliterating verse, but when the host “saugh it was tyme, he clapte his handes two, / And farewel! Al oure revel was ago (1203–4.” The absence of alliteration in the next few verses is underscored by its reappearance in lines 1207–8, “But in his studie, ther as his **b**ookes **b**e, / They **s**eten **s**tille, and no wight but **th**ey **th**re.” The magician's book, like the poet's verse, holds the mirror up in which

Aurelius can see himself reflected, but it is a mirror that prettifies (in consort with the imagery of gilding that seems to turn everything in the tale into gold), and the alliterative ornamentation of the verse here calls attention to that parallel, a way of underlining the linguistic "artistry" by which the magic is achieved.[28] When the revel is done, so, too, is the alliterative ornament.

The tradition of the courtly alliterative blazon extends from the Harley lyrics of the early to mid-fourteenth century:

	Hire rode is ase rose that red is on rys;	Her complexion; small branch
	with lilye-white leres lossum he is;	cheeks; lovely she is
13	the primerole he passeth, the peruenke of pris,	daisy; periwinkle; value
	with alisaundre thareto, ache ant anys.	horse-parsley; wild celery

("Annot & John" in Brook 1956, 31)

–to the alliterative poems of Humphrey Newton, a gentleman poet of the late fifteenth and early sixteenth centuries, who writes of his mistress:

Su*m* tyme I lovwed a buerne in bveaute ful br*i*ght;	
She was tristy *and* tender, in truth for to tell;	
She wold salfe won of his sore, she is so semely in sight;	one
She is dight w*ith* diamou*n*des derworth, kercheff*es and* kell.	bedecked/hair-net

(Robbins 1950, 263)

Canacee makes salves "Of **h**erbes preciouse and fyne of **h**ewe / To **h**eelen with this **h**auk" (V 640–41), and the courtly mien of the Prioress is conveyed in a blazon decorated with alliterative ornament and consonance:

Ful semyly hir **w**ym*p*ul *p*ynched **w**as,
Hir nose **t**retys, hir eyen **g**reye as **g**las,
Hir mouth ful **s**mal, and ther*t*o **s**ofte and reed.
154 But **s**ikerly she **h**adde a **f**air *f*or**h**eed. . . . (I 151–54)

Far more often, however, it is the satiric blazon that features truly foregrounded alliterative ornament:[29] beautiful barnyard Alisoun, "a prymerole, a piggesnye"; or in the *Reeve's Tale,* Malkyn, the miller's daughter:

This **w**enche thi*kk*e and **w**el y**g**rowen **w**as,
With *k*amus nose and eyen **g**reye as **g**las,
3973 With **b**uttokes **br**ode and **br**estes **r**ounde and **h**ye.
But **r**ight fair was hire **h**eer; I wol nat lye. (I 3973–76)

The [r] and [h] phonemes of the last line here echo those of the preceding phrase as a kind of prosodic, bathetic anti-climax.

C. Prayer

Alliteration may well signal emotional heightening and the presence of liturgical collocation. In the York Cycle's Fishers and Mariners' play, for instance, Noah's opening prayer exhibits an unusual density of alliterative phrases:

That **l**ord that **l**eves ay-**l**astand **l**yff,
I **l**oue the **e**uer with **h**art and **h**ande,
That me wolde **r**ewle be **r**easoune **r**yffe,
Sex hundereth yere to **l**yffe in **l**ande.
Thre **s**emely **s**onnes and a **w**orthy **w**iffe
I haue euer at my **st**even to **st**ande.
(Beadle 1982, 62)

The alliterative "hail" prayer, common in the York plays, may be found in other contexts as well, as, for example, in the prayer to St. Robert of Knaresborough (late fifteenth century):

Hayle! **ch**eftane, **C**ristes aghen **c**onfessour,
Als **s**eruauntt of our **S**auiour;
Haile! **S**aintt Robert, thrugh **G**oddes **g**race
Pere and **p**atron of this **p**lace.
(Bazire, ed. 1953, 76)

So, for instance, the "Invocacio ad Mariam" of the Second Nun's Prologue has a substantial incidence of alliteration, both twice-struck within the line and running across lines (note, for instance the [k] alliteration):

Thow **M**ayde and **M**ooder, doghter of thy **S**one,
Thow **w**elle of **m**ercy, **s**ynful **s**oules **c**ure,
In whom that God for bountee chees to **w**one,
Thow **h**umble, and **h**eigh *o*ver **e**very **c**reature,
Thow **n**obledest so ferforth oure **n**ature,
That **n**o desdeyn the **M**a*k*ere hadde of **k**ynde
His Sone in blood and flessh to **c**lothe and **w**ynde.

The Prioress, too, begins her invocation with a certain alliterative gravity:

"O **L**ord, oure **L**ord, thy name how mervei**ll**ous
Is in this **l**arge world y**s**prad"–quod **sh**e–
"For noght **oo**nly thy **l**aude preci**ou**s
Par**f**ourned is by men of dignitee,
But by the mouth of children thy *b*ountee
Par**f**ourned is, for on the **b**rest **s**oukynge
Somtyme **sh**ewen they thyn heriynge.

"Wher**f**ore in **l**aude, as I *b*est kan or may,
Of thee and of the white **l**ylye **fl**our
Which that the **b**ar, and is a **m**ayde alway,
To telle a storie I wol do my *l***ab**our;
Nat that I may encressen hir honour,
For she hirself is honour and the roote
Of **b**ountee, next hir **S**one, and **s**oules **b**oote.

"O **m**ooder **M**ayde, O **m**ayde **M**ooder free!
O **b**ussh unbrent, **b**rennynge in **M**oyses sighte!"

Here, of course, relying largely on the rhetorical tropes of ploce and antimetabole, the language mirrors the generally emotional appeal associated with affective piety, particularly as connected with women. Elizabeth Robertson notes that "although it is unclear exactly what Chaucer himself may have known about feminine affective piety, he must have been aware of the emotional fervor of female meditation so prominent in late thirteenth and fourteenth century female mysticism in England and on the continent," concluding that "the Prioress's Tale may well have been the result of his observation of women's role in meditation" (Robertson 1990). Richard Rolle's alliterative prose in English and Latin might well serve as models for the stylistic heightening associated with affective piety:

> Alas, **s**wete Ihesu, how may a cristen **s**oule **s**e his lord **s**uffre so myche **p**eyne, that neuere tres**p**asside? / Thi **gr**intinge [moaning] & **gr**onynge, thi **s**orewinge & **s**ighynge, the ruthe [pitifulness] of thi chere **p**ersith myn herte. / The **c**rowne of al **bl**is, that **c**rowneth al **bl**issid, the **k**ing of alle **k**ingis, the **l**ord of alle **l**ordis, the **e**mperour of **h**elle, is now hound crowned with thornes . . . . (Rolle 1895, I: 98)

Elsewhere, of course, Rolle's prose resembles alliterative verse, as in the famous passage from *Ego dormio et cor meum vigilat*: "**R**obys & **r**iches **r**otes in the dyche. **P**ryde & **p**ayntynge **s**lake **s**alle in **s**orowe" (Rolle 1895, I: 53). Alliteration is only one trope of repetition that links the voices of the Prioress and Second Nun to the long tradition of male writing which conceived the female voice as spontaneously oral and eloquent.[30]

D. The Satiric Impulse

By the mid-fifteenth century, bourgeois poetry, particularly when associated with public occasion, had adopted the alliterative mode, as is indicated by the opening lines of the dedicatory poem on the Culham bridge at Abbington (the plaque, if not the verse itself, according to the record, set up by Richard Fannand, Iron-monger, in 1457):

Off alle Werkys in this Worlde that ever were wrought
Holy chirche is chefe, there children been chersid. cherished
For be baptim these Barnes to blisse been I brought,

Thorough the grace of god, and fayre refresshed.
Another blissed besines is brigges to make, bridges
There that the pepul may not passe after greet showres.
(Smith, ed. 1907–10, part V)

The unconscious risibility of these lines is grist for the satirist parodying one of the lower classes who aspires above his station, as in poems like the Tudor "Crosse Rowe" that begins:

A for Alyn Mallson that was armyde in a matt
and rode to rychmar for to fyght with a gnatt
B for bartem the baker that brostyn mutt he be
he claymed hys haeritage vpon the Pyllere.[31]

Stylistic fair game for the parodist and satirist,[32] Alan Mallson's grandfather must surely have been that original Flemish burgher-knight, Child Thopas, object of courtly affection (and derision):

Ful **m**any a **m**ayde, **b**right in **b**our,
They **m**oorne for **h**ym para**m**our,
Whan **h**em were **b**et to **s**lepe;
But **h**e was **ch**aast and no le**ch**our,
And **s**weete as **i**s the **b**rembul flour
That **b**ereth the rede **h**epe.

The beginning of the Second Fit particularly, with its invocation of "mynstrales" and "geestours" rides at an alliterative gallop roughshod over all the stylistic conventions typical of riming romances and alliterative long-line poems:

Yet **l**isteth, **l**ordes, **t**o my **t**ale
Murier than the **n**ightyngale,
For **n**ow I wol yow rowne
How **s**ir Tho**p**as, with **s**ydes **s**male,
Prikyng over hill and dale,
Is comen agayn *t*o **t**owne.

The apparently aimless "t" alliteration of "to my tale" in the first line finds its point in the submerged "t" alliteration of "to towne" in the last line–the tale of gallant questing over down and dale brings us finally not to high adventure but only back to town.

His **m**yrie **m**en co**m**anded **h**e
To **m**ake **h**ym bothe **g**ame and **g**lee,
For nedes **m**oste he fighte
With **a** ge**au**nt with **h**evedes three,
For para**m**our and jolitee
Of oon that shoon ful brighte.

The metrical imbecility of an over-determined stress alternation (what Gaylord 1979 has called "the under-riding effect . . . a comic monotony of metrical pace" [88]) is brilliantly underscored by vocalic alliteration: "With **á** ge**áu**nt with **hé**vedes thrée"–the indefinite article occupying a stress position as if to suggest that two-headed and four-headed giants are also thick on the ground in fairyland. (Chaucer does the same thing, as Gaylord notes, with "*An* Elf queene," "as if there were more than one lurking in the woods" [1989, 91])

"Do come," he seyde, "my **m**ynstrales,
And gees*t*ours for to **t**ellen **t**ales,
Anon in **m**yn ar**m**ynge,
Of **r**omances that been **r**oiales,
Of popes and of cardinales,
And eek of **l**ove-**l**ikynge."

They **f**ette hym **f**irst the **s**weete wyn,
And **m**ede eek in a **m**azelyn,
And **r**oial **s**pice**r**ye
Of gyngebreed that was **f**ul **f**yn,
And ly*c*orys, and eek *c*omyn,
With **s**ugre that is trye.

The two rime phrases, "love-likynge" and "ful fyn" are the only examples I have found in "Sir Thopas" of what may be the imitation of an alliterative clashing stress (the form of the B verse in which no unaccented syllable falls between staves, as, for instance, line 6 of *Sir Gawain and the Green Knight*: "Welneghe of al the wele in the west iles" [Tolkien and Gordon 1968, line 7]). Gaylord has observed of the romance diction of "Sir Thopas" that "even the matter of 'formulaic writing' is artistically handled, and imitated only up to a point. I have already mentioned words, phrases, and elements that bespeak popular poetry, and which are to be widely discovered in all sorts of works and authors. And yet a close study of the copious lists of formulas compiled by Albert C. Baugh from metrical romances of 'the matter of England' suggests that Chaucer has consistently availed himself of very little of what is common and predictable in such works as Guy of Warwick and Beves of Hampton" (1989, 97). If Chaucer did not lift the diction of "Sir Thopas" whole cloth from the riming romances, he nevertheless caught their characteristic use of tags as, for example, an infinitive in the second half-line preceded by a word beginning with the required alliterative sound, here, for instance, "whan hem were bet to slepe" (744) or "an elf-queene for t'espye" (799). There are also otiose tags like "in the place" (720, 781, 816,); "in londe" (887); and various permutations of "As I yow telle" (713, 728, 749, 758, 896). Oakden also notes a fondness for beginning a line with "For"–in the first two stanzas of the second fit, "For" begins three of the 12 lines (II:393).

Surely a high point of Chaucer's kind of artfulness with alliteration is his portrait of Pertelote in the *Nun's Priest's Tale*, in which alliterating, etymologically

French characteristics ("curteys," "discreet," "compaignable") alternate with traditional English collocations ("herte in hoold," "loken in every lith"), a linguistic pastiche that lends weight to John Trevisa's observation that "vplondisshe men wil likene hym self to gentil men and fondeth with greet besynesse for to speke frensce."[33] Such an alliterating potpourri of French and English puts us on the scent of Chaucer's droll oxymoron–a courtly chicken, an elegant fowl:

Curteys she was, dis**c**reet, and de*b*onaire,
And **c**ompaigna*b*le, and *b*ar hyr**s**elf so faire
*S*yn thilke day that **sh**e was **s**even nyght oold
That trewely she **h**ath the **h**erte in **h**oold
Of **Ch**aunte**c**leer, **l**oken in every **l**ith.

No less a courtier, Chauntecleer draws himself up to sing, not the courtly French aubaude (dawn song) that we might expect, but what sounds suspiciously, as Skeat says, like the alliterative refrain of a popular English song:

He **l**oved hire so that **w**el was hym ther**w**ith.
But **s**wich a joye was **i**t to **h**ere hem synge,
Whan that the brighte **s**onne gan to **s**prynge,
In **s**weete accord, "My **l**ief is faren in **l**onde!"–
For thilke tyme, as **I** have **u**nderstonde,
Beestes and **b**riddes koude **s**peke and **s**ynge.

And so in turn, the alliterative echo, "the blake beres, or boles blake," in Pertelote's mockery of Chauntecleer's nightmare, is designed to burlesque Chauntecleer's courtly pretensions, seemingly extinguished in light of his terrifying dream:

Right as the humour of **m**alen**c**olie
Causeth ful **m**any a **m**an in sleep to **c**rie
For feere of **b**lake **b**eres, or **b**oles **b**lake,
Or elles **b**lake develes wole hem **t**ake.
Of **o**there **h**umours koude I **t**elle also
That **w**erken **m**any a **m**an sleep ful **w**o . . .

Pertelote's foray into the alliterative style here is designed to explode Chauntecleer's manly style (also alliterative) and shame him by countering his dream with a stylistic echo of his earlier courtly self.

That domestic fowl who speak London English should parody the alliterative courtly high style is not altogether surprising, as the alliterative courtly poetry copied out on the back of St. Paul's Cathedral Chapter rent-roll, "A Bird in Bishopswood," attests:

And as I sat in my solas and alle thes syghtys sawe,
A bryd bode on a bough, fast me besyde,

The fayrest fowyl of fethyrs that I had say beforne;
Fyguryd in feturyys fourmyd so clene
That she nad lyme ne lyth that lakke myght hafe . . .
(Kennedy 1987)

Another use of alliteration for satiric ends may be found in "Swiche olde lewed wordes" that January uses to woo May in the *Merchant's Tale.* As echoes of *The Song of Songs,* January's English restores to the Latin the erotic meanings that had been carefully spiritualized by the glossators:

"Rys up, my **wy**f, my **l**ove, my **l**ady free!
The turtles voys is herd, my dowve sweete;
The **w**ynter is goon with alle his reynes **w**eete.
Com **f**orth now, with thyne eyen **c**olum**b**yn!
How **f**airer **b**een thy **b**restes than is **w**yn!
The gardyn is en**c***l*osed al a**b**oute;
Com **f**orth, my **w**hite **sp**ouse! **O**ut of doute
Thou **h**ast me **w**ounded **i**n myn **h**erte, O **w**yf!
No **sp**ot of thee ne knew I a*l* my *l*yf.
Com **f**orth, and **l**at us taken oure di**sp**ort;
I chees thee for my **w**yf and my con**f**ort."

Note especially here the alliterative linking of "spouse," "spot," and "sport" and the equivocal play of "spot" as referring both to blemish (echoing the Latin *macula,* and so the *sponsa*-as-*margarita,* who is immaculate) and to May's unexplored anatomy. This passage reads very much like a late fourteenth-century prose translation of *The Song of Songs,* particularly of the "mornynge song" which falls easily into alliterative half-lines:

the voys of the turtle   Is **h**erd in oure **h**erber,
That is thilk soule   That the Kyng of **h**evene
hath y *l*ad   Into his wyn-**c**eler
syngeth chast **s**onges   Of **l**ove-**m**ornyng
for hire **s**ynnes and for deth   Of Crist hir **m**ake.[34]

January's deployment of alliterative verse here echoes ironically against the earlier description of his wedding night and intensifies the irony of this later use of *The Song of Songs*:

The **br***y*de was **br**oght a**b**e*dd*e as **st**ille as **st**oon;
And **w**han the **b**e*d* was **w**ith the preest y**b**le*ss*e*d*,
Out of the chambre hath every **w**ight hym **d**re*ss*ed,
And Januarie hath **fa***s*te in armes take
His **fr**e*ssh*e **M**ay, his para**d**y*s*, his **ma***k*e.
He lulleth **h**ire; he *k*i*ss*eth **h**ire ful **o**fte;

With thi*kk*e **bru**stles of his **ber***d* un**so**fte,
Ly*k* to the **s***k*yn of **houn***dfyssh*, **sh**arp as **b**rere–
For **h**e was **sh**ave al newe in **h**is man**e**re–

One subtle effect of this passage is the dissonance it establishes between the conventional romantic prettiness of the poetry ("fresshe May" as "paradys") and the nasty, perhaps even brutish physicality of the act itself (the "houndfyssh" as both rapacious shark and coupling dog). This passage may be the finest example in Chaucer's verse of alliterative onomatopoeia; in the prick of the plosives and rasp of the sibilance one can feel, ruefully, May's morning bristle-burn.

The paradox of the alliterative style in the fourteenth century rests in the opposite uses to which it was put–both the high and low styles. Hence, Geoffrey Shepherd can define the alliterative style as potentially at odds with itself:

> It simplifies as well as intensifies, it produces the effect of idealization under the appearance of realism, the sense of a high style hoisted up out of colloquialism. It also betrays its susceptibility to parody, its tendency to collapse into patterned noise, into rant. (Shepherd 1970, 61–62)

Although Elizabeth Salter cavils with this as a description of alliterative long-line poetry (Salter 1983, 86), surely Shepherd hits the mark in describing the range of alliterative practices in Chaucer's poetry.[35] No better example of these extremes may be found in Chaucer than the juxtaposition in the *Clerk's Tale* of Griselda's patient composure with the Clerk's loss of both patience and equanimity in his "Envoy." If Griselda's use of alliteration, discussed earlier, speaks to her eloquence and mastery of the rhetorical situation, the Clerk's use of alliteration reveals his fear that language itself has betrayed him. Rising to ironic heights with an alliterative peroration that "quits" Griselda's own, he gives mock-advice to wives to be as unlike Griselda as possible, to use arrows of "crabbed eloquence" and "jalousie" to make their husbands "couche as doth a quaille":

If thou be **f**air, ther **f**olk been in pre**s**ence, (If A
Shewe thou thy vi**s**age and thyn a**pp**araille; then B)
If thou be **f**oul, be **f**re of thy dis**p**ence; (If not A
To gete thee **f**reendes ay do thy travaille; then C)
Be ay of chiere as **l**ight as **l**eef on **l**ynde, (Always D
And **l**at hym care, and **w**epe, and wrynge, and **w**aille! leads to E)

The final stanza of a double ballade with only three rimes (-ence, -aille, and -inde), these lines demonstrate the artful intersection of rime and alliteration, in which foregrounded "f" alliteration (as well as the split collocation "fair / foul") links lines 1207 and 1209, reinforcing the -ence rimes; and the continuation of "f" alliteration into 1210 makes the abab quatrain structure and the balance of clauses (if A then B; if not A, then C) that compose it clear. The "l" alliteration in the subsequent line marks out the unique -inde rime and, continuing on into the final line, links the last two lines with their cause and effect relationship (always D so that E), even as the -aile rime ties the final line back into the abab quatrain (B ["apparaile"] or C ["travaille"] will result in E ["waille"]). Here, too, alliteration seems a subtle device of characterization, for, at the very pitch of his sarcasm, the Clerk falls back upon three well-worn alliterative collocations, "foul / fair," "light as leef on lynde," and "wepe, and . . . waille." Taken together, these collocations may suggest the increasing verbal desperation and hackneyed character of the Clerk's portrait of "arch wyves." Finally, the Clerk's advice to follow "Ekko," who always answers "at the countretaille," has its prosodic counterpart in alliteration, which is, in some sense, a verbal "echo" just as the rimes here, "raille," "vaille" and "waille" are the final echo of that "countretaille" that is, at least according to the Lenvoy, every woman's last word. In another sense, the "countretaille" (counter-tale) is also the "Merchant's Tale," which follows, and which begins with the alliterating "Ekko"–"Wepyng and waylyng, care and oother sorwe" (IV 1213).

NOTES

[1]I wish to acknowledge my deep debt to Professor Alan Gaylord, whose generous reading of this essay did much to improve and clarify it.
On Shakespeare's alliteration, see Goldsmith 1989 and Pirkhofer 1963; on Spenser's, see Spencer 1898; on Dryden's, see Adams 1977; on Dante and Petrarch (and also Boccaccio), see Robey 1988. The early study of alliterative collocations in Chaucer's verse by McClumpha 1906 includes the apocrypha. It served as the basis for J.P. Oakden's study of Chaucer's use of alliterative phrases (Oakden 1930, 1935). Percy G. Adams' study, "Chaucer's Assonance," is marred by methodological problems (Adams 1972); see Finnie 1975.

[2]Transcribed from The Burghley Polychronicon (MS HM 28561, f. 24a) in the Huntington Library, San Marino, Calif., with the Library's kind permission.

[3]Paull Baum summarizes the prevailing attitude from ten Brink to Tauno F. Mustanoja: "Chaucer used alliteration as a conscious ornament only here and there. He seldom made it conspicuous . . ." (Baum 1961, 56). Such misprisions of Chaucer's prosody make possible, for instance, Sumner Ferris's assertion that there are "only three long alliterating passages in his poetry," adding a rime royal stanza from the Prioress's tale to the two battle descriptions: Ferris 1980.

[4]See, for instance, the excellent study by James I. Wimsatt, *Chaucer and his French Contemporaries*, especially the commentary on the *Prologue* to the *Legend of Good Women*: "Extended rhyme and alliteration strengthen the affinities to the French verse" (James Wimsatt 1991, 166).

[5]This is not to suggest that the alliterative long line did not provide a model for late fourteenth- and fifteenth-century poets. A.I. Doyle points out that fourteenth-century alliterative revival poems survive overwhelmingly in manuscripts of the fifteenth and sixteenth centuries (Doyle 1982, 88). See also Luttrell 1958 for evidence that the only extant copy of the *Destruction of Troy* was made c. 1540 by Thomas Chetham of Nuthurst, S. Lancs.); and it seems fairly certain that Humphrey Newton's "On clife that castell so knetered" (c. 1500), for example, is indebted in a limited way to *Sir Gawain and the Green Knight* (Robbins 1950). The west-country alliterative herbal whose opening lines, "Y wandryng ful wery and walkyng the wayes / In somer whan the schene sonne saylyd on hyghe" (1450–75), betrays as well its indebtedness to *Piers Plowman* (Wilson 1979). Malory, of course, draws on the English alliterative *Morte Arthure* for *The Tale of King Arthur and the Emperor Lucius.* Lawton demonstrates that in Cheshire and Lancashire in the fifteenth and sixteenth centuries there

existed an audience, mostly of lesser gentry affiliated with the Stanley family, whose taste for serious alliterative verse gave rise to the antiquarian form and style of Scottish Field (Lawton 1978). In the mid-sixteenth century, rimed alliterative long-line poetry was being written in the South and East as well, where it was not confined to celebrating martial exploits or great families. In particular, "Ielosy," a poem from the Blage MS., takes as its subject matter "cursyd Cupid, that foul faul hym euer, / blynd as a bytel, wythe his bowe in his hand" (Brewer 1965). There also seems to have been in southeastern England in the fifteenth century a use of alliteration for mnemonic purposes in such poems as the *ABC of Aristotle*, and this, too, was the subject of satire (Doyle 1982, 97). Newton also has an alliterative ABC poem: "A To Amerus to Aunterus, and Angur the not to oft. / B To bold ne to besy, / ne bourd not to brode" (Robbins 1950, 260), and the alliterative poem on plant names cited above is also alphabetical.

[6]"Geeste," too, of course, has its own complex history and needn't mean "alliterative verse" at all, as the "olde Romayn geestes" (II 1126) cited by the Man of Law suggest (see the discussion in Blake 1968). Nonetheless, opposed to rime and prose in Harry's comment, it is difficult to imagine what, other than alliterative verse, "geeste" might intimate in this context. Prose, at least, has been linked to rime royal in Stevens 1979.

[7]I here follow the broad definition of the term as "the repetition of the sound of an initial consonant or consonant cluster in stressed syllables close enough to each other for the ear to be affected. The term is sometimes also used for the repetition of an initial consonant in unstressed syllables . . ." (NPEPP 1993, 36).

[8]McClumpha first provided parallels between these passages and the romances *Kyng Alisaunder* and *Joseph of Aramathie* (McClumpha 1906, 51). F.N. Robinson (Chaucer 1957, 680) compared the passage in KnT to *Ywain and Gawain*; R.M. Smith 1936 made the case for *Ipomadon* and *Partonope of Blois*, a position critiqued by Parr 1945. Knight 1973, 127, finds similarities between the hunting scenes in KnT and *Sir Gawain and the Green Knight.*

[9]Despite their quite different approaches, Duggan and Cable come to very similar conclusions about the second half-line in alliterative long-line poems. See Cable 1988 and Duggan 1986.

[10]Everett 1955; she notes of "heterly" that it "belongs to the special vocabulary of alliterative writings," arguing for "the 'feel' of alliterative verse."

[11]All citations are to *The Riverside Chaucer* (Chaucer 1987). Alliterative stressed syllables are printed in boldface; alliterative syllables in unstressed position are printed in italic print. I have also included tertiary syllables in polysyllabic words when raised to ictus ("the marked or prominent position in the foot" [NPEPP, 554]; that is, syllables without lexical stress which occupy positions of metrical prominence in the line).

Chaucer was himself taken prisoner near Reims in 1360, although ransomed shortly thereafter, and this passage, which has no direct equivalent in Boccaccio, condensing as it does some 920 lines of Book Eight of the *Teseida*, perhaps reflects something of his own experience.

[12]Knight, *Ryming*, 1973, 156. In "Chaucer's Dainty 'Dogerel': The 'Elvyssh' Prosody of Sir Thopas," Alan T. Gaylord makes the same point about Chaucer's meter with relation to the riming romances; that is, it is not an imitation but "is, rather, gesturing towards a kind of poetic effect which came with an English birthright" (Gaylord 1979, 98).

[13]Finlayson 1967. The description of the battle occupies lines 3591–711 of the *Morte Arthure.*

[14]For a full treatment of the alliterative storm topos see Jacobs 1972 (for Chaucer, p. 699). To be sure, the ekphrasis of the temple of Mars in the KnT seems to hint at the association of storm and alliteration:

First on the wal was peynted a **f**orest ,
In which ther dwelleth neither man ne **b**est,
With **kn**otty, **kn**arry, **b**areyne trees olde,
Of **s**tubbes **sh**arpe and **h**idouse to bi**h**olde,
In which ther **r**an a **r**umbel in a **s**wough,
As though a storm *sh*olde **b**resten every **b**ough.

The hint here of an alliterative storm topos is not to be found elsewhere in Chaucer's poetry; see, for instance, the storm in the "Legend of Dido" in the *Legend of Good Women*, which is without significant phonological foregrounding of any kind:

> Among al this to rumbelen gan the hevene;
> The thunder rored with a grisely stevene;
> Doun cam the reyn with hayl and slet so faste,
> With hevenes fyr, that it so sore agaste
> This noble queen, and also hire meyne,
> That ech of hem was glad awey to fle.

[15]For a full description of Minot's prosody, see Osberg, *The Poems of Laurence Minot* (Minot 1996, 19–26).

[16]Following Dorothy Everett's lead, Blake suggests the influence on Chaucer of the tradition of alliterative religious prose (Blake 1969, 165).

[17]For the Harley lyrics, see the edition by Brook 1956; and Osberg 1984. For discussions of the continuity of the alliterative prose tradition, see not only the seminal study by R.W. Chambers, *On the Continuity of English Prose from Alfred to More and His School* (Chambers 1957), but also Dorothy Bethurum, "The Connection of the Katherine Group with Old English Prose" (Bethurum 1935) and Margery Morgan, "'A Talking of the Love of God' and the Continuity of Stylistic Tradition in Middle English Prose Meditations" (Morgan 1952).

[18]Cited incorrectly by Adams 1977, 5, as *De Rerum Natura* 6.21. Adams is concerned to show that English medieval and particularly Renaissance poets could find examples of alliteration in classical literature.

[19]Oakden's work is based on McClumpha's earlier collection of the alliterative phrases. McClumpha, however, included in his work poems now assigned to the Chaucer apocrypha–*The Flower and the Leaf, The Cuckow and Nightingale*, and *The Court of Love*, for instance. Of Oakden's 315 total phrases in Chaucer, 36 occur only in the apocrypha and are therefore to be excluded. Of these 36, 14 are unique to the apocrypha. Fourteen other phrases occur both in the apocrypha and in poems of the alliterative revival and the riming romances. Five occur only in the apocrypha and the alliterative revival poems; the final three occur only in the apocrypha and the riming romances.

[20]For the complex history of figures, tropes, and colors, see James J. Murphy, *Rhetoric in the Middle Ages* (Murphy 1974). The "schemata lexeos" and "tropi" listed here may be found in the *Barbarismus* of Donatus as well as the *Rhetorica ad Herennium*, Book Four, of Pseudo-Cicero; see Murphy, 36.

[21]This is certainly the case in the York plays, as noted by Garrett P.J. Epp: "the conventional association of alliteration with the high style, combined with its inherent dramatic power, make it a useful dramatic tool. Throughout the York Cycle, not just in the Passion sequence, different forms of the high style are used either to imitate passionate speech, or to elevate a line, character, or even pageant, and for a variety of reasons" (Epp 1989). It is interesting to compare Lydgate's use of the high style; in his "Ballade at the Reverence of Our Lady," he begs that an "auriat licour off Clyo . . . my stile redresse," and goes on with considerable alliteration:

> O closid gardeyn al void of weedes wicke,
> Cristallyn welle of clennesse cler consigned,
> Fructifying olyve of foilys faire and thicke,
> And redolent cedyr most derworthly ydyned,
> Remembyr of pecchouris that to the ben assigned,
> Or the wycked fend his wrath up on us wreche,
> Lantyrn of light, be thu oure lyfis leche. (Lydgate 1911)

Lydgate is elsewhere not much given to alliteration, although much of it here, to be sure, is the result of traditional collocations for the Virgin. Nonetheless, such phrases as "Vinarye envermailyd" and "mantel of myserycord" are surely expressions of the aureate style.

[22]Note also that the Chester Herod announces himself in extended alliterative verse: "I weld this world withouten weene; / I beate all those unbuxone b[een]e; / I drive the devills all bydeene / deepe in hell adowne," p. 164, lines 173–6. Unlike the York plays, the only other extensive use of rhythmical alliteration in the Chester plays is to be found in Play VII, where the shepherds and the boy speak in unrelentingly alliterative tail-rime. Buffoon kings asserting their authority in mock high style and buffoon shepherds clowning in low style speak the same stylized and satirized language in the Chester plays.

[23]Such formal alliterative address had a political and social function in the fifteenth century, as in Solomon's address to Henry the VII in the king's royal progress through York (1486):

> Moost prudent prynce of provid provision
> Ther premordiall princes of this principalitie
> Hath preparate your Reign the vij by succession
> Remytting this Reame as right to your roialtie
> Their of kinges conding of your consanguinitie
> ffull Roiall & Rightwise in Rule of ther liegence

Alternate verses preserved by the king's herald, add "And ful lordly thai execute the lawes of y' legence," completing the defective rime royal stanza (Jonston & Rogerson 1979, I: 148).

[24]Farmer 1986. It is worth noting that Melibee is brought to accept his wife's counsel "by cause of thy sweete wordes, and eek for I have assayed and preved thy grete sapience and thy grete trouthe" (VII 1113).

[25]The corresponding passage in *Il Teseida* is not particularly alliterative, although the hint may have been given Chaucer in II.32: "I **p**assi qua volgemmo, / e **p**orger **p**rieghi a te, **p**io signore, / di **t**ale ol**t**raggio con noi *p*ro*p*onemmo . . ." ["we turned our steps in this direction and resolved to make our plea about this outrage before you, merciful lord . . . ."]

[26]The thickening of alliteration at moments of emotional intensity can also be found in *Troilus and Criseyde*; see for instance the stanza that compares Criseyde's declaration of love in Book III to the nightingale's song:

> And as the **n**ewe abaysed **n**yghtyngale,
> That **s**tynteth first whan she by**g**ynneth to **s**ynge,
> Whan that she **h**ereth any **h**erde tale,
> Or **i**n the **h**egges **a**ny wyght **s**tirynge,
> And after **s**iker doth hire vois out **r**ynge,
> **R**ight so Criseyde, whan hire drede **s**tente,
> **O**pned hire **h**erte, and **t**olde hym **h**ire en**t**ente.

[27]Note that Theseus, too, is associated with an alliterative hunt, for which he is so eager "That in his bed ther **d**aweth hym no **d**ay / That he nys clad, and **r**edy for to **r**yde / With **h**unte and **h**orn and **h**oundes hym bisyde" (I 1676–78).

[28]Remarking the alliterative component of Aurelius's self-projection: "Thanne **c**ertes to my lady may I **s**eye, / '**H**oldeth youre **h**este, the rokkes been aweye'" (V 1063–64), and later "To bryngen hym out of his peynes **s**merte, / Or *w*ith a **s**werd that **h**e *w*olde **s**litte his **h**erte" (V 1259–60), Stephen Knight suggests that "alliteration subtly underlines the melodramatic nature of Aurelius's imagination at this stage of the story, and against this fantasy of himself his encounter with Dorigen will seem the more inadequate and comic" (Knight 1973, *Rymyng*, 195).

[29]So, too, when Sir Thopas envisions his "elf-queene," his speech breaks into alliterative decoration:

> "An elf-queen **w**ol I love, y**w**is,

For in this **w**orld no **w**omman is
　　　Worthy to be my make
　　　　　　In towne;
Alle **o**there **w**ommen **I** forsake,
And **t**o an elf-queene I me **t**ake
　　　By **d**ale and eek by **d**owne!"

Such alliteration is the result in part of traditional romance collocations like "worthy woman" and "dale and down."

[30]See Richard H. Osberg, "A Voice for the Prioress: The Context of English Devotional Prose" (Osberg 199b), in which I argue that Chaucer deploys the stylistic practices of this devotional prose to ventriloquise a "feminine" voice in the PrT.

[31]Buhler 1959. Satiric treatment of the lower classes using alliterating names can be found also in the list of cases called into court in "The Trial of Joseph and Mary":

Cok Crane and Davy Drydust,
Luce Lyere and Letyce Lytyltrust,
Miles the Myllere and Colle Crakecrust,
Bothe Bette the Bakere and Robyn Rede–

in *Ludus Coventriae*, XIV, lines 21–24 (Block 1922). Blake 1969 observes that "it is also possible that works in alliteration were beginning to be considered provincial at this time, as had certainly happened by the fifteenth century" (165). See also N.F. Blake, "Caxton and Courtly Style" (Blake 1968).

[32]In this I am somewhat at odds with J.A.W. Bennett, who argues in "Survival and Revivals of Alliterative Modes" that by the time James VI wrote about the "tumbling verse," it had come to be associated entirely with flytings (Bennett 1983). There is a good deal of evidence that as late as 1560, rhythmical alliteration in the high style was still used for ceremonial verse. See, for example, "ane new yeir gift to the quene mary / Quhen scho come first hame," composed in 1562; and "At matyne hours in middle of the nicht," dated 1568.

[33]Here "vplondish" seems a concept of provincial rustication, noted by the OED to mean in the sense of "rustic, rude, uncultivated, boorish." As Gaylord observes of the form of "Sir Thopas": "tail-rime . . . epitomizes the mingling and confusing of royal romance with the popular idiom, French wine with English sprouts" (1989, 103).

[34]This fourteenth-century translation is appended to a group of prayers, including one on the seven gifts of the Holy Ghost and the eight blessings of Christ. Printed in *Reliquiae antiquae* (Wright & Halliwell 1845, I: 38–42).

[35]True as well of the fifteenth century. Lois Ebin characterizes the fifteenth-century high-style poet: "the poet's effort leads man to truth, and his heightened style is seen as the medium which is most appropriate to his noble purpose" ("Poetics and Style in Late Medieval Literature," in Ebin, ed. 1984). Rhythmical alliteration certainly marks the high style of religious poems and poems of praise like Dunbar's "Welcome to the Lord Treasurer" or the welcoming "Hails" of the three kings in the York plays. Densely alliterative verse is also characteristic of the scurrility and the low style of Dunbar's *The Tretis of the Tua Mariit Wemen and the Wedo* or Octavian's ranting in the Corpus Christi plays.

James I. Wimsatt

Natural Music in Middle French Verse and Chaucer*

At the conclusion of W.B. Yeats's well-known lyric, *Sailing to Byzantium*, the aged speaker, having left behind the "dying generations" of the natural world, pictures himself "out of nature" and arriving at the "holy city of Byzantium." Once there, he declares, he will not take his "bodily form from any natural thing," but will assume a form like that of a bird made by goldsmiths from hammered gold and enameling–such a bird as serves "to keep a drowsy Emperor awake" or to sing "To lords and ladies of Byzantium / Of what is past, or passing, or to come." As Yeats presents it, the artistry that fashions his golden bird and its song has much more in common with the poetic process of Chaucer's French contemporaries (designed to please fourteenth-century lords and ladies) than with the Romantic art of Yeats himself; indeed, the bird and the song provide an excellent image for Middle French poetry, which I follow Eustache Deschamps in identifying as "natural music." In explaining natural music and its uses, this chapter provides a theoretical introduction to the subsequent historical survey of Chaucer's relationships to Middle French poetry.

The golden bird represents the poet "out of nature" that Yeats's speaker wishes to become, whose lyric is constant and immortal though its subject is the world of mutability. Yeats thus sets up an intriguing distinction between the form and manner of the verse on the one hand and its subject-matter on the other. It is not so much that the poetic process makes the world of change immortal, but rather that mutability is made to subserve the "artifice of eternity." In the *Prologue* to his poetry, Guillaume de Machaut sets up a distinction between manner and matter that is ultimately quite similar to that which Yeats makes between the immortal bird and the mortal subject it celebrates.

As the fully matured statement of the premier French poet and musical composer of the fourteenth century who more than anyone else established the mode, the *Prologue* is particularly important.[1] At its beginning the goddess Nature presents to the poet the skills needed for verse composition (Scens, Musique, and Rhetorique), and then the God of Love appears, bringing Machaut appropriate subject-matter (Dous Penser, Plaisance, and Esperance). The first gifts bear on the manner of the poetry and the second on the matter; these do not necessarily accord:

> Et s'on fait de triste matiere
> Si est joieuse la maniere
> Dou fait; car ja bien ne fera
> Ne gaiement ne chantera
> Li cuers qui est pleins de tristesse,
> Pour ce qu'il het et fuit leesse.[2] (V, 43–48)

> [And even though one writes about a sad subject, still the manner of the poem will be joyful; never will the heart which is full of sadness compose well or sing gaily, because it hates and flees joy.]

Even when Machaut's lover protests his sincerity, stating that in his sadness he must be truthful and write a sad song, we understand that the poet differs from his fictional counterpart.[3] The poet's verse and the bird's song, their gaiety immutable, find their subject in the mutable fortunes of the mortal world. However sad the subject, the poem will express joy.

Whether the "matiere" is happy or sad, Machaut states, when it is taken into the poem it becomes joyful. He thereby severs a connection between his own feelings and the feelings he represents within the poem. He also manifests no aim of stimulating the represented feelings in the audience. His stated object instead is to praise and please ladies (*Prologue* III, 24; V, 17–18, 177–78), and to reveal and glorify the benefits and honors that reside in Love.[4]

As with the song that the golden bird sings to a Byzantine court audience, Machaut's poems performed before the French courts find their subject-matter in the world of change–of happiness, apprehension, and sadness–but they purvey pure joy (*gaudium*), a quality of heaven, of a timeless sphere like Yeats's otherworldly Byzantium. It would not do, nevertheless, to speak of a strict division between the immutable and the mutable, since for both Yeats and Machaut the mutable subject becomes an integral part of the immortal songs. There is a difference between the poets' conceptions in that Machaut is more willing to rationalize his conception in Scholastic fashion than is the Romantic Yeats. For the latter, the song of the golden bird represents an ineffable ideal poetry; it cannot be described. But Machaut is specific: for him the poem is characterized by gaudium and produced by Scens, Rhetorique, and Musique (*Prologue*, ballade I). Scens "informs" the imagination ("engin"), and Rhetorique instructs in "versifying" and "metrifying," but Musique is the particular bearer of Joy. Machaut was the leading French musical composer of his time. When he speaks of "musique," however, he does not mean simply what we call music. In the *Art de dictier* Eustache

Deschamps, Machaut's disciple and celebrant, refers to both the accompanying melody of a poem and the sound system of a poem's words as "music." The sounds of the words he designates "natural music." Machaut composed many lyrics without supplying notation, and it seems clear that he, like Deschamps, thought of all such works as musical.[5]

"Natural music" as defined by Deschamps characterizes succinctly the distinctive quality of Middle French verse which exerted a major influence on Chaucer and through him on the English literary tradition. For the purposes of this study it is necessary to explore the significance of the term "natural music" at some length, but first I want to consider two other terms that I also call upon frequently, "lyric" and "lyrical."

LYRIC AND LYRICAL

In his essay "Lyrik und lyrisch," Emil Staiger generalizes that no "law of genre" is possible for the noun "lyric"/"lyrik" since the poems that have been identified as lyrics are too diverse. By contrast, he continues, the adjective "lyric(al)"/ "lyrische," when applied to literature, has a relatively unambiguous significance. The explanation that he offers for the apparent discrepancy is that the adjective "lyric(al)" is not related to the noun "lyric" as the adjective "iron"/"eisern" is related to the noun "iron"/ "eisen." Unlike the latter pair, in which the adjective implies the noun (an iron bar must be made of iron), the lyric poem does not have to be lyrical, and, inversely, lyrical characteristics are not found in lyric poems alone. Thus, epigrammatic poems, though commonly called lyrics, often are not lyrical, while the term is readily applicable to many literary texts like dramas and novels that are clearly not lyrics (Staiger 1974, 74).

Staiger is discussing the accepted usage of "lyrische" as applied to literature of every age. When I apply the noun "lyric" and the adjective "lyric(al)" to Middle French poetry here, I also use the terms in a nonspecialized way, in line with accepted usage among literary critics. The discrepancy between the adjective and the noun presents the same difficulty for the description of Middle French poetry as for literature in general. In the main the poems, long and short, are highly "lyrical" by almost anyone's definition; at the same time, a significant number of them conform to lyric versification, and are always called "lyrics," but are not lyric(al) in nature: political complaints, narratives of various kinds, humorous and bizarre pieces, witty dialogues.

"Lyric" and "lyrical" are nearly indispensable terms for this discussion of Middle French verse. While they are not medieval terms, criteria originating in medieval tradition support the category "lyric poem," if not the less specific adjective. Modern criteria for a lyric poem accord with explicit and implicit distinctions that the French poets and their scribes make in the rubrics, in their discussions of form, and in the way in which they organize their manuscripts. Most of the Middle French "lyrics" are distinguished by set forms, called formes fixes, and are labeled ballade, rondeau, virelay, lay, and chant royal (with other five-stanza forms). Poems in such forms are commonly grouped together in the manuscripts. Also logically classed as lyrics are other short poems of varying versification that are mixed in with the formes fixes in manuscript under headings like "complaint," "prayer," or such. Length is indicative but not controlling. Some rondeaux are only eight lines long, and some lays have as many as five hundred lines. At the same time, even when the content or length of some works does not exclude them from the category of lyrics, I do not so classify them if they have no fixed form and are never grouped with other lyrics in the manuscripts.

As applied to Middle French poetry in this study, therefore, the noun "lyric" is based on distinctions that the medieval poets and scribes saw as significant. While it does not predicate a set of invariable characteristics, it does provide a firm division between lyrics and non-lyrics; there is no question of a half-lyric or a near lyric. The adjective lyric(al), by contrast, as used here and commonly in literary discussions, allows all manner of degree; it is clear that Middle French court poetry in general is lyrical, but there are degrees in its lyricality, and many of the long poems are more lyrical than some works with the forms of lyrics. Notwithstanding, the adjective is closely related to the noun since the qualities designated by "lyric(al)" are those most characteristic of lyric poetry. In the great body of modern critical writing on the subject, there is a certain basic agreement about these qualities. Some of the recent discussions may clarify what I signify by the adjective.

The well-regarded *Handbook to Literature* provides a starting-point. In defining the lyric poem, the *Handbook* essentially characterizes lyricality. The lyric, it states, is a "brief subjective poem strongly marked by imagination, melody, and emotion, and creating a single, unified impression" (Holman and Harmon 1986, sv "lyric"). Like most such definitions this one presents problems of vagueness ("marked by imagination," "unified impression"), but it also identifies specific characteristics, thereby providing a useful list for discussion of lyricality: brevity, subjectivity, emotion, and melody.

Brevity is perhaps the most frequently cited trait of lyric, but in the main short length is a symptom of a more basic and essential characteristic, that which Northrop Frye identifies as "discontinuity," a term I use frequently in this book. In Frye's vision of literature as a territory in which the different genres have varying degrees of dominance, he sees the "lyrical area" as one in which the "sense of the discontinuous increases." In lyrical verse, he says, lines and stanzas keep interrupting, leading the reader away "from an ordinary experience in space or time, or rather from a verbal mimesis of it." Instead of a continuing narrative, the lyric provides a meditation or a discourse revolving around an occasion, either public, like a funeral, or private, "like drinking or lovemaking."[6] In Middle French poetry discontinuity is manifested most obviously in lines of set length, distinguished by complex rimes and gathered in firm stanza units; these provide divisions for a lyric discourse that is very light on narrative, in long poems as well as short ones, focusing on such occasions as the impending separation of lovers or the lady's acceptance of her suitor.

The traits of subjectivity and emotion (more precisely, subjective point of view and emotive content) are closely related. In Roman Jakobson's view, for instance, the lyric poem is "oriented toward the first person" and "intimately linked with the emotive function," typically representing the first-person speaker's feelings.[7] Jonathan Culler reminds us, though, that one ought not to think of the lyric utterance as primarily a realistic expression of feeling. "The methodological heritage of the New Criticism encourages us to focus above all on the complexities of the speaker's attitude" revealed in the poem. But that focus can lead to denigration of works of more self-conscious rhetoric, as those marked by the figure of apostrophe, which usually seem overwrought if read as naturalistic utterance (Culler 1985, 39). The stricture certainly applies to Middle French lyric, which is both rhetorical and conventional. Such poetry often becomes, in Jakobson's terms, "poetry of the second person," which is addressed pointedly to another, and "is either supplicatory or exhortative" (Jakobson 1987, 70).

W.R. Johnson's study of classical and modern lyric classifies lyric poems more sharply according to the object of the first-person speaker's discourse. Johnson sets up two main categories, "the I–You poem, in which the poet addresses or pretends to address his thought and feelings to another person," and the "meditative poem, in which the poet talks to himself or to no one in particular or, sometimes, calls on, apostrophizes, inanimate or nonhuman entities, abstractions, or the dead" (Johnson 1982, 3). In Johnson's scheme, the I–You poem is characteristic of classical verse, while the meditative type has come increasingly to dominate nineteenth- and twentieth-century lyric. Johnson clearly prefers, or at least finds healthier, the I–You type, made up of "lyrical discourse . . . the process by means of which the lyric poet describes (and so evokes) an emotion or complex cluster of emotions while simultaneously submitting that evocative description to dialectical scrutiny, to deliberation, to argumentation" (p. 197). In the modern meditative lyric, by contrast, the sense of audience within the poem is lost.

Though he does say that Shakespeare, Donne, and Herbert are among the "masters of lyrical deliberation" (I–You poetry), Johnson is little concerned with verse written between classical Latin times and the nineteenth century. He passes over medieval lyric in a paragraph, suggesting that it began "in what Sir Thomas Browne calls 'that vulgar and Taverne Musick, which makes one man merry, another sad,' and that reminds him of 'the sensible fit of that Harmony, which intellectually sounds in the eares of God'" (p. 5). The second part of the quotation represents a thoroughly medieval attitude, suggesting a formal concern that looks to transcendental experience, while the first part is less authentic, evoking the spurious association of tavern and church that modern imagination has ascribed to the Goliards. On balance, the I–You / meditative distinction is quite enlightening for Johnson's study of classical and modern poetry, but it has little to contribute to a definition of lyrics such as Machaut or Chaucer wrote. "Alas!" says Machaut, beginning a meditative type, "I have failed in my very sweet desire, / Because Fortune is contrary to me," and then "Alas!" in an I–You type opening, "I so much desire the time when I will see you, my very sweet one . . . that it seems to me . . . a hundred years since I saw your bright face" (Machaut 1973, nos. 121 & 123). Subjective, emotive expression characterizes both poems, and the effect seems much the same whether or not the addressee is specified.

The features of discontinuity and emotive subjective presentation characterize most Middle French court poetry, but they do not primarily account for its particular character and value. The discontinuity of the poems, resulting mainly from the non-narrative nature of the content, is disguised and counteracted by long clauses and artful transitions. Similarly, the emotions of the speaker are not a strong force in the work. While the emotional commitment of the speaker in a lyric like Yeats's *Sailing to Byzantium*, expressed through a highly original mythology, is a major factor in its effectiveness, for Middle French poems hyperbolic expressions of feeling are matters of convention. The speakers who suffer and rejoice in relentless superlatives are counters that serve the more distinctive values of the French work. These values are manifested primarily in its sound system, what the *Handbook* calls its melody. In Middle French verse, unlike most Romantic and modern lyric, discontinuity, subjectivity, and expression of emotion subserve this melody–this poetic music.

A usual characterization of the lyric emphasizes the importance of sound and refers to its musicality, as in the *Handbook*. A longer definition will note further that the lyre is responsible for the word, and remark that Greek and other primitive poetry was originally performed to the accompaniment of a harp. Some see this early connection of lyric with music as inorganic, and the divorce of music from lyric as a natural historical development, but almost all probing discussions find continuing significance in the association. For Northrop Frye, once a practicing music critic, the originary association of lyric with music has two integral consequences: it leads the verse away from ordinary language, from "sense into sound, from reason into rime, from syntax into echo, assonance, refrain, even nonsense syllables." Another consequence is that "the words do not resonate against the things they describe, but against other words and sounds" (Frye 1985, 34–5). In another formulation Tilottama Rajan, asserting the "monologic" tendencies of lyric in contrast to other literary genres, speaks of the conventions that "ask us to respond to poetry on the level of sound rather than content and as song rather than language." These conventions "allow the poem to unfold in a timeless and transcendental space." The consequence for Rajan is that "lyric, because of its proximity to song, is associated with a logocentrism that mutes the difference between language and what it signifies, whereas drama makes explicit the dialogic nature of language" (Rajan 1985, 199 & 203). Both Frye and Rajan suggest that meaning in lyric is more or less expendable. The German critic, Emil Staiger, also indicates that lyrical verse may sacrifice sense for sound. Such poetry is markedly "musikalisch," he states, "so much so that often the sense of the words seems less important than their sound. We understand lyrically in a direct manner, without the grammatical, logical, or perceptual relationships having to be clear" (Staiger 1974, 76).

The rhythmic sound patterns of lyric poetry assuredly are musical. And in the Middle French lyric more than in almost any body of poetry the sound system is dominant, making the term "music" appropriate. This does not mean, however, that verbal sense is made either unclear or irrelevant, as the critics' statements might suggest. Rather, as John Stevens says of Dante's conception of lyric, "It is not that the 'sound must seem an echo to the *sense*' but something more physical–'the sense must seem an echo to the *sound*' (Stevens 1968, 14). Middle French poetry conforms to this conception; it does not sacrifice sense to sound, but rather puts the sense in service to the sound. After treating somewhat cursorily modern insight into the relation of sound to sense in poetry, I will try to show just how this may be true through a discussion of Deschamps' conception of "natural music."

Recent treatments of lyric have tended to concentrate on aspects of point of view and subject-matter rather than the sound, which is often dismissed with vague commentary on the music of the verse. (Johnson 1982, for instance, is interested in the ethos of the speaker, in "praise and blame" and such matters, and very little in the sound.) When modern theorists do write about sound, the assumption is that the phonetics of a work ideally reinforces the sense, usually mimetically or expressively. Paul de Man finds Rilke most successful when "the play of sound seems mimetically to overcome contingency . . . as sound reinforces and determines meaning" (see Culler 1985, 46). Northrop Frye similarly finds mimesis, "imitative harmony," in the sound of a poem by Wyatt (Frye 1985, 34). Likewise, in the essay "Linguistics and Poetics," Jakobson argues against "phonetic isolationism," stating that "any conspicuous similarity in sound is evaluated in respect to similarity and /or dissimilarity in meaning" (Jakobson 1987, 87).

In these treatments of the relation of sound and sense, the implicit model is one that is inherent in structural descriptions of language. Analysis begins with the phonemes, significant units of sound, progresses to the morphemes, the clusters of phonemes that make bases and affixes of words, and then builds to the syntactical ordering of morphemes in sentences. This structural level is made to correlate with lexical meanings to convey the sense of an utterance. Such a model seems to accord very well with one's intuitive experience with everyday use of language. One has a meaning to convey, so one builds up sentences that will express this meaning; whatever the details of the construction of the sentences, the structure will subserve the content.

Literature, however, involves a specialized use of language. In Jakobson's useful schematization of the factors of verbal communication, the "poetic" function of language focuses on the message itself, this notably in contrast to the "referential" or "denotative" function (p. 66). Not that the "poetic" function supersedes the "referential"; in literature the poetic simply is emphasized. Umberto Eco, making use of Jakobson's analysis, notes that "Insofar as the aesthetic text has a self-focusing quality . . . its structural arrangement becomes one of the contents that it conveys" (Eco 1976). A use of language that focuses on the phonetic aspect of the message, then, will add to the contentual meaning.

The analysis appears unexceptionable; where Middle French poetry calls the analysis into question is in the tacit or expressed assumption that in successful poetry the added phonetic meaning is somehow designed to reinforce the semantic meaning and is successful in so far as it does: "The sound must seem an echo to the sense." Jakobson seems of two minds on the subject. One of his well-known analyses clearly illustrates this assumption that mimesis is the major consideration for effective phonetics. To illustrate how sound functions poetically as an adjunct to the sense, he cites the slogan of Dwight Eisenhower's election campaign, "I like Ike." He finds that "both cola of the trisyllable formula "I like / Ike" rime with each other, and the second of the two riming words is fully included in the first one (echo rime), / layk / – / ayk /, a paronomastic image of a feeling which totally envelops its object. Both cola alliterate with each other, and the first of the two alliterating words is included in the second: / ay / – / ayk /, a paronomastic image of the loving subject enveloped by the beloved object. The secondary, poetic, function of this campaign slogan reinforces its impressiveness and efficacy"(p. 70).[7] Jakobson describes what we might call a phonetic embrace, a synesthetic hug. Common phonetic analyses of poetry will stress comparable mimetic and expressive effects: the onomatopoeia of "whine" or "giggle," or the expressive effects of a "gloomy" series of back vowels or of an "angry" collection of consonant clusters, and so on. Such analyses applied to verse perhaps overemphasize local and limited effects of particular phraseology. The regular sound patterns that carry through a poem typically have much more important values that are formal rather than mimetic or expressive; this applies especially to Middle French "natural music."

Ideas that Jakobson expresses when he is talking about the semiotics of art suggest bases for a more global analysis of the sounds in a text, and are much more applicable to Middle French verse (and probably to verse in general). Here he does not allege expressive or mimetic values. Quoting approvingly Gerard Manley Hopkins' statement that "The artificial part of poetry, perhaps we shall be right to say all artifice, reduces itself to the principle of parallelism," Jakobson explains that as a feature of all artifice, parallelism "is the referral of a semiotic fact to an equivalent fact inside the same context"; the effect is self-referential. He sees this principle as relevant not only to poetry; of music he states that "In the musical art the correspondences of elements that are recognized, in a given convention, as mutually equivalent or in opposition to each other, constitute the principal, if not the only, semiotic value." He finds support in Stravinsky's repeated claim that "music is dominated by the principle of similarity," and in Schönberg's statement that "to compose is to cast a glance upon the theme's future" (pp. 451–3).

The principle of parallelism in sound dominates the Middle French *formes fixes* lyrics, which have stanzas of set length, mostly uniform line lengths and cesura, complex rime schemes with the same rime sounds used throughout the poem, and refrains of one or more lines for each stanza. In the terms of Jakobson's semiotic analysis, it seems quite appropriate to refer to these works as musical.[8] The medieval conception of music as a form of mathematics makes the idea even more apt and meaningful, for in this view the semantic content of the poetry can be seen as itself contributing to the music through abstraction and repetition, and the referentiality of both expression and content can be seen not only in modern terms as reflexive parallelism, but also in a medieval view as forming a symbolic entity that looks outward to a spiritual realm where weight, number, and measure reveal divine beauty.

NATURAL MUSIC

As Deschamps describes "natural music" in the *Art de dictier* (*Art of Writing Poetry*), it is simply the sound of the words of poetry. From his description, then, one gathers that all poetry has natural music, but of course poetry for Deschamps was primarily the Middle French form in which sound is privileged above other features. Other poetic modes do not similarly foreground sound. Especially since the eighteenth century, literary theorists, including the poets themselves, have treated the phonetics of verse as ancillary and subservient to the semantics. There is therefore particular appropriateness in reserving the label "natural music" in this study for the Middle French type and for describing Chaucer's verse in the same mode. Though only Chaucer's shorter poems may be seen as natural music unadulterated, almost all of his poetry partakes of it, especially that in stanzas. There is only an apparent paradox in the fact that much natural music never had musical accompaniment. In the fourteenth century, lyric texts lacking music became the rule, and, as we have seen, common usage in literary discussion warrants our talking about lyric texts as musical in themselves.

Deschamps' classification of poetry as a branch of music was not new. In his thirteenth-century *Parisiana Poetria*, John of Garland presented rhythmic poetry as a species of music, and the definitions in two French treatises that followed Deschamps' work show that his idea remained current through Middle French times.[9] It was more common to view poetry as rhetoric. The Provençal *Leys d'Amors* (1342), like Deschamps, prefaces its classification of poetry with a consideration of the Seven Arts, but it places poetry under Rhetoric, not Music.[10] And Dante's title for his treatise on poetics, *De vulgari eloquentia*, clearly allies vernacular verse with rhetoric (in *Convivio* II, xiv, 108, Dante also indirectly identifies rhetoric with poetry by associating rhetoric with the planet Venus); though, as we will discuss, music figures prominently in his definition of "poesis." The same alliance with rhetoric is found in the several late medieval French manuals for poets which Langlois appropriately calls "Arts of the Second Rhetoric."[11] Yet, whichever rubric for poetry was used, rhetoric or music, all of these medieval treatments of poetics place primary emphasis on the repetitive sound patterns, the quality that certainly motivated both Deschamps and John of Garland to identify poetry as music.

Deschamps' *Art de dictier* is poorly organized and fragmentary, and the thinking behind it often seems pedestrian, but the treatment of vernacular verse as "natural music" has both originality and considerable descriptive power, particularly for Middle French poetry. In Deschamps' usage, accompanying melody–what we commonly call music–is "artificial music," while the words of a poem–the text–make "natural music."[12] Of themselves, poetic texts are musical and able to stand alone: "Each of these two [types of music] is pleasant to hear by itself. The one may be sung without words with voice and art; likewise, the words of the poems may often be spoken in many places where they are willingly heard, where the melody of the artificial music would not always be appropriate, as between lords and ladies aside and in private; or natural music may be said and spoken from the mouth of a single person, or some book of these pleasant things read before someone who is sick, and in similar cases where the song performed would be out of place because of its loudness."[13]

Certain scholars have seen in Deschamps' "natural music" his excuse for not composing music for his lyrics as the poets conventionally had done. Numerous others have recognized it as more than a convenient excuse, but their conclusions often differ: some see him as asserting the independence of poetry from music, others posit a close alliance between the two.[14] The last view, I believe, is the accurate one; Deschamps is not rationalizing his personal inability, nor is he making poetry a separate art. He means just what he says; drawing on traditional ideas, supported by no less an authority than Dante, he is claiming that poetry– text by itself–is a kind of music. (See Stevens 1968; & 1986, 19–22.) This conceptual alliance of poetry and music provides an important key to understanding Middle French verse, especially in the light of the common medieval conception of music by medieval theoreticians.

According to their theory, music was an expression of mathematical ordering. Its abstract numerical quality generated Saint Augustine's influential statement, "Musica est scientia bene modulandi" / "Music is the science of good measurement." It was the most exact of the mathematical sciences and therefore a principle of creation, for God's mode of action was seen as mathematical, based in the biblical text, "Thou hast ordered all things in measure and number and weight" (*Wisdom of Solomon* 11:20). Music worked by cosmic principles, and was inherent in the perfectly harmonious movement of the heavenly bodies. Its source was in the empyrean, and angels were the consummate musicians. An important consequence of a mathematical conception of music is that mimetic or expressive properties were not attributed to music. It was only in the Renaissance that it generally was seen as directly representing ideas and embodying emotion.[15] John Stevens notes of song since the Renaissance that "when the words [of a song] express a mood, refer to an object, make a plea, we expect the composer to match them," but he doubts that "Machaut's songs ever embody such a relationship" (Stevens 1984, 111). This is at least relatively true for the whole mode, and it applies to both the natural and the artificial music–that is, to the sounds of the text as well as to the melody.

That the principle of a non-mimetic, non-expressive relationship of the sounds to the verbal meaning applies to the phonetics of the poetic text as well as to any musical notation provided for the text is a main tenet of this study. Musical presentation was especially important in the genesis of the main formes fixes (ballade, rondeau, virelay), since they originated as dance lyrics, and it had permanent effect on certain aspects of the versification. But while the major French poets after Machaut did not compose music for their works, and Machaut himself supplied no accompanying music for the greater part of his lyrics, the concept of music as number continued to rule the poetry.

Deschamps speaks of the powers of music to refresh the weary (Deschamps 1878, VII: 269)· and Machaut declares in his *Prologue*, citing the examples of David and Orpheus, that music has power to make men joyful, appease the wrath of God, and to move even inanimate objects (85–146); it is clear that they saw it as a powerful emotive force. Nevertheless, they do not suggest that music is directly representational in conveying either mimetic or expressive significance (see Stevens 1986, 386). For them, music's power lay in its mathematical ordering, which had a harmonizing effect on the vital spirits; its measure and proportion were internalized in the hearers and resulted in their calming and healing.[16] This comes through in Machaut's discussion of music in his *Prologue.* Consonant with his description of the "matere" of love poetry, he emphasizes the characteristic gaudium of music. Like Amour, it is inherently joyful: "Music is a science which encourages laughing and singing and dancing. It doesn't care for melancholy or for the man who broods on trivial matters . . . Wherever [Music] is, she brings joy" (85–91). The effect does not result from a lilting melody or a spirited rhythm, but rather because "everything about [music] is more exactly proportioned than in any other science" / "Tous ses fais plus a point mesure / Que ne fait nulle autre mesure" (99–100).[17]

Music assuredly was seen as suitable for entertainment indoors and out, but it was not seen as mere pastime. Its basis in number and proportion made it particularly suitable to prayers addressed to God, and characteristic of heavenly beings and heaven itself. Machaut speaks with admiration of the central role of music in the Mass. "Is there anything more worthy," he asks, "than to praise God . . . and His sweet mother . . . by singing?" He goes on to comment that the angels, saints, and archangels praise God in Heaven by their singing, which affirms that "Music is in Paradise" (101–25). The perfection of number, expressed in music, thus brings us close to the divine.

The mathematical nature of music and its consequent non-referential character indicate why Machaut and his contemporaries did not think it imperative to make the words comprehensible in their complex polyphonic arrangements, why in their music they did not evoke physical phenomena–the rushing of the wind, the clashing of armies, the calm of sunset–and why there was no attempt to imitate or stir the passions. To quote John Stevens once more (this time discussing a Machaut complainte), "It is unnecessary to make any cross-reference between the poem and the melody except *metrically* . . . There is no *referential* relationship between the two. Neither the mood, nor the ideas . . . nor the concepts of particular words, are the subject of musical attention" (Stevens 1984, 116–emphasis in original).

With such understanding of music in mind, we may summarize the nature of the verse Deschamps calls "natural music." As with melody, the sounds of the text are to be conceived in mathematical and abstract, as opposed to expressive and naturalistic, terms. The most prominent aspects of the verse and the verbal sound will be its regular divisions of pause, line, and stanza, and its regular phonetic repetitions, especially those of rime and refrain. The number of syllables per line will be absolutely consistent, the cesura very regular, and the complex rimes the same in each uniform stanza. The formal, mathematical quality of the versification will be abetted grammatically by a syntax whose phrases and clauses fit unobtrusively into line and hemistich, and semantically by highly conventional imagery and diction. The meanings carried by the words–by the sentences of the text–will tend to abstraction and frequently will be repetitive. In this fashion both syntax and sense become an adjunct to the patterns of the sound. Dragonetti describes similarly the semantics of the Old French chanson; the lyric fiction, he says, should lack "all traces of individuality, that thereby the sensibility of the listeners may be drawn by exclusive attention to the play of figures, of rhythm, and of song."[18]

NATURAL MUSIC IN FRENCH AND ENGLISH LYRIC POEMS

The highly formal fourteenth-century French lyrics, representatives par excellence of Deschamps' "natural music," have not appealed to modern tastes. However, the negative judgment of our time is based on norms that the medieval French writers would hardly have understood. Exactly what they were working for, well expressed in the term "natural music," can be approached by looking at a rather extreme example. Machaut's ballade "Douce dame, vo maniere jolie" has a particularly strong sound system. In addition to the requisites of the standard ballade form–three stanzas with the same rimes repeated throughout the poem, each stanza concluding with a refrain line–it employs an important special effect, celled "équivoque et retrograde," whereby each line begins with the sounds (in this case two full syllables) that ended the previous line:

Douce dame, vo maniere jolie
Lie en amours mon cuer et mon desir
Desiramment, si que, sans tricherie,
Chierie adès en serez, sans partir.
Partir vaut miex que d'autre souvenir
Venir peüst en moy, qui en ardure
Durement vif et humblement l'endure.

Dure à moy seul, de tous biens assevie,
Vie d'onneur plaisant à maintenir
Tenir m'estuet dou tout en vo baillie
Liement, et, pour joie desservir,
Servir vous vueil et mes maus conjoïr.
Joïr n'espoir, helas! et sans laidure
Durement vif et humblement l'endure.

Dur espoir ay, puis qu'Amours ne m'aïe.
Aïe à vous me convient requerir;
Querir ne l'os, pour ce qu'à m'anemie
Mie ne doy ma dolour descouvrir.
Couvrir en moy l'aim miex jusqu'au morir.
Morir me plaist, et, combien que me dure,
Durement vif et humblement l'endure.

(Machaut 1973, no. 58)

[Sweet lady, your pretty ways bind in love my heart and my desire desiringly, so that you will always be held dear for them without trickery, completely. [Even] parting is worth more than the thought of another can produce in me, who while burning live painfully and endure it humbly.

Hard to me alone, lady replete with all good, I must lead a life of honor happily, pleasant to maintain, wholly in your power, and to merit joy I wish to serve you and with you to take pleasure in my sufferings. I have no hope of having joy, alas! and without offending, I live painfully and endure it humbly.

A hard hope I have, since Love does not help me. I must ask help of you. But I dare not ask it, since I must not reveal my trouble to my enemy. I prefer to hide it in me until death. It pleases me to die, and, whatever the difficulty, I live painfully and endure it humbly.]

The seven-line stanza form used here, known in English as rime royal, is Chaucer's favorite. The retrograde arrangement, though, is not Chaucerian; as a matter of fact, it is hardly typical of its author, being the only ballade of Machaut–Chaucer's main French model–that uses the retrograde device.

Though it is in a sense atypical, I use the work as an example because the additional sound repetition emphasizes the phonetic qualities that constitute "natural music." In the *Art de dictier* Deschamps states that the retrograde/équivoque device makes "the strongest ballades possible to compose" / "les plus fors balades qui se puissent faire."[19] His phraseology suggests, correctly I think, that the sound repetitions at the beginning of the line fit in with and intensify in so far as is possible the other formal elements of the work. We might first consider the nature of this device and its contribution to the form of the lyric, and afterwards deal more generally with the rimes to which the repetitions are closely attached.

In Deschamps' usage, neither "équivoque" nor "retrograde" has its Modern French meaning. "Retrograde" for him means simply the immediate repetition of sounds, and "équivoque" means using the repeated sounds to produce a different sense; thus, "-lie" at the end of the first line is the ending of "jolie," but in the second line it is a verb meaning to tie or bind; "desir" in the second line is a noun, and in the following line it is the first element of an adverb. For the relationship between the repeated elements to be "équivoque," at the least there must be a change in the part of speech; beyond this requirement the connection of sense to meaning in the rimed sounds is entirely arbitrary. Thus, between the repeated sounds there is often no accord in the meanings, as in "bail*lie*" (10, power) and "*lie*ment" (11, gaily). Or the sense may even be opposed, as "tri*cherie*" (3, trickery) to "*chierie*" (4, dear), with the opposition having no special significance. The arbitrary relationship strictly accords with the aims of "natural music" as I have described it, in which no direct bond between the sound and the sense is cultivated. The echoing of sounds with no stable connection to the meaning serves to subordinate the semantic to the phonetic aspects of the language, the phonetic being in itself more distinctive in this poetry.

The retrograde repetitions, of course, also reinforce the line divisions, the rimes, and the refrains which are the essential and constant features of phonetic repetition in the ballades. By virtue of their relatively abstract meanings, the rime elements in these poems also help to make the phonetic independent of the semantic. For confirmation we can refer to the lyric at hand. Two of its three rimes, *-ie* and *-ir*, are simply grammatical endings, marking mainly nouns and infinitives, and in no case carrying lexical meanings. Only the third rime, *-dure*, sometimes acts as a stem. As a result, with most of the lines–seventeen out of twenty-one–the rime falls on a grammatical suffix, so that although we might assume that the rime will emphasize major words and point up meanings, the effect instead is to distract us from the important lexical elements and draw our attention to the sound pattern–the music. To make this point clear, we might look at a stanza of a Middle English lyric from the famous Harley 2253 manuscript (from the fourteenth century), for which the principles of versification are quite different from the French.[20] The individual lines make heavy use of alliteration, and the stanzas have in addition a uniform rime scheme:

Ichot a burde in boure bright	I know / maiden / bower
That sully semly is on sight	exceedingly comely
Menskful maiden of might,	noble / power [over us]
Feir and free to fonde.	beautiful / enjoy
In all this wurchliche won	splendid world
A burde of blod and of bon	
Never yete I nuste non	knew no one
Lussomore in londe.	more lovely
	(Luria & Hoffman 1973, #32)

Just as with the French ballade, the subject-matter here is the narrator's love for his lady. The English lover in this particular work is in a happier state than the Frenchman of the previous poem, but in both traditions the lovers run the gamut of emotion; they suffer, they praise the lady, and they live in bliss with about the same frequency and to the same degree.

Yet the versification of the two traditions is radically different. In this English lyric almost every important word–the nouns, adjectives, and verbs that carry major lexical meaning–is pointed up either by alliteration or by rime. Since the alliteration consistently falls on the first letter of the stems, and the rimes are mostly parts of monosyllabic stems, they serve to emphasize the semantic content and to bind the phonetic systems of the verse to the meaning. In the French poem, by contrast, there is little to help bring out the important lexical elements. There are comparably drastic differences in other aspects of the versification, in the matter of syllable count, and in the use of cesura. The lines of the French poem have exactly ten syllables to the line, and the cesura falls regularly after the fourth syllable (occasionally after the sixth, the standard alternative); the units of syntax are made to conform to the sound system. With "Ichot a burde" there is a flexibility that accommodates clauses and phrases of varying lengths; in this lyric, as is typical, there is no regular cesura and the number of syllables in the line varies from six to nine.

The English poem has a certain tumbling rhythm that would allow us to speak of its music, but not as readily as with the French work; and indeed it seems likely that the Middle English alliterative lyrics trace their ancestry to prose (see Osberg 1977). But the Romance lyric had always been musical, both in its traditional accompaniment of "artificial" music, and in the text's being considered musical of its very nature, as Dante testifies in *De vulgari eloquentia.*

In his unfinished treatise Dante deals at length only with the canzone form, but his discussion of the stanza applies well to the stanzas of the Italian ballada or the French ballade.[21] Dante says that the stanza is the basic unit of the canzone and has "a capacity for the whole art"; that is, if we know how to make the stanza, we know how to make the poem. He defines a stanza as "the combination of lines and syllables within the limits of a determined melody and in harmonic relation" (Dante 1973, 51); or, as another translation has it, "a stanza has a fixed music and numerical proportion, being a bounded structure of lines and syllables" (Stevens 1986, 21).

Whichever translation one follows, it is obvious that Dante considers melody and numerical proportion the important aspects of the structure. This is made more explicit in his further description of the stanza. He says that the stanza can have a single melodic line throughout, without repetitions, or it can have a pivot, a diesis, with repeated melodic parts lying on either side, or on both sides of the pivot. The "division of the melody," then, is a crucial matter (Dante 1973, 51–3). With the French ballade the same definition applies; what the French do fits into Dante's prescriptions, though with less freedom of variation. The French stanzaic melody is always divided by a diesis, and the first part, the "front," contains two exactly symmetrical sections, while the second part, the "cauda," almost always constitutes a single section. Thus, the front of a rime royal ballade (such as "Douce dame, vo maniere jolie") set to music has a text riming *ab* twice, with each *ab* having the same melody, and the cauda *bcc* has a single separate melody. The diesis, obviously, occurs at the end of line 4.

Dante assumes that a lyric text will accommodate a potential musical setting, but he says that melody is not essential to the form. To support this assertion, he notes that while a text may be called a canzone, the music cannot. The canzone proper therefore consists of "harmonized words for a musical setting" (p. 49), with the musical notation not itself required to fulfill the form. Deschamps' treatment of the Middle French lyrics accords well with such an assumption. There are various specific ways in which the text and melody of French fixed forms conform to each other and to Dante's description. In the case of the rime royal ballade with musical setting, isosyllabic and riming ababbcc, there are certain matters in which the musical notation and the structure of the text will be made to fit each other. The two *ab* sections will exactly match each other in melody, line structure, and rime, while the unduplicated bcc section will have a different, unrepeated melody. If the lyric lacks notation, the musical structure will still be present, implicit in the versification, marked especially by the rime.

Rime is a very prominent feature in the Romance lyric, and both Dante and Deschamps illustrate and discuss its use in detail. The rimes of a stanza, according to Dante, contribute particularly to "the sweetness of a whole unit in harmony." His phraseology suggests that rimed poetry possesses an independent musicality. Dante is precise about the proper use of rime, even beyond what has to do with the musical setting. Especially he recommends two additional conditions that rime royal, the favorite stanza of both Machaut and Chaucer, fulfills particularly well. One is the connection of the two parts of the stanza, the front and the cauda, which is effected by having "the first line of the last part . . . rime with the last line of the first part." This results, Dante says, in a "rather beautiful concatenation of the stanza itself." In rime royal, accordingly, the last line of the front, *abab*, rimes with the first line of the cauda, *bcc*. Dante further states that "the endings of the last lines will be arranged more beautifully if they fall into silence with a rime" (p. 58). Thus, he praises the effect of ending a stanza with two riming lines, as happens in rime royal.

Dante is not discussing ballade stanzas like rime royal, however. For him, the supreme lyric form was the canzone, the Italian version of the French grand chant courtois. Like the canzone and the Provençal canso in their linguistic habitats, the chanson reigned as the pre-eminent poetic form in France through most of the thirteenth century. In contrast to the ballade, the chanson had no set number of stanzas (there were commonly five or six), and there was no refrain. The fourteenth-century chant royal, which was not given a refrain till after mid-century, is the direct descendant of the grand chant; in the Middle French period it and all the related five-stanza formes fixes found their homes in the puy [civic literary society] and seldom were accorded musical accompaniment.

The absence of the repetitive refrain made the chanson text markedly less "musical" than the ballade, which became the reigning form at the Middle French courts after about 1300. The ballade and the related rondeau and virelay had originated in the thirteenth century as dance forms, and through mid-century were commonly set and sung to music. (For the early development of the ballade and the related formes fixes, see Lawrence Earp's important study, "Lyrics for Reading" [Earp 1991].) Ironically, the musical nature of the forms led to a decline in musical accompaniment for them, for the polyphonic musical settings which Machaut and others came to give them made the works unsuitable for dancing, and their difficulty ultimately discouraged all but very skilled composers from providing notation.

While the ballade form underwent an evolution throughout the fourteenth century, the development of the form in the latter part of the fourteenth century did not have important effect (except in connection with the envoy) on Chaucer, who modeled most of his lyrics and his stanzaic verse on the ballades of Machaut, which were mainly composed between 1340 and 1365. . . . To suggest the close relationship, and to illustrate further the "musical" traits of the verse of the two poets, we might compare a stanza of the Machaut ballade "Toute ensement" with a stanza of Chaucer's lyric *To Rosemounde*. Machaut's stanza, eight lines of decasyllables except for a seven-syllable fifth line, with an *ababccdd* rime scheme, is one of three that he most favors, and on occasion he sets it to music. I quote the first of the three uniform stanzas:

Tout ensement com le monde enlumine
Li biaus solaus, quant il rent sa clarté
Et que ses rais la froidure decline
Et fait venir les biens a meürté,
  Einsi le haut bien parfait
De ma dame vaint tout vice et deffait:
Par tout resplent sa vaillance et habunde
Mais de son bien, certes, c'est tout le monde.
(Machaut 1973, no. 204 [Machaut 1909, #196])

[Just as the fair sun lights up the world when it shines, and as its rays lessen the cold and make things ripen, even so the great perfect good of my lady overcomes all vice and defeats it: her excellence shines and abounds everywhere, and as for her virtue, indeed, it's the whole world.]

Like "Tout ensement," *To Rosemounde* is a ballade with stanzas of eight lines, but they are all uniformly decasyllabic. Chaucer employs the "Monk's Tale" rime scheme that both he and Machaut often used. The first stanza illustrates:

Madame, ye ben of al beaute shryne
As fer as cercled is the mapamounde,
For as the cristal glorious ye shyne,
And lyke ruby ben your chekes rounde.
Therwith ye ben so mery and so jocounde
That at a revel when that I see you daunce,
It is an oynement unto my wounde,
Thogh ye to me ne do no daliaunce.

We may think of the "natural music" of these texts as having two aspects: that which relates it to the "artificial music" which is a potential component of both, and that which is independent of melody. As regards the first, though no music was composed for either of these poems, both have an "underlying musical structure" (Machaut 1973, 18) stemming ultimately from the ballade's origins as a dance form. The prosodic structure is closely related to the potential musical form. The conventional musical organization of the stanza may be described as I I II.[22] Each I is usually two lines long, the two I's together forming the frons: the II is the remainder of the stanza, the cauda or tail. This organization of the melody conforms to the structure of meter and rime in the verbal text. The musical measures reflect the dependable regularity of the syllable count, and the music further conforms closely both to cesura and to line divisions. Thus, Machaut's music regularly observes cesura at the fourth syllable with rests and/or melismas (Gieber 1982, 2–6), and it consistently sets off the rimes at line ends with notes of extended duration and sometimes with preceding melismas and following rests (pp. 6–7).

The ballade stanzas of Machaut and Chaucer quoted above both display the potential musical form, though Chaucer's not quite as strictly as Machaut's. With both poems the first four lines form a frons (I I) riming *abab*, and the last four a cauda (II). Both lyrics, furthermore, have a completely regular syllable count, thereby facilitating the conformity of musical measure.[23] In the matter of cesura, however, while Machaut's poem comes close to absolute regularity, Chaucer's does not, particularly in the stanza quoted. In all but two of the twenty-four lines of "tout ensement" cesura occurs between the fourth and fifth syllables. *To Rosemounde*, by contrast, has nine variant cesuras. These occur in bunches, though, making for regularity; from line 8 to line 19 the cesura occurs consistently at the standard position, syllable 4. (Cesuras occur after syllables other than the fourth in *To Rosemounde* at lines 1–5, 7, 20–2; and in *Tout ensement* at lines 11 and 15).

Of course, all facets of the poetry's sound patterns, not only those that originate in the practices of the musical composers, are relevant to what Deschamps calls "natural music." Particularly important are the phonetic qualities of the words and the rimes, major subjects of the *Art de dictier*. After the introduction on the Seven Arts, in which he fixes verse in the classification of natural music, Deschamps proceeds to an analysis of the sound values of letters–mutes, liquids, vowels, semivowels, and so on–suggesting his high sensitivity to the phonetic quality. He employs the remainder of the treatise for a discussion of the various lyric types.

In his relatively unsystematic characterization of the lyric types, rime is the feature of versification that Deschamps refers to most frequently,[24] and an oral reading of Machaut's and Chaucer's poems suggests how important the rime sounds are for this kind of verse. Comparing the two poems, one may be impressed by Chaucer's command of rime in the face of his (generally valid) complaint about the scarcity of rime in English.[25] His rime sounds are more complex than Machaut's and he manages with fewer of them; the French poem uses four rime sounds, the English but three for a ballade of the same length. The French has an approximate alternation of masculine and feminine rimes (the alternation was recommended in the treatises), with some use of "rime consonant," vowel only, or vowel and consonant. All of Chaucer's rimes, being feminine, extend over two syllables; furthermore, and quite important to the effect, all of his include a nasal [n]. Machaut's poem utilizes a large number of nasals and sibilants, but his graceful, understated refrain has an effect entirely different from the repeated *o*'s and *e*'s in open monosyllables in Chaucer's "Though y*e* t*o* m*e* n*e* d*o* n*o* daliaunce."[26]

In the jaunty staccato of its refrain, as well as in some other aspects of the sounds of *To Rosemounde*, we may find a minor but marked expressive element that is not present in "Tout ensement" and is foreign to the "natural music" of the mode. Machaut's poem exemplifies this music. The sounds have little discernible expressive relationship to the sense of the words. The images and the diction are strictly conventional, their commonplace nature reducing their prominence *vis-à-vis* the sound. In the stanza quoted, for example, the well-worn images of light express the triumph of good. The lady is like the sun which overcomes the cold and ripens things; her goodness shines out and defeats all vice. Machaut's diction is likewise quite predictable; there is not a word in the stanza, indeed in the whole ballade, that surprises us. At the same time there are repetitions of the usual words that are almost incantatory. In accord with the poem's categorical praise and exaggerated comparisons, all three stanzas begin with *tout* or *tant* or both, leading in each case to conjunctions *com*, *quant*, and/or *que*; and then *tout* sounds again in the refrain lines. *Bien* in the refrain has four counterparts in the rest of the text; and in stanza 3 the simple possessive *son*, referring to the lady's various conventional qualities (onneur, douceur, pris, etc.), occurs six times in two series before its final utterance in the refrain. This repetition of almost empty words–words which because of their predictability or grammatical status carry minimal lexical meaning–contributes to a privileging of sound values over the sense.

Comparable promotion of sound over meaning may be found in the rimes in "Tout ensement." Most of the riming elements have negligible semantic content. The *-é* rime ending is a grammatical marker of either a noun or a past participle, and *-ait* is a grammatical suffix of a noun, a verb, or an adjective. The other two rime endings of the poem, *-ine* and *-onde*, are often part of the stem (*monde*), but they too serve as markers of verbs (dec*line*). The rime, then, tends to focus on abstract grammatical meaning rather than on the lexical meaning carried in the stems of the words.

In the relationship of the sounds to the meaning of the text, this poem is typical of the formes fixes lyrics. Although rime is a prominent feature, it often carries more abstract grammatical meanings, thereby working together with the strong rhythmic patterns to make a music of the text with which the verbal meanings are consonant and not competitive. The diction and images–conventional, unobtrusive, and often abstract–make the sense handmaid to the sound. To repeat John Stevens' words about Dante's conception, "It is not that the 'sound must seem an echo to the *sense*,' but something more physical–'the sense must seem an echo to the *sound*.'"

The sound patterns of Chaucer's *To Rosemounde*, it must be granted, are not always so neutral in relation to the sense as one would expect in a forme fixe poem. The metrics, as already noted, are generally regular. The language, too, conforms in large part to the type. There is a predictable recurrence of "so," "as," and "al," characteristic of the conventional hyperboles and similes of the poetry; one also finds predictable words and images, like "beaute," "shyne," and "mery"; "cristal," "ruby," "wound." At the same time there is humor in the staccato effect of the refrain, already discussed, and in some quaint diction and images, underlined by rimes on stem syllables: the bookish reference to the "mapam*ounde*"; the lady "so joc*ounde*" with her childish "chekes *rounde*" and "semy voys that ye so smal out twy*ne*," and in the next stanza, the hapless lover like a "pyk walwed in galaunty*ne*." In this case the sounds are expressive in that they emphasize the humorous content of the words. Through them Chaucer plays with the conventions of the poem in praise of the lady.

Chaucer does not habitually reflect his meaning in the sounds, either mimetically or expressively–though he does more than Machaut, as *To Rosemounde* suggests.[27] Furthermore, though we may find humor in the rimes of *To Rosemounde*, the intensive use of the devices of sound characteristic of Middle French poetry is not of itself humorous, either intentionally or unintentionally. Chaucer himself often uses exceptional sound effects without a humorous edge or other significant semantic implications. *Womanly Noblesse* provides a good example. Again, the first stanza illustrates:

So hath myn herte caught in remembraunce
Your beaute hoole and stidefast governaunce,
Your vertues al and yowre hie noblesse,
That you to serve is set al my plesaunce,
So wel me liketh your womanly contenaunce,
Your fresshe fetures and your comlynesse,
That whiles I live, myn herte to his maystresse
You hath ful chose in trewe perseveraunce
Never to chaunge, for no maner distresse.

The other two stanzas comparably utilize the same two rime sounds, both characteristically French suffixes, both extended, both incorporating sibilants. There are, then, twenty-seven consecutive line endings of *-aunce*, *-esse*, plus four more of *-aunce* in the envoy. Yet the ludicrous effect that seems guaranteed by such extravagance does not materialize. The sense, while serving the sound, is not subverted by it. Though there is a certain light tone in the poem that is implicit in the mode, it is not a comic piece like *To Rosemounde*. The poem's diction includes only the predictable words: "herte," "beaute," "noblesse," "trewe," etc., and it is filled with forty first- and second-person pronouns. Such elements acting with the versification produce an effective piece of "natural music."

To Rosemounde and *Womanly Noblesse* surpass the usual riming effect of the French ballade, yet they hardly go beyond the rime effects of the typical French lay and virelay, whose lengthy stanzas of short lines regularly have but two or three rime sounds, themselves often phonetically interrelated. It is perhaps no happenstance, then, that both of these ballades of Chaucer, with their complex rimes, find probable originals in virelays of Machaut. The virelay is the second type of lyric that Deschamps exemplifies in the *Art de dictier*. The form of the virelay (also called chanson baladée) normally requires three stanzas with an extended refrain of three to seven lines that opens and closes the poem and is also repeated between stanzas. The refrain and first stanza of Machaut's "Dame, le doulz souvenir," which, like *Womanly Noblesse* deals with the lover's sweet memory of his lady, illustrate the form:

Refrain: *Dame, le doulz souvenir*
Qu'ay nuit et jour
De vo parfaite douçour
Que tant desir
Me fait en joie languir

Et en dolour.

Stanza 1: Car quant je puis bien penser
Par doucement ramembrer
    Et à loisir
Qu'il n'a en vous point d'amer
Fors tout doulz a savourer,
    Et qu', au plaisir
De tous, des dames tenir
    Vous oy la flour
Et des bonnes la millour,
    Pas ne m'aïr;
Car en moy joie gringnour
    Ne puet venir.

Refrain: *Dame, le doulz souvenir, etc.*

(Machaut 1973, no. 276 [Machaut 1909, Chanson baladée 21])

[Lady, the sweet remembrance that I have night and day of your perfect sweetness, which I desire so much, makes me languish in joy and in sorrow.

For since I can well ponder by sweetly remembering at my ease that there is nothing bitter about you, but all is sweet to savor, and that, as all are pleased to say, you hold the flower of womanhood and are the best of the good, then I have no vexation; for greater joy could not come into me.

Lady, the sweet remembrance, etc.]

As is common in Machaut's virelays, there are two rime sounds in the refrain with a third added in the stanzas, all phonetically related: *-ir*, *-our*, *-er*. *Womanly Noblesse* has longer lines than most virelays, but it is probably as close as Chaucer gets in a whole poem to virelay form. It has but two rime sounds, closely related; its stanzas open with an *aabaab* rime scheme typical of Machaut's virelays; and its first two lines are virtually repeated at the end of the poem, as is the case with the multiline virelay refrain which appears at beginning and end (as well as between stanzas).

Anelida's complaint in *Anelida and Arcite* (Chaucer 1987, lines 211–350) is the other work by Chaucer that displays significant affinities to virelay metrics, especially by virtue of internal rimes in two of the stanzas (272–80, 333–41). These represent especially impressive technical achievements, again belying the scarcity of rime in English. We might look at six lines of the first of these stanzas, divided medially to point up the rime:

My swete fo,	why do ye so,	for shame?
And thenke ye	that furthered be	your name
To love a newe,	and ben untrewe?	Nay!
And putte yow	in sclaunder now	and blame,
And do to me	adversite	and grame,
That love yow most –	God, wel thou wost –	alwey?
		(272–77)

When the lines are cut off at the rime sounds, which provides a reasonable alternative format, each stanza produces twenty-seven short lines with an *aabccb*, etc., rime scheme:

> My swete fo
> Why do ye so,
> For shame?
> And thenke ye
> That furthered be
> Your name . . . .

The Machaut virelay quoted is very much like this; other virelays are even more like it.

Such a sequence also resembles stanzas of short lines found in the lays; however, the lay form features numerous varieties and mixtures of rime schemes and line lengths. To judge by his extant work, Chaucer never tried to compose anything like a lay, which Deschamps accurately calls "une chose longue et malaisiée a faire et trouver" / "a long and difficult thing to make and create." The song of Antigone in *Troilus* derives materials from Machaut's lays (see Kittredge 1910 & James Wimsatt 1976, 287–89), and it has something of the typical lay length; but its versification bears little relationship to the form.

Another type that has minimal relevance to Chaucer's practice is the complaint (though one might suppose otherwise, since manuscript rubrics consistently identify several of his pieces by that label), and he makes use of the language of several Machaut pieces called "complaintes." But even though the complaint is often mentioned in contemporary lists of lyric types, unlike the French types we have been discussing it has virtually no history as a musical form[28] and never achieved a standard versification of its own. Deschamps does not mention it in the *Art de dictier*. Machaut, like other poets, attaches the label "complainte" to works of various metrics. Nevertheless, his frequent use of a sixteen-line stanza with an *aaabaaabbbbabbba* rime scheme in poems he calls complaintes perhaps constitutes an attempt to identify this verse form with the type. In Chaucer's poetry the rime scheme is found in two stanzas in Anelida's complaint (256–71, 317–32).[29] But such other "complaints" as *Complaint of Venus*, *Complaint to His Lady*, and *Complaint to His Purse*, have stanzas related to the ballade. There are also no poems by Chaucer in the five-stanza forms particularly popular in the puys: chanson royale, pastourelle, and serventois.[30] In the *Art de dictier* Deschamps mentions such forms only in conjunction with a discussion of puy presentation (Deschamps 1878, VII: 290), giving one example (with the mistaken label "balade" in both manuscripts). With Chaucer the statement in the *Legend of Good Women* (F 423; G 411), crediting him only with ballades, rondeaux, and virelays among the various types, agrees rather closely with the extant evidence.

By a large margin the ballade was the most common of the French formes fixes in the fourteenth century; it was a staple for all purposes. As a consequence, in his *Art* Deschamps gives more examples of the ballade form than of any other. (In the *Art de dictier* Deschamps presents eight ballades, a chanson royal, three virelays, seven rondeaux, and several sections of a lay.). With Chaucer too, to judge from his extant work, the ballade was much the favored form, and its contribution to the metrics and rhetoric of his stanzaic work can hardly be overestimated. Nine of his short poems carry over into English the ballade versification complete, utilizing characteristic stanza forms, repeated rimes, and refrains; two of these are triple ballades.[31] Six more of his shorter poems incorporate a total of thirteen formally defined three-stanza units that have approximate ballade metrics.[32] The only other forme fixe that Chaucer takes over into English complete is the rondeau, which in the *Art de dictier* Deschamps exemplifies in both the eight-line form favored by Machaut and the thirteen-line form that Chaucer employs in two extant pieces.[33] Ballade, rondeau, and virelay are closely related forms.

Chaucer's stanzaic poems, long and short, commonly use the most popular ballade stanzas. Of the fifteen lyrics that comprise or incorporate ballades or near ballades, nine use rime royal (*ababbcc*) and three the "Monk's Tale" stanza (*ababbcbc*). Rime royal similarly was Machaut's favorite ballade stanza; of his 265 ballades, 138 are in rime royal. Machaut also used the Monk's stanza (for 7 poems), but Deschamps was its champion, writing 495 ballades that use it; it was also Granson's favorite (24 poems). There are larger implications of ballade versification for Chaucer's stanzaic works. In the light of his great debt to Machaut, his familiarity with the other French writers, and his metrical practice in the short poems, it is hardly daring to infer that the stanzaic form of his longer pieces in rime royal and the Monk's stanza–which include the *Parliament of Fowls, Troilus and Criseyde*, and five of the *Canterbury Tales*–develop from French ballade usage. Rather, it is surprising that there has not been more general agreement that these stanzas of Chaucer originate in the ballade.[34] For the versification of Chaucer's stanzaic works only the "Clerk's Envoy," the terza rima in *Complaint to His Lady* (23–39), and the tail-rime of the "Tale of Sir Thopas" lack antecedents in the formes fixes; and of these the "Clerk's Envoy", with its repeated rimes in *-ence* and *-aille*, is clearly related to them.

NATURAL MUSIC IN MACHAUT'S "REMEDE" AND CHAUCER'S "TROILUS"

The consummate representative of natural music among longer Middle French poems is Machaut's *Remede de Fortune*, and the most important English poem that has a substantial element of natural music is Chaucer's *Troilus and Criseyde*, though it is generally identified as epic and/or romance rather than lyric. These two long poems will serve here to exemplify natural music in extended verse. Both integrate lyric forms, and despite their narratives both have fundamental lyricality: to varying degrees they display the discontinuity, subjectivity, and emotive content that is characteristic of lyric, these features assisting the metrics, grammatical structure, and conventional content in creating impressive natural music.

Remede de Fortune can be seen as the archetypal poem among Middle French dits amoureux. It is a mirror of court life, and it incorporates an art of poetry and an art of love. The narrative upon which it builds this threefold summa is quite simple. The lover is the central figure and narrator. As is proper, he is a poet who spends his time writing lyrics in his lady's honor. The story gains its initial impetus from a lay of his, complete with music, which fortuitously and anonymously comes into the lady's hands. She has him read it and afterwards inquires who wrote it. Torn by emotion, unable either to acknowledge the work or to lie to her, he leaves abruptly and goes off to the Parc de Hesdin where he makes a long formal complaint against Amour and Fortune. Responding to the complaint, Lady Esperance appears and proceeds to console him with Boethian wisdom and two songs. Her long presentation, which is the central component of the poem, sufficiently encourages him that he returns to the lady's chateau. There he joins the carole the lady is participating in, and subsequently confesses his love; after careful questioning, she accepts him into her service. They participate together in the activities of the castle–Mass, dinner, musical entertainment, games–but fear of scandal keeps her from giving him any sign of favor. The poem ends with Amant in a state of suspended animation.

This uncomplicated story, typical of the mode, provides a basis for extensive lyric development, formal and informal. Lyric discontinuity is evident throughout. There are nine independent intercalated lyrics which interrupt the octosyllabic couplets, including the lover's lay and complaint, and the chant royal and ballade of Esperance. As Ernest Hoepffner has noted, the lyrics taken together embody a tableau of the principal types, one example of each, presented in order through the poem from the most to the least metrically complex. According to Hoepffner, Machaut's purpose was to act as a literary legislator for the time by setting up models of the types for others to follow (Machaut 1908, II: xxxiv–liv). This seems clear, but there is much more to the poem's lyric nature. In addition to the set pieces, the narrative provides a series of occasions for lyric development in discrete (discontinuous) passages of the couplets themselves. Indeed, in presenting in first-person narrative a typical lover's career, from uncommitted youth to acceptance by the lady to separation from her, it forms a cycle of the typical situations. One after another of them is suited to lyric development: the young man is assigned a lady by Amour; he praises her as his exemplar and guide; powerless to declare his love, he writes poems about his longing; he stands mute and embarrassed in her presence; despairing of Love's help, he complains against Fortune; he looks forward to Death, makes his will, is saved by Hope, resolves to declare himself, hesitates before her, at length makes his declaration; she tests him, then accepts him; he rejoices in Love, imagines that she is fickle, is reassured by her; yet, at the end, he still must endure separation. Each stage provides a lyric moment.

In addition to its full set of lyric forms and its cycle of lyric situations, a third dimension of the *Remede* as poetic lesson-book is provided by the Boethian dialogue of Lady Esperance and the lover (1608–2892). The presentation of Esperance is the core of the Art of Love of the *Remede*. Esperance treats extensively the problems that Fortune presents to the lover and she expatiates on the mysterious beneficence of the God of Love. In the course of the discussion, she develops many of the commonplaces of the love poetry: the least gift of the lady is worth more than the lover can merit; since the lady has all virtues she must have pity; the lover's confusion before the lady has shown him to her as true lover; and so on.

Much of the language derives from the *Roman de la Rose*, but the love affair is far from that of the *Roman*. The lover is shy and restrained, not importunate; his overt aim is to honor and serve the lady, not get her to bed; he abides by Bien Celer (Hide Well) in order to avert slander against the lady, not to conceal misbehavior. That Esperance's Art of Love finds its model in the Boethian discourse of Reason in the *Roman de la Rose*, rather than from the Ovidian lecture of the God of Love, is an index of the change in sensibility between the poems. The poetic locus of action is another major indicator of the difference. The Amant of Guillaume de Lorris operates in a cosmic garden of procreation; his ultimate aim is copulation. Machaut's lover moves in a castle and park so close to reality that it can be located on the map; his ultimate aim coincides with that of the poet–to honor the lady.

Love poems of all times claim to present real experiences of the speakers, but in this matter they obviously vary. Middle French poems were often written for patrons and about their experiences. The question of the relation to reality is explicitly broached in the *Remede* by the identification of the locale as Hesdin, site of the great palace and park that Jean le Bon frequented. If the place has a real location, then are the main figures simply ideals, or are they meant to represent real people? Because the lady is the center about which this poem and all the poetry turns, her identity perhaps is the key. Machaut concludes his general *Prologue* by emphasizing the centrality of the lady in his oeuvre:

> Or pri a Dieu qu'il me doint grace
> De faire chose qui bien plaise
> Aus dames; car, par saint Nichaise,
> A mon pooir, quanque diray,
> A l'onneur d'elles le feray.
> (*Remede de Fortune* is quoted herein from Machaut 1988)

[Now I pray to God that he give me grace to write something pleasing to ladies; for by Saint Nicaise, as far as possible, whatever I say, I say for their honor.]

The poet is to produce poems founded on the honor and praise of women. To accomplish this purpose he will embody in his depictions the admirable qualities of women. But where in his experience will the poet find his model, the counterpart to this exemplary lady? Will he find it in the pretty attendant with whom he carries on a more or less serious flirtation (Chaucer found his wife among Queen Philippa's damsels)? In the lady who presides (queen, princess, duchess)? Or in the idea of woman abstracted from the characteristic virtues of all the court ladies whom he knows and has heard about?

It seems clear that the abstracted idea of woman provides the characterization of the beloved lady of the poems; the descriptions are consistently of ideals that no actual lady would have fulfilled on all counts. At the same time, through an acrostic or a pun the poet sometimes lets us know that there is a real lady to whom the poem is directed and whom the idealized depiction more or less indirectly compliments. This actual person obviously might be anyone whom the poet fancies, but such evidence as we have suggests that in the case of the fourteenth-century poets the patroness most often is the poem's object: Bonne of Luxembourg, Blanche of Lancaster, Isabelle of York, Marguerite of Flanders, Anne of Bohemia, Isabelle of Bavaria. To increase the "louange des dames," the court poet writes about an ideal while honoring a grand lady. He typically has no thought of soliciting the lady's love in any milieu but that of the narrative, in which the usual Amant counterpart of the poet is at once more naïve and worthier than the writer is known to be. The conventions are so well established, the representation so idealized and stylized, that there is little chance of anyone's taking offense. There are, of course, no rigid rules about the real-life reference of a poem. At times, for instance, the first-person narrator of a lyric or dit is meant to represent a nobleman on whose behalf the poet composes his poem, as in Machaut's "Complainte VI." In that work an acrostic reveals that it was written for Pierre, King of Cyprus, and addressed (in all likelihood) to Marguerite of Flanders (see James Wimsatt 1970, 40–59). The basic intention would have been political instead of amorous, to gain the powerful lady's help for Pierre's crusade. Thus, while Marguerite doubtless was meant to see the lover's extreme expressions of distress as arising from a gentle heart like Pierre's, she was not expected to respond directly to him as suitor or lover, nor would she have thought of doing so.

In presenting Bonne of Luxembourg in the guise of the ideal lady (see Machaut 1988, 33–35), the *Remede* is quite in line with the custom of the Middle French mode. With the musical notation of seven fully developed lyrics, it also recapitulates the mode's history as it is bound up with notation. Even as regards narrative the work is allied with lyric, for the simple love stories that underlie the lyric genre are the genesis of the narratives of *Remede de Fortune* and dits amoureux like it. The longer narratives grow out of the conventional stories that the short poems predicate. Later dits with no formal lyric insertions and no music still participate in the line of development. Besides the conventional stories and rhetorical figures, they retain much of the "natural music" of the regular metrics, the complex rimes with heavy word-play, the repetitive diction, and the predictable narrative and exempla, all of which give them a euphonious and abstract character that may be called "musical." Almost any passage in the couplets of *Remede*, where there is neither music nor fixed form, shows these characteristics just as formal pieces do. We might instance the passage in which Amant describes the effects of his first sight of the lady, which anticipates the experiences of Chaucer's Black Knight and of Troilus:

Ainssi fist Amours par son art
Qui mains franc cuer doucement art
Que, quant premiers ma dame vi,
Sa grant biauté mon cuer ravi.
Et quant de s'amour fui espris,
Jonnes estoie et desapris,
S'avoie bien mestier d'aprendre,
Quant tel fait vouloie entreprendre.
Que dis je? Ains l'avoie entrepris,
Qu'ains conseil ne congié n'en pris
Fors a mon cuer et a ses yeus,
Qui en riant m'ont en maint lieus
Prié que par amours l'amasse
Si doucement, que je n'osasse
Leur veul refuser, ne peüsse.
Et mes cuers vouloit que je fusse
Touz siens, et je aussi le vouloie,
Et pour ce a eulz me conseilloie.
Si qu'ainssi fui, se Dieus me gart,
Pris par Doulz Ris et Douz Regart.
Et certainement, se je eüsse
Tant de bien en moy que je fusse
Aussi sages com Salemons,
Et fust miens quites tout li mons,
Et aussi preus comme Alixandres
Ou comme Hector, qui gaire mandres
Ne fu de li quant a valour,
Et sc'eüsse autretant d'onnour
Comme ot Godefroy de Buyllon,
Et la biauté qu'ot Absolon,
Et de Job la grant pasciensce,
L'estableté et la constance
Et de Judich et de Socratés,
Qui en .i. point estoit adés,
Car pour gaaingne ne pour perte
Ne se mouvoit, tant fust aperte,
Et avec ce l'umilité
Que Hester ot, et la loyauté
De Abraham, a verité dire
Ne peusse je pas sousfire
Pour dame amer de tel affaire.
Mais Amours le me firent faire
Qui m'i donnerent liegement,
Quant je la vi premierement;
Si que siens sans riens retenir

> Sui, quoy qu'il m'en doie avenir,
> Et serai, tant com je vivray,
> Ne jamais autre amour n'avray. (87--134)

> [Thus Love, by her skill, which gently enflames many a noble heart, caused my lady's great beauty to carry away my heart when first I saw her. When I was kindled by her love, I was young and inexperienced, and I had much to learn if I wished to embark upon such a course. What am I saying? I had already embarked upon it, having asked advice and leave only of my heart and her eyes, which often laughingly bid me so sweetly to love her that I dared not and could not refuse their wish. My heart wanted me to be hers entirely, and I too wanted it, and therefore I heeded their advice. Thus, God help me, I was captured by Sweet Laughter and Sweet Looks. Yet truly, if I were so gifted as to be as wise as Solomon, and if all the world were completely mine, and I were as valiant as Alexander or as Hector (who was scarcely less brave than he) and if I had as much honor as Godfrey of Bouillon, and the beauty of Absalon, and Job's great patience, and the steadfastness and constancy of Judith and of Socrates, who always held to one position, because he would not change it for loss or for gain, no matter how great; and if I had in addition the humility of Esther and the faithfulness of Abraham, in truth I would still not be worthy to love a lady of such rank. But Love made me do it, who made me her liege man when first I saw her; so I am hers without reserve, come what may, and will be hers as long as I live, nor shall I ever love another.][35]

The content here is reflective, descriptive, and hyperbolic, much more characteristic of lyric than of narrative. What is more, the passage fits together rhetorically and metrically as the lover's unified statement of the permanent effects of his first sight of the lady. It begins and ends with his declaring that Amour permanently changed him when she showed him the lady ("Ainssi fist Amours . . . quant premiers ma dame vi" [87–89]; "Mais Amours le me firent faire . . . Quant je la vi premierement" [128–30]), and in between he develops the themes of her worth and his unworthiness. In the versification the rimes are particularly notable; almost all are extended to more than one syllable ("aprendre" / "entreprendre"; "Alixandres" / "gaires mandres," etc.) with an occasional cleverness ("Dieus me gart" / "Douz Regart"). The heavily subordinated and co-ordinated syntax fits easily into the line units, with numerous enjambments that do little violence to them. The filiation of this passage to the sung lyric that is its ancestor, and its compatibility with such lyrics, is manifest. It is a fine example of "natural music," as is the comparable passage in the *Book of the Duchess* (1052–87). *Remede de Fortune* and the other dits amoureux in the same line of development are virtually made up of such passages.

Despite its alliances with the long narrative forms of epic and romance, Chaucer's *Troilus and Criseyde* partakes of the highly lyric dit amoureux. According to my analysis, *Troilus* has fifty-six developed lyric passages, amounting to 1,532 lines (of 8,238) that are essentially non-narrative; which might, with moderate alteration, be made into separate lyrics closely related to the formes fixes.[36] In the rime royal stanza form, in their diction and imagery, in their rhetorical orientation and logical development, and often in their very length, most of these passages are fine examples of natural music. Much of the remainder of the poem also shows filiations with the French. To call *Troilus* a collection of "lyric clusters" or a "sonnet sequence"[37] is hyperbolic but hardly perverse, as may be illustrated by setting a ballade of Machaut beside a passage from the opening of Chaucer's poem.

Machaut's "Plourez, dames" is quite typical of his ballades, and yet it has claims to special status as a work that Machaut particularly prized and that was well known both to his French successors and to Chaucer. Probably composed in the 1350's when Machaut was near the peak of his creative powers, it is one of but two lyrics that he esteemed so highly as to put it in three places in the complete manuscripts of his poetry: in his collection of lyrics without music, the *Louange des dames*; among the "balades notées" with music; and as an intercalated lyric in the late long *Voir-Dit*. Chaucer made use of this ballade most notably in the *Complaint of Mars*, and Deschamps clearly considered it a Machaut trademark.[38] Its subject is thoroughly conventional; like scores of formes fixes lyrics, it is concerned with the lover's prospective death. Because the generic lover was absolutely dependent on the lady and Amour, many occasions could threaten his life: the lady's refusal, his inability to see her or go to her, a prospective separation, her betrayal of him, malicious gossip about either of them, her death. In "Plourez, dames" the situation is not specified; the audience is told only that the speaker expects to die soon, though it is possible that help will materialize. The work as a whole is a request to ladies for their tears and prayers. In conformity with ballade form, the poem has three stanzas, each employing the same rimes and terminating with the same refrain. The first stanza shows its form, rhetorical approach, and general content:

> Plourez, dames, plourez vostre servant,
> Qui toudis ay mis mon cuer et m'entente,
> Corps et penser et desir en servant
> L'onneur de vous que Diex gart et augmente.
>   Vestez vous de noir pour my,
> Car j'ay cuer teint et viaire paly,
> Et si me voy de mort en aventure,
> *Se Diex et vous ne me prenez en cure.*
> (Machaut 1973, no.162; also Machaut 1909, # 229; and [with its music by Leo Schrade] Machaut 1908, III: 120)

> [Weep, ladies, weep for your servant, who has always put his heart and purpose, body and thought and desire into serving your honor; may God increase and augment it. Dress in black for me, for I have a stricken heart and a visage grown pale, and I see that I will die if God and you do not take care of me.]

In the two stanzas that complete the ballade the lover makes his will, leaving his heart to the ladies' protection, his flesh to the worms, and his possessions to the poor; but finally he suggests that since the ladies are so replete with good, they may still save him.

Conventional generic elements are found in all aspects of the representation in "Plourez, dames." The characters prominent in the poem are the standard narrator-lover, the collective ladies of understanding whom he addresses, and a deity who is both the God of Love and the Christian deity. The filiations of the poem to Christian prayer are obvious. The imagery comes from the familiar iconography of death and dying: weeping mourners, black garments, a will or testament, a death bed, prayers for the dying. The diction is highly conventional and repetitive, thereby creating parallel patterns of sound and meaning. There is an unusual degree of repetition of the personal pronouns; the first-person singular occurs twenty-one times in its various cases in the poem, the second-person plural fifteen times. The lexical patterning is also served by the repetition of nouns and verbs drawn from the poetic world of Amour: Dieus (seven times), plourez–plourant, servant, mis–met, cuer (four times), mort, parti–departi, and priez–depri. The restricted lexicon that results from convention and repetition compares in its statistical limitation to the phonetic design made up by consonant-vowel combinations or to the simple syntactic combinations that compose a grammatical pattern. In this way, representational elements make up an abstractable formal pattern congruent with that of the phonetic and grammatical schemes.

As in all Middle French lyrics, the pattern of sound is a notable feature. (In forms like the lay, virelay, and rondeau, in which the lines are often shorter, the refrains more extended and the rime endings fewer, the sound pattern is usually more obtrusive even than in the ballade.) Repetitions demanded by the ballade form include the use of the refrain and of the same rime sounds in the three stanzas. In "Plourez, dames" each of the four rimes appears six times. As was considered desirable, there is an alternation of masculine and feminine rimes.[39] Many of the rimes are extended; that is, they involve at least two syllables, as with rimes throughout on *-ente* and *-ure*. The identical rimes on "servant" in the first stanza and "depri" in the third stanza are both extended and équivoque. The rime is prolonged to three syllables in "ce parti" and "departi" in the second stanza. In addition to these phonetic matters involving the standard form of the ballade, Machaut makes further discreet uses of sound patterning throughout the poem. One notable aspect of this appears in the recurrence of the initial labials *p-*, *v-*, and *m-*. Together with an impressive number of verbs and nouns in the poem that begin with one of these labials ("plourez," "priez," "vestez," "vers," "viaire paly," "mis," "mort," etc.) are found many of the form words ("vostre," "vous," "vo," "pour my," "me voy," etc.). The labials also participate with other sounds in the substantial unobtrusive alliteration ("*M*on *c*uer *v*ous lais et *m*et en *v*o *c*ommant").

A major aspect of Machaut's lyrics is the fitting of the syntactic units to the metrical divisions of line and stanza in his verse, the apparent ease of the conformity obscuring an impressive grammatical variety and complexity. Sentences of all lengths occur in Machaut's ballades, but long sentences are much more common. His eight-line stanza usually is made up of two extended sentences, with the length achieved by liberal compounding and subordinating of clauses. In "Plourez, dames" each stanza has two complete sentences. In the first and third stanzas we find a typical structure, with the opening sentence ending at line 4, coincident with a break in the rime scheme and the underlying musical form.[40] As might be expected when long sentences are employed in verse, enjambments are not infrequent; in this poem there are six. At the same time, in Machaut's ballades the enjambment never involves unusual grammatical disjunctions, such as separation of preposition from object or adjective from noun. He avoids these assiduously.

In building his long sentences Machaut employs a multiplicity of syntactic structures. Thus, while convention and repetition conduce to uniformity in the diction, commonly an element of great variety, the patterns of syntax, by nature much more limited, are quite varied. The result is that image, lexicon, and syntax have comparable degrees of patterning and variety. The poem at hand makes use of many kinds of co-ordinating and compounding. At the same time, there is nothing fatiguing or awkward about the sentences. One does not stumble over them in reading, nor does one need to hear them repeated in order to comprehend them. For all of the apparent intricacy of syntax, Machaut's sentences have a smoothness and elegance that provides the major precedent for the ease of Chaucer's verse.

"Plourez, dames" offers a specific precedent for certain passages in Chaucer's poetry. One of these is the final tern of the complaint section of "Complaint of Mars" (281–98) in which Mars asks knights, ladies, and lovers for their pity. Another is Criseyde's "testament" (IV. 771–91) when she concludes that she will naturally die when she parts from Troilus. In both of these three-stanza set pieces the images also center on mourning and death; black clothes, holy tears, request for pity, and bequeathal of heart specifically evoke Machaut's lyric. But I want to concentrate here on comparing "Plourez, dames" with four stanzas from Book I of *Troilus*, where the congruencies are less specific and the important generic relationships stand out more clearly. The passage in question follows the three stanzas that open the poem, in which the narrator announces his subject (the "double sorwe of Troilus"), invokes the Fury, and acknowledges his inadequacies. He then petitions lovers, as Machaut had petitioned ladies, with a series of imperatives, ending with a statement that equates his act of composition with prayer:

> But ye loveres, that bathen in gladnesse,
> If any drope of pite in yow be,
> Remembreth yow on passed hevynesse
> That ye han felt, and on the adversite
> Of othere folk, and thenketh how that ye
> Han felt that Love dorste yow displese,
> Or ye han wonne hym with to grete an ese.
>
> And preieth for hem that ben in the cas
> Of Troilus, as ye may after here,
> That Love hem brynge in hevene to solas.

And ek for me preieth to God so dere
That I have myght to shewe in som manere
Swych peyne and wo as Loves folk endure,
In Troilus unsely aventure.

And biddeth ek for hem that ben despeired
In love, that nevere nyl recovered be,
And ek for hem that falsly ben apeired
Thorugh wikked tonges, be it he or she;
Thus biddeth God, for his benignite,
So graunte hem soone out of this world to pace,
That ben despeired out of Loves grace.

And biddeth ek for hem that ben at ese,
That God hem graunte ay good perseveraunce,
And sende hem myght hire ladies so to plese
That it to Love be worship and plesaunce.
For so hope I my sowle best avaunce,
To prey for hem that Loves servauntz be,
And write hire wo, and lyve in charite,
And for to have of hem compassioun,
As though I were hire owne brother dere.

It is remarkable that although they occupy a dominant place in the crucial introductory stanzas of the poem, these thirty lines contribute nothing to the exposition or the narrative. Their role is purely lyric. The passage is a self-contained set piece that keynotes lyric themes which run through the poem right to the Dantean conclusion, and which are enunciated repeatedly by all the main characters as well as by the narrator.

Like Machaut's ballade, the passage represents a type of love lyric common in Middle French verse, the prayer; more particularly, both examples are petitions expressed in quasi-Christian terms and forms, and addressed to initiates of love, asking them to assist lovers in their need and distress. Of course there are formal differences between the two; Chaucer's stanzas do not have a refrain or a consistent repetition of rimes. At the same time the origin of Chaucer's rime royal stanza is found in Machaut's ballade practice, and analysis of the imagery, diction, and syntax shows further basic affinities.

Chaucer's imagery and the figures invoked in the passage are standard fare in the French lyrics: in the world called up some few of the lovers find contentment, are pleasing to their ladies, enjoy heaven's solace, bask in happiness; most of them are enduring pain and woe, and they despair and suffer because of wicked tongues and long to leave the world; all of them are servants of Love, in need of prayers for grace, which will give them the strength to persevere in their calling. The narrator who refers to this world of Amour and who speaks on behalf of lovers is another relatively common figure in the lyrics. His deity seems both pagan and

Christian; he mentions prayers to "God" three times, but he also names "Love" as a presiding power five times. The diction is again remarkably repetitive: "ye" and "yow" echo through the first stanza, "hem" and "hire" in the last three. Forms of "love" occur seven times, and forms of "pray" and "bid" six times. None of the words are unusual; "plese", "ese", "despeyred", and "wo" are all repeated, and fortified by "pleseaunce"; "pite", "peyne", "apeyred", "grace", "adversite", etc.

The standard imagery and repetitive conventional diction again make it appropriate to speak of a pattern that matches the abstract design of the phonetics and the grammar. Though there is no refrain or consistent repetition of rime, the rime royal versification as Chaucer practices it here produces a marked phonetic configuration. The three rime endings that he intertwines in each stanza are predominantly extended rimes, and two rime sounds of the first stanza (*-ese*, *-e*) are repeated in the third and the fourth. The anaphoral ands and thats that begin almost half the lines, and the seven imperative *-eth* inflections that regularly recur, reinforce the repetitive effects of the rimes. Producing an effect comparable to the alliterating labials in "Plourez, dames," Chaucer uses numerous labial plosive p's and b's in important words and phrases like "bather," "drop of pite," and "despeired".

Chaucer's complex, flowing syntax is vital in the effect of the passage. Three of the four stanzas are made up of two sentences, the other of one.[41] Following Machaut's practice, all three sentence-endings within the stanzas come at the conclusion of lines in the middle of the stanzas, two of them at the metrical (and musical) hinge–that is, at the close of the *abab* section. The smoothness of the sentences masks impressive complexity. If we take the single sentence that makes up stanza 4, for instance, we find the sense flowing easily from the subject ("ye loveres") and a modifying clause ("that bathen . . ."), to a conditional clause ("If ony drop"), and thence to the two main verbs ("remembreth . . . and thenketh"), the first possessing a double object with complex modifiers ("Passed hevynesse . . . and . . . the adversite"), and the second leading to a concluding chain of three clauses. Undoubtedly, Chaucer learned much about building such sentences in emulating Machaut, whether consciously or not. The use of enjambment is symptomatic of the syntactical affinity: in Chaucer's four stanzas there are eight cases of enjambment, proportionately equivalent to the six of "Plourez, dames." By comparison, the other generally less skillful French lyric poets use briefer sentences with more end-stopping, while Boccaccio's *Il Filostrato* employs a more paratactic syntax with more enjambment, conducive to a brisk narrative pace.

As I have said, these four stanzas keynote the pervasive lyric element of the poem. They serve to blend the conventional features of an idealized world of Amour into the epic setting. The primary poetic values in the passage are those characteristic of works like "Plourez, dames," that is, of natural music. Representational features participate in the abstract patterning of the poem much as do phonetic and syntactic elements. In sum, Machaut's lyrics and dits provided Chaucer with a model of natural music which the English poet employed in all of his lyrics and much of his stanzaic work, *Troilus* most notably. In *Troilus*, of course, much goes beyond the Machauvian mode–the Troy story, the machinations of

Pandarus, the trappings of heroic verse. Yet the French contribution is never submerged. It remains prominent in the ballade stanza that Chaucer uses, in the large number of set pieces which with little alteration could be made into formes fixes lyrics, and in the character, dialogue, and behavior of the lovers.

NOTES

*Reprinted with permission from *Chaucer and His French Contemporaries. Natural Music in the Fourteenth Century* (Toronto: University of Toronto Press, 1991), pp. 3–42.

[1]Among the sometimes conflicting analyses of the *Prologue* are Hoepffner (Machaut 1908–21, I: 1ii–lv); Kelly 1978, 3–12; Calin 1974, 234–37; Brownlee 1984, 16–19; and Lukitsch 1983.

[2]Edited in Machaut 1908–21, 1–12 (quoted herein); and in Chichmaref, Machaut 1909, I: 3–13. The *Prologue* has 298 lines, including the four ballades that open it. The fiction of the work, in which Nature and Amour appear to Guillaume and provide him the wherewithal to write poetry, suggests that it preceded his other work; nevertheless, it was composed late in life (c. 1370) and reflects the knowledge that a career of writing had given him.

[3]See, e.g., Balade notée 32 in *Poésies,* in which the complaining lover declares, "Je ne say mon oeuvre contrefaire" (line 19). Chaucer's Mars follows this reasoning closely in *Complaint of Mars:* "If a wight shal pleyne pitously / Ther mot be cause wherfore that men pleyne" (lines 156–67). We understand that Machaut and Chaucer did not have to be suffering to compose effective complaints, though suffering was necessary to the poet-lovers in the fictions. Commenting on the sincerity of the earlier French poets, Robert Guiette remarks that they write not about "l'amour qu'ils vivent 'dans les faits' ou qu'ils ont vécu, mais l'amour idéal qu'ils pourraient vivre et comme ils pourraient le vivre selon les suggestions de la convention courtoise" (Guiette 1972, 43).

[4]The opening rubric of the *Prologue* states that the goddess Nature comes to Guillaume "volant orendroit plus que onques mais reveler et faire essaucier les biens et honneurs qui sont en Amours."

[5]Thus Lukitsch concludes that Machaut, even though Nature makes a threefold gift to him–Rhetorique and Scens, as well as Musique–thought of poetry as a kind of music: "All Machaut's remarks on the character of his poetry are in fact much more readily understood if we assume that he defines poetry as music" (Lukitsch 1983, 264).

[6]Frye 1985, 31–32. Frye also discusses the lyric at length in *Anatomy of Criticism* (Frye 1957, 246–50 & 270–81). For discontinuity as a characteristic of the long French *dit* see Huot 1987, 212–13, with references to Cerquiglini and Zumthor.

[7]Jakobson 1987, 70. For Jakobson, at least in translation, "emotive" and "expressive" are synonymous (66). In this study I aim to distinguish between these adjectives.

[8]In his analysis of the trouvère lyric, Robert Guiette makes a suggestive comparison of the medieval Romance lyric text to music, asking for a rediscovery of the "sens formel" of the lyrics. "One should read these chansons as one reads musical forms, in following their movements, relationships, and arrangements, but without neglecting the sense value of the theme and the expressive quality of the word-play and the arrangements. In the chanson one must consider the number or the formula, but perceive at the same time the incantatory power and the life, without which we would only have school exercises" (Guiette 1973, 43).

[9]"Rhythmic" (i.e., accentual) poetry contrasts with "metrical" (measured) verse. "Rithmica species est enim musice": *Parisiana Poetria* 1974, 6. Molinet, "L'Art de Rhétorique," in Langlois 1902, evidently follows John in stating, "Rethorique vulgaire est une espece de musique appellée richmique," and the anonymous author of "L'Art de science de rhetorique" (p. 265) also says much the same thing.

[10]*Leys d'Amours* I: 82. "E dizem que aquesta sciensa, en quant que toca bel ornat e bo de parlar, se fonda sobre rethorica." The *Leys* draws much of what it says about rhetoric from Brunetto Latini's *Trésor,* which places "li enseignemens de diteors" among the attributes of Rhetoric (Brunetto 1863, 9).

[11]Even the two that refer to rimed poetry as music call it "rhetorique vulgaire." The notion

of a "second rhetoric" was commonplace. Depending on the classifier's orientation, the first was either prose or Latin, and the second was either poetry or vernacular. (See Langlois 1902, i–iv.)

[12]Though the labels "natural music" and "artificial music" are not original with Deschamps, his distinction between them–spoken text versus sung text–evidently is new. We might nevertheless infer from the previous treatises how Deschamps arrived at his individualistic classification. The distinction between the two musics goes back to the ninth century, but the older formulations envision natural music as including more than spoken poetry. For the origins and earlier history of the concept, see Bower 1971. In the view of the influential Regino of Prum (d. 915), Bower notes, "Music exists on two levels: the natural, which embraces the music of the spheres, the harmony of the human body and soul, and music sung to the praise of God in the eight tones; and the artificial, music created by man, instrumental music consisting of five tones and two semitones" (22). Cassiodorus, though earlier than Regino, is somewhat closer to Deschamps. Stevens 1986 generalizes that Cassiodorus' "theoretical divisions apply to natural as opposed to artificial music, music of the human voice not of instruments. Vocal music is found both in song (sung poetry) and in speech" (378). See also Bower, 23.

[13]"Et neantmoins est chascune des ces deux plaisant a ouir par soy; et se puet l'une chanter par voix et par art, sanz parole; et aussis les diz des chançons se puent souventefoiz recorder en pluseurs lieux ou ilz sont moult voulentiers ois, et le chant de la musique artificiele n'aroit pas tousjours lieu, comme entre seigneurs et dames estans a leur privé et secretement, ou la musique naturele se puet dire et recorder par un homme seul, de bouche, ou lire aucun livre de ces choses plaisans devant un malade, et autres cas semblables ou le chant musicant n'aroit point lieu pour la haulteur d'icellui" (Deschamps 1878, VII: 272).

[14]The *Art de dictier* has been the subject of substantial scholarly attention. See especially Patterson 1935, I: 87–95; Dragonetti 1961, 49–64; Laurie 1964; and Varty 1965. The most recent discussion of Deschamps' concept of natural music is probably the most authoritative and provides precedent and support for important aspects of my argument (Stevens 1984, "'Music' of the Lyric"). The significance of the *Art* to Chaucer's concept of literature is treated by Olson 1973; see also Olson 1984, in which he credits Deschamps with more subtlety than he displays in the *Art de dictier* or elsewhere; e.g., at page 235 he deduces from Deschamps' failure to talk about functions of poetry beyond what he describes as "recreational" that Deschamps consciously excluded other functions. Considering the fragmentary system of the *Art*, Deschamps' failure to discuss a topic is minimally indicative. One might also note that Modern English "recreation" has rather narrow connotations as compared with the medieval French cognate "recreez" (from Latin "recreare"), which Deschamps employs in the *Art de dictier* (Deschamps 1878, VII: 269).

[15]The change in the mimetic and emotive relationship of music to text between the Middle Ages and the Renaissance is a basic point in two books by Stevens: *Music and Poetry* (Stevens 1961, esp. 33–38), and *Words and Music* (Stevens 1986, esp. 300–2); and throughout his inaugural lecture, *The Old Sound and the New* (Stevens 1982).

[16]In *Convivio* II, xiv, 110 Dante explicates the restful effects of music by referring to its actions on the "human spirits": "Music draws to itself the human spirits which are, as it were, mainly vapors of the heart, so that they almost cease from any action of their own, so undivided is the soul when it listens to Music; and the virtue of all the spirits is, as it were, concentrated in the spirit of sense which receives the sound" (Dante 1909).

[17]I might cite once more the interesting parallel found in Dante; in *Convivio* II xiv, 110 Dante speaks of the "sweetness" of music found in both words and song; he says that music "is wholly dependent on relation, as is seen in words arranged in harmony and in songs; and the harmony resulting from these is the sweeter in proportion to the beauty of the relation, which in that Science is especially beautiful, because this is its principal aim."

[18]Dragonetti 1960, 545. Though his study, like Guiette 1972, is based on an analysis of the Old French lyric, both works are relevant to analysis of the Middle French.

[19]Deschamps 1878, VII, 277: "Balade equivoque, retrograde et leonime. Et sont les plus fors

balades qui se puissent faire, car il couvient que la derreniere sillabe de chascun ver soit reprinse au commencement de ver ensuient, en autre signification et en autre sens que la fin du ver precedent" / "These are the most powerful [difficult?] ballades which can be made, for it is necessary that the last syllable of each line be repeated at the beginning of the following line, with another meaning and another sense than at the end of the line preceding." Though the meaning "difficult" is possible for "fortes," I translate it according to the more common sense, "powerful," since Deschamps discusses other lyric forms, such as the lay, that were more difficult to compose. But even if one sees "fortes" as pertaining primarily to difficulty of composition, the rationale for the effort would be the strength of the achievement.

[20]I develop more fully the comparison between the French syllabic and the Middle English alliterative tradition in "Chaucer and Deschamps' 'Natural Music'" (James Wimsatt 1991).

[21]The ballade (or ballada) stanza, to be sure, is tied more to the whole person than are the stanzas of the chanson (or canzone). Each of the ballade stanzas has the same refrain, and the form has a fixed number of stanzas (three).

[22]I follow Wilkins' introduction to *Louange*: "The underlying musical pattern of the ballade is I I II. . . . Normally, the two lines riming a b are set to the first music section, this then being repeated with lines three and four, also riming a b, since it is a fundamental rule that lines of verse set to identical music must have identical riming and metrical structure . . . . When Machaut composed no music for a poem the underlying structure is, of course, theoretical but nonetheless real" (Machaut 1973, 19).

[23]I assume Chaucer's "revel" in its position at the cesura will count one syllable ("rev'l"), and that necessary elisions will be made ("mery 'nd"). One also has to assume two silent terminal *e*'s for words in the succeeding stanzas of Chaucer's poem.

[24]Rime is not a major subject of discussion in Machaut's *Prologue*, though his use of rime there well illustrates its more importance. He does cite different types: "serpentine," "équivoque," "leonine," "croisie," "retrograde," "sonant," and "consonant" (Machaut 1908, V: 151–56). He does not explain his terms, and neither Deschamps nor other writers offer consistent explanations. In general, "sonant," "consonant," and "leonine" refer to varying extensions of the rime ending, with "sonant" signifying rime of the stressed terminal vowel only (also called "pauvre") or of vowel and consonant (examples from "Plourez, dames": "pour my" and "paly," "comm*ant*" and "reman*ant*"); "consonant," "riche," and "leonine" designate rimes that go beyond simple vowel-consonants to full consonant-vowel-consonant syllables, or vowel-consonant-feminine ending ("*vers*," "di*vers*"; "ent*ente*, ""augm*ente*"). There was no fixed label for further extensions of the rime ("c*e parti*," "d*eparti*"). "*Riche*" and "leonine" have taken on more specific meaning in modern usage. As already discussed, for the Middle French writers "équivoque" denotes rime of the same word with some change in sense ("vostre *servant*"; "en *servant*"). "Serpentine" perhaps signifies whole-line rime, very rare. Even more than with the retrograde-and-équivoque type, whole-line rime is more an ideal in the mind of the theoretician of natural music than a usual possibility. For definitions of the various terms, with references to the several treatises he edits, see Langlois 1902, "Table des noms propres et des termes techniques," 427–73.

[25]". . . to me it ys a great penaunce, / Syth rym in *English hath such skarsete*," etc. *Complaint of Venus,* Chaucer 1987, lines 79–80.

[26]J.B. Bessinger's reading of *To Rosemounde* on the recording, *The Poetry of Geoffrey Chaucer* (Caedmon TC 1226, 1967), illustrates well how the sounds of the refrain emphasize and fit in with the light spirit of the lyric.

[27]A good example of mimetic effects in the phonetics is found in the words of the duck and the goose in the *Parliament of Fowls*; see Chaucer 1987, especially lines 498–504 and 561–67.

[28]The only complaint for which Machaut provides music is that in *Remede de Fortune* lines 1193–1400. Neither he nor others followed up this musical composition.

[29]In line length Chaucer's stanzas are somewhat different from Machaut's. Every fourth line in Machaut's stanza has four syllables, while the other lines uniformly have either eight or ten. The lines in Anelida's complaint more or less reverse this scheme, with his fourth lines having ten syllables and the others eight.

[30]He wrote no five-stanza chansons unless, of course, they are lost or unidentified, as with the four French "Chançons Royaux" by "Ch" in the Pennsylvania manuscript. See James Wimsatt 1982, 1–35.

[31]Chaucer's single ballades are *To Rosemounde*, *Truth*, *Gentilesse*, *Lak of Stedfastnesse*, *Complaint of His Purse*, *Against Women Unconstant*, and *Legend of Good Women* F 249–69 (G 203–23). His triple ballades *Fortune* and *Complaint of Venus*, as well as his triple roundeau *Merciles Beaute*, were perhaps designed for musical settings. On the polytextual technique of presenting double or triple ballades musically, see Wilkins 1968, 125; and for its origins in motet practice, see Wilkins 1979, 10–16.

[32]The near-ballades include the five "terns" of the *Complaint of Mars* lines 164–298; the nine-stanza "Bill of Complaint" in *Complaint unto Pity* lines 57–119, divided every third stanza by a couplet riming on *-eyne* lines 76–77, 97–98, 118–19); the *Envoy to Scogan* (six stanzas), the *Envoy to Bukton*, *Womanly Noblesse*, and *A Ballade of Complaint* (ascribed).

[33]A single rondeau in the *Parliament of Fowls* (680–92), and a triple rondeau in *Merciles Beaute* (the attribution to Chaucer is safe, I believe).

[34]Among studies of Chaucer's versification, only Maynard 1934 registers a conviction that Chaucer developed the rime royal stanza from the French ballade; see especially 83–92. Maynard's study needs to be fortified by supporting data such as Wilkins and Poirion (1965) employ in their studies, and its description of the ballade is in part outdated. Baum 1961 exemplifies the still current uncertainty of scholars in stating that "no positive statement may be made" about whether Chaucer adopted rime royal from the ballade or developed it from an eight-line stanza form (48). Martin Stevens' "Royal Stanza" is similarly unsure about the debt of Chaucer's stanzas to the French (1979, 70a). Maynard shows that the designations "ballade and rime royal came to be practically synonymous," no doubt witnessing early recognition of the French origin of Chaucer's stanzas (88). See also Stevens 1979, 62–6 on the name "rime royal."

[35]*Remede de Fortune* is quoted herein from Machaut 1988 *Guillaume de Machaut: Le Jugement du roy de Behaigne and Remede de Fortune* (Wimsatt & Kibler).

[36]I have discussed at length the connection of *Troilus* with Middle French lyric in "The French Lyric Element" (James Wimsatt 1985). There are specific filiations between *Troilus* and *Remede de Fortune*. See Kittredge 1915 and James Wimsatt 1976.

[37]Robbins, "The Lyrics," in Rowland 1979, 382 thus characterizes *Troilus*. Comparably, in "The Vintner's Son" he refers to *Troilus* as "an intricate and closely worked *dit amoureux*" (in Kibler ed. 1979, 161).

[38]For Chaucer's knowledge of "Plourez, dames" see James Wimsatt 1978, 74. In the refrain line of one of his two ballades on Machaut's death, Deschamps appropriately echoes "Plourez, dames": "Vestez vous noir, plourez tous, Champenois / La mort Machaut, le noble rhetorique" (Deschamps 1878, I:244 [no. 123, lines 23–4]. See also Deschamps' ballade on the death of du Guesclin: II, 27–8 [no. 206, lines 9–10]).

[39]For the preference for alternation of masculine and feminine rimes, see Deschamps' *Art de dictier* (Machaut 1908, VII: 276) and the treatise of the Anonyme Lorrain in Langlois, ed. 1902, 202. The principle was often ignored.

40 In Stanza 2 the first sentence carries over to the middle of line 6. While such a break in the middle of the line is unusual, the length of the sentence is not. Indeed, many ballade stanzas, especially in the rime royal form, consist of a single sentence.

41 The analysis of Chaucer's rime royal stanza in Cowling 1926, expressed in terms of "pauses" and "half-pauses," is based on a study of all of Chaucer's stanzaic work. His conclusions suggest that the syntax of the four stanzas is typical of Chaucer's stanzas. Normally, says Cowling, the Chaucerian rime royal "is terminated by a full pause after the seventh line," and "there is usually one half-pause within the stanza, dividing it most often into a quatrain followed by a tercet" (312). Also relevant to this syntactic analysis is the comparison of Chaucer's *Troilus* stanza with Boccaccio's practice in the *Filostrato* in Wallace 1985, ch. 6.

Emerson Brown, Jr.

The Joy of Chaucer's Lydgate Lines

More than twenty years ago, in his indispensable essay on Chaucer's prosody, the editor of this volume lamented that "most contemporary criticism of Chaucer's art treats him *as a master in prose*" (Gaylord 1976, 30). That observation is no less true today, and so far as I can tell most contemporary teaching of Chaucer suffers from the same defect.

If Chaucer is a great poet and not simply a wise and witty fellow who happened to write in verse, teachers and readers of Chaucer need to attend not only to what he says but to how he says it. We need to attend especially to passages where Chaucer does things that could not be done as well, or at all, in prose. Inspired to do something about the lack Professor Gaylord describes and eager to offer talks for which oral delivery is useful (as it so rarely is in papers we dutifully read to one another at conferences), several years ago I lectured here and there suggesting some ways to get the poetry back into our appreciation of Chaucer.[1] One way involved Chaucer's so-called "Lydgate" or "broken-backed" lines. That part of the talk was so much fun to perform that I didn't write it up for publication until, with this volume, an unrefusable opportunity appeared.

Even though astute observers of the manuscript tradition have long recognized that Chaucer did, indeed, write Lydgate-like lines, editors of the most respected and widely used texts of Chaucer have persisted in perpetuating the distortions of Chaucer's rhythms that result from tidying up his verse to meet the later conventions of the English iambic pentameter line. As a result, such texts indoctrinate new readers into thinking of Chaucer as a poet writing, when he was careful enough to do so, the sort of line produced by Shakespeare, Milton, Wordsworth, and Tennyson. That's not bad company, but with such indoctrination, it is no wonder that those few readers of Chaucer who finally look at his poetry in a diplomatic edition of a reliable manuscript find some of his lines disturbingly out of place in the verse tradition in which they assume he belongs. As one thoughtful, conservative, and deservedly admired textual critic wrote to me:

> At all periods the best English poets have written a "performance rhythm," and Chaucer is one of them. What I don't like is the "Lydgate line" concept–Norman Blake has it too.... English verse has a melody; and some of us can hear it, after years of training to be sure, and some never can but have to scan. They are the ones who want to hypernormalize Chaucer's verse.

When those "years of training" include wide reading of later iambic pentameter poetry and Chaucer's verse in doctored texts, an unexpected conjunction of stresses is not likely to reveal the expected "melody." Thus Chaucer's editors can feel justified, indeed compelled, to overlook the authority of the best manuscripts and emend Chaucer's verse to bring it into harmony with the later tradition. In the process, they have not only altered what Chaucer wrote but weakened some of his finest lines.

It's not that Chaucer's poetry existed in a culture free of discord. Time and again the medieval world reveals a delight in bizarre incongruity, a willingness to play with established forms, an audacious capacity to detect hints of disorder in a putatively ordered and harmonious universe. This delight appears in the fantastic sculpture of Gothic cathedrals, in the Feast of Fools and wild Biblical parody of the Goliards, and in the anatomically remarkable activities carried out in the margins of medieval manuscripts. In a world that so rejoiced in unexpected, indeed, in grotesque, incongruity, one might expect to find a similar sense of play in the manipulation of poetic rhythms. Yet most modern editors have long labored under the assumption that the poet who could use the iconography of Pentecost to describe the twelve-fold division of a fart was too fastidious to have written a single "Lydgate line."

Before proceeding any further, I should explain what this term means. In 1891, J. Schick analyzed Lydgate's verse into five "principal metres" (Schick, liv). The third is the "peculiarly Lydgatian type, in which the thesis is wanting in the cesura, so that two accented syllables clash together":

```
 x    /     x  /        /  x  / x  /
Me thought I was ||  cast as in a traunce.
```

These two stresses at the cesura constitute the "Lydgate" or "broken-backed" line. Often Lydgate's versification is not easy to defend. In fact, for many of his lines it is probably wishful thinking to posit any coherent verse pattern at all, much less a felicitous one. But the issue here is not Lydgate's versifying skill but Chaucer's. If, as Schick claimed over a hundred years ago and as Derek Pearsall has affirmed, "Lydgate is entirely dependent on Chaucer in the choice of all his principal meters," and if the "broken-backed" line is among Lydgate's principal meters (as it indisputably is), then Chaucer wrote "Lydgate lines."[2] Lydgate, it is true, was appropriately modest about his metrical skills, but Chaucer was his model, and in his introduction to the *Siege of Thebes*, Lydgate praises Chaucer and does his best to establish himself as Chaucer's disciple and continuator. Here, if anywhere, we would expect Lydgate to imitate Chaucer's verse assiduously, and here "broken backed" lines abound:

> Of eche thyng / keping in substaunce (53)
> Voyding the Chaf / sothly for to seyn (55)
> The holy seynt / plenly to visite (71)
> (Lydgate 1930)

(For some further examples, see lines 81, 98, 102, 112, 117, 119, 142–43, 158, 160.)

Although Schick restricts his "peculiarly Lydgatian" lines to those with juxtaposed stresses at the cesura (as here), an awkward (to modern ears) jamming together of stressed syllables can occur elsewhere in the line, and Chaucer's editors smooth out those lines as well. The term "Lydgate effect" will refer to any such pair of stresses editors have removed from our awareness of Chaucer's metrical practices. The most reliable manuscripts record hundreds of places where Chaucer failed to adhere to later conventions of iambic respectability.

Over the centuries, editors and critics have found various ways to deal with these Lydgate effects. They have chided Chaucer for metrical crudeness and let it go at that. They have acknowledged the roughness of the verse, excusing it as inevitable given the barbarism of Chaucer's age, and have then gone on to praise him for being able to shine, although perhaps dimly, in such a dark world. Or they have assumed that Chaucer was a better (that is, more regular) versifier than the best manuscripts reveal, and they have touched up his lines wherever necessary to make them into respectable (that is, more regular) iambic pentameter. For a long time this third approach has prevailed in editions intended for students and for most scholarly work as well.[3] The trouble with this approach, as Eleanor Hammond pointed out long ago, is "the tendency to reason in a circle, to start from the assumption that Chaucer is 'impeccable,' and, after constructing a body of texts on that hypothesis, by eliminating or altering whatever seems incompatible, to deduce from them the original assumption of the impeccability of Chaucer." Hammond observed, ruefully, that "most authorities still refuse to accept the existence in Chaucer of the so-called 'Lydgate Line'" (Hammond 1908, 481). Most authorities are still refusing.

Even the best manuscripts are far from flawless. Still, although neither is the replica of Chaucer's own autograph copy that we all lust for, Chaucer's editors have long recognized that the Hengwrt (Hg) and Ellesmere (El) manuscripts are by far the best manuscripts of the Canterbury Tales, and the Hg text and the El variants are easily accessible in the Variorum edition of Hg (Chaucer 1979). Until recently, El was thought the better of the two. It contains unmistakably Chaucerian material missing in Hg; it presents the tales in a more coherent order; it is metrically smoother; and it contains the well-known pictures of the Canterbury pilgrims. But some scholars have long suspected that Hg–a less lavishly produced and less heavily edited copy written by the same scribe–is actually superior to El in those parts it contains. The Variorum edition of Hg and the labors of Variorum editors preparing the individual fascicles of the Canterbury Tales have firmed that suspicion into strong conviction. Derek Pearsall, for example, accepts Hg's readings over El's "on a variety of grounds," among them "[m]ore authentic metrical practice," as he explains:

> [S]tudy of the text as it is presented in Hg, and of the relation between Hg and other MSS., compels one to recognize that the metrical practice revealed in Hg is much more likely to be authentically Chaucerian. The freedom and generosity in the conception of the rhythmical possibilities of the pentameter, the audacity of variation and experimentation, and the subtle sense of the relation between rhetorical and syntactical impetus and rhythmical variation, as they may be deduced from Hg, are all positive characteristics of the creative poet at work, whilst the mending and smoothing of lines to produce a mechanically regular syllable count, at the expense of natural speech-rhythms, are likely to be characteristic of the improving scribe or editor. (Chaucer 1984a, 96)

In El, he notes, several variants "demonstrate a minute and pedantic care for metrical regularity" (98). Nonetheless, El agrees with Hg in recording a great many lines tainted by that dastardly Lydgate effect.

Finding an example of this Lydgate effect in Chaucer need take us no further than the eighth line of the General Prologue:

/ x x / x / / x / (x)
Hath in the Ram his half cours yronne[4]

The best manuscripts present the line as here, without the archaic weak adjective ending on "half" that most editors supply.[5] No one doubts that Chaucer often begins a basically iambic line with a trochee. But assuming that in the rest of the line weak stresses precede strong ones with relentless regularity leads to metrical gibberish:

/ x x / x / x / x /
Hath in the Ram his half cours yronnë

Obviously, this will not do. Perhaps to avoid such a disaster but more likely simply out of the conviction that Chaucer was too good a poet to cram two stresses awkwardly together on "half cours," with a few exceptions editors have overlooked the evidence of the manuscripts, accepted the variant found in the ever fussy Harley 7334 scribe and elsewhere, and stuck a final *-e* on "half," usually substituting *v* for *f*, to produce "halve," a phonetically defensible spelling but one found in none of the manuscripts.[6] There it is, a line of which Alfred, Lord Tennyson would have been proud:

/ x x / x / x / x / (x)
Hath in the Ram his halvë cours yronnë

Obviously, this is an improvement over the imaginary metrical horror above, but is it an improvement over what Chaucer most likely wrote, and is there a way to scan Chaucer's line that preserves the evidence of the manuscripts without destroying the meter? I believe there is, a technique that saves not only this line but many frequently emended lines throughout Chaucer's works. By treating "half" as a long syllable, as it is both in actual pronunciation and by the conventions of classical prosody, we can linger on that syllable, emphasizing its length and giving it a hovering effect (marked thus: /–), secure in the knowledge that the rhythm is moving along nicely without our tinkering and that the underlying meter and normal stress patterns need not be at odds, like this:

/ x x / x /– / x / (x)
Hath in the Ram his half cours yronnë

I prefer that line and have no trouble believing that Chaucer knew what he was doing when he wrote it, perhaps aware that the break in rhythm brings extra emphasis to the phrase "half cours." But whether we prefer this line or not, we should at least give it a sympathetic hearing.

After all, what evidence is there that Chaucer invariably wrote the sort of iambic pentameter lines that his editors supply? It's not that he is unconcerned about meter. Addressing his "little bok," *Troilus and Criseyde*, he prays "that non myswrite the,/ Ne the mysmetre for defaute of tonge" (5.1795–96). But "iambic pentameter" is our description of Chaucer's predominant meter–our description and perhaps our creation. As some theorists have suggested, Chaucer may have intended four principal stresses, two per half line. Rhetorical emphasis and normal speech patterns often support this approach, as seen in the opening lines of the *Canterbury Tales*:

/ x / x x x / x / (x)
Whan that Au(e)ryll with his shoures sootë
x / x / x / x x x /(x)
The droght of March hath percëd to the rootë

A few can be stretched to six:

x / x / x / x / x / x /
But soorë weptë she if oon of hem were deed (GP 148)

There are even times, generally late at night, when Chaucer's lines seem to sing with sixteen beats per line, leading me to suppose that he should be credited with inventing the twelve-bar blues, a hypothesis with which those who have heard these thoughts in public performance can hardly fail to agree. (You had to be there.)

Tastes and notions of correctness change. The Lydgatian "Hath in the Ram his half cours yronne" may sound crude and a-rhythmic to us, but to other ears it might, though a surprise in its metrical surroundings, fit into long-recognized and accepted verse forms. With stressed and unstressed syllables mentally converted to long and short ones to accord with classical prosody, those first seven syllables would constitute the so-called aristophanic verse, a verse made up of a choriam,

– x x – , and a bacchiac, x – –, a verse form found, for example, in Horace's "Lydia, dic, per omnes" (*Odes*, 1.8).

It would be risky to suggest that Chaucer consciously imitated classical Latin meter here, rounding off an aristophanic verse with an amphibrach in brilliant play against the underlying iambic pentameter. Less risky is it, however, to suggest that rhythms that Shakespeare and others have taught us to think of as crude were not necessarily crude to medieval poets and their audience, or that rhythms editors have imposed on Chaucer's verse might sound crude or square to him.

As we all realize, absolute metrical regularity is the death of poetry. No one would insist that all of Chaucer's lines must consist of five perfect iambs. Everyone accepts his so-called "headless line," as in the first line of the General Prologue, and his frequent use of a trochee as the first foot of a line. The problem is not that Chaucer departed from absolute metrical regularity–he would be unreadable if he didn't–but that he departed in ways many readers now find unacceptable. Otherwise reliable scribes keep jamming those stressed syllables together, and we find it difficult to keep the "beat."

Yet the "beat" is what great poets begin with. They know what the beat is. They have it in mind and know that their audience can sense its presence, but they don't cram it down our throats. If you want to hear musical meter gone wrong by a process of oversimplification similar to that of doctored texts of Chaucer, listen to a symphony orchestra try to play jazz. It will play the notes, perfectly measured out as written, but it doesn't swing. And the reason it doesn't swing is that it makes the beat too obvious by slamming right down on top of it instead of playing around it. A twentieth century practitioner of subtle rhythms had this to say about the beat:

> You don't play the beat where it is. You draw a picture away from the beat right up to its core with different notes of different sounds of the drum instruments so continuously that the core is always there for an open mind. While you make it live, now and then you go inside the beat, dead center, and split the core to the sides and shatter the illusion so there is no shakiness ever. If one tries to stay inside dead center or directly on top of the beat or on the bottom, the beat is too rigid on the outside where it is heard. The stiffness should only be felt inside the imaginary center of the exact tempo's core. (Charles Mingus, quoted in *The New Yorker* [June 18, 1979], p. 100.)

But how outrageously anachronistic to suggest that the comments of an American jazz musician can have anything to do with Chaucer! If Chaucer's sense of metrical propriety was simple and smooth enough to forbid two consecutive stresses where we don't expect them, then it is logical to assume that the rhythms of music in his time would also be simple and smooth, nothing remotely like the complex rhythms of bebop.

Had every feature of Chaucer's world been as crude and simple as we assume was true of the plumbing, then the idea that late fourteenth century music was equally simple might seem logical enough. But some fourteenth century music was not that simple at all. This is the period of the *Ars Nova* (taken from the name of a treatise by Philippe de Vitry), the *Ars Subtilior,* and, as at least one musicologist would have it, of the *Ars Subtilissima.* As Plato, Hitler, and Stalin, among many others, reveal, the respect that the totalitarian mind has for art does not necessarily encourage artistic innovation and freedom.[7] Musical innovation so alarmed Pope John XXII that he tried to put an end to it in the bull, *Docta sanctarum.* That was in 1322, but the trouble was just beginning.

With Philippe de Vitry, Guillaume de Machaut, and several other composers later in the century, tonal and rhythmic complexity increased to an extraordinary extent. Critics have been exploring the relationship between music and Chaucer's poetry for at least a century and a half, from the impressionistic ramblings of Leigh Hunt to the more hard-headed and historically based studies of recent decades. Far from being a daring hypothesis proposed by only a handful of modern musicologists, the complexity of fourteenth century music is duly noted in standard reference works, as, for example, here: "[Machaut's great Mass] combines solid tradition, in its isorhythmic foundations, with wild audacity, especially in its astounding rhythms and intervals" (*The New Catholic Encyclopedia,* 10.11). In his description of late fourteenth century mannerist style (*Ars subtilior*), Richard Hoppin describes a "polyphony in which the individual lines achieved a maximum of rhythmic independence"; in one traditional form, a "stable foundation [in the tenor] enabled the cantus to indulge in a wide variety of rhythmic complications, sometimes to the point of destroying all feeling of a consistent metrical organization" (Hoppin 1978, 475). In accord with Hoppin is David Monroe, one of the finest twentieth century performers of medieval music:

> [The late fourteenth century] *avant-garde* . . . produced works which in harmonic daring and rhythmic complexity have not been equaled until the twentieth century. . . [In one piece] the upper two parts indulge in vigorous hemiolas which are literally 'against the time'. . . . [In another] the composer seems to be attempting to cram into one piece all the notational subtleties and intricate cross rhythms of which music is capable. (Monroe 1973, 14)

Although the trend-setters and most famous names are from the continent, similar developments were occurring in England (Hoppin 1978, 508–10).[8] Given such variety and complexity in the music of Chaucer's contemporaries, it may be legitimate to wonder if one enthusiastic and influential defender of emending Chaucer's Lydgate effects fully grasped the essence of the problem when he complained to a roomful of Chaucerians that "some of you can't keep time to a five-beat line."

One word in particular provides interesting evidence concerning Chaucer's metrical practice. Lacking the time, patience, and expertise required for extensive data-crunching, I sought examples of a Lydgate effect involving a word that could, by its etymology, have a final *-e* and that appears often enough to give a good sample without appearing so often as to be overwhelming. What I found was a *host* of examples.

Middle English *ho(o)st(e), ost,* derives from Old French *(h)ost(e)*, the final *-e* of which would not have been pronounced by the fourteenth century (and was not part of the original etymon, deriving from Latin *hospes, hospitem*–the [h] had been lost in Old French pronunciation, but the spelling with "h" was returning since the twelfth century). Of course, the final -*e*'s that have been silent in French speech for centuries were, and are still, pronounced in French verse and song–one more reason, if one more is needed, to believe that some of the no longer spoken final -*e*'s in Chaucer's verse are to be pronounced as well.[9] Some twenty times in the Canterbury Tales a stressed "host" precedes a stressed syllable beginning with a consonant. All Chaucer had to do to avoid that Lydgate effect was add a final -*e* to "host." (It would have been "inorganic," i.e., non-etymological.) Did he add that -*e* or didn't he? Hg and El do not show a final -e in a single one of those lines. Yet modern editors disagree, spectacularly.

Aside from Manly and Rickert, the Variorum, and Blake, editors almost always smooth out "host" by adding a final -*e*.[10] And Manly and Rickert show little confidence in the manuscripts: "not even the earliest and best can be depended upon to represent Chaucerian usage in the matter of the final *e*"; Hengwrt, Ellesmere, and Corpus "almost never write 'Hoste' although the word is often disyllabic" (Manly and Rickert 1940, 3.421). Yet in rime position, Chaucer invariably matches "host" with uninflected Anglo-Saxon monosyllables: *boast, cost, ghost, most,* and *wost.* If Chaucer wrote a disyllabic "hoste," then either the excellent scribe who prepared Hg and El or some editor who worked over the text before it reached him systematically deleted every final -*e* on "hoste" that Chaucer had written. Scribes and editors add final -*e*'s all over the place, but why delete them? Simply in conscious or unconscious effort to make "host" conform to normal speech? But why delete the -*e* on "hoste" while faithfully transcribing hundreds of other -*e*'s that also were not pronounced? Simply in conformity to the scribe's own spelling habits, overruling his copy text with absolute consistency in a few dozen words scattered over thousands of lines in making two separate copies at different times? Why not follow a basic scientific principle and accept the simplest explanation: that the scribe wrote "ho(o)st" because he was faithfully following copy?[11]

In other manuscripts, "hostes" creep in, particularly in Harley 7334, whose scribe is also given to eking out lines by adding such dreary fillers as "ful" and "wel" (e.g., "Oure hoost saugh wel . . ." [A3128]; " . . . host ful leue . . . " [A3501]). But scholars have long recognized that Harley 7334 is of little value in determining what Chaucer wrote.

Try reading some of the unamended lines aloud, pausing to emphasize the first word in the Lydgate effect in the fashion suggested above. Read them aloud and *listen*:

x /– / x / x / x /
Oure hoost lough and swoor so moot I gon (MilT 3114)

x /x / x /– / x /
He seydë John myn hoost lief and deer(e) (MilT 3501)

x / x /x / x /– /x
Sire Clerk of Oxenford our Hoost saydë (ClkP 1)

As you become accustomed to giving that first syllable enough length to compensate for the felt absence of an unstressed syllable, it becomes more likely that Lydgate's "broken-backed" lines seem like wretched verse not because their meter is intrinsically ugly but because Lydgate uses it far too often and so mindlessly that it bears little relationship to what he is trying to say. Like many disciples, Lydgate may be slavishly imitating a form of his master's without grasping its proper use. Unlike Lydgate, Chaucer employed this pattern rarely enough so that it retains its surprise value and adds something to the line.

In performance, Chaucer (or any other reader) might focus reaction to the pattern by tone of voice. What it adds for us, as we read silently, depends on what voice we hear each time we read Chaucer. The point is not that a break in anticipated meter means some specific thing but that it encourages the reader to pause and think, something Chaucer so often invites us to do. When I read this next line, the voice I hear suggests that the Lydgate effect may gently distance the poet from his pilgrim narrator's obvious admiration for the Prioress:

x / x / x / x /– /
Her grettest ooth was but by Seint Loy (GP 120)

But whatever effect *Seint Loy* has, the editorial tinkering that eliminates it produces a line that is not only less interesting metrically but less rich in connotation:

x /x / x / x /x /
Hir grettest ooth was but by Seintë Loy

Similar in its subtle suggestion of the narrator's naïveté is:

x / x / x /x /– /x
Of cursing oght(e) ech gilty man dredë (GP 660)

If the best manuscripts follow copy exactly in this next example, Chaucer could be remarkably careful in indicating when he wanted the extra emphasis of a Lydgate effect and when he didn't. When the mysterious old man in the Pardoner's Tale first appears, the long stress on "old" unrelieved by an unstressed syllable urges a split second of extra attention to his age, as it contrasts with that of the insolent youths who confront him. That accomplished, Chaucer immediately returns to his usual stress pattern, perhaps further emphasizing the Lydgatian "old man" by contrast:

x /– / x x /x \ x /x
An old man and a pourë with hem mettë
x /x / x /x\ x /x
This oldë man ful mekëly hem grettë (PardT 713-14)

But for me, the mother of all Lydgate effects occurs at the climax of the Nun's Priest's Tale:

x / x /– / x / x /
And whan the fox saugh that he was goon (NPT *4608)

Pratt alone (Chaucer 1966) prints the line as Chaucer wrote it. Other editors substitute these dreary refinements:

x / x / \ x x / x /
And whan the fox saugh that the cok was gon

(for syllable count: Manly, Robinson, Baugh, Fisher, Benson); or

x / x / x \ x / x /
And whan the fox sawgh that he was y-gon
(Skeat; "was agoon," Pollard/Donaldson)

Without being indoctrinated to believe that Chaucer's verse scans like Tennyson's, it is difficult to imagine that experienced and sensitive readers could find either of these relentlessly regular lines superior to what Chaucer wrote.

We recall the scene. After several lines of essentially smooth iambics, the sudden break in rhythm at "fox saugh" surprises us at the exact moment when Chanticleer surprises the fox.[12] Nor is this the only startling yet apt break with iambic respectability in the Nun's Priest's Tale. Pertelote ends her comically protracted medical and pharmacological discourse with a detailed prescription to cure her husband's affliction. This passage is also in iambic pentameter, its smooth rhythms and learned terminology perhaps lulling us into forgetting that we are listening to a hen who has failed utterly to grasp the seriousness of her rooster's premonitory dream. Then she finishes her medical advice with a Lydgate-line of at least twelve syllables (with "merye is" we have a feminine rime with the previous "beryis"), followed by one that sounds to me like two dactyls followed by two iambs, a marvelous line that starts out almost as if it were bringing the dactylic hexameter of classical epic into the hunt and peck mock-epic world of the barnyard (with a fowlish intonation) :

x / /\– / x x x / x / x x
Of herb(e) yue growynge in oure yerd ther mery(e) is;

/ x x / x x / x / x /
Pekke hem vp right as they growe and ete hem in. (*4157-58)

If it is not clear by now that Lydgate-effects and other metrical surprises in the best Chaucer manuscripts belong there and merit attention, mere piling up of further examples will probably not help much. Instead, I would like to conclude by returning to the eighth line of the General Prologue.

An ingenious reader given to flights of interpretive fancy might be tempted to read much into Chaucer's delicate placing of the first Lydgate-effect in the Canterbury Tales. The words where that effect occurs, "half cours," appear almost exactly half way between the "Whan that April" that begins the General Prologue and the holy place ("Caunterbury") that is the pilgrims' goal. As the opening lines of the Prologue challenge us to learn the need and the way to move from spring weather, lovesick birds, and professional pilgrims to the blessed martyr's shrine, so the challenge of the fictional pilgrimage is to complete both that same journey to Canterbury and a parallel anagogical journey as well. This latter journey, implied from the outset, the good Parson finally makes explicit at the end, praying in his prologue that Jesus

> . . . for his grace wit me sende
> To shewe yow the wey in this viage
> Of thilke partfit glorious pilgrymage
> That highte Ierusalem celestial.

This is the journey that Saint Paul describes as, of all things, a *course:*

> For I am even now ready to be sacrificed; and the time of my dissolution is at hand. I have fought a good fight; I have finished my course (*cursum consummavi*); I have kept the faith (*2 Tim* 4.6–7).
>
> But I fear none of these things [the "bands and afflictions" awaiting him at Jerusalem], neither do I count my life more precious than myself, so that I may consummate my course (*cursum meum*) and the ministry of the word which I received from the Lord Jesus. (*Acts* 20.24).

Part of the challenge Chaucer accepted was finding a geographical, spiritual, and literary answer to a question that would not be grossly distorted if it were put in just these terms: how do you transform a half course and return (from the Tabard to Canterbury and back) into a whole course (from earthly existence to the heavenly Jerusalem)? How do you persuade pilgrims and readers that their proper movement is not circular and repetitive but linear? Chaucer captured the cyclical and hence non-teleological view of human history poignantly in the Stoical resignation of Egeus in the tale that begins the pilgrimage:

> This world nys but a thurghfare ful of wo
> 2848 And we been pilgrymes, passynge to and fro
> Deeth is an ende of euery worldly soore.

To the ancients, history is circular, lacking both beginning and end. In the pagan wisdom of Egeus, pilgrims can only pass "to and fro." But to Christians, "the wicked walk in circles" (*in circuitu, Psalm* 11.9), a passage Augustine uses frequently in his attack on those philosophers whose sempiternally repeated cycles of time deny both the creation and the end of human history (*City of God*, 12.13–16). Christian pilgrims should not pass "to" (Canterbury) and "fro" (back to the Tabard). On the highest level, their pilgrimage (and the one we take with them) should lead to "Jerusalem celestial" and end there.

In order, finally, to reveal unmistakably the presence of the anagogical in the literal, Chaucer had to leave his masterpiece incomplete, thwarting Harry Bailey's (and his own?) design for an outing of jolly tale-telling on both the journey outward and the return. Chaucer had to show that in the only terms that counted when the Parson's turn came round at last, Canterbury was not halfway through the course, was not the turning point in the race through life, but was the finish line. As the poem begins, the sun is at a halfway point. Although we don't know it yet, sitting as we are in the Tabard, ready to wend on our pilgrimage, we too are already at the halfway point–"nel mezzo del cammin di nostra vita." Like Dante's, our journey out is–*sub specie aeternitatis*–our journey home.

Needless to say, it would take a more confident (or foolhardy) critic than I to claim that the absence of a single final *-e* in one line encourages or even permits such wild speculation. I shall be more cautious and claim only that until our texts contain what the most dependable evidence indicates that Chaucer wrote, no such speculation is even possible. "Hath in the Ram his halfë cours yronne" is an ordinary, regular line. "Hath in the Ram his half cours yronne" is not. It may remind us of the delight in the unexpected that is so much a part of medieval life. It may remind us of the wild tonal and rhythmic complexity of late medieval music. It may even prod us to pause and think about half courses. If nothing else, it may fill our hearts with joy, as we tap our feet and hear–far off but distinct–Geoffrey Chaucer swing.

NOTES

[1]Those sites and occasions included South Atlantic Modern Language Association, Medieval Academy, the Five Colleges group at Amherst, and Rutgers–as part of the celebration honoring Alfred Kellogg at the time of his retirement.

I wish to take this opportunity to thank Fred C. Robinson, David Benson, Howell Chickering, and Professor Kellogg for encouraging my act.

[2]"The peculiarity of his metre, and in particular the hard core of broken-backed and headless lines, must therefore be attributed, again, to the elusive example of Chaucer" (Pearsall 1970, 62).

[3]The Variorum editors, cautious about emending *causa metri*, represent Chaucer's lines accurately, as does Norman Blake, persuaded that "whatever is not in [the Hengwrt manuscripts] may be considered spurious" (Blake 1979, 9–10). Those exceptions aside, Skeat, Pollard, Robinson, Donaldson, Baugh, Pratt, Fisher, and Benson are virtually identical in their sweeping removal of manuscript-supported Lydgate effects. I omit from consideration the many anthologies containing excerpts of Chaucer intended for classroom use. When not simply reproducing earlier doctored texts, such collections tend to simplify Chaucer's language even further.

[4]*Canterbury Tales* lines that appear in Hg are quoted from the Variorum facsimile (Chaucer 1979); other lines and all line numbers are from Benson's Chaucer 1987.

[5]Joining Hg and El are Petworth, Lansdowne, Harley 1758, and Selden. Bodley 686, Fitzwilliam, Harley 7333 and 7334, and Trinity Oxford have "his halfe."

[6]Skeat's comment is instructive: "in A8, the grammar and scansion require *half-e* not half; though, curiously enough, this correct form appears in H[1] only, among all the seven MSS" (Chaucer 1894, vol. 4, p. xviii). Aside from the editions rigorously faithful to Hg, the only noteworthy exceptions are Pratt's (Chaucer 1966) and, perhaps influenced by Pratt, Benson's (Chaucer 1987).

[7]Plato: "For a change to a new type of music is something to be aware of as a hazard of all our fortunes. For the modes of music are never disturbed without unsettling of the most fundamental political and social conventions, as Damon [of Athens, fl. 460 B.C.E] affirms and as I am convinced" (*Republic*, 4.424).

[8]The Old Hall manuscript "presents a synopsis of the musical genres and styles that were being cultivated in England at the turn of the century," among which, some "are written in

the complex meters and rhythms typical of late fourteenth century French music" (Yudkin 1989, 579).

[9]Although Southworth's theory that Chaucer's final e's were not pronounced was harshly attacked when it first appeared decades ago and has been further discredited since, unassailable refutation of it may finally have arrived (see Barber and Barber 1990 & 1991).

[10]In five instances some editors restrain from adding the final-*e*: Skeat, Baugh, and Fisher at Man of Law's Epilogue 1174, the latter two finding an additional syllable by substituting the manuscript variant "herkeneth" for "herkneth"; Baugh and Fisher at Wife of Bath's Prologue 850, and Skeat, Robinson, Baugh, Fisher, and Benson at Parson's Prologue 67. These exceptions can be wrenched into iambic respectability by pronouncing some final *-e* in the neighborhood (or by stressing "herkeneth" on the second syllable) but doing so results in absurdly unnatural stress patterns. Pollard always adds an *-e* and compounds the damage by marking it to be pronounced.

[11]Manly and Rickert would disagree: "it is not wise . . . to conclude . . . that because the spelling of the MSS having the best texts agree in general, these MSS reproduce the spelling of the original. It is far more likely that the agreement means that they were made by scribes who had received the same type of training" (1940, I.560).

[12]Pearsall retains the Hg/El version, as would be expected, and finds it acceptable even though it is "defective of a syllable" (Chaucer 1983, 253n). Still, the line is not quite a "good 'Lydgate line'," a standard that NPT *3970 achieves (130n).

Part Three:
Essays on Prosodic Practices

Winthrop Wetherbee

Theme, Prosody, and Mimesis in the *Book of the Duchess*

Perhaps the most useful description of the style of the *Book of the Duchess* is that of Wolfgang Clemen (Clemen 1964, 62–65). Throughout the poem, he observes, flights of rhetoric wrought to "the pitch of exaggeration" alternate, not always gracefully, with colloquial passages full of "sudden cries and pious ejaculations," vows, protestations, asides, and an elliptical syntax where relatives are "'swallowed' as it were, in the hasty and emotional pressure of the narrative."[1] Chaucer's versification is experimental in a complementary way: bold, pungent, and aiming always at "variety and urgency." Unlike the subtle fluency of Gower, whose dialogue preserves its animation without requiring us to supply so much as an exclamation point, reading aloud a Chaucerian passage like that which reveals the fact of the lady's death (BD 1298–1310) can leave one breathless.

The value of Clemen's response to Chaucer's style lies not so much in its general accuracy–in fact only a few passages in the poem answer faithfully to his description–but rather in its recognition of the complication created by sound, syntax and rhythm in a poem which, in its formal aspect, emulates the courtly elegance of the *dits* of Machaut and Froissart. As Clemen goes on to remark, the effect of this elaborate and vivid style on our response to the series of vivid pictures it serves to frame is hard to characterize: some essential point seems continually to elude us. I will be arguing in this essay that the elusiveness Clemen notes is an essential strategy of the *Book of the Duchess*, and that an important index to the poem's complex intention can be found in the seeming eccentricities of its verse. We are too often reminded that this is early work, "experimental" in a sense which tends to imply uncertainty or inconsistency. I will make no attempt to defend the metrics of the *Book of the Duchess* against any such charge of "immaturity," something which in any case seems to me impossible to define, nor will I try to mediate among critics who have sought to characterize the poem's line in terms of its relative indebtedness to the model of the *octosyllabe*, or to the primarily accentual meters of earlier Middle English verse.[2] There can be no doubt that, as James Wimsatt has argued, the "music" Chaucer would have discovered in Machaut and his French followers is something altogether different from what the alliterative tradition bequeathed to him, and that his prosody was strongly influenced by it (Wimsatt 1991b, 288–9; cf. Baltzer et al. 1991, 6–7, 136–47). Nevertheless, his verse remains different from that of his French contemporaries in fundamental ways which have to do largely with the rhythm and accentual patterns of English.[3]

There is no contradiction in saying that Chaucer wrote English verse in French forms, and to decide whether French or English models exercised the greater influence on him would require evidence we have not yet discovered. Instead I take for granted that Chaucer's metrical practice is that of a conscious artist, astutely responsive to the subtleties of the verse of his French contemporaries,[4] and well aware of the rhythmical possibilities afforded by a hybrid Franco-English diction. On this basis I will explore what I take to be his most significant manipulations of sound and rhythm, isolating such features as pacing, enjambment, and the use of hypermetrical lines, in order to demonstrate the correlation between the prosody of the *Book of the Duchess* and its most important themes. Much of what I have to say amounts to little more than an inventory of recurring phenomena which I have sometimes been content to define rather impressionistically, but my purpose is less to characterize Chaucer's verse technique in terms of standard prosody than to show that his own prosody in this early poem is conscious, intricate, and carefully adapted to the representation of the delicate psychological process the poem describes. Again and again metrical effects that may appear simply eccentric or accidental reveal themselves as calculated gestures, ways of calling attention to an underlying existential level of experience which the poem's formal rhetoric and conventions tend to obscure.

Like any argument about prosody, mine will rely largely on my empirical response to Chaucer's lines, and I will be even less concerned than most of the critics I cite with metrical "rules." Nonetheless I should note that my understanding of the tetrameter of the *Book of the Duchess* rests on certain assumptions. I would argue for a considerable flexibility in determining the metrical value of final *-e*. "Noble" has to my ear the value of a monosyllable in BD 435 ("That th**óugh** **Á**rgus the n**ó**ble cont**óu**r"), but is bisyllabic in 287 ("That n**ó**ble mán, the **Á**ffrikán"). On the other hand, I note that where final-*e* has inflectional value it is usually so disposed in the line as to assume syllabic value as well (Chaucer 1982, 68-70; Samuels 1972). My standard for the tetrameter occasionally requires the near conflation of syllables in determining quantity. Thus in BD 14 ("For s**ó**rwful ymáginá**á**cióun"), I hear the suffix "-ful" and the unstressed initial syllable of "ymaginacioun" as having together the metrical value of a single syllable, and I would grant the same license for more coarsely textured juxtapositions like those of weak final syllable and auxiliary verb in BD 101 ("So whán this **lá**d*y koude* h**é**re no w**ó**rd"), or weak final syllable and pronoun in 885 ("But whé*ther she* kn**é**w or knéw it nóght"). With due allowance for lines that lack an initial unstressed syllable (common also in the more obviously "regular" *House of Fame*) and for phrases that seem to read best as anapestic (a phenomenon in keeping with French practice, or that followed in the Middle English rendering of the *Roman de la Rose*), I hear the meter of the poem as basically tetrameter, basically iambic.

Song and the making of verse are important matters in the *Book of the Duchess*, and the passages which deal with these matters provide a good introduction to the intricacies of the poem's prosody. When Chaucer's dreamer-narrator comes upon the Man in Black, the Knight is engaged, as the conventional framing of the encounter would lead us to expect, in song:

> He made of ryme ten vers or twelve
> 464 Of a compleynte to himselve–[5]

A few lines later we hear these "ten or twelve" verses (in fact, eleven), but we can hardly be said to hear them performed:

> 470 Ful pitous pale and nothyng red,
> He sayd a lay, a maner song,
> Withoute noote, withoute song, . . .

The song is a solitary and private act. The Knight's extreme pallor, and the more elaborate analysis of his psycho-physical state a few lines later (487–513) , indicate that his utterance is the product of a genuine crisis. Artistry is incidental to its production. The narrator is offhand and vague as to the form and structure of a "maner song" produced "withoute note, withoute song," and thus very different from the elaborate lyric performances in the *dits* of Machaut and his followers. There, lyric is a vehicle of enlightened sympathy among sensitive and courtly interlocutors, but the song of Chaucer's Knight is so exclusively his own that its occasion, though twice made plain, seems entirely to elude the dreamer, and the song itself is quite forgotten in the wake of the inner crisis it precipitates in the Knight.

But for all their ostensible artlessness, the prosody of these lines is complex. In the earlier couplet (463–64), the long consonantal syllables that slow the first line set off by contrast the slackness of the vowels that begin the second. Combined with the weak syntactic link represented by the repeating prepositional phrases ("of rym," "Of a compleynte"), they produce a couplet that is effectively retrograde in its movement, suggesting the reluctant, almost involuntary character of the Knight's utterance. In the second passage (470–72) the alleged unmusicality of the Knight's words can seem to be either emphasized or contradicted by the clang of the *rime riche* on "song." The movement of "withoute note, withoute song" (472) is ponderous and heavily cesurated, but at the same time oddly sonorous, and the structure of the line in its very mechanical symmetry makes it a textbook example of the classic French *octosyllabe*. In all of these respects it provides a fitting introduction for a song which, though it has been cited as an example of "the inadequacy of riming octosyllables as a suitable vehicle for plangency" (Davenport 1988, 65), in fact shows plangency deliberately contained by a plain diction and an almost austere meter:

> "I have of sorwe so gret won
> That joye gete I never non,
> Now that I see my lady bryght,
> Which I have loved with al my myght,
> Is fro me ded and ys agoon. . . .
> "Allas, deth, what ayleth the,
> That thou noldest have taken me,
> Whan thou toke my lady swete,
> That was so fair, so fresh, so fre,
> So good that men may wel se,
> Of al goodnesse she had no mete!"

Though it is sporadic, and halting even at its most audible, there is a kind of music in these lines. The simple words and subdued rhythms suggest the style of Gower at its plainest,[6] but like the verse of Gower, the song is fully adequate to its purpose. The placement of "sorwe" and "joye" in the opening lines–lines that are spare yet precisely regular–gives both words their full syllabic value, and grounds the song in the timeless lyric opposition of *joi* and *dolor*, though here the delineation of these opposing forces is not, as in so many courtly lyrics, an end in itself. The fourth line, unique in its direct reference to the Knight's own feelings, is also the densest, most markedly consonantal line in the song, and in the wake of its urgent stresses the line that follows, and announces the Knight's loss, has the effect of a diminuendo. Lines 481 and 485 balance one another in structure as well as rime. In both, a syllable is "lacking," but in both the space this creates in the line is like a rest in music. The pause after "Allas" dictated by the rhythm of 481 is precisely echoed in 485 at the climax of the anaphora that ends in the enjambed phrase, "So good." This in turn resonates with the "goodnesse" which gives fullness to the final line of the song.

The artistry of the song is unobtrusive and, as the lines discussed above make clear, it eludes the narrator, whose characterization of it anticipates the lines in which the Knight himself will later describe his attempts at verse:

> Trewly I dide my besynesse
> To make songes, as I best koude,
> And ofte tyme I song hem loude;
> And made songes thus a gret del,
> Althogh I koude not make so wel
> Songes, ne knewe the art al,
> As koude Lamekes sone Tubal . . .

Here the intrusive recurrence of "songes" recalls the riming on "song" in 471–72. Together with the unexectedness of "loude" (which anticipates the "wodedowve upon the spray" of Sir Thopas), and the faltering rhythm and dull rimes of 1159–61, it serves to express the strain of the Knight's diffidence in the face of the challenge of "making" in the courtly way. The song the Knight finally allows us to hear (1175–80), utterly conventional in sentiment, its all too predictable rimes bound by a cumbersome aabbaa structure, is just the sort of earnest, self-conscious performance ("I not wher it were the werste") that we have been prepared for, and altogether different in kind from the "artless" simplicity of his earlier lyric.

We must keep many effects in mind as we respond to verse of this sort. To the extent that our expectations are conditioned by the conventions of the *dit*, we expect that the Knight's lyric utterances will be elaborately framed and stylistically complex; but his first, humble song, casually and almost prosaically introduced, and overshadowed immediately by the extended analysis of the Knight's inner crisis, defeats this expectation, and in so doing typifies the loose fit between convention on the one hand and the concrete effects of language and rhythm on the other that is one of the poem's most striking features (and one that will, of course, recur in countless forms in Chaucer's later poetry). Throughout the poem, Chaucer's verse achieves many of its effects through what can seem accidental divergences from its own norms, as if its rhythms were beyond Chaucer's power or that of his protagonists to control. In this respect, too, the poem's verse mirrors the experience it describes. Where the artistry of the *dit* consists in the careful manipulation of the relationship between "real" feeling and a form whose extreme artificiality is fully understood and openly acknowledged, both Chaucer's narrator and his knightly interlocutor seem awed, confounded, or at times confused by the conventions they are made to deploy.

In an inspired moment of unwitting insight, the dreamer refers to the Knight's unfolding of the history of his love as "shryfte wythoute repentaunce" (1114), a phrase which, though admittedly problematical, seems to me to express the essence of the Knight's experience, both as grieving lover and as poet. On the one hand, the Knight is doubtless in the position of a would-be penitent who cannot or will not repent his attachment to a worldly love, and so cannot hope to be shriven.[7] But at the same time, his narrative performance has the effect of "shrift," both insofar as he is relating what he feels to be the true history of this love, and in that at a deeper level he is undergoing a kind of therapy that leads in the direction of true absolution, by releasing him from his obsessive engagement with the lady's memory into the beginnings of a larger, incipiently religious appreciation of her value. The process is perceptible in the momentary insights which punctuate his recollections of her grace and beauty of manner: His lady is the embodiment of "mesure" (881–82), a torch diffusing its light with limitless generosity (963–65), the "soleyn fenix of Arabye" (982)–quasi-spiritual intimations which build to an explicit affirmation of her special relation to "trouthe":

Therof she had so moche hyr del –
And I dar seyn and swere hyt wel –
That Trouthe hymself over al and al
Had chose hys maner principal
In hir that was his restyng place.
Therto she hadde the moste grace
To have stedefast perseveraunce
And esy, atempre governaunce
That ever I knew . . .

The Knight descends from the strongly Marian image of lines 1002–04 to resume his review of the lady's social virtues, but his language remains charged with religious overtones,[8] and the sustained emphasis on the potentially spiritual significance of the qualities, set off by the firm meter and solemn rimes, make this passage unique in the poem.

The Knight of course remains strident in his refusal to acknowledge the implications of his rich intuitions and discover a virtue in the necessity of loss, and it is this that makes possible his communion with the dreamer-narrator, whose experience on his own less exalted level is hardly less paradoxical. Unlike the typical French narrator, highly refined despite his frequent lack of success in love, Chaucer's bookish insomniac hardly seems to belong to the world he describes; he is not clearly courtier, lover, or even poet, and his responses to the experience he narrates are generally those of the *homme moyen sensuel*, triggered by naive self-projection or stray bits of realistic observation. Alcyone disappears from the poem as concern for her sleepless sorrow is displaced by the narrator's preoccupation with his own; the net effect of the elaborate machinery of the Morpheus episode is to focus his desire for sleep; and the little whelp who "koude no good" (390) mirrors his active but aimless capacity for intuitive sympathy. There is a certain progression in all of this: As the narrator's confused and repetitive harping on his condition in the poem's opening lines somehow results in a gradual clarification, to the point at which the recognizable form of the sorrowing lover begins to emerge, so the figures of whom he reads and dreams enable us to chart his course toward the central encounter with the Man in Black. But in both cases he remains unaware of what is happening, so focused on his own situation and on the concrete circumstances of his dream experience that his progress occurs at a wholly subliminal level.

All of this is announced by the opening lines of the poem, where sound and rhythm convey both the psychological dynamics of the narrator's condition and the poem's awareness of its somewhat ambivalent intertextual engagement with the French tradition.

I have so many an ydel thoght
Purely for defaute of slep
That, by my trouthe, I take no kep
Of nothing, how hyt cometh or gooth,
Ne me nys nothyng leef nor looth.

Al is ylyche good to me –
Joye or sorowe, wherso hyt be –
For I have felynge in nothyng,
But as yt were a mased thyyng,
Alway in poynt to falle a-doun;
For sorwful ymaginacioun
Ys alway hooly in my mynde.

Derek Brewer cites these lines to illustrate Chaucer's deliberate adoption of a chatty, colloquial style, clearly demarcated from the smoother and more overtly sophisticated effects of Machaut and Froissart (Brewer 1966b, 2–7). But as Steven Guthrie notes, the promise of this prefatory manifesto is not borne out by the tone and diction of the poem as a whole, and even here the impact of Chaucer's assertive Englishness of tone and manner depends on our recognizing the Frenchness of the model from which he affects to be distancing himself.[9] In the diction of the passage, too, English and French are in dialogue. The perplexity conveyed by the narrator's downright English coexists in an uncertain relation with a psychological awareness capable of characterizing his "mased" state in more sophisticated terms, as "ymaginacioun" and "melancolie"– intuitions which show him in close touch with the idiom and psychology of his continental models (Kelly 1978, 45–46, 96–105, 219–22).

The rhythm of the passage sets off the numb, sluggish state of the narrator's feelings. The insistent repetition of "nothing" is itself suggestive of the blockage of articulate feeling we associate with "melancolye,"[10] and the effect is reinforced by the turgid consonantal movement of a line like "Ne me nys nothyng leef nor looth." The effect of the repetition of "**nó**thing" becomes almost paralytic in line 11, where heavy internal riming sets off the ponderous end-rime "no**thíng**," whose inert weight is further emphasized (after a slight syntactic disjunction) by the *rime riche* of "mased **thýng**." The nervous energy of the next two lines leaves us unprepared for the more solemn slowing-down that follows: the portentous flow of "For sorwful ymaginacioun"–a line which in Renaissance English might have passed as a pentameter[11]–is further extended by the long vowels of line 15, and suggests that an unveiling of the narrator's true state is imminent. But instead his preoccupation with sleep returns like King Charles's head.

Important to the effect of this passage is the way in which its more or less obsessive energy overflows the tetrameter line. We are made to feel the urgency of the narrator's concern with his insomnia by the burst of energy with which one line emerges from another. A hint of reluctance to probe his state of mind is audible in his assertion that his confusion is "**Purely** for defaute of slep" (BD 5), and the play on "nothing" discussed above begins with a similar abruptness in line 7. This is in fact a distinguishing characteristic of the narrator's lines. Enjambment, in the form of the isolation at the beginning of a line of a striking word or short phrase that bears a close syntactic relation to the previous line, is probably more prominent in the *Book of the Duchess* than in any other of Chaucer's poems, and provides a remarkably consistent index to his thematic purposes. We hear it working to more complex effect in BD 23 ("**Slepe**; and thus melancolye"), in which the obsessive force of the enjambed syllable is balanced by the slow unfolding, perhaps for the first time in an English poem, of "melàncoly'ë", so that the line neatly epitomizes the inner dialogue through which the narrator's condition is tentatively made plain. The halting progress of this revelation is epitomized in BD 35 ("The **sothe**; but trewly, as I gesse"), where the juxtaposition of the enjambed "sothe" with "trewly"–the one synonym denoting a truth the narrator claims is inexplicable, the other introducing its explanation–focuses the contradictory state of his thoughts. Similarly, the cheerful illogic with which pity for Alcyone leads his thoughts wholly out of the world of the poem and into a "tomorrow" for which the closed time-frame of the narrative would seem to have made no allowance, is emphasized by the overflow of "all the morwe/**Áftir**" (BD 99–100).

Enjambment provides a frame for Alcyone's presence in the poem. She is first brought before us in lines which convey her defining need for Ceyx by the use of an enjambed word which echoes an earlier end-rime with something of the effect of *rime riche*:

This lady, that was left at **hom**,
Hath wonder that the king ne cóm
79 **Hóm**, for it was a longe terme . . .

And her final abandonment of consciousness is marked by what is probably the most forceful enjambment in the poem:

With that hir eyen up she casteth
And saw **noght**. "Allas!" quod she for sorwe,
214 And deyede within the thridde morwe.

The poem's most elaborate use of the device occurs in the analysis of the Knight's inner state following his first song. A cluster of enjambed phrases emphasize the literal, physical nature of the process being described, as the blood rushes to the Knight's heart,

To wite eke why hyt was adrad
By kynde, and for to make hyt glad,
495 For hit ys membre principal
Of the body; and that made al
Hys hewe chaunge and wexe grene
And pale . . .

The crisis, offered as the Knight's involuntary response to his own lyric utterance, sets his situation in precise, radical contrast to that of the archetypal heart of the classic song of *fin amor*, the "chant qui vient du coeur" in the lyrics of the troubadours and trouvères (Zumthor 1972, 205–219). The enjambed words provide a series of firm reminders of the finite, material context in which the vital spirits minister to the suffering heart, circumscribing the process in a way which excludes any possibility of courtly mystification.

Other, seemingly more eccentric variations in the poem are harder to classify in terms of conventional prosody. One such is the occurrence of occasional hypermetrical lines which, as my printing of them is intended to show, can be treated as pentameters, and seem almost to require to be read this way. The first of these is the line in which the narrator turns from his brief, radically impersonal account of the disastrous outcome of Ceyx's voyage, to the situation of Alcyone:

76 Nów for to **spéke** of **Ál**cyóne, his wíf:

A few lines later the emotion that love inspires in "this noble wif" is conveyed in a similarly decasyllabic line:

87 For hím, a**lás**, she lóved álderbést.

And when the narrator awakens within his dream, the list of stories englazed in the window of his chamber includes this couplet of plausibly pentametric lines:

Of **Á**chillés and of kýng **Lá**medón,
330 And éke of **Mé**deá and of Jasón[12]

It is perhaps going too far to try to find a common function for these irregular lines. The first two in any case are from the portion of the poem (31–96) found only in Thynne's edition, and thus the possibility exists that they are spurious.[13] But if we accept that the passage as a whole is probably authentic, it becomes plausible that the hypermetrical character of these lines is authentic as well, since where a doubtful reading existed in his manuscript or manuscripts, Thynne would have tended to regularize the line.[14] The reading of lines 329–30 is the same in all the surviving manuscripts, and the fact that they are a couplet seems to me an argument, though hardly a conclusive one, that their parallel irregularities are deliberate and authentic.[15]

Assuming for the sake of argument that these four lines are indeed pentameters, how can we account for them? All four may be said to have a broadly heraldic function. In the case of Alcyone, they may remind us of the far larger, more operatic role assigned her in Ovid's version of her story *(Metamorphoses* 11.410–748), a role which Chaucer acknowledges but conspicuously declines to develop (84–87, 95–100, 215–17). The later couplet evokes the vast *Roman de Troie*, where love and heroism compete on the plane of world history. Again the suggestion is of a poetic universe grander than the Chaucer of this poem is prepared to engage. We may read these lines as we read the often elaborate classical references in Machaut and Froissart: they are a tacit acknowledgment by contrast of the more modest ambitions of one who, like the typical narrator of the *dit*, knows himself to be at best a lesser Guillaume de Lorris, one of the *petis servans* of love (Burrow 1983, 5–12).

One may still ask, of course, whether in writing these decasyllabic lines Chaucer would have felt himself to be invoking a higher strain. The French *decasyllabe,* surely Chaucer's first model for his pentameter (Guthrie 1995, 94–101), was at this stage almost exclusively a lyric meter, the vehicle of *ballade* rather than major narrative. We have no evidence that Chaucer had yet encountered the hendecasyllabic line of Boccaccio and Dante which was to confirm him as at once a writer of pentameter and the poet of large-scale narrative on classical themes. But the *Book of the Duchess* shows him everywhere concerned with contrasting effects of sparseness and density, extension and contraction, and it is entirely possible that his realization of the greater rhythmical and tonal capacities of the longer line was not so closely linked as is commonly assumed with his later discovery of the achievements of the *trecento* poets.

However we evaluate the quasi-pentameter that introduces Alcyone, a clear awareness of Ovid and a high degree of prosodic self-consciousness appear in the immediately preceding lines, which describe the fatal storm,

> Such a tempest gan to rise
> That brak her mast and made it falle,
> And cleft her ship, and dreinte hem alle,
> That never was founde, as it telles,
> Bord ne man, ne nothing elles.
> Right thus this king Seys loste his lif.
> Now for to speke of Alcyone, his wif. . . .

The terse, balanced phrases of the first couplet convey no hint of the elaborateness of the description of the storm in Ovid's narrative, a tour de force that aims to rival the opening scene of the *Aeneid.* The more informal lines that follow sustain the effect of brusque factuality, and the final fact, Ceyx's death, is conveyed by a line of eight heavily consonantal monosyllables which, set against the longer, lighter line which completes the couplet and shifts our attention abruptly to Alcyone, suggests the contrasting effects of spondaic and dactyllic movement in classical hexameter. Virtually every detail of the prosody of the passage attests to Chaucer's concern to emphasize the utter separation of the sphere within which Alcyone's emotions are dominant from the hardly more violent world of physical necessity and destruction.

Still harder to characterize, but constituting a distinctly recognizable technique, are what I think of as the "extra" lines in the poem, syntactically independent units which appear like sudden afterthoughts to sharpen the effect of a descriptive passage. Their meter is notably regular, its firmness serving to set off their precise and evocative phrasing:

> And throgh the glas the sonne shon
> Upon my bed with bryghte bemes,
> With many glade gilde stremes;

And eke the welken was so fair–
Blew, bryght, clere was the ayr . . . .

The third line of this passage is wholly gratuitous in terms of the information it conveys, and the passage as a whole can seem no more than an exercise in *amplificatio.* The point is in the heightened sensory effect of the "extra" lines. The lightly and tritely alliterative movement of the second line is complemented by the long, rich sounds of the third, as brightness by warmth. A syntactic shift renders the lines of the second couplet (339–40) radically separate from one another; and this disjunction sets off the effect of spontaneous pleasure conveyed by the three luminous adjectives, "Blew, bryght, clere," which stand out in contrast to the mere prettiness of the fair welkin of the previous line, as the vividness of "bryght" in this line contrasts with its wholly conventional effect three lines earlier. Here as so often in the poem the conventional and conventionally programmed perceptions of the dreamer are seen to overlie an instinctive, involuntary responsiveness that unobtrusively informs his lines. In the same way, as if discovering the fact for the first time, he observes of the burgeoning forest foliage, "Swetnesse of dew had mad hyt waxe" (415), a line which, once its crisp and vivid diction has been clearly *heard,* is hard to forget. It is a similarly unexpected burst of insight that makes the Knight declare, amid the hyperbole of his account of his lady's face, "And every day hir beaute newed" (906).

The Knight is once again the beneficiary of a generous prosody in the last passage I will discuss, lines spoken by himself which recall the moment when he first beheld his lady, and that explain his decision to devote himself once and for all to her service:

"I wil anoon ryght telle thee why.
    I sawgh hyr daunce so comlily,
Carole and synge so swetely,
Laughe and pleye so womanly,
And loke so debonairly,
So goodly speke and so frendly,
That certes y trowe that evermor
Nas seyn so blysful a tresor."

As the Knight summons up the vision of the dancing, singing maiden, his lines mime the suspensive effect of memory, "turning" on the same rime through three successive couplets,[16] and the rime-words ("cómlily," "swétely," wómanly") perform a stately dance of their own. Here for a moment prosody and therapy have become as nearly as possible one and the same.

NOTES

[1]On these aspects of the style of BD, see, e.g., Kiser 1991, 13–14, who notes that the narrative of the Knight of BD is punctuated by 47 assertions of his veracity; on Chaucer's treatment of relatives, see Roscow 1981, 118–19.

[2]Baum 1961, 28–33, emphasizes that Chaucer 's ear for English verse rhythm is strongly conditioned by earlier, more distinctively English and in some cases more colloquial verse, so that his line falls "midway between the syllabism of the French octosyllabic and the freedom (or incompetence) of the minstrels' work." See also Robinson 1971, 176–85. Baum's "midway" view is challenged by Malone 1968, who is at pains to show that the poem's meter owes much more to the Germanic metrical tradition, as defined by ten Brink and others, than to the example of French octosyllabic verse: "The basis of Chaucer's metrics in BD and HF was the long line familiar to us in OE poetry" (81). But while Malone shows that BD can indeed be scanned in terms of the Germanic metrical tradition, and often cites good philological evidence for his reading of a particular line, he does not demonstrate, as he claims to have done, that the model of the French octosyllabic line, which his essay in fact simply ignores, is therefore irrelevant.

[3]Wimsatt acknowledges the difference this makes (Baltzer et al. 1991, 145–46), but still argues for the primacy of French "natural music" in shaping Chaucer's line.

[4]Guthrie 1987 shows that Machaut's line exhibits far more variation than the binary, regularly cesurated *octosyllabe* of earlier periods, and contrives to incorporate the movement and phrasing of natural language, tendencies which may well have provided a starting point for Chaucer's experimentation in BD. Even Robinson, in most respects the strident champion of an "English" Chaucer, acknowledges that Chaucer's aim is to write a poem recognizably in the French tradition (Robinson 1971, 178), though he is vague about the model French verse might have provided (239–43).

[5]*Book of the Duchess*, 463–64. Here and throughout, I follow the text of *The Riverside Chaucer* (Chaucer 1987).

[6]On the "plain style" in Gower, see Ricks 1983, who notes Gower's ability to achieve complex effects with words like "thing," "soft," "cold." Much of what Ricks says about the plain style can be applied to the lyric of Chaucer's Knight.

[7]This is argued by Diekstra 1981, 224–25, who also provides a review of interpretations of BD 1112–14.

[8]On the diction of these lines, see Phillips 1982, 162.

[9]Guthrie 1995, 103. See also Guthrie1987, 66–67, where he shows that Machaut's line not only exhibits far more variation than the binary, regularly cesurated *octosyllabe* of earlier periods, but contrives by various means to incorporate the movement and phrasing of natural language, tendencies which may well have provided a starting point for Chaucer's experimentation in BD.

[10]See Kelly 1978, 195–96, for illustrations of the psychology of melancholy in Chaucer's poetry.

[11]"For **só**rrowfúl imági**ná**tión," cf. Chapman's "**Sí**lently **glí**ding éxha**lá**tións" (*Bussy d'Ambois* 2.2.159).

[12]As with "**Á**lcyone" (BD 65, 76, 145, 220, 264, 1327), so in the case of "Achilles" and "Medea" my scanning requires placing the accent on the first syllable. Though there are exceptions, this is in fact Chaucer's normal practice. For "**Á**chilles" see HF 398, 1463; Troilus 2.416; MLT 198; NPT 3148 (4338). For "**Mé**dea" see BD 726; HF 401, 1271; MLT 72; LGW 1395, 1629, 1652, 1663.

[13]For the argument that lines 31–96 should be considered spurious until more convincing evidence for their authenticity comes to light see Blake 1981. His textual arguments are answered by Phillips 1986. As further evidence that the lines are genuine, Phillips notes echoes of Chaucer's known French sources, verbal correspondences to Gower's version of the Ceyx-Alcyone story (written presumably some years after Chaucer's), possible echoes in fifteenth-century poets, and phrasing which appears to be echoed later in the poem. A brief rejoinder, Blake1986, deals mainly with the textual evidence adduced by Phillips, but also dismisses the correspondences she cites between BD and other poems as too general to be persuasive.

[14]This is in fact what modern editors have generally done. Skeat, F. N. Robinson and other modern editors before Benson omit "Alcyone" from 76 (Robinson considered it a gloss that

had strayed into the text), and "alas" from 87. See Benson's textual notes in *The Riverside Chaucer* (Chaucer 1987, 1136–37).

[15]Again on metrical grounds, most editors have omitted "kyng" in 329. And it is of course possible to partially normalize 330 by accenting "Medea" on the second syllable or treating it as bisyllabic.

[16]The most nearly comparable example of sustained rime that I have found in Chaucer is *Troilus and Criseyde* 5.1786–90, where the effect is that of Dante's *terza rima,* and serves to set off the triad of "comedye"/"tragedye"/"poesye."

David Wallace

The Making of *Troilus and Criseyde*[*]

Having formed some general estimate of Chaucer's attitude towards the *Filostrato,* we may now concentrate upon the detailed business of his *makinge.* Chaucer's general restructuring and amplification of the *Filostrato* need not detain us here: this subject has been considered by a succession of scholars, and their findings have been intelligently summarized and improved upon by Robert Payne (*Key of Remembrance* 177–88). We will seek, rather, to observe the fine details of Chaucer's reactions to the language, syntax and prosody of the Italian poem. Few critics would doubt the value of such close comparative analysis, although some might question the feasibility of applying it to the works of medieval authors.[1] The vagaries of manuscript transmission certainly impede the process of detailed verbal comparison: for we cannot definitively establish what Boccaccio wrote (no autograph *Filostrato* having yet come to light), what Chaucer read, or even what Chaucer himself composed. Such uncertainties do not threaten the general conclusions reached in our last chapter: but the limitations that they impose here must be acknowledged at the outset. It would be foolhardy to hang a thesis upon a single, isolated correspondence of phrasing or syntax. For this reason we will accumulate large numbers of correspondences, juxtaposing–for the most part–complete stanzas of the two poems. The editions of Branca (*Opere di Boccaccio*) and of Robinson (*Works of Chaucer*) are employed throughout.[2]

Despite such limitations, the enterprise of this chapter is, I believe, essential if our understanding of Chaucer's engagement with Italian writings is to make further progress: for nobody, to my knowledge, has ventured to estimate just how good Chaucer's grasp of Italian was.[3] We might surmise that Chaucer, as a career diplomat and civil servant, would necessarily have been an accomplished linguist (Ruggiers, 161) although doubts have been raised (Harbert, 145–48) concerning his abilities as a Latinist. Comparative studies of the *Filostrato* and the *Troilus* might have yielded some estimate of Chaucer's abilities as Italianist, but such work has been impeded by R.A. Pratt's article of 1956 (Robinson drew attention to these "new discoveries of Professor Pratt," 812). Pratt proposes that Chaucer, in composing *Troilus and Criseyde,* availed himself of a French prose translation by a certain (presumably fourteenth-century) Beauvau d'Anjou. (The fact that Chaucer might have employed a French intermediary in working with the *Filostrato* does not, of course, prove that his knowledge of Italian was defective.[4]) But Carla Bozzolo 1973 has more recently argued a most convincing case for attributing the *Roman de Troilus* to Louis de Beauvau, an attribution previously advanced by Hauvette, Chiurlo and Marletta. Bozzolo (29–33) assigns the *Roman* to the period 1442-58 . Barry Windeatt, on investigating Pratt's arguments, finds that "the evidence for any use of Beauvau by Chaucer remains insubstantial in quantity and quality"(*Chaucer* 1984b, 19).

Comparative study of the *Filostrato* and *Troilus and Criseyde* suggests that Chaucer's understanding and appreciation of Boccaccio's language was extraordinarily acute. Many of the passages examined in the previous chapter support this proposition; subsequent investigation will, I hope, further establish that Chaucer–unlike many of his modern critics–was a serious student of the Italian language, not just a cheerful dilettante.[5] It appears that Chaucer, in reading the *Filostrato,* was concerned not simply to catch the drift of a given stanza, but to analyze and worm his way into the language from which the stanza is fashioned. Before transforming the *Filostrato,* Chaucer understood what the *Filostrato* meant.[6]

Robert Payne does not consider the *Filostrato's* contribution to the style of the *Troilus;* he implies that Chaucer put the Italian work back on the shelf once he had extracted a "rough structure" from it. Payne speaks of Chaucer "tossing aside all but 2750 lines of the *Filostrato's* 5704, compressing those into 2580, and then adding some 5660 more lines, either of his own or (more often) borrowed from Boccaccio or someone else" (Payne, 176). Such statistics, coupled with the suggestion that Chaucer casually discarded over half of the *Filostrato* before beginning serious elaboration of the *Troilus,* are misleading. I shall argue that the *Filostrato* never left Chaucer's desk, or his imagination, until the English poem was complete; its contribution to the *Troilus* is much more substantial than has hitherto been recognized.

In this chapter we will examine how Chaucer utilizes the phrasing and syntax of the *Filostrato* and how he employs the narrative pattern of the Italian poem to orientate the progress of his own narrative. Consideration of the techniques which Chaucer employs in amplifying stanzas from the *Filostrato* affords further opportunities to discover what Chaucer found congenial in his source. Similarly, consideration of what Chaucer chose to abbreviate or reject highlights aspects of the *Filostrato* that the English poet found inappropriate. Boccaccio's attitude towards versification (particularly the extraordinary counterpointing of syntax against meter which generates or is generated by the distinctive prose-like movement of his verse) caused Chaucer considerable misgivings: we shall see that at certain moments the English poet turns instinctively to the *Rose,* to its French derivatives and to the *Commedia* for some stable models of prosody (and for a more assured control of courtly vocabulary). Finally, having compared the *Filostrato* and the *Troilus* with a typical tail-rhyme romance, we will assess the relationship of *Troilus and Criseyde* to the traditions of illustrious and popular literature that have been outlined in these six chapters.

Chaucer's understanding of and engagement with the *Filostrato* manifests itself in a variety of ways: three of his adaptations on a single theme–wisdom–offer an initial indication of the intelligent flexibility of his response.

In I, 9,2, Boccaccio refers to Calcàs as an "antiveduto saggio"; in I, 79, Chaucer refers to Calkas as a "forknowynge wise." Chaucer understands that Boccaccio intends "saggio" as a noun rather than as an adjective; he translates it by employing the substantive "wise." Chaucer further appreciates how Boccaccio has created a compound adjective in combining the participle "veduto" with the prefix "anti"; he similarly combines prefix and participle in "forknowynge," a participial adjective which is apparently new both to Chaucer's writings and to the English language.[7]

Later on in Book I, Troilus (like Troiolo) imagines how he will be derided for falling in love:

> "Che si dirà di te intra gli amanti
> se questo tuo amor fia mai saputo?
> di te si gabberebbon tutti quanti,
> di te direbbono: 'ecco il provveduto . . .'"(I, 51, 1–4)

> "What wol now every lovere seyn of the,
> If this be wist? but evere in thin absence
> Laughen in scorn, and seyn, 'Loo, ther goth he
> That is the man of so gret sapience . . .'"(I, 512–15)

Chaucer follows the first line of the Italian quite closely, although he personalizes and individualizes ("every lovere seyn") Boccaccio's impersonal construction. In the preceding stanza, Chaucer had employed the verb *japen* to translate Boccaccio's "gabbare" (I, 508; I, 50,4); here he varies his translation by rendering "si gabberebbon" as "Laughen in scorn." Chaucer neatly concentrates the full sense of Boccaccio's second line into four monosyllables; he thereby wins space for an expansion of the phrase "ecco il provveduto." Although the term "provveduto" is employed substantively, it is constructed in the same way as "antiveduto," combining a prefix with a past participle. In translating it, Chaucer might have employed his recent coinage "forknowynge," or have coined something similar: yet he chose not to do so; perhaps he wished to avoid any association (even for ironic effect) of Troilus and Calkas. His expansion, which sounds no internal echoes, renders Boccaccio's phrase most diligently: "Loo, ther goth he" gives dramatic colour to "ecco," and the whole of the following line is taken up with his interpretation of "il provveduto."

In Book II, the English hero follows his Italian counterpart in resolving to write to his beloved:

"Allora" disse Troiol: "Fatto sia
il piacer tuo; io vado e scriveraggio,
ed Amor priego, per sua cortesia,
lo scrivere e la lettera e 'l viaggio
fruttevol faccia." E di quindi s'invia
alla camera sua, e come saggio
alla sua donna carissima scrisse
una lettera presto, e cosi disse: (II, 95)

Quod Troilus, "Depardieux, ich assente!
Sith that the list, I wil arise and write;
And blisful God prey ich with good entente,
The viage, and the lettre I shal endite,
So spede it; and thow, Minerva, the white,
Yif thow me wit my lettre to devyse."
And sette hym down, and wrot right in this wyse. (II, 1058–64)

Chaucer follows Boccaccio's structuring of the stanza quite closely here: Troilus, like Troiolo, graciously accepts the advice that he has been offered, resolves to go and write a letter, prays for success and then prepares himself to write. By compressing the rather diffuse narrative action of Boccaccio's final three-and-a-half lines into just one line, Chaucer is able to extend Troilus' speech and to squeeze in a fresh detail. At first glance, this detail–a rapid invocation to Minerva which comes almost as an afterthought–owes nothing to Boccaccio: Chaucer often inserts passing references to classical figures into Boccaccio's narrative framework. But here, Chaucer's mini-invocation may well have been inspired by a phrase in the *Filostrato.* Boccaccio's hero, we are informed, writes wisely, "come saggio"; Chaucer's hero prays to the goddess of wisdom for "wit my lettre to devyse."

Chaucer's most striking departure from the Italian in this stanza comes with his substitution of "God" for "Amor." This change sharply juxtaposes Christian and pagan terms of reference as God and a Roman goddess are appealed to within the space of a single stanza. Such juxtapositions are not uncommon in the *Troilus:* but it is difficult to explain why Chaucer was moved to make this particular substitution. It may be that his mind was deflected into the Christian sphere by Boccaccio's gracious phrase "Fatto sia/ il piacer tuo," which recalls "fiat voluntas tua" from the *paternoster;* this may also account for Troilus exclaiming "Depardieux" ("by God"), an interjection which occurs nowhere else in the poem. All this must remain speculation. We can, however, be more confident in assuming that Chaucer's viage translates Boccaccio's "viaggio"; "viage" is therefore likely to mean "journey" (that of the letter to Criseyde), rather than "enterprise" (as Davis, *A Chaucer Glossary* suggests: see *viage* [2]).

These three examples of Chaucer's writing on the theme of wisdom all testify to his fine understanding of phrases from the Italian text, although they reflect this understanding in differing ways. The first example sees Chaucer evolving a concise but complex phrase which matches an Italian original; the second sees him electing to expand a similar Italian phrase; the third sees a simple Italian phrase triggering Chaucer's independent powers of invention. Parallels analogous to our third example afford the most generous scope for critical ingenuity: but more precise verbal parallels provide more reliable evidence of Chaucer's comprehension of the Italian text. And, in fact, simple parallels of phrasing, at first glance unremarkable, often conceal much ingenuity on Chaucer's part:

> ". . . i' 'l taccio per lo meglio . . ."
> ". . . I hide it for the beste." (II, 3,8; I, 581)

This comes close to being an exact translation: but we should note Chaucer's rendering of "taccio" as "hide." English has no verb corresponding to the Italian *tacere* (or to the Latin *tacere,* the French *faire* or the German *schweigen);* "taccio" must be translated by a phrase such as "I keep silent." By employing the verb *hyden,* Chaucer is able to keep the shape of Boccaccio's clause and to round off his stanza with a simple, emphatic phrase.

The first three stanzas of *Filostrato* VII occasion comparably simple yet highly intelligent translations from Chaucer:

> Troiol, sì com'egli è di sopra detto,
> passava tempo . . . (VII, 1, 1–2)

> This Troilus, as I byfore have told,
> Thus driveth forth . . . (V, 1100–1)

Boccaccio's opening line, with its dense subordinate clause, is imbalanced: its syllables divide 2+9. Chaucer restores proportion to the line by dividing it 4+6. He adopts the narrative formula of Boccaccio's subordinate clause: but, characteristically, he both simplifies and personalizes it. He goes on to convert Boccaccio's colorless phrase "passava tempo" ("he passed the time") into a phrase whose formulaic associations invite us to view the *aventure* of Troilus in a more detached manner.[8] Chaucer's usage of narrative formulae here raises the curtain on a fresh episode in his story; it also sees him linking up with Boccaccio's stanzas after having worked independently for over one hundred lines.[9]

In reading Boccaccio's next stanza, Chaucer came across the past participle "beffati"; this he translates by employing the past participle "byjaped." Here, as often, it is necessary to consider these phrases in context to appreciate fully the neatness and economy of Chaucer's translation:

> E così stetter mezzo dì passato,
> beffati spesso dalla lor credenza,
> sì come poi mostrava esperienza. (VII, 2, 6–8)

And thus byjaped stonden for to stare
Aboute naught this Troilus and Pandare. (V, 1119–20)

Chaucer often takes pains to conclude a stanza with a weighty, well-defined couplet. Here he cuts the prediction of future action in Boccaccio's final line, and wins further definition for his couplet by switching, momentarily, to the present tense. "And thus byjaped" neatly fuses "E così" from the sixth line of Boccaccio's stanza with "beffati" from the seventh.

The next stanza of the *Troilus* furnishes two further examples of Chaucerian economy: each of its monosyllabic asseverations ("for aught I woot," "so trowe I") provides an adequate translation of an Italian phrase and saves Chaucer three syllables:

Troiolo disse: "Anzi mangiare omai,
per quel ch'io posse creder, non verrebbe:
elle penrà a disbrigarsi assai
dal vecchio padre piu che non vorrebbe,
per mio avviso; tu che ne dirai?
Io pur mi credo che ella sarebbe
venuta se venire ella dovesse,
e s'a mangier con lui non si ristesse." (VII, 3)

To Pandarus this Troilus tho seyde,
"For aught I woot, byfor noon, sikirly,
Into this town ne comth nat here Criseyde.
She hath ynough to doone, hardyly,
To wynnen from hire fader, so trowe I.
Hire olde fader wol yet make hire dyne
Er that she go; God yeve hys herte pyne!" (V, 1121–27)

Boccaccio's third and fourth lines are not easy to translate: "disbrigarsi" ("to disentangle oneself") and "penare" ("to experience difficulty") are not common verbs, and the positions of "assai" and "non vorrebbe" in the line–dictated by exigencies of rime–are potentially confusing.[10] But Chaucer evidently understood the meaning of these lines; he adapts them most skillfully in V, 1124-55.

Chaucer's couplet arouses complex sensations in the reader. Troilus paints a vivid picture of a pathetic "olde fader" who is determined to dine with his daughter: yet, the reader appreciates, the true pathos here lies in Troilus' energetic self-deception. Boccaccio provides suggestions for all this, but in dividing them between his first and last lines he dissipates much of their pathetic potential. By rendering "anzi mangiare" as "byfor noon," Chaucer saves Boccaccio's suggestions for his couplet; and once again, Chaucer's couplet is splendidly concentrated and well-defined.

Chaucer's translation of *Filostrato* VII, 29 provides a further impressive example of his resolution to build climactically towards a memorable couplet. Here, as often, the autonomy of Boccaccio's couplet is much eroded by enjambment and elision:

"Oh me, Criseida, qual sottile ingegno,
qual piacer nuovo, qual vaga bellezza,
qual cruccio verso me, qual giusto sdegno,
qual fallo mio o qual fiera stranezza,
l'animo tuo altiero ad altro segno
han potuto recare? Oh me, fermezza
a me promessa, oh me, fede e leanza,
chi v'ha gittate dalla mia amanza?" (VII, 29)

"O, my Criseyde, allas! what subtilte,
What newe lust, what beaute, what science,
What wratthe of juste cause have ye to me?
What gilt of me, what fel experience,
Hath fro me raft, allas! thyn advertence?
O trust, O feyth, O depe aseuraunce,
Who hath me reft Criseyde, al my plesaunce?" (V, 1254–60)

Chaucer's translations of Boccaccio's terms here are so intelligent and precise that they might almost have served as a glossary for a fourteenth-century English reader of the *Filostrato*. Chaucer translates "sottile ingegno" by forming a noun from the adjective "sottile" which corresponds to the sense of the substantive "ingegno": *subtilte* invariably has associations with mental ingenuity in Chaucer. "Newe lust" crisply translates "piacer nuovo"; "beaute" translates "bellezza." Chaucer drops "vaga" (one of Boccaccio's favorite adjectives)[11] to introduce "science" (one of Chaucer's favorite nouns)[12] and to create a three-fold pattern of appeal which matches and balances that of the stanza's penultimate line. Chaucer flattens the two-fold appeal of Boccaccio's third line into a single question, but his phrase "wratthe of juste cause" splendidly combines the senses of "cruccio" and "giusto sdegno." "Gilt of me" neatly renders "fallo mio"; "fel experience" intelligently interprets "fiera stranezza," its choice of adjective being particularly apt.[13] Up to this point–the end of the fourth line–Chaucer has kept pace with Boccaccio's stanza. Boccaccio's object, verb and complement have not yet been reached; if Chaucer is to secure the relative autonomy of his couplet, he will need to compress these into his next line. Chaucer achieves such compression with great assurance: his choice of "raft" as verb and "advertence" as object is quite inspired.

Of the three qualities which feature in Chaucer's penultimate line, "feyth" directly translates "fede" while "trust" and "depe aseuraunce" correspond more loosely to "fermezza/ a me promessa" and "leanza." The couplet, once again, brings a subtle shift of emphasis from Chaucer. Whereas Troiolo continues his appeal to Criseida, Troilus' appeal drifts away from any fixed point of address. Troilus, momentarily, speaks into a void. This subtle shift is beautifully accompanied by a modulation between the first four syllables of the fifth line and the first four of the seventh; the verb *reven is* employed again to fine effect.

I would like to draw attention to one last detail of this particular Chaucerian translation: whereas Troiolo opens his apostrophe with "Oh me, Criseida," Troilus begins "O my Criseyde." The change is slight. It may be that Chaucer's text had "mia" for "me," or that Chaucer misunderstood: but it seems highly likely that Chaucer would have recognized "Oh me" (and its variant forms)[14] as an exclamation approximating to the English "allas"; and, in fact, we find that two of Boccaccio's usages of the exclamation in this stanza bring forth an "allas!" from Chaucer. I think it probable that Chaucer consciously decided to insert the possessive adjective "my" into V, 1254; if we juxtapose the opening of his previous stanza with its Italian counterpart,[15] we may deduce what provoked him to do this:

> "La tua Criseida, oh me, m'ha ingannato,
> di cui io piu che d'altra mi fidava,
> ella ha altrui il suo amor donato . . ." (VII, 26,1–3)

> "My lady bryght, Criseyde, hath me bytrayed,
> In whom I trusted most of any wight.
> She elliswere hath now here herte apayed." (V, 1247–49)

This juxtaposition elicits a most striking contrast: whereas Troiolo disassociates himself from Criseida in speaking (to Pandaro) of "la tua Criseida" ("your Criseida"), Troilus speaks of "my lady bryght." With such a change, Chaucer repudiates Troiolo's repudiation of his beloved. Chaucer's wish to emphasize the continuing selfless devotion of Troilus to Criseyde also accounts, I would suggest, for the reappearance of the possessive adjective in V, 1254. It accounts for the suppression of the self-referential quality of Troiolo's "fermezza/ a me promessa" (VII, 29,6-7). It may also account for the translation of "altrui" (VII, 26,3, "another person") as if it were "altrove" ("elsewhere") in V, 1249. The thought that Criseyde may have bestowed her love "elliswhere" is painful but comfortingly vague; it shields Troilus from the more painful admission that Criseyde has taken another man.

Chaucer's adaptation of *Filostrato* IV, 80 follows Boccaccio's initial appeal to experience and adheres to the general development of Boccaccio's argument: but only one Chaucerian phrase represents a studied imitation of the Italian. This phrase, however, is splendidly effective: Chaucer sets it like a jewel at the center of his stanza:

> Ma come noi veggiamo ch'egli avviene,
> che l'una donna l'altra a visitare
> ne' casi nuovi *va* se le vuol bene,
> così sen venner molte a dimorare
> con Criseida il giorno, tutte piene
> di pietosa allegrezza, ed a contare
> le cominciaron per ordine il fatto,
> com'ella era renduta, e con che patto. (IV, 80)

> But as men seen in towne, and al aboute,
> That wommen usen frendes to visite,

So to Criseyde of wommen com a route,
For pitous joie, and wenden hire delite;
And with hire tales, deere ynough a myte,
Thise wommen, which that in the cite dwelle,
They sette hem down, and seyde as I shall telle. (IV, 680–86)

Boccaccio's oxymoron "pietosa allegrezza" finely captures the conflicting feelings of the women who visit Criseida: although they pity her for having to leave Troy, they are stimulated by their own company and excited by their role as social commentators. Chaucer shows his admiration for Boccaccio's phrasing in speaking of the "pitous joie" of the Trojan women.

The register and flavor of Chaucer's phrasing often reveals a subtle understanding of the Italian text even when it does not represent a *verbum pro verbo* translation:

Saziar non si poteva il giovinetto
di ragionar con Pandaro . . . (III, 63, 1–2)

This is o word for al; this Troilus
Was nevere ful to speke of this matere . . . (III, 1660–61)

A Chaucer Glossary glosses the phrase "ful to speke" as "sated with talking," recording it as an instance (apparently unique in this sense) of Chaucer's usage of the adjective *ful.* Chaucer was evidently influenced here by Boccaccio's association of *saziare* (a verb usually associated with eating) and *ragionare.*

The primary meaning of the Italian noun *pensiero* is "thought; idea" (*Cambridge Italian Dictionary*, I, 555): but *il pensiero* is usually–especially in poetic contexts–an unhappy process. Chaucer understood the sad overtones of Troiolo's "pensiero"[16]:

Aveagli già amore il sonno tolto,
e minuito il cibo, ed il pensiero
multiplicato sì che già nel volto
ne dava pallidezza segno vero . . . (I, 47,1–4)

And fro this forth tho refte hym love his slep,
And made his mete his foo, and ek his sorwe
Gan multiplie, that, whoso tok kep,
It shewed in his hewe both eve and morwe. (I, 484–87)

Boccaccio's first three lines are patterned and structured by a sequence of three past participles. This sequence is generated by the auxiliary verb which features in the stanza's opening phrase ("Aveagli") and is subsequently understood by ellipsis. Chaucer adopts Boccaccio's three-fold patterning, but avoids verbal auxiliaries and employs three independent verbs: *reven*; *maken*; *ginnen.* Despite this change, Chaucer's lines still owe much to the Italian: "love" ("amore") remains the subject of his main clause; a similar clausal subordinator ("that"; "sì che") introduces the dependent clause at a similar point in the stanza. English monosyllables prove, once again, most economical: for example, although Chaucer requires six words to translate the awkward phrase "minuito il cibo," his paraphrase costs only six syllables. It is interesting to note that Chaucer again elects to fill the space that such economy wins him not with extra narrative detail but with phrases which enhance the illusion of an easy-going narrative style: "and fro this forth"; "whoso tok kep"; "both eve and morwe."

The presence of certain phrasings in *Troilus and Criseyde* may best be accounted for–and their meaning more securely established–by referring to the *Filostrato.* The scientific and dialectical connotations of the term "discese" employed in *Filostrato* VI, 12,5 are preserved by the English "descendeth" (V, 859)[17]; the noun phrase "un accusarla" in IV, 69,3 inspires "hire accusement" (IV, 556), a phrase containing a substantive which occurs nowhere else in Chaucer's writings. The usage of the verb *convenirsi* in a rhyming position at II, 111, 1 probably accounts for the impressive presence (unique in the *Troilus*) of the adjective "covenable" in II, 1137; the adjective "molesta" in IV, 102,6 certainly inspired what is the only verifiable Chaucerian usage of the verb "moleste" (IV, 880).[18] The phrase "con cambiata/ faccia"–which troubles the modern translator (see Fs IV, 4,5-6 and Havely, pp. 57, 201)– is straightforwardly rendered by Chaucer as "with a chaunged face" (IV, 68). The highly unusual participial adjective "malvissuto" (IV, 38,1– it does not appear in Decameron; it is not listed in Cambr. Ital. Dict.) inspires the coinage "myslyved" (IV, 330). In III, 349, Chaucer's remarkable consideration of sighs ("sikes") as "richesse" borrows from Boccaccio's "sospir . . . a gran divizia" (III, 11,5). This last Chaucerian adaptation forms part of a close and sustained engagement with an Italian stanza:

Chi poria dire intera la letizia
che l'anima di Troiolo sentiva,
udendo Pandar? Ché la sua tristizia,
com' più parlava, più scemando giva.
Li sospir, ch'egli aveva a gran divizia,
gli dieder luogo e la pena cattiva
si dipartì, e '1 viso lagrimoso,
bene sperando, divenne gioioso. (III, 11)

Who myghte tellen half the joie or feste
Which that the soule of Troilus tho felte,
Heryng th'effect of Pandarus byheste?
His olde wo, that made his herte swelte,
Gan tho for joie wasten and tomelte,
And al the richesse of his sikes sore
At ones fledde; he felte of hem namore. (III, 344–50)

Here, as often, Chaucer begins by imitating Boccaccio quite closely; he then proceeds to elaborate his stanza more independently, although details from the

Italian text figure in this elaboration. To appreciate just how closely Chaucer adheres to the letter and spirit of the Italian stanza, we may compare his handiwork with that of a modern translator:

> "Who could describe all the joy that Troiolo felt in his heart as he listened to Pandaro? For the more he heard, the further his grief diminished. He gained respite from the sighs that had overwhelmed him, his desperate suffering was allayed, and his sad looks were cheered by hopes of happiness." (Havely, 47)

Clearly, if Chaucer had worked from a prose text similar to that of Havely, his verse would have differed markedly from the stanza he derives from the *Filostrato.*

The modern translator makes "Troiolo" the subject of a first subordinate clause; he translates "anima" ("soul") as "heart" and tucks this away in a locative phrase; he transforms the present participial phrase "udendo Pandar" into a temporal clause featuring a perfect verb. Chaucer correctly translates "anima" as "soule" and follows Boccaccio in making "the soule of Troilus" ("l'anima di Troiol") the subject of his subordinate clause. Correctly translating "udendo" as "heryng," he upholds Boccaccio's usage of the present participle.

Havely catches the sense of Boccaccio's next sentence: but whereas Boccaccio has "com' più parlava" (with Pandaro actively talking), Havely has "the more he heard" (with Troiolo actively listening). This change of verb is dictated (I presume) by the desire to concentrate upon Troiolo; similar reasoning accounts for a change at the beginning of the next sentence, where "He" (Troiolo) supplants "Li sospir" as initial subject. Such changes combine to draw us away from the Italian stanza, for Boccaccio concentrates not upon the hero but upon the hero's parts and attributes: his soul; his sadness; his sighs; his wretched pain.[19] Chaucer follows Boccaccio's choice of emphasis; as "Troiolo" is nowhere the subject of a sentence in the Italian stanza, so "Troilus" ("he") does not figure as subject in the English until the intensification of the final half-line.

Modern translations of the *Filostrato* (bound by the constraints of modern syntax and vocabulary) inevitably obscure many of Chaucer's diligent imitations of Boccaccio's phrasing and syntax. For example, the present participial constructions which are one of the *Filostrato's* most distinctive attributes exert an important, if limited, influence on the syntax, style and prosody of the *Troilus:*

> <u>Immaginando affanno né sospiro</u>
> <u>poter per cotal donna esser perduto</u> . . . (I, 35,1–2)

"He imagined that neither trouble nor suffering for such a lady's sake could be wasted . . ." (p. 28)

> <u>Imaginynge that travaille nor grame</u>
> <u>Ne myghte for so goodly oon be lorn</u> . . . (I, 372–73)[20]

Present participles in English and Italian perpetually tempt poets with the offer of an easy rime: Chaucer yields to this temptation much less often than Boccaccio, but occasionally (as here) he follows the Italian initiative:

> Così adunque andandosi gabbando
> or d'uno or d'altro Troiolo, e sovente
> or questa donna or quella rimirando . . . (I, 26, 1–3)

> Withinne the temple he wente hym forth pleyinge,
> This Troilus, of every wight aboute,
> On this lady, and now on that, lokynge . . . (I, 267–69)

Boccaccio's opening line juxtaposes two present participles: although Chaucer converts the first of these into a simple past tense, he nevertheless captures the reflexive quality of Boccaccio's "andandosi gabbando."

In III, 1534-40 Chaucer follows Boccaccio in introducing his stanza with a past participle ("Tornato"; "Retorned") and his couplet with a present participle ("pensando"; "Thynkyng"). Chaucer's fine stanza owes as much to Boccaccio's syntactic framework as it does to his phrasing:[21]

> Tornato Troiol nel real palagio,
> tacitamente se n'entrò nel letto
> per dormir s'el potesse alquanto ad agio,
> ma non gli poté sonno entrar nel petto,
> sì gli facean nuovi pensier disagio,
> rammemorando il lasciato diletto,
> pensando seco quanto piu valea
> Criseida, che el non si credea. (III, 53)

> Retorned to his real paleys soone,
> He softe into his bed gan for to slynke,
> To slepe longe, as he was wont to doone.
> But al for nought; he may wel ligge and wynke,
> But slep ne may ther in his herte synke,
> Thynkyng how she, for whom desir hym brende,
> A thousand fold was worth more than he wende. (III, 1534–40)

Chaucer's stanza is expertly organized into three parts. The first follows the Italian quite closely. In the second, anaphora augments the effect of rime in forming a tightly concentrated center to the stanza from which the couplet may flow. And although the second half of the sixth line carries the sense of Boccaccio's sixth line, the couplet flows most beautifully; the potential of Boccaccio's final cramped and hurried half-line is fully realized.

Of course, Chaucer often chose to go against the patterns of Boccaccio's syntax. In his next stanza, for example, Chaucer eschews Boccaccio's usage of the present participle; in the stanza after this he introduces a present participle where Boccaccio employs the present tense:

> El giva ciascuno atto rivolgendo
> nel suo pensiero e 'l savio ragionare . . . (III, 54,1–2)
>
> And in his thought gan up and down to wynde
> Hire wordes alle, and every countenaunce . . . (III, 1541–42)
>
> grazie infinite ne rende ad Amore . . . (III, 55,4)
>
> Thonkynge Love he so wel hire bisette . . . (III, 1552)

Chaucer's first translation here draws upon an earlier triumph in rendering awkward phrasing:

> seco nel cor ciascuna paroletta
> rivolvendo di Pandaro . . . (II, 68,3–4)
>
> And every word gan up and down to wynde
> That he had seyd . . . (II, 601–2)

Here we may consider how Chaucer imitates Boccaccio (upholding his choice of present participle) in concluding one stanza and in beginning the next:

> pensando che amore a molti aperto,
> noia acquistava e non gioia per merto.
>
> Ed oltre a questo, assai più altre cose . . . (I, 36,7–37,1)
>
> "–for he thought that a love that was made known to many people would reap sorrow rather than joy as its reward. And he also thought of trying a great many other ways . . ." (p. 28)
>
> Remembryng hym that *love* to wide yblowe
> Yelt bittre fruyt, though swete seed be sowe.
> *And over al this, yet muchel more* he thoughte . . . (I, 384–86)

It is difficult to decide whether or not the two couplets here should be underlined. Chaucer's fine metaphoric language greatly improves upon the plainness of Boccaccio's *sententia:* yet the Italian text provides Chaucer not only with a *sententia* for elaboration,[22] but also with a present participle by which such elaboration may be tethered grammatically to the main body of the stanza. The modern translation again conceals the correspondence of present participles. It also obscures the similarity between the opening phrases of the next stanza by translating "oltre" as if it were "anche." This is especially unfortunate as Chaucer's translation of "Ed oltre a" is, like that of "rivolvendo" in II, 601, re-employed at a later point in the narrative:

> "Ed oltre a ciò, questa città si vede
> piena di belle donne e graziose . . ." (IV, 48,1–2)

> "And moreover this city appears to be full of lovely and graceful women . . ." (p. 62)

> "And over al this, as thow wel woost thiselve,
> This town is ful of ladys al aboute . . ." (IV, 400–1)

Turning to another episode from the *Troilus,* we find that Chaucer in fact settled on a satisfactory translation of the prepositional phrase "oltre a" at an early point in his narrative. These lines furnish us with a further fascinating example of Chaucer's adaptation of a Boccaccian present participle:

> Piacendo questa sotto il nero manto
> oltre ad ogni altra a Troiol . . . (I, 30,1-2)

> "Since this lady in the black cloak pleased Troiolo above all others . . ." (p. 27)

> She, this in blak, likynge to Troilus
> Over alle thing . . . (I, 309–10)

Boccaccio's use of participles, then, excites a variety of responses from Chaucer; it seems evident that Chaucer considered each usage with the same discriminating respect that he shows for all aspects of Boccaccio's syntax. Chaucer's close analysis of the Italian text is again evident in his imitation of phrases from I, 30,1-2. Here he adopts the constituent parts of Boccaccio's lines but reorders them; elsewhere he sometimes follows Boccaccio's ordering remarkably closely:

> Nell'opere opportune alla lor guerra
> egli era sempre nell'armi il primiero . . . (III, 90,1–2)

> "He was always the foremost in furthering the campaign on their side with feats of arms." (p. 56)

> In alle nedes, for the townes werre,
> He was, and ay, the first in armes dyght . . . (III, 1772–73)

Robinson's punctuation suggests that Chaucer's lines may be divided into five constituent parts: we find that the order of these parts corresponds exactly to that of the equivalent phrases in the Italian. However, when Boccaccio's phrasing and syntax prove intractable Chaucer shows himself quite willing to depart from them:

> Di Pandar crebbe allora la pietate
> ed il disio di ciò voler sapere,
> Ond'el seguì: "Se la nostra amistate . . ." (II, 4,1–3)
>
> "With that Pandaro's pity increased at that–as did his desire to find out the truth–and so he replied: 'If our friendship. . .'" (p. 31)
>
> This Pandare, that neigh malt for wo and routhe,
> Ful ofte seyde, "Allas! what may this be?
> Now frend," quod he, "if evere love or trouthe . . ."(I, 582–84)

Chaucer here avoids getting into the kind of tangle that the modern translator finds himself in by recasting Boccaccio's syntax and by entering into direct speech a line earlier than the Italian: what Boccaccio reports of Pandaro, Pandarus expresses for himself. Such ingenuity from Chaucer is not uncommon: he often improves upon his source simply by converting reported action into speech (for example, Fs VII, 10,6–7 and T&C V, 1170), or vice versa:

> "Cost piangendo, in amorosa erranza
> dimoro, lasso, e non so che mi fare . . ." (IV, 70,1–2)
>
> Thus wepyng that he koude nevere cesse,
> He seyde, "Allas! how shal I, wrecche, fare ?" (IV, 575–76)

The stanzas immediately preceding these lines are given over to the speeches of Troiolo and Troilus. Chaucer follows the pattern of Boccaccio's "Così piangendo" in IV, 575 but ducks momentarily out of direct speech: he probably wished to avoid the somewhat maudlin spectacle of a hero reporting upon his own "wepyng."

Chaucer's understanding of the Italian text manifests itself in adaptations of difficult or idiomatic passages. Chaucer finds a delightfully appropriate English equivalent for Pandaro's *sotto voce* comment in VII, 10, 7-18 (V, 1174-76) and evidently understands Boccaccio's usage of the idiom *avere gola a* in IV, 32,5 (IV, 285).[23] Here he clearly understands the grammatical function of the term "tanto":

> "Oh," disse Pandar "com'hai tu potuto
> tenermi tanto tal foco nascoso?" (II, 9,1–2)
>
> "'Oh–' said Pandaro, 'how could you have kept so ardent a passion as this concealed from me?'" (p. 31)
>
> "How hastow thus unkyndely and longe
> Hid this fro me, thow fol?" quod Pandarus. (I, 617–18)

Havely apparently takes "tanto" to be an adjective premodifying the noun "foco" (which he translates as "passion"). Chaucer sees "tanto" as an adverbial phrase (in which "per" and "tempo" are understood by ellipsis). Maintaining the ellipsis, Chaucer translates "tanto" with the adverb "longe." Chaucer's reading of the line is the correct one: "tal" is the adjective which premodifies "foco," not "tanto."

Another correct interpretation of the term "tanto" figures in Chaucer's adaptation of the dense and difficult couplet which concludes Troiolo's apostrophe to Death ("Morte"):

"tu n'uccidi ben tanti oltre al volere,
che ben puoi fare a me questo piacere." (IV, 62,7–8)

"Syn that thou sleest so fele in sondry wyse
Ayens hire wil, unpreyed, day and nyght,
Do me at my requeste this servise:" (IV, 512–14)

Boccaccio's apostrophe expires in a rush of words: Chaucer, we have noted, generally favors a more measured, recapitulative couplet; here he transfers Troiolo's petition to the head of his stanza and dilutes its breathless compactness. At other times, however, he is pleased to imitate the dense quality of Boccaccio's phrasing:

. . . sì com'egli avviene
che colui ch'ama mal volentier crede
cosa ch'accresca amando le sue pene . . . (VIII, 7,2–4)

". . . for it is usual for a lover to be reluctant to believe anything that will add to his sufferings in love." (p. 98)

For with ful yvel wille list hym to leve,
That loveth wel, in swich cas, though hym greve. (V, 1637–38)

Boccaccio introduces his sententious appeal to experience with the familiar formula "sì com'egli avviene." In the *Troilus,* such weighty utterances are most often housed in the couplet; Chaucer–doubtless alerted by Boccaccio's introductory formula–transfers Boccaccio's *sententia* from the main body of the stanza to its appropriate place. In a footnote, Havely argues against the interpretation of earlier translators (see Griffin & Myrick 1967) who

. . . assume that *mal* modifies *ama,* and translate: "he who loveth ill, willingly believeth . . ." But *male* is well attested in the sense of "not" or "hardly" (GDLI, *male* [advb.], 15). Cp., for example, Inf. XVIII, 52. (p. 204)

I feel sure that Havely is right here: but for confirmation we may turn to the *Troilus.* Chaucer translates the phrase "colui ch'ama" as "hym . . . / That loveth" and "mal volentier crede" as "with ful yvel wille list . . . to leve." Chaucer evidently takes "mal" in the sense that Havely suggests to be appropriate; and yet his paraphrase still manages to incorporate the literal flavor of "mal" that the earlier translators include and Havely obscures. Here, as often, modern translators of the *Filostrato* would be well advised to look to Chaucer for guidance.

I hope that the foregoing analyses have helped substantiate my claim that Chaucer understood Boccaccio's language extraordinarily well. The *Filostrato* may initially have commended itself to the English poet through the strength and originality of its plot: but its syntax and phrasing also came to exert a considerable influence on the elaboration of the *Troilus.*

In chapter III, we considered the way in which Chaucer in the *Troilus* develops the fiction of following Lollius, an ancient author whose role corresponds to that of Ilario in the *Filocolo.* At the surface of his fictional world, Chaucer purports to be translating from ancient Latin: but beneath its surface we discover him energetically practicing translation from modern Italian. Posture and practice seemingly constitute distinct aspects of Chaucer's creative enterprise; the gap between them is never apparently bridged. But here, at least, we can consider these aspects in the closest juxtaposition:

> "<u>se Calcas per ambage</u> e per errori
> <u>qui non ci mena</u> . . ." (VI, 17,3–4)
>
> "And <u>but if Calkas lede us with ambages,</u>
> That is to seyn, with double wordes slye,
> Swiche as men clepen a word with two visages . . ." (V, 897–99)

Considering *Troilus* I, 1065–71 in chapter 5, we observed Chaucer reacting to his Italian source by invoking the guidance of a Latin rhetorician, Geoffrey of Vinsauf; here, on discovering an impressive Latinate noun in the Italian ("ambage"), he poses as one who glosses a Latin term, employing a suggestive formula ("that is to seyn"–familiar from *Boece*–to enhance the effect. Neither of these reactions to the *Filostrato* halts or detracts from the development of the narrative action. The earlier example can be taken simply as a passing reflection on Pandarus' thoughtful plotting of Troilus' love suit. The later example, which glosses a difficult or unfamiliar word, acquires dramatic appropriateness in being spoken by Diomede, a man who characteristically shows himself sensitive to the fact that Criseyde, in passing over to the Greeks, is embracing an unfamiliar culture.

As we have seen, Chaucer introduces many new words to English in translating from Boccaccio's Italian: but, typically, he draws attention to his translation practice only in appropriating a word of high Latin pedigree. There seems little doubt that he *did* recognize "ambages" as a noun of Latin origin; he may have recalled it from Vergil's *Aeneid:*

> Talibus ex adyto dictis Cumaea Sibylla

horrendas canit *ambages* antroque remugit,
obscuris vera involvens . . . (VI, 98-100)

"With such words the Cumaean Sibyl sings from her shrine her fearsome enigmas
and echoes booming out from the cavern, enfolding the truth with darkness . . ."

Here "ambages" fall from the mouth of the Cumaean Sibyl: discovered in such a context, the term offers impressive suggestive potential to a poem that seriously concerns itself with the problem of truth and true speaking in a pagan world. The *Troilus* is one such poem; the *Commedia*[24] is another:

Né per ambage, in che la gente folle
già s'inviscava pria che fosse anciso
l'Agnel di Dio che le peccata tolle,
ma per chiare parole e con preciso
latin rispuose quello amor paterno . . . (Par XVII, 31–35)

"Not in enigmas, in which the foolish people
were once entangled before the slaying
of the Lamb of God who takes away sins,
but in plain language and in precise
terms that paternal love replied . . ."

A similarly sharp distinction between the languages of pagan fiction and of Christian truthfulness is drawn by Chaucer in concluding both the *Troilus* and *The Canterbury Tales.*

Boccaccio's employment of the term "ambage" may, then, have sent Chaucer to Dante and from Dante to Vergil; it may have sent him to a text (perhaps glossed) of the *Aeneid;* it may have sent him to a French translation of a Latin text.[25] Whatever the case, or combination of cases, the range of possibilities opened up by Boccaccio's "ambage" stands as fitting testimony to the rich potential of his text as a Chaucerian source.

In 1355, Pierre Bersuire employed "ambages" as a French noun in translating Livy from Latin into French.[26] In composing the *Troilus,* Chaucer is similarly concerned to expand his native lexicon, and thereby to increase the creative potential of the English language: he too attempts to introduce "ambages" to his vernacular. The considerable contribution made by Boccaccio's vocabulary and phrasing to this process of lexical expansion is nowhere acknowledged by Chaucer. And on the only occasion that Chaucer draws attention to his introduction of a new word to the English language in *Troilus and Criseyde* he disguises his indebtedness to the Italian by affecting the pose of a glossator of Latin. The fact that "ambages" took root in French and fell upon stony ground in English might be seen as offering Boccaccio some measure of historical revenge and of poetic justice.[27]

Chaucer's fundamental indebtedness to the *Filostrato*'s narrative framework is readily apparent from a brief examination of the table of parallels provided by F.

N. Robinson.[28] Many divergences in sensibility and attitude (much discussed by English critics) set the English poet apart from Boccaccio: but for all that, Chaucer continues to employ stanzas from the *Filostrato* until his *Troilus* is virtually complete; Book V reveals parallels with the Italian work as impressive and sustained as any in Book I (compare Fs VII, 10 and T&C V, 1170–76, Fs VIII, 14 and T&C V, 1688–94). The *Troilus* does not "grow away from" its Italian source. The pattern of the *Filostrato*'s "tale" (I, 263) is firmly imprinted on Chaucer's mind. When he excurses from his source, this pattern is not forgotten; he can generally be observed to be moving *away from* or back *towards* Boccaccio's poem. The *Filostrato* orientates the progress of *Troilus and Criseyde* from start to finish.

Chaucer's first sustained digression from his source comes with the insertion of seven stanzas (I, 218-66) between imitations of *Filostrato* I, 25 and I, 26. But in fact, the English poet begins to move away from Boccaccio's text even in translating the opening line of I, 25:

> O ciechità delle mondane menti. . .

> O blynde world, O blynde entencioun! (I, 211)

The term *entencioun* occurs far more frequently in *Boece* than anywhere else in Chaucer's writings: its presence here lends philosophical precision to Boccaccio's somewhat vague exclamation at worldly blindness and adumbrates the discussion of natural law which follows. This discussion is first conducted in a comic vein with the example of "proude Bayard" (I, 218), but is then more seriously applied to the case of Troilus. For four stanzas Chaucer develops a didactic, authorish posture in preaching to his audience of lovers on the "ensample" (I, 232) of Troilus. Two important (and closely associated) strains of imagery are delicately introduced during this excursus: that of Fortune's wheel (I, 215-16) and that of the navigational imagery which describes how Troilus' heart is steered (I, 228). Employing such imagery, Troilus attempts (tragically) to forge a link between his love for Criseyde and the force which orders the universe (see I, 416; III, 1291; IV, 282; V, 641). Having moved a considerable distance from his source text, Chaucer spends an entire stanza in realigning himself with it. The distinction that he draws here between "my tale" and "other thing collateral" is most instructive:

> But for to tellen forth in special
> As of this kynges sone of which I tolde,
> And leten other thing collateral,
> Of hym thenke I my tale forth to holde,
> Bothe of his joie and of his cares colde;
> And al his werk, as touching this matere,
> For I it gan, I wol therto refere. (I, 260–66)

From this it seems that Chaucer appraised the *Filostrato* much as we have suggested: as a source providing an excellent story-line ("tale") which may be embellished, expanded and supplemented from time to time with incidental authorial commentary ("other thing collateral").[29] It is a notable feature of the *Troilus* that Chaucer most often speaks and poses as an *auctour* when working away from his Italian source. Poised to embark on his lengthiest and most ambitious departure from the *Filostrato* (III, 442-1309, the very heart of the *Troilus*), Chaucer seems almost overwhelmed with authorial self-consciousness: he confesses his own uncertainties (III, 442-48), nervously discusses his own strategy of writing (III, 491-504) and makes several references to "myn" (imaginary Latin) "auctour" (III, 502-03, 575-78).

Having worked away from the *Filostrato* for well over one hundred stanzas, Chaucer rejoins it with remarkable ease:

> Lungo sarebbe a raccontar la festa,
> ed impossible a dire il diletto . . . (III, 31,1–2)
>
> Of hire delit, or joies oon the leeste,
> Were impossible to my wit to seye . . . (III, 1310–11)

He then proceeds to employ (to a greater or lesser extent) every one of Boccaccio's next thirty-four stanzas (III, 32-65; III, 1310-1680). It seems that even in setting out for uncharted territory in III, 442 Chaucer definitely envisaged rejoining the *Filostrato.* Chaucer often terminates a sustained bout of independent elaboration by hooking up most emphatically with his source text as if to orientate himself and draw breath:

> "Ben puoi dunque veder ch'Amor t'ha posto
> in loco degno della tua virtute;
> sta' dunque fermo nell'alto proposto
> e bene spera della tua salute,
> la quale io credo che seguirà tosto
> se tu col pianto tuo non la rifiute.
> Tu sei di lei ed ella di te degno,
> ed io ci adoprerò tutto '1 mio 'ngegno." (II, 24)
>
> "And sith that God of *Love* hath the bistowed
> In place digne unto thi worthinesse,
> Stond faste, for to good port hastow rowed;
> And of thiself, for any hevynesse,
> Hope alwey wel; for, but if drerinesse
> Or over-haste oure bothe labour shende,
> I hope of this to maken a good ende." (I, 967–73)

Having worked independently for eleven stanzas (I, 890-966), Chaucer reestablishes contact with his Italian source here most decisively;[30] and yet, remarkably, no flaw appears in the seamless garment of Pandarus' discourse. The craft which Chaucer employs in rejoining the *Filostrato* is sometimes exquisitely subtle: earlier in Book I, in the space of a single line, he realigns himself with Boccaccio's narrative while yet sounding a final echo of the wheel of Fortune imagery that has been developed over his last three stanzas (I, 834-54)

> " . . . orsù, lascia 'l tapino
> pianto che fai . . . " (II, 16,5–6)

> "Lat be thy wo and tornyng to the grounde . . . " (I, 856)

Between terminating one "Parte" of his *Filostrato* and beginning another, Boccaccio habitually outlines and introduces the next phase of his narrative in a lengthy rubric. Chaucer, we have noted, builds such authorial reflections into the fabric of his poem. On four occasions,[31] Chaucer ignores Boccaccio's structural divisions and continues his narrative without a break. These continuations are finely crafted: for example, having imitated the final stanza of the *Filostrato's* fifth "Parte," Chaucer proceeds directly to an imitation of the first stanza of *Filostrato* VI. Once again, Chaucer wins fresh impetus and dramatic force for his narrative by transferring and recasting Boccaccio's reported action into direct speech:

> Dall'altra parte in sul lito del mare,
> con poche donne, tra le genti armate,
> stava Criseida, ed in lagrime amare
> da lei eran le notti consumate . . . (VI, 1,1–4)

> Upon that other syde ek was Criseyde,
> With wommen fewe, among the Grekis stronge;
> For which ful ofte a day "Allas!" she seyde,
> "That I was born! Wel may myn herte longe . . ." (V, 687–90)

The ghostly presence of the *Filostrato* may sometimes be discerned beneath Chaucer's narrative surface even when the English poet appears to have put the Italian text to one side. In beginning Book II, Chaucer develops his narrative independently for almost three hundred lines. Halfway through this independent development, however, we find:

> Quivi con risa e con dolci parole,
> con lieti motti e con ragionamenti
> parentevoli assai, sì come suole
> farsi talvolta tra congiunte genti . . . (II, 35,1–4)

> So after this, with many wordes glade,

And frendly tales, and with merie chiere,
Of this and that they pleide, and gonnen wade
In many an unkouth glad and dep matere,
As frendes doon whan thei ben mette yfere . . . (II, 148–52)

I think it likely that Chaucer consciously referred to the *Filostrato* at this point: for he is influenced here not by the cadences of Boccaccio's language, but simply by the details of his narrative. Chaucer's imagination rarely seems to have been swayed simply by the rhythms of Boccaccio's verse.[32] (The cadences of the *Commedia,* however, exerted a continuous influence on the young Boccaccio: his opening line here is obviously (if not consciously) modeled on *Inferno* XVIII, 91).

In the midst of Chaucer's lengthiest independent elaboration we encounter a most unexpected (and hitherto unnoticed) borrowing from Boccaccio's text:

ora i polsi fregando ed or la faccia
bagnandogli sovente, come accorte
persone, s'ingegnavan rivocare,
ma poco ancor valeva l'adoprare. (IV, 19,5–8)

"Now speke to me, for it am I, Criseyde!"
But al for nought; yit myght he nought abreyde.

Therwith his pous and paumes of his hondes
They gan to frote, and wete his temples tweyne . . . (III, 1112–15)

Here it seems most likely that Chaucer deliberately resorted to his Italian source text in order to appropriate a number of narrative details. The passage he imitates forms part of the *Filostrato*'s fourth "Parte": Troiolo, having heard the Trojan parliament pronounce that Criseida should be handed over to the Greeks, faints, wounded with "alto duol" (IV, 18,8); Priamo, Ettore and his brothers attempt to revive him. Chaucer evidently found such high public melodrama–worthy of a popular romance–inappropriate: but he judged such a collapse fitting when transferred to the private drama played out at the center of his poem. Clearly, then, Chaucer had read ahead in the *Filostrato* very carefully before embarking on his greatest independent excursus.

Having considered the ways in which Chaucer introduces and concludes extensive digressions from his source, I would like, briefly, to draw attention to a technique that he characteristically employs in more restricted amplifications of Boccaccio's text. This technique is quite simple: Chaucer sometimes expands an *ottava* by dividing it into two parts and devoting a stanza to each part. I have been able to identify twenty-nine examples of this technique.[33] Their distribution is interesting: eight of them occur in the first three Books of the *Troilus,* and the other twenty-one in the last two. This suggests that Chaucer may have evolved the technique in the actual process of composing his poem.[34] The distribution of examples in *Troilus* IV and V usefully draws attention to the parts and qualities of the

Filostrato that Chaucer found admirable and amenable: for it seems reasonable to assume that Chaucer would only have expanded his source in this way when he was happy with its potentialities. Two examples from the middle of Book IV–where such expansions are densely distributed–bear this out:

> Ne potea ritenere alcun sospiro,
> e tal fiata alcuna lagrimetta
> cadendo, dava segno del martiro
> nel qual l'anima sua era costretta; (IV, 84, 1–4)

> For which no lenger myghte she restreyne
> Hir teeris, so they gonnen up to welle,
> That yaven signes of the bittre peyne
> In which hir spirit was, and moste dwelle;
> Remembryng hir, fro heven into which helle
> She fallen was, syn she forgoth the syghte
> Of Troilus, and sorwfully she sighte. (IV, 708–14)

> ma quelle stolte che le facean giro,
> credevan per pietà la giovinetta
> far ciò, ch'avesse d'abbandonar esse,
> le quali esser solean sue compagnesse. (IV, 84,5–8)

> And thilke fooles sittynge hire aboute
> Wenden that she wepte and siked sore
> Bycause that she sholde out of that route
> Departe, and nevere pleye with hem more.
> And they that hadde yknowen hire of yore
> Seigh hire so wepe, and thoughte it kyndenesse,
> And ech of hem wepte eke for hire destresse. (IV, 715–21)

In the space of a stanza, Boccaccio moves from considering the outward manifestations of Criseida's grief to reporting the way in which these signs are interpreted by the circle of women that surrounds her. Chaucer, respecting the balanced structure of this *ottava,* allots a stanza to each of its two equal parts. He imitates Boccaccio's first four lines of external description very closely and then, typically, moves inwards to consider Criseyde's secret thoughts. Although the last three lines of Chaucer's stanza depart from the *Filostrato,* their syntax and prosody exhibit powerfully Boccaccian characteristics: a present participle introduces the dependent clause; enjambments and mid-line pauses unsettle the equilibrium of the lines. For once, the firm articulation of the Chaucerian couplet is eroded; Chaucer successfully conveys the inner agitation of his heroine.

In his next stanza (IV, 722–28), Chaucer simply expands Boccaccio's succinct portrayal of Criseida's female companions (IV, 85). Boccaccio rarely succeeds in evoking pathos through lyricism: but here–and elsewhere–he creates a most poignant effect by dramatic means in surrounding private grief with a social circle. Chaucer much admired this section of the *Filostrato*: he closely imitates all eight of the *ottave* following the rubric at IV, 78 and devotes two stanzas to IV, 79 (IV, 666–79) as well as to IV, 84. He ends by adopting Boccaccio's assessment of the effect that the words of these foolish women have on the heroine:

> . . . né erano altro che grattarla
> nelle calcagne, ove il capo prudea . . . (IV, 85,5–6)
>
> But swich an ese therwith they hire wroughte,
> Right as a man is esed for to feele,
> For ache of hed, to clawen hym on his heele! (IV, 726–28)

Chaucer's refined (or mock-refined) rendering of Boccaccio's epigrammatic colloquialism testifies further to his exceptional abilities as an Italianist. Boccaccio's lines here are redolent of the *cantare* manner[35]; in fact the whole of this colorful, rapidly-narrated episode owes much to the *cantare* ("a tradition of popular narrative in ottava rima which has much in common with the English tradition of tail-rime romance"; Boitani & Mann, eds. 1986, 31). The *ottava* at IV, 8I employs the quadripartite structure typical of the *cantare* stanza in reporting the various reactions of the Trojan women to Criseida's imminent departure. Chaucer found this congenial: the first six lines of his equivalent stanza (IV, 687-93) adhere closely to the structure and content of Boccaccio's *ottava.* A four-part *ottava* facilitates the task of a translator or adapter by offering its ideas in simple two-line units.[36] In his final expansion of an *ottava* into two stanzas (V, 1744-57), Chaucer adopts three ideas from a quadripartite Boccaccian stanza (VIII, 25,1-4, 7-8) and casts one aside (VIII, 25,5-6). The brusque and summary manner in which Boccaccio orders events in VIII, 25 proves congenial to Chaucer because, at this late stage of the narrative, he is earnestly attempting to detach himself and his emotions from the story of Troilus. Earlier on, however, Chaucer characteristically endeavors to smooth away the rough edges of Boccaccio's narrative manner and to slow its somewhat hectic rate of development:

> Chi potrebbe giammai narrare appieno
> ciò che Criseida nel pianto dicea?
> Certo non io, ch'al fatto il dir vien meno,
> tant'era la sue noia crude e rea. (IV, 95,1–4)
>
> How myghte it evere yred ben or ysonge,
> The pleynte that she made in hire destresse?
> I not; but, as for me, my litel tonge,
> If I discryven wolde hire hevynesse,
> It sholde make hire sorwe seme lesse

Than that it was, and childisshly deface
Hire heigh compleynte, and therefore ich it pace. (IV, 799–805)

Ma mentre tai lamenti si facieno,
Pandaro venne, a cui non si tenea
uscio giammai, e 'n camera sen gio
la dov'ella faceva il pianto rio (IV, 95,5–8)

Pandare, which that sent from Troilus
Was to Criseyde–as ye han herd devyse
That for the beste it was acorded thus,
And he ful glad to doon hym that servyse–
Unto Criseyde, in a ful secree wise,
Ther as she lay in torment and in rage,
Com hire to telle al hoolly his message . . . (IV, 806–12)

Although he asks "how" rather than "who" ("chi"), Chaucer adopts Boccaccio's employment of an inexpressibility topos couched in terms of an answered question. In extending this topos over an entire stanza, Chaucer personalizes its reflective quality. Once again, such reflections may be read as a private commentary on his source: for Boccaccio *does* attempt to render the heroine's "pleynte," albeit not in full ("appieno," IV, 95,1). In the two stanzas preceding IV, 95, Boccaccio's heroine berates her absent father and bewails her own state. Chaucer makes no use of these verses, which are certainly cliché-ridden and woodenly melodramatic: little better, in fact, than the "compleynt" of Dido in *The House of Fame,* 300–60, a passage which the mature Chaucer could hardly have recalled without some embarrassment (identified as a "compleynt" in 362):

"Oimè lassa, trista e dolorosa,
ch'a me convien porter la penitenza
del tuo peccato! Cotanto noiosa
vita non meritai per mia fallanza.
O verità del ciel, luce pietosa . . ." (IV, 94,1–5)

"Woe is me, abandoned, sad and grieving,
for it falls to me to do penance
for your sin! Such a vexatious
life I did not deserve through fault of my own.
O heavenly truth, piteous light . . ."

"Allas!" quod she, "my swete herte,
Have pitee on my sorwes smerte,
And slee me not! goo nought awey!
O woful Dido, wel-awey!" (HF 315–18)

The sudden arrival of Pandaro in the second half of *Filostrato* IV, 95 certainly makes Boccaccio's usage of the inexpressibility topos seem somewhat perfunctory: Boccaccio again seems to be writing "with rakel hond" (T&C I, 1067). By reflecting on the way in which a "litel tonge" may "childisshly deface" a "heigh compleynte," Chaucer fills out his first stanza and postpones the arrival of Pandarus until his second. In this second stanza, Chaucer states his subject immediately ("Pandare") but does not reach his main verb ("Com") until the beginning of the final line. He is content to devote most of the intervening space to a résumé of past events; this is introduced by a phrase ("as ye hen herd") which confirms his intimacy with his auditors.

Chaucer sometimes exploits the space created by the expansion of a single *ottava* into two stanzas by introducing classical material: in I, 704–07 he introduces proverbial lore, (possibly derived from Ovid or Seneca) and in III, 374–75 a reference to Achilles; in IV, 299–301 he refers to Oedipus ("Edippe") and in V, 599–602 to Juno's hatred of the Thebans. But as a rule, Chaucer seems content simply to expand his text along the lines mapped out by the *Filostrato:* again, it is as if he wishes to do justice to Boccaccio's fecund (sometimes riotous) powers of invention.

Chaucer demonstrates as much skill in abbreviating his source as he does in amplifying it. In Book V, for example, we see him reducing a sequence of eight *ottave* from *Filostrato* VII (18–25) to five stanzas of rhyme royal (1212–46). Here, as often, it is instructive to consider what Chaucer cuts from his source. In VII, 2I, for example, Priamo (in a tone of voice which recalls the affective, *cantare*-like simplicity of the *Ninfale fiesolano*) entreats his son Troiolo to disclose the cause of his misery: "Dilmi, figliuolo . . ." (VII, 21,7). Such pathos does not suit Chaucer here: he deprives Priam of direct speech and fuses VII, 21 with VII, 22. Similarly, many of Criseida's final words to Troiolo in *Filostrato* IV are found unfitting for the *Troilus*. Much is cut and much compressed: for example, the first three *ottave* of Criseida's expatiation on the "evil things" ("cose ree," IV, 147,6) that may follow as consequences of Troiolo's flight from Troy (IV, 147–49) are packed into a single English stanza (IV, 1555–61); and in the stanza following, Criseida's frothy circumlocutions are supplanted by a crisp, argumentative style that reminds us that Criseyde is the niece of Pandarus:

> "As alday happeth after anger game . . .
> ....
> "For hastif man ne wanteth nevere care." (IV, 1563,1568)

Three stanzas later, Criseida's long-winded (pseudo-courtly) style again contrasts with Criseyde's incisiveness:

> "Ed oltre a questo vo' che tu riguardi
> a ciò che quasi d'ogni cosa avviene:" (IV, 152,1–2)

> "And in addition to this I wish you to take notice
> of that which holds in almost every case:"

"And forthi sle with resoun al this hete!" (IV, 1583)

Criseyde supports her case in this stanza with three pithy proverbs, whereas Criseida begins a rambling, two-stanza embroidery of a theme ("familiarity breeds contempt") derived from Andreas Capellanus (Boccaccio 1964, II, 862, n. 90). Seven stanzas later, Criseida launches another polite appeal (adapted from Dante's appeal to Vergil in *Inferno* XXVI, 66); Chaucer again naturalizes the artificial, pseudo-courtly quality of Boccaccio's language:

"Ond'io ti priego, se 'l mio priego vale . . ." (IV, 160,1)

"Therefore I pray you, if my prayer be of value . . ."

"Forthi with al myn herte I yow biseke . . ." (IV, 1632)

Chaucer seeks out and fuses the essential content of *Filostrato* IV, 160–1, in simple, unaffected language (IV, 1632–38). We may observe, here, the technique of amplification discussed above employed in reverse: Chaucer derives a single stanza from two *ottave*. Incidences of this pattern of abbreviation are not, however, numerous enough to warrant much discussion; it seems more germane to conclude this brief section by re-emphasizing the notable contribution made by English monosyllables to the cause of economy in translation:

E fatto questo, con animo forte
la propria spade del fodero trasse,
tutto disposto di prender la morte,
acciocché il suo spirto seguitasse
quel della donna con sì trista sorte,
e nell'inferno con lei abitasse,
poi che aspra fortuna e duro amore
di questa vita lui cacciava fore. (IV, 120)

And after this, with sterne and cruel herte,
His swerd anon out of his shethe he twighte,
Hymself to slen, how sore that hym smerte,
So that his soule hire soule folwen myghte
Ther as the doom of Mynos wolde it dighte;
Syn Love and cruel Fortune it ne wolde,
That in this world he lenger lyven sholde. (IV, 1184–90)

Chaucer's seven-line stanza contains nine words more than Boccaccio's *ottava.* Chaucer's economical employment of monosyllables is augmented by skillful powers of compression. The essence of Boccaccio's third line is captured in just three words ("Hymself to slen"). Boccaccio's next two lines are rendered in one: Chaucer transforms the phrase "quel della donna" into "hire soule" and inserts this into the middle of his fourth line; he cuts "con sì trista sorte," a weak phrase which serves to supply Boccaccio's third "a" rime. Chaucer now has three lines in which to translate the last three lines of the *ottava;* he elects, characteristically, to classicize Boccaccio's infernal vision by introducing the ancient (and Dantean) figure of Minos.

In incorporating ideas from *Filostrato* III, 78 into his *prohemium* to Book III, Chaucer packs more words into his seven lines than Boccaccio can fit into eight. Skillfully compressing each of Boccaccio's first three ideas, Chaucer gains the effect of *anaphora* on "Ye." Having disposed of Boccaccio's first five-and-a-half lines in just over three lines, Chaucer is able to rearrange and develop the ideas introduced by the Boccaccian relative adverb "once" in a more leisurely fashion:

> Tu 'n unite le case e le cittadi,
> li regni e le province e 'l mondo tutto
> tien', belle dea; tu dell'amistadi
> se' cagion certa e del lor caro frutto;
> tu sola le nascose qualitadi
> delle cose conosci, onde il costrutto
> vi metti tal, che fai maravigliare
> chi tua potenza non sa ragguardare. (III, 78)

> Ye holden regne and hous in unitee;
> Ye sothfast cause of frendshipe ben also;
> Ye knowe al thilke covered qualitee
> Of thynges, which that folk on wondren so,
> Whan they kan nought construe how it may jo
> She loveth hym, or whi he loveth here,
> As whi this fissh, and naught that, comth to were. (III, 29–35)

This juxtaposition reminds us that whereas the mature Chaucer is a skilled and experienced versifier, the youthful Boccaccio has yet to discover his métier as a prose writer. As we have noted, Boccaccio's respect for the restraints of poetic form is somewhat limited: his first main verb here arrives with a sudden thump ("tien"), and his positioning of "onde" is particularly awkward. It is ironic that *Troilus and Criseyde* has so often been discussed as if it were a novel (and especially ironic that Meech should have contributed to such discussion; p. vi): for much of Chaucer's translating of the *Filostrato* is analogous to a movement from prose to verse.[37]

The language of the *Filostrato* repeatedly endeavors to break loose from the conventional constraints of verse and to develop a prose-like impetus. For example, although the first two lines of IV, I3 are end-stopped, the rest of this stanza develops its argument with scant reference to line-endings, an argument which is extended (as in III, 78) with an awkwardly-positioned "onde." And although the first two lines of VII, 6 are end-stopped, the rest of this stanza (which features a sequence of four mid-line copulative "e"s) is governed by a prose-like logic. Having pursued his argument across a line-ending, Boccaccio often elects to catch his breath by coming to a dead halt in the first half of the subsequent line: to this end he favors terms with a heavily-stressed final syllable such as "incominciò" (see, for example: IV, 15,3; IV, 50,2; VII, 51,7; VIII, II,3 & 7). He is fond of separating the subject of a lengthy sentence from the main verb and of filling the intervening space with subordinate clauses introduced (most typically) by relative pronouns such as "il quale"[38]; in IV, 112 he rounds off an extraordinary prose-like stanza by rhyming "i quali" with "vostri mali." Chaucer exhibits great skill in containing the flow of Boccaccio's ideas within tighter (or more conventional) constraints of versification. Some *ottave,* however, lie beyond his powers of redemption:

> Pandaro, presa la lettera pia,
> n'andò verso Criseida, la quale
> come 'l vide venir, la compagnia
> con la quale era lasciata, cotale
> gli si fé 'ncontro parte della via,
> qual pare in vista perla orientale,
> temendo e disiando; e' salutarsi
> du lunge assai, poi per le man pigliarsi. (II, 108)

> "Pandaro, having taken the pious letter,
> went off towards Criseida, who
> on seeing him coming, having left
> the company with which she was, she
> went along part of the way to meet him,
> who seems like an oriental pearl to look at,
> fearing and desiring; and greeting one another
> from afar, they then took one another by the hands."

This clumsy and confusing stanza, with its glut of personal and relative pronouns, is not much improved by the *cantare-style* simile in its sixth line which, in rhyming "orientale" with "la quale" and "cotale," provides Boccaccio's third "b" rhyme. Such *ottave* are not a rarity in the *Filostrato:* Boccaccio seems particularly prone to drop into a prose-like rhythm when shifting his protagonists from place to place or when chronicling a quick succession of events. Chaucer reacts to such stanzas in varying ways. He aligns himself with the first line of *Filostrato* II, I08 in II, 1093 but goes on to elaborate and enliven his stanza quite independently. He passes over four prosaic, business-like stanzas in which final arrangements are made for Troiolo's nocturnal encounter with Criseida (III, 21–24), but keeps determinedly abreast of four stanzas in which Troiolo's fears about Criseida's disloyalty are confirmed (VIII, 8–11; V, 1646–73). In adapting (rewriting and versifying) certain prose-like Boccaccian *ottave* Chaucer takes great pains:

> E questo detto, il suo Pandaro prese
> per mano, e 'l viso alquanto si dipinse

con falso riso, e del palagio scese,
a varie cagion con gli altri finse
ch'eran con lui, per nasconder l'offese
ch'el sentiva d'amor; ma poi ch'attinse
con gli occhi di Criseida la magione
chiusa, sentì novella turbagione. (V, 51)

"And having said this, his Pandaro he took
by the hand, and his face he somewhat painted
with a false smile, and left the palace,
and trumped up various excuses with the others
who were with him, to hide the suffering
that he was feeling from love; but when he reached
with his eyes of Criseida the mansion
closed, he felt new perturbation."

And therwithal, his meyne for to blende,
A cause he fond in towne for to go,
And to Criseydes hous they gonnen wende.
But Lord! this sely Troilus was wo!
Hym thoughte his sorwful herte braste a-two.
For, when he saugh hire dores spered alle,
Wel neigh for sorwe adoun he gan to falle. (V, 526–32)

This *ottava* is drawn from one of the areas of *the Filostrato* that Chaucer most admired, or made most use of; even though no exact verbal correspondences arise when it is juxtaposed with the Chaucerian stanza quoted above, there is no doubting the appropriateness of this juxtaposition. In his first five-and-a-half lines, Boccaccio packs a prodigious quantity of information into a string of short clauses which show scant respect for line-endings; he then introduces a longer clause with a tortuous and confusing word order before squeezing in one last short clause. The word which bears most weight in this *ottava is* the "ma" which introduces a turn in the argument analogous to that in a well-made sonnet. A more disciplined poet would not, perhaps, have left such a vital conjunction stranded in mid-line. Chaucer, in seeking to improve on Boccaccio's stanza, might have elected to make his turn in the couplet, as he does elsewhere in V, 27. But, with a characteristically explosive authorial ejaculation, he turns earlier rather than later; this allows him to surround the crucial information in his penultimate line with two lines of emotional intensification. The whole of Chaucer's stanza, constructed line-by-line, exhibits great poetic balance and control; his first three lines offer a splendid and economical digest of the information piled up in the first five-and-a-half lines of Boccaccio's *ottava.*

Chaucer makes intelligent use of many *ottave* whose prose-like qualities inhibit extensive literal imitation. He sometimes selects a single motif from an Italian stanza as a starting point for his own poetic elaboration. In IV, 115 Boccaccio devotes an entire stanza to describing the sighs, cries and tears of his lovers; he tells us in his final line that these tears "amare fossero oltre lor natura." Chaucer tells of tears that "bittre weren, out of teris kynde" (IV, 1136) before going on to develop an exquisite comparison with the tears of Myrrha ("Mirra"). In similar fashion, he passes over most of the apostrophic melodrama of *Filostrato* IV, 62 before lighting on an idea couched in its couplet and making this the starting point for his own more balanced and thoughtful poetic development (IV, 512-18).

Chaucer persistently endeavors to divert the prose-like current of Boccaccio's language into more conventional poetic channels. He frequently substitutes proper nouns for personal pronouns and curtails the processions of relative pronouns which stretch out Boccaccio's sentences. So in beginning his Book III *prohemium,* Chaucer follows Boccaccio (III, 74) in enjambing between his first two lines (and in entering into a first subordinate clause) but then terminates his sentence at the end of his second line. Boccaccio, typically, extends his period with a "dal quale" in the second half of his second line. This necessitates further enjambment; continuing his period right through the *ottava,* he reaches his main verb in his final line.

The prose-like rhythms which permeate Boccaccio's *ottave* vitiate attempted adaptations of epic similes from Dante and Vergil: Boccaccio proves unable to hold the balance between two halves of a comparison. In *Inferno* XII, 22-25 Dante (likening the movement of the Minotaur to that of a wounded bull) creates a delicate equilibrium by balancing "Qual è" at the beginning of one tercet with "vid' io" at the beginning of another. Chaucer, following Boccaccio's appropriation of the Dantean passage (IV, 27), matches "Right as" with "Right so" (IV, 239-42); in the *Troilus,* as in the *Commedia,* two lines separate these clinching phrases. In the *Filostrato,* however, the whole structure of the simile seems close to collapse. Boccaccio begins by adapting the Vergilian formula "non aliter" ("Né altrimenti") and reaches the second half of his comparison in his fifth line: but his second "clinching phrase" is surrounded by so much enjambment that it offers little resistance to the momentum of a prose period in full spate. Nine stanzas before this, (IV, 18) Boccaccio's attempt to adapt a simile from *Aeneid* IX, 435–37 ends in similar disarray. On this occasion he balances "Qual" against "tale" in his fourth line: but he leaves this "tale" stranded in mid-line and, incredibly, fails to end-stop a single line of his *ottava* until his final line where, once again, he finds his main verb. Chaucer passes over this *ottava:* but he upholds Boccaccio's choice of rhetorical form (epic simile) and theme (natural decay) in turning to a Dantean simile which features bare autumnal branches (*Inferno* III, 112–17; IV, 225-31). Chaucer again respects Dante's construction of the simile by balancing phrases at the beginning of his first and fourth lines ("Come," "And as"; "similemente," "Lith Troilus"). Chaucer enhances the balance and stability of his stanza by alliterating and by repeating "biraft"; the second appearance of this participial adjective yields an internal rime with "ilaft." Chaucer charges his stanza with a metamorphic suggestiveness in describing the way in which Troilus is bound "in the blake bark of care" (IV, 229). In his final line, however, he takes the trouble of anchoring such poetic virtuosity to the immediate facts of his narrative. Directed by Boccaccio to Dante, Chaucer builds upon Dante's example to achieve one of the most accomplished stanzas of the *Troilus:*

And as in wynter leves ben biraft,
Ech after other, til the tree be bare,
So that ther nys but bark and braunche ilaft,
Lith Troilus, byraft of ech welfare,
Ibounden in the blake bark of care,
Disposed wood out of his wit to breyde,
So sore hym sat the chaungynge of Criseyde. (IV, 225–31)

In discussing the verse of Machaut and Chaucer, James Wimsatt observes that "in court poetry the forces of disorder and dissolution could be kept under control within the tight constraints of form and convention" (J. Wimsatt 1975, 18). The *Troilus* takes shape within such constraints: the *Filostrato,* however, sees a simultaneous slackening of the outer constraints of prosody and of the inner constraints of courtesy:

"Io credo certo ch'ogni donna in voglia
vive amorosa, e null'altro l'affrena
che tema di vergogna; e s'a tal doglia
onestamente medicine piena
si può donar, folle è chi non la spoglia . . ." (II, 27,1–5)

"I believe for certain that every woman in desire
lives amorously, and nothing else reins her back
but fear of scandal; and if to such pain
a full dose of medicine might honestly
be applied, he who does not strip off such pain is crazy . . . ."

Pandaro's argument here, developed without regard for line-endings, debases (drags down from a higher to a lower social level) the language of *amour cortois.* Such debasement is a characteristic feature of a work in which the term "cortese" itself is (as in the *cantare* tradition) pressed into service as a decorative epithet affording a convenient rime. Troiolo awaits Criseida:

"La donna cortese
tosto verrà, ed io sarò giocondo . . ."(III, 25,6–7)
"The courteous lady
will soon be here, and I'll be cheerful . . ."

Boccaccio employs terms such as "valore" and "valorosa" with great frequency and little precision. At their most intimate moment, his lovers experience "l'ultimo valore" of love, whereas Troilus and Criseyde "Felten in love the grete worthynesse" (III, 32,8; III, 1316). Pandaro urges that no woman is ""più valorosa"" than Criseida; it inevitably follows (through exigencies of rime) that none is "più graziosa": Pandarus maintains that no woman is "more bountevous/Of hire estat" nor "more gracious/ For to do wel" (II, 22,1,3; I, 883–84, 885–6). The *Filostrato's* imperfect control of courtly terminology complements its imperfect versification: both imperfections attest to a lack of *mesure,* the vital quality which governs the social and poetic procedures of the *Troilus*:

> So when it liked hire to go to reste,
> And voided weren thei that voiden oughte,
> She seyde . . . (II, 911–13)

Chaucer's measured, unhurried lines here create (particularly through the delicate balance of "voided weren" against "voiden oughte") a sense of a world in which social proprieties are scrupulously (but unostentatiously) observed. This sense is strengthened just five stanzas later when Troilus, under the pressure of intense emotion, restrains himself from questioning Pandarus until such proprieties have been observed and secrecy is ensured:

> With al the haste goodly that they myghte,
> They spedde hem fro the soper unto bedde;
> And every wight out at the dore hym dyghte,
> And where hym liste upon his wey him spedde.
> But Troilus . . . (II, 946–50)

Once again, Chaucer's evocation of a social order in which such domestic procedures are quietly observed is complemented by the unhurried development of his end-stopped lines: Boccaccio's enjambments belong to a different world. Pandaro, in lecturing Troiolo, explicitly insists on the importance of secrecy: news of Criseida's sexual compliance must not find its way "into the vulgar mouth" ("alla bocca del vulgo," II, 25, 5). But such solicitude simply forms part of a practical strategy of seduction: the young Boccaccio's insensitivity to the spiritual dimension of secrecy compares with that of the *canterino* who struggled with *La Chastelaine de Vergi.*

At critical moments in the development of their courtship, Troiolo and Criseida are each persuaded by the brute force of Pandaro's crude arguments (see II, 29,1-3; II, 55, 1–64). At comparable moments, Chaucer turns instinctively away from Boccaccio towards the French poets he had admired and imitated since his youth. In Book I, for example, Pandarus concludes a vigorous assault against Troilus' wanhope by appropriating arguments from the *Roman de la Rose* (20859–63; I, 810–12) and from Machaut's *Remède de Fortune* (1636-48; I, 813-19). Such arguments prove effective:

> Of that word took hede Troilus . . . (I, 820)

In II, 820-931 Criseyde is similarly moved by the persuasive force of Antigone's song: the arguments and the lyricism which make her better disposed towards love are developed from a set of Machaut lyrics which "includes two lays, two balades, and a virelai" (J. Wimsatt 1976, 291–he examines the song and its sources in some detail). Later in Book II Chaucer puts his schooling in the figurative language of the *Rose* to good use in revealing the inner workings of his heroine's psyche where Boccaccio confines himself to the description of externals:

> Poi si [Pandaro] partì, ed ella dall'un canto
> della camera sua, ove più rada
> usanza di venire ad ogni altro era,
> a scriver giù si pose in tal manera: (II, 120,5–8)
>
> "Then he left, and she in a corner
> of her room, to which most infrequently
> was there occasion for anyone else to come,
> set herself down to write in such a way:"
>
> And into a closet, for t'avise hire bettre,
> She wente allone, and gan hire herte unfettre
> Out of desdaynes prison but a lite,
> And sette hire down, and gan a lettre write . . . (II, 1215–18)

Four stanzas later Pandarus employs the language of the *Rose* in referring to Criseyde's desire to maintain "the forme of daunger" (II, 1243); a little later he imagines a debate between Kynde and Daunger staged within Criseyde's mind (II, 1373–76); and finally, as Troilus and Criseyde consummate their love, Chaucer himself steps in to ward off "thow foule daunger" and "thow feere" (III, 1321). The "daungerous" behavior of Criseyde is largely modeled on that of Machaut's ladies, as are her subtle powers of argument, her rhetorical skill and her penchant for proffering momentous oaths of loyalty. Troilus' agonized inner conflicts recall those of certain Machaut heroes, as does his abiding concern to discover "trouthe" in his lady.[39]

Machaut and the poets of the *Rose* also provide Chaucer with models of versification and with a fund of poetic motifs for the incidental embellishment of his work.[40] Their influence in the *Troilus* makes itself felt even when Chaucer appears to be following Boccaccio. In V, 218–45, for example, Troilus' complaint borrows material from Boccaccio (V, 20–21, 24-25) but develops it in a restrained and formal manner that is reminiscent of the French poets. Boccaccio's popular epithets are rejected ("misero dolente," "cuor del corpo mio," "lasso più ch'altro," "o dolce bene," "o caro mio diporto," "o bella donna," "o dolce anima mia") or refined beyond recognition: "dolce anima bella" becomes "my righte lode-sterre" (V, 25,1; V, 232). Boccaccio's brightest ideas are developed within tighter bounds of versification:

> ". . . ore abbracciando
> vado il piumaccio . . ." (V, 20,5–6)
>
> "And graspe aboute I may, but in this place,
> Save a *pilowe*, I fynde naught t'enbrace." (V, 223–24)

Anguished, semi-rhetorical questions appear in every Chaucerian stanza and anaphora is employed to fine effect. Chaucer end-stops every line until the middle of his final stanza, where his sudden departure from the norm (V, 242–45) proves brilliantly effective: the balance and restraint of Troilus' complaint is broken by one final anguished outburst.

In previous chapters we have considered ways in which the *Roman de la Rose* precedes the *Commedia* as an extended vernacular narrative. In passing from the poets of the *Rose* and their continuators, Chaucer's personal poetic evolution traces, in a sense, this historical movement. James Wimsatt rightly insists that Chaucer did not abandon the French love poets on discovering the Italians (J. Wimsatt 1976, 277); I would reinforce his point by proposing that Chaucer's apprenticeship among French texts actually primed him, in many ways, for his encounter with the *Commedia.* We discover, in examining the *Troilus,* that Chaucer often turns from Boccaccio towards Dante and the French poets for similar reasons: for a more sophisticated, first-hand understanding of *curteisie* and for standards of versification which might attest to such understanding.

In adapting the *Rose,* the poet of *Il Fiore* (perhaps Dante himself) launched a forthright attack against "i borghesi" (CXVIII, 5&10), the mercantile and entrepreneurial class that had encroached upon traditional aristocratic domains, forcing the nobility into debt and reducing them to the level of basket-makers (CXVIII, 8). La Vechia voices the essential wisdom of this world in which everything is for sale: she instructs Bellacoglienza in the art of feminine "mercatantia" (CLVII, 8) until her disciple is fit and willing to "far mercato" (CXCIV, 5). La Vechia, like the merchants of medieval Italy, makes much use of courtly language: the term "cortese" is frequently on her lips, and concepts such as "franchezza" are subtly redefined.[41] The *Filostrato,* composed within a Florentine merchant colony, undoubtedly perpetuates this popular debasement of aristocratic language. Its appropriation of Dantean phrasings contributes to this process. The unreflective enthusiasm for the *Commedia* evident in the *Filostrato* (and in numerous *cantari* and other popular pieces) would not, one feels, have amused the great poet. It certainly would not have amused Petrarch, who (in writing to Boccaccio in 1359) lamented the fact that Dante's verse was "acclaimed and declaimed . . . by 'ignorant oafs in taverns and market places.'" (Foster 1984, 29–translating a passage from *Familiares* XXI, 15). *Troilus and Criseyde,* however, attests to a mature, deeply-meditated feeling for the *Commedia* (and for the art of poetry) which even Dante (if not Petrarch) might have admired. Certain Dantean scenes cast long and subtle shadows over the *Troilus*: Chaucer (as an author of romances) was undoubtedly alive to the moral issues raised by a reading of *Inferno* V; and his reading of the first nine tercets of *Inferno* XXX certainly alerted him to ways in which the disaster of Thebes foreshadows that of Troy.[42]

The sophisticated ways in which Chaucer adverts to the *Commedia* in fashioning his *Troilus* contrast markedly with the cheerful robustness of Boccaccio's usage of Dante. The Dantean tercet which Chaucer so carefully incorporates into his final stanza (*Paradiso* XIV, 28–30) is squeezed by Boccaccio into a single line and allowed no especial prominence (II, 41, 4). Chaucer does, however, occasionally follow Boccaccio's initiative in mining the *Commedia* for more routine poetic requirements: in III, 1688-94, for example, he draws upon two inexpressibility topoi from different areas of the *Paradiso* (XIX, 7–9; XXIV, 25–27). The *Filostrato's* forthright adaptation of Dantean effects was, I believe, of especial interest to Chaucer in demonstrating how a tale of secular love might be embellished and ennobled without losing its fundamental romance character. For the narrator of *Troilus and Criseyde* often speaks with two distinct voices:

> Now let us stynte of Troilus a stounde . . .
>
> And thus he dryeth forth his aventure. (I, 1086,1092)
>
> Owt of thise blake wawes for to saylle,
> O wynd, o wynd, the weder gynneth clere;
> For in this see the boot hath swych travaylle,
> Of my connyng, that unneth I it steere. (II, 1–4; cf. Purg I, 1–3)

Here Chaucer ends the first Book of his *Troilus* as a romancer[43] and begins the second as a follower of Dante. Such shifts in authorial identity are a characteristic feature of Chaucer's poem. In the stanzas following the *prohemium* to Book III, for example, Chaucer works hard to recover his posture as an unpretentious romancer. (In *Anelida and Arcite* he was, apparently, unable to effect such a recovery after Anelida's lengthy *compleynt*). He enlivens the ending of his first narrative stanza with an authorial exclamation; five stanzas later he slackens the pace of his narration by rhyming his couplet with two romance tags:

> God leve hym werken as he kan devyse! (III, 56)
>
> His resons, as I may my rymes holde,
> I wol yow telle, as techen bokes olde. (III, 90-91)

In III, 106 Troilus addresses Criseyde as "wommanliche wif," a phrase which he employs again in III, 1296. Criseyde reminds us that she is a romance heroine by warning Troilus that although he is a "kynges sone" he will enjoy no more "sovereignete" over her in love than she deems appropriate (III, 169–72). Six stanzas later Chaucer closes one narrative episode and opens another by employing one of his favorite forms of tag phrase[44] and by shifting his scenery with the ostentation typical of a romancer:

> . . . it joie was to here.
>
> Now let hire wende unto hire owen place,
> And torne we to Troilus ayein . . . (III, 217–19)

The form of this tag phrase may be compared with a line from *Amis and Amiloun*; the same tail-rime romance provides a parallel to the deliberate change of scene engineered by Chaucer in III, 218 (and in II, 687–9, III, 1583–86, and V, 195–96) and combines this with an authorial interjection reminiscent of III, 56:

That semly was on to se. (534)

Lete we sir Amiloun stille be
With his wiif in his cuntre–
God leue hem wele to fare–
& of sir Amis telle we . . . (337–40)

Derek Pearsall has suggested that *Amis and Amiloun* "has some claim to be regarded as the typically best English romance." (Pearsall 1965, 110). *Amis,* the *Troilus* and the *Filostrato* have much in common which sets them apart from the *Commedia.* Their authors cultivate an easy-going narrative manner: they employ recapitulatory formulae, repeat phrases or entire lines and predict the future outcome of present actions.[45] The rimes of the *Commedia* strive for perpetual, ingenious variety: these authors ease their task of rhyming by introducing numerous references to sources, religious oaths, stock phrases and standard epithets. Chaucer takes full advantage of the fact that his heroine's name rimes with *seyde.*[46] He employs variations of the romancer's simile "stille as any ston" on five occasions in the *Troilus* and rimes on *ston* six times (II, 600; II, 1494; III, 699; IV, 354; V,1729. II, 600; II, 1228; II, 1494; III, 891; IV, 354; IV, 467). He rimes on *two* on over twenty occasions; these include the romance tags "eyen two" (III, 1352, IV, 750) and "armes two" (IV, 911). Chaucer turns to Petrarch for his first *Canticus Troili*: but in the latter part of his poem Troilus' song is often that of Amis:

His song was, "Waileway!" (984)

For which his song ful ofte is "weylaway!" (IV, 1166)

(The term "weylawey" is used on thirteen occasions, the first being in III, 304.)

The author of *Amis,* like Chaucer and Boccaccio, makes effective use of internal debate[47]; and he too chooses to accentuate the isolated misery of his heroine by surrounding her with cheerful female companions (Belisaunt sends the maidens away on the arrival of Amis, 565–67:

Vp hir ros that swete wight,
In-to the gardine sche went ful right
With maidens hende & fre.
The somers day was fair & bright,
The sonne him schon thurch lem of light,
that semly was on to se.

Sche herd the foules gret & smale,
the swete note of the nightingale
Ful mirily sing on tre;
Ac hir hert was so hard ibrought,
On loue-longing was al hir thought,
No might hir gamen no gle. (529–40)

In such a stanza we may discern a "hierarchy of semantic features" (Culler 1975, 53): some elements are more essential to the development of the story than others. These less essential elements (often located in the shorter lines) make the art of poetic composition less exacting; they also allow the audience momentary relaxations of concentration. Chaucer and Boccaccio seem similarly determined to cultivate an easy-going narrative manner which will not over-tax their auditors. This presents a radical contrast to the demands exacted from the solitary reader who struggles to follow Dante through his great poem. There are no inessential phrases, no momentary resting-places, in the *Commedia;* the faint-hearted reader is actively encouraged to abandon his attempt to read the poem (see Par II, 1–9).

Chaucer's choice of the *Filostrato* as the source of his great *tragedye is* unlikely to have been a happy historical accident. Chaucer's knowledge of Italian was, we have noted, extraordinarily good: he knew just what he was choosing (and, presumably, paying for) in adopting Boccaccio's poem. The author of the *Filostrato,* Chaucer would have realized, shares his reverence for Dante: but he also shares his fondness for a tradition of stanzaic narrative which draws much of its peculiar vigor from popular, oral-derived origins. Chaucer's discriminating adherence to the style and conventions of the English romances was, it would seem, a matter of deliberate choice.[48] In the final Book of the *Troilus* Chaucer leans especially heavily upon the conventions of romance: it is as if he wishes to push his protagonists (brought to imaginative life by his artistry) back into the world of artifice.[49] To this end he elects to follow Boccaccio's summary, *cantare*-like account of Troiolo's death, emitting a cry ("weilawey") and a pious exclamation ("save only Goddes wille!") that are quite typical of an English romancer:

. . . e dopo lungo stallo,
avendone già morti più di mille,
miseramente un dì l'uccise Achille. (VIII, 27,6–8)

". . . and after much delay,
having already killed off more than a thousand,
one day Achilles wretchedly killed him."

But weilawey, save only Goddes wille!
Despitously hym slough the fierse Achille. (V, 1805-6)

This couplet provides one ending to the story of Troilus; the remaining nine stanzas provide another which bears witness to Chaucer's highest artistic pretensions.[50] The very last of these stanzas sees Chaucer turning to Dante: it is the *Commedia,* Chaucer suggests, that stands before him as his pattern of versification, of style and of Christian propriety:

> Quell' uno e due e tre che sempre vive
> e regna sempre in tre e 'n due e 'n uno,
> non circunscritto, e tutto circunscrive . . . (Par XIV, 28–30)
>
> Thow oon, and two, and thre, eterne on lyve,
> That regnest ay in thre, and two, and oon,
> Uncircumscript, and al maist circumscrive,
> Us from visible and invisible foon
> Defende, and to thy mercy, everichon,
> So make us, Jesus, for thi mercy digne,
> For love of mayde and moder thyn benigne.
> Amen.

NOTES

[*]Reprinted with permission from *Chaucer and the Early Writings of Boccaccio* (Woodbridge, Suffolk: D.S. Brewer, 1985), Chaper 6, pp. 106–40.

[1]Problems associated with the close reading of medieval texts are identified and discussed in Spearing 1972, 1–27.

[2]For explanations of editorial practice, see Branca, II, 839–44; Robinson, pp. xl–xli, 905-6. The list of variant readings in Robinson may be supplemented by those in Root 1926. All textual parallels adduced by my comparisons of Fs [*Il Filostrato*] and T&C [*Troilus & Criseyde*] have been checked against (and are upheld by) the new Windeatt text of the *Troilus* 1984, always excepting obvious differences in editorial punctuation and spelling.

[3]Windeatt 1983 has provided materials which help in forming such an estimate; see also his *New Edition* 1984, 163–83.

[4]It seems that T. S. Eliot was influenced by the Temple Classics translation of Inf XV in composing *Little Gidding:* see Bennett 1974, 65-66. This does not prove that Eliot's Italian was defective.

[5]For a vigorous example of modern dilettantism, see Ian Robinson 1972, 248–65.

[6]As we shall see, Chaucer's understanding of Boccaccio's Italian sometimes surpasses that of the *Filostrato's* most recent (and most competent) English translator, N. R. Havely.

[7]See OED, foreknow (b); MED for(e-knouen).

[8]"Thus driveth forth" echoes a phrase in V, 680 and recalls I, 1092 . . . , a line which is repeated at V, 1540.

[9]The last readily identifiable parallel in phrasing came with VI, 31,1 and V, 989. (The phrase "of which he was ful feyn" (V, 1013) may owe something to "fu assai caro" (VI, 32,2); "seco venne pensando" (VI, 33,7) may have inspired Chaucer's use of the present participle in "Retornyng in hire soule ay up and down" [V, 1023]).
I shall argue below that when Chaucer rejoins Boccaccio's text after having elaborated his narrative independently, he often rejoins it most emphatically: here he makes continuous and extensive use of the first eleven stanzas of *Filostrato* VII.

[10]We cannot, of course, straightforwardly equate our own difficulties with those of Chaucer. As Chaucer's word order was highly flexible, comparable flexibility in the *Filostrato* may not have troubled him. But the two verbs in question do seem to have been comparatively rare: *penare* does not feature in the *Commedia* (although it appears nine times in the *Decameron*);

disbrigare appears only once in the *Commedia* (albeit in the memorable context of *Inferno* XXXIII, 116) and does not appear in the *Decameron.*

[11]The adjective *vaga,* which has a broad range of application, appears forty-four times in the *Decameron;* the phrase "vaga bellezza" appears at III, 8,25; IV, Intro 3I; X, 8,78.

[12]*Science* is featured forty-five times in Chaucer's writings (including nineteen usages in *Boece).* In the *Troilus* it appears only twice (I, 67; V, 1255). In speculating that "science" may have drawn Criseyde's attention away from him, Troilus is probably thinking of the influence of Calkas, "That in science so expert was . . ." (I, 67).

[13]ME *fel* derives from OF *fel,* "fierce, savage"; its range of meaning corresponds closely to that of the Italian *fiera.*

[14]The form "oh me" occurs once in the *Commedia (Inf* XXVIII, 123) and "omè" five times. The form "oimè" occurs frequently in the *Decameron,* and in the *Canzoniere* too (but not as frequently as Petrarch's imitators lead one to expect).

[15]The Italian counterpart is VII, 26. Chaucer makes no use of VII, 28. In VII, 27, Troiolo interprets his own dream; Chaucer saves this stanza until V, 1513–19 and makes Cassandra the interpreter.

[16]Chaucer's understanding was doubtless aided by the fact that ME *thought* could have similarly distressful overtones (which modern English *thought* has lost): see OED, *thought* (5).

[17]Compare the meanings of *descenden* and *discendere* given by MED (7) and by *Grande Dizionario della Lingua Italiana* (9).

[18]*Covenable* features most prominently in scientific and theological contexts (see MED, *covenable* [1-6]); all but two of the verifiably Chaucerian usages occur in prose works. The verb "moleste" appears in Rom 5274.

[19]See also Chaucer's translation of Fs III, 53,4 (III, 1538 . . .) where "slep" ("sonno") is accorded a similarly active role.

[20]For another close Chaucerian imitation of an Italian stanza beginning with a present participial phrase, see IV, 127–30 (and Fs IV, 12,1-3).

21Compare also Fs IV, 83, T&C IV, 701–7; Fs IV, 69,1–3, T&C IV, 554–6. In translating Fs IV, 69,3 Havely (p. 64)–but not Chaucer–misses Boccaccio's sudden switch to the present tense.

[22]Boccaccio's *sententia* was a popular commonplace (see Branca, *Opere di GB,*II, 849). It is featured as the thirteenth of the "rules of love" in *De Amore* II, viii: "Amor raro consuevit durare vulgatus." See Andrea Capellano 1947, 358–59.

[23]"Gola" means "throat"; "avere gola a qualcosa" means "to have an appetite for something, to desire something." The expression is still current although, curiously, it is not listed in *Cambr. Ital. Dict.*

[24]*Ambages* is not a rare noun in classical Latin: see Glare, *Oxford Latin Dictionary, ambages. It* occurs three times in the *Aeneid:* I, 342; VI, 29,99. Dante employs the term "ambage" only once in the *Commedia;* there seems little doubt that, in doing so, he is thinking of *Aeneid* VI, 99.

[25]For the idea that Boccaccio sometimes signposts Chaucer back to Dante, see Bennett 1983, 94–109). . . . I can see nothing in the context of Fs VI, 17,3-4 which might have done this, excepting the word "ambage" itself. Bersuire's Livy translation (discussed below) is the kind of French text that might possibly have served Chaucer here.

[26]See Guilbert 1971, Vol I, XCIII and *ambages.*

[27]T&C V, 897 is the only incidence of *ambages* recorded by MED. OED records a number of incidences (none earlier than 1520), but notes that "there has been a growing tendency to look upon it as merely L[atin]" *(ambage).*

[28]See Chaucer 1957, 813. I have found Robinson's table to be substantially correct in its particulars; it has been of great use. Some additions and amendments are offered in my 1983 article, 202.

[29]The ensemble of "tale" and "other thing collateral" bears an interesting relationship to the concept of *conjointure* established by Chrétien de Troyes in opening *Erec et Enide. Conjointure* (a term adapted from a well-known passage of Horace's *De Arte Poetica)* means "a whole made out of several parts" or simply "arrangement"; as such, "it is not a substitute

for the *conte,* but something which a skillful poet can and must superimpose upon it" (Vinaver 1971, 36–37). See also Kelly 1970.

[30]For further notable examples of sedulous imitation following independent elaboration, compare: Fs II, 128,6–8, T&C II, 1321–23; III, 5, III, 239–45; III, 11, III, 344–50; IV, 137, IV, 1422–28.

[31]Compare: I,57–II,1 & I, 540–553; V,71–VI,1 & V, 680–93; VI,34–VII, 1 & V, 1093–1106; VII,106–VIII,1 & V, 1555–68.

[32]In VI, 533 Chaucer's "non hardyment" owes more to the musicality of Boccaccio's verb phrase "non ardirai" than it does to the literal sense: but such an instance is rare. The noun "hardyment" appears nowhere else in Chaucer.

[33]The twenty-nine examples that I have been able to identify are listed below. Where possible I have indicated in brackets the way in which Boccaccio's *ottava* is divided up by Chaucer. The presence of "1/2" simply indicates that Chaucer divides Boccaccio's ideas somewhere other than at the end of a line. In several cases (indicated with an asterisk) Chaucer reorders the sequence of Boccaccio's ideas.

Filostrato	*Troilus & Criseyde*	
I, 8	I, 64–77	
I, 28	I, 288–301	(3 + 5)
II, 13	I, 701–14	(3 + 5)
II, 33	I, 1044–57	(5 + 3)
II, 118	II, 1191–1204	(4 + 4)
III, 15	III, 372–85	(*)
III, 16	III, 386–99	(5 + 3)
III, 40	III, 1394–407	(4 + 4)
III, 94	IV, 1–14	(3 + 5)
IV, 4	IV, 57–70	(4 + 4)
IV, I3	IV, 134–47	(4 1/2 + 3 1/2)
IV, 30	IV, 260–73	(5 + 3)
IV, 34	IV, 295–308(	3 + 5)
IV, 68	IV, 561–74	(4 + 4)
IV, 75	IV, 617–30	(4 + 4)
IV, 79	IV, 666–79	(*)
IV, 84	IV, 708–21	(4 + 4)
IV, 95	IV, 799–812	(4 + 4)
IV, 96	IV, 813–26	(6 + 2)
IV, I07	IV, 918–1	(6 + 2)
IV, 118	IV, 1156–69	(*)
IV, 131	IV, 1331–7,1345–51	(2 1/2+ 5 1/2)

(between these 2 stanzas translating IV, 131, Chaucer inserts a stanza translating IV, 134)

V, 22	V, 281–94	(5 1/2 + 2 1/2)
V, 33	V, 386–99	(3 + 5)
V, 50	V, 512–25	(5 1/2 + 2 1/2)
V, 57	V, 589–602	(6 + 2)
V, 70	V, 666–79	(*)
VI, 15	V, 876–889	(4 + 4)
VIII, 25	V, 1744–57	(4 + 4)

[34]In T&C I, 64-77 Chaucer spreads the ideas of Fs I, 8 over two stanzas rather than dividing them up and developing them separately as he does later in the *Troilus;* consequently, these two early stanzas prove somewhat repetitive.

[35]See Branca in Boccaccio 1964, II: 860, n. 59. But see also Par XVII, 129, where Cacciaguida urges Dante to write a vision that will set readers of bad conscience scratching: "e lascia pur grattar dov'è la rogna."

[36]See, for example, Fs IV, 40 where the *ottava's* quadripartite structure is (as in many *cantare* stanzas) accentuated by the use of anaphora. Chaucer passed over all four ideas in this *ottava* of lyric complaint.

[37]Chaucer's rendering of the *Filostrato* often brings an increase in expressive vehemence and intensity: see Windeatt 1977–78. It is important to emphasize that Chaucer often achieves such intensification by compressing loose Italian arguments into single lines: for example, in translating Fs IV, 50 in IV, 435–41 he achieves expressive vehemence but avoids enjambment.

[38]See, for example: I, 40; V, 6. Chaucer sometimes separates subject from main verb to great poetic effect: see CT I, 1–12.

[39]On Criseyde, see J. Wimsatt 1976, 285–7; on Troilus, see 279–82, 284–86.

[40]For example: T&C IV, 519–20 adapts RR 6352–53;V,1373–79 adapts some of the paradoxes piled up in RR 4263–4300; IV, 1–11 borrows from the account of Fortune in Machaut's Le Jugement dou Roy de Behaingne 684–93.

[41]La Vechia's advice on discerning the true purposes of a correspondent is remarkably similar in spirit to that offered by the author of a treatise for novice merchants . . . : "O s' alcun ti mandasse alcuno scritto,/ Sì guarda ben la sua intenzione,/ Ched e' non abia fintamente scritto" (CLXXI, 9–11; Corti 1952). For examples of "cortese," see *Fiore* CXLII, 4; CXLIII, 13; CXLV, 1; CXLVI, 7 (Castets 1881). For "franchezza" (and the argument that women are "franche nate"), see CLXXXIII.

[42]For evidence of Chaucer's familiarity with these passages, see T&C III, 988–990 (Inf V, 103); III, 1625–28 & IV, 481–83 (V, 121–23); IV, 1538–40 & V, 599–602 (XXX, 1–4).

[43]Peter Haidu observes that "the basic narrative vocabulary of romance is *avanture*" ("Introduction" to Haidu 1974, 4]).

[44]For similar phrases, see: T&C II, 817, III, 1228; PF 175. The phrase "that joye it was to here" supplies a rime in LGW F 140 and a complete tail in *Sir Thopas* (VII, 768).

[45]Typical recapitulative phrases are: Fs III, 4,1 ("com' è detto avanti"); T&C III, 1394 ("of whom that I yow seye"); A&A 901 ("as y you say"). In Fs I, 38,7 Boccaccio repeats a line (I, 26,7) "secondo gli usi canterini" (Boccaccio 1964, II, 849, n. 21); in I, 31,1 he repeats a phrase from the final line of the preceding stanza, an expedient which is also "di tradizione canterina, per aiutar la memoria di chi recitava" (n. 23). T&C II, 637 closely resembles SqT V, 558 . . . A&A 265–66 repeats the couplet at 229–30. For predictions of future narrative developments–which Branca (Bocaccio 1964, II, 863, note 10) again denotes as characteristic "della tecnica narrative popolaresca e dei cantari"–see Fs V, 14,7–8 and VI, 8 (which Chaucer imitates in the stanza V, 764-770). See also T&C III, 1383–86 and A&A 1354–56 (which anticipates 2131–32).

[46]On the habitual use of predicate formulae which feature *seyde* in the ME romances, see Wittig 1978, 19-20; on predicate formulae in general, see Duggan 1973, 108–9.

[47]See A&A 637–51, 1273–84, 2281–2304 and above, pp. 98–100. In A&A 1273 the indecisive knight is (like Pandarus in V, 1729) "stille so ston."

[48]John Burrow observes that "Gower stands off from the [popular English romance] traditions so generously represented in the work of Chaucer" (Burrow 1971, 29–my addition in brackets).

[49]The set-piece descriptions of Diomede, Criseyde and Troilus in conventional romance terms in V, 799-840 inevitably distance us from these characters. This distancing effect is continued when the narrative proper resumes in V, 840: Diomede, pressing on with his seduction, is said to be "as fressh as braunche in May" (V, 844; and see V, 847, 848 and 854).

[50]This brief account of the ending of T&C, which necessarily concentrates upon stylistic register, may be supplemented by the fine article by Bonnie Wheeler, "Dante, Chaucer and the Ending of *Troilus and Criseyde*" (Wheeler 1982).

Charles A. Owen, Jr.

Chaucer's Witty Prosody in the General Prologue

The wit in prosody, as Alan Gaylord has shown in what he calls the "elvyssh" prosody of Sir Thopas (Gaylord 1979), is almost always dependent on context and meaning; it includes not just the humorous but the ingenious, the unexpectedly patterned. Rhythm in patterns of sound can even include rhetorical and grammatical considerations. These observations have special relevance for poetry like Chaucer's, with its avoidance of system and its tendency to test meaning. When some thirty years ago I published an article on Chaucer's prosody called "'Thy drasty rymyng . . .'" (Owen 1966), the title itself suggested the indirection inherent in the subject.[1]

This indirection has many aspects. It includes Chaucer's level of awareness. Did he consider himself to be writing decasyllabics or what we call iambic pentameter? The answer can only be a highly qualified one. He certainly knew the decasyllabics of his French contemporaries with the fixed cesura after the fourth syllable. His experience as an English poet had also led him to a thorough understanding of the differences between the two languages, of the possibility of using stress rather than syllable-count plus cesura as the metrical principle for line length.[2] The five-stress line was not, of course, an absolute. Five equal stresses in a line were rarely possible. Muted stress, trochees, and spondees all occur and contribute, especially when combined with a syncopation of the rhythmic design. The stress pattern in English decasyllabics became with Chaucer's experience an instrument to experiment with in an unlimited way. Instinct and conscious intent combined to create the lines we read. He knew he could substitute freely and could lengthen or shorten his lines by a syllable or two. In much of his poetry he was not trying for special effect, simply for a sense of measured, not monotonous language. This sense gave the special prosodic effect when it did occur the impact of surprise, of wit.

The other measure of his lines (in addition to stress and syllable count) was rime.[3] Rime could be relatively unobtrusive, simply the mark of line-ending. But it was always a matter of conscious choice. It could become, as in much contemporary French poetry, an independent test of skill and ingenuity. The French names–rime riche, leonine, retrograde–testify to rime's importance. Rime-schemes rather than content came to identify ballades, virelais, rondeaux.[4] The couplet in which Chaucer wrote most of his narrative poetry was the simplest of forms. It did not dictate elements of style or content. It made possible experiment, versatility, a wide range of effect. Normally Chaucer did not emphasize the couplet form. He built up periods of thought, ending sometimes at the end of a couplet, frequently in mid-couplet, occasionally in mid-line. As a result the closed couplet, even more often the single line, stood out in its contexts.

Enhanced rime also became a choice for various kinds of effect. The choice of the word "nyghtertale" (97) would not have occurred, had it not been that it was to serve as enhanced rime-word (rime-word I use for the first line's end in a couplet, rime for the second's) for the rime "nyghtyngale." This identical-plus-rime for the last two stresses is rare but not unique in Chaucer's practice. We get also rime-plus-identical "be served . . . reserved" (187 f), identicals "hethenesse . . . worthynesse" (49 f.), rime riche "seke . . . seeke" (17 f.), and near-identicals "space . . . pace" (35 f.).[5]

Rime (as well as stress) influences pronunciation. Words in poetry sometimes have their accents affected by metrical stress and especially by their use as riming syllables, invariably in stress position. The single line "Trouthe and honour, fredom and curteisie" (46) gives some examples. Stress influences the second syllable of "honour" but not of "fredom," while rime gives additional stress to the penultimate syllable of "curteisie." Striking evidence of the influence of rime comes in the sequence of rime-words from 109–13: "visage . . . usage . . . bracer . . . bokeler . . . daggere." This evidence of the special quality words in poetry acquire from their context justifies studying them closely. Chaucer especially repays such study, because he is constantly challenging the reader with new rhythms, new sound patterns, new indirections, new ways of testing value, of mocking excess, of imitating speech and action.

Part IV of my article "'Thy drasty ryming . . .'," on the decasyllabic couplet, included instances of what might be considered witty prosody from the General Prologue,[6] but none from the introductory section, before the pilgrims' portraits. I should like first to concentrate on that section of 42 lines before going into greater detail with the portraits.

The opening (1–42)

Let us consider the noble opening period, lines 1–18. The obvious prosodic features include the internal rime ("swich-which") in lines 3 and 4; the two run-on lines, 7 and 16; the four consecutive heavily feminine rimes on -ages, -ondes from 11 to 14; the spondaic effect in the first two syllables of line 12; the pronounced alliteration on str- in 13 accompanied by nd- and n-dominance from 12 to 16, including the internal rime in the last two stresses of 14; similar rimes (-ondes, -ende) from 13 to 16, and near-internal-rimes in the run-on "Of Engelonde," 16; the near-internal-identicals ("hooly", "holpen") and the rime riche ("seeke") of the last two lines; finally the syntax-defining openings of lines 1, 5, 12, "Whan", "Whan", "Thanne." All of these features participate in the underlying ingenuity that weds sound and meaning in the passage.

In this respect we must pay some attention to the relationship between syntax and line-structure. The first four lines are subordinated by the first "Whan" and include the subject of the subordinate clause (in line 1), the predicate (in line 2), a parallel predicate (in line 3), a clause subordinate to the second predicate (in line 4), the "swich-which" internal rime with normal word order reversed helping to establish the elided subordination ("Of which vertu engendred is the flour"). The words "Whan Zephirus eek" start off the parallel but shorter (2½-line) second clause, line 5 having an almost exactly parallel subject to the first one and 6 having a predicate that runs over into 7. The third subordinate clause (introduced simply by "and") continues the grammatical acceleration, completing itself wittily in 1 ½ lines with the first riming verb in the passage "yronne." The alert reader recognizes that the "half cours" the young sun has run is his second (April), not his first (March); in other words that we're twice as far in the Ram as we might have thought.[7] The riming verb "yronne" closes a series of strikingly active verbs, a delight in and a celebration of the forces in nature and simultaneously a delight in and a celebration of the power of language to express these forces: water in showers pierces to the root and bathes in "licour"; the breeze's breath "inspired hath" (first use in English with this added meaning of breathing through) "the tendre croppes"; the young sun runs his fifteen daily rounds that move him also in the zodiac (only a half-course and backward at that). Is one of the slant meanings of these lines that the sun, for all the speed of his daily running, finds himself further and further behind in the zodiac?[8]

The grammatical acceleration, noted in the first three clauses, appears to continue when the fourth and last parallel clause (again introduced by "and") gives a complete subject and predicate in the single line 9. But it turns out to have merely postponed its more vivid meanings to subordinate (10) and sub-subordinate (11) lines. The sub-subordinate line, "So priketh hem nature in hir corages" has the form of an independent clause, and indeed in a sense not just the one or two previous lines but all ten lines are the result-clauses the construction signals grammatically. The first word in line 12 "Thanne" makes clear that we have completed the temporal context with the strongly feminine rime-word "corages" and that we are about to find out what this long series of subordinations has led up to.

The length of the first two syllables (a spondee), the verb-subject reversal, and the grammatical completeness, "Thanne longen folk to goon on pilgrimages," make this line (12) and especially the word "longen" stand out. A number of observations crowd in at this point to define the implications, liminal and sub-liminal, of this crucial line and this crucial word. The "corages-pilgrimages" rime seals the role of nature in the longing of people for movement at the same time that it helps to contrast the birdlike ("priketh") with the implications for people in the word "longen." The ensuing two lines, grammatically dependent on "longen" even as they elide it, define it further with the rich sound of "straunge strondes/To ferne halwes kowthe in sondry londes." There is a gradual shifting in these seven lines of the main clause, reflected in the words "specially" and "ende". The period is winding down. It carries with it in the -nd- of the rimes (13 to 16) and the -end and -ond of the run-on (16), sounds associated with the longing. But we are coming to the end and the purpose, up from inner longing to what can be seen. "Pilgrimages," longest word in the passage and riming with "corages," is in part premonitory; "Caunterbury," almost as long, specifies the where:

> The hooly blisful martir for to seke,
> 18 That hem hath holpen whan that they were seeke.

The rime riche on "seeke" has abrupt sound and meaning: it brings us back from desire for the "straunge" and distant to the world of illness and obligation and established institutions. The consoling, the redeeming implications of "hooly blisful" and "holpen" (note the internal near-identical, reinforced by the heavy stresses) only partly balance the final emphasis of "seeke" (which receives with "hol-" one of the two heavy stresses in the line).

The "corages-pilgrimages" rime is striking enough in sound, meaning, and position to call attention to itself when it recurs a few lines later in singular form, carrying with it "wenden" and "Caunterbury" and characterizing the I-narrator, at his first appearance, as a pilgrim of "ful devout corage." As earlier, observations and qualifications crowd in. This second verse paragraph starts with the verb "Bifil," sudden and specific. Details of time and place fill the first two lines, a day in the spring, the Tabard, Southwerk, all subordinated by the last three words that of course include the rime, "as I lay." The passiveness of "lay" and the seriousness of "ful devout corage" give way to the activity of the noun clause, subject of "Bifil": the nighttime arrival of the "Wel nine and twenty"–pilgrims, it is true, "That toward Caunterbury wolden ryde." The emphasis, however, given by the two successive run-ons (25, 26), is on their diversity ("sondry folk") and "felaweshipe." These characteristics absorb the attention and the energies of the narrator as, in the second sentence, after two main clauses and a subordinate clause of description, we get the hyperbole, "So hadde I spoken with hem everichon" (note the strong adverb-verb-subject sequence)

> That I was of hire felaweshipe anon
> 33 And made forward erly for to ryse
> To take oure wey ther as I yow devyse.

The fellowship has thus not only taken over the narrator's "corage," but his grammar as well: the "I" and "hire" (32) become "oure" (34). The dance of the pronouns continues in 34 with "I" and "yow," in the narrator's first address to the reader. The wit here is clearly not just in the prosody but in what the prosody supports: the contrast in rhythm between the first two verse paragraphs, the first one dominated by the main verb, long waited for, "longen", the second by the first word, the main verb (again), "Bifil . . ."; the way the "nine and twenty" enliven the picture with their entry and their run-ons; the linking of the paragraphs through repetition of key words, "pilgrimage. . . corage" (rime-words), "wenden," "Caunterbury" (twice); the speed with which fellowship leads to the forword "erly for to rise / To take oure way" (shift from "hire" to "oure" in mid-sentence).

The opening of the third and final of the verse paragraphs continues the address to the reader, the emphasis moving from "felaweshipe" to diversity with the promise of a portrait for "ech of hem" (run-on). It provides a striking contrast with the first two verse paragraphs. Instead of "Whan that" (with the long subordination) or "Bifil" (abrupt main verb), we get a whole half line of function words, "But nathelees whil." There follow three lines of rationalization, at the end of which comes the "yow" that determines the level of discourse: a continuation of the address to the reader first indicated in the last words of the second verse paragraph. Meanwhile we have the near-identicals for the first couplet, "space-pace," rime-words that will be used on several other slant occasions in the Prologue. Why this long self-justification? What is the time and space he tells us he has, "Er that I ferther in this tale pace"? The answers are not simple.

If the narrator has time and space, it is because nothing is happening until the time for the "forword" to be observed, the early rising and the taking of "oure wey." Ostensibly the pilgrims are sleeping, and the narrator can take the opportunity (in an almost conspiratorial way) to convey to the audience everything he knows about each of them. Does the line "That slepen al the nyght with open ye" make ever so slight a resonance at this point? Certainly the narrator is sleeping as pilgrim at the same time he is awake addressing the audience.

Real time and space of course have the narrator before his audience (or the writer before his blank leaves) with perfect freedom to tell the audience whatever he pleases. In addition to ostensible time and space and conspiratorial converse, we get accordance to "resoun" (rime word) to justify telling us "al the condicioun/ Of ech of hem" (run-on).[9] Chaucer's awareness of the task he has set himself, twenty-some portraits one after the other, before anything in the way of "tale" has occurred, constitutes the undertext of these eight lines.[10]

At the end of the portraits the "clause" (rime word, 715) in which we have learned "Th'estaat, th'array, the nombre, and eek the cause / Why that assembled was this compaignye . . ." turns out to have taken no time at all:

> But now is tyme to yow for to telle
> How that we baren us that ilke nyght,
> Whan we were in that hostelrie alyght;
> And after wol I telle of our viage
> And al the remenaunt of oure pilgrimage.

The portraits are as it were a subordinate clause. The time they have taken up is narrator's time. The space is writing space. Address to the audience subsumes all forms of discourse. The narrator can abandon narrative to explain himself whenever he wants. He can also set and reset the clock. He can return to the night at the Tabard, the night when the narrator established fellowship with the pilgrims and agreed to rise early for the "viage." He can introduce the Host and the "remenaunt," the plan for storytelling, for which the Host is responsible. "Clause," "Viage," "Remenaunt of oure pilgrimage," emphasized prosodically, constitute in the slant terms of the narrator what we know as the Canterbury Tales.

Rhetoric, grammar, meaning, all contribute to the witty prosody that marks the first 42 lines of the Prologue and prefigures, as we shall see, some of the effects in the portraits. The lines that move from measured formality to colloquial intimacy repay a second reading; in the words of Alan Gaylord, they "encourage meditation."[11] Chaucer's use of sound patterns in the portraits is constantly varying. Ordinarily his rimes simply help to measure his verse, but occasionally they stand out and they frequently give emphasis to meaning, especially when sounds are repeated internally. The same goes for alliteration and assonance, for run-on lines, for the movement or omission of the cesura. For each of the portraits I will try to pick out the special prosodic effects. In the case of the Knight this means concentration on the first eight lines and the final seven.

The Knight

Does the tautological use of "first" with "begynne" (final rime word) at the end of the introduction merely betray the narrator's eagerness to accept his challenging task, and does his repetition of it in the very next rime ("first bigan") transfer this eagerness to the Knight's riding "out" (run-on, 45) at the start of his career to a lifelong dedication? This dedication finds expression after the run-on in the climax of the first four-line sentence: ". . . he loved chivalrie,/Trouthe and honour, fredom and curteisie" (46). The first two sentences, each four-line, have "worthy man" to end the first line and "evere honoured for his worthynesse" to end the eighth, with "Ful worthy" to start the second sentence. "Worthy" occurs twice more in the portrait, the last time conceding only to the alliterated adjective "wis" (note near-identicals, "were wor-", "was wis"). To return to the portrait's first eight lines, the second sentence stresses space, the world-wide extent of his activity in the rime-stressed spondaic negative superlative "no man ferre" and the twofold "cristendom . . . hethenesse,"[12] before returning to time, "evere honoured," in the final line.

I find I must mention the alliteration that leads up to the final seven lines: "worthy . . . wys" (68), "meeke . . . mayde" (69):

> He nevere yet no vileynye ne sayde
> In al his lyf unto no maner wight.

The quadruple negative,[13] reinforced by the spondaic effect of "no vil- . . . no maner", leads up to the positive single-line summary, the power of the words validated by all that has come before, enhanced by what Alan Gaylord has called the "residual trochee-ness" of the three adjectives:

72 He was a verray parfit gentil knyght.

Then comes the "But," and the word to the reader that we are shifting to clothing–anticlimax if ever there seemed to be one. His horses' precedence (74) compounds the effect. The word "bismotered" (76; first use of the word according to MED) stands out, sound and meaning, the second overtly critical word in the portrait (the first was when he fought for a pagan against another pagan, evidence that the narrator will not hold back the negatives). Do the implications of "Al bismotered" justify the "But"?

For he was late ycome from his viage
78 And wente for to doon his pilgrymage.

Thus the last rime of the portrait, "pilgrimage," that figured twice in the introduction and will figure twice again at crucial moments (A 724 and I 50), transforms the external smut to a further mark of the knight's "corage" (rime word for the previous two pilgrimages), to the absence not just of "vileynie" but of vanity in his make-up, to a witty authenticating of his worth.

The Squire

The Knight's influence extends over the next two portraits, of his son a squire, and of his servant the yeoman. The presence of both and of only the two (see line 101 f.) confirm the meaning given "bismotered" by the final couplet of the Knight's portrait. The Squire's identity as a "lovyere and a lusty bacheler" starts the "l-" alliteration that links love and "lokkes," suggesting the varied surfaces–qualities, activities (note all the verbs), and clothing–the portrait (and the man) are so rich in; including the near-by chyvachie (compare the Knight's world-wide "chivalrie"):

And born hym weel as of so litel space
88 In hope to stonden in his lady grace.

Space here means time but suggests also the limited space of his world,[14] filled as we learn in the rime by concern for "his lady grace." The fashionable clothing and the multifarious activities (eight verbs in three lines, 94–96) include the line of summary, "He was as fressh as is the month of May"; they lead up to the drama of the last four lines:

So hoote he lovede that by nyghtertale
He sleep namoore than dooth a nyghtyngale.
Curteis he was, lowely, and servysable,
100 And carf biforn his fader at the table.[15]

The hyperbole of sleepless passion, mocked (and celebrated) in the identical-plus-rime of the line endings, only seems to continue in the line of courtly qualities; the word "carf" blunter than "curteis" brings us up short; the prominent final -f leads to "biforn his fader." This final line has an effect similar to that of the final couplet in the Knight's portrait. The implied scene at table turns what we had expected to be mere courtly love into a sign of mutual respect (compare the later picture of the Franklin and his son in the Squire-Franklin link).

The Knight's Yeoman

In the rhythm of the grouping of portraits the fact that the Knight had "servantz namo / At that tyme, for hym liste ride so" (102) gives the Yeoman meaning that will resonate in the next group of portraits, as Chaucer originally planned it (note the linking by rime not just of Yeoman-Prioress but of the two groups). The actual description of the Yeoman has a repetitiveness, reflected in the "grene" (103, 116) that begins and ends the riming in his portrait. "Grene" also initiates the assonance on long-*e* that sets off the "sheef of pecok arwes, bright and kene" that we later learn "drouped noght with fetheres lowe" (107). The "yemanly" dressed tackle makes up almost the entire portrait, each item attaching itself with the four-times repeated "he bar," each time prosodically stressed by more than one alliterated *b*-. The one verb other than "bar" applies not to weapons but to the "Cristopher on his brest"; its "sheene" riming with the final green of his "bawdryk" and implying that he kept it as "yemanly" dressed as his "gay bracer" and his "gay daggere," (forced rime-words in successive couplets, 111–14). The consistent praise with its subtle prosodic emphasis has a witty indirection that prepares us for the final line of summary and gives the portrait an interest the narrator does not find overwhelming in the Yeoman: "A forster was he, soothly, as I gesse." (117)

The Prioress

The first of a new group, the Prioress, is linked by rime to the narrator's guess about the Knight's Yeoman. The group she heads is perhaps the richest of all prosodically. Originally, she was to have had four subordinates traveling with her:

> Another Nonne with hire hadde she
> 164 That was hire chapeleyne, and preestes thre.

This entourage for the Prioress was meant to contrast with the military group marked by the Knight's austerity. The substitution of Monk and Friar for two of the three priests maintained the contrast between military and religious groups, but no longer is the Prioress's entourage a contrast of four to the Knight's two. Of course portraits of Second Nun and Nun's Priest, clearly intended in the final plan, would presumably have made comparison of the two groups more complex (see the references in note 10).

Praise of the Prioress's manners dominates the first nineteen lines of the portrait, with rimes playing at first an important part in the order: manner of smiling (first!)

"symple and coy" suggests manner of swearing "but by Seinte Loy"; manner of being called, "madame Eglentyne" (for the Mother Prioress?), suggests manner of singing "service dyvyne": "Ful weel . . . . ful semely"; then we get the three lines on speaking French "ful faire and fetisly" (minimally rimed on the adverbial "-ly")–

> After the scole of Stratford atte Bowe,
> For Frenssh of Paris was to hire unknowe.

The delightfully provincial Stratford atte Bowe (not just Stratford) establishes the rime for "unknowe."

The meaning of "scole" continues to resonate in the first line of the ten devoted to the Prioress at table: "wel ytaught was she with alle." It is not table but more specifically "At mete" where "She leet [internal rime; assonance with later rime word] no morsel [spondaic effect, "no mor-"] from hir lippes [alliteration, labials] falle / Ne wette hir fyngres [short vowels] in hir sauce [long diphthong] depe; / Wel koude she carie a morsel and wel kepe [repetition, with syncopation of stress, of wel plus /k/-sound; see also alliterative "carie"] / That no drope ne fille upon hire brest [two successive stresses in "no drope"; last two of four negatives stressing fastidious avoidance of the unspeakable–sauce-drop on her breast, indeed–and leading up to the general positive]. / In curteisie was set ful mochel hir lest" [line of summary: 132]. There follow four further lines of her specific handling of food, the first three epitomizing her prim proprieties:

> Hir over-lippe wyped she so clene
> That in hir coppe ther was no ferthyng sene
> Of grece, whan she dronken hadde hir draughte.

The spondaic effect ("no ferth-") followed by the run-on, assonance, early cesura ("Of grece") add a prosodic shiver to the fastidious avoidance, while the strong alliteration on dr- plus the back vowels ("dronken . . . draughte") give body to her appetite for what's actually in the cup.

After the ten lines of specific encounters with food the narrator turns to the more general aspects of her demeanor. Numerous *and*'s (six in five lines) accentuate her dedication to courtliness, "desport . . . plesaunt . . . port, / And peyned hire to countrefete cheere / Of court . . . estatlich . . . digne of reverence." The insistence, the too-muchness, finds in addition a slight metrical equivalence in the extra syllable "and to been" (40) and the stress on initial "And" in "And to ben holden" (141).

The initial "But . . ." (142) and the narrator's overt presence in "for to speken" signal the change from surfaces to "conscience." The shift from stress to length in "so char-" and "so pitous" (spondees?) lends additional weight to the weight of meaning in the words themselves; the alliteration on /w/ ("wolde wepe"), the grammatical climax in line 144 of a result-clause (dependent on the *so*'s with that elided), seem to be taking us to something really important when the rime "mous" explodes in a deflating epiphany, extended for us in the run-on "Kaught in a trappe." The dead or wounded mice and pet dogs dominate her emotional life in a plethora of /d/'s starting with "deed," running through the rimes "bledde . . . fedde . . . breed . . . deed" (145–48), changing to strong alliteration on "sm-" and internal rime in the last two stresses: "Or if men smoot it with a yerde smerte" (149). The final line of summary gives an ironic shortness to the portrait's discussion of "hire conscience":

> 150 And al was conscience and tendre herte.

Furthermore, "tendre herte" has taken over the rime-emphasis (cf. 142).

The portrait ends with twelve lines on clothing and appearance, emphasizing a conventionally romantic delicacy, as at the beginning of her portrait, with modifiers like "semyly, tretys, fetys," enhanced on three occasions by the almost contradictory "ful" (note "ful smal," 153). The exception comes in three lines, introduced by "But sikerly . . . ," revealing her span-broad forehead, "For hardily she was nat undergrowe" (156). Here the subliminal meanings of "hardily" and the succession of three longs, "was nat un-" give the understatement a prosodic counterweight. The effort to minimize her awkward size reflects the lightness of the whole portrait's praise for not quite the right qualities, the slight misfit between vocation and vita. The sheen of her rosary and the pendant brooch complete the gentle satire with the internal rime of "small coral," the alliteration of "gauded al with grene," the assonance followed by a spondee of "brooch of gold ful sheene" (a fourth "ful"), the identicals for rime in the final couplet, enhanced by the internal rimes (on both "-it" and "a") and the assonances:

> On which ther was first write a crowned A
> 162 And after *Amor vincit omnia.*

Prosodic richness wittily underlines the decorative import of beads and brooch and the multiple meanings that can be (have been) inferred from the Latin motto.[16] The liveliness of the ending contrasts with the neutrality of the previous portrait, the Yeoman's, despite the use of some of the same elements (note the fourth "he bar," 116, and "she bar," rime for 158, the Yeoman's Cristopher and the Prioress's beads-hung brooch, and the use of the "grene-sheene" rime, 115 f., 159 f.).

The Monk

The second portrait in the religious group quickly (165-171) takes the Monk, "An outridere," out riding literally with a rich series of sound-meaning enhancements ("a fair for the maistrie . . . A manly man to be an abbot able . . . stable . . . men myghte his brydel heere / Gynglen in a whistlynge wynd als cleere . . . chapel belle"). That the stable where he keeps "Ful many a deyntee horse" chimes with the Monk's being "abbotable" throws lurid light on the institution he practices his "maistrie" in. After the seven lines with their vivid sense of how men "heere" the

Monk, we get a striking combination of the "pace-space" near-identical rime-pair and a vehemently ungrammatical sweeping away of monastic rule:

Ther as this lord was kepere of the celle
The reule of Seint Maure or of Seint Beneit
By cause that it was old and somdel streit–
This ilke Monk leet olde thynges pace
And heeld after the newe world the space.[17]

The apparent subject, given in the single line (173) with subordinate clauses in the single lines before and after, receives additional emphasis from the assonance of the repeated "Seint" with the rime-sound "-eit". The abandonment of the subject "The reule . . . ," in favor of "This ilke Monk," earlier called "this lord," gives the (un)grammatical equivalent for the enormity of his actions. Again "space" has an important temporal dimension. But literal holding of space in the sense of dominating wherever he is, sweeping away older things like grammar, recurs throughout the portrait and justifies the single-line summation of him as "a fair prelaat" (204). Institutional arrangements contribute a further element of the undertext. Holding space and making it productive constitute the rationale for the cell of which the Monk is "kepere." His contempt for "olde thynges" (including any expectation that as a Monk he would "keep to" his cell) finds reflection in his riming of "pulled hen" with "hooly men," "cloystre" with "oystre," and in the mocking agreement of the narrator:

And I seyde his opinion was good.
What sholde he studie and make hymselven wood
Upon a book in cloystre alwey to poure
Or swynken with his handes and laboure
As Austyn bit? How shal the world be served?
Lat Austyn have his swynk to hym reserved.

What we hear from both participants in this putative dialogue is the double sound of the Monk's voice, in his own words and in the narrator's mocking imitation-celebration. The two rhetorical questions, for which the answers are the opposite of what the Monk's rhetoric requires, the recurrence of "cloystre" which encloses the scorn of the Monk's "oystre," the series "swynken . . . Austyn bit . . . Austyn . . . his swynk," the rime-plus-identical of "be served–reserved" (where the *re-* should receive at least a pitch emphasis), the rhythmic rush over muted stresses, over even the extra syllable in 184, to the sudden midline stop "As Austyn bit?", with the contrasting shortness of the second three-stress rhetorical question, help to celebrate the Monk's reckless rejection of the rule in favor of the "newe world."

It is to this new world that we return in the final 19 lines of the portrait. "Therfore" marks the transition to hunting, good food, fine clothes, the satisfactions of the abundant life. The Monk's contempt for his vows needs no further mention. Alliteration, assonance, single line summaries help to convey the affluent self-indulgence. As in the first seven lines there is almost a total absence of negatives (see "no cost" and "nat pale" below):

> Grehoundes he hadde as swift as fowel in flight;
> Of prikyng and of huntyng for the hare
> Was al his lust, for no cost wolde he spare.

His physical radiance receives a sounding tribute:

> His heed was balled that shoon as any glas
> And eek his face as he hadde been enoynt.
> He was a lord ful fat and in good poynt,
> His eyen stepe and rollynge in his heed,
> That stemed as a forneys of a leed.

The portrait ends as if exhausted by its unmonastic exuberance with three single-line observations, the first a negative, that sets up alliterations (/p/ and /b/) and assonances, even internal rimes and identicals ("-at," "pale"), with runs of long and unstressed syllables and at the end a dying three-syllable feminine rime-word:

> He was nat pale as a forpyned goost.
> A fat swan loved he best of any roost.
> His palfrey was as broun as is a berye.

The evident prosperity of the monastery supports a lordly lifestyle, which the Monk, "a fair prelaat," "to been an abbot able," will only augment.

The Friar

The Monk's contempt for his vows is more than matched by the Friar, the final figure in the clerical group. Again we hear the sound of the man's voice, this time an insinuating sweetness, that perverts his office and seduces others for his own pleasure and profit. This voice expresses itself variously throughout the portrait in the words he chooses, in the way they are placed, in his efforts to justify (to himself?) his behavior toward rich and poor, in the ballads he sings, finally in his mannered speech:

> Somwhat he lipsed for his wantownesse
> To make his Englissh sweete upon his tonge.

The Friar's preeminence (expressed in a negative superlative) in "daliaunce and fair langage" prepares us (rime as well as reason) for the innocent-sounding "ful many a mariage" he has made "Of yonge wommen at his owene cost" and for the line of summary that brings to an end the first movement of the portrait

(208–14) with a witty and riming confirmation of institutional and personal corruption: "Unto his ordre he was a noble post" (214).

The second movement (215–32) quickly directs itself to the Friar's perversion of confession, that sums itself up in a final couplet:

> Therfore in stede of wepynge and preyeres
> Men mote yeve silver to the povre freres.[18]

This movement proceeds from point to point punctuated by the appearance of sweet reasonableness, but actually repeating four times the Friar's approval of money in place of repentance. We start with the word that he was "ful wel biloved and famulier" with all the best people, especially the "worthy wommen of the toun,"

> For he hadde power of confessioun
> As seyde himself moore than a curat
> 220 For of his order he was licenciat.

Three more "For"s (225, 227, 229) open lines leading to the final couplet's "Therfore" (231), confirmed by a continuation of the comforting ecclesiastical rime-sounds: "confessioun . . . absolution . . . penaunce . . . yshryve . . . (he dorste mak avaunt) . . . repentaunt." The words, as the narrator tells us, paraphrase for the most part the Friar's own. The fact that they appear only in rime position accentuates the importance he places on sound rather than meaning:

> Ful swetely herde he confessioun
> And plesaunt was his absolucioun.
> He was an esy man to yeve penaunce
> 224 Ther as he wiste to have a good pitaunce.

The emphasis of vowel-sound (assonance) points up the meanings in two of the three words, "swetëly" (221, prosodically drawn out in three syllables), "plesaunt" (222), "esy" (223). The pliancy of "esy" qualifies both the giving and the penance, being in its turn qualified by the "Ther as" subordination, especially in the delightful ambivalence of "good pitaunce" (where "good" means good–big and "pitaunce" means small extra ration)–with the resonance of the whole couplet defining "an esy man." Only as we approach the concluding "Therfore" does a temporary recognition of crude reality break through: "For many a man so hard is of his herte . . . " (229; note the succession "man- . . . man . . . hard . . . herte").

The Friar's "power of confessioun" works on the purses rather than the consciences of both men and women. From the portrait's first characterization of him as "a wantowne and a merye" his special involvement with women has been apparent. The end of the confession section seems directed at men primarily. The balance is redressed in the next seven lines by the word of his "typet . . . ay farsed ful of knyves / And pynnes for to yeven faire wyves" (234), the "murye note" of his music (235 f.), his prize-winning ballads (237), and his fine health (238 f.)–random details that show the ease of the Friar's freedom from vocational concern. They show as well the freedom from system on the part of the narrator, a delight in challenging us to assimilate his observations.

Hard-heartedness might be ascribed to the Friar himself in his attitude toward the sick and the poor, developed in a 16-line passage (240–255). This passage, which begins with his refusal to associate with sick people and female beggars, ends with his charming a farthing out of a destitute widow. In its course it imitates and mocks his attitude, so at variance with his vocation (poverty, chastity, humility), employing sound-effects and grammar as well as meaning, at times even recording the Friar's thoughts in a kind of interior monologue. For instance we get in the first three lines (240-2) the alliterations on /t/ and /b/ and the exaggerated rime with internal chiming on the feminine suffix "-estere"; the series "everich (241) . . . swich (243) . . . sike (245) . . . swich (247) . . . riche" (248); the reversal of order in two successive sentences (243-247), which makes us wait for the infinitive subjects, each taking up a single line:

> For unto swich a worthy man as he
> Acorded nat as by his facultee
> To have with sike lazars aqueyntaunce.
> It is nat honest, it may nat avaunce
> For to deelen with no swich poraille . . . .

This passage of internal monologue generates a rhetoric of indignant protest at the very thought of dealing (note the spondees) "with no swich poraille" (rime-word, the rime coming on the French suffix, dismissing as a whole class the very people his vows should associate him with, and further diminished by the rime, "vitaille," a class of things).[19] We have experienced the redefinition by context of the value words "worthy" (243), and "honest" (246), a redefinition that reaches its climax with the lines:

> And over al ther as profit sholde arise
> Curteis he was and lowely of servyse.
> Ther nas no man nowher so vertuous.

Line 250 of course recalls the Squire's 99, but "Curteis," "lowely," and "servyse" are drained of all positive meaning by the preceding 249 with "profyt" and "aryse." The climax comes in line 251 with "vertuous," a triply negatived superlative,[20] preceded in the line by /n/-alliteration, long open-/o/ assonance, and two spondees, to mark the distance between context and meaning.

Two single lines of summary follow the 16-line passage that ends with the Friar charming his "ferthyng" from the destitute widow: the first on the Friar's skill in raising money, the second a surprisingly crude statement of his sexual play: "And rage he koude as it were right a whelp" (257). As if to correct a false impression, the last twelve lines emphasize his helpfulness on "love-dayes," his careful grooming, his lisping, and the twinkle in his eyes after singing to his own accompaniment on the harp. With regard to the grooming, Lawrence Besserman (1979) has persuasively argued a witty reference to the divided papacy:

For ther he was nat lyk a cloysterer
With a thredbare cope as is a povre scoler
But he was lyk a maister or a pope;
Of double worsted was his semycope
That rounded as a bell out of the presse.
Somwhat he lipsed . . . .

The "thredbare cope" prepares in sound for the simile to "a pope," with emphasis on two in "double" and "semi" and the repetition in the rime, "cope." This simile-laden passage ends by wittily denying in the Friar's lisp any extension of the bell image to sound.

It is perhaps to bring the clerical group to a close with emphasis on the attractive surfaces of Friar-maister-pope. The three portraits we have in this second group certainly present a decline in morality, from the Prioress's tender-hearted "cheere of court" through the Monk's lordly pursuit of the "newe world" to the Friar's perverse seduction of others for his own profit and pleasure. The ironic contrast with the three portraits of the military group is one we make rather than the narrator. His apparent enthusiasm for all his fellow-pilgrims, expressed at times (as in the Friar's-virtue line) with prosodic salvos, keeps us alert and helps to keep all six portraits fresh in the memory. Like the smut that wittily confirms the Knight's worthiness, the praise of the regular clerics has an ironic effect; in the case of the Friar especially, the claims of moral virtue startle us tn their context, which wittily drains the value words of all but a tittle of their meaning.

The order of the portraits in the Prologue has the spontaneity observable within the portraits. Groups of pilgrims cut across the ordering according to social status, which has at best only a vague and fitful validity: we do indeed begin with the Knight and end with the "churls." But the positioning of the Man of Law and the Franklin hardly does justice to their status. In the end the grouping of pilgrims will perform a mnemonic function, though the basis for the groups is far from systematic. What is systematic, as we shall see: the groups come in twos.

The Merchant

The next two portraits are of single pilgrims, the Merchant and the Clerk, contrasting figures in their manner of speech and in their attitude toward wealth. The Merchant we hear in his commerce-centered entrepreneurship:

His resons he spak ful solempnely,
Sownynge alwey th'encrees of his wynnyng.
He wolde the see were kept for anything . . .

Here the reversal of stress on the word "spak" (for the third foot, not with a cesura immediately before) prefigures the next line with its four two-syllable words working against the iambic stress-pattern, the last one, the gerund "wynnyng," forcing the rime sound on *-ing*–an example of what speaking "resons" solemnly sounds like.

> This worthy man ful wel his wit bisette
> 280 Ther wiste no wight that he was in dette . . .
> For sothe he was a worthy man with alle
> 284 But sooth to seyn I noot how men hym calle.

The six /w/'s in the first couplet (279 f.) give prosodic emphasis to the portrait's double use of "worthy." Having the appearance of worth, the sound of worth, forsooth, is about as far as the *sothe* will permit one "to seyn."

The Clerk

The Clerk on the other hand, that "unto logyk hadde longe ygo," had a "leene" hors, and himself "nas nat right fat" (with further assonance in the rime-pair rake-take; 286–8). We learn of him not that he was "worthy" specifically, but that he "Ne was so worldly for to have office" (292). The two-line summary in which the narrator tries to mock his willingness to spend all his money on books rather than high living–

> But al be that he was a philosophre
> 298 Yet hadde he but litel gold in cofre

–registers quite differently from similar efforts in the portraits of the Monk and the Friar, registers in fact as digressive and irrelevant in the context of the Clerk's disposal of and gratitude for what he is given to live on. His manner of speech resounds in the single-line summation (remarkable for its syncopated stress pattern) of his devotion to study:

> 303 Of studie took he moost cure and moost heede,

and then in the associated description of his manner of speech itself:

> Noght o word spak he moore than was neede
> 305 And that was seyd in forme and reverence
> And short and quyk and ful of hy sentence.
> Sownynge in moral vertu was his speche
> And gladly wolde he lerne and gladly teche.

Despite his laconic habits, his speech does not avoid repetitions for emphasis: "moost . . . moost . . . moore" (303 f; note the spondaic effects associated with the second "moost" and with the first four words of 304), "gladly . . . gladly" (308; note the use of the final couplet as a summing up and compare 307 with the "Sownyng" line in the Merchant's portrait). Note, too, how "quyk" gives a witty addition of life to "short" (306). The Clerk not only survives the narrator's lame joke at his expense; he emerges ironically from the narrator's reluctance to praise and stands out as the model for the scholar-teacher in the final line of his portrait.

The Man of Law

The next pilgrim is the most important in social status since the Knight; his title, "A Sergeant of the Lawe," fills most of the first line (309); his frequent presence at the Parvys fills all of the stress-light second; his presence on pilgrimage, finally indicated at the beginning of the third, is followed by a vague indication of his importance, "ful riche of excellence." The alliterated pair of adjectives, "war and wys," that fill the last three syllables of the portrait's first line prefigure in their interaction two instances in the portrait of wittily paired lines, where the second drains as mere semblance the claim to value of the first:

> Discreet he was and of greet reverence–
> 313 He semed swich, his wordes weren so wise.

This first instance is not a couplet, but the second line not only undercuts the first in meaning, it connects grammatically only through the heavily stressed "swich," an internal rime with "ryche" (311). Prosody further picks out with /w/- alliteration and the extra syllable in "weren" the spondaic "so wise" (note also "swich"), not to mention the repetition of the alliterated rime word, "wys." The second instance of the second line of a pair draining the value from the first interrupts the details of his land-purchasing and his legal skills with a sudden closed couplet:

> Nowher so bisy a man as he ther nas
> 322 And yet he semed bisier than he was.

Here the rimes are especially witty, the negative "nas" bringing to an end the assertion of value, while the positive "was" seals the deflation. By denying that his purchasing could be "infect" (rime with "in effect"), or that a man could "pynche at his writyng" (first use of pinch in this meaning, probably a pun on Pinchbek, an actual Sergeant of the Law; see Manly 1926, 151–57), the portrait suggests his pinched attitude toward land ownership. Does the Man of Law's self-importance outweigh his professional eminence? The portrait clearly raises but does not answer the question.

The Franklin

In his "compaignye" is another distinguished man, the Franklin. Together they constitute a "land and law" group. They would certainly take precedence over most of the other pilgrims. The Franklin's portrait contrasts with the Man of Law's by putting off to the final six lines all reference to his official functions; these include having been the King's chief administrative officer in the shire (sheriff). The portrait concentrates instead on his attitude toward food and drink. After hearing about his beard, white as a daisy (332), and his complexion, "sangwyn" (333), we get the startling specificity: "Wel loved he by the morwe a sop in wyn." The rimes stress the interconnections: the next line reverts to the general, "To lyven in delit was evere his wone," but note "lov- . . . lyv- . . . -lyt" and the rimes "-wyn . . . wyn . . . wone". The sounds seem to be telling us the Franklin is all of a piece. The metaphor of the next three lines sums it up:

> For he was Epicurus owene sone
> That heeld opinioun that pleyn delit
> 338 Was verray felicitee parfit.

His essence through and through finds witty definition in the unmetrical nine-syllable line, where the stress pattern gives unusual weight to the confirming adjectives "verray" and "parfit" (used previously of the Knight, 72) and where the light "felicitee" gathers up the implications of "To lyven in delit" and "pleyn delit." The portrait gives the Franklin's gratification of his senses, his indulgence in pleasure, a philosophical celebration. Does the morning sop in wine portend a self-centered sybarite?

The next two lines begin the process of tempering the Franklin's epicureanism:

> An housholdere and that a greet was he.
> 340 Seint Julian he was in his contree.

The weight of "housholdere" is confirmed in the heavily stressed adjective, "greet." The very next line, "His breed, his ale was alweys after oon" (341), makes clear the quality of his hospitality, "so plentevous" that

> 345 It snewed in his hous of mete and drynke
> Of alle deyntees that men koude thynke.

The rigor of his gourmet tastes, which include raising his own fish, his own fowl, draws from his land and from his cook the best they have to offer. The contrast of "snewed" with the pinching of his companion is clear (Chaucer's use of both words, "pinche" and "snewed," is unusual; see MED.) His "felicitee parfit," derived from "pleyn" delight, involves a level of control, of discipline; it includes sharing the good things the land provides with others.

It also includes in the end performing his duties as landholder, presiding at "sessiouns," serving in parliament and as "contour" (whatever that was)–"Was nowher swich a worthy vavasour" (360, final line of summary, a negative superlative). The fullness of the Franklin's delight makes possible his sober and generous stewardship. His self-indulgence in the morning sop of wine, his anger at his cook's neglect, temper the quality of his worthiness. The question of how much has given critics a witty challenge.

The Guildsmen

The rhythm of the portraits becomes witty in itself with the second of the two middle groups of portraits. It contains the largest group of pilgrims so far, a Haberdasher, a Carpenter, a Weaver, a Dyer, a Tapestry-maker, and a Cook. The first five are Guildsmen. Non-victuallers all, the Guildsmen can be covered in a single portrait, since they were "clothed alle in o lyveree / Of a solempne and a greet fraternitee" (364). Not only were their knives, belts, and pouches "chaped noght with bras / But al with silver" (367), but each seemed "a fair burgeys / To sitten in a yeldehalle on a deys" (370).

> Everich for the wisdom that he kan
> 372 Was shaply for to been an alderman.

Nothing in the meaning or the sound has quite prepared us for the word "shaply," nor for the way the wives, also indistinguishable, take over the portrait for the last five lines (374–8).

The meagreness of the portrait, 18 lines for five people (or ten if you count the wives), finds explanation in the other member of the group, their cook. Belonging to a great fraternity gives any insecurities they might feel a protective coloring. They not only eat together; they provide their own food. Their exclusivity accounts for the distance from which the narrator sees them. The portrait of the Cook seems to be listing all his skills at his trade. The single line, "Wel koude he knowe a draughte of Londoun ale" (382), sneaks in consumption, as no doubt the Cook did, in the midst of preparation. In the pattern, "Wel koude he," it actually prepares for the next couplet's "He koude" plus six verbs of culinary activity. "But greet harm . . ." signals the only other break from cookery in the nine-line portrait, a closed couplet (385 f.) informing us of his unappetizing "mormal." Everything we learn about the Cook reflects on the Guildsmen's exclusivity. Do the 27 lines for the group of six pilgrims comment ironically on their "shaply" self-importance?

The Shipman

There follow the portraits of three single pilgrims. The first, the Shipman's, has very little prosodic emphasis to accompany the startling things we learn about him. Two separate lines of summary sandwich the information about his depredations on the Chapman's wine (alliteration of "draughte" and "drawe" in a short line[21]). The second of the two lines, "Of nyce conscience took he no keep" (398, rime for "whil that the chapman sleep") almost lulls us into missing the meaning in the innocent-sounding:

> If that he faught and hadde the hyer hond
> 400 By water he sente hem hoom to every lond.

Word order gives some emphasis to "By water," and the alliteration on /h/ prepares for "hoom." "But of his craft . . ." introduces the final ten-line section, mostly devoted to his navigational skills and his detailed knowledge of "havenes" (407), of in fact "every cryke" (409) in the opposite coast, knowledge that we presume he put to some use, remembering "If that he faught . . . ." A couplet interrupts with qualities exercised in no routine wine-trade:

> Hardy he was and wys to undertake;
> 406 With many a tempest hadde his berd been shake.

Beard-shaking is a new and wittily impressive measure for the strength of tempests. The indirection of our knowledge of the Shipman is reflected at the beginning in the narrator's "For aught I woot he was of Dertemouthe" (389). In the last line we are given with more certainty the name of his barge, "The Maudelayne" (410).

The Physician

The "Doctour of Phisik," second of the three single pilgrims, gets the immediate accolade of an impressive negative superlative, "In al this world ne was ther noon hym lik" (472). The next line, "To speke of phisik . . ." limits the scope to professional concerns, but note the way the stress and internal rime pick out the two syllables of "phisik." After eight lines of detail about his medical skills, we get the single line of summary, "He was a verray parfit praktisour" (422, cf. the two previous uses of "verray" and "parfit," 72 and 338). Only four lines interrupt the paean to the physician's skills that culminates in the impressive six-line list of authorities ancient and modern that "Wel knew he." These four lines signal their qualification with an initial three-syllable feminine rime:

> 425 Ful redy hadde he his apothecariës
> To sende hym drogges and his letuariës
> For ech of hem made oother for to wynne–
> Hir frendshipe nas nat newe to bigynne.[22]

The triple alliteration, the double negative, and the spondee ("nat newë") in a single-line independent clause (428) give prosodic emphasis to an amusing understatement, with the euphemism, "frendship," applied to this age-old conniving for profit. The only other departures from the stress on professional skills come at the end when we learn first of his attention to diet, his comically placed single-line neglect of the "Bible" (rimed, feminine and deadpan, with "norissyng and digestíble"), his richly colored and silk-lined clothing, and, in the final four lines, more about his love of gold. These four lines start with the wittily ambiguous assertion that "he was but esy of dispence" (cf. use of "esy" in the Friar's portrait, 224) and end with the joke (using the same rime sound as the clothes couplet two lines back) about gold's use as a "cordial": "Therefore he lovede gold in special" (444, cf. with joke on gold in Clerk's portrait, 297 f). The reverse-stress on "Therefore" is a hearty-hollow emphasis, a wry poke in the ribs.

The Wife of Bath

The last of the independent pilgrims is the Wife of Bath. In the first lines, after the detail of her deafness, "and that was scathe" (446), the transnational "haunt" (unusual word in rime-position) of her clothmaking, "swich" that "She passed hem of Ypres and of Gaunt" (448, note the three-stress line), shrinks geographically to the parish-wide negative superlative, "In al the parisshe wif ne was ther noon" (449), and the delightful vignette of precedence at the offering that ends with her "out of alle charitee" (452, note the contrast of beginning and ending, "in . . . out", "al . . . alle," and the geographical ironies). The six lines that follow of clothing and appearance, governed not by system but by effect on the narrator, skip from top, "Hir coverchiefs" (453), to bottom, "Hir hosen" (456), and back up to "Boold was hir face" (458). They lead to the single-line summary, "She was a worthy womman al hir lyve" (459).

As if to explain her lifelong worth, the first word of the next line, the plural "Housbondes" waits until the rime for its surprising number, "fyve." The possible ambiguity of the "Withouten" that brings up the subject of other lovers in youth (461) loses its uncertainty in the following line, "But thereof nedeth nat to speke as nowthe" (462, note the n-alliteration, the unusual word "nowthe"). Four lines devoted to the extraordinary range and frequency of her travels (note the strongly alliterative "straunge strem" and the way the word order emphasizes "thries" and the place-names) end with the line of summary, suggestive of two simultaneous meanings (the literal provides opportunity for the figurative, prepared for by the "oother compaignye in yowthe," 461):

467 She koude muchel of wandrynge by the weye.

Note the muting of the first and fourth stresses to pick out the three important words and reinforce the alliteration. Further details of appearance– "Gat-tothed" (468), and her easy seat on her ambler (469); and clothing– "Y-wympled wel" (470), her hat "As brood as is a bokeler or a targe" (471), a foot-mantel (472), a pair of sharp spurs (473), lead to a single line and a closed couplet that celebrate, at the end of the portrait, her jocularity and her knowledge of the art of love:

In felaweshipe wel koude she laughe and carpe.
475 Of remedies of love she knew per chaunce
For she koude of that art the olde daunce.

The final rime pair, "knew per chaunce . . . olde daunce," discounts any suggestion that the art of love came to the Wife of Bath through books. The Wife projects an amusing preeminence professionally and personally.

The Parson

The Parson and the Plowman, brothers traveling together, recall the father-son pair with which the portraits began. The Parson's portrait is the second longest and one of the strongest, building up its picture patiently, fusing two image-clusters (gold-iron-rust, shepherd-sheep-shit) as it suggests the sound of his voice. In the beginning, in the middle, and at the end we get the bold generalizations on which the portrait is built; at the beginning "a povre Persoun of a Toun,"

> But riche he was of hooly thought and werk.
> He was also a lerned man a clerk. . . .

The poor-rich antithesis governs much of the first half of the portrait. We see him loath to "cursen" for his tithes but rather giving to "povre parisshens"

> Of his offryng and eek of his substaunce.
> He koude in litel thyng have suffisaunce.

The rime words "substaunce . . . suffisaunce" underscore in their sound sequence the paradox of his richness. Similarly, we experience the way context defines the meaning of distance (compare the travels of Knight and Wife of Bath), as "he ne lefte nat . . . / . . . to visite" the farthest in his wide parish whenever they needed him, in all weathers "Upon his feet and in his hand a staf" (495). The staff suggests the image of the good shepherd behind the second bold generalization and much of the second half of the portrait:

> This noble ensample to his sheep he yaf,
> That first he wroghte and afterward he taughte.

At this point we pick up the tone of his voice:

> Out of the gospel he tho wordes caughte
> And this figure he added eek therto
> That if gold ruste, what shal iren do?
> For if a preest be foul, on whom we truste,
> No wonder is a lewed man to ruste,
> And shame it is if a preest take keep
> A shiten shepherd and a clene sheep.

The contrast with the Friar's utterance is striking. The Parson's plain speaking focuses on two centers of power. The first is the figure, "if gold ruste, what shal iren do?" (spondee, followed by the "what" that turns the whole sentence into a question, strong enough to cast its unspoken answer across the next four lines; the first two lines pick up "ruste" in their near-identical rimes, ". . . truste . . . to ruste"). The second center of power comes at the climax in the word, "shiten," the Parson's way of startling us into a realization of what has happened only too often to the pastoral ideal ("shiten shepherde" forces two figures together into an alliterative pair, prepared for by "shame" and continued in the "clene sheep" at the end of the line; note the four "sh-"s and the four long "-ee-"s). The pastoral image continues for ten more lines, including a vignette of what the Parson did not do, i. e., rent out his benefice, abandon his flock to the wolf, and settle for a lucrative job in London–the implication being that this was not uncommon behavior for priests. In contrast , "He was a shepherd and noght a mercenarïe" (514, single line of summary with three-syllable feminine rime).

The next twelve lines move from the standards he set for his own conduct to the moderation of what he expected from others. To the sinful, he was "nat despitous / Ne of his speche daungerous ne digne [alliteration on /d/ and /sp/], / But in his techyng discreet and benigne [note the less stressed /d/ and the subtle rime-enhancement of "ne digne" in "benigne"]. / To drawen folk to hevene by fairnesse . . ." [516–19, /d/ and /f/, stress on "fair-"]. But the "obstinat . . . of heigh or lough estat [522–again, subtle rime-enhancement], / Hym wolde he snybben sharply for the nonys" (523; word order, stress-reversal, and /h/ help place the weight of "snybben" on "Hym"). And so:

> A bettre preest I trowe that nowher noon ys[23]

(single-line, double-negative assonance-rich superlative with two-word identical for rime). "Ne maked him a spiced conscience" (526) startles with "spiced" (compare the "nyce conscience" the Shipman doesn't have, 398) even as it stresses the balance, the down-to-earth good sense of the Parson, and prepares for the final couplet's thematic generalization:

> But Cristes loore and his apostles twelve
> He taughte; but first he folwed it hymselve.

The wit in the Parson's portrait is not humorous-satirical; as in the Knight's portrait, it comes from making virtue interesting. It consists in finding the oppositions and balances essential to his performance as priest, the "povre-riche" opposition, the "wroghte . . . taughte" balance, the pithy sound of his voice: gold rusting, "iren," the "shame" of the "shiten shepherd," the "snybbing" of the obstinate and the avoidance of a "spiced" conscience. These oppositions, in this balance, have prosodic emphasis. The Parson's portrait has no description of appearance or clothing; it devotes itself exclusively to his performance as priest. His character shines through performance. We hear his voice; we see him in action; we experience him in the language of his portrait. Prosody supports this effort, as surely as it aids in the mocking of excess and in the exposure of evil.

The Plowman

His brother, the Plowman, receives only thirteen lines of description. The second line, "That hadde ylad of dong ful many a fother" (530), places him, in its emphasis on "dong," at the least savory of his tasks involving hard physical labor. Here is a "shiten" man, living in charity. The next five lines give in small compass the commitments he lives by, that transform the earth he works:

A trewe swynkere and a good was he
Lyvynge in pees and parfit charitee.
God loved he best with al his hoole herte
At alle tymes, thogh him gamed or smerte,
And thanne his neighebor right as hymselve.

Word order and the spondaic effect ("God loved") contribute to the power of these lines (note also the sequence, "good . . . /Lyv . . . . / God lov-"). The Plowman carries out the second of the two great commandments (535) by the threshing, diking, and delving he does "For Cristes sake, for every povre wight" (537). The tithes he pays "Bothe of his propre swynk and his catel," imply a "suffisaunce" resembling his brother's. The two portraits reinforce each other. The emphasis in the second on "swynk" and on verbs of physical hard labor show the Plowman at work in the "dong," no less dedicated than the Parson to a brotherhood that transcends family.

The last group of pilgrims are the rascals, those left over, named for us by Chaucer and including himself. The finality of "ther were namo" (544) suggests that as for the Second Nun and the three priests Chaucer was not originally planning portraits for them (see references in note 10). Most critics consider them the "cherles" from the characterization given two of them in the Miller's Prologue. They would come near the bottom in most categories of value.

The Miller

The first, the Miller, "a stout carl", receives a portrait that keeps returning to his crude physical make-up: "Ful byg he was of brawn and eek of bones" (546), "At wrastlynge he wolde have alwey the ram" (548). It turns out that he is a kind of ram himself:

He was short-sholdred, brood, a thikke knarre;
Ther was no dore that he nolde heve of harre,
Or breke it at a rennyng with his heed.[24]

The weight of the first two lines: internal identicals ("was . . . was") at the first stresses, spondaic effect at the second stress in each line ("short-shold- . . . no dore"), the cross-riming in the sequence "shold- . . . brood . . . no dore . . . nold-," the plethora of consonants in the first line to imitate his rugged physique, the double negative heaving off hinges in the second line—this weight of the first two lines sets up for the sudden speed of the third line with its stress on the three syllables, "brek . . . ren . . . heed" to give the physical shock at the word "heed" a prosodic shock as well. The portrait further celebrates the Miller's crude physique with the run-on and early cesura of "A werte," a two-stress archaic pair of "nosethirles" ("blake"), and a set of similes comparing his features to those of animals and common things ("a spade," "a greet forneys"). At the end we learn that he was "a janglere and a goliardeys" (560 f.), a quite normally dishonest blue-and-white-garbed Miller, and a bagpiper ("And therwithal he broghte us out of towne" 566).

The Manciple

The Manciple turns out to be a much more gentle rascal than his fellow churls. The narrator goes so far as to call him "A gentil Maunciple" in his first three words. The portrait is dominated by a rhetorical question:

> Now is nat that of God a ful fair grace
> That swich a lewed mannes wit shal pace
> The wisdom of an heep of lerned men?[25]

The answer would seem to be as rhetoric requires, Why yes, of course. We have already learned of his skill in purchasing, that he "wayted so in his achaat / That he was ay biforn and in good staat" (572, note the spondaic last foot). It is only when we finish our study of his more than thrice ten masters, ten lines in a twenty-line portrait, and learn in a final triumphant line of summary, "And yet this Manciple sette hir aller cappe" (586, internal rime on -et plus the condensed archaic idiom "hir aller" and the pick-up from the previous line of a two-stress rime "falle or happe . . . aller cappe"), that we realize the extent of the mockery implicit in the question. Half his life is apparently spent in his careful scrutiny of this "heep" (his word no doubt) of learned men. That his success in cheating such a distinguished group contributes so much to his amour propre makes the "ful fair grace" of God a crushing standard.

The Reeve

The Reeve has only one master to manage but a work force under him that numbers many. His physical appearance dominates the first six lines of the portrait. The description starts with the words "sclendre coleric." Is the unnecessary -c- in sclendre an indication of its close association with the choler of his basic nature? Certainly, the way he shaves and keeps his hair has a muted effect, compared to the final two lines of the section:

> Ful longe were his legges and ful lene
> Ylyk a staf–ther was no calf ysene.

The repetition of "ful," the second one (as in 153) approaching an oxymoron, the alliteration on /l/, the near internal rime "staf. . . calf," give prosodic emphasis to his dessicated boniness. This is the last we hear of his physical make-up, but the detail is striking enough to recur to mind, as we shall see, at two later points in the portrait (605, 621). Other indications of his appearance are like the already noted references to shaving and hair-style. They receive little prosodic emphasis. They all seem to reflect an effort on his part to appear harmless: the rusty blade he carries (618), his "long surcote of pers" (617) "tukked . . . aboute" like a friar (621), the shadowed isolation of his "wonynge" (606 f.), and the "ful good stot" he rode called Scot (615 f.). A sudden change brings us the carpentering skills he learned in youth (613 f.); they provide an innocent contrast with what we learn in the rest of the portrait about his conduct as a Reeve.

The Reeve is presented as in complete control, on good terms with his lord, whom by covenant (internal rime with the gov- of "governynge," 599) he has reported to directly since the lord came into his estate, and whose gratitude (and even gifts) he has won by giving and lending him "of his owene good" (611). The secret of his success receives subtle confirmation in rime-sound:

> Wel koude he kepe a gerner and a bynne;
> Ther was noon auditour koude on him wynne.
> Wel wiste he by the droghte and by the reyn
> The yeldynge of his seed and of his greyn.

The repeated "Wel," the word "kepe," the spondaic "noon aud- . . . him wyn-," the sequence "wyn- . . . wis-," the three-stress rhythm of the last two lines linking bin-keeping, weather, and harvest–these all prepare us to hear "reyn" in "greyn," to see him as knowing without apparent effort how much grain there should be. The consequence of the Reeve's skills, seen in the list of what the lord leaves in his exclusive "governynge" (597–601), makes its greatest impact on those who work with and under him:

> Ther koude no man brynge hym in arrerage.
> Ther nas baillif, ne hierde, nor oother hyne,
> That he ne knew his sleighte and his covyne.
> They were adrad of hym as of the deeth.[26]

The chorus of negatives of different semantic force invites some comment. The first line is a negative absolute, its meaning reinforced by the four consecutive strong syllables, "no man brynge hym." The three negatives of the second line sweep bailiff and herdsman into servitude with "oother hyne" and serve as double negative with the fourth negative "ne," reducing the chicanery of all three groups to the positive "knew" of the Reeve's knowledge. They lead up to the summary of the terror he inspires, invoking in the final word, "deeth" (note the alliterative "adrad of") a fusion of the powerful allegorical figure, reinforced by the double-meaning (in "deeth") of plague.

The imagery of his associates' dread implies an importance the rest of the portrait does not support. His skill at detecting "sleighte and covyne" has for those he exposes a supernatural aura, but the limited scope of his operations shows him to be a petty scoundrel. The final thing we hear about him is wittily appropriate: "And evere he rood the hyndreste of oure route." The alliteration on /r/ and the hint of subservience in "hyne" (see previous rime-word of line 603) call attention to the dual attraction this position holds for him, serving his affected humility and at the same time his instinct to keep under scrutiny all his fellow-pilgrims. His secretive, suspicious isolation does not pass entirely unnoticed. A choleric sensitivity to unintended (?) insult will expose him far more generally in the storytelling.

The Summoner

The Summoner's portrait begins with a distasteful account of his visage that lasts 13 lines, slides into the sound of his voice as he disports himself in taverns for 11 lines, then takes up for 16 lines his good fellowship, including the doctrine he teaches on the archdeacon's curse and the narrator's shocked rejection of it. The portrait ends with three lines devoted to his influence on young people, and three lines on his garland and his cake. The portrait mirrors in its diffuseness the careless irresponsibility of its subject.

The revolting account of his skin disease opens the portrait and includes a single line of summary making his "visage" frightening to children (628). His futile efforts to cure the disease serve only to aggravate it:

> Ther nas quyk-silver, lytarge, ne brymstoon,
> Boras, ceruce, ne oille of tartre noon,
> Ne oynement that wolde clense and byte,
> That hym myghte helpen of his whelkes white
> Nor of the knobbes sittynge on his chekes.

The negatives dominate all five lines here; they render with prosodic force the futility of efforts at cure. The first line with its two negatives, its short /i/'s, its syncopated stresses involving spondees for the second and final feet, the second line's internal riming with the first line, "nas . . . -ras", "-targe . . . tartre," the resumption of overt negatives in the series "ne oil- . . . noon . . . Ne oyn-," the wishfulness in the "wolde" and the resort to extremities in the "byte"–these lead up to the frustration of the word "helpen" that can chime with "whelkes white" (the three strong stresses in the line) without effect on them nor on the stressed "knobbes sittynge on his chekes" of the next line. The effort at external remedy finds further aggravation of his disease in his rich diet, with the rime-word "chekes" reflected internally in the following line, the syncopated rhythm and the combination of assonance and internal rime picking out for emphasis "Wel lov- . . . garleek . . . and eek lekes /. . . . strong wyn reed as blood" (635, note relation with the opening "fyr-reed"). The stress-cluster in the last five words serve at once to characterize the Summoner's reckless gusto and the narrator's ironic emphasis.

The wine-drinking slips naturally into the sound of his voice, as under the influence he speaks and cries "as he were wood" (636). The next ten lines record his tavern-voice, featured prosodically by the stress-heavy "no word but Latyn" (638, a mispronunciation riming with "wyn"); the three successive lines with "-er-" in mid-line ("termes . . . lerned . . . herde," 639–41); the pair of lines not a couplet, "And eek ye knowen wel how that a jay / Kan clepen 'Watte' as wel as kan the pope" (642f., "jay" and "pope" jangle their difference, with the pope saying "watte"–like a jay or the Summoner?–having a comic impact); and ending "Ay 'Questio quid iuris' wolde he crie" (646). This mindless flaunting of law-Latin leads seamlessly to two lines of summary:

> He was a gentil harlot and a kynde;
> 648 A bettre felawe sholde men noght fynde.

From this point on, "gentil" harlotry, called repeatedly good fellowship (650, 653), takes over the portrait as we learn how the Summoner encourages the misconduct, especially the sexual misconduct, he should as the archdeacon's agent be summonsing to punishment. He of course practices what he permits: "excuse hym atte fulle" (451) suggests the digression, "Ful prively a fynch eek koude he pulle." As the narrator devoted ten lines to the Summoner's tavern-Latin, he now spends ten lines on his "teaching" about the archdeacon's "curs." The prosody invites a number of observations. The series "good felawe / . . . . noon awe / . . . caas . . . ers- . . . curs" introduces the lame joke on the riming "purs," the word occurring in three successive lines, each time earlier, until the telegraphed punch-line, "'Purs is the ercedekenes helle,' seyde he." The joke draws the narrator's indignant comment as we turn from "purs" back to "cursing" (riming "dede" with "drede", 659 f.)[27] :

> For curs wol slee right as assoillyng savith
> And also war hym of a Significavit.

The final "curs" (the sixth "-urs" in seven lines) introduces a series of /s/'s with the strong feminine ending "savith" preparing for the Latin "Significavit" that starts off well but doesn't quite complete the feminine rime, and reduces the spiritual "curs wol slee" to an anticlimactic physical imprisonment. This unique resort on the narrator's part to overt moral disapproval lacks the power to expose of the approval he sometimes lavishes on his scoundrels.

The last six lines of the portrait combine a surprise on the Summoner's influence with two details of his flamboyant good fellowship. That the two disparities are interrelated comes as a shock:

In daunger hadde he at his owene gise
The yonge girles of the diocise
And knew hir conseil and was al hir reed.

The power of these words is unmistakable: "daunger" points to instinctive levels of behavior between the sexes, "diocise" to his wide-spread influence; "gise" and "girles" foreshadow the willing intimacy in the "knew hir conseil and was al hir reed." That the Summoner's loud and showy permissiveness can dispel the revulsion at his "cherubynnes face" speaks volumes for the venal appeal of the good fellowship that dominates the end of the portrait and is reflected in the trivial ornament of garland and cake (destined to play their part in the Physician-Pardoner link).[28] The minor hell ("tartre" and "brimstoon," 419 f.) he makes for himself and jokes about with his companions (458) has the attraction for teen-agers of a safe rebellion, sanctioned as it is by an officer of the ecclesiastical court. It curiously foreshadows where the Friar will attempt to send summoners when he volunteers to tell a tale.

The Pardoner

The Summoner's companionship with the Pardoner, featured in the first six lines of the Prologue's final portrait, flaunts in the song they sing "Ful loude" their defiance of a moralistic society. The word "gentil," applied to a third of the "cherles" (cf. "A gentil Maunciple" 567, "a gentil harlot" 647, and a "gentil Pardoner" 669), throws a questionable aura over what follows. "That streight was comen fro the court of Rome" (671) receives a kind of derisive echo in the title of the song, " 'Com hider, love, to me'," with its repetition of "com-," its two-word off-rime (stress on "me" in the title but not in the rime), and its sexual implications. These implications are reinforced by the "stif" in the Summoner's "burdoun," the trompe of his voice compared to that (we later hear) of the Pardoner's, "as smal as hath a goot" (riming with the "al hoot" of his pardons "comen fro Rome"), and in fact with most of what we hear of the Pardoner's physical make-up, and especially the line of summary that brings the first half of the portrait to an end:

691 I trowe he were a geldyng or a mare.

The narrator spends an inordinate time on the Pardoner's hair; it's as if it were extremely important to get its quality and the effort he makes to arrange it just right:

This Pardoner hadde heer as yelow as wex
But smothe it heeng as dooth a strike of flex;
By ounces henge his lokkes that he hadde,677
And therwith he his shuldres overspradde
But thynne it lay by colpons oon and oon.
But hood for jolitee wered he noon
For it was trussed up in his walet.
Hym thoughte he rood al of the newe jet;
Dischevelee save his cappe, he rood al bare.

The first three lines form a unit marked by the "hadde" constructions at either end, the riming similes and the repeated "heeng." The next four lines have the two corrective "But"s for the middle lines with, in the first, the dominant /n/ sounds leading to identicals for the last two stresses, and in the second, the wait for the rime to discover that hood for "jolitee" he wore "noon." Each thing we hear is qualified, added to, or corrected. The striking idiom "al of the newe jet" has had its meaning deflated by the initial "Hym thoughte." The single long word, "Dischevelee," set off by the cesura, with the French word for hair as its root and a French suffix making it a past participle, stands alone with only the most general grammatical function to indicate the effect so carefully aimed at in all nine lines: casual disarray. For a second time "he rood al" is pre-deflated, "save his cappe . . . bare." In all this effort to create a contradictory appearance, the substance is minimal, and like the wax and flax to which his hair is compared, separated from its living source.

The next seven lines give us details, seemingly miscellaneous but most of them related to what we've already heard. The first line, however, despite the internal rime with "bare" in "Swich glarynge eyen . . . as an hare" seems a departure, the one vital unqualified detail–the Pardoner as haunted, fugitive? But the "vernycle" is sewed to his cap (685); the "walet" holds hood as well as pardons from Rome (687); his voice (688) we heard in the opening song; and the absence of beard (689 f.) relates to his sparse hair. The details with the repetition of "hadde" (684f., 688f.) add up, as we have seen, to an "I trowe he were" (not "he was"). Are we to assume that the essential man no longer exists?

"But of his craft" there can be no question: "Ne was ther swich another pardoner" (693). The form here is familiar: the negative superlative. The substance of the Parson's "bettre preest" line (the closest previous negative superlative, 524) is lacking. The Pardoner is unique in the way he practices his craft. What that way is, becomes clear as we hear about his relics:

> For in his male he hadde a pilwe-beer
> Which that he seyde was Oure Lady veyl.
> He seyde he hadde a gobet of the seyl
> That Seynt Peter hadde whan that he wente
> Upon the see, til Jhesu Crist him hente.
> He hadde a croys of latoun ful of stones
> And in a glas he hadde pigges bones.

The use here of the "he hadde"s and "he seyde"s has a wittily climactic import. In the first instance we learn both the reality and the contrast of the Pardoner's claim for it. In the second instance, what "He seyde he hadde" takes three lines, a laconic but vivid picture of Christ's rescue of Peter when he "wente" (run-on) upon the sea. The run-on here receives emphasis from the non-iambic pattern of the first four feet. For the last two relics we get only the reality, with no connection with religion for the final one, just "pigges bones." That he can pass off as religious relics pigs' bones to those who keep pigs supererogates any specification of his claim.

The next six lines, three closed couplets, featuring at least one alliterated pair of words in each couplet, complete the picture of his craft as Pardoner:

> But with thise relikes whan that he fond
> A povre person dwellynge upon lond,
> Upon a day he gat hym moore moneye
> Than that the Person gat in monthes tweye;
> And thus with feyned flaterye and japes
> He made the person and the peple his apes.

The run-on in the first couplet to the first of the alliterative pairs emphasizes the activeness of "fond" and the helplessness of its object, the poor parson. The "whan that" has the sense of whenever. The second couplet contrasts the time elements at beginning and end at the same time that it also highlights the second alliterative pair, "moore moneye." The third alliterative pair, "feyned flaterye," signals the double duplicity of the Pardoner's actions, while the alliterated /p/'s get echoed in the final word of the last couplet. What the three couplets add up to is that the Pardoner has no reality as a Pardoner at all. He is a consummate mountebank of false relics, contemptuous of the people he makes "apes" of, isolated by the intensity of his avarice, subversive of the function he purports to perform. Pardons give him entree to what he really enjoys doing, pretending to piously preach.

Another closed couplet, the fourth in a row, makes a transition to the Pardoner in church (note the similarity of the rime-sound "-aste" to "japes . . .apes" of the previous couplet). The first line is remarkable for its absence of substance; again we get an alliterative pair: "But trewely to tellen atte laste." Does it prepare us sufficiently for the claim in the second line, which outdoes the Monk's fair prelacy (204) but not quite the Friar's superlative virtue (251)?

> 708 He was in chirche a noble ecclesiaste.

The last six lines present the Pardoner in church. They lead up by a series of steps to the thing he does best, to the thing he most enjoys doing: "Wel koude he rede. . . / But alderbest he song an offertorie [three-syllable feminine rime, ending the string of closed couplets]; / For wel he wiste, whan that song was songe . . ." (alliterative pair plus near-identical pair). All is anticipation. As at the beginning, we have the Pardoner in song (710, 711, 714), this time ready to preach

> and wel affile his tonge
> To wynne silver, as he ful wel koude;
> 714 Therefore he song the murierly and loude.

Another "therefore"!–made steely through syntax and satiric logic. Observations crowd in at this point: the word "affile" for what he does to his tongue, with the run-on "To wynne silver" emphasizing his addiction; the word "murierly," grammatically concocted to fit the rhythm and giving his merriment an undefined spill-over plurality; the repetitions of the verb and adverb to project the singing at beginning and end of the portrait; the loudness of the Pardoner's insubstantiality; the preparation in the portrait for what the poet has already created, the performance as "preacher" in the Pardoner's Tale.[29]

The long but incomplete series of portraits is at an end. The rhythm of the grouping, which the two missing portraits would not change, can be seen retrospectively to have implications beyond the ones already noticed. The surprise of a subgroup within the final group of churls, disclosed to us only at the beginning of the last portrait, has special impact. In a work written in couplets, but not dominated by the couplet form, closed couplets tend to stand out (as they do in the last portrait). Similarly with the grouping of portraits. The Knight–Squire at the beginning, the Merchant–Clerk (single pilgrims but contrasted), the Man of Law–Franklin, the Guildsmen–Cook (witty pairing of five and one) in the middle, the Parson–Plowman originally at the end but now supplanted, the Summoner–Pardoner now at the end–the couplings have meaning beyond the meanings of the separate portraits. The pairs at beginning and end have special impact. The tried and tested worthiness of the Knight and the promise of his son the Squire, the effective charity in action of the two brothers, the Parson and the Plowman, had given a foundation of stability, health, and value to the society projected. The company of churls, self-serving, dishonest, but in positions of minor influence, shaded without shaking the ground. The final pair noisily celebrate their partnership in subversion. The influence of the Summoner on the young in the diocese, revealed at the end of his portrait, and the success of the Pardoner in disrupting whole communities–strongly suggested in the Prologue but not fully revealed until his performance as storyteller–end the account of a society on a note of deception, subversion, and disease. Association with the Church gives the two men power to prey on others. What we experience at the end is also the noise and insubstantiality of evil. The misused power tempts but does not compel others. What it does lead to inevitably is isolation, illness, a kind of half-life for the misusers of power. The final pair diminishes and infects, it does not threaten to destroy, the society depicted.

We return to the story of the pilgrimage in the last 144 lines of the General Prologue. These lines naturally fall into three sections. The first, which we have already noted in part, is the longest address to the audience in The Tales of Caunterbury (715–46).[30] The second involves the Host's role at the Tabard the night the narrator joined the company of pilgrims, especially his exchange with the group (747–821). The third section is not really part of the General Prologue despite the rime-link to it (821 f.). Lines 822–58 constitute the head-link for the Knight's Tale. They should properly be labeled as such.

Chaucer's Apologies

The long address to the reader starts out, as we have seen, making a more-than-

672-line-long "clause" of what will be, when complete, the twenty-four portraits;[31] it also sets the clock back to "How that we baren us that ilke nyght . . ." (721). It then turns to two apologies the narrator makes to his audience. Both are ironic, both challenge the audience to critical alertness. The first (much the longer) points to the nature of fiction; it might be seen as the culmination of the wit that informs so much of the Prologue, indeed so much of Chaucer's poetry.

It is important to realize that the whole address to the reader takes place within the fiction. In other words it is part of the autobiographical fragment in the life of the narrator, who is partially at least Chaucer incognito (the Man of Law in his head-link can refer to the poet's works from a haughty critical stance with no apparent knowledge that Chaucer is one of his listeners). But it is also Chaucer the performer, incognito only to the fictional pilgrims, not to the audience he is reading his works to, the readers he is writing his works for. This audience is very much aware that what they are being entertained by is in large part a fiction, that the apology for repeating exactly what people say is in effect a slant claim for the truth in fiction, that the responsibility for the words they hear when a character speaks separates Chaucer the creator from Chaucer the creature within his own fiction. Ostensibly the narrator is asking his audience not to attribute it to his "vileynye,"

Thogh that I pleynly speke in this mateere
To telle yow hire wordes and hir cheere
Ne thogh I speke hir wordes proprely.
For this ye knowen al so wel as I:
Whoso shal telle a tale after a man
He moot reherce as neigh[32] as evere he kan
Everich a word, if it be in his charge,
Al speke he never so rudeliche and large,
Or ellis he moot telle his tale untrewe,
Or feyne thyng, or fynde wordes newe.
He may nat spare althogh he were his brother,
He moot as wel seye o word as another.
Crist spak hymself ful brode in hooly writ
And wel ye woot no vileynye is it.
Eek Plato seith, whoso kan hym rede,
The wordes moote be cosyn to the dede.

The fiction that it is not a fiction dominates the literal meaning of this passage. The problem of language is paramount. But it is seen in the passage in terms of what people say, their words, their speaking, their telling tales. Note in the first three lines "speke . . . / To tellen . . . wordes . . . / . . . Ne thogh I speke hir wordes proprely" (where "proprely" wittily excludes all reference to propriety, precisely what is being violated as he speaks their words properly, i. e. exactly, please forgive him).[33] Note the way the references to language continue: "al so wel . . . / Whoso shal telle a tale . . . He moot reherce as neigh as evere he kan / Everich a word. . . ." The seeming redundance of "a" creates a Chaucerian idiom that accentuates the strained linking of universality ("everych") and singularity ("a word"); it stands out further because of its climactic position as object delayed by a subordinate clause after the verb (the intervening clause means wittily the smallest space possible). Note also the sound "evere" three words back, the position at the beginning of the line, the reversal of stress in "Everych," and the heavy cesura following "word": "Everych a word" resonates beyond its literal meaning, and encapsulates the issues raised by the passage.

We continue with more references to language: "Al speke he never [note the third "ever"] . . . / Or ellis he moot telle his [note internal rime: "ellis. . . telle his"] tale untrewe [the /t/'s] / Or feyne thyng [like a fictional autobiography?] or fynde wordes newe" (note the /f-n/'s). These three unacceptable alternatives to "Everych a word" have witty critical resonance. They are in fact (even telling a tale "untruly") what we are experiencing as we read our narrator's account. The word "spare" assumes that repeating a man's words is a kind of exposure, and "brother," unexpectedly intimate, reflects the narrator's pose of naive simplicity, carried to a climax in the next line's suggestion that one word is as good as another–the inadvertent contradiction of all that the narrator has been saying. The citing of Christ as example for Chaucer's literary practice has a wittily blasphemous dimension (possible only to the pose of simple innocence in Chaucer's narrator). Plato's dictum that words should bear close relationship to the deed they describe comes almost as an afterthought; the omission of a syllable after "seith" creates a heavy cesura, the pause or take-in of breath before the interpolated recognition that not many people can read Plato; only then do we get as the final line the cousinship of words and deed. This can have the specific meaning of onomatopoeia; or it can extend to the subject of this essay, the many ways in which "Everich a word" can by sound, rhythm, grammar, rhetoric more fully "telle the tale."

The apology prepares for the range of voices and levels of discourse the portraits have made possible. It anticipates in both meaning and language the more sophisticated apology in the Miller's head-link, where the impending series of fabliaux raises the issue immediately. Chaucer's claim not to be responsible for the "everich a word" has a deeper level of responsibility. He must do justice to the "sondry folk" he has created. He must give the impression of repeating what they said. "To telle his tale untrewe" would be not to improve the tale consciously (which the poet invariably does), but to make it conform throughout to the poet's proprieties of diction and verisimilitude, rather than to the putative speaker's. To "feyne a thyng" would be to impose on the fictional "reality" things that do not carry out the fiction.

Of course feigning things (creation) and finding new words ("as neigh as ever he kan" to "the dede") is what the poet is constantly up to. Creating a fiction in which he can participate on the level of his creatures imitates God's (as Christ's) practice on a deeper level than language. His role of observer and narrator, ultimately of storyteller like his fellow-pilgrims, gives him no power over them. Within his creation they are enfranchised to do and especially to say things he would not. Thus Chaucer the performer in his partly ironic apology for plain speaking comes to the aid of Chaucer the poet in the poet's effort to imitate the world he knows and lives in. In addressing the audience from within the fiction, he alerts them, challenges them to the evaluation and judgment of what he will report–"everych a word." Truth in fiction imitates the truth of experience. The paradoxical freedom of creatures (in fiction as well as in the world) establishes a foundation for value. It also enfranchises the poet to "reherse" and the audience to experience and enjoy without the inhibiting consequence of the actual. The denial of fiction behind this naive apology gives witty resonance to the values inherent in the telling of tales, whatever the level of their fictionality, to the responsibilities and freedoms of all involved, those who tell, those told about, and those who hear (or read).

The second apology is much shorter, ultimately less important. The narrator asks forgiveness for not setting "folk in hir degree / Heere in this tale, as that they sholde stonde." (745) He thus calls attention to the order of the portraits. A systematic arrangement according to social rank would interfere with the mnemonic advantage of the groupings and might lead to an expectation of system throughout the work, an imposition of thematic similarity for groups of tales (as in the *Decameron*), rather than the spontaneously generated orderings we get (in both portraits and tales). To ascribe to his own shortwittedness the actual ordering of the portraits indirectly flatters the poet's own wit. The ironic appeal to the audience's understanding brings the section to a stand on the identical "–stonde."

The Host

The ensuing section, the last of the real General Prologue, introduces the Host, first in a seven-line "portrait" (751–57) and then dramatically by presenting his part in the colloquy with the pilgrims in direct quotation. The narrator's short description of him prepares us for his dominance of space: "A semely man . . . / For to been a marchal in an halle . . . / Boold of his speche, and wys, and wel ytaught / And of manhod hym lakkede right naught" (751–52, 755–56). His manhood and mastery remind us of the Monk. The portrait ends by emphasizing the Host's somewhat self-serving mirth, as it slips into direct discourse:

Eek therto he was right a myrie man,
And after soper pleyen he bigan
And spak of myrthe amonges othere thynges,
Whan that we hadde maad oure rekenynges,
And seyde thus: "Now lordynges trewely
Ye been to me right welcome hertely;
For by my trouthe, if that I shal nat lye,
I saugh nat this yeer so myrie a compaignye
Atones in this herberwe as is now.
Fayn wolde I doon yow myrthe, wiste I how.
And of a myrthe I am right now bythoght
To doon yow ese, and it shal coste noght."

Ingratiation, mirth, and claims of sincerity vie for dominance in the Host's speech. He calls them "lordinges," rimes "trewely" with "hertily," and has a whole line, "For by my trouthe, if that I shal nat lye," postponing flattery of their mirth with protests of sincerity. Despite the superlative nature of their mirth, expressed negatively with three time limitations, he would like to increase it, if he knew how–then quite suddenly ("myrthe" and "now" repeated), he knows how. What started him off on mirth was collecting their "rekenynges"; he ends on the note of reassurance: the mirth will cost nothing.

Chaucer is giving us, if not "Everych a word," a good sampling of the Host's speech. The Host's voice establishes his presence. We are not surprised that he asks the "myrie" company's assent before he divulges the details of his plan for their added mirth: "Hoold up youre hondes withouten moore speche" (783); or that he keeps before them the question of money: the prize-dinner will be at "oure aller cost" (799; note the disingenuous "oure"). He will not charge them for riding with them and being their guide (804); any one who dares "withseye" his judgment "Shal paye al that we spenden by the weye" (806). So infectious is his "cheere" that the pilgrims (in imitation?) direct him to set a price for the prize-dinner (815).

By the end of the section the Host has not only established himself as controlling space at the Tabard, he will exercise authority (and dispense mirth) on the road to Canterbury and back. He has converted the pilgrims to storytelling; he has made them rivals in a contest of which he will be the judge; he has insured their return to the Tabard for a prize-awarding final dinner. He has taken unwittingly the leading role in the narrator's segment of autobiography, and made of it a frame story. The principal events in it will be narratives; the climax will be the Host's decision as to who has told "Tales of best sentence and moost solaas" (798). His authority makes him a kind of co-author. Not only judge, but at the pilgrims' request "reportour" of their tales as well, he clearly has no inkling of the report he is at this very moment, as we read the narrator's account, figuring in.[34]

The wit in this section is in our hearing the Host's voice, our sensing the motivations under the habitual bonhomie, our seeing him as a character in the narrator's effort at undistorted reporting, the whole projected through the irregular regularity of decasyllabic couplets in Chaucer's fiction that purports not to be a fiction.

In the Prologue as a whole, the couplets, the single lines, the repetitions of words and sounds, the rhythmic variety, the experiments with audience expectation in respect to word order, grammar, and rhetoric, have helped to keep the level of attention high, have given witty emphasis, have at intervals provided elements of wit to the verses. There has been little repetition of effect. Enhanced rime for instance has served a variety of purposes, mocking the Squire's exaggerated passion ("nyghtertale / . . . nyghtyngale" 97 f.); reflecting the Monk's contempt for Austyn and his swink ("be served / . . . reserved" 187 f.); giving force to the application of the Parson's image-cluster, gold-rust-iron ("truste / . . . to ruste" 501 f.); stressing the triviality of the Manciple's triumph ("falle or happe / . . . aller cappe" 585 f.). Some portraits–the Prioress's, the Pardoner's–have throughout subtle prosodic reinforcements; others, like the Shipman's, have relatively few. But the Shipman's "By water . . ." (400) has a witty delayed meaning that combines indirection and direction, prosodically emphasized as the first words in the second line of a closed couplet, with the further emphasis of word order in the sentence. The closed couplet only occasionally figures in Chaucer's prosody, but worth remembering is its witty prominence in the Man of Law's portrait, especially the "nas / . . . was" rime (321 f), and the series of three with their alliterative pairs that describe the Pardoner's exploitation of his relics (701–6). The single line, usually a line of summary (but note the Franklin's love of a morning sop of wine, 334), occurs in almost all the portraits. The single word also stands out–"bismotered" (76), "pynche" (326), "shaply" (372), "Dishevelee" (683)–to point out only a few of the examples. It might be proper to end this summary by recalling the wittily drained "proprely" (729) and the wittily enriched "longen" (12).

The Prologue has by no means exhausted the capacity of Chaucer's fiction for surprise. The portraits do not limit; they enable. The audience will base its willing suspension of disbelief on the storytelling rather than the events within the stories. The range of narrators will open up for Chaucer possibilities he has not experienced before in variety of genre and levels of style. He will be able to challenge his auditors, his readers, to take seriously what they have previously regarded as beneath serious attention. Slantness of meaning so richly exploited in the Prologue will provide opportunities for experiment in all the relationships–between the pilgrims, between the stories they tell: especially between the pilgrims and the stories they tell. Developing these opportunities will put off indefinitely and, as it transpired, long beyond Chaucer's ability to settle, questions of consistency, final ordering, and completion.

But no matter how quiet their author's bones may lie, his lines continue to surge into life with a movement and a meaning of their own.

NOTES

[1]My position on Chaucer's prosody is closest to that of Gaylord as set forth in "Scanning the Prosodists: An Essay in Metacriticism" (1976). The 1979 article on Sir Thopas parallels and extends brilliantly the prosodic analysis in Part II of "'Thy Drasty Rymyng. . ." Calling the prosody "elvyssh" anticipates my use of the word "witty." For my earlier work on the portraits of the Prologue, see chapter III of Owen 1977, and the essay in the Elizabeth Salter Memorial, Owen 1983. This present essay extends my contribution to Jost 1994, which dealt with the first 42 lines of the Prologue. Quotations from Chaucer will be from the Riverside Chaucer (Chaucer 1987), except for the punctuation, which will be much reduced, and except for instances where the Hengwrt, Manly-Rickert, or Variorum text differs as discussed in footnotes.

[2]The difference is especially important with octosyllabics, which in English become four-beat but in French remain eight-count, the longest line without cesura. Variations in word length give French octosyllabics rich rhythmic potential in contrast to the English four stresses that, tending to break in the middle, develop an unpleasant regularity. For discussion of line-length and cesura in French, see Lote 1951, I, 83–116 & 213–33.

[3]I have adopted Alan Gaylord's spelling (rime, riming) as more appropriate when speaking of Chaucer.

[4]See Lote 1951, II, 111–75, for the different kinds of rime in medieval French poetry.
[5]Rime riche is a special case of what I call identicals. It involves two words that sound the same but have different meanings or grammatical functions. Identicals involve complete syllables. The single vowel as rime is thus both an identical and a rime.
[6]See Owen 1966, 555–60, where the Man of Law's couplet A321f., the Squire's identical-plus-rime A97f., single lines for Squire A92, for Friar A214 and A251, and the more complex sound patterns in the Prioress's, the Monk's, the Friar's, the Parson's, and the Summoner's portraits are discussed.
[7]Line 8, short a syllable, throws prosodic emphasis on "half cours." The Riverside edition chooses correctly, I think, the El–Hg reading in place of "halve cours" favored by most modern editors.
[8]See B 295 ff., "O firste moevyng. . . ," which recognizes the contrary movement of the unfixed stars in the zodiac. Malcolm Andrew, ed. of the Variorum Critical Commentary and Explanatory Notes to the GenProl (Chaucer 1993, Part 1B), tells me that I am the first to suggest the daily running of the "yonge sonne" as included in "his half cours."
[9]Riverside (Chaucer 1987) has "And whiche they weren" for 40, though El, En^1, and Hg lack the final -n:

> And whiche they weere and of what degree,
> And eek in what array that they weere inne . . .

I would read line 40 as having a syncopated rhythm, with "whiche" as two syllables, emphasizing its importance as substantive, and "weere" as one. Manly (1926), reads "weere" as two syllables, the pause before "and" protecting it from elision. My reading would not have a pause before "and". This is an instance where the Skeat-Robinson-Riverside reading has eliminated awareness that a question affecting prosody can be raised. I find myself remembering the Riverside reading and having to make an effort to remember that the "-n" is probably not Chaucer's.
[10]For the number of portraits Chaucer intended at different stages of his planning for the whole work, see Owen 1961 and Owen 1983. Chaucer may originally have planned as few as fourteen portraits. See also my chapter II on "The Development of the Canterbury Tales" in Owen 1977, and my essay on beginnings and endings in Owen 1992.
[11]Gaylord 1992, 87. He makes the point that a Chaucer portrait "is only partially received when it is heard . . . it needs to be read in a book . . . . Chaucer comes to write books-of-talking for the solitary reader" (90 f.).
[12]Riverside's adoption of the El reading, "in hethenesse," supported by most of the other manuscripts, seems questionable. I prefer the more colloquial (and metrical) Hg reading.
[13]Both Hg and El readings have a quadruple negative. Here the Hg "Ne nevere yet no vileynye he sayde" has the support of only Ch for beginning with "Ne."
[14]The Hg "in so litel space" has far less manuscript support than the El "of. . . ," which seems to me clearly the better reading. I also prefer the El "lovyere" earlier in line 80, not only because it has better manuscript support from non-southern scribes, but because it is the more difficult reading, more likely to have been altered by scribes.
[15]The Riverside "sleep," line 98, receives no comment, though "slepte" appears in Hg, El, and other manuscripts. "Sleep" appears in Ha^4, Cp, a, and To, each of which represents a different one of the five textual traditions Manly-Rickert and the Variorum recognize for this part of the Canterbury Tales. As the more unusual form of the past tense, it strikes me as probably the correct reading, more likely to be changed intentionally or inadvertently by a scribe. See the use of "sleep" later in the Shipman's portrait, line 396, where it is protected as rime-word.
[16]I take the reading from Hg-Ch-Ha^4, supported by a (Dd out), for line 161. The Riverside "write," adopted without comment from Skeat and the Robinson texts, has prevailed also with Fisher, but has little support in the manuscripts. Whether we retain "ther" as Manly-

Rickert do or omit it as in the Variorum, the two stresses on "first writ-" followed by the two unstressed syllables place prosodic emphasis on "a crowned A." Gaylord 1992, 89 ff., makes these final lines of the Prioress's portrait the first example of his critique of dramatic enactment as the way to experience Chaucer's poetry fully. He speaks of "this well known sequence of cunningly sprung lines, each one a kind of trigger to release many meanings, each one glancing off the others with refractory sparkle." He later uses a closer analysis of lines 132–50 to demonstrate what he means by the "'more bookish' kind of reading aloud I call 'recital'" (96). See also his "After the Forme of My Writynge: Gower's Bookish Prosody" (Gaylord 1993) for his distinction between Chaucer's and Gower's prosodies.

[17]Riverside takes line 172 as belonging with the jingling of the Monk's bridle bells, rather than the way he rules the cell. Robinson (Chaucer 1957) and Blake (Chaucer 1980) have it right in my view. The Monk is lord-keeper in the line; the point about the relative importance for him of hunting and religious observance has already been vividly made in the bell-sounds. "Ther as" makes a fresh start.

[18]Worth noting is the way the Summoner uses the "freres-preyeres" rime four times in his mocking imitation of the Friar's voice as he has his friar lecture the bed-ridden Thomas on the advantages of being associated with such a God-favored group as friars (D1863-1947). In Thomas's angry reply, his first rime-pair is "yeres-freres."

[19]"Poraille" lumps together poor people, making it possible for the Friar to distance himself from them in a single word. MED has a number of 14th-century examples, none of which has the dismissive tone of the Friar's portrait.

[20]Riverside keeps the Skeat-Robinson reading from Ellesmere, "nas," though the Hg "was" has better manuscript support. I accept here the Riverside reading, because of the "was" in both the line preceding and the one following. Line 251 is definitely a single line, shocking in its context. The negatived verb helps set it off from its neighbor lines, a typical Chaucer slanted-indirection.

[21]Skeat got "y-drawe" from Gg, used by Robinson and the Riverside without comment, though the textual evidence is overwhelmingly for "drawe."

22 Hengwrt adds an extra "his" before "drogges" that throws the meter off (a 14-syllable line with the *-n* on "senden"). Ellesmere also provides the "nas" in place of Hg's "was" and the spelling "nat" in place of "noght." The latter two may well be right in Hg. Manly & Rickert have the Ellesmere readings. We need to be aware that we are making choices in readings like these.

[23]This line has two variants with strong manuscript support. For "that" Hengwrt with the support of Ha[4] has "ther"; a with wide manuscript support omits the word. The omission is perhaps the hard reading. All three readings are possible. M-R chose the Hg reading, though one might have expected them to pick the omission.

[24]Some manuscripts (including the independent Gg and To) have "Ther nas" for the beginning of line 550. Riverside has "nas," having inherited it from Skeat and a mistaken reading of Ellesmere in Furnivall's Six-Text Print. Hg, El, and a agree on "was."

[25]Hengwrt with the support of only four manuscripts from the large general group has "ful gret grace."

[26]Hengwrt, Gg and a number of manuscripts in the large group leave out the "ne" before "hierde" in line 603.

[27]Line 660 reads "Of cursyng oghte ech gilty man drede" in almost all the manuscripts, including all the independent ones. M-R think "him" or "to" before "drede" are scribal efforts to mend the meter. Each appears in a few manuscripts of the large group. If "him," favored by some modern editors (Robinson, Pratt, and Riverside), is accepted, the rime is further augmented: "in dede. . . him drede" 659 f.

[28]As Gordon Hall Gerould pointed out (1952, 57), the "alestake" the Pardoner refers to is more likely the garland the Summoner is wearing, rather than an actual tavern, C 321. The "draughte of corny ale" C 456 and the "cake" C 322 he gets from his companion.

[29]The Pardoner's Prologue and Tale belong probably to the same period as the "marriage

group" of tales, influenced as both are by the treatise on Penitence and the Seven Deadly Sins (the Parson's Tale). See Dempster 1953. It was probably the performance as storytellers of the Pardoner and Summoner that led to Chaucer's decision to do portraits of the churls.

[30]The Retraction appended to the treatise on Penitence and the Seven Deadly Sins, which, in my view, became a part of the Canterbury Tales after Chaucer's death, is of course a longer address to the reader; hence my use of Chaucer's title for the work (as in the Retraction): The Tales of Caunterbury.

[31]Portraits for the Second Nun and the Nun's Priest are lacking. Critics like to imagine that Chaucer would not have worried about the missing portraits, or for that matter the missing tales either. Larry Benson in the Riverside Edition paraphrases his earlier conclusion (Benson 1981, 116) that "unfinished, unpolished, and incomplete as *The Canterbury Tales* may be, Chaucer is finished with it" (Chaucer 1987, 22). The evidence seems to me to point to renewed engagement and commitment. See my essay in the *Chaucer Yearbook* (Owen 1992), with references to earlier work.

[32]Riverside prints "ny" (Ellesmere) in place of "neigh" (Hengwrt) in line 732. Manuscript evidence seems to favor the Hg reading. Gg hedges with "nyh." "Ny" would be the more unusual spelling and, if what Chaucer intended, would have the advantage of having a small word represent the smallest space. Chaucer seems to have used "ny" several times in Melibeus and the Parson's Tale. Hg has "ney" in B 2568, 2562, 2566; "ny" in B 2585, 2735. El has "ny" throughout except 2558, "neigh." El has "ny" in I836. See also line 20 of the Complaint to his Purs.

[33]"Proprely" (line 729) was used in the fourteenth century with the meaning "according to proper conduct, decorously," 5b in MED (see also 6a). Examples in addition to Chaucer include the *Romance of William of Palerne* and Gower.

[34]This projection of an ending quite different from the one projected in the Parson's Prologue involves a change in the over-all plan not generally recognized. The end projected in the Parson's Prologue is for a collection of stories, not for a storytelling contest. See my essay in the *Chaucer Yearbook* (Owen 1992). Most critics view the change as a diminution, but they keep the prize-awarding dinner, as if it were compatible with the Parson's Prologue. Chaucer would have been compelled to choose between the two endings. In my view he already had. There were loose ends and contradictions in many of the fragments. Chaucer had not yet gotten around to correcting them and organizing the fragments in an ordering. He may well have had one in mind. But he had an enormous amount of writing still to do when death or a final illness put an end to his literary activities.

Howell Chickering

Comic Meter in the *Miller's Tale*[*]

Chaucer's major poems are usually read primarily for their stories and only secondarily, if at all, for their poetry. Critics in this century have rightly been fascinated by long-standing problems that arise from his methods of narration. "At all times," Stephen Knight wrote in 1973, Chaucer "has been recognized as a fine storyteller and a master of description. The remarkable thing about all these views of Chaucer is that they could be just as valid if he had written in prose: very little criticism treats him as a man working with the special methods and the special powers of the poet" (Knight 1973, vii). In 1987 Robert M. Jordan pointed out again that "interpretive criticism of *The Canterbury Tales* has tended to overlook the primacy of the medium as Chaucer's instrument of poetic expression" (Jordan 1987, 57). This situation continues today, as Derek Pearsall has pointed out with some acerbity: "Though it might easily slip one's mind, given that nine-tenths of the critical writing on Chaucer never mentions the fact, Chaucer's poetry is written in verse, and the way we read that verse and respond to its musicality, whether in our heads or when reading aloud, is presumably an important part of our reading of and response to its meaning" (Pearsall 1991, 41).

I heartily agree with Pearsall, and would go one step further: reading Chaucer's works as verse ought to be the critic's first order of business. As a poet, Chaucer necessarily thought, felt, and imagined in lines, couplets, stanzas, as well as in larger units of narrative verse. He had no other choice. As a medieval storyteller he expected to make sentences by making lines. With the exception of the *Tale of Melibee*, it was in fact the only way he told a story. It follows that this management of narrative and character is inextricably bound up with his management of his verse form. Therefore our first responses to Chaucer's text should be to its formal poetic features and to how their most immediate effects create meaning.[1] This is not a new approach to Chaucer's poetry; among Pearsall's one-tenth of criticism there have been some splendid studies that examine Chaucer's special powers as a poet.[2] My contention is only that we should be doing more such criticism, and doing it more fundamentally, in order to be better readers of his poems.

The *Miller's Tale* provides a good example. Everyone agrees that it is one of the funniest stories in the English language. But how is it funnier for being told in couplets? Would it be less funny in prose? Much has been written about its plot, characterization, imagery, diction, and rhetorical features that survive translation into modern prose–but only Jordan, to my knowledge, has directly addressed the effect of the couplets at the tale's several narrative climaxes.[3] Those are inspired moments of high bawdy to which I will return below, but there are also other ways in which Chaucer's verse form contributes to his poetic meaning. In the hands of a good poet, form is less a limitation than an energizing opportunity to make meanings that wouldn't be there in prose. Our expectation that the poet's lines will rime in couplets creates a whole new set of possible meanings. Each rime-word marks off a small segment of narration (the line), and each couplet thus puts together two narrative segments with similar final sounds. Putting the two together affects the sense of both lines in the couplet. It may make them parallel, or identical, or sharply contrasting, or simply different. One reason the *Miller's Tale* is a great poem is because Chaucer so thoroughly exploits the comic possibilities of his basic verse form. The present essay cannot be an exhaustive treatment, but I hope it will at least demonstrate that the meter and rime of Chaucer's couplets create particular comic effects that could not be gained through any other form of language, and that they are synergistic with the rest of his rich provocations to "outrageous and unquenchable" laughter (Coghill 1967, 99).

First it is worth considering why so little attention, relatively speaking, has been paid to the local effects of Chaucer's verse even though claims are continually made for his greatness as a poet. Deficiencies in our current methods of literary education might be indicted, as well as general trends and trendiness in recent criticism, but I leave animadversions on such developments to those who have traced them with the irony they deserve. (See for example Fromm 1991 and Park 1991). I think the reasons particular to Chaucer studies fall under three headings. Scholarly uncertainty about the precise nature of Chaucer's pronunciation and prosody has been a chronic affliction from the Renaissance down to this day, and while it has not kept readers and reciters from appreciating Chaucer's poetic effects, it has promoted a cautious silence about his metrics (for the various definitions of Chaucer's meter, see Mustanoja 1979 and Gaylord 1976). The second reason that critics talk so little about the effects of Chaucer's versification is probably the influence of the dominant book on the subject, Paull F. Baum's *Chaucer's Verse*, which tends, of all things, to downplay Chaucer's specifically poetic achievement:

> Chaucer was first of all a narrative poet. His main interest, and ours, is in the story and its adjuncts, the people and surroundings, which make the story something more than a bald and unconvincing narrative. The 'poetry' is therefore diffused. It is infrequently concentrated into separable parts and passages which, so to say, float the reader over level stretches and at times lift him above them. Yet all nar-

> rative poets have liked to heighten the narrative and refresh the reader, here and there, with fine things, purple inlays, which are meant frankly as embellishments. In Chaucer many of these are subdued inconspicuously to the mean level. But when he wanted something special, or one came to him as it were spontaneously, he could indulge the reader very beautifully. (Baum 1961, 80)

It is hard to improve on Alan Gaylord's tart assessment of this influential conception: "It represents a version of Chaucerian criticism which is a reaction to hypermodernism, and hence imputes merit to a poetry characterized as un-intense, uncomplex, straightforward, often plain, even careless." Baum takes Chaucer's basic line to be a series of five iambs but allows it much flexibility, and "it is this conservative sense of ease which keeps Baum's practical criticism so persuasive." Of the passage quoted above, Gaylord exclaims, "What's purple is 'poetry'; that gray stuff in between is Chaucer's 'verse.' The dichotomy strikes me as absurd if taken as a general principle, occasionally half-way accurate, quite often dead wrong" (Gaylord 1976, 33, 34, & 35). I fully agree. Chaucer the poet is more than an embellisher, just as he is more than a raconteur. But in today's academy–thanks partly to Baum, partly to a hyper-postmodernism he did not live to see–it has become easier to talk about the rhetoric of his poetry or its narrative structure than about its texture and rhythms as verse, especially if his poetic effects are regarded as usually "subdued inconspicuously to the mean level." The third factor deflecting attention from Chaucer's poetic form is his own extraordinary management of it. He is so skillful in the disposition of his lines and rimes that sometimes, even for considerable stretches of text, we can forget that we are reading poetry at all. The action, characters, and speeches seem to be set before us with the vividness of life itself. Chaucer's capacity to make his medium seem transparent may explain why Baum attended only the purple patches and saw the rest as gray. Yet, as readers have always known, Chaucer achieves an astonishing range of effects in the couplet form. (For an excellent brief account of Chaucer's use of the couplet, see Owen 1966, 555–63; for a longer treatment, Masui 1964.) If at times the effect is the almost complete subordination of the verse form to the sense of his sentences, that does not mean we should therefore ignore it. Indeed, how he accomplished that minor miracle is well worth our attention.

Definitions of Chaucer's meter can become so torturous that the practical critic recalls Saintsbury's observation with delight:

> You may call a thing an octosyllable, or an iambic dimeter, or a four-beat verse, but the *thing* is the same and unmistakable. So, too, . . . [is] the great staple metre of the *Canterbury Tales*, whether you call it "riding rhyme," or "heroic couplet," or "rhymed decasyllables," or "rhymed five-beat lines," or anything else that the wit or the perversity of man has invented or may invent. (Saintsbury 1906, I: 169)

A. C. Spearing was perhaps imprudent when he wrote that the basic line "in nearly all *The Canterbury Tales* is the same as that of Shakespeare's blank verse or Pope's heroic couplets: the iambic pentameter," but I must confess that I always use this anachronistic term myself when I explain Chaucer's versification to students.[4] Perhaps it may be allowed to stand if we do not mean by it Pope's strict decasyllabics, and if we allow for the flexibility found in the manuscripts and enacted in performance.[5] Chaucer's pentameter line normally has ten syllables but can vary from nine to eleven syllables. If we give the syllables the accents they would have in phrases of normal speech, usually five stresses will emerge when we read the line aloud with natural emphasis. Usually the rhythm is iambic, but now and then, especially at the beginning of a line, or after a mid-line pause, it may be trochaic. There may be one or more cesuras, varying in placement, or none at all, depending on the syntax and sound-texture of the line. Often an interior stress (usually the fourth but sometimes the second or third) will be quite light and may not be heard in conversational recitation. Occasionally anomalous lines do not fit these norms. This unexceptional account of Chaucer's meter is all we need to appreciate what he could do with it.

Chaucer first used couplet rimes in this meter for narrative purposes in the *Legend of Good Women*, although as Saintsbury justly points out he had already written more than a thousand couplets in the rime royal stanzas of the *Troilus*.[6] Already in the *Legend* he could build extended verse paragraphs that move through the couplets with continual syntactic variation in a "literary-colloquial register" (Gaylord 1983, 314). In this, as in his earlier octosyllabic poems, he shows his enormous capacity to adapt and transform his more enclosed and end-stopped metrical model, which in the case of the pentameter couplet was surely Machaut's decasyllabic couplet in lyric set-pieces.[7] In the diction of his French models as well as in earlier and contemporary popular English poetry, Chaucer found tag formulas and fixed rime pairs. His colloquial tags are suggestive of oral delivery ("I dar wel seyn," "there nis namor to seye"), and some of his standard rime pairs ("wif" / "lif," "sorwe" / "morwe") already had stock thematic value in earlier English verse (Crosby 1938, 421–4; and Sudo 1969).

These received conventions stayed with him throughout his career but, as Eleanor P. Hammond wrote long ago, "the medium in which Chaucer's padding formulae and expletives are carried is of so firm and flavored a quality that our attention is not diverted by them. They . . . often seem formulae only when we have disengaged them from their context" (Hammond 1927, 88). Similarly, other Middle English poets rimed often by assonance only, but Eric G. Stanley has shown that in comparison to them Chaucer is an extremely accurate rimer (Stanley 1988). He is also very resourceful and diverse, riming with equal ease on Latinate learned words ("proporcioun" / "exaltacioun" [Prologue to the *Parson's Tale*, 9–10]) and short colloquial ones ("of this" / "ywis" [*Nun's Priest's Tale*, 2767–68]). He found clanging, repetitious rimes in French[8] and assonantal rimes in English, then, and transcended both, forging a new kind of couplet while at the same time inventing the earliest version of the English iambic pentameter line. As Michio Masui remarks in the fullest study to date of Chaucer's riming practices, Chaucer may "have been the first poet [in English] to consider the rime-scheme seriously and to put his principles of riming into practice from every point of view . . . not only acoustic, but structural, semantic, and stylistic as well" (Masui 1964, 304).

Charles Owen claimed that "what we experience in Chaucer's use of the couplet is what we experience in his poetry as a whole, a freedom from system or repetitive form" (Owen 1966, 563). More recently, in ascertaining Chaucer's meter directly from the manuscripts, Derek Pearsall has noted "the freedom and generosity in the conception of the rhythmical possibilities of the pentameter, the audacity of variation and experimentation, and the subtle sense of the relation between rhetorical and syntactical impetus and rhythmical variation" that "are surely positive characteristics of the creative poet at work" (Pearsall 1987, 57 & 51). However, perhaps because Chaucer's iambic pentameter has been regarded as "almost a *de novo* creation" (Baum 1961, 11), critics have been loath to focus on Chaucer's use of the couplet, preferring instead to track what Matthew Arnold called "his divine fluidity of movement." They forget that the same Arnold who denied Chaucer "high seriousness" said in the same magisterial tone that Chaucer's fluidity was not due to his metrical liberties: "It was dependent upon his talent. Others with a like liberty do not attain the fluidity of Chaucer" ("The Study of Poetry": Arnold 1889, 31).

For the most part, critics have sailed on the tack taken by H. S. Bennett: "We shall reach no vital results . . . so long as we are content to examine his work in single lines, and to discuss his variations within the line or the couplet. We must escape from the line, as Chaucer did, and see the wider movement and the way in which sentences and paragraphs were built up" (H. Bennett 1947, 89). Here Bennett, perhaps purposely, blends his metaphor for Chaucer's verse paragraphs with the critic's own escape from the necessity for close reading. It may strike the lover of poetry as a harsh irony that Bennett, writing in the influential Oxford History of English Literature, treated Chaucer's basic expressive instrument of meter and rime as though it were unimportant. But there is plenty of warrant for Bennett's focus on the larger rhythms of the poetry, and ever since Robert O. Payne's seminal examination of Chaucer's poetics as a response to medieval rhetorical traditions, critics have concentrated with great profit on the larger rhetorical aspects of Chaucer's poetry.

One question such a focus raises is Chaucer's own attitude toward "the central belief, in rhetorical theory, that poetry is the art of clothing the already discovered truth in fitting language" (Payne 1963, 57). Like his "deere maister soverayn" Geoffrey de Vinsauf, Chaucer usually refers to his own poetic practice as turning a story into verse, and the emphasis of the medieval rhetoricians on the artificiality of composition has led some critics to insist that there is no such thing as "organic form" in Chaucer's poetry (see esp. Jordan 1967 and Brewer 1975). This is a salutary correction of a New Critical assumption that has been too often applied ahistorically, but we must not assume, because Chaucer speaks of verse as cloaking a subject or a "sentence," that he *wrote* in a manner that kept the two apart. Although theorists like Boccaccio and Geoffrey de Vinsauf regarded poetry as a garment that veils spiritual truth, the latter also treats it as a material to be molded like wax, and thus emphasizes the palpability, not the transparency, of the poetic medium.[9] Chaucer's rhetorical molding of his poetry often calls as much attention to itself as to its "message"; witness the *Nun's Priest's Tale*, where the "chaf" becomes the poem's true literary "fruyt." In his actual practice, he did more than merely pour the wine of old stories into new bottles shaped like couplets. Sometimes his verse may be only a vehicle that carries meaning as on a flatbed, "withouten doute," but on other occasions his form and meaning may be splendidly joined.

These occasions of artistic integration are not as infrequent as Baum thought, and have been praised by scholars writing about quite different aspects of Chaucer's "art poetical." For instance, Dorothy Everett, looking at the first stanza of the *Parliament of Fowls*, concluded that "the rhetorical devices used here are not, as it were, appended to the fabric of the stanza: they are themselves the fabric" ("Art Poetical": Everett 1955, 154). In her study of the imagery of the fabliaux, Janette Richardson found that "in a number of the separate tales Chaucer does reveal a unique awareness of the aesthetic whole and . . . his handling of imagery within these tales contributes significantly to the essential unity of each" (Richardson 1970, 58). Writing about Chaucer's parody in *Sir Thopas*, Alan Gaylord observed that "like all good poets, his telling is a showing: his prosody is a way-of-doing what is significant" (Gaylord 1979, 101). And Michio Masui limited his discussion of Chaucer's use of "rimes for a humorous effect" to punning rimes like "cordial" / "in special" (*General Prologue*, 443–44) because he saw the full range of Chaucer's rimes as integrated into the whole effect of his poetry's technique and meaning (Masui 1964, 283–86 & 304).

All this suggests that we can confidently approach the *Miller's Tale* expecting that its basic poetic form will contribute to its meaning. Before examining the special comic effects of Chaucer's rime and meter, I want to look briefly at their more normative contribution to narrative meaning. Any full conception of Chaucer's poetic achievement must include his creation of a conversational voice that emerges from the verse form without calling attention to that artifice. Tauno F. Mustanoja takes Chaucer's "greatness as a metrical artist" to be "the easy flexibility with which he resolves the conflict between his meter and the natural prose rhythm of living speech," while Nevill Coghill points out that his control of narrative pace in the couplet form is due to his "special skill in carrying or turning the meaning on the rhyme-word, for the rhyme-word is generally a climax in sense as it is in sound" (Mustanoja 1979, 70; and Coghill 1967, 129). These accounts of Chaucer's metrical talent emphasize the congruence between his poetic form and the contours of the speaking voice, or at least the illusion of a speaking voice.[10] Its frequent occurrence should not blind us to the fact that Chaucer made this congruence happen; it did not merely occur.

In the *Miller's Tale*, he unobtrusively melds the couplets with the cadence of the sense right from the start. I quote from the *Variorum* edition of Hengwrt, removing the modern punctuation. Since the virgules in Hengwrt are scribal and do not regularly mark cesuras, I omit them as well. This presentation of the text is thus fairly close to what a medieval reader would have faced in trying to articulate Chaucer's text, and offers salutary ear training. The sentence demarcations will be evident both from the sense and from Chaucer's use of cesuras and end-stopped lines.[11]

Whilom ther was dwellynge in Oxenford
A riche gnof that gestes heeld to bord
And of his craft he was a carpenter
With hym ther was dwellynge a poure scoler
Hadde lerned art but al his fantasie
Was turned for to leere astrologie
And koude a certeyn of conclusions
To demen by interrogacions
If that men axed hym in certein houres
Whan that men sholde have droghte or ellis shoures
Or if men axed hym what [sholde] bifalle
Of every thyng I may nat rekene hem alle

There are no prior traditional or thematic relationships between the rime-words of the first couplet, which by its easy enjambment undoes the sentence's inversion of main subject and verb. The conversational tone is enhanced by the initial trochee ("Whilom") and the very lightly (or even un-) stressed "ther was."[12] In the second line, which by contrast is fully iambic, we take in the sense of "that gestes heeld to bord" so readily that it hardly feels like an inversion for the sake of rime, and the whole line can be read without any pronounced cesura (the *Variorum* itself does not introduce a comma). Meter and sense conjoin in the third line to push the little words "And of" into iambic stress, because "of his craft" means "as to (or concerning) his occupation"; that less than exalted trade of "carpenter" then receives two stresses (the last one quite light) to complete the line and the sentence.

This "riche gnof," a stock figure from Old French fabliaux, is set against his conventional opponent, "a poure scoler," not only by their two adjectives but also by the exact metrical echo of the first line in "With hym ther was dwellynge." Chaucer might easily have put the scholar in the carpenter's house using various other phrases, but this parallelism and the repeated verb "dwellynge" firmly yoke them together as opposed forces in the coming narrative. As rimes, "carpenter" and "scoler" are a species of light rime quite common in Chaucer.[13] They meet Chaucer's rime requirement of like sounds at the end of lines, without asking us to hear the pairing of those sounds as "a climax in sense." As we will see, Chaucer can easily bring the sense of rime-sounds into high prominence when he wants to gain particular effects, but in this and the following couplet the roots of the four rime-words do all necessary narrative duty, presaging the scholar's use of "astrologie" to play upon the carpenter's "fantasie." (Here not in the sense of "fancy, desire," but as "imagination" or "delusion." See Ross in Chaucer 1983, 132–and cf. line 3835.)

The diction of the next couplet rime is Latinate and technical, with both words only recently domesticated into English.[14] "Of conclusions" and "interrogacions" fill the last three beats of each line with a mock-pompous solemnity and a loud rime on "–[s]ions." At the same time, this sonorous gesture toward the Oxford learning of the "scoler" seems to arise naturally out of the grammatical deployment of these two phrase-objects in a sentence that eventually extends to nine lines, winding its way through the next two "if" clauses with the ambling grace of confident exposition. The first "If that" takes a spoken trochaic stress, then two lines later "Or if" introduces the repeated "men asked hym" with an equally natural iamb: the contours of the metrical emphasis exactly follow the easy contemplation of the giddily widening possibilities of Nicholas's predictions. The contrast in dictional levels between "interrogacions" and "asked" also points to the intellectual levels of Nicholas and John–the funnier because in context it seems that "interrogacions" has some special astrological meaning but, so far as we know, it did not (Chaucer 1983, 133). Perhaps Chaucer also already had "Nowelys flood" in mind when he rimed "shoures" with "houres" in the next couplet, since he uses the rime of "hour" / "shour" again at lines 3519–20 when Nicholas first tells John about "Noes flood."[15]

Certainly the metrical and dictional doublings of the "ther was dwellynge" and "if men axed hym" clauses (3187–90 and 3195–97), despite their air of casual elaboration, are not chance alignments. A few lines ahead at "Allone withouten any compaignye" (3204) Chaucer deliberately recalls and parodies Arcite's line from the *Knight's Tale*, in one of what Alcuin Blamires has aptly called his "narrative resonances" (Blamires 1987, 64–69). We ought to expect that such vibrations of meaning will be found in his poetic texture as well as in his thematic and narrational echoes. This opening passage comes to an end with a fine colloquial flourish that may have a further resonance of its own. Coghill's observation about "turning the meaning on the rime-word" applies well to "what sholde bifalle" when it is matched with "I may nat rekene hem alle" and we think ahead to the series of completely unexpected events that will conclude the tale. The heavy cesura of the last line acts as a full stop, allowing Chaucer to utter a short new sentence that completes the sense of the verse-paragraph. Perhaps it is not too fanciful to suggest that in the rhythms of the enjambed and rapid "what sholde bifalle/ Of every thing," and then the narrator's curt dismissive comment, we can hear the germ of John's later anxious gabbling and Nicholas's peremptory replies.

This should suffice to show not only that the tale's opening exposition is much enhanced by Chaucer's unobtrusive "natural" use of his poetic form, but also that what Mustanoja calls the "easy flexibility" of his meter is conjoint with his long-range narrative purposes. (Knight also analyzes the opening sentence briefly, and points to Chaucer's rhythmic variety within the "straightforward narrative" of lines 3307–11 [Knight 1973, 31 and 33].) Right after this quiet beginning, other poetic effects begin to ring more strongly in our ears. They illustrate the range of Chaucer's typical manipulations of rime and meter in the tale. Some are broad, some subtle.

> This clerk was clepyd hende Nicholas
> Of derne love he koude and of solas
> And therto he was sleigh and full privee
> And lyk a mayde[n] meke for to see

As his diction does more generally, some of Chaucer's rimes enhance his characterizations, serving as cues or commentary, happy grace-notes played against the broader melody of the plot. Much has been written about the poem's diction, particularly the epithet "hende" for Nicholas, which begins here as a parodic use of a worn-out courtly term meaning "courteous, gracious, gentle," and then takes on all its other possible meanings in subsequent situations: "pleasant," "clever," "dexterous," "handy," with the last having a lewd application in line 3276. Often several meanings are present at once, as in the final scene, where it means both "near at hand" and "clever," with disastrous results (See Beichner 1960; E.T. Donaldson 1970; Stillwell 1955; and Chaucer 1983, 133–34). Chaucer conducts similar comic explorations of semantic fields in his epithets of "sely carpenter" for John and "joly" or "jolif" for Absolon.[16] They make a sort of teasing game that he plays with his readers, where we are invited to guess which meanings will be appropriate in which context, and thus pay close attention to possible nuances. This poet's word game so well suits the storyteller's aims that Paul Beichner could write of the "high organic unity" of the poem, in which Chaucer "has made it appear that the plot was created for the [characters], and not that they were created for the sake of the fabliau plot" (Beichner 1960, 127).

What I will call Chaucer's epithetic rimes operate in much the same way. "Nicholas" is almost always rimed with either "solas" as here, or with "cas" or "allas," while "Absolon" is rimed repeatedly with "anon" and "wo bigon." All these rime words anticipate or refer to some aspect of the plot. Upon rereading the poem, they gain the delicious flavor of anticipated comedy as we savor Chaucer's "exquisite preparation" for the action through his word choices (the quoted phrase is from *Chaucer's Bawdy*: Ross 1972, 172, concerning "Goddes pryvetee"[3164]). Like the epithetic adjectives, they also help fix the characters' traits in our minds, so that their stock attributes seem specific to the action of this one story. All three of the male characters eventually have occasion to say "allas" as the result of Nicholas's tricks. He sets up an elaborate "cas" but one that he cannot see the end of ("He saugh nat that," as John says of the clerk who fell in the marl-pit [3461]). The "solas" of "derne love" that he has his mind and hands on from the outset finally comes to pass in the "busynesse of myrthe and [of] solas" at line 3654, whereas Absolon's "solas" (3335) is never anything more than brewhouse entertainment. Absolon is first "wo bigon" in his love-longing for Alisoun (3372, 3658) and then more truly woebegone in the denouement. And all the twists of the plot that involve the humiliation and revenge of Absolon happen "anon."

Chaucer had used thematic rime-pairs before in *Troilus*, particularly "Troye"/"joie" (31 times!), "routhe"/"trouthe," "serve"/"disserve," and "mente"/"entente," as well as "name"/"fame" in *The House of Fame* (Masui 1964, 278–83; Sudo 1969; Stokes 1980; and Windeatt 1992 , 358–9). While he did not invent the device (he found "Troie"/"joie" and "nature"/"creature" ready-made in French poetry), nonetheless in *Troilus* he deployed his leitmotif rime-pairs so as to bring out an "ironic and poignant" resonance which, as Barry Windeatt says, allows the reader to explore the relation between the rimed terms "in a way that contributes to the poem's analysis of love and the lovers" (pp. 358–59). This was an enormously creative use of traditional materials, and we should not be surprised to see him putting the same technique to comic purposes. His thematic riming of course derives from traditional collocations, as Ruth Crosby showed long ago (Crosby 1938, 421–24). Shortly after this passage we see rimes that point up the underlying stereotyped ideas about marriage that make the story go:

This carpenter hadde wedded newe a wyf
3222 Which that he lovede more than his lyf

3225 For she was wilde and yong and he was old
And derned hymself been lyk a cokewold

Men sholde wedden after hir estaat
3230 For youthe and elde is often at debaat

This sort of riming sounds like folk wisdom and helps account for our sense that the story is an earthy proverb come to life. Like Chaucer's other dictional choices, it also can have metaphorical or commentative force. The conventional "wyf"/"lyf" rime is a good example. Five of the six times "wyf" appears in the tale in final position it is rimed with "lyf" and the rime-pair is spoken by the poet, Nicholas, John, and Alisoun, all in remarks that point up the character of anxious old John, for whom Alisoun is life itself, or else that redound upon Alisoun's almost edible sexual desirability. In the *Canterbury Tales* generally a wife may be the jewel in a man's life or the thorn, depending always on context, and Chaucer used the rime-pair so frequently that he surely meant it to have thematic significance, asking us to explore the variable (and often ironic) relationship between the rimed terms in different stories.[17]

Chaucer seems to have renovated every conventional device or technique that he used in the *Miller's Tale*. Even the alliterative cliché of the simile "And lyk a mayde[n] meke for to see" has an ironic point–Nicholas is no meek maiden when he starts to "pleye" with Alisoun–and it takes on a further twist if we are willing to see hints of a parody of the Annunciation in the portrait of this clerk who sings "Angelus ad virginem" (see Rowland 1970). But Chaucer could also get much broader effects when fitting similes into couplets, as we see in the tour de force of his *effictio* of Alisoun (3233–70: for the rich critical response, see Chaucer 1983, 142–52). After a much enjambed beginning and a focus on her clothing worthy of any portrait in the *General Prologue*, he introduces a veritable fusillade of similes as the description draws toward its close:

3255 Ful brighter was the shynyng of hir hewe
Than in the Tour the noble yforged newe
But of hir soong it was as loude and yerne
As any swalwe sittyng on a berne
Therto she koude skippe and make game
3260 As any kyde or calf folwynge his dame
Hir mouth was sweete as bragot or the meeth

Or hoord of apples leyd in hey or heeth
Wynsynge she was as is a ioly colt
Loong as a mast and uprighte as a bolt
A brooch she baar upon hir loue coler
As brood as is the boos of a bokeler

Here are no less than eight similes in six closed couplets, each ending a sentence with its second rime, a feature which is even more obvious to the ear without modern punctuation (Knight 1973, 32 also notes the congruence between Chaucer's rime and syntax here). This is not an unusual way for Chaucer to frame similes (witness *Knight's Tale*, 1655–56), but it is his practice to be more expansive, as in *Knight's Tale*, 1638–48 or *Parliament of Fowls*, 442–45, and nowhere else does he line up so many in such short compass. Here Alisoun's hue is like a new coin (and "for she was of towne," Absolon later "profred meede" [3380]); her song (to be compared to the two clerks') as lively as a sparrow's, a symbol of lechery; her skipping like a young calf's; her mouth like mead or apples; her skittishness like a colt's (cf. line 3282 and the Wife of Bath's "coltes toothe," D 602); her height like a mast; her posture straight as an arrow; her brooch the size of a shield-boss. This train of comparisons is an incongruous mixture of positive, neutral, and negative traits comparable to Chaucer's technique of disarranging ready judgments in the *General Prologue* portraits (see Mann 1973, 190–201). But here at first the similes command our attention more than the attributes they express. It is easier to envision a newly minted "noble" than "the shynyng of hir hewe," and easier to imagine a swallow's song than to know what Alisoun might sing. We see a kid or calf gamboling, not Alisoun dancing. Then the balance between the two sides of the comparisons stabilizes as the list goes on. Her mouth is compared to three country edibles, and we know equally the sweetness of kisses and apples. We see her large brooch as though it were in fact a boss. The overall effect, as in the *effictio* as a whole, is to make Alisoun seem part of the rustic environment she is compared to, and to align her human lasciviousness with the natural animal activities of the barnyard.

By casting these comparisons in closed couplets, Chaucer uses the properties of his form to give further artistic order to his similes. As Coghill noted, each rime can be a small climax in sense as well as sound. The first and second rimes of each couplet establish, and then meet, the expectation of a significant repeated sound. The first lines of all but the "colt" / "bolt" pair are run-on in their sense; their syntax reaches beyond the line-end while still asking for a slight pause on the rime-word so that we can register the sound that will be matched when the couplet (and sentence) closes. This formal shaping of these similes gives them an apothegmatic quality; as with Pope's couplets, we admire the trim way they are said as much as their humorous sense.[18] Chaucer's care in making these rimes calls further attention to the interrelatedness of his poetic language throughout the poem: "yforged newe" connects lexically with Absolon's trip later on to the forge of Gervase, and the "kyde or calf folwynge his dame" presages his crooning to Alisoun that "I moorne as dooth a lamb after the tete" (3704). This flourish of similes in the *effictio*, then, draws attention to itself in several ways, allowing us to call to mind other areas of the poem with an aesthetic joy that is more than mere happy anticipation, and sensitizing us to every sort of word choice the poet makes (how deliciously expressive of Absolon's squeamishness is the later rime "rubible"/"quynyble" [3331–32]). As we will see, the couplet form also helps stabilize and energize the turns of the narrative, making them feel both more surprising and more inevitably right.

The lewd parody of courtly wooing that follows is wildly silly, and especially hilarious in the pacing of its action, but how is it funnier for being in meter and rime?

> Now sire and eft sire so bifel the cas
> That on a day this hende Nicholas
> Fil with this yonge wyf to rage and pleye
> Whil that hir housbonde was at Osneye
> clerkes been ful subtil and ful queynte
> And pryvely he caughte hire by the queynte
> And seyde ywis but if ich have my wille
> For derne love of thee lemman I spille
> And heeld hire harde by the haunche bones
> And seyde lemman love me al atones
> Or I wol dyen al so God me save
> And she sproong as a colt dooth in the trave
> And with hir heed she wryed faste awey
> She seyde I wol nat kisse thee by my fey
> W[h]y lat be quod ich lat be Nicholas
> Or I wol crye out harrow and allas
> Do wey youre handes for youre curteisye
> This Nicholas gan mercy for to crye
> And spak so faire and profred hym so faste
> That she hir love hym graunted atte laste
> And swoor hir ooth by Seint Thomas of Kent
> That she wolde been at his comaundement
> Whan that she may hir leyser wel espie
> Myn housbonde is so ful of ialousie
> That but ye waite wel and been pryvee
> I woot right wel I nam but deed quod she
> Ye moste been ful derne as in this cas
> Nay therof care thee noght quod Nicholas
> A clerc hadde lutherly biset his while
> But if he koude a carpenter bigyle
> And thus they been acorded and ysworn
> To waite a tyme as I have told biforn
> Whan Nicholas hadde doon thus everydel
> And thakked hire upon the lendes wel
> He kiste hir sweete and taketh his sautrye
> And pleyeth faste and maketh melodie

Unpunctuated, the first line of this passage demonstrates how playable Chaucer's meter is when it comes to our hearing cesuras, even in such a free-wheeling colloquial address to the pilgrim audience. The *Variorum* edition places only one comma after the second "sire," while *The Riverside Chaucer* sprinkles four commas amid the first five words. The single-pause rendition sounds like the Miller trying to get the attention of only one of his betters (the Knight?) by repeating his title of address, whereas performing the line with a triple pause before the main cesura gives an elaborately heavy emphasis to the Miller's attempt to engage the "gentils" in his lewd harlotry. In its most expanded paraphrase it might run, "Now then, you sir here, and again, you sir over there." Neither scansion has medieval authority, and neither is wrong. We may choose whichever better suits our view of the poem. It is a characteristic of Chaucer's art to engage the reader actively in the constructive work of bringing the text to dramatic life, even in such small metrical details. To a degree, this is a kind of "undecidability," but undecidable among only a limited number of options; we can't, for instance, make the epithetic rime of "cas" end-stopped, but must enjamb both it and "Nicholas" as the sentence rolls "prively" toward his "hende" gesture.

The subsequent rimes act like the key words in a series of punch-lines. Who could divine that Chaucer would rime the cleverness of clerks with the very same word in a lewd pun?[19] According to Freud's model of jokes, when suppressed "dirty" material pops into consciousness unexpectedly, we laugh because libidinal energy is suddenly released (Freud 1963). The model has its limitations, but it holds true for the several other lewd rimes quoted below. Clearly, the reader's expectation that Chaucer's couplets will rime contributes to the surprise of his wordplay. The *rime riche* upon "queynte" is even funnier, of course, because the device was a much-admired grace of French courtly poetry. The next two rimes are comic in different ways. Courtly lovers "spille" or "die" for their ladies after long love-suffering, but Nicholas will expire unless he has his "wille" "al atones." Middle English "spille" does not have the double meaning of Renaissance "die," but since it also means spilling something, it takes on the *double entendre* of "ejaculate" from its context. In the next couplet the quick alliterations on "h" and "l" and the use of the low word "lemman," instead of "lady deere" or at least "swete herte," add to the tincture of silliness heard in the snappy "haunchebones" / "al atones." Not only is the gesture funny in itself but the two-word second rime spills out of Nicholas's mouth with absurd rapidity.[20]

When Alisoun springs "as a colt dooth in the trave" we make several comic connections. The simile reminds us that she is as "wynsynge" as a colt (3263) and gives a very exact visual image of a horse suddenly bucking in a shoeing frame. But the couplet also closes just as Nicholas finishes speaking (presumably he still has hold of her), and her startled animal response is thus linked to his blasphemous asseveration. She turns away "hir heed," but not her body, and the heavy cesural emphasis on "heed" almost gives her response a flirtatious quality, as indeed does "I wol nat kisse thee," where sense and rhythm make "kisse" the most heavily stressed word. He has her by the crotch, and her response is to say that she will not kiss him. This version of the "olde daunce" begins to look like a medieval *lambada.*

In the next two lines, again rimed epithetically on "Nicholas," each stressed word offers a possibility of richly theatrical posturing. Every reader must become an actor here, choosing among various possibilities that will link the stressed words into articulated lines. We can see this in the quite different treatments of the couplet in the *Variorum* and *The Riverside Chaucer*. The *Variorum* (Chaucer 1983) follows Hengwrt and Ellesmere MSS. in reading "ich" in line 3285 and punctuates thus:

> "Wy, lat be, quod ich! Lat be, Nicholas,
> Or I wol crye, 'Out, harrow, and allas!'"

The Riverside Chaucer (Chaucer 1987) emends "ich" to "she" and turns Alisoun's proposed three-word scream into two separate cries:

> "Why, lat be!" quod she. "Lat be, Nicholas,
> Or I wol crie 'out, harrow' and 'allas'!"

These two versions have quite different qualities of tone and nuance, though their general sense is the same. Thomas Ross, the editor of the *Variorum*, feels that the manuscript reading "ich" intensifies Alisoun's protest, but his punctuation is confusing ("lat be,–quod ich, lat be!" would better suit his view) and Manly and Rickert point out that "ich" and "sche" are easily confused in Middle English orthography (Chaucer 1983, 157). I think I prefer the emended "quod she" which not only keeps the telling of the tale in view, but also calls into question exactly how sincerely she means "lat be"; the distancing effect of the speaker's cue intensifies her mock-modesty. Ross's version of her threat, however, seems to me funnier than *The Riverside Chaucer*'s, which basically has her warning Nicholas, "First I will say one thing, and then I will say another thing," whereas Ross has her naively linking her outcries together with an "and" even while she would utter them. These two lines, then, are playable in the extreme when done aloud, and the stressed words can be given a variety of comic emphases. One must choose to articulate only one option in performance, but we can entertain the whole range of possibilities in our minds when reading silently, which enriches our appreciation of an already hilarious moment.

The final line of Alisoun's speech is wonderfully ludicrous. "Take your hands off my private parts," she says in effect. A strong cesura follows, and then she gives her compelling reason: "for youre curteisye," as though Nicholas had approached her courteously in the first place. We might also consider what would be lost if the gist of this line were to be said in other words, such as "Tak of youre handes," instead of "Do wey." Chaucer's "wey" echoes both the sound and sense of "wryed faste awey," a pleasing intensification, while at the same time we hear it echo the rime-word "fey." If the *Miller's Tale* is in one sense a blasphemous parody or religious burlesque, as various critics hold, then this echo of Alisoun's conventionally pious "fey," and her capitulation to Nicholas moments later, both suggest that her faith, like Nicholas's, is only in salvation by sex. This is confirmed by Chaucer's choice of sound-texture when the diphthong of "awey"–"fey"–"wey" reappears as a rime-sound at the beginning of the next narrative segment, lines 3307–11, when Alisoun goes "on an hali*day*" to the parish church, her forehead washed till it is "bright as any *day*." There she will work "Cristes owene werkes"–clearly ironic, since she gives Absolon a bad case of "love longynge." Even in the most minute choice, of "do wey" over "tak of" for instance, we can see Chaucer's rimes, texture, and sense all working together artistically.

Against her call to "curteisye" Nicholas "gan mercy for to crye," in a couplet that links two different actions together. Quite frequently Chaucer uses the couplet this way when switching speakers or topics; we see it again in the next "cas" /"Nicholas" rime, and it plays an important part in the denouement, where it is put to special ends.[21] It only takes one more couplet for Nicholas to press his case successfully, a piece of comic timing funny in itself which Chaucer improves on by using the tired courtly cliché of "she hir love hym graunted atte laste." The "so faste" / "atte laste" rime firmly guides the pace of the comic action, and in "profred hym" perhaps we may also see Nicholas pressing not only his courtly suit, but his physical self upon her. Presumably they are holding this conversation while he is still holding on to her, since we are not told he ever took his hands away for courtesy, and he has yet to "thakke" her "upon the lendes wel." What Chaucer has done in fashioning such lines is not only swiftly sketch a ribald scene with the raucous emphases of a burlesquehouse comedian; at the same time, he has found a way to express the theme of the sacred vs. the profane, to conduct a critique of social pretensions and shopworn literary language, and to leave much unsaid about the action while stimulating the reader's comic imaginings of it. In addition, his language is of a piece with the whole poem: the loaded thematic words "privee" and "derne" found throughout the poem occur here as Alisoun warns Nicholas of her husband's jealousy. To create all these effects in so short a space can only be the work of a poet, not a teller of funny stories.

There may be a larger point here as well. Chaucer's passing dictional joke about Alisoun's agreeing to be at Nicholas's "comaundement"–scarcely an adherence to the Ten Commandments–is connected by its rime to Thomas à Becket, to whose shrine the pilgrims are journeying in the frame-tale. While it may be especially appropriate for Alisoun to swear by a saint locally revered in Oseney (Chaucer 1983, 158), the phrase "Seint Thomas of Kent" also has the commentative or meta-narrative effect of lifting us momentarily out of the sharply focused world of the tale, to make whatever ironic comparison we will between the two levels of narrative. Chaucer does this more than once in the course of the Canterbury Tales, often by creating "narrative resonances" between tales, and I think a good reading of any one tale will try to attend to his characteristic effect of inviting comparison by juxtaposition. Riming itself, by its nature, offers a similar invitation at a technical level, and when Chaucer's use of rime itself becomes like meta-narrative, it can tell us something more general about the poet's view of the unending and unstable joys of comparison.

But not every rime in even so artful a poem as the *Miller's Tale* will sustain the weight of such speculations. I make no aesthetic case for the choice of "everydel" at line 3303, for instance. It can't be true that Nicholas "had thus done everything" that he wanted to, or there would be no need to dupe carpenter John. By this quite vague rime-word Chaucer is only preparing for the wonderfully patronizing and expectant gesture of the next line, "And thakked hire upon the lendes wel." This is "riding rime" slowing to a walk, but it picks up immediately in the next couplet, where Chaucer saw his chance to lay four nearly parallel verbs into two lines in order to reinforce narrative closure, while at the same time foregrounding the theme of sexual melody (ironically set against the rime-word "sawtrye"),[22] as well as making the rhythm of the couplet dramatically embody its sense. Like Nicholas's crying mercy in lines 3288–89, we may hear the polysyndeton of the "And" clauses with or without cesuras, but I think that to run them on rapidly while reading either passage aloud would be to lose the sense of Nicholas's excited sexual anticipation. I imagine that Chaucer hoped his readers would play both passages with heavy cesuras for their full dramatic effect.

Chaucer's metrical effects, after all, are intended to make use of the reader's expectation of regularity, against which we can hear variations. John Hollander points out that "actual lines of iambic pentameter, because they can't simply repeat identical pairs of syllables, have individual and particular rhythms which depart from the metrical pattern slightly. It is in this variation that the sound of poetry lives" (Hollander 1989, 6). For example, at lines 3747–48 in the denouement two quite regular iambic pentameter lines occur as a couplet. They are as close to identical in their stress-patterns as is possible, but the difference in their rhythm is pronounced and in a sense inexorable:

> Who rubbeth now who froteth now his lippes
> 3748 With dust with sond with straw with clooth with chippes

The rhythm of the first line perfectly expresses Absolon's agony of humiliation by its repetition of the two synonymous verbs held suspended in the moment by the open vowel of "now" in the second and fourth stresses. The next line releases all that pent-up energy, obsessively using the "with" construction over and over for all five iambs in the line. Absolon is so desperate to scrub off his humiliation, he will use all the substances he can find, and ends with the incongruous "chippes," riming (as well as scrubbing) against "lippes." This is high metrical comedy. It fits Absolon's prior characterization perfectly, and has been long prepared for. In fact, one could write (and I hope someone will) another whole article about the poetic means by which Absolon is characterized.

Let us look more closely at the denouement to see how the couplet form helps Chaucer shape his narrative. There, at the very top of his form, Chaucer engages in creative activity that is quintessentially *playful*, producing a rich variety of comic effects that utilize all aspects of his art. Even though my account will focus only on his meter and rime, through them we can see that his playfulness conduces to what can only be called our aesthetic bliss, even, or especially, in the passages that contain the broadest humor in the poem. As E.M.W. Tillyard said some fifty years ago, in the finale Chaucer "gets beyond the social bounds of comedy and impels the reader's mind to exult and to expand as it does in enjoying the very greatest art" (Tillyard 1934, 92).

This Absolon doun sette hym on his knees
And seyde I am a lord at alle degrees
For after this I hope ther cometh moore
Lemman thy grace and swete bryd thyn oore
The wyndow she undooth and that in haste
Have do quod she com of and speed thee faste
Lest that oure neghebores thee espye
This Absolon gan wipe his mouth ful drye
Derk was the nyght as pych or as the cole
And at the wyndow out she putte hir hole
And Absolon hym fil no bet ne wers
But with his mouth he kiste hir naked ers
Ful savourly er he were war of this
Abak he sterte and thoghte it was amys
For wel he wiste a womman hath no berd
He felte a thyng al rogh and longe yherd
And seyde fy allas what have I do
Te hee quod she and clapte the wyndow to
And Absolon gooth forth a sory paas
A berd a berd quod hende Nicholas
By Goddes corpus this gooth faire and wel
This sely Absolon herde every del
And on his lippe he gan for anger byte
And to hymself he seyde I shal thee quyte
Who rubbeth now who froteth now his lippes
With dust with sond with straw with clooth with chippes
But Absolon that seith ful ofte allas
My soule bitake [I] unto Sathanas
But me were levere than al this town quod he
Of this despit awreken for to be
Allas quod he allas I ne hadde ybleynt
His hote love was coold and al yqueynt
For fro that tyme that he hadde kist hir ers
Of paramours he sette noght a kers
For he was heelyd of his maladye
Ful ofte paramours he gan defye
And weep as dooth a child that is ybete

Poor Absolon. In line 3730 the complete thought just fills the five stresses of the end-stopped line:

This Absolon gan wipe his mouth ful drye

The anticipation expressed by the pause at the line-end is heightened by the rime-word "drye." Absolon is, as we know, "somdel squaymous / Of fartyng" and certainly doesn't want to drool on his "sweete bryd" at their very first romantic kiss. Right after this, Chaucer deploys his cesuras so as to build up comic anticipation to an almost unbearable pitch. The narrative idea of the sentence beginning "Derk was the nyght" stretches across not one but five lines, and Chaucer has arranged the sentence phrases so they fit exactly into the half-lines created by the heavy cesuras in the first and third lines. The cesura of the second line is very light; we're not sure if we should read "out" with "wyndow" or with "she," and so we don't pause long in the middle of the line. There is thus a delicious metrical delay even as the sentence moves forward:

Derk was the nyght as pych or as the cole
And at the wyndow out she putte hir hole
3733 And Absolon hym fil no bet ne wers . . . .

Chaucer keeps all these lines end-stopped until he gets to his climactic rime-word, "ers," which is also the key word at this first of several narrative climaxes, and at that point he makes the line run right on to the cesura in the next line:

But with his mouth he kiste hir naked ers
3735 Ful savourly er he were war of this

Even while we hear "ers" completing the rime, the line rushes right over its final word, not stopping until it lands on "ful savourly." The meter thus gives a double emphasis to the single comic event. It is all the funnier because "squaymous" Absolon with his dry lips has given Alisoun a hearty kiss on the nether parts, and it happens in a poetic form that emphasizes the suddenness of the act while also lingering on the telling of it. Chaucer can only obtain this double effect by writing in verse.

What is even funnier is that it has already happened and Absolon isn't even aware of it: "er he were war of this." The completion of the sentence with "of this" requires Chaucer to continue with another rime, allowing him to add climax to comic climax. Notice more particularly exactly the way in which Absolon still isn't fully aware of what has happened, although Chaucer and his readers already know:

Abak he sterte and thoghte it was amys
3737 For wel he wiste a wormman hath no berd
He felte a thyng al rogh and longe yherd
And seyde fy allas what have I do

These four lines are all end-stopped. They are four segments of one comic idea–Absolon's realization of what he has done–and each could be a complete sentence in itself. When Chaucer thought of the sense of these four lines, he knew he would have to rime the middle two as a couplet, and he had to decide which of those two lines to put first. He could have reversed them and still have made perfect sense within the demands of his poetic form (for a discussion of coordinate parataxis in the poem, see Jambeck 1975). Then they would sound something like this:

> Abak he sterte and thoghte it was amys
> He felte a thyng al rogh and longe yherd
> [And] wel he wiste a womman hath no berd
> [He] seyde fy allas what have I do

This version is not as good, however. What has been lost is Chaucer's understanding of his character at this point, and his genius in conveying that understanding to us subtly, even within these broad comic strokes. He knows that, for an Absolon, one's physical sensations and one's thoughts about them don't really fit together. Absolon thinks he's a great "paramour," and he is anything but. So Chaucer stays inside Absolon's "thoghte" for the first line, as the character struggles to fit idea and reality together: "Well, I kissed her lips, but women don't have beards–what on *earth* can be going on?" Then, once we see the concrete image of "berd" at the line-end, we can immediately think of how the pubic triangle is shaped like a beard. Then, and only then, does Chaucer give the sensory details of what that beard feels like when Absolon kisses it. Not only does this order of the two lines make Alisoun's "berd" more real to our senses, it also keeps us focused on exactly how–with a long double-take–Absolon comes to realize what he has kissed. That is why the order of lines as Chaucer wrote them is funnier than my more logical and sequential rearrangement.

Another major poetic effect in this passage is Chaucer's use of the couplet to link one discrete sentence or event to the next. As noted earlier, elsewhere Chaucer frequently uses couplets for narrative linkage, and Kaluza's "rime-breaking" seems quite the wrong term for this shaping device, though he defines it much as I do.[23] I would prefer to call them simply "linking couplets." If we look back at the rime-pairs "espye" / "drye," "do" / "to," and "paas" / "Nicholas," we see Chaucer yoking together parts of his narrative that, as Robert Jordan puts it, want to fly apart (Jordan 1967, 195). Marvelously unexpected incongruities are being forced together by the couplet form:

> And Absolon gooth forth a sory paas
> A berd a berd quod hende Nicholas

By "a berd" Nicholas means of course "a joke," but to us the word also signifies the lower "berd" that so puzzled Absolon in his ruminations just prior, which Nicholas doesn't know about. Our readerly perception of this extra meaning, and of this discrepancy, is an extra pleasure due to Chaucer's wordplay in part, but it also derives from the couplet yoking the two different narrative segments together.

This comic violence of form, if I may call it that, is one of the ways in which Chaucer poetically creates the effect of ever-mounting comedy, of piling climax upon climax, joke upon joke. I am not alone in thinking that one of the funniest rimes in the entire poem is not on "ers" or "fart" or "queynte," but on those two little words "do" and "to":[24]

> And seyde fy allas what have I do
> Te hee quod she and clapte the wyndow to

That rime, clapped shut itself by the poet's own wonderfully exuberant energy, expresses everything about Absolon, and about Alisoun's view of him. The couplet puts the nether kiss in a frame of reference that implies all of their elaborate characterizations in the first part of the tale. And, while the comedy of character is perhaps always the richest source of humor, it is also worth pointing out that this couplet itself not only contains its formal rime "do"/"to," but also the internal rimes "Fy,"/"I," "Te hee"/"she," and "al*las*"/"c*la*pte" (Knight 1973, 35, also points to this line but notes only "Te hee"/"she" as an internal rime). It is a rich moment of comedy made richer by its extravagant texture of sound.

This linking of disparate narrative elements by couplets goes hand in hand with a narrowed focus on the present action, and abrupt shifts of viewpoint. As Jordan has so well put it, several times we are moved from one side of the shot-window to the other, without syntactic links but within the couplets (Jordan 1967, 193–96). This is a powerful use of the couplet as a narrative device. It reaches its acme at the end of the tale, and is accompanied by the poetic explosions of a number of loaded words that Chaucer has built into earlier parts of the poem. We already know that "kisse" is loaded, since it has played a crucial part in the comedy thus far, but upon a first reading of the tale we have no inkling that Nicholas will want to get into the act as well. Chaucer drafts him into service with an insouciant air. What could be more natural than that he has to perform a natural function? But when Chaucer places hende Nicholas against Absolon's pretended desire to kiss Alisoun a second time, his offer of a bribe, and that red-hot coulter in his hands, we suddenly have, within the limited and highly artificial space of one couplet, the very strongest kind of comic narrative expectation:

> This wol I yeven thee if thow me kisse
> 3798 This Nicholas was risen for to pisse

We don't expect this narrative development at all, enhanced as Jordan points out by the complete semantic contrast between "kisse" and "pisse," and we are doubly delighted.

> This Nicholas was risen for to pisse
> And thoghte he wolde amenden al the iape
> 3800 He sholde kisse his ers er that he scape

And up the wyndow did he hastely
And out his ers he putteth pryvely
Over the buttok to the haunche bon
And therwith spake this clerk this Absolon
Speke swete [bryd] I noot noght wher thow art
This Nicholas anoon leet fle a fart
As greet as it hadde been a thonder dent
That with the strook he was almoost yblent
And he was redy with his iren hoot
And Nicholas [amydde] the ers he smoot
Of gooth the skyn an handbrede aboute
The hoot cultour brende so his toute
That for the smert he wende for to dye
As he were wood for wo he gan to crye
Help water water help for Goddes herte
This carpenter out of his slomber sterte
And herde oon cryen water as he were wood
And thoghte allas now cometh Nowelys flood
He sette hym up withoute wordes mo
And with his ax he smoot the corde atwo
And down gooth al he foond neither to selle
Ne breed ne ale til he cam to the celle
Upon the floor and there aswowne he lay[25]

Notice that line 3800 has six stresses: "He shóldë kíssë hís érs | ér that he scápë" (to fail to hear a spondee before the cesura would be to miss the plain emphasis of the sense), while the next three lines, though each has ten syllables, scan rapidly with only four audible stresses each ("-ly" won't take full stress). This tucking-in of the accents squeezes the sense, as though one held it in one's fist, only to release it again into full pentameter in the next two couplets:

He sholde kisse his ers er that he scape
And up the wyndow did he hastely
And out his ers he putteth pryvely
Over the buttok to the haunche bon
And therwith spake this clerk this Absolon
Speke swete [bryd] I noot noght wher thow art
This Nicholas anoon leet fle a fart
As greet as it hadde been a thonder dent
That with the strook he was almoost yblent

The last two couplets (3805–8) contain several sorts of explosions. In "swete bryd," we hear an echo of line 3726, "Lemman thy grace and swete bryd thyn oore," and we might even imagine that we can hear an unsaid "swete berd" as well. As for "I noot noght wher thou art," Nicholas gets quite exactly located by the rime-word "fart," while on the other side of the window stands poor Absolon who earlier on was "squaymous / Of fartyng."[26] The poetic explosion of meaning in the next couplet is synesthetic: Chaucer mixes three physical senses together to create an epic breaking of wind, the equivalent of a thunderbolt from the hands of Zeus, perhaps even the last trump of the Apocalypse, something of such astounding violence that it can only be answered by Absolon branding Nicholas right smack on the rear. In "yblent" (3808) we can hear an echo of "ybleynt" in the earlier couplet at lines 3753–54, in which the pun on "queynte" was part of the idea of hot love being cooled with water:

> Allas quod he allas I ne hadde ybleynt ("turned away")
> His hote love was coold and al yqueynt ("quenched")

What we won't remember, though, is that John the carpenter is sleeping in his tub, up in the rafters nearby. Chaucer uses another linking couplet:

> Help water water help for Goddes herte
> This carpenter out of his slomber sterte

Chaucer chose "herte" instead of his much more usual "sake" because he was thinking ahead to "sterte," as he did in *Knight's Tale*, 951–52; probably he also wanted to recall the sound of that very painful "smert" in line 3813. Everybody knows that the *Miller's Tale* has two story-lines in it, but because of what Tillyard called the "obliquity" of its plot and what folklorists call its "suspended plot-element," no one remembers the carpenter when reading this part of it for the first time, or even upon repeated rereadings.[27] The intensity of Chaucer's focus on the sexual and scatological material, and on the humiliation and revenge of Absolon, makes us completely forget old John. Yet the moment has been elaborately prepared for, even in the local texture of the language.

Nicholas's word "water" gives us a subtle reminder of who might have been dreaming about flood waters; and the word "herte," through its echo of "smert," recapitulates the farting and branding. When the poem is read aloud, this moment when the two plots come together in the "herte"/"sterte" couplet usually gets an even bigger laugh than either the nether kiss or the branding. Part of our laughter is at ourselves, happily acknowledging that like the characters, we have been masterfully tricked (thus Bratcher and von Kreisler 1971, 332–33; and Dane 1980, 216). It is, as Jordan says, principally an aesthetic laughter, expressing our amazement and delight that "the disparate parts of the narrative now fall marvelously together, converging with the plummeting carpenter at the feet of Alison and Nicholas" (Jordan 1967, 196).

Since this couplet brings both plots together, we might think of it as the riming of the two lines of narrative. And if, in the study of narrative, we can contemplate stories riming with each other, then this is surely the most surprising and satisfying narrative rime in English literature. Tillyard compares the "abstract significance" of the plot at this moment to "that of good music or of the best Byzantine mosaics" (Tillyard 1934, 92). The suspended plot-element that falls into place at the end is a common feature in the medieval and modern analogues, but no one would make a remark like Tillyard's about any of them, because nowhere else in the tradition of this tale-type is the manner of telling the story so well fused with its matter. Even the Flemish version contemporary with the *Miller's Tale*, also in verse and the closest analogue in folkloric terms, does not connect the two plot-elements via its own couplet form.[28]

In considering this climactic couplet where the two plot-lines intersect, I am moved to reflect more generally about Chaucer's desire to put things together, to recycle, to redefine. He is always doing it in the *Canterbury Tales*. For instance, in the *Miller's Tale* he requotes lines from the *Knight's Tale* in upside-down contexts: Arcite's tragic outcry is quoted in the description of Nicholas as a single lodger, and the Knight's metaphor for his storytelling becomes in the Miller's mouth the real "oxen in my plough" by which he swears he is no cuckold (see further Dean 1969). The love-triangle of two men and one woman is told first in the genre of high romance in the *Knight's Tale*, and then in the low style of the fabliau. While it would be an exaggeration to say with R. A. Shoaf that "*The Miller's Tale* is, in effect, a pun on *The Knight's Tale*," nonetheless there is great merit in approaching Chaucer's narrative designs through the sounds of their articulation. Chaucer's sense of what Shoaf calls "juxtology" is pervasive throughout the *Canterbury Tales*, operating at the level of puns, rime words, some of which are puns themselves ("queynte" [3276]), as well as through plot composition, and through the comparisons and contrasts of whole tales and their tellers.[29]

In fact, Chaucer seems to have had an inexhaustible interest in making comparisons of all sorts: of individual words in different contexts, of lines, of characters, of stories, of ideas. I wouldn't be surprised if the very idea of "quyting"–in its meaning of "matching" or "comparing"–arose out of Chaucer's constant fashioning of couplets (how many thousand?), which may have led him from a poet's technical awareness of sameness and difference to a more global awareness of how to play one story ironically against another. But this is quite unprovable, and not the main point of my demonstration. I hope, rather, simply to have shown that Chaucer's handling of meter and rime are essential to the comedy of the *Miller's Tale*, and that the more closely we pay attention to them the funnier the poem becomes.[§]

NOTES

[*]Reprinted with permission from *Chaucer Yearbook* 2 (1995): 17–47.

[1]As Alan T. Gaylord urged more than fifteen years ago in "Scanning the Prosodists: An Essay in Metacriticism": "We need to put versification back into the glossary of those who have regularly discussed Chaucer's style. Expressive variation, metrical complexity, and what Fussell calls 'density' are all pleasant and interesting subjects, and since they require that close attention be given to poetry, their pursuit should be encouraged" (Gaylord 1976, 76). I am pleased to acknowledge a general debt to the scholarship and attitudes of that essay, and to Gaylord's subsequent work on Chaucer's prosodic practices.

[2]A representative list: Dorothy Everett, "Chaucer's 'Good Ear,'" and "Some Reflections on Chaucer's 'Art Poetical,'" in Everett 1955; Paull F. Baum, *Chaucer's Verse* (Baum 1961); A. C.

Spearing, *Criticism and Medieval Poetry* (Spearing 1972); Michio Masui, *The Structure of Chaucer's Rime Words* (Masui 1964); Charles A. Owen, Jr., "'Thy Drasty Ryming'" (Owen 1966); Charles Muscatine, "*The Canterbury Tales*: Style of the Man and Style of the Work" (Muscatine 1966), esp. pp. 89–104; Eric G. Stanley, "Stanza and Ictus" (Stanley 1968); Stephen Knight, *Rhyming Craftily* and *Meaning in Chaucer's Poetry* (Knight, both 1973); John Leyerle, "The Heart and the Chain" (Leyerle 1974); Alan T. Gaylord, "Chaucer's Dainty 'Dogerel'" (Gaylord 1979); Mark Lambert, "Telling the Story in *Troilus and Criseyde*" (Lambert 1986), esp. p. 63 ff.; and Barry Windeatt, "To rym wel this book til I have do" (Windeatt 1992).

[3]Jordan 1967, 194–97. Knight gives a good brief sketch of the whole range of the tale's special poetic features in *The Poetry of the Canterbury Tales,* Knight 1973, 31–36. A thorough survey of the criticism is provided by the introduction and critical apparatus of Thomas W. Ross's indispensable *The Miller's Tale* in *A Variorum Edition* (Chaucer 1983). Ross notes that "there is still a need for an analysis of the poetic effects other than diction in the tale" (p. 48).

[4]"Chaucer's Language," in Spearing 1965, 100. Suzanne Woods gives essentially the same account of Chaucer's meter as I do here, although she would prefer to call it "decasyllabic verse" instead of "iambic pentameter," which she sees appearing in its stricter Renaissance form only with Surrey (Woods 1984, xi, 41–2, & 47).

[5]Pearsall 1991 describes and defends the metrical variations found in the manuscripts, using examples from the *Nun's Priest's Tale.* He cites two twelve-syllable examples of "the apparently irregular versification sanctioned by Hengwrt and Ellesmere" (p. 56), both of which I scan with five stresses, distributed freely to reinforce their dramatic meaning: "And in this cárt héerë | he lýth gápying ùpríght" (B 4232, VII 3042), where a triple anacrusis leads to a spondee before the cesura; "But hérkneth | to that ó màn fîl a grét mervaíllë" (B 4266, VII 3076), which opens with an amphibrach (often punctuated by an exclamation point), then follows its cesura with an anapest. I find it interesting that even these "metrically unusual" lines (Pearsall) can be described by modern prosodic terminology.

For variations in performance by competent readers, and some of the questions they pose for criticism, see *Chaucer Aloud*: Bowden 1987, 3–19, 50–76, 114–53, 172–84, and 254–82; "Unpunctuating Chaucer": Chickering 1990, 105–8; "Imagining Voices: Chaucer on Cassette": Gaylord 1990; and the review of Bowden's book in Gaylord 1989.

[6]Saintsbury 1906, I: 163. It seems indisputable that Chaucer already had a clear conception of a pentameter line in *Troilus.* Barry A. Windeatt has recently shown that the evidence of the manuscripts is that Chaucer "aimed to write decasyllabic lines with a generally alternating pattern of stress," tolerating "great variations on the pattern by comparison with later poets working in the same metre." It might be thought that such play in the metrical form makes it no meter at all, but Windeatt shows that "the many devices of variation in stress pattern that Chaucer deploys in no sense overthrow the prevailing metre"–see "Metre" in his edition: Chaucer 1984, 55, 61, and 62.

[7]Gaylord 1983, 314; and "Chaucer's Early Translations from French": Weiss 1982. Scholarship has been slow to confirm Skeat's surmise that Chaucer's narrative couplet came from Machaut's lyric decasyllabics (Chaucer 1894, 6: lxii), but in recent years James I. Wimsatt has shown the profundity of Chaucer's indebtedness to such French sources. See *Chaucer and His French Contemporaries*: JamesWimsatt 1991.

[8]Chaucer was undoubtedly referring to this feature of contemporary French poetry when he complained in *The Complaint of Venus* that "rym in Englissh hath such skarsete" that it was "a gret penaunce" to translate "word for word" the triple ballade of Oton de Grandson; see Owen 1966, 533–34.

[9]For this view and the references to Boccaccio and Geoffrey de Vinsauf, see Jordan 1987, 12–13 & 16–17. For further discussion on Chaucer's views as seen through his actual practice, see in Payne 1963, ch. 2, "Chaucer on the Art of Poetry," pp. 60–90.

[10]H. Marshall Leicester, Jr., in "The Art of Impersonation: A General Prologue to the *Canterbury Tales,*" claims that the text itself generates the illusion of living speech: "It is writ-

ten to be read, but read as if it were spoken. The poem is a literary imitation of oral performance" (Leicester 1980, 221). All the more reason, then, to attend the particulars of its poetic form.

[11]Ellesmere MS. readings appear in brackets. Pearsall's "Chaucer's Meter" (Pearsall 1987, 51–54), argues for preferring the meter of the manuscripts over the smoother version that appears in most editions, and for preferring, on balance, Hengwrt over Ellesmere; see also Ross in Chaucer 1983, 59. I follow their choice of base-text but also share the reservations of Ralph Hanna III about the very concept of a "best text" and about the blanket superiority sometimes argued for Hengwrt over Ellesmere. See his "Problems of 'Best Text' Editing" (Hanna 1987). On the question of the virgules, see Killough 1982.

The quotations in the present essay are unpunctuated following the position taken in my "Unpunctuating Chaucer," (Chickering 1990): when reading Chaucer's text closely for its poetry, it is best to encounter it without the editorial pre-reading encoded by modern punctuation. A glance at the text as printed in *The Riverside Chaucer* (Chaucer 1987) will show the extent of regularization, disambiguation, and interpretive voicing in our standard reading edition.

[12]Scansion varies notoriously with each reader's performance aloud, and no two readers are likely to hear the same line exactly the same way, especially if one's scansion admits an intermediate level of intonation between fully stressed and unstressed. In this essay, I offer only my own audition of the lines, not an authoritative interpretation, which the status of Chaucer's text itself puts beyond final proof. At the same time, there is much that readers do agree on, and by taking my metrical cues mainly from Chaucer's sense I hope to have made convincing determinations.

[13]For such light rimes on words whose stress varies depending on their position in the line, see Davis, "Language and Versification," in Chaucer 1987, xxxi. Perhaps the most frequently encountered stress-variable word is "manere." The second syllable of "scoler" is again stressed when it occurs in rime position at *General Prologue*, 259–60 ("cloysterer' / "povre scoler") and *Romaunt of the Rose*, 6359–60 ("now forster" / "now scoler"), but its first syllable is stressed when it occurs inside the line at *Reeve's Tale*, 4002 and *Romaunt of the Rose*, 5950.

[14]The *MED* shows "conclusioun" entering the language in the 1380s, with citations from the Wycliffe Bible, Gower, and Chaucer, who uses it frequently, often referring to a rhetorical conclusion. "Interrogacioun" is attested early only here in the *Miller's Tale*, although it was a common enough Latin word in writs and philosophical disputations. Ross takes "conclusions" as "experiments" (Chaucer 1983, 133), while *The Riverside Chaucer* follows Robinson's Chaucer 1957 and Skeat's Chaucer 1894 in glossing it as "the technical term for propositions or problems." Either meaning serves in context.

[15]Chaucer uses the same threefold collocation of "houres," "shoures," and "droghte" in *Squire's Tale* 117–18, the only other instance in his works. This astrological wet-dry antithesis was surely conventional (cf. *General Prologue*, 1–2), and likely enough the rime pair was as well. It would appear that he used such formulas not by reflex, but only when they suited his expressive purposes.

[16]Reed 1962; & Silar 1990. There is a similar thematic loading of double meanings in "derne" and "privee" here as well; see Neuss 1974 & Chaucer 1983, 134.

[17]In the so-called Marriage Group alone, Chaucer rimed "wyf" with "lyf" all thirteen times it appears as a rime-word in the Prologue to the *Wife of Bath's Tale* and the tale itself, nine out of ten times in the *Franklin's Tale*, and ten out of fourteen times in the *Merchant's Tale*. Chaucer's riming practice says something about his conception of Griselda, too, insofar as in the *Clerk's Tale* "wyf" appears no less than 38 times, but only once in the line-end position, again rimed with "lyf" (162). Griselda was not a wife to be associated with life by poetic convention, it would seem.

[18]W. K. Wimsatt, Jr., describes Pope's couplets as introducing a strong surprise in sense by using parallel syntactic structures that rime on different parts of speech. In a rather unfair comparison (apples and oranges, not apples and bragot), he sets Chaucer's often light rimes

against Pope's practices, with Chaucer's at the weak end of a scale in which rime-sounds and rime-sense mutually reinforce each other. I have to agree that generally Chaucer uses rime more as a narrative vehicle than for such strong formal effects, but it is pleasant to think that this passage gives Wimsatt the lie, however briefly. See his "One Relation of Rhyme to Reason": W. K. Wimsatt 1954.

[19]I think the best translation of the second "queynte" would be "the lovely' as a substantive, or if one seeks an equivalent in modern American slang perhaps "the yumyum." It is a fairly transparent euphemism that immediately collapses into ME "cunte" as soon as we hear it as a pun–see Ross in Chaucer 1983, 153–54, and Ross 1972, figs. 7–9, for a brief history of commentary on this pun and medieval depictions of the gesture. For a full list of the occurrences of "queynte" in Chaucer's works, see Ross 1972, 175–84. Larry D. Benson offers many arguments that "queynte" never directly means "cunt" in Chaucer, in part because it works as a pun here (Benson 1984, 42). For rebuttals, particularly concerning *Troilus* 5.543, see Fleming 1990, 1–44; and Delany 1992, who examines the controversy over "queynte" in the context of a theoretical and historical discussion of medieval obscene puns.

[20]Compare the even funnier pairs "cynamome" / "speketh to me" (3699–3700) and "com pa me"/"to blame" (3709–10); see further Chaucer 1983, 221–22, 224. Riming one word against two was not *ipso facto* a comic effect for Chaucer, however. Much depends on the pace and sense of the couplet. See Masui 1964, 28–30, for a list of such rimes. "Fro ye" rimed against "Troye" and "joie" in the first stanza of *Troilus* is a good example of the uncertain tonal status that this device can have.

[21]Masui 1964, 218–22, calls it "rime-breaking," following Kaluza's term *Reimbrechung*, and notes 32 instances in the *Knight's Tale*. Chaucer also uses it frequently in the *Reeve's Tale*.

[22]Owen 1966, 560–61, notes the repetition of the rime-pairs "ringe"/"singe" and "sautrye"/"melodie" throughout the poem. Nicholas originally uses his psaltery to sing "Angelus ad virginem," but now after this burlesque of the Annunciation, his making "melodie" becomes a sexual symbol, to reappear as a rime when he and Alisoun are abed in lines 3651–56. Throughout the poem, music and religion are tied together ironically, blasphemously, parodically. See further Gellrich 1974; Kaske 1962; Rowland 1974; Reiss 1964 and 1970.

[23]Kaluza defines it as "die Verlegung einer stärkeren Satzpause am das Ende des ersten der beiden ein Reimpaar bildenden Verse";–quoted from *Chaucer-Handbuch*, p. 208, by Masui 1964, 218.

[24]Coghill 1967, 99, calls the second line of the couplet "perhaps the funniest line in the funniest story in the world"; Ross in Chaucer 1983, 229, hears it as "the cruelest titter" in the tale.

[25]Ross in Chaucer 1983, 241, argues powerfully for preferring the Hengwrt reading "in" over the Ellesmere "amydde" at line 3810, adducing several analogues in which the coulter or spit is thrust up the joker's anus. Having argued for metrical flexibility in Chaucer, I can scarcely quarrel with the "in" reading on the ground that it gives the line only four stresses. But I print the Ellesmere reading, somewhat diffidently, on the grounds that it makes better sense when taken with the next two lines, where "toute" means "rump," not "anus," and a hand's breadth of flesh is burnt off.

[26]For the role of scatology in the poem, and an analysis of how Chaucer makes it more scatological than its nearest analogue, see Beidler 1977.

[27]See Tillyard 1934, 86–92, on obliquity. Bratcher and von Kreisler 1971 explain the technique of the suspended plot-element both here and in several modern analogues. For reflections on our recapitulation of our original responses to literary and dramatic works, see Appendix 1, "On the Persistence of First Impressions," in Booth 1983, 121–25.

[28]Text and translation of the Flemish poem, "Dits van Heilen van Beersele die de .iii. jaghede te spele," are printed in Bryan & Dempster 1941, 112–18. It is the only contemporary analogue to contain all three of the Aarne-Thompson motifs found in Chaucer: the kiss, the flood, and the branding.

[29]Shoaf 1988, 55. See further his excellent discussion of the theoretical significance of John's unwitting pun, "Nowelys flood," pp. 53–55.

§Earlier versions of this paper were delivered at SUNY-Binghamton in 1989 and at Southern Methodist University in 1992. I thank all respondents for their comments, the members of the Five College/UConn Chaucer faculty seminar for their helpful suggestions, Nancy Mason Bradbury for her critical reading of the penultimate draft, and my colleague William H. Pritchard, as always, for his good ear.

Stephen Knight

The Nun's Priest's Tale*

Most critical accounts of "The Nun's Priest's Tale" have been fairly limited in range; they usually praise its mock-heroic wit and its breadth of reference, but hesitate to investigate more deeply its possible meaning or the details of its construction. Two well-known critics have, however, gone further and have imputed a specific meaning to the tale. J. Leslie Hotson has expounded it as a political allegory about Chaucer's contemporaries, but he does recognize the mock-heroic character of the tale as well, and says that the contemporary references would add:

> . . . a subtlety of touch-and-go allusion to contemporary events of the first order, and give the matchless tale a new zest.
>
> (Hotson 1924, 781)

In a more single-minded reading Mortimer J. Donovan regards the tale as a Christian allegory; he takes the animal plot as a pure fable and allows little value to the mock-heroic interpretation of the poem, saying firmly that as a whole it is "a sermon on alertness to moral obligation."(Donovan 1953, 498) In comparison with other tales, relatively little has been said about the story-teller; this may be partly because the priest is barely mentioned outside his tale and its links, and so Arthur T. Broes and R. M. Lumiansky have had to depend on internal evidence for what light they have cast on this issue. As a result both have based their findings on rather speculative and thin arguments.[1]

Since the tale has been so widely praised, it is surprising that so little has been said about its mechanics. The structure has not been discussed at all; this seems especially odd since its similarities to "The Pardoner's Tale"–a long theoretical discussion and then brisk action–and the clear juxtaposition of views at the end would seem to invite structural analysis, especially in the light of R. M. Jordan's stimulating book, *Chaucer and the Shape of Creation* (Jordan 1967).

Several writers have discussed topics close to an assessment of the poem's style, without dealing directly with it. Karl Young and Robert A. Pratt have investigated the sources of the rhetorical references and John M. Manly used the tale as an opening exemplum in his famous lecture (Young 1943–44; Pratt 1949; Manly 1926). Manly felt that in it Chaucer showed the natural conclusion of his "gradual release" from the rhetoricians; C. S. Baldwin took a sterner view of the author's treatment of his authorities, saying that he "pillories" Geoffrey of Vinsauf (Baldwin 1927, 110). Recent critics have seen Chaucer's relationship with his rhetorical masters as more complex than this. Dorothy Everett has reminded her readers of Chaucer's enigmatic character, and E. T. Donaldson suggests that rhetoric is, in a way, the true topic of the tale (Everett 1955, 174; Donaldson 1971, 146–50). I shall return to these two critics later, for their comments are important and should be considered in the light of what is to be argued here.

Only a few critics speak in any detail about the poem's style and none of these says very much. Charles Muscatine treats this tale last of all in his discussion of *The Canterbury Tales* and while he does describe the stylistic changes that occur in it, he gives none of the detailed comment that is so impressive in his handling of *Troilus and Criseyde* and "The Miller's Tale." He treats the tale as an epitome of the mixed style that he has previously explicated in Chaucer, and consequently much of his comment is general (Muscatine 1969, 237–43). The remarks that John Speirs makes are also general, but this is in keeping with his approach, tending as he does to sum up a passage's tone and effect without any extensive detailed analysis (Speirs 1951, 185–93); more detailed comments on the tale are given by D. J. Brindley in an article which follows fairly closely Speirs's methods with Chaucer, and which makes some perceptive comments (Brindley 1964). R.W.V. Elliott gives a brief but lucid summary of the poem's style in his account of this and "The Pardoner's Tale" (Elliott 1965, 19–25). All of these writers state or imply that at certain points Chaucer does exploit his stylistic powers to create or emphasize his effects, but none of them, with the partial exception of Donaldson, attempts to offer a critique that could be summarized. Rather they make a series of interesting points, and these will be referred to as they become relevant in the course of this chapter.

The fact that these critics have said little about the poetics of this tale might suggest that there is little to say, and this would seem to be confirmed by those who have edited it most fully. Sisam makes a few shrewd comments on Chaucer's tags and line-fillers (Chaucer 1927, 30–31); Coghill and Tolkien appreciate some high points and discuss some of the commoner rhetorical figures (Chaucer 1959, 7–30 & Appendix, 46–50). The most recent editor, Maurice Hussey, speaks more directly about his view of the tale "as poetry." He notes several simple effects of repetition and some characteristics of orally-delivered poetry, mentions some apparently irregular lines and then says that now ". . . we are to consider the wider effects of the poetry, since we have seen that the verse is not devised to yield the utmost only to close critical scrutiny" (Chaucer 1965, 32). In Hussey's view the nature of the poetry here is the same as that summed up by A. C. Spearing when he describes the characteristics of *The Book of the Duchess*:

> The "poetry," one might say, is not even noticeable locally; by calling attention to single lines in the passage I have maltreated it. That is not how it works; its most important effects are cumulative. (Spearing 1972, 16)

I have been arguing in these chapters, often explicitly and always implicitly, that Chaucer does frequently write with close attention to the detailed effects of his poetry, and so it would seem necessary to contradict this view of "The Nun's Priest's Tale," especially as it is widely held to be among the most expert pieces of Chaucer's later poetry. Happily, it is very easy to assert that a close reading does not, to use Spearing's word, "maltreat" the poem: there is a good deal of highly skilled detailed writing that has either gone unnoticed or has not been fully appreciated.

"The Nun's Priest's Tale" is the last in a wonderfully varied group. Before it come "The Shipman's Tale," "The Prioress's Tale," Chaucer's tales of Sir Thopas and Melibee and "The Monk's Tale." Apart from the sign of uncompleted revision in "The Shipman's Tale" (where he speaks like the Wife of Bath, lines 12–19) it is a finished and varied group. The coarse vigor of the Shipman is answered by the elegant religiosity of the Prioress; Chaucer's own tales are in fine contrast with each other and his serious tale seems to expose a moral threadbareness in both the Monk and the Prioress. The Nun's Priest to some extent "quites" the Monk, as several critics have shown (see Watson 1964). In its highly aware intelligence and assured reference to practically every literary genre in medieval England, "The Nun's Priest's Tale" is a worthy end to this brilliant and subtly related sequence.

The link before the tale is short, but in it we find both the sense of interplay and tension that is created in the group as a whole and also the stylistic subtlety of Chaucer's most artful poetry. The Knight begins by interrupting the Monk, though he seems to have waited for a decent moment to speak–the Monk's analysis of tragedy with regard to Croesus makes a reasonably apt conclusion to his gloomy discourse, though he clearly does not mean it as one. The Knight's opening words demonstrate a tone that is clearly appropriate for interrupting a pilgrim of some importance:

> "Hoo!" quod the Knyght, "good sire, namoore of this!
> That ye han seyd is right ynough, ywis,
> And muchel moore; for litel hevynesse
> Is right ynough to muche folk, I gesse.
> I seye for me, it is a greet disese,
> Whereas men han been in greet welthe and ese,
> To heeren of hire sodeyn fal, allas!" (Chaucer 1957)

Caution and tact are suggested by the many pauses as well as by the oblique syntax; with great politeness the Knight blames himself for finding the tale oppressive. The tactful style implies much about the Knight himself, and about the respect due to the Monk. As the Knight goes on, though, he describes a more positive type of story without pause or qualification:

"And the contrarie is joye and greet solas,
As when a man hath been in povre estaat,
And clymbeth up and wexeth fortunat,
And there abideth in prosperitee.
Swich thyng is gladsom, as it thynketh me,
And of swich thyng were goodly for to telle."

In the context of this firm and flowing passage the parenthetic "as it thynketh me" is a statement of confidence, not one of cautious qualification, and the passage shows how the Knight, typically, has managed to assert his quiet but forceful personality.

The Host, a less polite assessor of personalities, now speaks with less tact and less fluency:

"Ye," quod oure Hooste, "by seinte Poules belle!
Ye seye right sooth; this Monk he clappeth lowde.
He spak how Fortune covered with a clowde
I noot nevere what; and als of a tragedie
Right now ye herde, and, pardee, no remedie
It is for to biwaille ne compleyne
That that is doon, and als it is a peyne,
As ye han seyd, to heere of hevynesse.

As in his remarks to the Monk before his tale, the Host does not judge him worthy of much politeness–his tone to the Prioress is very different, for example. The word "clappeth" is bluntly rude, and the effect of the run-on "I noot nevere what" is damningly dismissive. The Host's frequent use of enjambment here does not give an ornate tone as it can in some other speakers; rather, as in Ector's use of it, the effect is to break up the ordered quality that regular verse can have. The pauses and the varying rhythms of the lines help to create the colloquial effect. In keeping, the syntax is very simple, for there is no subtle subordination here. The repeated "and als" and the colloquial running-on of the lines create an effect very like that of the sequences of loosely linked co-ordinate clauses typical of much medieval English prose.

So the Host dismisses the Monk in a speech-style which proclaims a plain man having little patience with folly, especially when it is contrasted with that of the Knight. The Host rambles on into another loosely connected sentence:

"Wherfore, sire Monk, or daun Piers by your name,
I pray yow hertely telle us somwhat elles;
For sikerly, nere clynkyng of youre belles,
That on youre bridel hange on every syde,
By hevene kyng, that for us alle dyde,
I sholde er this hen fallen doun for sleep,
Although the slough had never been so deep;
Thanne hadde your tale al be toold in veyn."

He has need of the summarizing final line here, for the sentence has maundered to a rather obscure close–it is a passage that students often find tricky to translate into the "good modern English prose" of examination rubrics. The Host here shows none of the crisp organization and forceful vocabulary of the Knight at his most fluent, and none of the tact of him at his most pausing; but the Host is not being as rude as he is elsewhere (to the Franklin, for example), and the following lines show an attempt to placate the Monk:

"For certeinly, as that thise clerkes seyn,
Whereas a man may have noon audience,
Noght helpeth it to tellen his sentence.
        And wel I woot the substance is in me,
If any thyng shal wel reported be.
Sir, sey somwhat of huntyng, I yow preye."

The Host fits in a few learned terms–"sentence," "audience," and "substance"–presumably to humor the Monk, and tries to move him on to a topic he ought to describe well.[2] The Monk briskly refuses and so the Host turns to another cleric; here he feels no need for persuasion and adopts a different tone, forceful and imperative singular (Lumiansky notes "the patronizing tone and content of this speech; 1953, 901):

"Com neer, thou preest, com hyder, thou sir John!
Telle us swich thyng as may oure hertes glade.
Be blithe, though thou ryde upon a jade.
What thogh thyn hors be bothe foul and lene ?
If he wol serve thee, rekke net a bene.
Looke that thyn herte be murie everemo."

The Priest assents; he strikes a humble note:

"Yis, sir," quod he, "yis, Hoost, so moot I go,
But I be myrie, ywis I wol be blamed."

He accepts the Host's authority so readily and offers so much servile agreement in two lines that, in the light of the tale to follow, it is hard to avoid thinking that his words imply a judgment on the Host's bossy manner. This may be to read a lot into the link, but Chaucer invites such reading. This link, like so many others, is rich with implication; the speeches indicate that the pilgrims are constantly making judgments about each other, and these judgments are subtly implied in the manner in which they speak. The Host's style of speech is many-sided, and his assessment of a person is shown in several aspects of his style, not merely in the well-known variation between "ye" and "thow." But other characters also participate in these little dramas, and their speech can also imply judgments.

These links are the most advanced form of Chaucer's mimetic art; there is very little direct description–here we are just told that the Host is "rude and boold" in speech to the Priest and we are given a final assessment of the Priest as "sweete" and "goodly." Both characters demonstrate these qualities in their styles of speech.

A lot goes on in the links of this group of tales, and this one is typical of the general effect of them; they emphasize the tension between the pilgrims and, consequently, between the tales. Without them it would be hard to say whether Chaucer really meant the tales to interact, but on the evidence of the links this is plainly his purpose, though it may not be his only purpose–the tales are at the same time self-sufficient. But after a link like this one we are prepared to look for effects deriving from the juxtaposition of the tales and, important to this study, our ears are attuned to different styles of speaking and we expect different styles to have differing implications. As in all the links where we find this "roadside drama," so well described a good time ago by Kittredge (1915, 146–218), the style of the speaker is central to his meaning, and this should bring us to read–or listen to–"The Nun's Priest's Tale" itself with heightened awareness and expectation.

The tale opens in a simple manner, giving us undecorated information:

A povre wydwe, somdeel stape in age
Was whilom dwellyng in a narwe cotage,
Biside a grove, stondynge in a dale.
This wydwe, of which I telle yow my tale,
Syn thilke day that she was last a wyf,
In pacience ladde a ful symple lyf,
For litel was hir catel and hir rente.

The lines move along steadily, notable neither for fluency nor jerkiness; the diction is not ornate, but nor is it brusque in manner, for there is a reasonable number of two-syllable words and French-derived terms. In the last line the narrator pauses over the widow's income: the word "catel" is a little surprising in this humble context, for its normal uses are different. It and "rente" are generally used of a more elaborate system of life. Though both are French, they are reasonably common in Chaucer and in earlier texts, though the fact that about half the occurrences of "catel" are from "The Parson's Tale" and *The Romaunt of the Rose* may imply a learned ambiance. But any possible irony in this slightly elaborate description is, for the moment, muted, for the narrator goes on to speak about the widow's simple mode of life in a simple style:

By housbondrie of swich as God hire sente
She foond hirself and eek hir doghtren two.
Thre large sowes hadde she, and namo,
Three keen, and eek a sheep that highte Malle.

This is rather plainer than the opening lines; the style now creates more fully the simplicity of this humble scene as the narrator lists the animals with scrupulous care. The fact that it is the sheep who is named may prepare us subliminally for a beast-fable, but the basic effect is that these lines are fully in sympathy with the widow's life. The scene might be being set for a story of moral virtue, like the opening of "The Clerk's Tale." In this context the use of the words "catel" and "rente" might seem a little odder than before, and as the narrator continues the reason for their use becomes clear. If it is to be a moral tale, it is not to be a simple, low-key one, for in the next lines the possible ironies of "catel" and "rente" are reinforced by a series of words whose ambiance is more clearly inappropriate to this scene:

> Ful sooty was hire bour and eek hir halle,
> In which she eet ful many a sklendre meel.

The words "bour" and "halle" belong to a type of building quite different from humble cottages. The hall is, of course, the great hall of the medieval house and the "bour" is the ladies withdrawing room which, at this time, would only be found in really large houses: the grandeur the words imply is well seen in a house like Penshurst Place. The irony here is clear enough, but a number of editors have missed the important point that it is a one-room cottage–bower and hall are one. We would expect this of a humble cottage at this time in any case, but the fact that both "rooms" are sooty clarifies the point–a real "bour" would not contain a fire. To add weight to this joke, in Chaucer the word "bour"has a genteel connotation, and the same appears true of the word "sklendre."[3] The humility of the window's state is treated ironically in the vocabulary, and in this context "catel" and "rente" seem to have taken on an ironic quality as well. The narrator now raises this little joke into a major motif, for the next passage showers us with a series of elaborate gastronomical terms:

> Of poynaunt sauce hir neded never a deel.
> No deyntee morsel passed thurgh hir throte;
> Hir diete was accordaunt to hir cote.

The account found in all the histories of the language, that elegant foods bear French names, here springs into poetic life, and the setting of the food terms in the same place in each line stresses the effect with an easy skill. The following lines enlarge the joke, pointing out that if you use French names for fine foods you also have to use French names for the physical problems they cause:

> Replecciooun ne made hire nevere sik;
> Attempree diete was al hir phisik,
> And exercise, and hertes suffisaunce.
> The goute lette hir nothyng for to daunce,
> N'apoplexie shente nat hir heed.

Again the lines are skillfully constructed, the French names for disorders tend to come early in the line and a good balance is maintained between the two halves of the line. This gives a firm clarity to the negative-positive balance in the argument. The skilled jesting with language is now dropped for a while, but it has had an important effect. Not only has this been an interesting and lively description of country simplicity, it has also introduced the mock-heroic to the tale; the language used has directed a certain amount of mockery at the areas where these elaborate words are used without being inappropriate–here, on the other hand, is not only simplicity, but health as well.

The final sequence of this description returns to the simple style:

> No wyn ne drank she, neither whit ne reed;
> Hir bord was served moost with whit and blak,–
> Milk and broun breed, in which she foond no lak,
> Seynd bacoun, and somtyme an ey or tweye;
> For she was, as it were, a maner deye.

The mild note of mockery towards courtliness is maintained, as we are told that the widow is quite satisfied with this diet, and the style of the lines very satisfyingly acts out the plainness of her life. There is no enjambment, no elaborate diction, and here we do find that simple monosyllabic note which was not present in the opening lines of the description. The simple rime words press the point– "blak"/"lak" and "tweye"/"deye" and the extra pause and rather bathetic comment of the final line bring the whole description to a slow and fading close. The whole passage is just one more example of the remarkable richness Chaucer can produce from a formal description: it is not as dense with implication as the description of Alisoun in "The Miller's Tale" but it is a little masterpiece. The poor widow is convincingly created. Muscatine remarks on "the husbanding of sensory effect" in this passage and Brindley talks of the "unassuming realism of the widow's style," (Muscatine 1969, 239; Brindley 1964, 149), but there is more than this here. Within the description there is an indication of, and a preparation for the varying tones the tale is to demonstrate. This is brought about by the subtle modulation of the style throughout this passage and by the manipulation of the vocabulary in particular.

The narrator moves on to another description which is to be, in visual terms, very different, but the ground-bass of which has already been sounded in the ironic use of ornate language in the widow's description. First we read simply:

> A yeerd she hadde, enclosed al aboute
> With stikkes, and a drye dych withoute,
> In which she hadde a cok, hight Chauntecleer.

Reading the tale for a second time, it sounds very like a farmyard equivalent of a defended position–this may be an accident, but if so it is a happy one, for this selection of detail fits in well with Chauntecleer's chivalric presentation. At first his description is merely hyperbolic:

> In al the land, of crowyng nas his peer.
> His voys was murier than the murie orgon
> On messe-dayes that in the chirche gon.

But the simile is not only a *superlatio* [hyperbole], it is a most dignified sort of simile and the word 'orgon' is itself a lofty term to use (see Karpf 1930, 124–27). The next couplet continues this note:

> Wel sikerer was his crowyng in his logge
> Than is a clokke or an abbey orlogge.

As so often in Chaucer, the similes do not merely state a comparison; the object used in comparison implies something about the subject of the simile. To describe Chauntecleer we need a union of the grandeurs of the medieval church and the subtleties of medieval technology–and ornate language is a *sine qua non.* Even a 'clokke' will not do: the word 'orlogge' is enlisted for a more fitting comparison–and Chauntecleer still overgoes it. The word 'logge' also appears to dignify Chauntecleer, for it probably has a chivalric connotation.[4] The rest of the discussion of Chauntecleer's crowing continues the *superlatio*, of thought and of style:

> By nature he knew ech ascencioun
> Of the equynoxial in thilke toun;
> For when degrees fiftene weren ascended,
> Thanne crew he, that it myghte nat been amended.

The confidence and vigor of his crowing are finely expressed: after the elaborate language the blunt "Thanne crew he"is delightfully judged, and the rest of the line seems to have rather a lot of stresses, asserting in its firm sound just what it says.

The physical description of Chauntecleer that follows also shows this high humor and uses more ironic language to characterize this magnificent cock:

> His coomb was redder than the fyn coral,
> And batailled as it were a castel wal;
> His byle was blak, and as the jeet it shoon;
> Lyk asure were his legges and his toon;
> His nayles whitter than the lylye flour,
> And lyk the burned gold was his colour.

The description has been discussed elsewhere and critics have explained the multiple joke–the elegance of the similes and the rhetorical correctness of the *effictio* [brief sketch] (see Muscatine 1969, 239; Elliott 1965, 21; and the notes on the passage by Hussey [Chaucer 1965] and by Coghill & Tolkien [Chaucer 1959]). That the language is so grand and the organization so decorous is one side of the joke: that it is, apparently, an accurate picture of the most gorgeous of farmyard birds is the other side (Boone 1949). It is one of the high moments of Chaucer's work, and the effect derives largely from the witty selection of epithet and simile. But, especially in the light of this study, it is interesting to note the suggestion of dignity and formality that is given as the lines group into something very close to a *repetitio* [repeating a word at the opening of successive clauses] with *compar* [clauses or phrases with similar length and structure]. There is a brief stiffening and elevation in the sound of the verse which brings out finely the excellent joke.

The language of romance is sustained as the narrator moves on to the rest of the household:

> This gentil cok hadde in his governaunce
> Seven hennes for to doon al his plesaunce,
> Whiche were his sustres and his paramours,
> And wonder lyk to hym, as of colours.

The mock-heroic language is plain enough, but here we also have a trick which is to recur in the tale and whose effect depends upon poetic subtlety. Embedded in this passage is one piece of information which subverts the whole edifice of lofty language–the hens were his sisters as well as his paramours. But this reference is skated over, the narrator runs on quickly in the only three-line sentence we have had for about twenty lines; he seems to want only to tell us about the color of the hens. The organization of the lines throws the emphasis quite away from the startlingly animal detail that Chauntecleer's court–and we must by now call it that–was incestuous. This teasing effect recurs almost at once.

Pertelote is, as has frequently been noted, a properly courtly lady:

> Curteys she was, discreet, and debonaire,
> And compaignable, and bar hyrself so faire,
> Syn thilke day that she was seven nyght oold,
> That trewely she hath the herte in hoold
> Of Chauntecleer, loken in every lith . . . .

The sentence builds up grandly to the climactic enjambment and the closing conventional phrase "loken in every lith." But again, a deflatingly realistic piece of chicken-life has been hurried over. A week is young indeed for a courtly lady to be beloved, but more acceptable for a chicken. As before, the narrator plants the jolting fact in the middle of his grand sentence, and the effect is to prevent the lofty language from asserting its nobility: the style remains mock-heroic because of this, and the poem is not allowed to assume the sort of seriousness that this style might lead us to expect. The characters may be described like lords and ladies and may act a little like lords and ladies, but we are prompted to remember that they are nothing but chickens. The issue seems important to the poet at this early stage, for after a few lines he makes the point again. We hear of the two lovers singing, in the proper language of the lyrics:

But swich a joye was it to here hem synge,
Whan that the brighte sonne gan to sprynge,
2879 In sweete accord, "My lief is faren in londe!"

But then the narrator says:

2880 For thilke tyme, as I have understonde,
Beestes and briddes koude speke and synge.

The remark breaks the fantasy of the story once more. An ingenious commentator could impute it to that well-known naïve narrator whom Chaucer often uses as a stalking-horse; I think it is not necessary to be so complicated. The remark fits in with the other references that specify the mock-heroic tone of the poem and it may well serve another fairly simple function: it is quite common for the narrator of a tale to speak in his own voice at the end of a section. This presumably had a lot to do with the exigencies of reading aloud a long story–both "The Knight's Tale" and Troilus and Criseyde have many of these moments. And this point does mark the end of the opening sequence of the tale, for now there is to be some action.

The poetic skills that have been quite clear in this opening are still to be found in the next sequence, though I think they are shown differently. So far, the main weight of the poetic subtlety has been in the imaginative choice of language, though sometimes the organization of the lines has given added point to this and sometimes effects have been implied by the prosody alone. In the following sequence I believe Chaucer uses a subtle modulation of style in a major way, to give Chauntecleer and Pertelote contrasting personalities.

When Pertelote hears Chauntecleer groaning in his sleep her reaction is affectionate, but crisp:

She was agast, and seyde, "Herte deere,
2890 What eyleth yow, to grone in this manere ?
Ye been a verray sleper; fy, for shame!"

His reply is a little different:

And he answerde, and seyde thus: "Madame,
I pray yow that ye take it nat agrief.
By God, me mette I was in swich meschief
2895 Right now, that yet myn herte is soore afright."

Both speakers use the polite plural and both begin with a lofty vocative. "Herte deere" and "Madame" are both firmly stressed and provide the rime, so drawing our attention to the extreme politeness of these birds. But Chauntecleer lacks the sharp tone and brisk style of Pertelote; this difference is first seen in the contrast between "She was agast, and seyde" and the slacker "And he answerde and seyde"–and the longer syntactical units of Chauntecleer's lines continue the same note. He uses one enjambment, where the ends of her lines fall heavily. It would be an adventurous criticism which confidently found a marked character difference in these two short passages alone, but as the tale continues we find that the contrast sketched here is made stronger.

As Chauntecleer goes on, enjambment seems a motif of his style:

> "Now God," quod he, "my swevene recche aright,
> And kepe my body out of foul prisoun!
> Me mette how that I romed up and doun
> Withinne our yeerd, wheer as I saugh a beest
> Was lyk an hound, and wolde han maad areest
> Upon my body, and wolde han had me deed."

The opening two lines are reasonably crisp, though the comma at the end of the first line represents a light pause at most, but then the lines are strongly run on; this no doubt makes more emphatic the final monosyllabic "wolde han had me deed" but also gives a curious fluency, perhaps a volubility to the lines. But Chauntecleer does not always speak in this way; the dramatic ending to this passage is pursued in the next lines where he gives a vivid account of the mysterious "beest":

> "His colour was bitwixe yelow and reed,
> And tipped was his tayl and bothe his eeris
> With blak, unlyk the remenaunt of his heeris;
> His snowte smal, with glowynge eyen tweye.
> Yet of his look for feere almoost I deye."

There is one enjambment here, but the effect of the run-on "With blak" is rather crisp and cannot be said to continue the flowingly run-on effect of the previous passage (Kökeritz 1954, 946, sees *rime riche* in 2903–04, but it hardly gives the sequence an ornate tone). Throughout Chauntecleer's speech we will find these two tones: sometimes he speaks in a general and fluent manner, moving with grace and speed, while at other times he is more dramatic and impressive; he uses both styles skillfully to be a convincing speaker. But even at his most dramatic and forceful his tone is different from Pertelote's normal style. He is always elegant and poised, but her verse is more broken up by pauses, is not run on, and she conveys a business-like, common-sense note:

> "Avoy!" quod she, "fy on yow, hertelees!
> Allas!" quod she, "for, by that God above,
> Now han ye lost myn herte and al my love.
> I kan nat love a coward, by my faith!
> For certes, what so any womman seith,
> We alle desiren, if it myghte bee,
> To han housbondes hardy, wise, and free,

And secree, and no nygard, ne no fool,
Ne hym that is agast of every tool,
Ne noon avauntour, by that God above!"

Each line ends firmly, and very few of them are without some pause. The pauses fall differently in each line and so we do not get a measured, repetitive effect; instead it is a direct, forceful and rather pungent style–clear, straight speaking to match the strong feelings that she has on the topic. She has firm opinions, crisply expressed, and they are informative and factual. They may be *sententiae*, but they are not sententious, in the modern sense of the word. As she goes on the style remains forceful. The lines are still end-stopped, full of specific nouns and clear adjectives and the rhythms are constantly changing. The speech cannot be intoned: it has to be punched out, just as she punches out clear opinions and reams of information:

"Swevenes engendren of replecciouns,
And ofte of fume and of complecciouns,
Whan humours been to habundant in a wight.
Certes this dreem, which ye han met to-nyght,
Cometh of the greete superfluytee
Of youre rede colera, pardee,
Which causeth folk to dreden in hir dremes
Of arwes, and of fyr with rede lemes,
Of rede beestes, that they wol hem byte,
Of contek, and of whelpes, grete and lyte."

There is one enjambment here, as line 2929 runs on to "Of arwes," but this does not establish a fluid tone as does enjambment in Chauntecleer's speech; the run-on phrase is short and the effect is to emphasize this beginning of Pertelote's list of the contents of choleric dreams. There is some complex language here, for she is learned and controls the vocabulary of dream lore. The speech continues in this way, full of good sense and information, ending with a charmingly detailed account of medieval laxatives:

"A day or two ye shul have digestyves
Of wormes, er ye take youre laxatyves
Of lawriol, centaure, and fumetere,
Or elles of ellebor, that groweth there,
Of katapuce, or of gaitrys beryis,
Of herbe yve, growynge in oure yeerd, there mery is;
Pekke hem up right as they growe and ete hem yn."

Once again a few lines are run on, and once again the effect is to stress the pauses in this careful, packed speech (just previously, lines 2946–67 are another example of this); the rugged rhythms of the lines emphasize the firm effect–the last two lines are especially deliberate.

In tone, then, Pertelote's long speech is forceful, even aggressive; it masses information and advice in crisp language, learned when it needs to be but never anywhere near high style. Her Latinisms are particular and necessary, not general and decorative. In total concord with this style is the fact that her speech has a closely worked argument. She states: (1) You have acted in a cowardly manner, fearing a dream. (2) Dreams are not to be feared. (3) This is because they derive from disordered humours. (4) Treatment is available for this condition. (5) Therefore, taking the treatment, "Dredeth no dreem" (line 2969).

Speirs has summed up Pertelote:

> Pertelote is the practical wife. She ascribes a purely physiological cause and significance to dreams and advises a laxative. She has a wealth of knowledge of medicine, of remedies and herbs, at her finger-tips.
>
> (Speirs 1951, 187)

This is true, but Speirs does not note that it is the driving, blunt style of her speech that creates this impression as much as anything else; if she spoke differently we would read her personality differently. The speech she has made seems in many ways to conflict with the description of her as "Curteys," "discreet, and debonaire" and makes these terms seem even more ironically unfitting. Of course, the heroine of romance is often presented as a healer–it is the one act of which she seems capable, in many romances–but she heals by laying on of hands and by mixing unspecified magical potions. Pertelote is a very down-to-earth version of this–and here may be yet another joke in the tale. If it is, the poetic control of the tale helps to make the joke, as it helps to shape her whole personality.

Chauntecleer seems to have experienced this sort of thing before, because he is neither daunted nor persuaded by her; he replies with great politeness:

> "Madame," quod he, "graunt mercy of youre love."

And he embarks on a refutation. That it is necessary to quote his opening words at length immediately suggests something about the type of answer he is making:

> "But nathelees, as touching daun Catoun,
> That hath of wysdom swich a greet renoun,
> Though that he bad no dremes for to drede,
> By God, men may in olde bookes rede
> Of many a man moore of auctorite
> Than evere Caton was, so moot I thee,
> That al the revers seyn of this sentence,
> And han wel founden by experience
> That dremes ben significaciouns
> As wel of joye as of tribulaciouns
> That folk enduren in this lif present."

It is one long elaborate sentence, with subordinate phrases and clauses running here and there. The elaborate syntax and the extended utterance are quite opposed to Pertelote's style. Another marked difference is that where she used Latinisms as the specific names of objects, Chauntecleer uses them as abstract nouns, and they tend to fall as rime words to stress their elaborate nature. Her long words were functional parts of her lines, his advertise themselves more. The complex language is in keeping with his scholarly– even scholastic–approach: he immediately takes up her one "auctorite" and refutes it. But his refutation needs examining: she referred to Cato and quoted briefly from him. Chauntecleer in reply gives the opinion of a number of unspecified authorities, and gives it in indirect speech–he is neither exact nor convincing. The argument of this opening sentence is vague and the fluent floridities of its style seem to have little content. But Chauntecleer is satisfied that the point has been nailed down, for he goes on:

> "Ther nedeth make of this noon argument;
> The verray preeve sheweth it in dede."

These assured lines lead into his *exempla*, and his confidence sounds quite hollow against the swift-moving scholarly banalities of his opening refutation. It is a simple enough joke–the husband assumes his pretensions to knowledge will satisfy the little woman. It is Chaucer's control of poetic style that shapes the joke so well; the narrator does not have to prompt the reader, for character is created in speech here just as it was in the link before the tale.

We would associate long-windedness with the bombastic opening Chauntecleer has given us, and he does not disappoint. He embarks on his "verray preeve" (which incidentally has nothing to do with dreams of joy, though he has just raised this topic in line 2980). His opening line has a note of imprecise scholarship in it, but he is now in his dramatic mode and moves quickly on:

> "Oon of the gretteste auctor that men rede
> Seith thus: that whilom two felawes wente
> On pilgrimage, in a ful good entente;
> And happed so, they coomen in a toun
> Wher as ther was swich congregacioun
> Of peple, and eek so streit of herbergage,
> That they ne founde as muche as o cotage
> In which they bothe myghte ylogged bee."

The syntax is still extended, but the effect of subordination is not as marked as it was in his general opening remarks. The passage starts off with a good deal of enjambment, but this does not have as convoluted an effect as before because here there is a narrative moving onwards and a series of active verbs.

The muted enjambment we find here would seem to be a transitional device, for as the *exemplum* continues it settles down into a purely end-stopped style. This may be because it would be hard indeed to tell a direct and straightforward *exemplum* in an elaborate and roundabout style, but Chaucer does let Chauntecleer begin to speak in a florid style and only then makes him talk simply. We have seen already that Chauntecleer can talk with directness–he is not all hot air, as the story will finally show, or perhaps we should say he commands a variety of hot airs. This change of style demonstrates that he has more than one way of impressing his audience, for now he starts on a skillfully told, gripping *exemplum.*

Elsewhere we have seen Chaucer merging one style into another, and this is what he seems to be doing here. The effect is to show that Chauntecleer can be persuasive and dominating, though the validity of this domination will be questioned by another change of style before long. Perhaps another effect–and it may be an important one to Chaucer the craftsman–is to vary the stylistic surface of this poem again. The full effect of this change may be hard to assess, but it is there, for now Chauntecleer leaves his vague and general manner and falls quickly into the dramatic recounting of his story, straightforward and speedy: the movement is simple and there is at least one active verb in every line:

> "And so bifel that, longe er it were day,
> This man mette in his bed, ther as he lay,
> How that his felawe gan upon hym calle,
> And seyde, 'Allas! for in an oxes stalle
> This nyght I shal be mordred ther I lye.
> Now helpe me, deere brother, or I dye.'"

The *exemplum* proceeds in this manner, seeming to speed up as it goes along; the syntax becomes extended at times, though never convoluted, for the movement is a quick one from line to line and enjambment is used only twice and then for stress. The first instance of this illustrates the speed of movement as well:

> "This man gan fallen in suspecioun,
> Remembrynge on his dremes that he mette,
> And forth he gooth–no lenger wolde he lette–
> Unto the west gate of the toun, and fond
> A dong-carte . . . ."

The grisly aspect of the murder is thus stressed and enjambment is used again for this effect shortly afterwards:

> "The people out sterte and caste the cart to ground,
> And in the myddel of the dong they founde
> The dede man, that mordred was al newe."

This climax of the *exemplum* epitomizes its direct swift style. But if we are impressed by this, we are soon checked: immediately Chauntecleer switches styles and we are reminded of his bombastic side. He offers a rhetorical *conclusio* [pithy statement in conclusion]:

> "O blisful God, that art so just and trewe,
> Lo, how that thou biwreyest mordre alway!
> Mordre wol out, that se we day by day.
> Mordre is so wlatsom and abhomynable
> To God, that is so just and resonable,
> That he ne wol nat suffre it heled be,
> Though it abyde a yeer, or two, or thre.
> Mordre wol out, this my conclusion."

Chauntecleer is aware of this as a formal conclusion and he makes the style appropriate. He opens with *exclamatio* [expression of grief or indignation] and moves on with *sententiae* [truisms, maxims], he multiplies epithets in an elevated manner–"just and resonable," "just and trewe"–and offers a pair of really ornate epithets in "wlatsom and abhomynable": according to the dictionaries the Germanic word would have been quite as rare as the Latinate one at this time. (Chaucer only uses "wlatsom" twice–here and in "The Monk's Tale"–perhaps another touch of parody.) The second line opens with a vowel assonance that almost amounts to a hoot in "Lo, how that thou," the word "Mordre" is used in *traductio* [repetition of the same word with different meanings] here, and it is the subject of a fine *sententia* in line 3052 that is repeated in the closing line. There is *repetitio* in the placing of "Mordre" three times at the head of the line, and there is a stylish control in the line "Though it abyde a yeer,or two, or three." It is a well–modeled piece of verse; a seventeenth century printer might have been tempted to put one of those disembodied pointing hands in the margin, and perhaps the improving rubric 'Sentence' beside it as well.

The preceding passages should have advised us to be cautious about what Chauntecleer is saying–is it really as important as it sounds? And if we consider for a moment, this high point has an implicit comic quality. The finely presented conclusion has, in fact, only a tangential relevance to the topic, for he has been talking about dreams, not murders, and his floridity leads him astray here. The point is made clearer when Chauntecleer returns to his story; he races though the final events in a totally contrasting style and ends with an anti-climactic, but fully relevant conclusion:

> "And right anon, ministres of that toun
> Han hent the carter and so soore hym pyned,
> And eek the hostiler so soore engyned,
> That they biknewe hire wikkednesse anon,
> And were anhanged by the nekke-bon.
> Heere may men seen that dremes been to drede."

Chauntecleer has previously carried himself away with his party-piece on murder and here has to return jerkily to his topic. His stylistic powers seem fine, but his conceptual control is not so good. There may well be another irony, in support of this, in the next lines. He goes on with another story, saying:

> "And certes in the same booke I rede,
> Right in the nexte chapitre after this–
> I gabbe nat, so have I joye or blis–"

His insistence that he tells the truth makes it all the more likely that this is another indication of his shaky scholarship and his willingness to cast up a cloud of words, for as Coghill and Tolkien remark, this story does not follow the previous one in the source. It would be a recherché point, but then in many ways it is a recherché tale and Chaucer does seem to draw attention to the assertion.

The second *exemplum* is a reworking of the theme of the first, and it similarly begins with a long, flowing sentence:

> "Two men that wolde han passed over see,
> For certeyn cause, into a fer contree,
> If that the wynd ne hadde been contrarie,
> That made hem in a citee for to tarie
> That stood ful myrie upon an haven-syde . . . . "

Then the *exemplum* simplifies its style and continues in a quick and compact manner. The change from an extended to a simple syntax is not perhaps as marked as it is in the first *exemplum*, but it is there and it does to some extent support the tonal characterization of Chauntecleer as a naturally long-winded person who can "perform" dramatically at times. The third *exemplum* is on the same theme, and although these *exempla* do not advance the argument at all this in itself should not make us question their validity. The building up of exemplary proof is a perfectly acceptable form of medieval argument, and because it seems like a move from the very particular to the very general a modern reader should not therefore assume Chaucer has no time for it. Manly's description of exemplary argument as an "astonishing fad" is too peremptory (Manly 1926, 104), but Chaucer does seem sensitive to the possible misuse of exemplary argument–the Pardoner is one example; in "The Franklin's Tale" he shows Dorigen going nowhere at great length with a series of *exempla*; and here he chooses to give this method of arguing to the wordy Chauntecleer and a different method to the clear-headed Pertelote.

The stylistic nature of the third *exemplum* strengthens this impression; in it Chauntecleer's bombastic nature emerges very clearly. This *exemplum* is not told in the swift, rather objective style of the other two. It is heavy with enjambment, a motif of Chauntecleer's florid style:

> "His norice hym expowned every deel

His sweven, and bad hym for to kepe hym weel
For traisoun; but he nas but seven yeer old,
And therfore litel tale hath he toold
Of any dreem, so hooly was his herte."

The learned condescension of Chauntecleer is obvious:

"By God! I hadde levere than my sherte
That ye hadde red his legende, as have I."

The reference to his "sherte" brings back all the ludicrous aspect of the learned cock, and a specifically comic context is recreated–if we have forgotten it–to enrich the moment as Chauntecleer reels off a list of learned authorities in his support.

It seems then, that although *exempla* may be perfectly acceptable, as in "The Tale of Melibee," there is a possibility of abuse and there may be a comic aspect to them. The first leads into flowery irrelevance, the second reminds us of this briefly and the third demonstrates clearly the speaker's pretentious personality. His conclusion has a similar note:

"Shortly I seye, as for conclusioun,
That I shal han of this avisioun
Adversitee; and I seye forthermoor,
That I ne telle of laxatyves no stoor,
For they been venymous, I woot it weel;
I hem diffye, I love hem never a deel!"

Chauntecleer's words are formal and stylish in construction. The placing of the word "adversitee" is especially artistic, and Naunin identifies *contrarietas* [arguing by contraries] in line 3156 (Naunin 1929, 42). It is a formal "defiance," and the speaker shows learning and nobility. The fact that it is laxatives he faces so nobly is in itself comic enough–Chaucer seems to have found the whole topic of excretion as funny as English comedians still find it–and the whole joke is summed up in the ambiguous word "diffye," meaning both the lofty challenge and the simple act of digestion. Once more the comedy is given its fine point by the delicate modulation of the style and the skilled selection of language.

In the following sequence the comedy develops strongly, setting out more boldly in action the comic implications made so far. In spite of his lengthy arguments, Chauntecleer ignores his dream and flies down, because Pertelote transmits courage to him. The lines that summarize this have a real comic vigor:

"For whan I see the beautee of youre face,
Ye been so scarlet reed aboute youre yen,
It maketh al my drede for to dyen."

And Chauntecleer's explanation demonstrates his shoddy scholarship and his confident bombast:

> "For al so siker as *In principio,*
> *Mulier est hominis confusio,*–
> Madame, the sentence of this Latyn is,
> 'Womman is mannes joye and al his blis.'"

Where Pertelote used her learning in a practical way, Chauntecleer uses his–it is less than he pretends–to assert his dominance. Donaldson says that "rhetoric here is regarded as the inadequate defense that mankind erects against an inscrutable reality" (Donaldson 1970, 149). I feel this is to be too serious, as I shall argue later, but Donaldson certainly sees the effect of the rhetoric that Chaucer places in the rooster's mouth.

This strongly marked sequence of comic implication is followed by action which creates physically the mock-heroic follies so far only stated in description and revealed in speech:

> And with that word he fley doun fro the beem,
> For it was day, and eke his hennes alle,
> And with a chuk he gan hem for to calle,
> For he hadde founde a corn, lay in the yerd.
> Real he was, he was namoore aferd.
> He fethered Pertelote twenty tyme,
> And trad hire eke as ofte, er it was pryme,
> He looketh as it were a grym leoun,
> And on his toos he rometh up and doun;
> Hym deigned nat to sette his foot to grounde.

The regal notions that Chauntecleer has of himself are objectified in the farmyard; it is a brilliantly funny piece of observation, and the narrator mulls over the joke pleasantly:

> Thus roial, as a prince is in his halle,
> Leve I this Chauntecleer in his pasture,
> And after wol I telle his aventure.

Like the "leoun" simile, the word "halle" calls up the ironic effects of the opening part of the poem, "pasture" is a dignified name to give to running round after "a corn," and "aventure" itself is a word from the chivalric context. We are reminded of the verbal play that has gone before, but this passage is not notable for its poetic effects: its achievements are those of the comic imagination and they do not depend on poetic modulation to imply effect. The style is supple and polished, and the stressed repetition of "He" and "hym" assists the note of *superlatio,* but the mainspring of the comedy here is not prosodic.

The Nun's Priest has said that he will now get down to the story, but he continues it in that teasing manner that runs strongly throughout this tale,[5] for Chauntecleer's morning crow is approached with a wonderfully elaborate passage.

Like the previous action, it is the working-out of an element in the original description of him. The whole passage has to be quoted to show the effect:

> Whan that the month in which the world bigan,
> That highte March, whan God first maked man,
> Was compleet, and passed were also,
> Syn March bigan, thritty dayes and two,
> Bifel that Chauntecleer in al his pryde,
> His sevene wyves walkynge by his syde,
> Caste up his eyen to the bright sonne,
> That in the signe of Taurus hadde yronne
> Twenty degrees and oon, and somwhat moore,
> And knew by kynde, and by noon oother loore,
> That it was pryme, and crew with blisful stevene.

If you read the passage aloud it is a test of breath control; "caste" is the first verb of any weight, in the seventh line, and the construction of the sentence will not allow you to pause properly until the end. The structural figure of *circuitio* [a mode of amplification] is excellently illustrated here (the figure of *amplificatio* that is missing in "The Manciple's Tale"), and the joke expands with this complication: only a massively elaborated sentence will do to explain the circumstances under which this cock will give his morning crow.

The action slowly gets under way: the narrator frequently turns aside to comment to his audience in an ironic manner, and the variety of tone that he can encompass makes these moments the sharper. Thus he somberly remarks:

> For evere the latter end of joye is wo.
> God woot that worldly joye is soone ago.

And he mockingly adds that a "rethor" might "saufly" write this down as a "sovereyn notabilitee"–the elaborate phrase contrasts vividly with the mournful stresses of the sententia itself and suggests just that learned pomposity that is the topic of the joke.

The fluency of the narrator's comments strengthens the joke when he stops to make a rhetorical mountain out of a fox lying in some cabbages:

> O false mordrour, lurkynge in thy den!
> O newe Scariot, newe Genylon,
> False dissymulour, of Greek Synon,
> 3229 That broghtest Troye al outrely to sorwe!

It is not startling stuff; we know Chaucer can write like this, and the effect is not as complex as some of the earlier poetry in this tale where the rhythms and diction were prompting us towards attitudes to the speaker. The stylistic powers used towards the end of this tale are those of a great writer on holiday. Chaucer spreads himself; he makes fun of most sorts of medieval literature from romance to theology, and his poetry flows quickly and unostentatiously along as the narrator moves from joke to joke, from ironic reference to ironic reference. But if Chaucer is on holiday he is still a great poet, and a clear sign of this is that he provides us with two magnificent set-pieces.

In the first he amplifies the joke we have already seen, the idea of which is to build a rhetorical monument to an incident in this farmyard narrative. Chauntecleer approaches his doom and a sober moral is immediately drawn:

> This Chauntecleer his wynges gan to bete,
> As man that koude his traysoun nat espie,
> So was he ravysshed with his flaterie.

The point is driven home with all the pausing, weighty elaboration of the "Allegoria" at the end of a medieval fable:

> Allas! ye lordes, many a fals flatour
> Is in youre courtes, and many a losengeour,
> That plesen yow wel more, by my feith,
> Than he that soothfastnesse unto yow seith.
> Redeth Ecclesiaste of flaterye;
> Beth war, ye lordes, of hir trecherye.

The final, crucial action in this sequence races past in co-ordinate clauses:

> This Chauntecleer stood hye upon his toos,
> Strecchynge his nekke, and heeld his eyen cloos,
> And gan to crowe loude for the nones.
> And daun Russell the fox stirte up atones,
> And by the gargat hente Chauntecleer
> And on his bak toward the wode hym beer,
> For yet ne was ther no man that hym sewed.

At the end the monosyllabic subordinate clause breaks the chain of action and gives a momentary pause.[6] After it, the storm of rhetoric breaks. The series of apostrophes opens with exclamatio and repetitio and there follows, as Naunin engagingly describes it, 'ein ganze Kette von Apostrophen' ["a whole chain of Apostrophes"; Naunin 1929, 38]:

> O destinee that mayst nat been eschewed!
> Allas, that Chauntecleer fleigh fro the bemes!
> Allas, his wyf ne roghte nat of dremes!
> And on a Friday fil al this meschaunce.

The last line here is now elaborated in an apostrophe to Venus, filled with ornate language, which builds up to an *interrogatio* [use of a question] in the last line:

O Venus, that art goddesse of pleasaunce,
Syn that thy servant was this Chauntecleer,
And in thy servyce dide al his poweer,
Moore for delit than world to multiplye,
Why woldestow suffre hym on thy day to dye ?

The diction is appropriately elaborate and the syntax extended–the style of the paragraph rises to the height decorous for an address to Venus, and its elaboration seems fully in key with its ingenious discussion about the motivation of Chauntecleer's sexuality. The style is just what is needed for the joke to be an excellent one, and building upon this flourishing passage is the charming reference to "Gaufred, deere maister sovereyn" in the following lines.

Dorothy Everett has said ". . . if, as we read the *Nun's Priest's Tale*, we laugh too heartily and unthinkingly at the rhetoricians, there is a danger that Chaucer may be laughing at us" (Everett 1955, 174). The tone of this passage shows the wisdom of her remark; Chaucer is not mocking Geoffrey, rather he is self-indulgently flourishing rhetorical language in a holiday mood. If the style here were crude and limping, making "rhetoric" seem banal or bathetic, we might well say this was a determine of satire on the rhetoricians. But the style is easy, confident: the playfulness is that of a master. And indeed, he does not spend too long using his best rhetorical style in a comic cause, for as this long *apostrophe* continues the comedy is more of imagination and action than of language. The *apostrophe* to Geoffrey is widely regarded as the rhetorical sensation of the tale, but in fact it is not very ornate. There is a little elevated diction in it– "sovereyn," "compleynedest," "sentence"–and there is an *interrogatio* in line 3346. But if we are looking for a parody of rhetoric this will disappoint, and this may well be why Speirs said this apostrophe "anticlimaxed" the others, though he does not give reasons (Speirs 1951, 191).

This muted tone is maintained in the next apostrophe: the hens are presented as classical matrons, but the language is quite restrained. The style is flowing, it is true, but there is little decoration:

But sovereynly dame Pertelote shrighte
Ful louder than dide Hasdrubales wyf,
Whan that hir housbonde hadde lost hys lyf,
And that the Romayns hadde brend Cartage.
She was so ful of torment and of rage
That wilfully into the fyr she sterte,
And brende hirselven with a stedefast herte.

The word "sovereynly" is witty, for it means both that she shrieked the most and implies that she did it in queenly fashion, and the passage moves swiftly along, so swiftly that many an inattentive student has thought it is Pertelote who immolates herself. Chaucer's playing with high rhetorical style here has been brief; at first the style is carefully modeled to make the joke, but he feels no need to sustain the elaborate style once the point is established.

A longer passage of bravura poetry follows, when the farmyard chase occurs. This has often been discussed as a masterpiece of vigor and speed, and little comment is needed here (see Brindley 1964, 154–55; Robinson, 1971, 146; Muscatine 1969, 240; and the notes by Hussey [Chaucer 1965] and by Coghill & Tolkien [Chaucer 1959]). Not only stylistic brilliance is shown, but also that imaginative humor and subtlety that have typified the whole tale:

Ran Colle our dogge, and Talbot and Gerland,
And Malkyn, with a dystaf in her hand;
Ran cow and calf, and eek the verray hogges,
So fered for the berkyng of the dogges
And shoutyng of the men and wommen eeke,
They ronne so hem thoughte hir herte breeke.

Talbot and Gerland are rather aristocratic dogs' names, traditional for hunting dogs, and set against the humble name Colle they touch lightly the mock-heroic note again; the narrative sleight of hand of "oure dogge" strengthens the immediacy of the scene, and not only is the animal world of the farmyard mobilized, but we actually see into their thoughts: the narrator is suddenly empowered to tell us what the pigs were feeling. A lightly carried, but very real skill makes the scene intensely vivid. Chaucer's power to embody the meaning of a scene in the poetry is well illustrated in the final lines:

Of bras they broghten bemes, and of box,
Of horn, of boon, in whiche they blewe and powped,
And therwithal they skriked and they howped.
It semed as that hevene sholde falle.

After these spectacularly noisy lines Chaucer moves easily and undemonstratively to the end; the *conclusio* of the tale is a muted and thoughtful one, as varying interpretations of the tale are offered. Cock and Fox see it as a simply moral lesson advising them to cautious action in the world; the Priest himself speculates quizzically about its doctrinal possibilities; the Host's limited capacity has only grasped the vulgar bits–although the validity of this final link has been questioned,[7] its effect is clear enough as the tale stands. None of these views is given prominence, neither by direct statement nor by tonal implication, and most commentators have agreed that Chaucer saw an enigma as the only fit way of ending this most subtle of tales.

This quiet ending is, of course, in itself a piece of poetic modulation: the absence of spectacular effects here might tell us as much as the silence of the dog in the night-time told Holmes in "Silver Blaze." I believe this quiet close and the fading of spectacular rhetoric in the famous series of apostrophes show that Donaldson was overserious when he argued the thematic importance of rhetoric in the tale, saying that here we find that:

> . . . rhetoric enables man to find significance both in his desires and in his fate, and to pretend to himself that the universe takes him seriously.
>
> (Donaldson 1970, 149)

It is an appealing argument, and a well-presented one; he goes on to say "And rhetoric has a habit, too, of collapsing in the presence of simple common sense," which could be taken as an explanation of the quiet end (though Donaldson does not say this). But the fading of the rhetoric in the mock apostrophes and the quiet end of the tale make me believe that rhetorical writing is just one of the aspects of learning that Chaucer gently mocks in this festival tale, and I cannot see that this play anywhere has an implicitly moral side, except to warn us not to take ourselves too seriously.

The quiet ending is in part a return to normality after the pyrotechnics of the tale and partly a plain assertion that a story can be allegorized in a number of ways: there is a knowing simplicity in the Priest's tone as he finally speaks that makes the learned complexities the tale has presented seem hollow. In this respect the poetry at the end of this tale is as subtly evocative of the whole meaning of the tale as is the grand close to *Troilus and Criseyde* and the complex mixture of tones which ends *The Parlement of Foules* and "The Knight's Tale."

Not all of Chaucer's poems are, in stylistic terms, as complex and as successful as are these, nor does Chaucer always seek to create a highly-wrought poetry where meaning and style are inextricably united. That he does often do so has been the thesis of this study, and it is because I would value this type of poetry so highly that I would judge *Troilus and Criseyde* as Chaucer's finest work, and one of the finest in the language: in it extended and subtle meaning is transmitted in exquisitely judged and finely modulated poetry. But such a judgment starts from the premise that meaning-implying poetic modulation is the finest type of poetry, and this premise is not absolute. When we have shown that Chaucer can write like this and can satisfy the most exacting taste in this type of poetry, we should then note that he does not always write in this way. Just as to ignore Chaucer's poetic art has been, in the past, an error, it would be equally foolish to imagine that the poetic mastery outlined here is the only important thing about his work. It is all too easy to be obsessed by one's own arguments and one's own inclinations, and to believe no more needs to be said. Having this in mind, I would finally like to suggest that with a full understanding of Chaucer's power as a poet we can go on and see the other fine things his work has to offer, and we can go on more confidently because a comprehension of this basic and pervasive poetic skill will help us to understand and evaluate the many other aspects of his expansive genius.

NOTES

[*]Reprinted with permission from *Rymyng Craftily. Meaning in Chaucer's Poetry.* Sydney: Angus and Robertson (Publishers) Pty Ltd, 1973. Chapter 5, pp. 206–35.

[1]In "Chaucer's Disgruntled Cleric," Broes argues that the Priest mocks the Prioress throughout his tale (Broes 1963); in "The Nun's Priest in *The Canterbury Tales*" Lumiansky feels the basis of the tale to be the difference between the Priest's real personality and the one the Host imputes to him (Lumiansky 1953).

[2]The word "reported" may also be a learned term here; Chaucer only uses the verb five times and the noun "reporter" once. The OED records him as the first to use it in English.

[3]Although of OE origin, the word "bour" is not common in Chaucer; it appears in the conventional phrases "bright in bour" (Thopas, 1932) and "byrde in bour" (RR, 1014); it appears three other times in collocation with "halle"; it is used twice in "The Miller's Tale" with apparent ironic effect (cf. remarks on this in Donaldson 1971) and once in "The Wife of Bath's Tale" (line 300) where it also appears to have a genteel connotation.

The word "sklendre" occurs six times, three of them referring to a lady's slimness (Cl 1198, Mch 1602, RR 858). When the Reeve is described as a "sclendre colerik man" this may point towards the Miller's questioning of his masculinity. The other reference, Mk 3147, seems neither to support nor contradict the notion that the word has a romance connotation.

[4]At the time of writing the MED has not inched its way as far as "logge"; the existing dictionaries suggest a general sense of "rough shelter" which would seem, prima facie, appropriate enough for a cock. But the OED also lists "hut, booth, tent, arbor" as meanings. These tend towards the chivalric, and on several occasions the word is used in romances to mean the rough shelter the hero makes in the forest for his lady and himself. It is of French origin and Chaucer only uses it once (the verb "logge" appears four times, but it has no notion of "roughness" or chivalry, and it has its own noun, "loggynge" appearing once). The word may well have chivalric connotations, then, and if this were so it would give point to the only word in this passage without a specific implication.

[5]Sisam has commented very sensibly on this: "For he is both entertaining them and teasing them with suspense and irrelevance: he keeps an eye on them all the time, gauging to a nicety how far he can go without spoiling their pleasure, cajoling them with a promise, or muffling a protest by protesting first" (Chaucer 1927, xxx).

[6]Chaucer only uses "gargat" here; it also appears in *Kyng Alisaundre* and as a knightly surname. The word seems to be of exotic origin–OED suggests Italian or Spanish–and so this is one more dignification of Chauntecleer.

[7]See Robinson's note (Chaucer 1957); Lumiansky 1953 argues, convincingly I think, for the validity of the end-link.

WORKS CITED

Adams, Percy G. 1972. "Chaucer's Assonance." *JEGP Journal of English & Germanic Philology* 71: 52–39.

——. 1977. *Graces of Harmony: Alliteration, Assonance, and Consonance in Eighteenth-Century British Poetry*. Athens: University of Georgia Press.

Amis and Amiloun. 1937. Ed. MacEdward Leach. Early English Text Society. Original Series 203. Oxford: H. Milford, Oxford University Press.

"Ane new yeir gift to the quene mary." 1562. Scottish Text Society n.s. 22. pp. 235–42.

Andrea Capellano. 1947. *Trattato d'Amore; "De amore" libri tres. Testo latino del sec. XII con due traduzioni toscane inedite del sec. XIV*. Ed. Salvatore Battaglia. Rome: Perella.

Arnold, Matthew. 1889. "The Study of Poetry." In *Essays in Criticism: Second Series*. London and New York: Macmillan. pp. 1–55.

Ashby, George. 1899. *Poems*. Ed. Mary Bateson. Early English Text Society 76. London: Oxford University Press.

"At matyne hours." 1568. Scottish Text Society n.s. 22. pp. 131–32.

Baldwin, C.S. 1927. "Cicero on Parnassus." *PMLA* 43: 106–12.

Baltzer, Rebecca A., Thomas Cable, & James I. Wimsatt, eds. 1991. *The Union of Words and Music in Medieval Poetry*. Austin: University of Texas Press.

Barber, Charles & Nicolas Barber. 1991. "The Versification of *The Canterbury Tales*: A Compter-based Statistical Study, II. Leeds Studies in English 22; 57–83

Barney, Stephen A. 1993. *Studies in Troilus. Chaucer's Text, Meter, and Diction*. East Lansing, Michigan: Colleagues Press.

Battaglia, Salvatore. 1961–66. *Grande Dizionario della Lingua Italiana*. 18 vols. Turin: Unione tipografico-editrice torinese.

Baum, Paull F. 1961. *Chaucer's Verse*. Durham: Duke University Press.

Bazire, Joyce, ed. 1953. *The Metrical Life of St. Robert of Knaresborough*. Early English Text Society o.s. 228. London: Oxford University Press.

Beadle, Richard, ed. 1982. *The York Plays*. London: Edward Arnold.

Beaver, Joseph C. 1971. "Current Metrical Issues." *College English* 33: 177–97.

Paul E. Beichner, Paul E. 1960 (1948). "Characterization in *The Miller's Tale*." In *Chaucer Criticism: The Canterbury Tales*. Ed. Richard J. Schoeck and Jerome Taylor. Notre Dame: University of Notre Dame Press. pp. 117–29.

Beidler, Peter G. 1977. "Art and Scatology in the *Miller's Tale*." *Chaucer Review* 12: 90–102.

Bennett, H.S. 1947. *Chaucer and the Fifteenth Century*. Oxford History of English Literature.

No. 2, pt. 1. Oxford: Clarendon Press.

Bennett, J.A.W. 1974. "*Little Gidding.* A Poem of Pentecost," *Ampleforth Journal* 79, Pt. I: 60–73.

——. 1983. "Chaucer, Dante and Boccaccio," in Boitani, ed. 1983, 89–113.

——. 1983 "Survival and Revivals of Alliterative Modes." *Leeds Studies in English* 14: 26–43.

Benskin, M. & M.L. Samuels, eds. 1981. *So meny people longages and tonges.* Edinburgh: Authors.

Benson, C. David & Elizabeth Robertson. 1990. *Chaucer's Religious Tales.* Cambridge: D.S. Brewer.

Benson, Larry D. 1981. "The Order of The Canterbury Tales." *Studies in the Age of Chaucer* 3: 77–120.

——. 1984. "The 'Queynte' Punnings of Chaucer's Critics." *Studies in the Age of Chaucer, Proceedings.* No. 1: 23–47.

Besserman, Lawrence L. 1979. "Chaucer and the Pope of Double Worstede." *Chaucer Newsletter* 1, i:15 f.

Dorothy Bethurum, Dorothy. 1935. "The Connection of the Katherine Group with Old English Prose." *Journal of English and Germanic Philology* 34: 553–64.

Blake, N.F. 1968. "Caxton and Courtly Style." *Essays and Studies* n.s. 21: 29–35.

——. 1969. "Chaucer and the Alliterative Romances." *Chaucer Review* 3: 164-65.

——. 1979. "The Relationship between the Hengwrt and the Ellesmere Manuscripts of the *Canterbury Tales.*" *Essays and Studies,* n.s. 32 (1979): 1–18.

——. 1981. "The Textual Tradition of *The Book of the Duchess.*" *English Studies* 62: 237–48.

——.. 1986. "*The Book of the Duchess* Again." *English Studies* 67: 122–25.

Blamires, Alcuin. 1987. *The Canterbury Tales: The Critics Debate.* Atlantic Highlands, NJ: Humanities Press International.

Bliss, A.J. 1962. "The Appreciation of Old English Metre." In *English and Medieval Studies Presented to J.R.R. Tolkien.* Ed. N. Davis & C.L. Wrenn. London: Allen & Unwin. pp. 27-40.

Block, K.S., ed. 1922. *Ludus Coventriae.* Early English Text Society e.s. 120. London: Oxford University Press. Rpt. 1960.

Boccaccio, Giovanni. 1964– . *Tutte le opere di Giovanni Boccaccio.* 12 vols. Ed. Vittore Branca. Milano: Mondadori.

Boitani, Piero, ed. 1983. *Chaucer and the Italian Trecento.* Cambridge: Cambridge University Press.

—— & Anna Torti, eds. 1984. *Medieval and Pseudo-Medieval Literature.* Cambridge: D.S. Brewer.

—— & Jill Mann, eds. 1986. *The Cambridge Chaucer Companion.* Cambridge: Cambridge University Press.

Boone, Lalia P. 1949. "Chauntecleer and Partlet Identified." *Modern Language Notes* 64: 78–81.

Booth, Stephen. 1983. *King Lear, Macbeth, Indefinition, and Tragedy.* New Haven: Yale University Press.

Bowden, Betsy. 1987. *Chaucer Aloud: The Varieties of Textual Interpretation.* Philadelphia: University of Pennsylvania Press.

——. 1988. *Listeners' Guide to Medieval English: A Discography.* Garland Reference Library of the Humanities, 912. New York: Garland.

Bower, Calvin. 1971. "Natural and Artificial Music: The Origins and Development of an Aesthetic Concept." *Musica Disciplina* 25: 17–33.

Bozzolo, Carla. 1973. *Manuscrits des traductions françaises d'oeuvres de Boccace. XVe siècle* . Padova: Antenore.

Bratcher, James T. & Nicholas von Kreisler. 1971. "The Popularity of the *Miller's Tale.*" *Southern Folklore Quarterly* 35: 325–35.

Brewer, Derek S. 1963. [Review of Baum 1961.] *Review of English Studies* 14: 397–98.

——. 1965. "An Unpublished Late Alliterative Poem." *English Philological Studies* 9: 84–88.

——— , ed. 1966a. *Chaucer and Chaucerians; critical studies in middle English literature.* University: University of Alabama Press.

——— . 1966b. "The Relationship of Chaucer to the English and European Traditions" In Brewer, ed. 1966a. pp. 2–35.

——— . 1975. "Gothic Chaucer." In Brewer, ed. 1975. pp. 1–32.

——— , ed. 1975. *Writers and their Background: Geoffrey Chaucer.* Athens, Ohio: Ohio University Press.

——— . 1982. "The Grain of the Text." In Carruthers & Kirk, eds. 1982, pp. 119–127.

Bridges, Robert. 1921. *Milton's Prosody with a chapter on accentual verse & notes.* Rev. final ed. Oxford: Oxford University Press.

Brindley, D.J. 1964. "The Mixed Style of the Nun's Priest's Tale." *English Studies in Africa* 7: 148–56.

Broes, Arthur T. 1963. "Chaucer's Disgruntled Cleric: *The Nun's Priest's Tale. PMLA* 78: 156–62.

Brogan, T.V.F. 1981. *English Versification, 1570–1980: A Reference Guide with a Global Appendix.* Baltimore & London: Johns Hopkins University Press.

Brook, G.L., ed. 1956. *The Harley Lyrics. The Middle English Lyrics of M.S. Harley 2253.* Manchester: Manchester Univ. Press.

Brown, Emerson, Jr. 1978. "Chaucer, the Merchant, and Their Tale: Getting Beyond Old Controversies: Part I." *The Chaucer Review* 13: 141–56.

——— . 1979. "Chaucer, the Merchant, and Their Tale: Getting Beyond Old Controversies, Part II." *The Chaucer Review* 13: 247–62.

——— . 1980. "Diverse Folk Diversely They Teach." In Gibaldi, ed. 1980, pp. 63–75.

Brownlee, Kevin. 1984. *Poetic Identity in Guillaume de Machaut.* Madison: University of Wisconsin Press.

Brunetto Latini. 1863. *Li Livres dou Trésor.* Ed. P. Chabaille. Paris: Imprimerie Impériale.

Bryan, W.F. & Germaine Dempster, eds. 1941 (1958). *Sources and Analogues of Chaucer's Canterbury Tales.* Rpt. Atlantic Highlands, NJ: Humanities Press.

Buhler, Curt F. 1959. "A Tudor 'Crosse Rowe'," *JEGP Journal of English & Germanic Philology* 58: 248–50.

Burnley, David. 1982. "Inflexion in Chaucer's Adjectives." *Neuphilologische Mitteilungen* 83: 169–77.

Burrow, John. 1971. *Ricardian Poetry.* New Haven: Yale University Press.

——— . 1983. "The Portrayal of Amans in *Confessio Amantis.*" In Minnis, ed. 1983, pp. 5–24.

Butterfield, Ardis. 1991. "Lyric and Elegy in The Book of the Duchess." *Medium Ævum* 60: 33–60.

Cable, Thomas. 1972. "Timers, Stressers, and Linguists. Contention and Compromise." *Modern Language Quarterly* 33: 227–39 .

——— . 1988. "Middle English Meter and Its Theoretical Implications." *The Yearbook of Langland Studies* 2: 47–69.

——— . 1991. *The English Alliterative Tradition.* Philadelphia: University of Pennsylvania Press.

Calin, William. 1974. *A Poet at the Fountain: Essays on the Narrative Verse of Guillaume de Machaut.* Lexington: University Press of Kentucky.

——— . 1987. "Machaut's Legacy: The Chaucerian Inheritance Reconsidered." *Studies in the Literary Imagination* 20, 1: 9–22.

Cambridge Italian Dictionary: See Reynolds, Barbara.

Carruthers, Mary J. & Elizabeth D. Kirk, eds. 1982. *Acts of Interpretation . . . in Honor of E. Talbot Donaldson.* Norman, OK: Pilgrim.

Castets, Ferdinand, ed. 1881. *Il Fiore. Poëme italien du XIIIe siècle, en CCXXXII sonnets imité du Roman de la Rose par Durante.* Montpellier: Soc. pour l'Étude des Langues Romanes.

Cawley, A.C., ed. 1969. *Chaucer's Mind and Art.* Edinburgh & London: Oliver and Boyd.

Chambers, R.W. 1957. *On the Continuity of English Prose from Alfred to More and His School.* Early English Text Society, e.s. 191a. London: Oxford University Press.

Chatman, Seymour. 1960. "Comparing Metrical Styles." In Sebeok, ed. 1960, pp. 149–72.
——. 1965. *A Theory of Meter.* Janua Linguarum. Series Minor, #36. London: Mouton & Co.
——, ed. 1971. *Literary Style: A Symposium.* New York: Oxford University Press.
——, & Samuel Levin, eds. 1967. *Essays on the Language of Literature.* Boston: Houghton Mifflin.
Chaucer, Geoffrey. 1798. *The Canterbury tales of Chaucer: to which are added an essay on his language and versification, and an introductory discourse, together with notes and a glossary.* Ed. Thomas Tyrwhitt. 2 vols. 2d ed. Oxford: Clarendon Press.
——. 1869–77. *Canterbury Tales.* The Six-Text Print. Ed. Frederick J. Furnivall. The Chaucer Society. London: N. Trubner & Co.
——. 1878. *A Parallel-Text Edition of Chaucer's Minor Poems.* Ed. Frederick J. Furnivall. The Chaucer Society. London: N. Trubner & Co. Part II, pp. 164, 166.
——. 1882. *Chaucer's Troilus and Criseyde. A Parallel-Text Print.* Ed. Frederick J. Furnivall. The Chaucer Society. First Series, 63, 64. London: N. Trubner & Co.
——. 1894. *The Complete Works of Geoffrey Chaucer.* Ed. W.W. Skeat. 6 vols. London: Oxford University Press.
——. 1894–95. *Three More Parallel Texts of Chaucer's "Troilus and Criseyde."* Ed. Frederick J. Furnivall. Chaucer Society Publications. First Series, 87, 88. London: N. Trubner & Co. (Rpt. 1967.)
——. 1898. *The Works of Geoffrey Chaucer.* Globe Edition. Ed. Alfred W. Pollard, William S. McCormick, et al. London: Macmillan. (Rpt. 1899, 1901, 1953.)
——. 1899–1900. *The Complete Works of Geoffrey Chaucer: Edited from Numerous Manuscripts.* Ed. Walter.W. Skeat. 7 vols. 2d ed. Oxford: Clarendon Press.
——. 1926. *The Book of Troilus and Criseyde.* Ed. Robert K. Root. Princeton: Princeton University Press.
——. 1927. *Chaucer: The Nun's Priest's Tale.* Ed. K. Sisam. Oxford: Clarendon Press.
——. 1928. *Canterbury Tales.* Ed. John M. Manly. New York: Holt.
——. 1957. *The Complete Works.* Ed. F.N. Robinson. 2d ed. Boston: Houghton Mifflin; 1966. London: Oxford University Press.
——. 1959. *The Nun's Priest's Tale.* Ed. Nevill Coghill & J.R.R. Tolkien. London: Harrup, 1959.
——. 1963. *Chaucer's Major Poetry.* Ed. Albert C. Baugh. New York: Appleton/ Meredith.
——. 1965. *The Nun's Priest's Prologue and Tale.* Ed. Maurice Hussey. Cambridge: Cambridge University Press.
——. 1966. *The Tales of Canterbury.* Ed. Robert A. Pratt. Boston: Houghton Mifflin.
——. 1975. *Chaucer's Poetry: An Anthology for the Modern Reader.* Ed. E. Talbot Donaldson. 2d ed. New York: The Ronald Press.
——. 1978. *"Troilus and Criseyde," Geoffrey Chaucer: A Facsimile of Corpus Christi College Cambridge MS 61.* Ed. M.B. Parkes & Elizabeth Salter. Cambridge: D.S. Brewer.
——. 1979. *Geoffrey Chaucer, The Canterbury Tales: A Facsimile and Transcription of the Hengwrt Manuscript, with Variants from the Ellesmere Manuscript.* Paul G. Ruggiers & Donald C. Baker. Norman: University of Oklahoma Press.
——. 1979–80. Parkes, M.B. & Richard Beadle, eds. *Poetical Works: Geoffrey Chaucer: A Facsimile of Cambridge University Library MS Gg.4.27.* 3 vols. Norman, OK: Pilgrim Books.
——. 1980. *The Canterbury Tales by Geoffrey Chaucer: Edited from the Hengwrt Manuscript.* Ed. N.F. Blake. London: Edward Arnold.
——. 1982. *The Book of the Duchess.* Ed. Helen Phillips. Durham: Durham and St. Andrews Medieval Texts.
——. 1983. *The Miller's Tale.* Ed.Thomas W. Ross. *A Variorum Edition of the Works of Geoffrey Chaucer. The Canterbury Tales.* Vol. II, pt 3. Norman: University of Oklahoma Press.
——. 1984a. *The Nun's Priest's Tale.* Ed. Derek Pearsall. *A Variorum Edition of the Works of Geoffrey Chaucer. The Canterbury Tales.* Vol. II, pt 9. Norman: University of Oklahoma Press.

——— . 1984b. *Geoffrey Chaucer, 'Troilus & Criseyde': A New Edition of 'The Book of Troilus.'* Ed. B[arry] A. Windeatt. London & New York: Longman.

——— . 1985. *The Canterbury Tales.* Ed. Derek Pearsall. London: Allen & Unwin.

——— . 1987. *The Riverside Chaucer.* Ed. Larry Benson et al. Third Edition ["Robinson III"]. Boston: Houghton Mifflin.

——— . 1989. *The Complete Poetry and Prose of Geoffrey Chaucer.* Ed. John H. Fisher. 2d ed. New York: Holt, Rinehart and Winston.

——— . 1993. *The General Prologue. Variorum Edition of the Works of Geoffrey Chaucer.* Vol. II, Part 1A & 1B. Norman: University of Oklahoma Press.

The Chester Mystery Cycle. 1974, 1986. Ed. R.M. Lumiansky & D. Mills. Early English Text Society. s.s.3, 9. Oxford: Oxford University Press.

Chickering, Howell. 1990. "Unpunctuating Chaucer." *Chaucer Review* 25: 96–109.

——— . 1995. "Comic Meter and Rime in the *Miller's Tale.*" *Chaucer Yearbook* 2: 17–47.

——— . 1998. "Chaucer by Heart." In *Under Criticism. Essays for William H. Pritchard.* Ed. David Sofield & Herbert F. Tucker. Athens: Ohio University Press. pp. 91–108.

Chisolm, David. 1977. "Generative Prosody and English Verse." *Poetics* 6: 111–54.

Chomsky, Noam & Morris Halle. 1968. *The Sound Pattern of English.* New York: Harper & Row.

Clemen, Wolfgang. 1964. *Chaucer's early poetry.* Translated by G.A.M. Sym. New York, Barnes & Noble.

Clemoes, Peter. 1952. *Liturgical Influence on Punctuation In Late Old English and Early Middle English Manuscripts.* Occasional Papers: #1. Cambridge: The Department of Anglo-Saxon.

Coghill, Nevill. 1967. *The Poet Chaucer.* 2d ed. Oxford: Oxford University Press.

——— . "Chaucer's Narrative Art." In Brewer, ed. 1966. pp. 114-39.

Conner, Jack. 1974. *English Prosody from Chaucer to Wyatt.* Janua Linguarum. Series Practica, 193. The Hague: Mouton.

Corti, Gino. 1952. "Consigli sulla mercatura di un anonimo trecentista." *Archivo storico italiano* 110: 114–19.

Cowen, Janet M. "Metrical Problems in Editing '*The Legend of Good Women*'." In Pearsall, ed. 1987, Pp. 26–33.

Cowling, G.H. 1926. "A Note on Chaucer's Stanza." *Review of English Studies* 2: 311–27.

Crosby, Ruth. 1938. "Chaucer and the Custom of Oral Delivery." *Speculum* 13: 413–32.

Crystal, David. 1969. *Prosodic Svstems and Intonation in English.* Cambridge: Cambridge University Press.

Culler, Jonathan. 1985. "Changes in the Study of the Lyric." In Hosek et al., eds. 1985. pp. 38–54.

Dane, Joseph A. 1980. "The Mechanics of Comedy in Chaucer's *Miller's Tale.*" *Chaucer Review* 14: 215–24.

Dante Alighieri. 1909. *Convivio.* Trans. William Walrond Jackson. Oxford: Clarendon Press.

——— . 1973. *Literary Criticism of Dante Alighieri.* Ed. & trans. Robert S. Haller. Lincoln: University of Nebraska Press.

Daunt, Marjorie. 1947. "Old English Verse and English Speech Rhythm." *Transactions of the Philological Society for 1946.* pp. 56–72. London: David Nutt.

Davenport, W.A. 1988. *Chaucer: Complaint and Narrative.* Woodbridge, Suffolk: D.S. Brewer.

Davis, Norman et al. 1979. *A Chaucer Glossary.* Oxford: Oxford University Press.

Dean, Christopher. 1969. "Imagery in the *Knight's Tale* and the *Miller's Tale.*" *Medieval Studies* 31: 149–63.

Delany, Sheila. 1992. "Anatomy of the Resisting Reader: Some Implications of Resistance to Sexual Wordplay in Medieval Literature." *Exemplaria* 4: 7–34.

Dempster, Germaine. 1953. "A Period in the Development of the Canterbury Tales Marriage Group and of Blocks B2 and C." *PMLA* 68: 1142–59.

Deschamps, Eustache. 1878–1904. *Oeuvres complètes.* Ed. le Marquis de Quex de Saint-Hilaire and Gaston Raynaud. 11 vols. Société des Anciens Textes Français. Paris: Firmin Didot.

Dictionary of National Biography. 1885– . Ed. Leslie Stephen. London: Smith, Elder.

Diekstra, F. 1981. "Chaucer's Way with his Sources: Accident into Substance and Substance into Accident." *English Studies* 62: 215–36.

Dilligan, Robert J. & Karen Lynn. 1973. "Computers and the History of Prosody." *College English* 34: 1103–23.

DNB. See *Dictionary of National Biography.*

Donaldson, E.Talbot. 1948. "Chaucer's Final -e." *PMLA* 63: 1101–24.

———. 1949. "Chaucer's Final -e." *PMLA* 64: 609–10.

——— . 1950. "The Idiom of Popular Poetry in the Miller's Tale." *English Institute Essays 1950.* Rpt. in Donaldson 1970. pp. 13–29.

——— . 1966. "The Psychology of Editors of Middle English." *English Studies Today 4* (Rome). Rpt. in Donaldson 1970. pp. 102–18.

——— . 1970. *Speaking of Chaucer.* New York: Norton.

——— . 1972. "Chaucer and the Elusion of Clarity." In *Essays and Studies 1972 in Honor of Beatrice White.* Ed. T.S. Dorsch. New York: Humanities Press. pp. 23–44.

——— . 1975. "The Manuscripts of Chaucer's Works and Their Use." In Brewer, ed. 1975, 85–108.

——— . 1981. "Adventures with the Adversative Conjunction in the General Prologue to the *Canterbury Tales;* or, What's Before the *But?*" In Benskin & Samuels, eds. 1981. Pp. 355–66.

Donovan, Mortimer J. 1953. "The *moralite* of the Nun's Priest's Sermon." *Journal of English and Germanic Philology* 52: 498–508.

Doyle, A.I. 1982. "The Manuscripts." In *Middle English Alliterative Poetry and its Literary Background.* Ed. David Lawton. Cambridge: D.S. Brewer

Dragonetti, Roger. 1960. *La Technique poétique des trouvères dans la chanson courtoise.* Bruges: De-Tempel.

——— . 1961. "'La poesie . . . ceste musique naturele.' Essai d'exégèse d'un passage de l'*Art de dictier* d'Eustache Deschamps." In *Fin du Moyen Age et Renaissance.* Mélanges . . . Robert Guiette. Antwerp: Nederlandische Boekhandel.

Duggan, Hoyt N. "The Shape of the B-Verse in Middle English Alliterative Poetry." *Speculum* 61: 564–92.

——— . 1988. "Final *-e* and the Rhythmic Structure of the B-Verse in Middle English Alliterative Poetry." *Modern Philology* 86: 119–45.

Duggan, Joseph. 1973. *The Song of Roland: Formulaic Style and Poetic Craft.* Berkeley: University of California Press.

Earp, Lawrence. 1991. "Lyrics for Reading and Lyrics for Singing in Late Medieval France. The Development of the Dance Lyric from Adam de la Halle to Guillaume de Machaut." In Baltzer et al., eds. 1991, pp. 101–32.

Ebin, Lois, ed. 1984. *Vernacular Poetics of the Middle Ages.* Studies in Medieval Culture 16. Kalamazoo: Medieval Institute Publications.

Eco, Umberto. 1976. *A Theory of Semiotics.* Bloomington: Indiana University Press.

Eliason, Norman E. 1972. *The Language of Chaucer's Poetry. An Appraisal of the Verse, Style, and Structure. Anglistica* XVII. Copenhagen: Rosenkilde and Bagger.

Eliot, T. S. 1917. "Reflections on *Vers Libre.*" In Gross, ed. 1966. pp. 227–33.

Elliott, Ralph W.V. 1965. *The Nun's Priest's Tale and the Pardoner's Tale.* New York: Barnes & Noble, 1965.

——— . 1974. *Chaucer's English.* The Language Library. London: Andre Deutsch.

Epp, Garrett P.J. 1989. "Passion, Pomp, and Parody: Alliteration in the York Plays." *Medieval English Theatre* 11: 150–61.

Esch, Arno, ed. 1968. *Chaucer und seine Zeit: Symposion fur W. F. Schirmer.* Buchreihe der *Anglia* 14. Tübingen: Niemeyer.

Everett, Dorothy. 1955. "Chaucer's 'Good Ear.'" *Essays on Middle English Literature.* Oxford: Clarendon Press. pp. 139–48.

——— . 1955. "Some Relections on Chaucer's 'Art Poetical.'" *Essays on Middle English Literature.* Oxford: Clarendon Press. pp. 149–74.

Fairclough, H. Rushton, trans. 1922. *Virgil, with an English translation by H. Rushton Fairclough.* London: W. Heinemann; New York: G. P. Putnam's Sons. The Loeb classical library.

Farmer, Sharon. 1986. "Persuasive Voices: Clerical Images of Medieval Wives." *Speculum* 61: 517–43.

Ferris, Sumner. 1979. "A Hissing Stanza in Chaucer's 'Prioress's Tale.'" *Neuphilologische Mitteilungen* 80: 164–8.

Fifield, Merle. 1973. *Theoretical Techniques for the Analysis of Variety in Chaucer's Metrical Stress.* Ball State Monograph #23, Publications in English, #11. Muncie, Indiana: Ball State University Press.

Finlayson, John. 1967. "*Morte Arthure*: The Date and a Source for the Contemporary References." *Speculum* 42: 624–38.

Finnie, W. Bruce. 1975. "On Chaucer's Stressed Vowel Phonemes." *The Chaucer Review* 9: 337–41.

Firth, J. R. 1948. "Sounds and Prosodies." *Transactions of the Philological Society.* pp. 127–52. Rpt. in Palmer, ed. 1970. pp. 1–26.

Fleming, John V. 1990. *Classical Imitation and Interpretation in Chaucer's Troilus.* Lincoln: University of Nebraska Press.

Foster, Kenelm. 1984. *Petrarch. Poet and Humanist.* Edinburgh: Edinburgh University Press.

Fowler, Roger, ed. 1966. *Style and Language. Linguistic and Critical Approaches to Literary Style.* London: Routledge and Kegan Paul.

——— . 1966. "Linguistic Theory and the Study of Literature." In Fowler, ed. 1966. pp. 1–28.

Freeman, Donald C. ed. 1970. *Linguistics and Literary Style.* New York: Holt, Rinehart & Winston, Inc.

Freud, Sigmund. 1963. *Jokes and Their Relation to the Unconscious.* Trans. James Strachey. New York: W. W. Norton.

Fries, Udo. 1985. *Einführung in die Sprache Chaucers: Phonologie, Metrik und Morphologie.* Tübingen: Niemeyer.

Fromm, Harold. 1991. *Academic Capitalism and Literary Value.* Athens: University of Georgia Press.

Frye, Northrop. 1957. *Anatomy of Criticism.* Princeton: Princeton University Press.

——— . 1985. "Approaching the Lyric." In Hosek et al., eds. 1985. pp. 31–7.

Fussell, Paul. 1979 [1965]. *Poetic Meter and Poetic Form.* Rev. ed. New York: Random House.

Gaylord, Alan T. 1967. "*Sentence* and *Solaas* in Fragment VII of the *Canterbury Tales:* Harry Bailly as Horseback Editor." *PMLA* 82: 226–35.

——— . 1976. "Scanning the Prosodists: An Essay in Metacriticism." *Chaucer Review.* 11: 22–82.

——— . 1977. [Review of Knight 1973.] *Speculum* 52: 148–50.

——— . 1979. "Chaucer's Dainty 'Dogerel' : The 'Elvyssh' Prosody of Sir Thopas." *Studies in the Age of Chaucer* 1: 83–104. [Rpt. in Jost, ed. 1994.]

——— . 1983. "Dido at Hunt, Chaucer at Work." *Chaucer Review* 17: 300–15.

——— . 1989. [Review of Bowden 1987.] *Speculum* 64: 670–74.

——— . 1990. "Imagining Voices: Chaucer on Cassette." *Studies in the Age of Chaucer* 12: 215–38.

——— . 1991. "From Dorigen to the Vavasor: Reading Backwards." In *The Olde Daunce: Love, Friendship, Sex, and Marriage in the Medieval World.* Ed. Robert R. Edwards & Stephen Spector. Albany: State University of New York Press. pp. 177–200.

——— . 1992. "Reading Chaucer: What's Allowed in 'Aloud.'" *Chaucer Yearbook.* I : 87–109.

——— . 1993. "'After the Forme of My Writynge': Gower's Bookish Prosody." *Mediaevalia* 16: 257–88.

Gellrich, Jesse M. 1974. "The Parody of Medieval Music in the *Miller's Tale*." *JEGP Journal of English & Germanic Philology* 73: 176–88.
Gerould, Gordon Hall. 1952. *Chaucerian Essays*. Princeton: Princeton University Press.
Gest Hystoriale of the Destruction of Troy. In Gibbs, ed. 1966.
Gibaldi, Joseph, ed. 1980. *Approaches to Teaching Chaucer's "Canterbury Tales."* New York: The Modern Language Association of America.
Gibbs, A.C., ed. 1966. *Middle English Romances*. York Medieval Texts. Evanston: Northwestern University Press.
Gieber, Robert L. 1982. "Poetic Elements of Rhythm in the Ballades, Rondeaux and Virelays of Guillaume de Machaut." *Romanic Review* 73: 1–9.
Giegerich, Heinz J. 1985. *Metrical Phonology and Phonological Structure*. Cambridge: Cambridge University Press.
Glare, P.G.W., ed. 1968–82. *Oxford Latin Dictionary*. Oxford: Oxford University Press.
Glowka, Arthur Wayne. 1991. *A Guide to Chaucer's Meter*. New York: University Press of America.
Goldsmith, Ulrich K. 1989. "Words out of a Hat? Alliteration and Assonance in Shakespeare's Sonnets." In *Studies in Comparison*. Ed. Hazel E. Barnes, et al. New York: Peter Lang. pp. 11–30.
Grande Dizionario della Lingua Italiana: see Battaglia, Salvatore.
Gray, Douglas & E.G. Stanley, eds. 1983. *Middle English Studies Presented to Norman Davis*. Oxford: Clarendon Press.
Griffin, Nathaniel E. & Arthur Beckwith Myrick, transls. 1967 [1929]. *The Filostrato of Giovanni Boccaccio: A Translation with Parallel Text*. London: Oxford University Press. (Reprinted NY, 1967).
Gross, Harvey, ed. 1979 (1966). *The Structure of Verse: Modern Essays on Prosody*. Rev. ed. New York: Ecco Press.
Guilbert, L. et al., eds. 1971–78. *Grand Larousse de la langue française*. 7 vols. Paris: Larousse.
Guiette, Robert. 1972. *D'une poésie formelle en France au Moyen Age*. Paris: Nizet.
Guthrie, Steven. 1987. "Machaut and the Octosyllabe," *Studies in the Literary Imagination*. 20: 55–75.
---. 1987. "Prosody and the Study of Chaucer: A Generative Reply to Halle & Keyser." *Chaucer Review* 23, 1: 30–49.
---. 1991. "Meter and Performance in Machaut and Chaucer." In Baltzer et al., eds., 1991. pp. 72–100.
---. 1995. "Dialogics and Prosody in Chaucer." In *Bakhtin and Medieval Voices*. Ed. Thomas J. Farrell. Gainesville: University Press of Florida. pp. 94–108, 204–7.
Haidu, Peter, ed. 1974. *Approaches to Medieval Romance*. Yale French Studies 51.
Halle, Morris & Samuel Jay Keyser. 1966. "Chaucer and the Study of Prosody." *College English* 28: 187–219.
--- . 1971. *English Stress. Its Form, Its Growth, and Its Role in Verse*. New York: Harper & Row.
--- . 1971. "Illustration and Defense of a Theory of the Iambic Pentameter," *College English*. 33: 789–820.
Hammond, Eleanor Prescott. 1908. *Chaucer. A Bibliographical Manual*. New York: Macmillan.
--- , ed. 1927. *English Verse between Chaucer and Surrey*. Durham, NC: Duke University Press.
Hanna, Ralph, III. 1987. "Problems of 'Best Text' Editing and the Hengwrt Manuscript of *The Canterbury Tales*." In Pearsall, ed. 1987. pp. 87–94.
Harbert, Bruce. 1974. "Chaucer and the Latin Classics." In Brewer, ed. 1975. pp. 137–53.
Havely, N.R., ed. & transl. 1980. *Chaucer's Boccaccio: Sources of Troilus and the Knight's and Franklin's Tales*. Woodbridge: D.S. Brewer; Totowa, NJ: Rowman & Littlefield.
Hayes, Bruce. 1983. "A Grid-Based Theory of English Meter." *Linguistic Inquiry* 14: 357–93.
--- . 1984. "The Phonology of Rhythm in English." *Linguistic Inquiry* 15: 33–74.

Hollander, John. 1975. *Vision and Resonance. Two Senses of Poetic Form.* New York: Oxford University Press.

——. 1989. *Rhyme's Reason.* Rev. ed. New Haven: Yale University Press. 1989.

Holman, C. Hugh & William Harmon, eds. 1986. *Handbook to Literature.* 5th ed. New York: Macmillan.

Hoppin, Richard H. 1978. *Medieval music.* The Norton introduction to music history. New York : W.W. Norton.

Hosek, Chavia et al., eds. 1985. *Lyric Poetry: Beyond New Criticism.* Ithaca: Cornell University Press.

Hotson, Leslie J. 1924. "Colfax *vs.* Chauntecleer." *PMLA* 39: 762–81.

Huot, Sylvia. 1987. *From Song to Book: The Poetics ofWriting in Old French Lyric and Lyrical Narrative Poetry.* Ithaca: Cornell University Press.

Jacobs, Nicolas. 1972. "Alliterative Storms: A Topos in Middle English." *Speculum* 47: 695–719.

Jakobson, Roman. 1979. "Toward a Description of Macha's Verse." Trans. Peter & Wendy Steiner. *Selected Writings,* Vol. 5. Ed. Stephen Rudy and Martha Taylor. New York: Mouton. pp. 433-85.

——. 1987. *Language in Literature.* Ed. Krystyna Pomorska and Stephen Rudy. Cambridge: Harvard University Press.

Jambeck, Thomas J. 1975. "Characterization and Syntax in the *Miller's Tale.*" *The Journal of Narrative Technique* 5: 73–85.

Jefferson, Judith A. 1987. "The Hoccleve Holographs and Hoccleve's Metrical Practice." In Pearsall, ed. 1987. pp. 95–109.

Jespersen, Otto. 1900. "Notes on Metre." In Chatman & Levin, eds. 1967, pp. 71-90; and Gross, ed. 1979. pp. 105–28.

John of Garland. 1974. *The Parisiana Poetria.* Ed. Traugott Lawler. New Haven: Yale University Press.

Johnson, W.R. 1982. *The Idea of Lyric: Lyric Modes in Ancient and Modern Poetry.* Berkeley: University of California Press.

Jones, Charles. 1972. *An Introduction to Middle English.* New York: Holt, Rinehart and Winston, Inc.

Jones, Dorothy Richardson. 1992. *"King of Critics." George Saintsbury, 1845–1933, Critic, Journalist, Historian, Professor.* Ann Arbor: University of Michigan Press.

Jonston, Alexandra F. & Margaret Rogerson, eds. 1979. *York: Records of Early English Drama.* 2 vols. Toronto: University of Toronto Press.

Jordan, Robert M. 1967. *Chaucer and the Shape of Creation: The Aesthetic Possibilities of Inorganic Structure.* Cambridge: Harvard University Press.

——. 1987. *Chaucer's Poetics and the Modern Reader.* Berkeley & Los Angeles: University of California Press.

——. 1987. "Todorov, Vinsauf, and Chaucerian Textuality." *Studies in the Age of Chaucer, Proceedings* no. 2, p. 57.

Jost, Jean, ed. 1994. *Chaucer's Humor: Critical Essays.* New York: Garland.

Jungmam, Robert E. 1983. "'Amor vincit omnia' and the Prioress's Brooch." *Lore & Language* 9: 1–7.

Karpf, Fritz. 1930. *Studien zur Syntax in den Werken Geoffrey Chaucers.* I. *Weiner Beiträge zur Englischen Philologie* 55: 1–148.

Kaske, Robert E. 1962. "The Canticum Canticorum in the *Miller's Tale.*" *Studies in Philology* 59: 479–500.

Kean, P.M. 1983. "Chaucer an Englishman Elusively Italianate." *Review of English Studies* n. s. 34: 388–94.

Kelly, Douglas. 1970. "The Source and Meaning of *Conjointure* in Chrétien's *Erec* 14." *Viator* I: 179–200.

——. 1978. *Medieval Imagination: Rhetoric and the Poetry of Courtly Love.* Madison: University of Wisconsin Press.

Kennedy, Ruth. 1987. "'A Bird in Bishopswood': Some Newly-Discovered Lines of Alliterative Verse from the Late Fourteenth Century." In *Medieval Literature & Antiquities: Studies in Honour of Basil Cottle.* Ed. Myra Stokes & T.L. Burton. Woodbridge, Suffolk: D.S. Brewer. pp. 71–87.

Kibler, William W., ed. 1976. *Eleanor of Aquitaine: Patron and Politician.* Austin: University of Texas Press.

Killough, G.B. 1982. "Punctuation and Caesura in Chaucer." *Studies in the Age of Chaucer* 4: 87-107.

Kiparsky, Paul. 1975. "Stress, Syntax, and Meter." *Language* 51: 576–616.

---. 1977. "The Rhythmic Structure of English Verse." *Linguistic Inquiry* 8: 189–247.

Kiser, Lisa J. 1991. *Truth and Textuality in Chaucer's Poetry.* Hanover, NH: University Press of New England.

Kittredge, George Lyman. 1891. *Observations on the Language of Chaucer's Troilus.* Chaucer Society, 2d series, 28. London: Kegan Paul.

--- . 1910. "Antigone's Song of Love." *Modern Language Notes* 245: 158.

--- . 1915. "Chaucer's *Troilus* and Guillaume de Machaut," *Modern Language Notes* 30: 69.

--- . 1915 "Guillaume de Machaut and the *Book of the Duchess," PMLA* 30: 1–24.

--- . 1946 (1915). *Chaucer and His Poetry.* Cambridge: Harvard University Press.

Klausenberger, Jurgen. 1970. *French Prosodics and Phonotactics: An Historical Typology.* Beihefte zur Zeitschrift für romanische Philologie 124. Tübingen: Max Niemeyer Verlag.

Knight, Stephen. 1973a. *The Poetry of the Canterbury Tales.* Sydney: Angus and Robertson.

--- . 1973b. *Rymyng Craftily. Meaning in Chaucer's Poetry.* Sydney: Angus and Robertson.

Kökeritz, Helge. 1954. "Rhetorical Word-Play in Chaucer." *PMLA* 69: 937–52.

--- . 1961. *A Guide to Chaucer's Pronunciation.* New York: Holt, Rinehart & Winston. [Rpt. 1979, University of Toronto Press.]

Kurath, Hans et al., eds. 1954– . *Middle English Dictionary.* Ann Arbor: University of Michigan Press; London: Oxford University Press.

Lambert, Mark. 1986. "Telling the Story in *Troilus and Criseyde.*" In Boitani & Mann, eds. 1986. pp. 59–73

Langendoen, D. Terence. 1968. *The London School of Linguistics: A Study of the Linguistic Theories of B. Malinowski and J. R. Firth.* Research Monograph #46. Cambridge: M.I.T. Press.

Langlois, Ernest, ed. 1902. *Recueil d'arts de seconde rhétorique.* Paris: Imprimerie Nationale.

Lass, Roger & John M. Anderson. 1975. *Old English Phonology.* Cambridge: Cambridge University Press.

Laurie, I.S. 1964. "Deschamps and the Lyric as Natural Music." *Modern Language Review* 59: 561–70.

Lawton, David A. "Scottish Field: Alliterative Verse and Stanley Encomium in the Percy Folio." *Leeds Studies in English* n.s. 10: 42–57.

Leicester, H. Marshall, Jr. 1980. "The Art of Impersonation: A General Prologue to the *Canterbury Tales.*" *PMLA* 95: 213–24.

Lewis, C.S. 1938. "The Fifteenth-Century Heroic Line." *Essays and Studies* 24: 28–41.

Leyerle, John. 1974. "The Heart and the Chain." In *The Learned and the Lewed: Studies in Chaucer and Medieval Literature.* Ed. Larry D. Benson. Harvard Studies in English, 5. Cambridge: Harvard University Press. pp. 113–45.

Las Leys d'Amors. 1919–24. Ed. Joseph Anglade. Bibliothèque Méridionale. First series 17. 4 vols. Toulouse: Edward Privat.

Lote, Georges. 1951. *Histoire du Vers Francais.* Vols. I (1949) & II (1951). Paris: Editions Boivin.

Lotz, John. 1972. "Elements of Versification." In W. Wimsatt, ed. 1972. pp. 1-21.

Lukitsch, Shirley. 1983. "The Poetics of the *Prologue*: Machaut's Conception of the Purpose of His Art." *Medium Ævum* 52: 258–71.

Lumiansky, R.M. 1953. "The Nun's Priest in *The Canterbury Tales.*" *PMLA* 68: 896–906.

Luria, Maxwell S. & Richard L. Hoffman, eds. 1974. *Middle English Lyrics.* New York: Norton.

Luttrell, C.A. 1958. "Three North-West Midland Manuscripts." *Neophilologus* 42: 38–50.
Lydgate, John. 1911. *The Minor Poems of John Lydgate.* Ed. Henry Noble MacCracken. Early English Text Society e.s. 107. London: Kegan Paul, Trench, Trübner & Co.
——— . 1930 (for 1920). *Lydgate's* "Siege of Thebes." Ed. Axel Erdmann & Eilert Ekwall. Early English Text Society, e.s. no. 125. London: Oxford University Press.
Lynn, Karen. 1978. "Chaucer's Decasyllabic Line: The Myth of the Hundred-Year Hibernation." *Chaucer Review* 13: 116–27.
McClumpha, Charles Flint. 1906. *The Alliteration of Chaucer.* Leipzig: Grimme & Trömel. Rpt. 1970.
Machan, Tim William, ed. 1991. *Medieval Literature. Texts and Interpretation.* Binghamton: Medieval & Renaissance Texts & Studies 79.
Machaut, Guillaume de. 1908–21. *Oeuvre.* Ed. Ernest Hoepffner. 3 vols. Société des Anciens Textes Français. Paris: Firmin Didot.
——— . 1909 (1973). *Poésies lyriques.* Ed. Vladimir Chichmaref. 2 vols. Rpt. Geneva: Slatkine.
——— . 1973. *La Louange des dames.* Ed. Nigel Wilkins. New York: Barnes and Noble.
——— . 1984. *The Judgment of the King of Bohemia.* Trans. R. Barton Palmer. New York: Garland.
——— . 1988. *Le jugement du roy de Behaigne;* and *Remede de fortune.* Ed. James I. Wimsatt & William W. Kibler; music ed. Rebecca A. Baltzer. Chaucer Library. Athens: University of Georgia Press.
McJimsey, Ruth B. 1942. *Chaucer's Irregular -E.* Morningside Heights, NY: King's Crown Press of Columbia University Press.
Magnuson, Karl & Frank G. Ryder. 1970. "The Study of English Prosody: An Alternative Proposal." *College English* 31: 789–820.
——— . 1971. "Second Thoughts on English Prosody." *College English* 33: 198–216.
Malone, Kemp. 1968. "Chaucer's 'Book of the Duchess': A Metrical Study." In Esch 1968. pp. 72–95.
Manly, John M. 1926. "Chaucer and the Rhetoricians." *Proceedings of the British Academy* 12: 95–113.
——— . 1926. *Some New Light on Chaucer: Lectures Delivered at the Lowell Institute.* New York: H. Holt & Co.
Manly, John Matthews & Edith Rickert, eds. 1940. *The Text of the Canterbury Tales.* 8 vols. Chicago: University of Chicago Press.
Mann, Jill. 1973. *Chaucer and Medieval Estates Satire.* Cambridge: Cambridge University Press.
Masui, Michio. 1964. *The Structure of Chaucer's Rime Words. An Exploration Into The Poetic Language of Chaucer.* Tokyo: Kenkyusha.
Maynard, Theodore. 1934. *The Connection between the Balade, Chaucer's Modification of It, Rime Royal, and the Spenserian Stanza.* Washington: Catholic University of America Press.
MED: see Kurath, Hans.
Meech, Sanford Brown. 1969 [1959] *Design in Chaucer's 'Troilus.'* Syracuse: Syracuse University Press.
Minkova, Donka. 1987. "The Prosodic Character of Early Schwa Deletion in English." In *Papers from the 7th International Conference on Historical Linguistics.* Ed. A.G. Ramat et al. Amsterdam & Philadelphia: Benjamins. pp. 445–57.
Minnis, A.J., ed. 1983. *Gower's Confessio Amantis: Responses and Reassessments.* Woodbridge, Suffolk: D.S. Brewer.
Minot, Laurence. 1989. *The Poems of Laurence Minot: 1333-1352.* Ed. Thomas Beaumont James & John Simons. Exeter: University of Exeter Press.
——— . 1996. *The Poems of Laurence Minot.* Ed. Richard Osberg. TEAMS Middle English Texts Series. Kalamazoo: Western Michigan University.
Morgan, Margery. 1952. "'A Talking of the Love of God' and the Continuity of Stylistic

Tradition in Middle English Prose Meditations." *Review of English Studies* n.s. 3: 97–116.
Morte Arthure: A Critical Edition. 1984. Ed. Mary Hamel. New York: Garland.
Murphy, James J. 1974. *Rhetoric in the Middle Ages.* Berkeley: University of California Press.
Murray, James A.H. et al., eds. 1933– . *The Oxford English Dictionary.* Oxford: Clarendon Press.
Muscatine, Charles. 1963. *The Book of Geoffrey Chaucer: an account of the publication of Geoffrey Chaucer's works from the fifteenth century to modern times.* San Francisco: Book Club of California.
——. 1966. "The Canterbury Tales: Style of the Man and Style of the Work." In *Chaucer and Chaucerians: Critical Studies in Middle English Literature.* Ed. Derek S. Brewer. University: University of Alabama Press.
——. 1969. *Chaucer and the French Tradition.* Berkeley: University of California Press.
Mustanoja, Tauno F. 1979. "Chaucer's Prosody." In Rowland, ed. 1979. pp. 58–77.
Naunin, Traugott. 1929. *Der Einfluss der mittelalterlichen Rhetorik auf Chaucers Dichtung.* Bonn: Bonn thesis.
Neuss, Paula. 1974. "*Double-entendre* in *The Miller's Tale.*" *Essays in Criticism* 24: 325–40.
The New Catholic Encyclopedia. 1967–79. Prepared by an editorial staff at the Catholic University of America. New York: McGraw–Hill.
[NPEPP 1993] *New Princeton Encyclopedia of Poetry & Poetics.* 1993. Ed. Alex Preminger & T.V.F. Brogan. New York: MJF Books.
Oakden, J.P. 1930, 1935. *Alliterative Poetry in Middle English.* 2 vols. Manchester: Manchester University Press. Rpt. 1968.
OED: see Murray, James A.H.
Ogura, Mieko. 1979. "Metrics of Chaucer: An Analysis Based on the Kiparsky Theory," *Lexicon* 8: 1–15.
Olson, Glending. 1973. "Deschamps' *Art de Dictier* and Chaucer's Literary Environment." *Speculum* 48: 714–23.
——. 1984. "Toward a Poetics of the Late Medieval Court Lyric." In Ebin 1984. pp. 227–48.
Osberg, Richard H. 1977. "The Alliterative Lyric and Thirteenth-Century Devotional Prose." *JEGP. Journal of English & Germanic Philology* 76: 40–54.
——. 1984. "Alliterative Technique in the Lyrics of MS Harley 2253." *Modern Philology* 82: 125–55.
—— ed. & transl. 1990. *Sir Gawain and the Green Knight.* Series IV. English Language and Literature, vol 112. New York: Peter Lang.
——. 1996a. "The prosody of Middle English *Pearl* and the alliterative lyric tradition." In *English Historical Metrics,* ed. C.B. McCully & J.J. Anderson. Cambridge: Cambridge University Press. pp. 150-74.
——. 1996b. "A Voice for the Prioress: The Context of English Devotional Prose." *Studies in the Age of Chaucer* 18: 25–54.
Owen, Charles A., Jr. 1961. "The Twenty-Nine Pilgrims and the Three Priests." *Modern Language Notes* 76: 391–98.
——. 1966. "'Thy Drasty Rymyng . . .'." *Studies in Philology* 63: 533–64.
——. 1974. [Review of Robinson 1971.] *Speculum* 49: 148–51.
——. 1977. *Pilgrimage and Storytelling in the Canterbury Tales: The Dialectic of "Ernest" and "Game."* Norman: University of Oklahoma Press.
——. 1983. "Development of the Art of Portraiture in Chaucer's General Prologue." *Leeds Studies in English* n.s. 14: 116–33.
——. 1991. *The Manuscripts of the Canterbury Tales.* Chaucer Studies, 17. Suffolk: Brewer.
——. 1992. "The Canterbury Tales: Beginnings (3) and Endings (2+1)." *Chaucer Yearbook* 1: 189–212.
——. 1994. "Chaucer's Witty Prosody in the General Prologue, Lines 1-42." In Jost, ed. pp. 261–70.
Palmer, F.R., ed. 1970. *Prosodic Analysis..* London: Oxford University Press.
Palmer, R. Barton, ed. 1999. *Chaucer's French Contemporaries: The Poetry/Politics of Self and Tradition.* New York: AMS.

Park, Clara Claiborne. 1991. *Rejoining the Common Reader.* Evanston: Northwestern University Press.

Parr, J. "Chaucer and Partonope of Blois." *Modern Language Notes* 60: 486–7.

Patterson, Warner F. 1935. *Three Centuries of French Poetic Theory.* 3 vols. University of Michigan Publications in Language and Literature. Ann Arbor: University of Michigan Press.

Payne, Robert O. 1963. *The Key of Remembrance: A Study of Chaucer's Poetics.* New Haven: Published for the University of Cincinnati by Yale University Press.

Pearsall, Derek, ed. 1962. *The Floure and the Leafe.* London and Edinburgh: Nelson.

——— . 1965. "The Development of Middle English Romance." *Medieval Studies* 27: 91–116.

——— . 1970. *John Lydgate.* London: Routledge and Kegan Paul; Charlottesville: University Press of Virginia.

——— . 1977. *Old English and Middle English Poetry.* Routledge History of English Poetry. Vol. I. London: Routledge & Kegan Paul.

——— , ed. 1979 (1978). Piers Plowman *by William Langland ; an edition of the C-text.* Berkeley: University of California Press, 1979. York medieval texts : 2d ser. (orig. 1978).

——— . 1991. "Chaucer's Meter: the Evidence of the Manuscripts." In Machan, ed. 1991. pp. 41–57.

——— , ed. 1987. *Manuscripts and Texts: Editorial Problems in Later Middle English Literature.* Cambridge: D.S. Brewer; Wolfeboro, NH: Boydell & Brewer.

——— . 1997. *John Lydgate (1371-1449): A Bio-Bibliography.* Victoria, BC: University of Victoria, 1997.

PEPP 1974. See *Princeton Encyclopedia* 1974.

Phillips, Helen. 1986. "The Book of the Duchess, Lines 31–96: Are They a Forgery?" *English Studies* 67: 112–21.

Pirkhofer, Anton M. 1963. "'A Pretty Pleasing Picket'—On the Use of Alliteration in Shakespeare's Sonnets." *Shakespeare Quarterly* 14: 3–14.

Poirion, Daniel. 1965. *Le Poète et le prince: l'evolution du lyrisme courtois de Guillaume de Machaut à Charles d'Orleans.* Université de Grenoble Publications de la Faculté des Lettres et Sciences Humaines 35. Paris: Presses Universitaires de France.

Pope, M.K. 1961. *From Latin to Modern French.* Manchester: Manchester University Press.

Pratt, R.A. 1949. "The Classical Lamentations in the *Nun's Priest's Tale.*" *Modern Language Notes* 64: 76-78.

——— . 1956. "Chaucer and *Le Roman de Troyle et de Criseida,*" *Studies in Philology* 53: 509–39.

Priestly, J.B. 1924. *Figures in Modern Literature.* London: John Lane The Bodley Head Ltd.

*Princeton Encyclopedia of Poetry and Poetics.*1974. [PEPP 1974] Ed. Alex Preminger, Frank J. Warnke, and O. B. Hardison, Jr. Enlarged ed. Princeton: Princeton University Press.

Pyle, Fitzroy. 1973. "Chaucer's Prosody." *Medium Ævum* 42: 47-56.

Rajan, Tilottama. "Romanticism and the Death of Lyric Consciousness." In Hosek et al., eds. 1985. pp. 194–207.

Reed, Mary B. 1962, "Chaucer's Sely Carpenter." *Philological Quarterly* 41: 762–9.

Reiss, Edmund. 1964. "Chaucer's Miller, Pilate, and the Devil." *Annuale Mediaevale* 5: 21–5.

——— . 1970. "Daun Gerveys in the *Miller's Tale.*" *Papers on Language and Literature* 6: 115–24.

Reynolds, Barbara, ed. 1962, 1981. *The Cambridge Italian Dictionary.* 2 vols. Cambridge: Cambridge University Press.

Richardson, Janette. 1970. *Blameth Nat Me: A Study of Imagery in Chaucer's Fabliaux.* The Hague: Mouton.

Rickert, Edith, Clair C. Olson & Martin M. Crow, eds. and compilers. 1948. *Chaucer's World.* London: Geoffrey Cumberledge. Rpt. Columbia University Press.

Ricks, Christopher. 1983. "John Gower: Metamorphosis in Other Words." In Minnis 1983. pp. 25–49. Rpt. in Ricks, *The Force of Poetry* (Oxford University Press, 1984), pp. 1–33.

Robbins, Rossell Hope. 1950. "Poems of Humphrey Newton, Esq., 1466–1536." *PMLA* 65: 249–81.

——— . 1979. "The Lyrics." In Rowland, ed. 1979. pp. 380–402.

——— . "'The Vintner's Son': French Wine in English Bottles." In Kibler, ed. 1976. pp. 147–72.

——— , ed. 1959. *Historical Poems of the XIV and XV Centuries.* New York: Columbia University Press.

——— , ed. 1976. *Chaucer at Albany.* New York: Burt Franklin.

Robertson, Elizabeth. 1990. "Aspects of Female Piety in the Prioress's Tale." In Benson & Robertson 1990. pp.145–60.

Robey, David. 1988. "Alliteration in Dante, Petrarch, and Tasso: A Computer Analysis." In *The Languages of Literature in Renaissance Italy.* Ed. Peter Hainsworth et al. Oxford: Clarendon Press. pp. 169–89.

Robins, R. H. 1970. "Aspects of Prosodic Analysis." *Proceedings of the University of Durham Philosophical Society* I, Series B(Arts), No. 1, pp. 1–12. In Palmer, ed. 1970, pp. 188–200.

Robinson, Ian. 1971. *Chaucer's Prosody, A Study of the Middle English Verse Tradition.* Cambridge: Cambridge University Press.

——— . 1972. *Chaucer and the English Tradition.* Cambridge: Cambridge University Press.

——— . 1975. *The New Grammarian's Funeral.* Cambridge: Cambridge University Press.

Rolle, Richard. 1895. "Meditations on the Passion." In *Yorkshire Writers: Richard Rolle of Hampole.* Ed. C. Horstman. 2 vols. New York: Macmillan.

Roscow, G.H. 1981. *Syntax and Style in Chaucer's Poetry.* Cambridge: D.S. Brewer ; Totowa, NJ: Rowman & Littlefield. Chaucer Studies 6.

Ross, Thomas W. 1972. *Chaucer's Bawdy.* New York: E. P. Dutton.

Rowland, Beryl. 1970. "The Play of the *Miller's Tale*: A Game within a Game." *Chaucer Review* 5: 140–46.

——— . 1974. "Chaucer's Blasphemous Churl: A New Interpretation of the *Miller's Tale*." In Rowland, ed. 1974. pp. 43–55.

——— , ed. 1974. *Chaucer and Middle English Studies in Honour of Rossell Hope Robbins.* Kent, Ohio: Kent State University Press.

——— , ed. 1979. *Companion to Chaucer Studies.* Revised ed. New York & Oxford: Oxford University Press.

Ruggiers, Paul G. "The Italian Influence on Chaucer." In Rowland, ed. 1979. pp. 160–84.

Saintsbury, George. 1906–10. *A History of English Prosody from the Twelfth Century to the Present Day.* 3 vols. London: Macmillan.

——— . 1910. *Historical Manual of English Prosody.* London: Macmillan. Rpt. & ed. Harvey Gross, NY: Schocken Books, 1966.

Salter, Elizabeth. 1983. *Fourteenth-Century English Poetry: Contexts and Readings.* Oxford: Clarendon Press.

Samuels, M.L. 1972. "Chaucerian Final -e." *Notes and Queries* 217: 444–48.

Schipper, Jakob. 1910. *A History of English Versification.* Oxford: Oxford University Press.

Sebeok, Thomas A., ed. 1960. *Style in Language.* Conference on Style, Indiana Univ., 1958. Cambridge: Technology Press of MIT, jointly with New York: John Wiley & Sons.

"A Selective Bibliography of Recent Work in English Prosody." 1977. *Style* 11: 136–70.

Shakespeare, William. 1944. *The Sonnets.* Ed. Hyder Edward Rollins. A New Variorum Edition of Shakespeare. 2 vols. Philadelphia & London: J.B. Lippincott.

Shapiro, Karl & Robert Beum. 1965. *A Prosody Handbook.* New York: Harper & Row.

Shepherd, Geoffrey. 1970. "The Nature of Alliterative Poetry in Late Medieval England." *Proceedings of the British Academy* 56: 57–76. Rpt. in *Poets and Prophets: Essays in Medieval Studies By G. T. Shepherd.* Ed T.A. Shippey and John Pickles. Cambridge: D. S. Brewer, 1990. pp. 173–92.

Shepherd, Stephen H.A., ed. 1995. *Middle English Romances.* New York: Norton.

Shoaf, R.A. 1988. "The Play of Puns in Late Middle English Poetry: Concerning Juxtology." In *On Puns: The Foundation of Letters.* Ed. Jonathan Culler. Oxford: Basil Blackwell. pp. 44–61.

Silar, Theodore I. 1990. "Chaucer's Joly Absolon." *Philological Quarterly* 69: 409–17.

Smith, L.T., ed. 1907–10. *The Itinerary of John Leland in or about the years 1535–1543.* Parts I–XI. London: G. Bell.
Smith, Martin Ferguson, ed. 1975. *De rerum natura* by Lucretius; with an English translation by W. H. D. Rouse; rev. and new text, introd., notes, and index by Martin Ferguson Smith. Cambridge: Harvard University Press. The Loeb classical library; 181.
Smith, R.M. 1936. "Three Notes on the Knight's Tale." *MLN* 51: 318–21.
Smithers, G.V. 1983. "The Scansion of *Havelok* and the Use of ME *-en* and *-e* in *Havelok* and by Chaucer" In Gray & Stanley, eds. 1983. pp. 195–234.
James G. Southworth. 1954. *Verses of Cadence. An Introduction to the Prosody of Chaucer and His Followers.* Oxford: Basil Blackwell.
——— . 1962. *The Prosody of Chaucer and His Followers. Supplementary Chapters to* Verses of Cadence. Oxford: Basil Blackwell.
——— . 1964. "Chaucer's Prosody: A Plea for a Reliable Text." Rev. version rpt. in Cawley, ed. 1969. pp. 89–96.
Spearing, A.C. 1965. "Chaucer's Language." In Maurice Hussey, A. C. Spearing, and James Winny. *An Introduction to Chaucer.* Cambridge: Cambridge University Press.
——— . 1972. *Criticism and Medieval Poetry.* 2d ed. London: Edward Arnold.
Speirs, John. 1960 [1951]. *Chaucer the Maker.* Rev. ed. London: Faber & Faber.
——— . 1958. *Medieval English Poetry: The Non-Chaucerian Tradition.* London: Faber and Faber.
Spencer, Virginia Eviline. 1898. *Alliteration in Spenser's Poetry: Discussed and Compared with the Alliteration as Employed by Drayton and Daniel.* Zurich: Inaugural dissertation.
Staiger, Emil. 1974 [1952]. "Lyrik und lyrisch." In *Zur Lyrik-Diskussion.* Ed. Reinhold Grimm. Wege der Forschung 111. Darmstadt: Wissenschaftliche Buchgesellschaft. pp. 75–82.
Stanley, E.G. 1968. "Stanza and Ictus: Chaucer's Emphasis in *Troilus and Criseyde.*" In Esch, ed. 1968. pp. 123–48.
——— . 1988. "Rhymes in English Medieval Verse: From Old English to Middle English." In *Medieval English Studies Presented to George Kane.* Ed. Edward D. Kennedy, Ronald Waldron, & Joseph S. Wittig. Wolfeboro, NH: D. S. Brewer. pp. 19–54.
——— . 1989. "Chaucer's Meter after Chaucer, I: Chaucer to Hoccleve." *Notes and Queries* 36: 11–23.
Stevens, John. 1961. *Music and Poetry in the Early Tudor Court.* London: Methuen.
——— . 1968. "Dante and Music." *Italian Studies* 23: 1–18.
——— . 1984. "The 'Music' of the Lyric: Machaut, Deschamps, Chaucer." In Boitani & Torti, eds. 1984. pp. 109–29.
——— . 1986. *Words and Music in the Middle Ages: Song, Narrative, Dance and Drama, 1050–1350.* Cambridge: Cambridge University Press.
Stevens, Martin. 1979. "The Royal Stanza in Early English Literature." *PMLA* 94: 62–76.
Stillwell, Gardiner. 1955. "The Language of Love in Chaucer's *Miller's* and *Reeve's Tales* and in the Old French Fabliaux." *JEGP Journal of English & Germanic Philology* 54: 693–99.
Stokes, Myra. 1980. "Recurring Rhymes in *Troilus and Criseyde.*" *Studia Neophilologica* 52: 287–97.
Sudo, Jan. 1969. "Some Specific Rime-units in Chaucer." *Studies in English Literature* [Tokyo] 45: 221–36.
Sutherland, Ronald. 1958. "Structural Linguistics and English Prosody." *College English* 20: 12–17.
Tarlinskaja, Marina. 1984. "Rhythm-Morphology-Syntax-Rhythm." *Style* 18: 1–26.
Teager, F.E. 1932. "Chaucer's Eagle and the Rhetorical Colours." *PMLA* 47: 410–18.
ten Brink, Bernhard. 1901. *The Language and Metre of Chaucer.* 2d ed. Rev. Friedrich Kluge, trans. M. Bentinck Smith. London: Macmillan.
Tillyard, E.M.W. 1934 (1948). *Poetry: Direct and Oblique.* 2d ed. Rpt. London: Chatto and Windus.
Tolkien, J.R.R. & E.V. Gordon, eds. 1967. *Sir Gawain and the Green Knight.* 2d ed. rev. by Norman Davis. New York: Oxford University Press.
Turville-Petre, Thorlac. 1982. "The Lament for Sir John Berkeley." *Speculum* 57: 332–9.

Tyrwhitt, Thomas. 1798. "An Essay on His Language and Versification." *The Poetical Works of Geoffrey Chaucer.* 2 vols. Rpt. with corrections. Oxford: the Clarendon Press.

Varty, Kenneth. 1965. "Deschamps' *Art de Dictier.*" *French Studies* 19: 164–68.

Vinaver, Eugène. 1971. *The Rise of Romance.* Oxford: Clarendon Press.

Wallace, David. 1983. "Some Amendments to the Apparatus of Robinson's *Works of Chaucer.*" *Notes and Queries* NS 30: 202.

——— . 1985. *Chaucer and the Early Writings of Boccaccio.* Chaucer Studies 12. Woodbridge: D.S. Brewer.

Watson, Charles S. 1964. "The Relationship of the *Monk's Tale* and the *Nun's Priest's Tale.*" *Studies in Short Fiction* 1: 277–88.

Weiss, Alexander. 1982. "Chaucer's Early Translations from French: The Art of Creative Transformation." In *Literary and Historical Perspectives of the Middle Ages.* Ed. Patricia W. Cummins, Patrick W. Conner & Charles W. Connell. Proceedings of the 1981 Southeast Medieval Association Meeting. Morgantown: West Virginia University Press. pp. 176–82.

Wetherbee, Winthrop, ed. & transl. 1973. *The Cosmographia of Bernardus Silvestris.* A translation with introd. and notes. New York: Columbia University Press

——— . 1984. *Chaucer and the poets: an essay on Troilus and Criseyde.* Ithaca: Cornell University Press.

Wheeler, Bonnie. 1982. "Dante, Chaucer and the Ending of *Troilus and Criseyde.*" *Philological Quarterly* 61: 105–123.

Wickham, Glynne. 1959. *Early English Stages.* 2 vols. New York: Columbia University Press.

Wilkins, Nigel. ed. 1968. *One Hundred Ballades, Rondeaux and Virelais.* Cambridge: Cambridge University Press.

——— , 1979. *Music in the Age of Chaucer.* Cambridge: D.S. Brewer.

Wilson, Edward. 1979. "An Unpublished Alliterative Poem on Plant-Names from Lincoln College, Oxford, MS. Lat. 129 (E)." *N&Q* 224, n.s. 26: 504–8.

Wimsatt, James I. 1968. *Chaucer and the French Love Poets: The French Background of the "Book of the Duchess."* University of North Carolina Studies in Comparative Literature no. 43. Chapel Hill: University of North Carolina Press.

——— . 1970. *The Marguerite Poetry of Guillaume de Machaut.* University of North Carolina Studies in the Romance Language and Literatures, no. 87. Chapel Hill: University of North Carolina Press.

——— . 1975. "Machaut's *Lay de Confort* and Chaucer's *Troilus and Criseyde.*" In Robbins, ed. 1976. pp. 11–26.

——— . 1976. "Guillaume de Machaut and Chaucer's *Troilus and Criseyde.*" *Medium Ævum* 45: 277–93.

——— . 1978. "Guillaume de Machaut and Chaucer's Love Lyrics." *Medium Ævum* 47: 68–87.

——— . 1982. *Chaucer and the Poems of "Ch" in University of Pennsylvania* MS *French 15.* Chaucer Studies 9. Cambridge: D.S. Brewer.

——— . 1985. "The French Lyric Element in *Troilus and Criseyde.*" *Yearbook of English Studies* 15: 18–32.

——— . 1991a. "Chaucer and Deschamps' 'Natural Music.'" In Baltzer et al., eds. 1991. pp. 132–50.

——— . 1991b. *Chaucer and His French Contemporaries: Natural Music in the Fourteenth Century.* Toronto: University of Toronto Press.

Wimsatt, W.K., Jr. 1954. "One Relation of Rhyme to Reason." *The Verbal Icon: Studies on the Meaning of Poetry.* Lexington: University of Kentucky Press.

——— . 1970. "The Rule and the Norm: Halle and Keyser on Chaucer's Meter." *College English* 31: 774–88.

——— , ed. 1972. *Versification. Major Language Types.* New York: MLA, New York University Press.

Windeatt, Barry A. 1977. " 'Most conservatyf the soun': Chaucer's *Troilus* Metre." *Poetica* (Tokyo) 8: 44–60.
——— . 1977–8. "The 'Paynted Proces': Italian to English in Chaucer's *Troilus*." *English Miscellany* 26–27: 7–103.
——— . 1983. "Chaucer and the Filostrato," in Boitani, ed. 1983. pp. 163–83.
——— . 1984. "Thomas Tyrwhitt." In *Editing Chaucer. The Great Tradition*. Ed. Paul G. Ruggiers. Norman, OK: Pilgrim Books. pp. 117–43.
——— , ed. 1984. *'Troilus & Criseyde.'* See Chaucer 1984b.
——— . 1992. "To rym wel this book til I have do." *Oxford Guides to Chaucer: Troilus and Criseyde*. Oxford: Clarendon Press. pp. 354–59.
Wittig, Susan. 1978. *Stylistic and narrative structures in the Middle English Romances*. Austin: University of Texas Press.
Wolfe, Patricia M. 1972. *Linguistic Change and the Great Vowel Shift in English*. Berkeley: University of California Press.
Woods, Suzanne. 1984. *Natural Emphasis: English Versification from Chaucer to Dryden*. San Marino: The Huntington Library.
Wright, Thomas, ed. 1859. *Political Poems and Songs Relating to English History*. 2 vols. London: Longman.
——— & James Orchard Halliwell, eds. 1845. *Reliquiae antiquae*. 2 vols. London: J.R. Smith.
Young, George. 1928. *An English Prosody On Inductive Lines*. Cambridge: Cambridge Univ. Press.
The Year's Work in English Studies. 1974 (for 1972.) Vol. 53. Published for The English Association by The Humanities Press, N.Y.
Young, Karl. 1943–44. "Chaucer and Geoffrey of Vinsauf." *Modern Philology* 41: 172–82.
Yudkin, Jeremy. 1989. *Music in Medieval Europe*. Englewood Cliffs, NJ: Prentice Hall.
Zumthor, Paul. 1972. *Essaie de poétique médiévale*. Paris: Editions du Seuil.